ACCLAIM FOR FRED KAPLAN'S

THE SINGULAR
MARK TWAIN

"Refreshing. . . . Full of new material." —*St. Louis Post-Dispatch*

"Lively. . . . Clemens feels whole because Kaplan takes the time to show him in so many different settings and situations."
—*The Oregonian*

"Comprehensive. . . . Thoroughly researched. . . . Highly readable."
—*Fort Worth Star-Telegram*

"A vividly detailed account. . . . Kaplan clearly shows the connection between Twain's writing and the people and events that surrounded his life." —*Library Journal*

"Ultimately, Kaplan's major contribution may be in what he has taken out of the Twain mythology. No longer will Twain be referred to as an inspired primitive." —*Houston Chronicle*

"[Kaplan] has researched more fully and completely than any other has been able to do before. . . . Deeply detailed . . . rich with anecdote, facts and the humor that filled the man we have come to know as Mark Twain."
—*Times Record News* (Wichita Falls, TX)

FRED KAPLAN

THE SINGULAR
MARK TWAIN

Fred Kaplan is Distinguished Professor of English Literature at
Queens College and the Graduate Center of the City University
of New York. He is the author of the critically acclaimed biographies *Gore Vidal*, *Henry James*, *Dickens*, and *Thomas Carlyle*,
which was nominated for a National Book Critics Circle Award
and a Pulitzer Prize. He has held Guggenheim and National En-
dowment for the Arts Fellowships and was a Fellow of the National Humanities Center. He lives in Boothbay, Maine.

THE SINGULAR

MARK
TWAIN

To Howard
Best,

To Howard

Best!

[signature]

THE SINGULAR

MARK TWAIN

A BIOGRAPHY

FRED KAPLAN

ANCHOR BOOKS

A Division of Random House, Inc.

New York

FIRST ANCHOR BOOKS EDITION, AUGUST 2005

Copyright © 2003 by Fred Kaplan

The Library of Congress has cataloged the Doubleday edition as follows:
Kaplan, Fred, 1937–
    The singular Mark Twain : a biography / Fred Kaplan.—1st ed.
        p.   cm.
    Includes bibliographical references and index.
        1. Twain, Mark, 1835–1910. 2. Humorists, American—
    19th century—Biography. 3. Authors, American—19th century—
    Biography. 4. Journalists—United States—Biography.
    I. Title.
    PS1331.K317 2003
    818'.408—dc21
    [B]   2003043558

Anchor ISBN: 1-4000-9527-1

Author photograph © Daniel Reilly
Book design by Fritz Metsch

www.anchorbooks.com

Printed in the United States of America
10 9 8 7 6 5 4 3 2 1

To Talila and Andrew
May you grow to love Mark Twain
And the world of Books

CONTENTS

———◆———

THE SINGULAR

MARK
TWAIN

INTRODUCTION

He was named Samuel Langhorne Clemens at his birth on November 30, 1835. He became Mark Twain in February 1863, when he chose that odd but now familiar and resonant phrase as his pen name. Literary history has made much of it. Biographers and psychological critics have found significance in a man who, in creating an alternate self, calls himself "Twain." To his family he was always Sam or Samuel and occasionally Sammy; his wife had a pet name for him that was hers alone; his children called him "Papa." For legal purposes he was Samuel L. Clemens. When he became world-famous toward the end of his first decade under a literary pseudonym, he was known to his readers as "Mark Twain."

Gradually he himself began to elide the distinction between, even to merge, the two identities. By his middle age, very few people called him Sam, mostly those with whom he had been intimate before he became famous. Often he signed private letters "Mark Twain." Many of his friends called him "Mark." The world knew that the man in the white suit with the halo of white hair and the ever-present cigar or pipe was Mark Twain. The man and the pseudonym had grown comfortable with each other. In that sense, Clemens/Twain increasingly became a single figure, even to himself. Though the name suggests division, the reality tended toward unity.

Sometimes preoccupied with twins, with doubles, with separations—increasingly with loss—always concerned about his public image, he never felt inward or outward uncertainty about who he was or what he represented. "Twain" was both a trope and a joke. "When I was born I was a member of a firm of twins," he told his Lotos Club audience in New York in 1901, though he was not. "And one of them disappeared." He was Samuel Clemens until 1863, and often Mark Twain thereafter. The writer and the man became inseparable as a shorthand reference. But in his lifetime, they were essentially inseparable anyway.

Mark Twain is "singular" in three senses: (1) he is a unique figure in American literature who looms above all others as the most widely quoted and recognized, always envisioned as the quintessential American writer; (2) the writer and the man, despite the two names, are a unified personality; and (3) he is like no other nineteenth-century American literary figure in that his name alone brings to mind images and issues that are at the heart of American cultural history, that are central to a definition of America in the nineteenth century as well as today.

A deservedly praised and influential biography of Mark Twain's adult years held that Samuel Clemens/Mark Twain was a split personality, Clemens embodying the self-servingly conventional and materialistic Victorian side, and Twain the imaginative, iconoclastic side. It was a useful way to dramatize some of Twain's inconsistencies, and it appealed to the psychological models current in mid-twentieth-century America. It was not, though, the whole story of the phenomenon of Clemens/Twain. In historical fact, Samuel L. Clemens and his pseudonym "Mark Twain" denote a unified Victorian American to the extent that any human being can be unified, no more and no less complicated, let alone divided, than many of his contemporaries. His pseudonym does not embody an attempt to escape from his other self, or a fundamental internal division. Although he was a man of many inconsistencies, they do not add up to a split personality; on the contrary, they are an expression of the usual way in which people in Western culture, particularly in the nineteenth and twentieth centuries, respond to the pressures of daily life and play out their multiple desires and allegiances.

In this biography, until Samuel Clemens reaches the age of twenty-eight in 1863, I refer to him by his name at birth; thereafter as Mark Twain or simply Twain. Some Twain scholars have argued that "Mark Twain" as a name exists only as a single entity, an artificial construct that should not be divided into a first and a last name. But in the late twentieth century, "Twain" became a last name. American common sense usage makes anything else seem awkward and pedantic.

And that singular name has come to stand for much more than his individual life. Mark Twain is one of those rare instances in which the uniqueness of an historical figure has become emblematic of wide-ranging, deeply resonating issues. As an American writer, Twain is singular in that throughout his life and almost a hundred years after his death the articulation of only his name evokes unforgettable historical and emotional images, ideas, and actions. He is a cultural signifier. The European and American nineteenth century has a short but impressive list of such figures, among them Napoleon, Lincoln, Dickens, Marx, and Freud. But only one nineteenth-century American writer has that sort of name recognition. Like those of the other historical figures on any such short list, his name instantly evokes and is inseparable from issues so important that they have helped shape our view of ourselves and of our national self-definition. In the phrase of his good friend William Dean Howells, he is "the Lincoln of our literature." His name has taken on epic, almost mythic proportions.

In his literary works, Mark Twain had his fingers to the pulsebeat of who we were and are and made that available to us in ways that make it possible to say, as a metaphor, that Mark Twain wrote aspects of America into existence. Of course, it would still be there if he had never existed. But it would stand in our minds in a different way. He changed our view of ourselves, and there is an entity called "Mark Twain's America," whether one uses the phrase or not. That America is one we recognize as ours even in the twenty-first century, and images from Twain's writings help us to see it. *Tom Sawyer, Life on the Mississippi*, and *The Gilded Age* frame the issues and the images of the country versus the city, of the change from an idealistic, aesthetically attractive and pastoral Jeffersonian America to the post–Civil War, urbanized, industrialized, and corrupt Gilded Age; Twain's version of Hannibal, Missouri, became the archetype of small-town American pastoral life; *Roughing It* and other works provide a grid for America's preoccupation with East versus West and with our sometimes destructive love/hate relationship with nature—the tension between American idealism and American materialism, between the desire for a moral community and the desire to get rich, individually and collectively. The American fascination with inventions and the interplay between greed and creativity, between commercialism and art, he embodied in his life and writings. *Innocents Abroad* captures the special flavor of American religious hypocrisy and puritan narrowness; *A Connecticut Yankee in King Arthur's Court* epitomizes American can-do capitalism, our love affair with technology, and the dangers of technology run amok and its potential to destroy civilization. In a series of scalding essays late in the nineteenth and early in the twentieth century, Twain took up the cudgels against McKinley and Roosevelt's transformation of the old American republic into an imperial power, and on one inescapable central issue, race, he not only provided images but helped shape the ongoing debate. *The Adventures of Huckleberry Finn* still raises hackles, especially of those who cannot read its ironic use of the word "nigger." Twain strongly believed that white America owed reparations to black America: "Whenever a colored man commits an unright action," he wrote to a friend in May 1883, "upon his head is the guilt of only about one tenth of it, and upon your heads and mine and the rest of the white race lies fairly and justly the other nine tenths of the guilt." No other American writer has shown us ourselves so vividly and enduringly.

CHAPTER ONE

THE BEST BOY YOU HAD

1835–1847

1.

Two people dominated the early years of Samuel Clemens, one a warm presence, the other a cold absence. His mother, Jane Lampton Clemens, bore her burdens with cheerful lightheartedness and energetic imagination. She loved Fourth of July parades as much as she enjoyed funeral processions. Apparently she had a sense of fun but, according to her son, no sense of humor at all. She had a mincing, sharp tongue. She was incapable of recognizing wit or irony. His father, John Marshall Clemens, bore his burdens in melancholy and silence; he said very little to any of his children, and what he said reinforced his austere manner. He was not in favor of mischief, even childish mischief. He seemed not to find it easy to laugh, and neither parent was physically affectionate. Their eldest son recalled that at the death of one of their children they had kissed, a singular memory. The only time Sam Clemens ever saw any member of his family touch another, let alone embrace, was when John Marshall Clemens, on his deathbed, called his daughter to his side and put his arms around her. And though of course he and the family could not know it, when Samuel Clemens was born, John Marshall Clemens had most of his life behind him. He died at the age of almost forty-nine, when Sam was eleven years old. As a small boy, Sam had learned to keep out of his father's way. Now his father stayed permanently out of his.

When Mark Twain's paternal grandfather's family came to America from England is unclear, though probably no later than the mid-eighteenth century. His grandfather, Samuel B. Clemens, makes his first appearance in the historical record in Virginia in October 1797, in preparation for his marriage to Pamela Goggin. Nothing certain is known about him or his family before that date. The family believed that Clemens and Clements were the same family in England and that a Clements ancestor had served on the tribunal condemning Charles I to death. It was a trump card that the anti-aristocratic Mark Twain liked to throw down on the table of other people's pretensions, especially since his riposte had a radical and humorously bloody edge to it.

Jane Clemens, at least privately, enjoyed boasting that her family had aristocratic lineage. Many of the American Lamptons came to believe, without evidence except a similarity in name, that they were related to the English Earls of Durham. For many of the Lamptons it was not a tentative belief. At best, the main use the Clemens ancestry had in a boasting contest, once one put aside the king killer, was that a spurious argument could be made that the Virginia Clemenses were FFV (belonged to the First Families of Virginia), and thus the nineteenth-century Clemenses were akin to colonial royalty. "My mother knew all about the Clemenses of Virginia, and loved to aggrandize them to me," Twain recalled. But the record is clear that they were nothing of the sort. In fact, the longest and most distinguished lineage can be traced on Samuel Clemens' grandmother's side. The Goggin family, whose ancestors were tradespeople in England in the sixteenth century, came to Virginia in the seventeenth century and married into a Quaker family, the Moormans. The Moormans rose from farmers to wealthy planters. In 1775 Charles Moorman manumitted thirty-three of his slaves. In 1773, his daughter, Rachel Moorman, Twain's great-grandmother, married a non-Quaker, Stephen Goggin, Jr., whose father, an Anglican, had emigrated from Queen's County, Ireland. Their daughter, Pamela Goggin, born in 1775, married Samuel B. Clemens in Bedford County in 1797, the first recorded appearance of any Virginia Clemens. Of their five children, John Marshall Clemens was the first.

In 1802, Samuel B. Clemens paid $1,000 for four hundred acres in Bedford County, Virginia. In the summer of 1804, he sold all the land, part of it to his friend Samuel Hancock, and settled in the newly formed Mason County of West Virginia, where he bought a 199-acre farm. The next year, as he was taking part in a house-raising, a log being pushed up an incline slipped backward and crushed him to death against a tree stump. John Marshall was five years old. His mother moved her five children to Kentucky, where she had been invited to keep house for her brother, though she had been left some land in West Virginia and about a half-dozen slaves. In 1809 she married Simon Hancock, nephew of the friend who had bought some of Samuel Clemens' Virginia land, who had been her suitor before she had married.

Young John Marshall, born August 11, 1798, apparently did not have a warm relationship with his stepfather, who required that his wife's children by her first marriage repay him for his costs in raising them. At eleven years of age he began work as a clerk. In 1821, court commissioners liquidated Samuel Clemens' remaining estate, consisting mostly of ten slaves. Pamela renounced her share in favor of her children. John Marshall paid his stepfather $884.33 out of his share and shortly afterward liquidated the rest of his indebtedness. Soon he began to study law under a Columbia, Kentucky, attorney, and he was licensed to practice in 1822.

An attractive, fun-loving belle of the ball in Columbia, Jane Lampton was proud of her family and happy with life. On the maternal side, her ancestors were Montgomerys and Caseys, Protestants from Queen's County, Ireland, who migrated to Virginia and then to Kentucky. Her mother, Jane Montgomery, was the daughter of a distinguished Revolutionary War colonel. Her father, Benjamin Lampton, brought the Earls of Durham distinction to the marriage.

In 1818, when Jane Lampton was fifteen, her mother died. Her father remarried the next year. Jane's Columbia life continued to have its social pleasures, including recreation on the party and dancing circuit to as far away as Lexington. In 1823, according to a story she told her son, she fell in love with a shy young man who lived in a nearby town. He seemed to be in love with her, and everyone they knew, she thought, was aware of the relationship. The mores of the time, though, made it difficult for them to be alone together. Jane hoped for the opportunity. When her uncle tried to arrange that they be alone, she rejected his clumsy attempt as embarrassing. Soon after, her suitor, convinced that Jane had rejected him, so she thought, left Kentucky. Eager to show the world that she was not disappointed by his departure, and apparently in a pique, she accepted a proposal of marriage from John Marshall Clemens.

That they had known each other for some time is clear. The lawyer under whom John Marshall clerked was her cousin. Jane's uncle headed the Columbia volunteer fire department to which John Marshall belonged. Her father and uncle employed young Mr. Clemens to act as their agent in selling property in Tennessee. It is not clear, though, that they were anything more than acquaintances, and the austere, gaunt-looking, hard-working John Marshall Clemens was not likely to have flirted with Jane, nor she with him. She later claimed that she did not love him in the least. But, with or without love, the marriage proceeded, and with the usual consequences.

Married in May 1823, she gave birth, in July 1825, to their first son, Orion. Soon after, the young lawyer, with wife and baby, moved to the town of Gainsboro in undeveloped Jackson County in north-central Tennessee's Cumberland Mountains, just south of the Kentucky border, where Jane's cousin, Dr. Nathan Montgomery, lived. Perhaps they went for John Marshall's health; he may have been tubercular. There he struggled unsuccessfully to earn a living as a lawyer and had only modest success as the owner of a general goods store. In 1827, Jane gave birth to a daughter, Pamela, in Jamestown, Fentress County, Tennessee, a little east of Gainsboro. In 1831 they moved to nearby Pall Mall, almost on the Kentucky border. It was a far cry from Columbia, let alone the civility and culture of Lexington, and Jane Clemens was to do very little more dancing in her life. In late 1828 she gave birth to a son, Pleasant Hannibal, who lived for three months; in 1830 a daughter, Margaret; in 1832 a son, Benjamin.

The topic of entitlement now began to have even added cogency in the Clemens-Lampton household. In the late 1820s and early 1830s, John Marshall bought for about $400 approximately seventy thousand acres of land in Fentress County, south of Jamestown. The cost and the amount of land are estimates based on family oral history. The soil was poor and the terrain hilly; access was limited to dirt paths. John Marshall, though, envisioned the press of heavy immigration one day making the land valuable. Probably some of the initial purchase was made with the last of his inheritance from his father; additional parcels were purchased over many years. Apparently John Marshall expended with each purchase all the cash he had and bought again when he had accumulated more. At his death, he put his hope in the future value of the land to his descendants. He died "house poor," scraping for dollars, but his descendants, he expected, would be rich. His children lived, more or less, under his injunction never to sell. At different times the Tennessee land became for them, especially for Sam, a bitter joke, a psychological albatross, and an unheeded reminder of the destructiveness of unrealistic and uncontrollable dreams of wealth.

The Clemens family had a hardscrabble existence in Tennessee. Times were hard, and America was in transition. Industry and foreign trade were beginning to become profitable, and manufacturers in New England and owners of fertile land in Virginia did well. But people at the edge of the wilderness, earning their living by farming in rocky, soil-poor country or by providing goods and services to their rural communities, usually lived poorly. Cash was scarce. The barter system prevailed, if one had something to barter. And President Andrew Jackson's successful attempt to close the Bank of the United States, the most stable bank in the country, dried up credit and drained cash from the national economy. In 1834 there was a nationwide financial crash. Small loans became almost impossible to get. Twain believed that before the crash his father was worth not less than $3,500 separate from the value of the land, afterward "less than one-fourth of that amount." With most of John Marshall's cash tied up in non-income-producing land, the family lived at a level far below what it considered its due. There was no legal business, and the grocery and general goods store barely managed, so they took in boarders. What to do? Where to go? John Marshall was "a proud man, a silent, austere man, and not a person likely to abide among the scenes of his vanished grandeur and be the target for public commiseration."

In the late 1820s, Jane's father, Benjamin Lampton, a successful farmer and storekeeper in Columbia, had visited Missouri, which, in 1821, had become the twenty-fourth state as one of the conditions of the Missouri Compromise: Missouri had been admitted as a slave state, Maine as a free state. John Marshall Clemens had inherited eight slaves, seven of whom he had sold for economic reasons. One slave girl remained to help in the household. Jane Lampton's family had of course owned slaves, and Jane was used to household and field slaves, though slavery was not the economic basis of farming in Kentucky to the extent it was further south. But it was an integral part of the lives and minds of Samuel Clemens' parents; the Lamptons, like most visitors and migrants from southern states, found Missouri's slave-state status familiar and congenial. One of Benjamin's brothers had settled in Boone County, Missouri, about five years before. John Quarles, married to Jane's favorite sister, a shopkeeper, a farmer, and also an ex-Virginian, decided to strike out for Missouri also.

Four hundred miles northwestward from north-central Tennessee to St. Louis, one went on foot or horseback or by wagon to the Ohio River on the Kentucky-Ohio border, and from there by flatboat to St. Louis. And that was, by and large, far enough. Beyond Missouri were the territories, the prairies, vast emptiness, huge deserts, high mountains, Indian country and Mexican possessions, Texas and California. Few travelers and fewer migrants went that far, because there was little economic motivation to do so. Missouri, which was far enough away, had good soil and ample water.

With his wife and ten children, John Quarles made the journey. So too did Benjamin Lampton, with his second wife and their children. Both families settled in the small town of Florida, Missouri, in Monroe County, eighty-five miles northwest of St. Louis, about forty-five miles from the Mississippi River, where they opened a grocery and general goods store. Florida had been laid out in 1831 on high ground between the forks of Salt River. Like thousands of new towns, it was more hope than reality: the settler's desire for community, the real estate agent's dream of wealth. Population, about one hundred people. There were a few sawmills on the unnavigable river, the houses were made of logs, the few streets unpaved. America west of the Mississippi was still on paper, so to speak, diagrams and drawings on entrepreneurial maps. Settlers and profiteers bought and sold promises and hope. Each new town imagined itself a great metropolis of the future. Land scams abounded. Settlers who bought property sight unseen often found something very different from what they thought they had purchased.

In early 1834, when Quarles arrived, Florida looked promising. There was the expectation that the Fork River would be made navigable. There was fine "straight-grained" timber. The land was fertile, much of it government owned and cheap. Unlike John Marshall, Quarles was outgoing, good-humored, and optimistic. A Mason and free-thinker, as was his brother-in-law, he carried his unconventionality lightly, with jokes, hearty hospitality, and humorous tall tales. The store he founded was successful, a popular gathering place for residents and travelers. Soon he wrote to his Tennessee relatives about the attractions of Missouri. He urged his brother-in-law to make a new start. Life in north-central Tennessee was flat, stale, certainly unprofitable. Jane probably was eager to be reunited with her favorite sister. Soon John Marshall Clemens sold everything but the seventy thousand acres and whatever of use they could take with them. He may have had as much as a thousand dollars in cash. In spring of 1835, with the three youngest children in a small carriage drawn by two horses, and the others, including the slave girl, on foot, they set out northward to Columbia, Kentucky, where they visited family and old friends. Then to the Ohio River, where they took a steamboat to St. Louis. With a cholera epidemic devastating the city, they decided to go on immediately. At the beginning of June, they arrived in Florida, Missouri. The Quarleses welcomed them with open arms. Jane Clemens probably was not aware that she was about one month pregnant; the infant had been conceived in transit. Six months later, on November 30, 1835, she gave birth to a son, whom they named Samuel Langhorne Clemens.

2.

Jane Clemens had lost one infant after a three-month struggle, and she thought it likely she would lose this one too. "A lady came in one day and looked at him she turned to me and said you don't expect to raise that babe do you. I said I would try. But he was a poor looking object to raise." The first winter threatened to be his last. No doubt they kept him well wrapped and close to the fireplace in their rented two-room clapboard house on South Mill Street, where the baby had been delivered by a local doctor. Apparently there was no life-threatening illness, but the infant was fragile and ate poorly. When he got through the first year, then the second, his odds improved considerably.

What John Marshall did for a living in Florida is not entirely clear, except that initially he worked with his brother-in-law in his grocery and general goods store, apparently as his partner. Within a year or so John Marshall set up his own similar store close by, where his eldest son, Orion, then eleven, became the clerk. Perhaps both men assumed there was room in a growing town at a crossroads of trade for two such stores. In any case, John Marshall's real hope was to start practicing law again. As he had done in Tennessee, he began using his cash and perhaps his credit to buy land. Within weeks of arrival, he purchased two parcels from the government, 120 acres east of town and, further east, 80 acres of timber on the border of Monroe and Ralls Counties. Two weeks later he bought from the government another 40 acres. In September 1835 he bought three acres between this last parcel and the center of town, on North Mill Street, where he hoped someday to build a substantial house. How much he paid for each parcel is unknown, but government property often went from twenty cents or so to two dollars an acre. Still, it was an extraordinary flurry of acquisition by a new man in town whose sources of future income were yet to be determined. It suggests that John Marshall saw himself as having gotten in on the ground floor. The Salt River, he thought, would open to Mississippi River traffic. More settlers would come, building plots would be in demand, timber would be valuable. In May 1836, he paid his father-in-law $1,050 for a house on East Main Street.

One of the town's most accomplished residents, with an education that made him a likely leader, John Marshall was appointed in 1837 to head a board of sixteen commissioners to sell stock in the Salt River Navigation Company, whose mission it was to dredge, deepen, and clear the river. In February 1837, he chaired a state-incorporated commission to promote a railroad from Florida to Paris, Missouri, the Monroe County seat. That same year he and John Quarles became trustees of the newly created Florida Academy, probably the first local school. In November 1837, he was sworn into office as a judge in the Monroe County Court, an elected four-year position, mainly probating wills, at a salary of two dollars a day while court was in session. Nonetheless, another countrywide financial recession beginning in 1837 and lasting until 1840 made times hard. The family's needs were provided for by the profits from the store and whatever John Marshall earned as a lawyer. And also from the sale of wagons that he built himself: apparently he was inventive, mechanical, and facile with his hands. He now had enough money to build a house in the north side of town. There, in July 1838, Henry, the last child of the family, was born. But before Sam was four, and soon after Henry's first birthday, the family was on the move again.

By 1838 it was clear that the river would never be made navigable and the railroad would not be built. Florida would be cut off indefinitely from access to the county seat, to the Mississippi, to St. Louis, and beyond, and people and freight would be limited to dirt roads. Though the land was rich, water and good timber plentiful, John Marshall was not a farmer. As a lawyer, he needed clients. They were not plentiful even in more thriving towns; in Florida they were few and far between. As a store owner, he needed customers. Perhaps the death in August 1839 of his nine-year-old daughter, Margaret, from "bilious fever," played a role in the timing of the family's departure. It shocked and pained her parents, and it may have emotionally confirmed what reason had already told them was the best thing to do. Three months later John Marshall sold his property in Florida and in Monroe County. He moved his family thirty miles eastward, to Hannibal, Missouri, in Marion County, a new riverside town between two bluffs overlooking the Mississippi.

Until his death, in March 1847, John Marshall fared just well enough to keep his family decently, though far less well than he and they had anticipated. Hannibal, indeed, had its attractions for those in Florida, including its close proximity and especially its promise as a river port. Other Florida residents moved there at the same time as the Clemenses, including their family doctor and the local schoolteacher. It was a likely place to go, a lateral move, so to speak. John Marshall hoped that Hannibal would become the chief commercial center of northeast Missouri. When the Clemenses arrived, it was already, comparatively, a metropolis, with about 450 people, four times the population of Florida.

The town had been plotted in 1819 and incorporated in 1838. Land was offered cheaply to prospective settlers. A mail service was established. Local Indians were driven away. By 1839 it had a newspaper, a bookstore, a school, a few churches, a tannery, a tobacco factory, sawmills, pork slaughterhouses, and freight agents, and it was on its way to becoming the shipping port for the rich farmland to the west. John Marshall had guessed correctly: Hannibal had a future. Within eight years of his arrival, the population had reached 2,500. Stagecoaches went three times a week in every direction. Except during the winter months, daily steamboats brought mail from St. Louis. Illinois was a short ferry ride away. Traffic came downriver from as far away as Minnesota. St. Louis was only 130 miles downstream, and Memphis, Vicksburg, and New Orleans were in a clear line of descent. Transportation eastward was available at the meeting of the Mississippi and the Ohio at Cairo, Illinois. The river seemed both king and queen. Its enemy, the railroad, was still in its infancy.

John Marshall bought a quarter of a city block in the heart of town. It contained a number of wood frame structures at the corner of Hill and Main Streets, including one suitable as a store, another, the Virginia House, a small hotel, adequate as a family residence. He had paid a Hannibal

speculator, Ira Stout, $7,000 for the property, $5,000 of which he had gotten from Stout for the 160 acres of farmland, the 326 acres of timberland,
and the house he owned in Florida. Probably only about $2,000 in cash
changed hands. Some of the $2,000 shortfall he may have made up with
most of his available cash; $747 he borrowed from James A. H. Lampton, a
Florida resident and Jane's half-brother, the son of Benjamin Lampton and
his second wife; $250 he borrowed from James Clemens, Jr., a wealthy St.
Louis resident who believed he was a distant cousin. And he bought on
credit about $2,000 worth of goods from a St. Louis merchant to stock the
general store he soon opened on Main Street, one block above the wharf
and the river. Either John Marshall had overpaid for the property or the
property soon lost value, as events were to reveal. It's likely that he neither
got independent assessments of fair market value for the land he bought or
sold nor attempted to bargain on either end of the transaction. He was now
at least $3,000 in debt, with little to no cash on hand. His fifteen-year-old
son, Orion, was to run the store. John Marshall was to be on the ready for
legal business. One or both of his endeavors needed to show profits quickly,
but neither did.

While four-year-old Sam was finding out what a rich childhood he
could have in Hannibal, his parents and two oldest siblings were discovering how restrictively painful their financially pinched life would be. It
made John Marshall edgy and more withdrawn than he had ever been,
even though, as he had been in Florida, he soon became one of the town's
leading citizens. In September 1841 he sat on a circuit court jury; probably in 1844 he was elected justice of the peace, which included acting as
coroner and assisting in court functions, for which he was paid on a per
item basis. From summer 1844 to summer 1845, he chaired committees
for civic improvements such as paving roads, bringing a Masonic college to
Hannibal, and creating the Hannibal Library Institute, of which he would
soon be president, with 70 stockholders and 450 books. Deeply respectful
of education, in 1845 he paid for and attended a series of twenty lectures
on grammar taught by a traveling professor and, for the benefit of Orion,
who was working in St. Louis, took down "the substance of every lecture
as I have done this, and forward them to you, as punctually as I may find
safe hands to carry them to you." That Clemens was anticlerical had no
harmful effect on his civic prominence. As justice of the peace, he
presided over the town's first murder trial in September 1843. He ended a

disturbance in his courtroom by banging a violent defendant on the head with a hammer. In November 1846 he became a candidate in the August 1847 election for clerk of the circuit court.

From the start, though, John Marshall's legal shingle did not attract much attention. And the rental property on the Clemenses' one quarter of a city block was often vacant. In 1841 John Marshall transferred the title to James Kerr, the St. Louis merchant from whom he had bought merchandise on credit. A year later the entire property, divided into smaller parcels, was sold for $3,920, little more than half what Clemens had paid for it. The family moved, in 1847, to a modest clapboard on a small lot on Hill Street that James Clemens, the St. Louis lawyer, had bought for $330. The general store did poorly, at best. Orion, a preoccupied reader who loved to speculate and argue about political and religious issues, was taken out of the store and apprenticed to the local newspaper. Paying for any further education beyond the local school was out of the question, though John Marshall wished he could buy the *Hannibal Journal* and put Orion in charge, a gift to his undergifted son. Instead, Orion was sent in 1842 to St. Louis to learn to be a printer. His father's "meagre pickings" as justice of the peace sustained the family, but barely. Ira Stout, the speculator who had outsmarted John Marshall in 1839, had apparently also inveigled him into standing surety for a loan. When Stout defaulted, he left Clemens with another small debt. Desperate, John Marshall took a steamboat into the Deep South in early winter 1842, where he may have tried to dispose of his one remaining slave, though the "Charley" for sale may indeed have been a horse, since the trade produced only ten barrels of tar. The cost of the expensive trip became another debit in the family's account book. Jane Clemens later reproached John Marshall for the waste of money. With a "hopeless expression," he responded, "I am not able to dig in the streets."

To his children John Marshall seemed always tacitly to convey the message that he was silently suffering unwarranted slings and arrows. They were not to talk about it, and they were not to touch. "Stern, unsmiling," his son was to write, he "never demonstrated affection for wife or child. . . . Ungentle of manner toward his children, but always a gentleman in his phrasing—and never punished them—a look was enough, and more than enough." Throughout their shared years in Hannibal, Sam Clemens felt that his father was not only a stranger but a repressive reproof to his boyhood life. He seemed an enemy to fun and high spirits, with a sharp tongue and a narrow legal mind. In addition, John Marshall suffered from "mysterious illnesses," one of which may have been tuberculosis. Each spring, he had painful attacks of what he called "sunpain," whatever that was. For as long as his children knew him, he daily took doses of a patent medicine that he bought by the carton, a widely used remedy of now unknown content for assorted ills, which perhaps created its own set of pathological side effects more damaging than any benefits it provided. Thin and gaunt, unable to rise beyond daily economic struggle, no matter what he tried, John Marshall stiffened even more than his native rigidity required. Many years later, Sam said of his father, "My own knowledge of him amounted to little more than an introduction."

3.

For the first four years of Sam Clemens' life in Florida, and then for some ten more in Hannibal, Jane Clemens hovered over her sickly son. A firm believer in homeopathic medicine, she thought doctors a last resort. In Hannibal in those days "every old woman was a doctor, and gathered her own medicines in the woods." Jane was especially fond of castor oil, with molasses added to make the noxious taste more palatable. Water cures had become fashionable, and Jane Clemens liked to try new remedies. Remembering a time when he was about nine years old, Twain later recalled, "my mother used to stand me up naked in the back yard every morning and throw buckets of cold water on me, just to see what effect it would have. . . . And then, when the dousing was over, she would wrap me up in a sheet wet with ice water and then wrap blankets around that and put me into bed. I never realized that the treatment was doing me particular good physically. But it purified me spiritually. For pretty soon after I was put into bed I would get up a perspiration that was something worth seeing. Mother generally put a life preserver in bed with me. And when finally she let me out and unwound the sheet, I remember that it was all covered with yellow color."

But the homeopathic remedies or the water cure didn't always work. Sometimes "they left me so low that they had to pull me out by means of the family doctor." Jane called her former Florida neighbor, Dr. Meredith, who concocted his own remedies, often calomel and rhubarb rubs followed by bleeding and mustard plaster applications. Fortunately, nature's recuperative powers often saved the patient. When these "scientific" methods proved unavailing, Jane Clemens put her faith, as did many, in folklore and magic. For dental problems, they went to a "faith doctor" whose specialty was toothaches. There was also an "Indian doctor" who performed wonders with charms and incantations. There was almost no possible remedy that Jane Clemens would not try, though she usually kept her perspective and psychological sharpness about herself and her increasingly fractious son. The castor oil and the cold water may have been as much agents of punishment as cure. "I asked my mother about this . . . in her eighty-eighth year. . . . 'I suppose that during all that time you were uneasy about me?' 'Yes, the whole time.' 'Afraid I wouldn't live?' After a reflective pause . . . 'No—afraid you would.' "

Death seemed a continuous threat, first because of Sam's frailness and then as a reality imprinted on his consciousness by life history and religious psychology. A sleepwalker from an early age, he would act out his nightmares, and once came in a trance into the sitting room and tried to sit on one of Orion's boots. Another time, having dreamt that robbers were stealing his sheets and blankets, he stripped them from the bed and hid them. Then he awakened, cold and crying. When his brother Benjamin died at ten years old in May 1842, Sam held his mother's hand by the side of the corpse as she moaned uncontrollably. Jane Clemens made each child feel the dead boy's cheek to try "to make them understand the calamity that had befallen." Her church taught that sin permeated the human character and community. Unlike her husband, she was an active Christian, mainly Presbyterian, though she would attend any church that interested her or was convenient.

Though Jane's churchly interests were more social than theological, frontier Calvinism dominated her family's mentality and was the hallmark of Hannibal's views about ultimate issues. Very few doubted that sinners would be punished by the hand of a rigorous God, that he controlled circumstances and natural forces as instruments of his righteous wrath. In Hannibal, Jane Clemens at first attended the Old Ship of Zion, a Methodist church in a shabby little brick building by the public square, where Sam went to the basement Sunday school. In 1843, she joined the Hannibal Presbyterian Church, with a steeple high above North Fourth Street. Sermon rhetoric was hortatory and hot, in the inflated evangelical style. Fire and brimstone were imminent. Satan was real, and he visited Hannibal often.

Jane insisted that her children attend church regularly, and by the time Sam was six he was aware of sin and his own sinfulness. Vulnerable both to Satan and ministerial rhetoric, he felt guilty for his feelings and thoughts. Any deviation from strict adherence to the Ten Commandments and Calvinistic mores would be punished. Sin flourished in the rough, often blasphemous tongues of the townsmen, whom Sam began to emulate. Sin was in his own mind, partly because some sinful things, such as inattention in church, disobeying adults, practical joke playing, tricking other people for his own advantage, and lying to escape blame, were unavoidable. His mind just did it. His tongue worked on its own. His impulses were irresistible. As became a young sinner, Sam had a special interest in Satan. He asked his Sunday school teacher questions about Eve in the garden, wondering "if he had ever heard of another woman who, being approached by a serpent, would not excuse herself and break for the nearest timber." Twain recalled, "He did not answer my question, but rebuked me for inquiring into matters above my age and comprehension."

Though in later years he may have exaggerated the extent of his boyhood skepticism about religious claims and given them a humorous edge, undoubtedly his emotional vulnerability and tendency toward intellectual questioning coexisted uneasily. The former he associated with the terrors of the night, the latter with daylight reassurances. In the dark he feared that Satan would come to claim him as his own. In the daylight, he had the resources to deal with his Sunday school teacher. He had been "meditating a biography" of Satan, with whom he had an almost sympathetic fascination inseparable from terror, "and was grieved to find there were [no] materials." His teacher cheered him up "by saying there was a whole vast ocean of materials. . . . Yet he made me put away my pen; he would not let me write the history of Satan. Why? Because, as he said, he had suspicions—suspicions that my attitude in this matter was not reverent. . . . He said that anyone who spoke flippantly of Satan would be frowned upon by the religious world and also be brought to account." Often, in fear and trembling, during the dark hours, Sam Clemens agreed with him.

"Special judgment" explained seemingly unwarranted deaths. One of his playmates fell from a flatboat on which he had been playing and drowned. It was on a Sunday. That seemed to Sam and his friends no accident. "Being loaded with sin, he went to the bottom like an anvil." None of the boys in Hannibal slept that night. They were all, so to speak, "loaded with sin." Under his bedclothes that night, as a violent storm thundered, Sam quivered in fear. It seemed likely that he would be next. Thunder and lightning, emissaries of God's wrath, terrified him. He cursed the drowned boy for calling special attention to Hannibal, since the punishing angel, once in the vicinity, might decide to look around for other equally deserving boys. News of the death of one of the town drunks, Injun Joe, came "just at bedtime on a summer night, when a prodigious storm . . . that turned the streets and lanes into rivers caused me to repent and resolve to lead a better life. . . . Satan had come to get Injun Joe." Grim theological pummelings, the adult world's explanatory key to all life's miseries, were continuous. If things went wrong, you were to blame. You had offended an all-powerful God whose ways were beyond human understanding. God used death as his exemplary weapon to remind sinners to keep to the straight and narrow. Willfully self-expressive, Sam tried to keep in balance what seemed to him the two powerful forces of life, communal religious prohibitions and his instinctive delight in confrontation, in opposition, in defiance, in thinking and doing it his way.

On the one hand, he had a sense of leading an undeservedly charmed life; on the other, he worried that one day the balance would be righted and he would get what was coming to him. In 1844, as he was playing on a log supposedly attached to a raft, it tilted him into Bear Creek. A nonswimmer, he was about to go down for the third time when a slave woman who happened to come by grasped his fingers, the only part of him above water, and pulled him out. A week later, he was about to drown again. A local apprentice "plunged in and dived, pawed around on the bottom and found me, and dragged me out, emptied the water out of me, and I was saved again. I was drowned seven times after that before I learned to swim— once in Bear Creek and six times in the Mississippi." Everyone thought him "a cat in disguise." He began to believe that some people are born lucky, some not. When he made bad decisions later in life, he often made bad situations worse because he "couldn't shake off the confidence of a life time" in his luck.

Sometimes it seemed better to get the worst over with than to live in uncertainty. Impulsive and impatient, he had little tolerance for waiting. On one occasion he pursued resolution with almost suicidal determination. The incident is recounted twice, once placing it in 1845, when he was almost ten years old, the other in the summer of 1847, four months after his father's death. In both accounts Hannibal was afflicted with a measles epidemic. Jane Clemens, fearing that Pamela or Sam or Henry would get the near-fatal disease, took every conceivable precaution to prevent her children becoming infected. "For a time, a child died almost every day. The village was paralyzed with fright, distress, despair. Children that were not smitten with the disease were imprisoned in their homes. . . . There were no cheerful faces, there was no music, there was no singing but of solemn hymns, no voice but of prayer, no romping was allowed, no noise, no laughter, the family moved spectrally about on tiptoe, in a ghostly hush. I was a prisoner. My soul was steeped in this awful dreariness—and in fear. . . . Life on these miserable terms was not worth living, and at last I made up my mind to get the disease and have it over, one way or the other."

Sneaking into the house of his friend Will Bowen, sick with measles, he went upstairs, undetected, and crept into bed with Will. Suddenly Mrs. Bowen discovered him. Frightened, furious, she pulled him out, scolding him ferociously and sending him home. Determined, he tried again. Will was too sick to notice that he had a companion. When once more Mrs. Bowen discovered him, he was sure it was too late. Soon he had the measles, and for two weeks he seemed about to die. The doctor gave up on him. The tearful family gathered at his bedside to see him off. "They were all crying, but that did not affect me. I took but the vaguest interest in it, and that merely because I was the center of all this emotional attention and was gratified by it and felt complimented." The doctor put small sacks of hot ashes all over him. To everyone's astonishment, he started to get better and was soon entirely well.

4.

Sam was gradually discovering that a segment of the community was not getting what a just society should provide. But it was a slow awakening, not to be realized in any articulated overview until he was an adult, though his later intellectual awareness of slavery as an evil institution had its seeds in his sympathy for the black people of his Hannibal world. "In my schoolboy days I had no aversion to slavery," he later wrote. "I was not aware that there was anything wrong with it." As a slave state, Missouri took seriously the laws of contract and property that governed the status of slaves. In 1841 John Marshall Clemens had no hesitation, as foreman of a jury, sentencing three Illinois abolitionists to twelve years in prison for an attempt to "steal" slaves. In 1844, when John Marshall sued to collect a debt, "he had the sheriff seize a nine-year-old slave girl and sell her at public auction to satisfy the judgment." On the Missouri side of the river, slaves were slaves; on the Illinois side, they were subject to recapture as fugitives. And to the north and west were free states and territories. Of course not everyone on the Missouri side approved of slavery, and not everyone on the Illinois side did not. In the main, though, people accepted the customs and the laws of the towns and states in which they lived. And Hannibal, in which slaves composed one fourth of the population, had no use for abolitionists. Most of its residents, like the Clemens family, had come from slave states. "Kind-hearted and compassionate" as he recalled his mother being, he thought "she was not conscious that slavery was a bald, grotesque, and unwarrantable usurpation." Southern churches preached that slavery was sanctioned by the Bible and God. To favor emancipation was to be a traitor to both God's law and man's.

As a border state in a temperate climate, Missouri, especially north of St. Louis, had less pro-slavery fervor than the Deep South and less economic need for slaves. Though Missouri's pro-slavery ideology might have been widespread, Missourians in general felt less compelled to dehumanize slaves as individuals. There was indeed a slave market in Hannibal where they were regularly sold when an owner needed money, especially when an estate was being settled. But selling slaves away from their families was frowned on. You had the legal right to do it, but it wasn't the right thing to do. "The 'nigger trader,' " Mark Twain later reminisced, "was loathed by everybody. He was regarded as a sort of human devil who bought and conveyed poor helpless creatures to hell—for to our whites and blacks alike the Southern plantation was simply hell; no milder name could describe it. If the threat to sell an incorrigible slave 'down the river' would not reform him, nothing would—his case was past cure." Twain remembered seeing "a dozen black men and women chained to one another, once, and lying in a group on the pavement, awaiting shipment to the Southern slave market." Slave traders made regular sweeps through Hannibal, looking for slaves to buy or runaways to reclaim, and the riverboats going south to St. Louis, where there was a major market, and then all the way downriver, often carried human cargo.

When he could no longer afford to own slaves, John Marshall hired them from their owners by the year, usually from farmers like his brother-in-law, John Quarles. The children of slaves were slaves, so reproduction was encouraged. The Clemens household hired a young girl to do the housework, a grown woman to cook and wash, and "an able-bodied man" for heavy work. They were never too poor for that. And frontier democracy deemphasized wealth; the Clemenses could hold their heads up high by virtue of John Marshall's professional stature. "There were grades of society—people of good family, people of unclassified family, people of no family. Everybody knew everybody, and was affable to everybody, and nobody put on any visible airs; yet the class lines were clearly drawn and the familiar social life of each class was restricted to that class." Slaves were classless, beyond caste; everyone could associate with them, within the rules for such associations. A free black person, though, was an abomination, an affront to both class and nature. On the one hand, any touch of black blood, no matter how small, made a person black. On the other, mulattos were commonplace, the result of black-white sexual relations, one of the defining elements of American slave culture. Hannibal's was "mild domestic slavery," Twain recalled, "not the brutal plantation article. Cruelties were very rare, and exceedingly and wholesomely unpopular. . . . It is commonly believed that an infallible effect of slavery was to make such as lived in its midst hard hearted. I think it had no such effect. . . . I think it stupified everybody's general humanity, as regarded the slave, but stopped there." Still, even slaves in Missouri attempted to escape northward to safety. There were safe houses and the Underground Railroad, though the river, a conduit to freedom, flowed in the wrong direction. From free state to free state the law was inconsistent. National law required the return of slaves, but not every community or individual obeyed. On the Hannibal side of the river, the law was rigorously enforced. Not so in Illinois. In the summer before his twelfth birthday, Sam and a friend found the corpse of a fugitive slave.

And there were vicious incidents, a number of which he could never get out of his mind. When he was ten years old, he saw a man throw a "lump of iron-ore at a slave-man in anger, for merely doing something awkwardly—as if that were a crime. It bounded from the man's skull, and the man fell and never spoke again. He was dead in an hour . . . Nobody in the village approved of that murder, but of course no one said much about it." Once his father, whom he believed a kind and decent man, had whipped their house slave "for impudence to his wife—whipped her with a bridle." During the eleven and a half years of their lives together, John Marshall whipped his son only twice, once for lying, and both times lightly. But Sam frequently saw his father cuff their "harmless slave boy, Lewis, for trifling little blunders and awkwardnesses." Another young slave, hired by John Marshall, who had been separated from his Maryland family, had the habit of "singing, whistling, yelling, whooping, laughing" all day. The noise got on Sam's nerves. One day, having lost his temper, he went to his mother in a rage and said he "couldn't stand it, and *wouldn't* she please shut him up. The tears came into her eyes and her lip trembled," and she said that when poor Sandy sang it showed that he was not remembering his faraway family, but that when he was silent he was thinking of them, " 'and I cannot bear it. He will never see his mother again. . . .' It was a simple speech . . . but it went home, and Sandy's noise was not a trouble to me anymore."

From the summer of his seventh year in 1843 to the summer of his twelfth, he spent summers and some weekends during other seasons at John Quarles' farm, near Florida, some of the happiest days of his childhood. Good food, outdoor exercise, and loving company helped him overcome his sickly start in life. There, playing with his cousins and nurtured by the domestic warmth and comparative affluence of the Quarles household, his respect and affection for black people flourished. They were a vital part of the farm's life, both in the house and in the fields. He never saw a black person mistreated there, and he never saw a black person there who did not carry himself or herself with dignity and self-respect. "It was on the farm," he wrote late in life, "that I got my strong liking for [the black] race and my appreciation of certain of its fine qualities."

To Sam Clemens, the black world was fascinating. It had a freedom from puritan narrowness that he longed to have. With a keen ear, he enjoyed the sounds of black speech, exotically strange and comfortably familiar. Black folklore he found entertaining and powerful, its superstitions embodiments of folk wisdom, its connection with magic a riveting avenue into the mysterious. Black culture's combination of Christianity and superstition caught his attention, a retelling of the Bible that made it both contemporary and transcendent. "In the little log cabin [on the farm] lived a bedridden white-headed slave woman whom we visited daily and looked upon with awe, for we believed she was upward of a thousand years old and had talked with Moses. The younger negroes credited these statistics and had furnished them to us in good faith . . . we believed that she had lost her health in the long desert trip coming out of Egypt and had never been able to get it back again. She had a round bald place on the crown of her head, and we used to creep around and gaze at her in reverent silence, and reflect that it was caused by fright through seeing Pharaoh drowned." He too believed in the power of the story. Storytelling was one of the features of the slave world that impressed him most. John Quarles' trusted older slave Daniel, known as "Uncle Dan'l," "whose head was the best one in the negro quarter, whose sympathies were wide and warm, and whose heart was honest and simple and knew no guile," served as patriarchal mentor to the farm children. Long after Uncle Dan'l was dead, Twain recalled that, "spiritually," he had kept him "welcome company" over the years. He had "staged him in books under his own name and as 'Jim,' and carted him all around—to Hannibal, down the Mississippi on a raft, and even across the desert of Sahara in a balloon." At night, as they gathered around the fireplace in the kitchen, Uncle Dan'l told the wide-eyed children stories from his vast repertoire. "I can see the white and black children grouped on the hearth, with firelight playing on their faces . . . and I can feel again the creepy joy which quivered through me when the time for the ghost story was reached."

The farmhouse, a long rambling structure, was made constantly lively by the family's nine children and by visitors. It took its tone from the warm relationship between Patsy, Jane Clemens' sister, and her husband. Quarles himself was a paragon of conviviality. Their table, in summers set in the semiopen passageway between house and barn, overflowed with good things for the palate, their variety and healthfulness imprinted in Sam's mind with a sharpness that evoked in later years some of Mark Twain's most vivid descriptions. Upstairs, the children bunked together. In the summer, cool country breezes kept them comfortable. In the winter, they went up the bare wooden staircase from the kitchen where they had been listening to Uncle Dan'l's stories around the fire, taking "the turn to the left above the landing" to the bed under "the rafters and the slanting roof," with "the squares of moonlight on the floor, and the white cold world of snow outside, seen through the curtainless windows . . . how snug and cozy one felt under the blankets." He also remembered "how very dark that room was, in the dark of the moon, and how packed it was with ghostly stillness when one woke up by accident away in the night, and forgotten sins came flocking out of the secret chambers of the memory." But, at the farm, sleep returned quickly and daylight came.

During the summer, with his Quarles cousins, he attended a country schoolhouse about three miles from the farm, with twenty-five or so boys and girls. During lunch recess outdoors, they ate the farm-fresh food Aunt Patsy had packed for them. It was the pleasantest school he ever went to, as he recalled. Undoubtedly the workload was light, the games fun. Not far from the farmhouse, beyond the orchard, was a stand of trees set up as swings on which the children swooped skyward and then down and up again. A short walk away was a huge meadow, opening out onto a prairielike landscape. Country life was to young Sam a tactile paradise: "the wild blackberries . . . the taste of maple sap . . . how a prize watermelon looks . . . the crackling sound it makes when the carving knife enters its end . . . the look of green apples and peaches and pears on the trees . . . the look of an apple that is roasting and sizzling on a hearth in a winter's evening." And the summer lightning was not as threatening as it was in Hannibal, not an instrument of God's wrath sent to punish him for his sins. Away from his father's house, he felt less vulnerable, less self-critical. There were, though, some things about life at the Quarleses' that he liked less than others, particularly the night hunts for raccoons and possums "through the black gloom of the wood" where "the game was treed . . . then the lighting of a fire and the felling of the tree, the joyful frenzy of the dogs and the negroes, and the weird picture it all made in the red glare." And clubbing to death endless numbers of pigeons from among the millions who weighed down and broke tree branches during the pigeon season. And rising early, which all his life he objected to and rarely did, to hunt squirrels, prairie chickens, and wild turkeys in the chilly, dismal light.

5.

Like the boys he played with, Sam regularly imagined faraway adventures and great triumphs amid dangers. Hannibal had ample "let's pretend" scenery and sites: the bluffs on either side of town, one rising to Holliday's Hill, the other to the lover's leap. Bear Creek and the river were for swimming in summer, skating in winter. Jackson's Island was for escape into adventures, faraway exploration. One day he and his closest friend, Will Bowen, pushed a large boulder into motion; it rolled down Holliday's Hill, almost killing someone. At Bear Creek the boys swam naked; at Jackson's

Island they camped and pretended they were in the wilderness, the "terri-tories." With John Briggs he raided fruit orchards. John Robards and John Garth, whose sister Helen he adored, were part of the gang, boys given to escapades that sometimes got them in trouble, especially practical jokes that had some helpless townsperson as victim. One playmate, Tom Blankenship, was from the other side of the tracks, "ignorant, unwashed, insufficiently fed; but he was as good a heart as ever any boy had. His lib-erties were totally unrestricted. . . . We liked him; we enjoyed his society. And as his society was forbidden us by our parents . . . we sought and got more of his society than of any other boy's." Jane Clemens heard frequent complaints about her son, and evasive, self-justifying, and often funny ex-planations and excuses from him. Meanwhile, the steamboats on the river provided Sam with endless opportunities for dreaming about the glories of being a captain or, even better, a pilot, of voyaging to distant places that he had learned about in school. When a steamboat whistle announced an im-minent arrival, townspeople rushed to the dock, some with goods to be transported, others eager to be part of the excitement. Often the boys would swim out to "the annual procession of mighty rafts" that came down the river and "have a ride."

His boyhood adventures and rebellions were precisely that; some, though, edged into lifelong habits. Whiskey had only a minor appeal. Smoking, though, enthralled him. In Hannibal, cheap cigars cost ten cents a hundred. Tobacco fields flourished nearby, and the cost of smoking a pipe was limited to acquiring an inexpensive corncob. His friend John Garth's father, who owned a cigar factory, "also had a small shop in the village for the retail sale of his products. He had one brand of cigar which even poverty itself was able to buy. . . . It was called 'Garth's damnedest.' " Chewing tobacco was almost free, smoking and chewing widespread, at all ages and for both sexes. The guardians of rectitude preached against it; it was a dirty vice, a step down the slippery slope toward degeneration and damnation. But nobody considered it bad for one's health, except, perhaps, if you were tubercular. Jane Clemens warned her children against it. John Marshall believed that children should not smoke. That and its widespread popularity among his peers were enough to impel Sam to smoke as soon as he could and as often as he could. When his father asked him if he smoked, he lied. To his astonishment, he was believed, a lesson in the credulity of his parents and adults in general that increased his appreciation of his power to deceive. Behind fences and trees, in town, in the woods, alone or with other boys, smoking gradually became less an adventure and more a habit, the start of a lifelong submission to the pleasures of nicotine. Occasionally something motivated him to attempt reform. In spring 1850, he joined the Cadets of Temperance, a national organization, pledging not to smoke. In exchange, he received a red sash to wear around his waist. The desire to possess the sash had been his sole motivation for joining. Twice a year the cadets paraded. He remained steadfast until he "had gathered the glory of two displays—May Day and the Fourth of July. Then I resigned straightway. . . . I had not smoked for three full months. . . . I was smoking, and utterly happy, before I was thirty steps from the lodge door. I do not know what the brand of cigar was. It was probably not choice, or the previous smoker would not have thrown it away so soon. . . . I smoked that stub without shame." He was happily himself again.

By the time Clemens was fourteen one of the greatest adventures of American nineteenth-century history was under way. He and the other boys dreamed of joining the forty-niners' pursuit of gold in California. They played gold-mining games, searching, as they had done before, for buried treasure. Now, though, they had a material focus, a place to which they too might go and then return home with trunkfuls of gold to dazzle those they had left behind. When John Robards' father took him westward that year, the townspeople watched his cavalcade depart: "We were all on hand to gaze and envy when he returned, two years later, in unimaginable glory— for he had traveled. None of us had ever been forty miles from home. But *he* had crossed the continent. He had been in the gold mines, that fairyland of our imagination." When an older schoolmate, Reuel Gridley, joined the infantry company raised in Hannibal to fight in the Mexican War, Sam yearned for such high adventure. From an early age, travel seemed to Sam the epitome of adventure and glory. And in such distant places, like the gold fields, one could leave behind Hannibal's limitations. One could prove oneself worthy of esteem and at the same time get rich. Imaginary voyages were prelude to real travel.

Sam's education came mostly from experience and reading; the schools he attended were educationally thin. From an early age he avidly read anything he could get his hands on. Like Orion, he was eager to argue views and opinions with anyone. Orion developed an intense passion for telling the world how it might be a better place, Sam for telling the world what was wrong with it. Orion was serious, Sam full of games, mischief, and fun. At age four and a half, he attended Mrs. Horr's school in a log cabin on Main Street, which taught young children of both sexes. On the first day he broke one of the rules. Warned that the second infraction would produce punishment, he could not resist breaking another. A stern New England lady, Mrs. Horr sent him to get a switch. "I was glad she appointed me, for I believed I could select a switch suitable to the occasion with more judiciousness than anybody else," he later wrote. He returned with something short and light; it was not satisfactory. He was sent out for a better. He returned with a slightly more effective switch. Disgusted, Mrs. Horr appointed "a boy with a better judgment than mine in the matter of switches . . . and when he returned with the switch of his choice I recognized that he was an expert."

On his first day of class, Mrs. Horr read the daily selection from the New Testament, a lesson indicating that those who prayed hard enough would receive what they asked for. One of his classmates had a slab of gingerbread, a piece of which Sam very much wanted. He closed his eyes and prayed. Nothing happened. He tried again. When he opened his eyes, the gingerbread was in easy reach, and its owner was looking away. "In all my life I believe I never enjoyed an answer to prayer more than I enjoyed that one; and I was a convert, too. I had no end of wants and they had always remained unsatisfied up to that time, but I meant to supply them and extend them now that I had found out how to do it." Disappointment followed. Prayer soon disappeared from his daily, even weekly, rituals. When his mother, troubled about this, questioned him about the change, he burst into tears, confessing that he had "ceased to be a Christian. She was heartbroken, and asked me why. I said it was because I had found out that I was a Christian for revenue only and I could not bear the thought of that. It was so ignoble. She gathered me to her breast and comforted me. I gathered from what she said that if I would continue in that condition I would never be lonesome."

In Mr. Dawson's upper-level one-room school the children ranged from twelve years to young adulthood. Since literacy was a value often observed in the breach, it was not unusual in frontier schoolhouses to have twelve-year-olds alongside twenty-year-olds who desired to learn to read, doing the same lessons, grammar, composition, spelling, reading, recitation, history, arithmetic, and geography. Everyone had the right to attend the "common" schools, paid for by town taxes, though many did not or did so sporadically. At a Hannibal town meeting, someone proposed shutting down the common school. "An old farmer got up and said: 'I think it's a mistake to try to save money that way. It's not a real saving, for every time you stop a school you will have to build a jail.'" The oldest pupil was twenty-five-year-old Andy Fuqua, the youngest, seven-year-old Nannie Owsley. John Robards' brother George was "eighteen or twenty years old, the only pupil who studied Latin . . . slender, pale, studious . . . his long straight black hair hanging down below his jaws like a pair of curtains on the sides of his face." Sam's hair, like his brother Henry's, was thickly curled. Among the students were the first Jews he had ever seen. "It took me a while to get over the awe of it. To my fancy they were clothed invisibly in the damp and cobwebby mold of antiquity. They carried me back to Egypt, and in my imagination I moved among the Pharaohs and all the shadowy celebrities of that remote age."

Every week he recited, with dramatic emphasis, a poem from the class reader. His classmates mumbled in a monotonous singsong, usually the same two or three selections week after week from Byron, Thomas Campbell, and Felicia Hemens. "Give me liberty or give me death" was a passionately declaimed class favorite, the students more at ease with prose than poetry. Imitation and rote were the dominant pedagogic values. "There was not a line of original thought or . . . expression," Twain told a Hannibal High School graduation class sixty years later. "It would have been thought that there was something the matter with a boy or girl who would attempt such a thing."

Both in and out of school he regularly fell in love. He fell in love with girls his age; he fell in love with older women. He actively wooed a girl who lived down the street. Timid, he began the practice that might overcome shyness until shyness itself became a strategy. "Mary Miller . . . was the first one that furnished me a broken heart. . . . I soon transferred my worship to Artemisia Briggs. . . . When I revealed my passion to her she did not scoff at it. She did not make fun of it. She was very kind and gentle about it. But she was also firm, and said she did not want to be pestered by children. And there was Mary Lacy . . ." Laura Hawkins, whom he had a crush on, was transformed into *Tom Sawyer*'s Becky Thatcher and her name used for a character in *The Gilded Age*. As a writer, in private letters and in published works, Twain was to be limited by characteristic

Victorian reticence about discussions of sexual matters. But the young Sam Clemens was always falling in love with girls; his desire had both its sentimental and erotic elements; and the Mark Twain of later years reveals between the lines of his prose and sometimes explicitly that the natural activities of the sexualized body were a part of his life and his consciousness. What sexual activities he and the other boys of Hannibal engaged in he does not say, though he later remarked that masturbation is the birthright of every Protestant American boy.

6.

A desire for approval and applause started early, perhaps an attempt to impress his unimpressible father, probably to have his mother's love affirmed. At school, he dazzled his teachers with his quick intelligence and his friends with his cleverness and irrepressible mischief-making. He always had ideas, a commodity in short stock in his Hannibal world, some from books, many from his imagination, and he was charmingly affable. With hazel-gray eyes, a slim, medium-sized frame, and a pale complexion that rose into redness at his mass of curly hair, his appearance was pleasant, even attractive. Supported by his own and other peoples' opinion of him, he had high hopes for his future, though he had no ambition, during his Hannibal years, to be anything particular. At Mrs. Horr's school he was provided at a very young age with a leap forward into self-confidence and ambition. "Inspired by something which she honestly took to be prophecy, [Mrs. Horr] exclaimed in the hearing of several persons that I would one day be '*President of the United States, and would stand in the presence of kings unabashed.*' I carried that around personally from house to house, and was surprised and hurt to find how few people there were in that day who had a proper reverence for prophecy, and confidence in it. But no matter— the circumstance bedded in my memory for good and all." His mother, sometimes weary of his mischief-making, worried that his impulsiveness would get him into serious trouble, not high office. No doubt he was, for better and worse, the lively one of the household.

And there were hardly any limits to how far he would go to distinguish himself as special. Jealous of other boys who outclassed him or who had distinctions with which he could not compete, he was always hungry for praise and aware of the power of pretense and illusion. In May 1850, a mesmeric performer came to Hannibal to demonstrate his powers before a paying audience. Soon he was the talk of the village. Sam was at "the age at which a boy is willing to endure all things, suffer all things short of death by fire, if thereby he may be conspicuous and show off before the public"; so, as he later wrote, "when I saw the 'subjects' perform their foolish antics on the platform and make the people laugh and shout and admire, I had a burning desire to be a subject myself." He succeeded in being chosen, determined to outdo one of his peers who had performed successfully. "Upon suggestion I fled from snakes, passed buckets at a fire, became excited over hot steam-boat races, made love to imaginary girls and kissed them, fished from the platform and landed mud cats that outweighed me." He soon defeated his rival. For "Hicks was born honest, I without that encumbrance. . . . Hicks had no imagination, I had a double supply. He was born calm, I was born excited. No vision could start a rapture in him and he was constipated as to language, anyway, but if I saw a vision I emptied the dictionary onto it and lost the remnant of my mind into the bargain." Sam astounded the audience, which included his mother, night after night with his feats. He drove all rivals from the stage.

One day he played hooky and went fishing, on the rationale that if he were damned, as seemed likely, he might as well be punished for doing something pleasurable. When he returned, darkness had set in. The family would be at home. His father would see what he had been doing and where he had been. Punishment would certainly follow. Instead of going home, he climbed through the window of his father's nearby office, where John Marshall conducted his affairs as justice of the peace and coroner, and made himself comfortable. It was a good place to sleep the night and avoid punishment, temporarily. He did not know that the corpse of a man who had been stabbed to death lay on the floor. As his eyes grew used to the darkness, he thought he saw "a long, dusky, shapeless thing stretched upon the floor." He stared at it intently. "The moonlight came through the window and slowly moved its brightness . . . toward the gray object." It came nearer and nearer. "With desperate will I turned again and counted one hundred, and faced about, all in a tremble. A white human hand lay in the moonlight! Such an awful sinking at the heart—such a sudden gasp for breath! I felt—I can not tell what I felt. . . . The pallid face of a man was there, with the corners of the mouth drawn down, and the eyes fixed and glassy in death! . . . I went away from there. I do not say that I went away in any sort of hurry, but I simply went—that is sufficient. I went out at the window, and I carried the sash along with me. I did not need the sash, but it was handier to take it than it was to leave it, and so I took it."

It became a favorite story of his, with variations and embellishments, remembered in private, narrated in public. "That man had been stabbed near the office, and they carried him in there to doctor him, but he only lived an hour. I have slept in the same room with him often, since then—in my dreams." The story became in his mind and memory inseparable from his father's death, less than four years later, a dramatic, readily useable analogue.

The estrangement between father and son had kept Sam as much out of his father's presence as possible. John Marshall probably was too preoccupied to notice, struggling always to earn a living. He had debts to pay off, including money he still owed to the persistent Ira Stout. And there was also some money owed him, which he kept trying to collect, in vain. When his effort in September 1846 to sell the Tennessee land failed, he sold some of the family furniture to pay a note that was due. That same November he became a candidate for circuit court judge, with some likelihood that he would be elected the next August and collect a salary that would put his finances back on a sound footing. The family was still living in the large white house on the corner of Main and Hill. On March 11, 1847, John Marshall went to attend court in Palmyra. On his return, a sleet storm chilled him to the bone. Soon his lungs were racked. Pneumonia set in. Jane and Pamela nursed him. Dr. Meredith applied his skills and medicines, such as they were, but nothing helped. Orion returned from St. Louis to be of whatever assistance he could, but soon the family knew they were on a death watch. If Twain's "Villagers" can be trusted, his father implored the family to hold on to the Tennessee land, and then put his arms out to embrace Pamela, named after his own mother. She clung to him for a moment. He had nothing to say to his wife or other children. On March 24 the Presbyterian preacher came and asked him, "Do you believe in the Lord Jesus Christ, and that through his blood only you can be saved?" "I do," he said. Ten minutes later he died.

"In a burst of 'heart-wringing' grief and remorse for past disobedience," Sam, just four months beyond his eleventh birthday, "stood beside his father's coffin and promised his mother 'to be a better boy,' with the understanding in return that he could quit school and soon begin life as a faithful and industrious man." Jane Clemens apparently agreed to Dr. Meredith's request for an autopsy. With his eye to the keyhole, Sam saw the procedure. Dr. Meredith would have been especially interested in John Marshall's lungs. That night the eleven-year-old boy retrogressed to his earlier sleep-walking. The next afternoon John Marshall was taken by his family and friends to be buried in the Baptist cemetery north of town. "Even the *Democratic Gazette* eulogized this stalwart Whig for his 'public spirit,' his 'high sense of justice and moral rectitude.'" A month before his own death in 1910, Mark Twain wrote to his only surviving child, "My father died this day 63 years ago. I remember all about it quite clearly." He always declined to say much about it, let alone provide any details, but he did comment that his father's death left the family in "exceedingly straightened circumstances." It also left him with no way ever to reconcile with his father. Sam was to remain in Dawson's school, which he attended irregularly, for much of the next year. But, at the same time, he was apprenticed to become a printer like his brother, a notable comedown from the professional status of his father. John Clemens' death marked the end of Sam Clemens' childhood. Soon he and his family were to leave Hannibal forever.

7.

Strong-willed, mischievous, inventive, Sam Clemens flourished in Hannibal, the town that Twain transformed through selective representation into a national myth, the epitome of small-town, pre-industrial America. Except for the reminder of damnation that spoke in the thunder and lightning, he seems as a child to have looked mostly on the cheerful side. The real Hannibal, of course, had drunks, murderers, wife beaters, and madmen. He saw that also. Mark Twain's *Tom Sawyer* presents the bright side of that Missouri town. *Huckleberry Finn* contains some of its shadows, particularly slavery and Pap Finn, based on Jimmy Finn, the town drunk who lived in the tannery yard with the hogs and "died a natural death in a tan vat, of a combination of delirium tremens and spontaneous combustion." *Life on the Mississippi* presents a bucolic portrait of Hannibal slumbering in the summer sun, but it also contains, in a lower and less emphasized strain, occasional glimpses of its "characters," the bullies, the drunkards, the madmen that Sam Clemens and his friends teased and often ran from. Later in his literary life, the portrait darkened. Hannibal's citizens in *Pudd'nhead Wilson* are a mixed and fallen lot, slavery pervasive and vicious. But Twain himself never flinched from a realistic awareness of Hannibal. In "Villagers," though some of the names are changed, most of the residents are recognizable, including members of Twain's own family. Many lives are encapsulated in devastatingly brief, matter-of-fact, realistic accounts of all the things that can go wrong with any human life.

His ten years or so in Hannibal provided Twain with a complex treasure out of which he created many of the literary works for which he is best known. And in those years Sam Clemens/Mark Twain was formed by the young boy's interaction with the sights, the sounds, and the people he lived among. It was a world from which he desperately wanted approval. Early on, he gave up on his father. His mother provided the constructive parenting. She was someone he could count on. No matter what troubles he caused her, he felt certain that he would never alienate her. Her love provided the security that made possible his satiric stance in life and in literature. And when, in 1853, at seventeen years of age, he was restlessly ready and eager to leave Missouri, it was to his mother to whom he swore that he would neither smoke nor drink, the two vices to which she felt he was most susceptible. With Sam's energetic high spirits, she feared the worst might happen. An adventurous life could be dangerous to the body and the soul. From New York he wrote to her with his characteristic combination of sincerity and ironic humor, "You will doubtless be a little surprised, and somewhat angry when you receive this, and find me so far from home; but you must bear a little with me, for you know I was always the best boy you had, and perhaps you remember that people used to say to their children— 'Now don't do like Orion and Henry Clemens but take Sam for your guide!' " It wasn't true. They all knew that Henry, the youngest, was the best boy she ever had. But Sam, tongue in cheek, made his claim. On the one hand, he was the creative troublemaker of the family, its dissenting voice. On the other, he wanted his mother to love him, if not best, than at least very much. He would have been happy to have it both ways.

CHAPTER TWO

THE FIFTY-DOLLAR BILL

1847–1857

1.

Through a telescope at the top of a newly opened 350-foot-high observation tower, the tallest man-made structure in the western hemisphere, Samuel Clemens looked down, in late August 1853, with pleasure and wonder at the panorama of America's largest city. The tower's height exceeded that of the spires of its nearest rival, Trinity Church, by 112 feet. The final part of his ascent had been by steam-powered elevator, one of the new miracles of the age. The tower stood adjacent to the Crystal Palace, America's first world's fair, whose cavernous halls the starry-eyed Clemens had just wandered through, fascinated by the inventions and products on exhibit. The Croton Reservoir, at Forty-second Street and Fifth Avenue, was a few streets away. In the distance, to the south, was New York's teeming industrial, commercial, and social life; its northern terminus was Fourteenth Street and Union Square. This was still Walt Whitman's pre–Civil War New York, the Manhattan of Henry James' childhood. Lower down, Sam Clemens could see the building in the newspaper district in which he had found work as a printer, where from the fifth floor he gazed each day at the Battery and the bay beyond, amazed at the "forest of masts" flying "all sorts of flags." He could also recognize the area around the boardinghouse in which he had rented a roach-infested room. To the east and west, he could see the two rivers; to the north, the urban imprint in the process of transforming Manhattan farmland into city streets.

A few weeks before, seventeen-year-old Samuel Clemens, restless to expand his life, had left Missouri, without telling anyone and with hardly any money. Out of work in St. Louis, doubtful that he could find employment there or anyplace nearby, he had taken a trip longer than any taken by anyone in his family since his ancestors had crossed the Atlantic. From St. Louis, in the August heat, he had crossed the Mississippi by steamer to Illinois, then by railroad to Springfield, by stagecoach to Bloomington, and by railroad to Chicago; from there he had traveled by rail to Monroe, Michigan, on Lake Erie, where he boarded a steamer to Buffalo; from Buffalo he took the railroad to Albany. Steaming down the Hudson, six days after having left St. Louis, he arrived in New York City at five in the morning on August 24, 1853, exhausted and exhilarated. He needed work immediately, which he soon found as a journeyman printer at low wages in a printing plant, lucky to get any employment at all in an overcrowded and underpaid trade. But, he wrote home to his mother, "the printers have two libraries in town, entirely free to the craft; and in these I can spend my evenings most pleasantly. If books are not good company, where will I find it?" As always, he was continuing his education.

2.

Economic necessity pressed hard. Jane Clemens had to watch every penny even more carefully than before. Pamela gave piano lessons. Orion returned to Hannibal, trying to earn money as a printer and then to establish himself as a small-town newspaper owner, beginning his replication of his father's pattern of vocational and economic failure. Henry was too young to work, just barely. John Marshall Clemens had left little to his family except the Tennessee land, which there would be numbers of attempts to sell. For some time these came to nothing, partly because the offers were insufficient, in one important instance because Orion declined to sell on moral grounds: the likelihood that the land would be used to grow wine grapes offended his teetotaling principles. The two older boys and Pamela recognized that they would be responsible for not only their own support but their mother's as well.

For Sam, John Marshall Clemens' most interesting bequest was his library, which the probate court listed as "1 large Bible, 2 small D(itto), Revised statutes and form books, Missouri Justice, Websters Dictionary, Woodbridge and Williams Geography, New Testament, Lots of school books, 6 volumes Nicholsons Encyclopedia, Missouri Digest, Journal of the Missouri Convention, 2 vols Law of Missouri, 4 vols Blackstone's Commentary . . ." During his Hannibal years these were the books most easily accessible to Sam. The assorted schoolbooks probably were those he used; it's unlikely that either Mrs. Horr's or Mr. Dawson's school provided textbooks. The Bible he had both forced and voluntary experience with, and it was to remain throughout his life one of the works with which he was most familiar. When he talked about its absurdities, inconsistencies, and immoral passages, he talked from knowledge. And the use and misuse of the Bible maintained a primary place in his sensibility and imagination, from his first travel book to his last fiction.

Sunday school, forced on him by his mother, as was church attendance, focused on scripture. Books from a small collection of morally sanctioned volumes were awarded as prizes to the boys who could memorize the most biblical verses. Sam's Sunday school teacher didn't seem to notice when he repeated the same five verses week after week, though his mother regularly perceived his impious infractions. When they accumulated, she made him go, as punishment and penance, to church on Sunday nights. Always suspicious, she tested him regularly, asking him what the text had been for that service. Selecting a passage for himself, he usually deceived her successfully.

Both wise and a wise-aleck, he was indeed in some ways a model student, quick to learn, eager to understand, and unrelentingly self-regarding. In *Tom Sawyer,* he made the case for his benign good heart. In effect, he argued that even his lies were redemptive. "Like Aunt Becky and Mrs. Clemens," he later believed, the world "can now see that Mark was hardly appreciated when he lived" in Hannibal and that "the things he did as a boy and was whipped for doing were not all bad, after all." Like Tom Sawyer, he became, as a young boy, a self-justifying fast-talker and obsessive storyteller.

Fascinated by oratory, he admired vigorous church sermons. In retrospect, he admitted that "the oratory was bombastic, full of gesticulation, pounding the pulpit, and all sorts of exterior suggestions of sense, combined with the utter absence of that quality," unlike the more controlled oratory that became fashionable in the latter part of his life. For some of his Hannibal years he believed that the highest calling he could rise to was the ministry, and he later remembered that he himself had "desired earnestly to stand in that Presbyterian pulpit, and give instructions," though somehow he "never had any qualification for it *but* the ambition." What most appealed to him was imagining himself in a position of hortatory authority, the center of admiring attention, especially that of those who may have doubted his distinctiveness. And he had the desire to instruct the world, though there were other ways to do this than the ministry. Unlike his classmates, he had a talent for recitation, for effective delivery of dramatic declamations, and he loved the opportunity to show how it should be done. All his life, he would be eager to perform and to claim that, with poetry especially, effective oral presentation was the best communication of the reader's cognitive interpretation. Literary critics were beside the point.

Other people's stories often fascinated him, and stories were all around him. Frontier humor in Hannibal relied heavily on accents and mimicry. Humorous narratives and tall tales about people's adventures and foibles were part of cracker-barrel and whiskey-jug culture. Jokes at other people's expense got even funnier in the telling and retelling. Embellishment was an art, and Sam discovered that he had a talent for it, even more for the reworking of things that actually happened than for independent creation. He loved to report on what he had seen, with a twist—the addition of humor, satire, pathos, and pedagogy. His genius was to be for elaboration rather than construction.

An enthusiastic listener, as were his classmates, he attended revival meetings that made regular sweeps through the Missouri countryside. Adapted to frontier conditions, they had by the 1840s become an American art form, combining religious fervor, fire-and-brimstone preaching, stories of moral and spiritual redemption, and some of the features of a county fair. They publicly staged, for edification and sometimes amusement, narratives of confession and character. Jane Clemens loved to attend. Hymns filled the air, the music of Christian spirituality and conversion. With a good ear and an aggressive singing voice, Sam was responsive to the music. Some hymns impressed themselves into his memory, occasionally transformed by this gift for elaboration into humorous variants. The hymns themselves often moved him, not as attestations of belief but as expressions of the human condition. Hymn-singing and profanity often went together. One of his favorites he would bang out on the piano in later years: "There was an old horse/ And his name was Jerusalem/ He went to Jerusalem,/ He came from Jerusalem./ Ain't I glad I'm out of the wilderness! Oh! Bang!" The songs that he loved most, though, were black spirituals, laments of sorrow and consolation sung by the slaves at John Quarles' farm. For him, their power far exceeded that of white Hannibal's church hymns. Even parodies of black voices had a special appeal. When in 1842 Hannibal saw its first minstrel performance, "it burst upon" him "as a glad and stunning surprise." Straitlaced Presbyterians refused to attend. Even Jane Clemens didn't go. But Sam and the other "worldlings flocked to them and were enchanted."

3.

In spring and summer of 1847 eleven-year-old Sam Clemens worked at odd jobs while attending Dawson's school. In one of a number of inconsistent recollections, Twain claimed that since his mother was tired of trying to keep him "out of mischief," she decided to put him into "more masterful hands than hers." So he was apprenticed to Henry La Cossitt, the proprietor of the *Hannibal Gazette,* where he began work as a printer's devil, sweeping the floor, running errands, restacking type, learning the printer's trade. Orion had set the example, and Jane Clemens probably gave little consideration to alternative apprenticeships. Eager to have his costs off her hands and his hands busy at something useful, she sent him the way of easy opportunity. He never blamed his mother, and later in life came to see it as one of a series of predetermined steps that eventually produced Mark Twain the writer. His education from then on was to be self-achieved. Apparently he thought that just fine. It meant, though, that most professional paths would be closed to him. Of course the example of his father's failure to sustain himself as a lawyer made white-collar professionalism unattractive anyway, and the decision pushed him in the direction of entrepreneurial self-advancement.

Soon he left the *Gazette* to work as an apprentice to Joseph P. Ament, the proprietor of the *Missouri Courier,* a Hannibal weekly. Pay was room, board, and some clothes, but no money. Though his own home was only a short distance away, his new situation was an immense change. Struggling with poverty, Jane Clemens may have had little reason or opportunity to

feel regretful. Indeed, she may have thought the work structure a good antidote to her son's waywardness. But if anyone other than Sam thought of
himself or the Clemenses as special, this could not have been seen as
other than a movement into the common. Parents of the middle or proprietary class did not readily put their children into trade apprenticeships.
Sam's main complaint appeared to be that, of the two suits due him each
year, one "always failed to materialize and the other suit was not purchased
as long as Mr. Ament's old clothes held out. I was only about half as big as
Ament, consequently his shirts gave me the uncomfortable sense of living
in a circus tent, and I had to turn up his pants to my ears to make them
short enough." Though Ament seems to have treated his three apprentices
with reasonable respect, his wife, who "had attained to that distinction very
recently, after waiting a good part of her lifetime for it," economized rigidly.
Meager provisions were sent down to the apprentices' basement table.
When they were "promoted from the basement to the ground floor and
allowed to set at the family table . . . the economies continued." Sam,
though, could go home daily, if he chose.

Apparently Jane Clemens kept a bed or even a bedroom for her exiled
son, and he went back and forth regularly. In June 1849, when a cholera
epidemic swept the Mississippi valley, she made clear to Sam that he was
still in her charge, heavily dosing him with Patterson's Patent Pain Killer.
He poured it into a crack in the floor of his room. "One day when I was doing this our cat came . . . and I looked at him and wondered if he might not
like some of that pain killer. He looked hungry, and it seemed to me that a
little of it might do him good. So I just poured out the bottle and put it before him. He did not seem to get the real effect of it at first, but . . . the
next minute he jumped to the window and went through it like a cyclone,
taking all the flower pots with him." One time, at least, when he dressed
up as a bear to play a part in a play at one of Pamela's parties for her
friends, the joke was on him. When he was spied changing into the costume and practicing, there came "a smothered burst of feminine snickers
from behind the screen!" Mortified, he fled, returning when the party was
over, the house absolutely quiet. Pinned to his pillow he found a note
which made his "face burn. . . . 'You probably couldn't have played bear,' "
it said, " 'but you played bare very well—oh, very very well!' " He never forgot the embarrassment, the "burning shame." In the summer of 1848,
Ament made him stay in the third-floor *Courier* office on an otherwise free

afternoon. "I had one comfort. . . . It was the half of a long and broad watermelon, fresh and red and ripe." But what to do with the shell? Soon he saw his brother Henry approaching on the street. "I poised the watermelon, calculated my distance, and let it go. . . . That shell smashed down right on the top of his head and drove him into the earth up to his chin. . . . I was deceived into believing that he didn't suspect me. . . . He was only waiting for a sure opportunity. Then he landed a cobblestone on the side of my head which raised a bump there so large that I had to wear two hats for a time."

In early 1850, yellow fever raged in Hannibal, and Pamela wrote to Orion, fearing that it would "carry off nearly half the inhabitants," if it did not "indeed depopulate the town." Consequently, even more residents were on their way to California in response to those who had left the previous spring and had written back that they were "making large fortunes." Orion was making next to nothing in St. Louis. In April, he traveled to Tennessee, where he sold family land for very little money. Sam did not bring home any cash at all. The *Hannibal Journal* was for sale. "I think," Jane wrote to Orion, "if you could get some of the printers in St. Louis that are doing well to buy the of[fice] and give you an intrust let you come up and take charge of the office, get some old person to assist a little in editing merely to have their name. . . . I could board the hands and you could have Henry. Sam says he can't leave Ament."

By summer, the deal for the *Journal* was done. Borrowing from a nearby farmer at ten percent interest, Orion paid five hundred dollars for the plant and its goodwill. Henry immediately began working at the newspaper, probably for no salary. Sam soon left his *Courier* apprenticeship to work for Orion at a salary of $3.50 a week. As an apprentice, he had been promised no cash and got none. At the *Journal,* he had been promised cash but also got none because Orion had none to pay him. In the hope of increasing circulation, he "reduced the subscription price of the paper from two dollars to one dollar. He reduced the rates for advertising in about the same proportion, and thus he created one absolute and unassailable certainty—to wit: that the business would never pay him a single cent of profit." Most of the 450 subscribers paid in kind, not cash. By late 1851, the newspaper was in serious trouble. "The office rent was cheap, but it was not cheap enough . . . so he moved the whole plant into the house we lived in, and it cramped the dwelling place cruelly. He kept that paper alive during four years. . . . Toward the end of each year he had to turn out and scrape for the fifty dollars of interest due. . . . And that fifty dollars was about the only cash he ever received or paid out. . . . The paper was a dead failure."

Still, for Sam, the family-owned newspaper had attractions. As regards pay, he was no worse off than he had been before. At Ament's, he had been only a printer's devil. On cold mornings, he built the fire. Year round he brought water from the village pump. He swept the office floor daily. He also picked up type from under Ament's stand. "If he were there to see, I put the good type in his case and the broken ones among the 'hell matter'; and if he wasn't there to see, I dumped it all with the 'pi' on the imposing stone. . . . I wetted down the paper Saturdays, I turned it Sundays. . . . I washed the rollers, I washed the forms, I folded the papers, I carried them around at dawn Thursday mornings." As the *Courier's* paperboy, he had regularly been bitten by some of the village dogs. His duties at the *Journal* office were much the same, but discipline was more lax. If there was "a barbecue, or a circus, or a baptizing," the boys knocked off work, making up short matter by duplicating advertisements or reprinting all-purpose general material. They kept a galley of it always on hand. Orion, though, was sometimes a hard taskmaster, years later acknowledging that he worked Sam hard: "and if he got through well I begrudged him the time and made him work more."

As editor and owner, Orion exalted in his position, and he preferred to function at the high level of politics, philosophy, and religion. An obsessive editorialist with profound convictions, he was, according to his brother's later recollections, "full of blessed egotism and placid self-importance. . . . He wrote with impressive flatulence and soaring confidence upon the vastest subjects. . . . He was always a poet. . . . And whenever his intellect suppurated, and he read the result to the printers and asked for their opinion, they were very frank and straightforward about it. They generally scraped their rules on the boxes all the time he was reading, and called it 'hogwash' when he got through." Orion, though, did not discourage easily. And Sam, to his delight, soon had opportunities, when Orion was away, to edit the paper and to provide reportorial copy for the *Journal's* pages.

When in January 1851 a fire broke out in a grocery store next to the *Journal* office, Sam had his first opportunity to break into print. The printer's apprentice who had already been the butt of a number of Sam's jokes, Jim Wolfe, discovered the fire. Fearing it would spread, he hastily removed some equipment from the office. Sam's humorous, ironic paragraph was published in the *Journal* anonymously the next week under the title "A Gallant Fireman." With a quick ear for colloquial speech and an eye for funny situations, Clemens described Jim's actions and words. "Being of a *snaillish* disposition, even in his quickest moments, the fire had been extinguished during his absence. He returned in the course of an hour, nearly out of breath, and thinking he had immortalized himself, threw his giant frame in a tragic attitude, and exclaimed, with an eloquent expression: 'If that thar fire hadn't bin put out, thar'd a' bin the greatest *confirmation* of the age!' " As was often to be the case, his journalism was less reportage than feature article and character sketch combined, an invention based on fact but not a statement of fact. Entertainment and amusement easily trumped literal truth, a common practice in mid-nineteenth-century American country newspapers that provided a variety of reading matter, from fact to fancy, reportage to entertainment, with humor particularly valued.

For whatever reason, he would not appear again in print until almost a year and a half later. It may be that Orion was not enthusiastic about encouraging Sam's interest in writing. In May 1852, he published a sketch anonymously in the *Boston Carpet-Bag,* a weekly specializing in popular humor. Perhaps he received some pay, but, even if not, publishing in a Boston magazine must indeed have seemed confirmation of his talent. Called "The Dandy Frightening the Squatter," it was the first manifestation of what literary historians later were to call the "matter of Hannibal," a brief tale about a savvy woodsman teaching a lesson to a dandy who arrives in Hannibal and attempts to show off by frightening the squatter. When the dandy drew out "a formidable looking bowie-knife," the squatter "calmly surveyed him for a moment, and then, drawing back a step, he planted his huge first directly between the eyes of his astonished antagonist, who, in a moment, was floundering in the turbid waters of the Mississippi." A stock situation, it had minimal humor. Its best literary moment is the concluding comment by the western straight puncher, " 'I say, yeou, next time yeou come around drillin' key-holes, don't forget yer old acquaintance!' " And it concludes, "The ladies unanimously voted the knife and pistols to the victor." Whether sixteen-year-old Sam Clemens had any idea that some readers might find the imagery phallic and the squatter a parody of the ideal of western masculinity, the sketch anticipates Mark

Twain's preference, even when drawing on literary stereotypes and tall-tale exaggerations, to establish his literary base in the world he knew and in daily life. A week after the appearance of "The Dandy," "S.L.C." published in the *Philadelphia American Courier* a brief sketch in the form of a letter called "Hannibal, Missouri," a selective town history with humorous touches. Seeing the two articles "in print was a joy which rather exceeded anything in that line I have ever experienced since," he later wrote.

When in September 1852 Orion left for Tennessee via St. Louis to try again to sell some of the Tennessee land and perhaps save his failing newspaper, he left the *Journal*, at least for one issue, in the hands of his brother, who happily accepted the charge. He took the opportunity to publish four of his own sketches in three issues between September 9 and 23, which suggests that Orion's absence made these publications possible. Three of the four are set in Hannibal—one is a contribution to an ongoing dispute with the editor of the *Hannibal Tri-Weekly Messenger* about the barking of stray dogs, another is a satire on that same editor's apparent attempt, after being jilted in love, to commit suicide, and the third, titled "Historical Exhibition—A No. 1 Ruse," is a comic, slightly vulgar story about a man who sells tickets to an exhibition he deceives people into thinking is sexually titillating, anticipating the "Royal Nonesuch" episode in *Huckleberry Finn*. Unlike those in any of his previous sketches, the characters are intended to be realistic, though his authorial pseudonyms for three of the four sketches, W. Epiminondas Adrastus Perkins and W. Epiminondas Adrastus Blab, are not. The fourth sketch, "Blab's Tour," is an alcoholic's paragraph-length statement about his retreat to Glasscock's Island, later to be called Jackson's Island.

Reservations about his publishing in the *Journal* may have been resolved by the appearance in November of "Connubial Bliss," about the troubles of marriage that bachelors escape and the threat of drunkenness to marital happiness. The following May he published a series of sketches and possibly even a poem or two in the *Hannibal Daily Journal*, which Orion had created on the notion that by publishing every day as well as weekly he would somehow make his publishing activities financially sound. Now, with more pages to fill, he gave Sam his own "Assistant's Column." He also had the idea that he might save the newspaper if he could convince a literary celebrity to write a story to appear serially. Orion "wrote East," Mark Twain recalled, "and felt out the literary marketplace, but he met with only sorrows and discouragements. He was obliged to keep within the limits of his purse, and that limit was narrowly circumscribed. . . . He offered a sum to all the American literary celebrities of that day, in turn, but, in turn, Emerson, Lowell, Holmes, and all the others declined." Finally, he located a relatively unknown professional writer who would provide not an original story but a translated one for the five dollars Orion offered. He sent the money. The story came. The *Journal* widely touted its acquisition. Circulation, though, increased only modestly. Payment still came mostly in kind, not cash. By early summer 1853, Orion was broke.

Two years before, in September 1851, Pamela Clemens had married William Anderson Moffett, a merchant from Virginia. After a wedding trip to Niagara Falls, Moffett opened a grocery commission business in St. Louis. It prospered, and the next September Pamela gave birth to her first child, a son, and then, in July 1853, a daughter. Early in June 1853, Sam Clemens, without remunerative work, and sensing the *Journal's* imminent demise, left Hannibal for St Louis. Apparently intending to hang on as long as he could, Orion advertised for "An Apprentice to the Printing Business! APPLY SOON." In September, the only payment he could make was to turn the newspaper over to his creditor. He had next to nothing left. Soon he left Hannibal for Muscatine, Iowa, where he hoped he might buy an interest in a country newspaper and have better luck.

In St. Louis, Sam looked for work in the newspaper trade and got a series of temporary jobs. Jane Clemens arrived with Henry and rented a modest house, probably assisted by the Moffetts. In August, out of work, Sam decided that he'd had enough of St. Louis for the time being. A few days after the middle of the month he left for New York. The Clemens family's Hannibal years were over.

4.

By October 1853, after six weeks in New York, Sam Clemens had "taken a liking to the abominable place." "It is just as hard on my conscience to leave New York as it was *easy* to leave Hannibal" he wrote, despite "villainous" lodgings and unfamiliar food, especially stale white bread instead of hot biscuits. He intended to winter in a warmer climate, if he could continue to find work as a printer. Two cities to the south seemed likely destinations in the near future, Philadelphia and Washington. Then, with colder weather, someplace farther still, though he had not yet given thought to where. For a short while, he considered Albany instead of Philadelphia. At work each weekday and much of Saturday, he struggled to keep up with prevailing typesetting standards for speed and accuracy, which were more demanding than in Hannibal or St. Louis, for the newspapers that the John A. Gray Company printed, including the *Knickerbocker*, the *Jewish Chronicle,* and an Irish paper, three worlds that Mark Twain was to know much of and have strong feelings about. Each workday he rose at six A.M. to be at his post at seven. In his free time he stayed away from his lodgings as much as he could, mostly walking, agog at New York's street entertainment, including the military companies and their bands, one or another of which seemed always to pop up wherever he strolled. When he had a little money, he went to the theater, where he delighted in Edwin Forrest's performance in *The Gladiator.* "The man's whole soul seems absorbed in the part he is playing; and it is really startling to see him." The marvels of New York amazed his small-town eyes: the size, the huge number of people, the variety of cultures and products, from sybaritic luxury to the popular wonders of the world's fair.

Regularly confronted with swarming poverty and licentious realities of a kind and to an extent that he had never seen before, he was warily fascinated. A small-town semi-southern boy, his assumption of white superiority and acceptance of slavery forged his response to some northern ways. At the courthouse in Syracuse, on his way down the Hudson, he had been reminded of "the infernal abolitionists" who had attempted in 1851, soon after the enactment of the Fugitive Slave Act, to free a runaway detained in legal custody. "I reckon I had better black my face," he wrote to his mother, "for in these Eastern States niggers are considerably better than white people." In 1853 he saw black people and foreigners through Missouri lenses. Soon after arriving in New York, he was struck by the city's "trundle-bed trash." Wherever he walked, he saw hundreds of such "brats." "Niggers, mulattoes, quadroons, Chinese, and some the Lord no doubt originally intended to be white, but the dirt on whose faces leaves one uncertain as to that fact. . . . To wade through this mass of human vermin, would raise the ire of the most patient person that ever lived." Neither western nor eastern Anglo-American readers would have found these comments offensive. With rare exceptions, those in every region of pre–Civil War America assumed that blacks were inferior and the mixing

of races was pernicious. Nativism was on the rise as an organized movement, with increasing political power and the occasional resort to lawless
suppression. Immigrants arriving in large numbers, particularly the Irish
and Chinese, made even the liberal-minded uneasy and most others resentful. As a seventeen-year-old boy from the provinces, Clemens handled
this aspect of his temporary new world easily. The homeless children on
the streets did not raise any questions of morality, justice, or Christian
charity for him any more than for most New Yorkers. He wrote home about
these unfortunates as if they were mostly a nuisance, not an issue. Generally, he wore his inherited prejudices comfortably.

Most evenings he spent at the Printers' Free Library and Reading
Room, a few streets from his boardinghouse; its collection of three thousand volumes was the largest he had ever seen. Though it cost a dollar to
qualify to borrow, on-site reading was free to anyone in the printing trade.
Letters came from home, particularly from Pamela in St. Louis, with news
of the family and complaints that he didn't write often enough. In response, he bristled that at least, unlike Orion, he was able to take care of
himself. "I shall ask favors from no one," he asserted. Occasionally he complained that his letters were not being responded to regularly by Pamela
and his mother, to whom he wanted to send money. And, he assured his
mother, he would return in April, to take her on a long-planned trip to Kentucky. Loneliness and independence he kept mostly in happy balance.
What he missed most, though, was conversation.

As he walked northward toward Union Square, past the center of mer-
chandising and elegance, through the Broadway theater district below
Fourteenth Street and then to the Forty-second Street world's fair site, sex
and sexual merchandise—street prostitutes, solicitations, brothels—were
unavoidable. Bars, dance halls, and theaters used barkers, street handouts,
and billboards. Liquor of every sort was readily available, alcoholism widespread, drunkenness frequently on public display as inebriated men
lounged and staggered. "I always thought the eastern people," he was to
write to Orion from Philadelphia, "were patterns of uprightness; but I
never before saw so many whiskey-swilling, God-despising heathens as I
find in this part of the country." There was "plenty of work to be had for
sober compositors," he told his mother. "I was only 15," he wrote years later,
"when she got me to promise that I would not drink intoxicants; it was not
a limitless promise. I was merely to bind myself until she voluntarily

released me. I kept it absolutely inviolate during 7 years, and then she set me free." His promise not to drink also may have implied foreswearing premarital sex. Probably he found New York's widely available sex for purchase neither appealing nor affordable, though he may have felt about sex the way he felt about liquor. "Many and many a person has been ruined forever by making a pledge of that sort; and that I escaped destruction was perhaps wholly due to the fact that the pledge was given to my mother. . . . The instant a person pledges himself not to drink, he feels the galling of the slave-chain . . . and if he be wise . . . he will go instantly and break that pledge."

When he tore himself away from New York, he discovered that he preferred Philadelphia, where he arrived about October 20, partly because he found the people congenial, the size of the city manageable, and its landmarks fascinating. However, his four-and-a-half-hour trip—by steamboat from Manhattan to South Amboy, New Jersey, by railroad to Camden, and by ferry across the Delaware—provided a serious scare. At the point where a fatal rail accident had recently occurred, his train came to a screeching halt, reversed itself, chugged backward half a mile, "switched off on another track, and stopped; and the next moment a large passenger train came round a bend in the road, and whistled past . . . like lightning." He mused, "If we had been three seconds later getting off that track . . ." Employment as a substitute printer at the *Philadelphia Inquirer* came quickly and proceeded pleasantly. Subbing was available every night, on the seven P.M. to three A.M. shift, allowing him to sleep until eleven in the morning, "loaf the rest of the day," and entertain himself at night, often at the theater, before going to work. On Saturday nights there was a "free-and-easy" at the saloons. "A chairman is appointed, who calls on any of the assembled company for a song or a recitation, and as there are plenty of singers and spouters, one may laugh himself to fits at very small expense." What got on his nerves, though, was people urging him not to be "downhearted" when he had "not had a particle of such a feeling" since he had left Hannibal. At work, he discovered that he was one of the few men who did not drink whiskey regularly and disappear on a drunken spree. On local buses, he noticed that it was the custom for a gentleman always to hand up a lady's money to the conductor. A lady sitting opposite him handed him her money, "which was right." "But, Lord!" he wrote "a

St. Louis lady would think herself ruined, if she should be so familiar with a stranger."

An energetic sightseer, he was delighted by Philadelphia. From the Exchange he took a stage to Fairmont Hill and walked through Fairmont Gardens. At the top of the Hill was the city reservoir, the high dam an awesome display of engineering and aesthetics. From there, he walked to the 350-foot-long suspension bridge spanning the Schuylkill River, the first of its kind in the country. To see the monuments to major events and leading figures in American history, he did not have to travel far. More than any city in America, Philadelphia made a patriot's heart beat faster. This young printer's beat with awesome pride at the grave of Benjamin Franklin, whose rise from printer to publisher, writer, and national patriot was a success story he would have been happy to emulate. At Independence Hall, he read the inscription on the cracked bell. At the old state house, he went to the east room where the Declaration of Independence had been signed. "When a stranger enters . . . for the first time, an unaccountable feeling of awe and reverence comes over him, and every memento of the past his eye rests upon whispers that he is treading upon sacred ground . . . he stands where mighty men have stood." Though the prose reveals the self-consciousness of likely hometown newspaper consumption, his emotion was not exaggerated. Characteristically, his awe did not suppress his humor. When he sat on a bench onto which Washington's and Franklin's names had been inscribed, he "would have whittled off a chip" if he had gotten "half a chance," he wrote to Henry and Orion. And he was outraged that the home of American independence now found it difficult to raise money for a proper memorial to its most famous citizen because, he explained, there were "so many foreigners" there "who hate everything American." At the office of what had once been Franklin's newspaper there was "at least one foreigner for every American at work," he remarked, still flying the nativist flag.

By early December 1853, he realized that he had missed his chance to go south, probably because the challenge of quickly finding a job wherever he went seemed formidable, perhaps insurmountable. Philadelphia itself remained attractive, despite the weather. Apparently he had some friends, probably from the printing plant. His usual outgoing congeniality encouraged casual conversations. His letters to Orion's *Muscatine Journal*, though, lost some of their personal verve. And he got only the pleasure of writing them, not the reward of payment. When he found he had to spend thirty dollars to purchase winter clothes, he apparently had no money for travel. Working nights, he complained, was "injuring" his eyes. If he had the money, he wrote Pamela, he "would come to St. Louis now, while the river is open." When Christmas approached, he kept up his sightseeing schedule, reporting to the *Journal* about his visit to the Germantown battlefield and his astonishment, as he plunged through crowded shops, at how expensive everything was by Missouri standards. "I asked a lady what the best turkeys were selling at. She replied that she had priced several fine ones, which were *seven dollars apiece!*" And they were "vanishing from the market as if by magic." If he shared Christmas dinner, or even had one, no mention of it survives.

Through January and the first half of February 1854, he kept to his work routine. He had enough money to afford going to Washington in February, a much anticipated visit, and Edwin Forrest's performance in *Othello* at the National Theater reminded him of how much he admired Shakespeare. Washington's public buildings, though, were as much "out of place" in Washington as *Othello,* "like so many palaces in a Hottentot village." A small, uninteresting town, Washington had streets that were mostly unpaved, its private buildings ramshackle wood or brick structures. Except on Pennsylvania Avenue, there were no gas lamps. On his first morning in Washington light snow began to fall. Then heavy snow. He "started toward the capitol, but there being no sidewalk," he "sank ankle deep in mud and snow at every turn."

Washington, though, had ballast as the capital of a struggling, expanding republic. And its political corridors buzzed with the promise of the riches that would come from the country's vast spaces and natural resources. The Mexican War had recently brought Texas and California into the Union. Western gold and silver glittered. The territories between Missouri and the Rocky Mountains and those expanses to the west and northwest from the Rockies to the Pacific were in the process of becoming states. When Clemens went to the Capitol, its dome not to be completed until after the Civil War, he observed the bitter debate in the Senate and the House about the Kansas-Nebraska Act, which would soon repeal the Missouri Compromise. A divided country slowly but inexorably moved toward civil war. In the Senate chamber, Michigan's Lewis Cass seemed "a fine looking old man; Mr. Douglas . . . like a lawyer's clerk, and Mr. Seward is a slim, dark, bony individual, and looks like a respectable wind would blow him out of the country." Thomas Hart Benton "sits silent and gloomy in the midst of the din, like a lion imprisoned in a cage of monkeys, who, feeling his superiority, disdains to notice their chattering."

After admiring the statuary and the paintings, Clemens left the Capitol and visited the Smithsonian Institute and then the Patent Office Museum, gazing admiringly at Franklin's printing press. As an expert in such matters, he appreciated "what vast progress" since Franklin's day had been "made in the art of printing!" The Washington Monument, the cornerstone of which had been laid in 1848, had risen to 153 feet; it had another 400 to go and would take four years more to complete, Clemens estimated, if Congress would appropriate the necessary money to supplement private contributions raised by a national subscription campaign. It would, in fact, not be completed until 1884, an ongoing project with fortunes that to some extent ran parallel with Mark Twain's, and which became a sort of prompt for Twain's comic-satiric interest in monuments of various sorts, including his own later proposal for a monument to Adam.

After four days in the capital, he returned to Philadelphia. Unable to resume his previous job, he went, in early March, to New York, looking for employment. A widespread depression in the printing trade, however, left him considering whether to return to St. Louis to stay with his sister or go to Muscatine, where he could join his mother and Orion's household. Perhaps there would be work for him at the *Journal,* or in St. Louis. Certainly, though, he wanted to see his mother, who had joined Orion as soon as he was set up in Muscatine, a thriving river port with 5,500 residents, 220 miles north of Hannibal and 310 miles from St. Louis. With his mother in residence, there was less sting for him in the return. So, in early April, "sitting upright in the smoking-car two or three days and nights," he returned to the Mississippi valley. When he reached St. Louis, he was exhausted. After visiting a few hours with Pamela, he "went to bed on board a steamboat that was bound for Muscatine. I fell asleep . . . at once, with my clothes on, and didn't wake again for thirty-six hours." Fortunately, it cost him nothing to stay with his family, and he spent much if not all of his two or three months in Muscatine relaxing and reading. It was as far north on the river as he had ever been. Later he remembered Muscatine particularly for an incident in which a lunatic cornered him in the fields: "[He] extracted a butcher-knife from his boot and proposed to carve me up with it, unless I acknowledged him to be the only son of the Devil." What he also remembered were the beautiful sunsets.

By early August 1854 he had left for St. Louis, where he got printing work on the *Evening News,* the paper he had worked on before leaving for New York. After a few days with the Moffetts, he boarded nearby with a family he knew from Hannibal, "a large, cheap place" where many students from a nearby commercial college lodged. Lynch mobs, hostile to immigrants, whom they blamed for the country's ills, terrorized the St. Louis streets, determined to destroy "foreigners." With a friend, Clemens went to the armory and enlisted as a volunteer policeman, though he himself had been heretofore moderately anti-immigrant. With two hundred other men, he got some hasty basic training. Characteristically, he didn't stay enlisted long. At about ten o'clock at night, while men were drilling at the armory, word came, he later wrote, that "the mob were in great force in the lower end of the town, and were sweeping everything before them. Our column moved at once. It was a very hot night, and my musket was very heavy. . . . I was behind my friend; so, finally, I asked him to hold my musket while I dropped out of sight and got a drink. Then I branched off and went home. I was not feeling any solicitude about *him* of course, because I knew he was so well armed, now, that he could take care of himself without any trouble. If I had had any doubts about that, I would have borrowed another musket for him."

Eager to be in print again, he wrote some sketches, which he hoped the *St. Louis Republican* would publish. His sketches seemed to him perfect, he later remembered, without need of a single revision. More than twenty years later he agreed with a friend from these St. Louis days: "You have described a callow fool, a self-sufficient ass, a mere human tumble-bug, stern in air, heaving at his bit of dung and imagining he is re-modeling the world and is entirely capable of doing it right. Ignorance, intolerance, egotism, self-assertion, opaque perception, dense and pitiful chuckle-headedness— and an almost pathetic unconsciousness of it all. That is what I was at 20." Confidently, he set out for the *Republican* office, his "brain full of dreams" and a "grand future" before him. "I knew perfectly well that the editor would be ravished with my pieces." Whether Clemens lost confidence when he got to the newspaper office or actually had the sketches rejected is unclear.

In mid-February 1855 he published the first of three "travel" letters in Orion's *Muscatine Journal*, impersonal items summarized from the two main St. Louis newspapers. Undoubtedly he was not paid for them. One item remarked on his attendance at a YMCA lecture by a controversial minister who had helped organize a Presbyterian church for blacks in St. Louis. Clemens thought him "an eloquent and interesting speaker." In another letter, he commented on the situation of a free black woman who had been arrested as a runaway slave because of her ignorance of stringent pro-slavery Missouri law. "She will doubtless be more careful in the future," he sententiously remarked. A paragraph let his Muscatine readers know that vicious Apache and Utah Indians were massacring whites: "unless a check is put upon them soon, terrible consequences will ensue." Two items in the February 16 letter had, though, the force of personal experience. When a livery stable near his lodgings went up in flames, he saw a reflected glow on his bedroom wall so bright that he could have read by it and heard "the shrieks of the poor horses as they madly struggled to escape." Another night he heard yelling in the street. When he went to investigate, a man was beating a woman with a barrel stave, driving her in front of him and cursing her vigorously. "And thus the gentleman amused himself until out of sight and hearing, and failed to stumble upon a single policeman." He was sorry "on this beast's account . . . that there is no purgatory for the brute creation." The equine beasts had suffered what the human beast deserved.

By spring 1855 Clemens had tired of St. Louis. He had companions at the boardinghouse and at work, some of whom he remembered affectionately years later. Pamela and her husband were hospitable, his niece and nephew amused him, and his mother visited from Muscatine. But he was preoccupied with what to do next. The romantic thought of becoming a steamboat pilot that had engrossed so many of his childhood days came to mind. He did not, though, have the money to purchase an apprenticeship. The previous December Orion had married Mary Eleanor Stotts, nine years his junior. A native of Keokuk, Iowa, a river town of 650 people on the Iowa-Missouri border, "Mollie" persuaded her husband to sell his share in the *Muscatine Journal* and move to her hometown, 214 miles north of St. Louis. His work in Muscatine could not support a family, and Mollie was to give birth to a daughter that September. In Keokuk they would have the advantage and company of her family, though not noticeably better financial opportunities. Two days after their arrival, Orion bought the Ben Franklin Book and Job Office, using much or all of what he had gotten for his share of the *Journal*. Probably he took on a debt to the seller.

Jane Clemens chose to move with Henry to St. Louis. Sam also could not have been eager to join his brother in Keokuk, but prospects had diminished in St. Louis, and Orion urged him northward. By mid-June 1855, Sam seems to have joined Orion, though clearly not intending to stay indefinitely. In mid-July, taking the steamer to Hannibal, he visited briefly, looking after some family business connected with the disposition of their Hannibal property. He also went to Florida, where the farm of happy childhood memory was in someone else's possession. John Quarles had sold it in 1852. In late 1855 he was to emancipate the great storyteller and companion of Sam's childhood, his "old and faithful servant Dann" who was in the "fiftieth year of his age." In St. Louis, Sam visited the well-to-do James Clemens, the "cousin" John Marshall had borrowed $250 from in 1839 and who had bought the small house in Hannibal that the Clemens family later rented. Sam hoped that James Clemens would help him through his contacts and money to become a cub pilot on a Mississippi steamboat. Alas, his "cousin" was of no help, and later wrote to Orion that illness had prevented him from recommending Sam to a friend who was "Pilot of one of the large boats." Anyway, he was of the opinion that Orion's brother "should stick to his present trade." Disappointed, Sam returned to Keokuk. For the time being, he had no place else to go and no money to get there.

From July 1855 to October 1856, Sam worked at the Ben Franklin Press, on the third floor of a commercial building on Main Street in Keokuk, with two short stints at a print shop across the river in Warsaw, Illinois. His brother Henry, whom he adored, came to Keokuk and worked alongside him. As usual, Orion agreed to pay handsomely, "five dollars a week and board." He most likely paid, with difficulty, board alone. Both Sam and Henry slept at the printing office. When Sam crossed the river to set type in Warsaw, it was for badly needed cash. The press required tedious work, including setting type for a city directory in which Sam humorously listed himself as an "antiquarian." He hated the job. And it did not provide, as it had in Hannibal, the opportunity to tinker and perhaps publish something of his own. Still, the printing trade gave him his first opportunity, in January 1856, to make a public speech at the Keokuk printers' banquet, honoring Benjamin Franklin's sesquicentennial birthday. It would not have been a demanding audience.

Though Orion's shop did not flourish, Keokuk bustled with commercial optimism, energized by the prevailing view that it was destined to be the most important river city between St. Louis and Davenport, Iowa. Gas lamps soon illuminated the main streets, some of which were paved. Three railroad lines were laying track toward the town, and in summer 1856 the first train arrived. With the population quickly doubling, real estate agents sold building lots as if they contained rich mineral deposits. Local people put money into land speculation. The building trades flourished, briefly. On one hand, the Mississippi's eleven-mile-long "Lower Rapids" forced river traffic to stop at Keokuk. On the other, a deep wide canal was being built to make the river navigable, which would speed traffic considerably but not benefit the town except during the construction period. Eventually, the railroad would make river transport generally uneconomical, but, during Clemens' stay, Keokuk bustled with the air and some of the substance of opportunity.

As usual, Sam had no difficulty establishing a social life. With tawny red hair, a prominent sharp-edged nose, and bright blue-gray eyes, he was more distinctive than handsome. He had his gift for conversation, a drawl that suggested downriver origins, and a desire for a life other than the tedium of the print shop. Even there he was apparently good-humored with Henry, loyal to Orion, and friendly with one of his coworkers who got paid, he later speculated, only in "uncashable promises." In quiet moments, he read whatever he could get his hands on—the three local newspapers, the three weeklies, and any books he could borrow. After his evenings at the New York Printers' Free Library, the local collection seemed minuscule. But hotels, even in towns like Keokuk, had small and sometimes varied libraries. Educated citizens, some of whom he became friendly with, had private libraries. He attended parties and soon knew most of the town's young people, including some young ladies, with whom he flirted. His likely attendance at music lessons with Keokuk's best-known music teacher, her studio one floor below the office of the press, was probably part of an effort to make himself more socially attractive. He had a rough, strong voice and could carry a tune, and his approach to the piano was harshly decisive. Keokuk's Mendelssohn Choral Society, in which Mollie's sister was a soloist, probably needed male voices. With Orion's wife, who helped him find his social bearings in a town she had lived in all or most of her life, he seems to have had an amicable relationship. Probably she introduced him to Ella Creel, actually his second cousin on the Lampton side, and Ella Patterson, Mollie's relative, both of whom he had crushes on. Keokuk's social life revolved partly around church. Years later he remembered that he had escorted one pretty seventeen-year-old. "I believe it was the first time I ever went to church; it was either the first time or the last time, I don't know which." In fact, it was neither first nor last, but the spirit of the remark was accurate. With his mother out of sight, church attendance had no appeal to him.

Through his sister-in-law, he became friendly with three daughters of the prominent Taylor family, all students at nearby Iowa Wesleyan University. Soon he had a crush on Annie Taylor. When she was away, they corresponded, and his one surviving letter is humorous, flattering, flirtatious, lengthy, and almost rises to the level of a courtship missive, especially in mid-nineteenth-century Iowa. "Ah, Annie," he told her, in response to her complaint about essay assignments in her classes, "I have a slight horror of writing essays myself; and if I were inclined to write one I should be afraid to do it, knowing you could do it so much better." Whether he was writing anything at all, other than trite verses in autograph albums, is unclear. He had, though, in June 1855, begun to keep a notebook, the start of a lifelong practice, of reminders, observations, ideas, and even French language exercises, which he wrote out and practiced. The entries were occasional. But some of them summarized items in his reading that interested him. Others were brief character sketches. "The Sanguine Temperament" he derived from a description of the four basic human temperaments in a popular series of lectures on phrenology. It became, in effect, his earliest self-portrait. "It is the burning, flaming, flashing temperament. Hence it hangs out its signs of fire in its red, blazing hair and countenance, its florid or sandy skin. It has blue eyes or gray . . . pliable, yielding muscles . . . great elasticity and buoyancy of spirit . . . impulsiveness . . . great warmth of both anger and love; it works fast and tires. . . . It loves excitement, noise, bluster, fun, frolic, high times, great days, mass meetings, camp meetings. . . . It is very sensitive and is first deeply hurt at a slight, the next emotion is violent rage, and in a few moments the cause and the result are both forgotten for the time being. It often forgives, but never entirely forgets an injury. . . . It has a ready tongue; is quick and sharp of speech . . . can cry and laugh, swear and pray, in as short a time as it would take some people to think once." Neither he nor his biographers were ever able to do better. And though nowhere does the notebook or its author say that he wants to be a writer, it is a writer's notebook.

Whatever his ambitions in spring 1856, they were framed in the terms of adventure. Restlessly bored, his temperament was characterized by its "readiness, and even fondness for change." Flirting with Annie Taylor would get him noplace, either sexually or maritally. In regard to the latter, his pocketbook was mostly empty, which made him an ineligible suitor. And what he wanted was adventure. He had a sense, he wrote to a lady friend in May 1856, of something great in store for himself. "Good-bye! a kind good-bye,/ I bid you now my friend, And though 'tis sad to speak the word,/ To destiny I bend." This "destiny," though, was more unformed and pliable than the sententious verse suggests. His desire to become a steamboat pilot had gotten him nowhere. He needed a sponsor, and none had been forthcoming. He had no money, either to pay for an apprenticeship or to travel anyplace of even moderate distance from Keokuk. With two friends, he fantasized about South America, applying his imagination to his reading, particularly to the first volume of a Navy Department report, *Exploration of the Valley of the Amazon* (1853–54). American southerners had for almost a hundred years hoped that Manifest Destiny would embrace Caribbean and South American colonies, "a tropical empire occupying the basins of the Amazon and the Mississippi and controlling the trade of the Pacific, populated by Negroes brought from Africa through a reopened slave trade." What riches would await him, he imagined, if he opened up "a trade in coca," which he had read was a vegetable with magical powers to sustain and nourish life. He could not get the idea out of his mind.

In early August, after one of his two coadventurers dropped out, he made plans to leave six weeks hence for New York. Orion had offered to give him "fifty or a hundred dollars in six weeks," an offer Sam discounted as unreliable, as it was. He wrote to Henry that their mother knew he was determined not to be left behind in New York but to go on directly. "I believe that the secret of Ma's willingness to allow me to go to South America lies in the fact that she is afraid I am going to get married! Success to the hallucination." Probably Annie Taylor was the lady Jane Clemens thought the likely bride. Her son, though, preferred adventure to marriage and had an imperial sense that he had his fortune to make in distant places.

Soon, though, the Amazon adventure was on hold. His potential traveling partner decided to stay at home, and the money for Clemens to make the trip was not forthcoming. In early October, he went to St. Louis, where he tried, without success, to borrow. He also saw his mother and sister, with whom he stayed. After attending the fair of the St. Louis Agricultural and Mechanical Association, he wrote a brief sketch, in the form of a letter, which the *Keokuk Post* and then the *Saturday Post* published toward the end of the month. At best, it put five or ten dollars in his pocket. When he returned to Keokuk in mid-October, eager to find out if another letter he had sent, under the pseudonym Thomas Jefferson Snodgrass, was to be published and to negotiate for some additional sketches, he was happy to learn that the editor liked what he had been reading. He agreed to publish additional travel letters from the young writer, probably at five or ten dollars each.

Fifty years later Twain wrote an account of his departure from Keokuk. "One day in the midwinter of 1856 or 1857 . . . a light dry snow was blowing . . . on the pavement, swirling this way and that way and making all sorts of beautiful figures. . . . The wind blew a piece of paper past me and it lodged against the wall of a house. . . . It was a fifty-dollar bill, the only one I had ever seen. . . . I advertised it in the papers and suffered more than a thousand dollars worth of solitude and fear and distress . . . lest the owner should see the advertisement." After four days, "I could endure this kind of misery no longer. . . . I felt that I must take the money out of danger. So I bought a ticket for Cincinnati and went to that city." As a story, it is emblematic of his belief for much of his life that luck would be with him and provide for him. The fifty-dollar bill was a ticket out of nowhere magically granted to one of nowhere's chosen creatures. Restless, eager to begin a new life, and hearing the call of the Amazon, he was given the means to go. Oddly, he chose to stop temporarily in Cincinnati, on the Ohio River that had brought his parents westward to the Mississippi. It may have been that the fifty-dollar bill was entirely mythic. It may have been that he needed to pause before he went on. It may have been that he had second thoughts about leaving the river.

5.

After arriving in Cincinnati in late October 1856, Clemens found work as a compositor at one of the leading printers. Cincinnati was not a promising place for a young man seeking his fortune. He knew no one, and he was not doing work that he particularly liked. With at least fifty dollars in his pocket, there would have been no need for that sojourn at all. Undoubtedly, though, he chatted as sociably with his coworkers as he always did. Indeed, he delighted in friendly arguments, especially about philosophical and theological issues, in which he played the devil's advocate. He struck up a friendship with a fellow boarder, a widely read autodidact who lent him books and with whom he had long talks about serious subjects. "A Cincinnati Boarding House Sketch," anonymously published as a travel letter in the *Keokuk Post*, presents an amalgam of theological arguments about the existence of God and soul, a satiric evocation of colloquial voices, personalities, and tall tales, including one about a ram and a farmer that, with variations, became one of his favorites. The participants are finally silenced when the "conversation [is] murdered by a pointless anecdote." The *Post* published two more such letters, under the byline of Thomas Jefferson Snodgrass, written as if by a country hick whose language, voice, and values reflect his provincial origins, an experiment that provided early and distant preparation for Twain's sophisticated later use of the colloquial first-person voice.

What he received for his Snodgrass letters, the last of which he sent to the *Keokuk Post* in March 1857, was no more than pocket money. He was for the time being stuck in place, and the way out was either east or west, east to the great cities he had visited in 1853 and the European world beyond, or west to still undefined adventure. Later, in various accounts of these months, he mentions Cincinnati at most in passing. Sometime he skips his residence there, as if it had never occurred. In one instance, he recalls inaccurately that in Keokuk in January 1857 he "lay aside" the compositor's "stick . . . to resume it no more forever." At the end of four months in Cincinnati, he made a choice. Eager to resume the life he had thought he was starting when he left Keokuk, he paid sixteen dollars for passage to New Orleans on the packet *Paul Jones*. He had thirty dollars left. In New Orleans, he hoped to earn passage to South America.

As the boat steamed away from Cincinnati in mid-February 1857, he basked in self-admiration. At last he was a "traveler." The *Paul Jones*, a run-down old steamer, had little to recommend it, and for days he had the main salon mostly to himself. Often he was on deck, his hat off, exultant and dreamy-eyed as the wind blew his hair, thinking of the "distant climes" he would visit. When the *Paul Jones* stopped to take on fuel, he remembered himself as a boy in Hannibal, hearing the whistle in the distance and running to see the much-admired big boats steaming into the dock. For all the years of his childhood he had thrilled to their arrival, their pilots among the most privileged, revered, and envied people in the world. Every boy with ambition dreamed of becoming one. With the sun blistering his face, he wished that "the boys and girls at home" could see him now. At Louisville, the *Paul Jones* got stuck on rocks in mid-river, where it remained four days. Consequently, the scheduled eight days to get to New Orleans became twelve. Often the crew cursed in exotic nautical terms, a specialized language that seemed to Clemens bracing and special. "I wished I could talk like that," he later wrote. When he tried to ingratiate himself with the envied first mate, he was put in his place. Creeping away, he courted "solitude for the rest of the day." Only the night watchman, who claimed to be the son of an English nobleman deprived of his inheritance, deigned to talk to him. "I sat speechless, enjoying, shuddering, wondering, worshipping." Later he was disappointed to learn that the man "had absorbed wildcat literature and appropriated its marvels, until in time he had woven odds and ends of the mess into the yarn, and then gone on telling it to fledglings like me, until he had come to believe it himself." Clemens was always, though, to have a soft spot for claimants, and for magical stories woven from the "odds and ends" of life.

Sometime after leaving Louisville, one of the two pilots, Horace Bixby, consented to let Clemens into the pilot house during his stints. From upstate New York, the thirty-one-year-old Bixby had come to the Mississippi at eighteen and worked himself up from the lowest position to pilot, licensed for any size steamer on the Lower Mississippi as well as on the Ohio. A smart, methodical professional, Bixby was known for his retentive memory, his explosive temper, and for being generous and fair. He never stayed angry long. A lively conversationalist, he may have found Clemens, who told him he was going to South America for his health, welcome company. At first the young man only watched. Soon he convinced Bixby to let him take the wheel in situations in which his inexperience would not be dangerous. And there could be little danger if Bixby remained in the pilot house. Perhaps Clemens raised, even if only indirectly, the possibility of his becoming a pilot. Perhaps Bixby allowed him to steer to assess his potential.

In New Orleans, on February 26, the two men parted company. Clemens, who had "nine or ten dollars," soon discovered that the next boat to the Amazon would not sail for a very long time, if ever. He needed an alternative plan. He searched for Bixby. Would he take him on as a cub pilot and, if so, how much would Sam have to pay him? Bixby was not keen on the idea. Though apparently he had concluded on the voyage down that the young man was capable, taking on an apprentice was a considerable responsibility. After some days of conversation, Bixby consented. The fee would be five hundred dollars—one hundred dollars down, the remainder payable from wages to be received. Clemens did not have a hundred dollars. Still, on the afternoon of March 4, 1857, when the *Colonel Crossman,* Bixby's ship for this New Orleans to St. Louis run, steamed away, Sam Clemens was standing next to his mentor. As they moved past the boats at the levee, Bixby turned to him and said, "Here, take her." Clemens took the wheel, his heart pounding.

CHAPTER THREE

THE RIVER

1857–1861

1.

With his hands on the wheel, silently cursing the mad pilot who had turned this responsibility over to him, twenty-one-year-old Sam Clemens steered the *Colonel Crossman* down the levee toward the open river. At one moment it seemed to him that he was "about to scrape the side off every ship in the line," they were so close. But soon he had a margin of safety. The volatile Horace Bixby, exploding into criticism of his apprentice's cowardice, took the wheel. Calming down quickly, he began to teach the young man about the river.

During the nine days the *Colonel Crossman* steamed upriver, Clemens received a concentrated tutorial in daytime and nighttime piloting. Every feature of the Mississippi, with its innumerable snags and sand bars, and the shorelines, expanding and contracting, became an object of intense scrutiny. Clemens was astounded by Bixby's ability to see what he himself could not, to know exactly where the boat was when he had no external clues to location. From moment to moment, changes in light and darkness, in an angle of observation, in conditions of weather, altered what had seemed one way to something quite different. Awakened at night to watch the pilot at work, in his mind he vengefully dared Bixby to locate a particular plantation when, as far as he knew, there were no guidelines or distinctions. In the darkness every stretch of shoreline seemed the same. Happily, he anticipated disaster. But Bixby steamed up to the Jones Plantation as if in broad daylight.

Each time he gave Sam the wheel, the apprentice got it wrong. "I either came near chipping off the edge of a sugar plantation, or I yawed too far from shore, and so dropped back into disgrace again and got abused." When Bixby told him that the river channel itself changed constantly through the pressure of water and the flow of silt, Clemens was aghast. He could hardly keep in mind the fixed points Bixby showed him now. When, soon after leaving New Orleans, Bixby saw that his apprentice was not taking notes, he said with exasperation, "My boy, you must get a little memorandum-book, and every time I tell you a thing, put it down right away. There's only one way to be a pilot, and that is to get this entire river by heart." Sam either borrowed or bought a ledger from one of the clerks, and, for the next three months, his literary output was a detailed river guide.

By the time the *Colonel Crossman* arrived in St. Louis in mid-March 1857, Clemens had "learned to be a tolerably plucky upstream steersman in daylight" and "had made a trifle of progress in night-work." He would not make more progress if he could not borrow the hundred dollars he needed to pay Bixby. First he went to his wealthy Clemens "cousin," James Clemens, Jr., but, as before, he got nothing. Fortunately, help came from home. His brother-in-law, whose St. Louis grocery was prospering, lent him the money. Sam made it a point not to tell his sister and mother that he "went on the river under a promise to pay Bixby $500" until some years after he had repaid the debt and obviated the possibility that they would criticize his judgment. He may have led them to believe that the entire cost was one hundred dollars. Swept up in the happy announcement that he "had decided to become a pilot . . . everyone," his niece Annie recalled, "was running up and down stairs and sitting on the steps to talk over the news." Sam would be fixed for life. They would all benefit. He might help Henry get a job. Jane Clemens would have another source of financial help, especially desirable since Orion seemed unable to provide even for his immediate family. The next month the irresolute older brother sold the Ben Franklin print shop and, in October, moved to Tennessee, where he attended law school, spending much of his time surveying what remained of the land inherited from John Marshall. In St. Louis, the Moffetts rented a larger house, joined by Henry and Jane. The Moffett home was to be Sam's St. Louis residence for the next four years.

For the return trip downriver, Bixby exchanged the *Colonel Crossman* for the more substantial *Crescent City*, a prestigious stalwart of the St. Louis–New Orleans route. "She was a grand affair," Twain later wrote, with a "sumptuous" pilot house where visiting pilots came to spin yarns. Eager to explore, Clemens inspected the boat from pilot house to boiler room, impressed by its size and power. Below, "fires were fiercely glaring from a long row of furnaces . . . over them were eight boilers. This was unutterable pomp." As the *Crescent City* steamed away at the end of April 1857, Clemens began, after his dispiriting experiences on the *Colonel Crossman,* "to take heart once more that piloting was a romantic sort of occupation after all." When the visiting pilots, on board to inspect the ever-changing "upper river" between St. Louis and Cairo, gathered in the pilot house, they regaled one another with stories. "Your true pilot cares nothing about anything on earth but the river, and his pride in his occupation surpasses the pride of kings." In his tutorial crouch, Sam listened, "a cipher in this august company."

But he had to learn the river, not stories. When night fell, he felt as perplexed as he had on the *Colonel Crossman*. The challenge remained the same. And, to his shock, topography that had appeared one way traveling upstream had, steaming down, different configurations. Bixby expected him to learn the day and night appearance of every landmark in both directions, every town, island, and bend, every snag, sand bar, reef, shoal, and woodpile, for the entire twelve hundred miles of a river that often changed abruptly, altered by rain, flood, falling trees, and stuck logs. And, during its annual high flood, it would look entirely different. The pilot had to know all this. Clemens marveled not only at Bixby's knowledge but at his nerve. When he steered the *Crescent City* into Hat Island at night, over sand bars and around rocks with the shallowest of draft, he seemed a man of heroic proportions, able to do the impossible. The leadsman called out the depth, each "mark" equal to six feet. Safety was "mark twain," or twelve feet of water beneath the ship. The boat "touched bottom," almost in the clutch of disaster. And then, with a sudden command from Bixby to give full steam, the *Crescent City* moved off the sand and into safety. It was a masterly performance.

With copybook in hand, Clemens made notes to remind himself of features that every pilot needed to know, increasingly unsettled, even frightened, by the range of information necessary to avoid disaster. "When I get so that I can do that," he told Bixby, at a moment of discouragement, "I'll be able to raise the dead, and then I won't have to pilot a steamboat to make a living. I want to retire from this business." "No," Bixby responded. "When I say I'll learn a man the river, I mean it. And you can depend on it, I'll learn him or kill him." Clemens gave Bixby many opportunities. After one particularly thick-headed incident, the older man summed up his apprentice's mental aptitude: "Well, taking you by-and-large, you do seem to be more different kinds of an ass than any creature I ever saw before."

But both ass and teacher stuck to their work and their arrangement. When he saw there was no arguing with Bixby, Clemens put on hold his deeply ingrained, self-protective contentiousness. Since Bixby was a worthy master, Clemens determined to be a worthy student. Little by little, he began to learn the river. Successful piloting, Bixby told him, "is an instinct. By and by you will just naturally know one [sight] from the other, but you will never be able to explain why or how you know them apart." In retrospect, Clemens found his best metaphor for describing the process in a comparison between piloting and reading. "The face of the water, in time, became a wonderful book," a living text of infinite interest to he who had mastered it. "I stood like one bewitched. I drank it in, in a speechless rapture. The world was new to me, and I had never seen"—let alone experienced—"anything like this." He began to balance happily the challenge of mastering the river with his response to its astounding beauty.

2.

When the *Crescent City* docked at the New Orleans levee in late May 1857, Clemens was exhausted. But he had more than two weeks to practice something he was already quite good at—sightseeing. Two things particularly fascinated him, the market and the cemeteries. The bright colors, the variety of tropical fruits, the plethora of every kind of produce from the kitchen, the farm, and the sea, sent his senses reeling with delight. The market was as much a display of people as of products, their multi-toned voices, their variety of skin tones, their diversity of languages: "groups of Italians, French, Dutch, Irish, Spaniards, Indians, Chinese, Americans, English, and the Lord knows how many more different kinds of people."

To him, the variety was an asset, the differences desirable, the community both tactilely sensual and raucously harmonious, his first experience with the American marketplace as a polyglot, multi-ethnic epitome of the national culture. His sheer pleasure in New Orleans was a step toward his gradual transcendence of Missouri slave culture provincialism and his increasing discomfort with xenophobia.

The cemetery was a mid-city necropolis with tombstones that told romantic stories, its flowers and vegetation turning it into a veritable garden of the dead. At the gravesite of a seventeen-year-old girl, where flowers were renewed daily though she had been dead five years, he remarked, "There's depth of affection!" He spent a half-hour watching chameleons at the gravesites, "strange animals, to change their clothes so often! I found a dingy looking one, drove him on a black rag, and he turned black as ink— drove him under a fresh leaf, and he turned the brightest green color you ever saw." The description was contained in a letter to Annie Taylor. That she had not answered his last letter, from Cincinnati, suggested that she was the chameleon who had changed her colors in regard to him. "You did write once, though, Annie, and that rather 'set me up.'" He had expected that she would continue to write to him. It was a tactful accusation of fickleness. And a lament that her "depth of affection" was shallow in comparison to that of the unseen hand that every day placed flowers on the grave of the seventeen-year-old girl.

Over the years he was to learn the art of flirting, but in his early twenties he was all sincerity and romantic innocence. And he had not gotten over his teenaged shyness. His Keokuk flirtations were behind him, Annie Taylor fading into the past. So too were Ella Creel and Ella Patterson. Thin, moderately muscular, slightly above average in height, he was used to exercising his body as well as his mind. By 1858, he was both delicate and rugged, attractive and masculine. And mostly grown up, though probably without any consummated sexual experience. On the river, in New Orleans, and to a lesser extent in St. Louis, he saw the visible signs of erotic life behind the transparent veils public codes imposed on private feelings. Rural Presbyterian puritanism had formed his moral life. He saw in his travels, though, that the world had many ways and other codes as well. His promises to his mother constrained him. "No Protestant child exists who does not masturbate," he later wrote. "That art is the earliest accomplishment his religion confers upon him." Alcohol was under control.

Tobacco was a necessity. Sex was more difficult to deal with. But falling in love was another story. In May 1858, in New Orleans, he met Laura Wright, the niece of a fellow pilot, and immediately fell hard.

She was both child and woman, with a purity that appealed to him. So too did her emerging womanhood, the charm and innocence of the Victorian archetype of the perfect wife. Not yet fifteen, "she was a very little girl, with a very large spirit, a long memory, a wise head, a great appetite for books," he remarked years later. Her innate wisdom transcended the limits of her experience. Her very nature was goodness; she was the kind of woman Clemens hoped he would one day marry, but at twenty-two and with so little to offer, he was not in a marriageable position. The daughter of a circuit court judge whose home was Warsaw, Missouri, 150 miles west of St. Louis, Laura Wright was on a holiday trip to New Orleans on her uncle's ship, the *John J. Roe*. Clemens was there, between assignments. When Bixby decided to work on the notoriously difficult Missouri River, he had made subcontracting arrangements in order to accommodate his apprentice. In July and August 1857, Clemens was on the *Rufus J. Lackland;* then August and September on the *John J. Roe;* in October the *William Morrison;* in November the *Pennsylvania;* December the *D. A. January;* in January 1858, the *New Falls City;* and, for the long stretch between February and June 1858, back again on the *Pennsylvania,* where Henry (whom Sam had sent to the hiring clerk in March) joined him in the lowly position of "mud clerk," working for room and board, his major duty to "receive or check off freight."

When Laura arrived with her uncle in New Orleans in May 1858, Clemens had five days in port before the *Pennsylvania* departed. They had one day together, after which they corresponded. Later, he made at least one visit to Warsaw, attempting to woo Laura and convince her parents that he was a desirable son-in-law, but he had no success. She remained, though, for a long time in his feelings and in his imagination as the object of his erotic longings. When in 1861 a new romantic interest complained to him that when he went to bed at night he "somehow always happened to think of Miss Laura" before he thought of her, he admitted that she was right. In 1864, Laura married. On May 6, 1885, he memorialized the date on which he had "parted from L."

In 1858, a licensed pilot earned $250 a month, a princely sum, but a cub received only room and food. In port, unless someone objected,

Clemens was able to sleep on his boat. An average round trip from St. Louis to New Orleans took about twenty-five days, with three to four in port at either end. In port, as the crew worked and the captain supervised, the pilot was free of responsibilites. So too was his apprentice. In St. Louis, Sam could rest his head and refresh himself at Pamela and Will Moffett's. In New Orleans, he was on his own. For pocket money, three dollars a night, he worked the night shift at the piers as a security guard, protecting cargo and huge stacks of wood that fueled the steamships' boilers. And he sometimes borrowed small sums from colleagues and friends, usually repaid from his New Orleans earnings. He owed Moffett one hundred and Bixby four hundred dollars, to be repaid from future salary, which he would begin to earn after the day he had learned his trade well enough to persuade two licensed pilots to sign his application to the government authority that regulated licenses. Two years in training, he had reason to believe, would suffice. There was no guarantee, but Bixby probably would not have kept him on if he had not been confident of his ability. No one, though, assessing his prospects, could have anticipated that events would soon make piloting an untenable profession. The new railroad through Mississippi, Tennessee, and Kentucky to the northern states was already decreasing steamboat passenger traffic. Soon it was to take away most of the cargo trade. Later, tugboats pulling barges made steamboats even less viable. And since by the 1850s most licensed pilots had an apprentice or two, there were more pilots in the pipeline than there were positions available.

Still, compared to his older brother, Sam seemed to have a golden future ahead of him. When Orion wrote euphorically from Tennessee about his great expectations, Sam replied, "I seldom venture to think about our landed wealth, for 'hope deferred maketh the heart sick.'" Soon Orion returned without having sold any of the family land. When Orion asked why he was not providing himself with pocket money by writing travel letters, Sam responded, "I cannot correspond with a paper, because when one is learning the river, he is not allowed to do or think about anything else." Certainly, though, he kept thinking about Laura Wright. In October 1859 he confessed to a family friend that everyone was well except himself—"I am in a bad way again—disease, Love, in its most malignant form. Hopes are entertained of my recovery, however." Laura Wright's contribution years later to the portrait of Laura Hawkins in *The Gilded Age* and her erotic appearance, in 1898, as his dream-sweetheart in "My Platonic

Sweetheart," attest to the permanent place she had in his imagination. The depth of his feeling was revealed in a note he wrote to a friend in 1906. "Here's a romance for you! Forty-eight years, 2 months and 1 day ago I parted from a sweetheart who was 14 years old, and since then I have never seen her nor exchanged a word with her—and to-day I got a letter from her! (I remembered the hand.) She is poor, is a widow, in debt, and is in desperate need of a thousand dollars. I sent it."

3.

Just after daybreak on Sunday, June 13, 1858, the *Pennsylvania,* with three hundred passengers and a crew of eighty, steamed toward Harrison's Woodyard, just above Ship Island, Mississippi. It carried 450 tons of cargo, principally wine, groceries, dry goods, and turpentine. Sam Clemens, who had served from the previous November until June 5 on the handsome, elegantly proportioned *Pennsylvania* under John Klinefelter, a "fatherly and indulgent" captain, was not aboard, but he knew both the pilots well. For George Ealer he had great respect and affection. An excellent chess player, Ealer played for love of the game, even with the ill-equipped apprentice. A Shakespeare enthusiast who knew the plays by heart, he recited aloud as he worked, interjecting pilot commands into his recitations, creating an undifferentiated stream of volatile language. Having recently read some of the literature produced by an outbreak of the who-wrote-Shakespeare disease, Clemens agreed with Ealer that Shakespeare, not Bacon, was the right man, though he infuriated the volatile Ealer by playing devil's advocate.

William Brown, to whose authority he had been subcontracted by Bixby, he hated. From their first meeting six months before, he knew that every minute he spent with Brown would be insufferably painful. Each time he was to come on watch with him, it would be with "dread in [his] heart." Middle-aged and somewhat deaf, a "malicious, snarling, fault-hunting, mote-magnifying tyrant," Brown peppered him with insulting questions and commands. An irascible bully, he constantly found or invented fault in his subordinate. Soon he took on fiendish proportions in Clemens' psychodrama. After every miserable watch, Sam went to bed with a happy task. "Instead of going over my river in my mind as it was my duty, I threw business aside for pleasure, and killed Brown. I killed him every night for months" in ways "that were sometimes surprising for freshness of design and ghastliness of situation and environment." If his sensitivity played a role in inventing the devil in Brown, his storytelling imagination played the decisive role in destroying him, a nightly ritual that allowed him to rise to face another day with his enemy.

Actually, he had come close to killing him early in June, as the *Pennsylvania*, twenty miles above Vicksburg, steamed toward New Orleans. The details of the episode are entirely dependent on Twain's own later account in *Life on the Mississippi*. Brown and Clemens were in the pilot house. Henry Clemens, on the hurricane deck, shouted up to Brown, on Captain Klinefelter's order, to bring the boat into a plantation landing a mile downriver. Brown did not acknowledge the request. Clemens heard it clearly. Perhaps the wind, or his partial deafness, prevented Brown from hearing it. As they went steaming by the plantation, the captain rushed to the pilot house and asked Brown whether or not Henry had transmitted the captain's order. "No," Brown said. "He came up here but he never said a thing." "Did he?" the captain asked Clemens. "Yes, he did," Clemens responded. An hour later Henry entered the pilot house to say, "I did tell you, Mr. Brown." "It's a lie!" Brown said. "You lie yourself," Clemens said. Brown ordered Henry out of the pilot house. As Henry stepped through the door, Brown, "with a sudden access of fury," picked up a piece of coal and sprang toward him. Sam picked up a stool and "hit Brown a . . . blow which stretched him out." He had "committed the crime of crimes." He had lifted his hand "against a pilot on duty." His piloting career, he imagined, was at an end.

If so, here was his chance to repay the older man for innumerable insults. Additional blows would not make his punishment heavier. Pouncing onto Brown, who was conscious, Sam pummeled him repeatedly. He could not remember afterward how many blows he had struck. "The pleasure of it," he later wrote, "probably made it seem longer than it really was." In his brief account to Mollie Clemens a few weeks after the incident, he reported that Brown collared Henry and "*struck him in the face! . . . Struck my little brother. I was wild from that moment. I left the boat to steer herself and avenged the insult.*" Captain Klinefelter ordered Clemens into his parlor for a hearing, where Clemens made no attempt to disguise what he had done. Klinefelter delivered his verdict: "You have been guilty of a great crime; and don't you ever be guilty of it again, on this boat. *But*—lay for him ashore! Give him a good thrashing, do you hear? I'll pay the expenses."

When Brown came off duty, he demanded that Clemens be relieved and then fired when the *Pennsylvania* reached New Orleans.

In his later version, Twain wrote that the captain found it expedient to comply. For the rest of the trip Clemens spent his time playing chess with George Ealer and listening to him recite Shakespeare. To Orion he wrote that the captain, who wanted to assign Brown to another boat when they reached New Orleans, proposed that Sam do the daylight piloting, Ealer the night shift. Never having had full responsibility as a pilot, afraid that he might "get into trouble," he declined. Since no position for Brown or a replacement pilot for the *Pennsylvania* could be found on short notice, Klinefelter kept Brown aboard, with the intention of discharging him when the *Pennsylvania* returned to St. Louis. He arranged passage for Clemens from New Orleans to St. Louis on the *Alfred T. Lacey*, due to depart on June 11. "Had another pilot been found" for the *Pennsylvania*, Brown would have been on the *Lacey*, Clemens on the *Pennsylvania*.

Sam expected to be reunited with Henry in St. Louis, where the story of how the loyal older brother had stood up for Henry, the darling of the family, would give great pleasure to everyone. And relief. Earlier, before leaving St. Louis for New Orleans on the *Pennsylvania,* Sam, so he later claimed, had dreamed that he had seen Henry's corpse, dressed in a suit of Sam's clothes, with a bouquet of white roses on his chest, with one red rose in the center. The corpse was in an open metal coffin supported by chairs in the sitting room. That last evening in St. Louis, Henry had shaken hands with everyone at the house before going off to his duties at the dock prior to departure. Kisses were not the Clemens custom. "These good-bys were always executed in the family sitting room on the second floor, and Henry went from that room and downstairs without further ceremony. But this time my mother went with him to the head of the stairs while he de-scended. When he reached the door he hesitated, and climbed the stairs and shook hands good-by again." When Sam awakened, he believed that what he had dreamed so vividly was real. Thinking that he could not bear to face his mother, he left the house. After walking a few streets, he ran back and bolted up the stairs. To his immense relief, there was no coffin in the sitting room. According to his niece, he told the family about the dream "before he went away," though some of the details varied from Mark Twain's account. "But the family were not impressed; indeed they were amused that he took it so seriously."

On the night before the *Pennsylvania* was to leave New Orleans, Henry joined Sam while he guarded dockside freight. It was a happy, chatty time for the brothers. They talked till midnight, and since they were not to sail together, Sam gave Henry advice: "In case of disaster to the boat, don't lose your head. . . . But you rush for the hurricane deck, and astern to the solitary lifeboat lashed aft the wheelhouse on the port side, and obey the mate's orders—thus you will be useful. When the boat is launched, give such help as you can getting the women and children into it, and be sure you don't try to get into it yourself. It is summer weather, the river is only a mile wide . . . and [you] can swim ashore without any trouble." Five minutes before the *Pennsylvania* left the levee, Sam said his last good-bye to his brother.

Two days later, at 6:15 A.M. on Sunday morning, a widower with his son and daughter were admiring the *Pennsylvania* as it passed. It may have been traveling at an excessive speed, perhaps engaged in attempting to beat another boat to St. Louis. Suddenly the boat exploded with a tremendous roar. Smoke obscured the view. As soon as it "cleared away," they saw the blackened wreck and heard hissing steam. The chimneys were entirely gone, "the superstructure from the wheels forward" demolished, the river "strewn with human beings and portions of the wreck." Many of those below, in the vicinity of the explosion, were either tossed up or crushed or scalded. Those above fell through the space that had opened or were hit by flying objects, killing or wounding them or tossing them overboard. Many were killed instantly. Others, crushed beneath twisted steel, moaned and begged for help. Some passengers and crew were completely unhurt, as if by a miracle. A few saved themselves, including a veteran of two previous steamboat explosions who, covering his nose and mouth until he almost suffocated, prevented the hot steam from scalding his lungs. In the pilot house, George Ealer saw the chimneys in front of him collapse. Muffling his face to avoid breathing steam, he fell forty feet to the top of one of the boilers that hadn't exploded. Hardly hurt, he quickly escaped into fresh air. Captain Klinefelter had strolled into the salon, having just been shaved, when the boat split in half a few feet in front of him. He was unharmed, but most of the ship's officers were killed. William Brown was blown into the river—his body never found.

When the explosion first occurred, Henry had been asleep in his cabin directly over the boilers. He was blasted into the air, then fell back down onto the hot steel. Something heavy fell on him. Still conscious, he crawled onto a mattress that floated him to a large raft hastily rowed from the wood yard out to the wreck. Apparently, he wanted to help in the rescue operation. For Henry, badly burned and internally injured, the next hours and days had the advantage of delirium and unconsciousness. With other survivors, he lay on the flatboat for eight hours in the burning sun. Within an hour of the explosion, as skiffs and other rescue vessels launched from shore approached the *Pennsylvania,* the barrels of turpentine in the hold gave way. Fire broke out, and within a minute the wreck was a flaming inferno.

Downstream, the raft and a yawl, overloaded with victims, including Henry, could not land. Precariously secured in the river, they waited for help. At midday a skiff brought bandages and linseed oil. At one P.M. the *Imperial* reached the flatboat and took the injured aboard. Other boats arrived. The temperature was now 100 degrees. It was decided that the seriously wounded were to be sent to Memphis. At four in the afternoon, Henry was transferred to the *Kate Frisby.* "From one end" of the boat "to the other lay, huddled together, the wounded, the dying and the dead." Doctors did the little they could. It took until three A.M. on Monday to get to Memphis, where other ships carrying the injured had already arrived. Henry, "senseless and almost lifeless," was carried to the Memphis Exchange, which had been transformed into an emergency hospital.

Within hours of the explosion, rumors flew upriver and down that an awful catastrophe had happened to the *Pennsylvania.* In St. Louis, the news reached William Moffett at his downtown store. At home, the maid told Pamela that her husband was downstairs in the parlor and wanted to see her. "We all felt it was odd my father should be home at that time," Annie recollected, "and send for her in this curiously formal way. My mother went down to the parlor. . . . My mother was crying. He had come with the news that the steamboat *Pennsylvania* had blown up, that Henry Clemens had been slightly wounded but that there was no news of Sam Clemens." The boys' mother was stunned. As the news went downriver, it met the *Alfred T. Lacey,* two days behind the *Pennsylvania.* Sam got word at Greenville, Mississippi, then read a newspaper account at Napoleon. Henry was listed among the injured. As the *Lacey* steamed upriver to Memphis, he saw the "floating bodies of victims."

On the evening of June 15, the *Lacey* docked in Memphis. With twenty borrowed dollars, Sam went straight to the makeshift hospital. The burn patients had been covered with white paint overlaid with raw cotton. The sight seemed both ludicrous and shocking. As soon as he saw Henry, scalded and emaciated, having inhaled steam, Sam knew his brother would die. Sinking down onto his knees, he was overcome with pain and guilt. If he had not fought with Brown, he would have been on the *Pennsylvania*. His luck may have saved him again, but Henry had had no luck at all. Like the other dying patients, he was kept heavily sedated. From the hospital, where Sam spent five semisleepless nights and days by his brother's bed-side, he telegraphed to St. Louis the news that Henry was not likely to re-cover. They already knew that the only Clemens aboard the *Pennsylvania* had been Henry. "Pray for me, Mollie, and pray for my poor sinless brother," he wrote to his sister-in-law. Throughout, Henry never became conscious enough to speak intelligibly. The experienced doctors devoted their attention to those with the best odds.

Late in the evening of June 20, a young doctor unexpectedly told Sam, to his unbelieving delight, that Henry would live. Since the moans of other patients might keep the boy awake, the doctor gave him an eighth of a gram of morphine. "They had no way of measuring the eighth of a gram," Twain, who had little confidence in doctors, wrote fifty years later, "so they guessed at it and gave him a vast quantity heaped on the end of a knife blade." Henry died a little before dawn on the next day. He was immedi-ately taken to the "dead-room." "We were not sorry his wounds proved fa-tal," Sam soon wrote in a tribute to his brother, "for if he had lived he would have been but the wreck of his former self."

After telegraphing the news to his family, he slept for a few hours. He was a wreck himself, though restorable. In the meantime, the charitable Memphis ladies who had distinguished themselves with an outpouring of every kind of help provided a metallic case for the "unpainted white cof-fin" into which Henry's body was placed. "When I came back and entered the dead-room Henry lay in that open case, and he was dressed in a suit of my clothing. I recognized instantly that my dream of several weeks before was here exactly reproduced." The one absent detail "was immediately sup-plied, for just then an elderly lady entered the place with a large bouquet consisting mainly of white roses, and in the center of it was a red rose, and she laid it on his breast." To an observer, Sam seemed "almost crazed with grief." The next day he brought the coffin to St. Louis, with a man whom the Memphis authorities insisted accompany him, so concerned were they about Clemens' fragile state. From Tennessee, Orion also returned to St. Louis.

On June 25, the family journeyed upriver with its youngest boy's corpse to Hannibal, where he had spent his childhood. He was buried beside his father in the Baptist cemetery. Neither Sam Clemens nor Mark Twain ever commented in writing on the funereal occasion. Jane Clemens, widowed for more than ten years, now had only three children alive. Her youngest living son did not miss his father, but he deeply and dearly missed Henry. Endlessly, Sam reproached himself for his brother's death. If he had not gotten him the job as mud clerk, the boy would still be alive. If Sam had not fought with Brown, the chain of events would have produced a different result. If Sam himself had been aboard the *Pennsylvania,* his brother might not have died. Perhaps the sinful brother would have perished instead. Certainly there was no justice in this world. And not, he believed, in any other.

4.

Two weeks later, in the middle of July 1858, the *Lacey* left St. Louis for New Orleans with Sam Clemens aboard. As the boat steamed past Vicksburg and then Harrison's Woodyard, every crew member would have had an idea of what Clemens was feeling. In those waters an important part of his past had died. With his older brother Orion, his relationship had always been tense, partly because Orion had conceived of himself as a substitute for John Marshall, a replacement father who could exercise authority over his younger brother. With Henry, Sam had been a benevolent older brother, and they had been playmates and roommates as children. Orion, ten years older, had not been a part of their daily lives in Hannibal until he had bought the *Journal,* and then he had been Sam's employer. On behalf of his mother, Sam had taken responsibility for Henry's well-being, and, in his own eyes, he had discharged that responsibility badly.

On board the *Lacey,* George Ealer offered the solace of Shakespeare and chess. With Bart Bowen, the other pilot, Sam talked about Henry and Hannibal days. Gradually, the absolute sting of Henry's death faded, though some of it would always remain. But it was not an incapacitating wound. At almost twenty-three years of age, Clemens was resilient, energetic, and capable of expressing himself effectively in his vocation and in his personal life. Henry's death changed him to the extent that it cast his general skepticism, his belief in randomness and luck, his rejection of Christian Providence and cosmic benevolence, into a deeper mold. His satiric tartness gathered extra sting; his humor was based increasingly on the cosmic insecurity behind the human absurd. He had already been in the process, now accelerated, of articulating his own sense of destiny and power. "What's the grandest thing in *Paradise Lost*," he soon wrote to Orion—"the Arch-Fiend's terrible energy. What was the greatest feature in Napoleon's character? His unconquerable energy. . . . And to-day, if I were a heathen, I would rear a statue to Energy, and fall down and worship it!" It was now Sam who was giving advice to Orion. "I want a man—I want *you*—to take up a line of action, and *follow* it out, in spite of the very devil."

What was surfacing into a credo of energy for himself was Satan's motto, *non serviam*. Satan was an attractive model, a cynosure of intellectual independence, the embodiment of his own commitment to think for himself, to make up his own mind about what was true. His words were an affirmation of Satan's claim in *Paradise Lost* that the mind makes its own heaven and hell. Although he might defer to authority if expedient, his mind was his own. He was to have, at most, only a small argument, if any at all, with Victorian propriety, and he would allow his satiric and deflationary tongue to go only so far, though sometimes it would be a considerable distance. But when it came to what went on in his own mind, he had begun to recognize no master but himself.

As the *Lacey* steamed southward, he was starting the final stage of his apprenticeship, a two-year period in which he was to earn his license and find himself mostly happy. That same summer of 1858 two other great events impressed him. "The first electric message . . . under the sea, by cable. It did not seem believable," he later recalled. A "wave of jubilation and astonishment . . . swept the planet." The earth was getting smaller. The heavens also put on a show of cosmic power, energy so great that it made earthly energy seem puny, a comet so bright that "more than once I read a newspaper by the light that streamed from that stupendous explorer of the glittering archipelagos of space." In August he went on the *John H. Dickey*, where he was to stay until mid-October, and then the *White Cloud* for the rest of that month, and on both boats he was under the tutelage of Sam Bowen, the youngest Bowen brother. Bixby, back from the Missouri, took him on the *New Falls City* and then the *Aleck Scott* from December 1858 to spring 1859.

In early April 1859, his apprenticeship over, he became a licensed pilot, with a salary of $250 a month. At the Pilots' Association office in New Orleans he was now a comrade and an equal. In St. Louis, to the Clemens family, he was a hero. In May, he was back on the *Alfred T. Lacey,* this time as pilot, with Bart Bowen his co-pilot. Less than one year after Henry's death, he had achieved his professional goal. Jobs came more readily. With good friends on the river and no black marks against him, he was in reasonable demand.

When in summer 1860, following orders, he ran the *City of Memphis* into another steamboat, the captain "shouldered the responsibility like a man." But when the *A. B. Chambers* ran aground, he was at the wheel and responsible. Co-piloting with Bixby, "running in the fog, on the coast, in order to beat another boat," he ran the *Alonzo Child* aground. It was a painful embarrassment; there was serious damage. Gradually he began to think that as a pilot he was "rather lucky than otherwise." He was still nervously concerned with getting the river right. With wheel in hand, he was never carefree. Often he took the conservative approach in situations in which better, more secure pilots, like Bixby and all three of the Bowens, would have performed more aggressively. There is no reason to believe that Clemens ever became more than an adequate pilot.

In later years, he glamorized his piloting days, the anxieties and insecurities having faded from memory. When he spoke about his river life to the Yorick Club in Melbourne, Australia, in 1895, he recalled, "At that time fog and dark nights had a charm for me. I didn't own any stock in that steamboat. And that is one of the very advantages of youth. You don't own any stock in anything. You have a good time, and all the grief is with the other fellows. Youth is a lovely thing, and certainly never was there a diviner time to me in this world. All the rest of my life is one thing—but my life as a pilot on the Mississippi River when I was young—Oh! that was the darling existence. There has been nothing comparable to it in my life since." Henry's death of course was not a memory he cared to impose on his reconstruction of that river life. And day in, day out, as apprentice and pilot, the level of anxiety, the fear that he would make a consequential mistake, made his feelings a complicated amalgam of happiness and misery. But the river was the stuff of personal and national legend, and legend demanded a certain sacrifice of truth.

As a cub and now as a licensed pilot he made the run from St. Louis to

New Orleans and back repeatedly, with a frequency and persistence that might have been tedious to someone less alert to self-education. Many of his spare hours he spent reading. But he had two additional texts to study, the river and its people. Aspects of the river landscape fed into the rich stream of literature and language available to him in the Romantic poetry he read. Ealer's Shakespeare and gradually his own became a regular supplement, a guide to his observations of people. The poet of human character had much to offer, as did, later, another of his favorite writers, Robert Browning, whose dramatic monologues he loved to recite. The river also provided Clemens with the living poetry of experience, the quirks and peculiarities, the anticipated and the unexpected characteristics of people. Fourteen years later, in "Old Times on the Mississippi," he was to emphasize what he had learned during the years he traveled from St. Louis to New Orleans. "I got personally and familiarly acquainted with about all the different types of human nature that are to be found in fiction, biography, or history. . . . When I find a well-drawn character in fiction or biography, I generally take a warm personal interest in him, for the reason that I have known him before—met him on the river."

Though St. Louis was home, it offered little more than the familiar. In December 1860, he applied to become a Mason, as his father and uncle had been, and was elected in February. New Orleans, however, had exotic appeal, including cultural attractions that made his heart beat a little faster as he steamed downriver. No matter what boat he was on, New Orleans was the destination, and the Crescent City contributed importantly to his education. In March 1859, he arrived on the *Aleck Scott* just as Mardi Gras began, "in blissful ignorance of the great day," as he wrote afterward to Pamela. It was his good luck, again. When he saw hundreds of men, women, and children dressed "in fine, fancy, splendid, ugly, coarse, ridiculous, grotesque, laughable costumes," it suddenly dawned on him: "This is Mardi-Gras!" Women in scant, alluring dress aroused him, though he put it in polite terms to his sister—"their costumes and actions were very trying to modest eyes." He was fascinated by the erotic atmosphere, the variety of shapes and the colorful appearances of human beings "representing giants, Indians, nigger minstrels, monks, priests, clowns,—birds, beasts—everything . . . that one could imagine." Its freedom appealed to his senses, arousing a pleasure nerve that Victorian bleakness sometimes dulled but never destroyed.

Strolling up St. Charles Street one evening, he joined a crowd waiting for "the grand torchlight procession of the 'mystic Krewe of Comus'" and managed to squeeze into an advantageous viewing position. After a number of false alarms, the parade began to appear in the distance. "Five thousand people near me were tip-toeing and bobbing and peeping. . . . Ever so far away down the street we could see a flare of light spreading away from a line of dancing colored spots. They approached faster . . . and here was the procession at last"—multicolored torches, an "endless line of hearts and clubs . . . led by a mounted Knight Crusader in blazing gilt armor . . . then the Queen of the Fairies . . . then the King and Queen of the Genii." To Clemens, this sensually exotic licentiousness seemed as much a part of the American experience as the genteel East Coast and the Presbyterian West. "I think that I may say that an American has not seen the United States until he has seen the Mardi-Gras in New Orleans."

America also meant the pursuit of fortune. In November 1860, Clemens bought eggs and apples in St. Louis, transporting them to New Orleans on the boat he was piloting. But, he wrote Orion, "the New Orleans market fluctuates." On his previous trip, eggs sold for forty cents a dozen. On his next, arriving with 3,600 dozen for which he had paid fifteen cents per, they sold for twelve and a half cents. So too with the apples. What to do? "We stored the infernal produce," he reported with disgust, "and shall wait for the market to fluctuate again." Imprudently, he was "deep in another egg purchase, *now.*" In one instance, after the deduction for his "egg speculation," only thirty-five dollars of his monthly paycheck remained. He had no way of knowing when he made the purchase in St. Louis what the New Orleans market price would be when he needed to sell. Still, risk was not a deterrent. In fact, it appealed to him. Risk provided excitement and possibility, the adrenaline rush that synthesized restlessness and fantasy. All around him, fortunes were being made, and lost. Newspaper columns overflowed with success stories, and bitter recollections of his father's failures probably intensified his ambition. The forty-niners had sent streams of gold eastward. American capital resources had increased considerably, and more foreign investors than ever before found American opportunities attractive. Everyone expected high rates of return.

In March 1861 Clemens took his mother and two friends, one a young woman from St. Louis, the other Ella Creel, as guests on a pleasure cruise to New Orleans. The captain of the *Alonzo,* celebrating his return to command after a long illness, had invited twenty to thirty couples on a river excursion, and he probably took Clemens' guests as his own, without cost to the young pilot. With a band on board, they were "a gay party." When not on duty, Sam flirted and danced. "Ma was delighted with her trip," he wrote to Orion, "but she was disgusted with the girls for allowing me to embrace and kiss them—and she was horrified at the Schottische," a polka, "as performed by Miss Castle and me." Perhaps she was still protecting her son from potential matrimonial advances. Though, as always, she carried her Presbyterian code with her, she was all in all delighted with the trip and especially, despite the heat, with her first visit to New Orleans. Sam happily took his ladies in a carriage around the Garden District, showing them the handsome residences. When the women were "hell-bent" on stealing some of the "luscious-looking oranges from branches which overhung the fences," it was his turn to teach his mother proper New Orleans manners. With three ladies on his arm, his own assumption of masculinity and his performance as a man of Victorian propriety allowed him to be both an excited flirt and his mother's loving son.

When he returned to St. Louis, escorting his sister Pamela, he went to see Frederick Church's huge painting *Heart of the Andes,* his brain "*gasping and straining with futile efforts to take all the wonder in.*" It may have brought to mind his fascination some years before with making his fortune in South America. Untrained and uninterested in the fine arts, he had little sense of painting as an art form or of its history and variety. What usually appealed to him depicted familiar and realistic things in accordance with popular taste. Or, as in the case of *Heart of the Andes,* bravura paintings with subjects exotic or sublime enough to appeal to his Miltonic sense of spectacle. Church's painting, which he went to see three times, was "the most wonderful beautiful painting which this city has ever seen," he told Orion.

In early 1861, in New Orleans, he visited a fortuneteller. A former Hannibal neighbor, Mrs. Holliday, a visitor to the family's St. Louis household and the prototype for the fictional Widow Douglas, thought he needed guidance and had told the fortuneteller about him. He had little inclination to believe in fortunetelling, but he had time, curiosity, and a nagging family friend to satisfy, as well as, apparently, some vocational ambivalence. He got, he thought afterward, his two dollars' worth, or so he wrote to Orion in an account of the session, which may have been shaped to express what was on his mind more than on the fortuneteller's. He earned his living on the water, Madame Caprell had said. He smoked too much; the family was short-lived on his father's side; his brother had an unbalanced character whereas his was unswerving; he had the best mind in the family; and he had overcome innumerable obstacles to rise to his present position. His "whole future welfare," according to Sam's account, depended on his getting married as soon as possible. "You can get the girl you have in your eye, if you are a better man than her mother," the fortuneteller advised. Apparently she had been told about Laura Wright.

But one of her observations did have startling force. "You have written a great deal; you write well," she told him, "but you are rather out of practice; no matter—you will be in practice some day." Writing, she concluded, was his true vocation. He was misplaced on the river. Indeed, at certain times he should stay away from water. His thirty-first year would be especially dangerous, she warned. Something other than piloting a steamboat was desirable, almost as a matter of life or death. Perhaps Clemens himself was writing the script. Anyway, Madame Caprell might have known from Mrs. Holliday about the sketches he had published in newspapers before becoming a cub pilot. But, since signing on with Bixby in 1857, Clemens had written very little. In August 1858, he had dashed off a sketch called "The Mysterious Murders in Risse," a tale of murder and revenge set in Germany, probably inspired by stories told to him by a crazy carpenter in his Hannibal childhood. He did not find a publisher for it. But, six months after becoming a licensed pilot in April 1859, he had resumed writing.

For some years now an elderly pilot, Isaiah Sellers, had been providing New Orleans newspapers, especially the *Picayune,* with river news, some of a general sort, usually practical information for the steamboat trade. Later, in *Life on the Mississippi*, Clemens recalled that Sellers signed his articles "Mark Twain," which Clemens claimed gave him the idea for his own pseudonym, though no record of Sellers' use of that signature has been discovered. Almost the same age John Marshall Clemens would have been had he lived, Sellers, in his early sixties, had impeccable credentials and geriatric authority, but his inclination to tell stories about his early days on the river made him an object of ridicule among the river men of a younger generation. To Clemens, who had sailed with him, Sellers seemed a sententious Polonius. In 1858, on the *William M. Morrison,* when Clemens was sent to awaken him, Sellers apparently either threw a boot at him or slapped him in the face. Personal injury may have been added to general dislike, and in March 1859 Clemens published in the *New Orleans Crescent*, under the heading "River Intelligence," a report from a fictional "Sergeant Fathom," an easily recognizable parody of Sellers. The piece was divided into two parts, the editorial voice introducing Fathom with gentle satire, then Fathom/Sellers providing in his own voice a burlesque account of his obsessive penchant for larding his narratives with precise details about the good old days. Upon reading it, Sellers was deeply hurt. Clemens had gotten his revenge. He had also gotten a publication in only his second return to writing in almost three years. Sellers had served Clemens well. But writing river news was not a living. Piloting was.

5.

When Confederate forces in Charleston Harbor fired on Fort Sumter in April 1861, Sam Clemens was aboard the *Alonzo Child* on his way to New Orleans. Though Louisiana, with most of the Deep South, had seceded from the Union in January, there had been until then no acts of war. With the attack in South Carolina, the watch-and-wait policy of temperate Southerners and of Lincoln's administration was no longer tenable. When Clemens arrived in New Orleans, despite a good deal of uncertainty about what the future held for a city dependent on river traffic, Southern patriotism and Confederate rhetoric were parading through the streets.

When the *Alonzo Child* left New Orleans after four days and returned to St. Louis, Sam Clemens would have been aware that he too soon would have to make a choice. St. Louis embodied the division that Missouri as a state contained. The southern portion leaned toward the Confederacy, the northern toward the Union, a microcosmic representation of the national division. With few exceptions, in St. Louis one could never be sure of anyone's affiliation. By now, the divisions that had been expressed in argument and rhetoric were being embodied in angry threats and incipient violence. Often the statewide division was replicated within divided families. True to her Kentucky roots, Jane Clemens felt deeply her Southernness, unreconstructed in regard to the appropriateness of slavery and the primacy of regional consciousness. Her idealistic oldest son advocated abolition and Unionism. Indeed, Orion, failing as a lawyer in Memphis, soon was on his way to St. Louis, which Union loyalists and the Republican leadership in Washington had determined to hold. Through his friendship with Edward

Bates, whose St. Louis law office he had clerked in and whose campaign to elect Lincoln he had aided, Orion hoped to get a government position. Newly appointed as Lincoln's attorney general, Bates was in a position to help. "It will be a great advantage to me to get some such office," Orion wrote to his brother. By late March he learned that he would be appointed secretary of the Nevada Territory. If Sam wanted a government clerkship, that probably could be arranged. What Sam wanted, for the time being, was to continue piloting, though that seemed increasingly unlikely, at least under circumstances he could accept.

On May 8 Clemens piloted the *Alonzo Child* into New Orleans, a city preparing for war. Southern gallantry and military skill would be quickly decisive, Southerners widely believed. Control of the Mississippi River would determine the war's outcome in the west. Fervently pro-Southern, the captain enlisted himself and his boat in the Confederate cause. After some refitting for military duty, the *Alonzo Child* would become a gunboat, patrolling from New Orleans to Vicksburg. Sam Clemens decided that he would excuse himself from service. His identification with the South was real, but it was the result of personal history and culture rather than intellectual or emotional conviction. In one sense, his long, slow regional drawl, more Kentucky than Missouri, was his most Southern characteristic. Though Jane Clemens had a passion for the South, her major concern was for her family; the reality of slavery she, and the Clemens family, could easily forgo.

Secession had never been popular in the Clemens family or in Hannibal. Orion's strong pro-Unionism did not distress his family and, to whatever extent Sam was a Southerner, he also had an intellectual and emotional identification with American national consciousness, with the United States. His Hannibal childhood had been filled with the symbols and rituals of the Union, from patriotic textbooks to annual Fourth of July celebrations. Southern self-consciousness had been more romantic myth than political activism. When he had traveled to the East, he had not felt himself in alien territory, despite his awareness of cultural differences. New York and Philadelphia he had found expressive of his personal and national identity. He was clear that he did not want to join the Southern navy. Waving good-bye to the *Alonzo Child,* he steamed northward as a passenger on the *Nebraska*—the last boat to get through the Union blockade.

In St. Louis he was without work. With minor struggle, the city seemed likely to remain under Union control, though nearby areas would be vigorously contested. In May and June 1861, Union and Confederate sympathizers in St. Louis were in the process of sorting themselves out. Attempting to steer the state toward the Confederacy, Missouri's new governor encouraged militia volunteers to organize themselves into pro-Southern units. As a licensed pilot, Sam Clemens was a potential asset to both sides. He did not want to serve in the Union forces, partly because of his Southern identification. He did not want to serve the Confederacy, partly because of his sense of national identity. But, as he stood on Southern soil, personal allegiance often seemed more important than issues. His friends and community mostly sympathized with the South. William Moffett announced that he would go to prison rather than fight against his brothers and friends if he were drafted into the Union army. One night, Annie Moffett remembered, "Uncle Sam and I were standing on the front steps . . . when a company of boys . . . passed," carrying a Confederate flag, "shouting 'Hurrah for Jeff Davis!' Uncle Sam called to them and asked if they wanted badges. Of course they answered yes. He asked me to run up to his room and bring down the ribbons I would find there. . . . I changed my allegiance almost daily, but I must have been on the Confederate side that day. . . . A very short while after . . . a boy eight or nine years old . . . was shouting, and waving a Union flag. Suddenly a gang of boys . . . set fire to the flag. Uncle Sam rushed from the house, rescued the flag, put out the fire and chased the boys away. . . . He loved his country's flag and all that it symbolized, and it hurt him to see even this cheap little flag insulted." At a minimum, it was emblematic of divided feelings and his own anxiety about becoming engaged in the conflict. "He was obsessed with the fear that he might be arrested by government agents and forced to act as pilot on a government gunboat while a man stood by with a pistol ready to shoot him if he showed the least sign of a false move. He was almost afraid to leave the house." He kept indoors as much as he could.

Restless and impatient, his nerves on ragged edge after weeks of keeping out of sight in St. Louis, he went in mid-June to Hannibal, ostensibly to collect a debt owed him by Will Bowen, who also could not practice his vocation and had returned to his native city to help his mother open a boardinghouse. Before he left, as Annie Moffett later recalled, a man came to the house in St. Louis and identified himself as Smith. "He had come with the wild project of forming a company. . . . Uncle Sam accepted at once." Perhaps he went to Hannibal with both interests in mind. Years before in Hannibal, as a boy of twelve, he had greeted with rapturous enthusiasm the call to arms for the Mexican War. He had had a "consuming desire" to heed it. Now, at twenty-five, he heard the bugle call again. Peer pressure probably pressed hard, and suddenly it must have seemed clear to him that he had to join with his Hannibal friends in the enterprise at hand. He was soon a member of an improvised militia, with no connection to any regular Confederate army group, called the Marion Rangers, after Marion County. It was, so to speak, a band of brothers, fourteen men, including Arch Fuqua, Sam Bowen, Ed Stevens, and John Robards, a militia with little equipment and leadership, which years later Mark Twain was to describe with comic, biting exaggeration and angry antiwar pathos in "The Private History of a Campaign That Failed." It contains the only, and undoubtedly partly fictional, account of the episode.

First the unit marched ten miles to New London, where an old veteran had them swear on the Bible allegiance to the Confederate cause. Then they went into training nearby, where they were visited by Ella Lampton, Sam's cousin, who thought them ludicrously unprofessional. Supplied by local farmers with horses and mules, they attempted exercises and maneuvers. Insecure, anxious, constantly attacked by rumors of enemy advances, they were mostly concerned about which direction to retreat in. Reacting to rumors exhausted them. None of them wanted to take orders from an equal, which remained the case even after they elected officers, as if military rank were determined by democratic procedures. Clemens found himself elected second lieutenant. Used to sleeping in comfortable beds, they found the woods and fields inhospitable. Food was scarce. On one exercise, mounted on a mule he had named Paint-Brush, Clemens almost drowned when the mule preferred to walk rather than swim across a river. One of his fellow soldiers recalled the occasion of an actual skirmish: "[We] mounted and rode away at full speed for our camp, leaving our lieutenant and 'Paint-Brush' far in the rear. The last we heard of him he was saying, 'Damn you, you want the Yanks to capture me!' " The irrepressible Sam Bowen cursed everything and everyone, including Clemens, in an unending torrent of invective. He cursed their situation even in his sleep. And they were always accompanied by fear. Faceless but formidable, the enemy was always, they worried, close by. For a while they camped at a farm. What they understood to be a Union force of undetermined but probably substantial size soon frightened them back into the security of the woods. Fortunately, the Union patrol turned out to be only a rumor.

By the second week, Clemens had an increasing sense of self-ridicule, of the heroic image of himself and his warrior brothers shrinking to a child-sized proportion. One night, so he later claimed, they confronted what seemed to them in the moonlight a Union soldier, the vanguard of a patrol, they assumed. They fired. He fell dead. When they examined him, they discovered that he was a civilian, and alone. Ashamed, Clemens had had enough. With a painful boil on his behind and his ankle aching from a fall from the second floor of a barn, he was irritable and miserable. He had, he decided, no "desire to kill people to whom [he] had not been introduced." Neither did his comrades. The Marion Rangers retreated west and south toward the town of Florida, familiar to Clemens from his boyhood days on his uncle's farm. Rumor reached them that a Union force was sweeping toward them, commanded, Twain later learned, by Colonel Ulysses S. Grant. The rumor was accurate. Having had more than enough and in no mood to fight against superior forces, the Marion Rangers disbanded. It was not difficult for Clemens to make the transfer from soldier to civilian; he had hardly been a soldier at all. Within a week, by early July, he was back in St. Louis.

It was not a comfortable place for a man with no work. The small fraternity of the Western Boatman's Benevolent Association kept an eye on one another. Some went to the Confederacy, others to the Union. His mentor, Horace Bixby, had enlisted in the Union navy. But to go to neither was unusual, certainly suspect. The military authorities, glancing down the roster of the Pilots' Association, would want to know the disposition of these valuable assets. In St. Louis, Clemens had good reason to keep out of sight, though on July 10 he appeared before his fellow Masons to receive his third degree as a Master Mason. He preferred lodge to church, and the enlightenment rationality of the Masons appealed to him enough so that he was not bothered by its "mysteries." Annie Moffett was disturbed that her uncle did not go to church: "I thought he needed a little religious instruction and started to tell him the story of Moses. Uncle Sam was strangely obtuse. . . . He said he knew Moses very well, that he kept a secondhand store on Market Street. I tried very hard to explain that it wasn't the Moses I meant, but he just couldn't understand." In general, though, whatever the attractions of Masonry, St. Louis was precisely the wrong place for Sam Clemens to be. Away from the river he would be less vulnerable. He had saved a thousand dollars, enough to travel—though not to sustain himself for more than six months.

In early July 1861, Orion Clemens received the instructions he had been eagerly awaiting since his commission as secretary of Nevada Territory had been affirmed. With his wife and daughter safely in the bosom of Mollie's Keokuk family, he was about to depart. Unfortunately, he had no advance against his salary for his travel expenses. Pamela or Sam would be the obvious source of money. Why shouldn't Sam help his brother by paying for his stagecoach fare, and, for that matter, come along himself? He could not stay in St. Louis. South, north, east—each of these directions had dangerous ideological and even military associations. Since 1849, when John Robards had marched out of Hannibal, his blond hair glamorously tousled by the wind, the faraway West had been an exotic and wonderful destination for young men to fulfill romantic dreams. California had been in everyone's mind, but recent reports of silver and gold deposits in the mountains not far from Carson City, where Orion would be situated, made Nevada or Washoe, as it was also called, equally compelling. Suddenly it seemed to make sense for Sam. Jane Clemens found it comforting that her two sons would be together and out of war's way. It would be for only about three months, they assumed, after which Sam would be able to resume piloting.

In mid-July, the brothers boarded the *Sioux City* at the St. Louis levee. It took them on a sleepy six-day trip up the Missouri to St. Joseph, on the Missouri-Kansas border, further west than either had ever been. At St. Joseph, Sam bought two tickets at two hundred dollars each, three hundred dollars in immediate cash and the final hundred due in thirty days, on the Central Overland and Pike's Peak Express. He was left with about eight hundred dollars, which needed to last until Orion received his first salary payment or until he himself could find a way to refill his wallet. When they discovered each passenger was limited to twenty-five pounds of baggage, they sent most of their possessions back to St. Louis. Orion "took along about four pounds of U.S. Statutes and six pounds of Unabridged Dictionary," Sam "a pitiful little Smith and Wesson's seven-shooter, which carried a ball like a homeopathic pill, and it took the whole seven to make a dose for an adult." Indeed, they knew little about the world to which they were going, though they got a better sense of it as soon as they entered the Concord coach, a "cradle on wheels" with leather shock absorbers that rocked rather than jolted the passengers. It was to be their crowded, claustrophobic home for the almost three weeks it would take to travel from Kansas to Carson City. On the second day, after a night at Cottonwood Station, they veered northwest, left the state of Kansas and entered Nebraska Territory. The younger of the two could not have imagined that he would not return for more than six years.

CHAPTER FOUR

THE MARK TWAIN LEDGE

1861–1864

1.

Twenty days after leaving Kansas the Clemens brothers were in Carson City, Nevada. By 1871, when he came to write *Roughing It,* Mark Twain had forgotten most of the details of the journey. Fortunately, he was able to refresh his memory by consulting a chronological account that Orion had kept. During the ensuing decade, he had traveled to so many places that his first stagecoach trip had lost its freshness; he also forgot because itinerary details rarely interested him. He had eyes mostly for character and story, for irony and paradox, the exotic and the unexpected, the culturally significant and the scenically beautiful. Later, Orion's journal gave him the framework on which to structure a partly factual, partly fictional narrative. Rocking and bouncing for twenty days in the Central Overland and Pike's Peak Express from St. Joseph to Cottonwood Station, Nebraska, from Fort Kearny on the Platte River to Fort Laramie, Wyoming, then through the South Pass to Great Salt Lake City, Utah Territory, and then across the Overland Pass to Carson City, Nevada, Sam Clemens apparently hadn't the slightest idea that one day he would want to write about this journey. Despite the travel letters and sketches he had written as a young printer and then as a river pilot, he did not consider himself a professional writer.

In his journal, Orion noted the sighting of their first jack rabbit, prairie wolf, and antelope; the change from farmland to prairie and from prairie to hill country; the muddy water of the Platte River; their first view of Indians, with buffalo skin wigwams; "an Indian child's grave on a scaffold about eight feet from the ground"; then the first cactus and "alkali water in the road, giving it a soapy appearance . . . the ground in many places appearing as if whitewashed." The Black Hills loomed. The first snow-covered mountains they had ever seen glittered in the sun "like settings of silver." At the Rocky Mountains' South Pass they were "902 miles from St. Joseph," which awed them. A Mormon wagon train seemed both indigenous and exotic. Union soldiers, who the day before had fired on "300 or 400 Utes, whom they supposed gathered for no good purpose," swaggered by them. On an early August afternoon, fifteen miles from Salt Lake City, "the most gorgeous view of mountain peaks" came into view. As they rocked on across the desert, the days were warm, the nights cold. On the sixteenth day, they descended Rock Canyon, to Carson Sink, "a beautiful lake." On August 14, they "arrived at Carson City . . . 1700 miles from St. Joseph."

While his failure to set down a contemporaneous record of the trip gave him greater freedom to reconfigure the past creatively, Twain found *Roughing It* a hard book to write precisely because of the novelty of creating, ten years later, a cultural and autobiographical narrative in the guise of a travel book. What Sam Clemens probably had at best only vague insight about in 1861, Mark Twain saw clearly in 1871. Ten years removed from the journey, Orion's record of when and where they had first sighted prairie dogs or how many days they had been out of St. Joseph when they came to the River Platte hardly mattered. What did matter was Sam's first encounter with Native Americans and with Mormons. When he first saw Native Americans, they were a curiosity; later, when he wrote about them, they were to him—and to the government—a blight to be extinguished. By 1871, the reality of Native Americans contrasted sharply with the idealistic image of the noble savage, of James Fenimore Cooper's literary red men. They were a shattered illusion, the one instance of an ethnic minority so alien and anti-Victorian and so much in the way of "progress" that Twain joined America at large in seeing nothing redeemable about them. Later, he was to admire and promote the legend of General George Custer.

The Mormons he was fascinated by. Though they get only bare mention in Orion's journal and seem hardly on Clemens' mind during his Nevada years, in *Roughing It* they are given star billing. A substantial part of a chapter represents, as if it were fact, a fictional account of a long interview with Brigham Young that a Mr. Johnson relates to Orion and Sam. The perilous religious and political history of the Mormons, overflowing into two appendices, became an important part of the narrative. Like many Americans, Twain found the only homegrown Anglo-American religious cult fascinating, its history part of his own concern with American values, with religious ideals and skepticism, with the attraction and the humorous possibilities of polygamy, and with the issues of nationhood that were part of the emerging consolidation of the United States as a single country from the Atlantic to the Pacific. Could this diverse country ever be genuinely united into a single entity?

In *Roughing It* Twain provided answers that his contemporaries wanted to hear. Whereas Orion's narrative takes them literally across the continental divide, Twain's highlights the mysterious unity of the East and the West. At the top of the divide, he writes, there is a spring, so their guide tells them, that sends water "through two outlets in opposite directions." This mythical spring seems the perfect image of the reality he and his readers desire as it sends one stream of water westward on a journey to the Gulf of California and the Pacific Ocean; the other eastward to the Yellowstone, the Missouri, and the Mississippi. Each, from the same source, travels thousands of miles through varied landscapes, uniting the country. The eastward-flowing stream continues, "traversing shoals and rocky channels, then endless chains of bottomless and ample bends, walled with unbroken forests, then mysterious byways and secret passages among wooded islands, then the chain bends again, bordered with wide levels of shining sugar-cane" to New Orleans, and finally, "after two long months of daily and nightly harassment, excitement, enjoyment, adventure, and awful peril of parched throats, pumps and evaporation, pass the Gulf and enter into its rest upon the bosom of the tropic sea, never to look upon its snow-peaks again or regret them." *Roughing It* is Twain's version, in words, of Frederick Church's painting *Heart of the Andes,* a spectacular, patriotic depiction of the American continent, with Twain's Mississippi Valley as its center. It was, in 1871, an affirmation of national unity that Sam Clemens, fleeing the Civil War in 1861, could not have envisioned in imagination or created in words.

2.

Carson City was "situated in a flat, sandy desert" surrounded by "prodigious mountains" with a vastness that made Clemens feel his soul expand "like a bladder." "Ultimately [you] find yourself," he wrote to his mother, "growing and swelling and spreading into a giant." Missouri had been nothing like this. His relationship to the landscape had to be newly conceived. From the surrounding heights, "you look disdainfully down upon the insignificant village of Carson . . . seized with a burning desire to stretch forth your hand, put the city in your pocket, and walk off with it." The air was thin, the sky infinitely high, the sun and shadows strikingly sharp. It was like being beamed down onto a strange planet where nothing like Missouri existed. The dominant color was a range of browns, from beige sand to dark mountains. In the treeless landscape, green was absent. "It never rains here, and the dew never falls. No flowers grow here, and no green thing gladdens the eye. The birds that fly over the land carry their provisions with them. Only the crow and the raven tarry with us."

Orion had brought his provisions with him, so to speak: his salaried position as secretary. Nevada was still officially a part of Utah Territory, and the secretary's responsibility was to work in conjunction with the newly appointed governor to lay the foundations of government, particularly the formation of a legislature. Nevada needed to become a territory before it could become a state. Edward Bates had not been imperceptive when, qualifying his recommendation, he had described Orion as "an honest man of fair mediocrity of talents & learning" who would do no worse than similar appointments. An inexperienced administrator, Orion soon clashed with the territorial governor, James Warren Nye, a New York City/Tammany Hall–bred politician whose ideas and practices differed from Orion's rigid Presbyterian mind-set. Orion tried to keep strict accounts. The governor juggled the ledger in order to keep cash flowing, sometimes into undeserving pockets, often into desirable political adjustments. Orion satisfied his accounts but not his constituency. If need arose under a category in which all funds had been dispersed, he considered it dishonest to transfer funds.

In 1861, Carson City, with a population of 1,500, was a dusty, windy town of ramshackle wooden structures and a few modest stone buildings. It offered an equitable climate and a location convenient to the mining settlements to the north, west, and south. Founded by Mormons extending the Utah domain westward, it had been transformed from farms and ranches into a commercial center by the discovery of silver ore in nearby Virginia City, which had a honeycomb of "ledges" permeating Davidson Mountain that came to be called the Comstock Lode, the single most valuable source of silver in the world. With alternating periods of boom and bust, Nevada's silver and gold, which had replaced California's as the main source of America's mineral wealth, helped finance the Union war effort and postwar expansion.

The second-highest government official in the territory, responsible for setting up a budget and governmental offices with twenty thousand dollars provided by Washington, Orion worked out of his bedroom. Outspoken about his pro-Union views, he immediately made enemies among Confederate sympathizers, but also among Unionists who thought Lincoln too inflexible in attempting an accommodation with the South. Washington, regularly behind in paying and petty about what were justifiable charges, expected Orion to reimburse it for disallowed expenditures. Generally, savvy officials did whatever was necessary to provide foolproof documentation. Orion, though, expected Washington to assume the probity of his procedures and the honesty of his accounts, especially his refusal to disguise, by mislabeling, necessary but irregular expenditures. When in 1862 the Treasury Department disallowed $1,330 incurred for printing official territorial documents, the bureaucratic machine began a ten-year process of cranking out threatening requests that he repay what it considered a debt. But when Washington took six months to send him his salary, he did not find it acceptable to borrow from one of his fat accounts to tide himself over. Behind his thick black beard, the elder Clemens was an inflexible Mosaic moralist.

Younger brother Sam, his eight hundred dollars dwindling fast, had, like the crow and the raven, to find his own provisions. But of two things he was certain. One: he had no intention of following one of the usual professions, such as law. "I have been a slave several times in my life, but I'll never be one again. I always intend to be so situated (unless I marry)"—

which seemed unlikely—"that I can 'pull up stakes' and clear out whenever I feel like it." Two: he was not going home until he was rich, even if that took more than three months. Fortunes were to be made. He wanted one. And the eyes of the homefolk were on him. He would not return without the wealth that would prove him estimable in their eyes.

Two weeks after arriving in Carson City, he traveled by horseback a hundred miles southeast to Aurora, eight thousand feet above sea level on the eastern slope of the Sierra Nevada in the Esmeralda mining district, near Mono Lake, on the Nevada-California border. Supposedly, gold and silver, hiding in "ledges," were to be had for the asking. Excited by Aurora's frenzied growth, he bought fifty "feet" at ten dollars each in the Black Warrior Gold and Silver Mining Company, paying a small fraction of the par value if he paid anything at all. A typical transaction, it was an "unprospected" claim, which meant there was reason to hope but no evidence yet to believe it contained valuable minerals. His down payment may have been his promise to pay for his shares in future labor. He gave little thought to the certainty that there would be later assessments to cover mining costs, an ordinary feature of such stock ownership. Certain that he was born lucky, Clemens believed that his luck and initiative would make him rich. He and Orion would be partners, share and share alike. Claims could be staked for just the price of the recording fee. Until one could record the claim, working it or simply being physically in possession sufficed. And the shotgun approach worked best. Stake as many claims as you can. If only one works out, you will be rich.

When Clemens arrived in Carson City, the basic industrial-economic configuration of Nevada mining was in place. He himself of course had no experience in mining of any sort. Like most miners, he rushed to where rumor declared valuable deposits existed. Sometimes as individual entrepreneurs, often with temporary partners, such miners staked out positions. Some had experience in placer mining, the process of searching for gold nuggets mixed with other ores, either in a river or at an exposed outcropping. Picks, shovels, sifters, food, clothes, a tent or a cave to sleep in, perhaps a mule or a horse, sufficed. This had been the California way, a low-investment business pursued mostly by undercapitalized individuals. Inexperienced miners expected silver or gold to catch their eye.

But in Nevada, the configurations of dark blue stone, indicating deeply buried deposits, required corporate arrangements to pay the high cost of deep tunneling, timber for shoring, machinery for pumping out underground water, and factories to pulverize, sift, and extract millions of tons of rock to release small amounts of precious metal. Capital came from San Francisco syndicates and banks, with San Francisco's stock market setting the value of Nevada mining companies. Most promising ledges, though, usually petered out or turned out not to exist at all. Or they moved underground onto someone else's land since Nevada mining law divided claims vertically. Lawsuits added heavily to the cost of business. Strenuous labor in the deep mines would, in the end, be the fate of most individual entrepreneurs, their dreams of wealth usually reduced to day-labor.

From September 1861 until April 1862, Clemens played out his career as an actual miner. Even at the end of 1861, with a firmer grasp of the reality, he still felt that he might strike it rich. In mid-December he journeyed on his "infernally lazy" horse to Humboldt County, Nevada, 175 miles from Carson City, accompanied by a friend from Keokuk days, William Clagett, the newly appointed notary public of Humboldt, and two new friends, a blacksmith from Carson City and a Maine-born lawyer turned journalist who had come to Nevada via California. The companionable men, their two-horse wagon burdened with 1,800 pounds of provisions (including ten pounds of tobacco, two dogs, ten packs of cards, and a copy of Dickens' *Dombey and Son,* which Clemens read with pleasure), took eleven days to slog to Unionville, a recently laid out town of five hundred people in the Buena Vista mining district. During a two-week visit, he helped his friends get settled, looked around at mining prospects to become active when the mills would start operation in the spring, and licked his lips over how cheap cost of shares in promising ledges. The three men built a log cabin to bunk in. Then, with two other new friends, one of them Captain Hugo Pfersdorff, the codiscoverer of the mining district, Clemens returned to Carson City.

His best hope, he gradually concluded, was speculative investing, trading "feet" rather than digging with pick and shovel. During the next three months his mind was almost entirely on ledges, ledges in Humboldt, Virginia City, and Aurora: how many feet could be bought at what price with what promise of return. One scheme after another flew upward in the happy rhetoric of greed, partly for self-deception but also to keep up the confidence of his Missouri family, to whom he had promised great riches. When his Esmeralda partner reported favorably on the likely earnings of their shares in the "Horatio and Derby," he assured his mother, "If nothing goes wrong, we'll strike the ledge in June—and if we do, I'll be home in July, you know." Like most of the miners, he was homesick. Meanwhile, his descriptions of Nevada life were so upbeat that his mother and sister proposed that they join him to see the wonders for themselves. If Moffett would come quickly, he responded, he would promise him profitable investments. But his mother or sister must take the comparatively easy, though still dangerous, route by sea to California. And he cautioned that they should realize that his "sanguine temperament" was given to exaggeration, and that his effusions over the likelihood of acquiring wealth from the mines needed to be taken with a grain of salt. He could not, though, restrain his compulsive optimism. All that was needed, he assured them, was capital. Fortunately, he had "convinced Orion that he hasn't business talent enough to carry on a peanut stand." "So, you see," he continued, "if mines are to be bought or sold, or tunnels run or shafts sunk, parties have to come to me—and me only. I'm the 'firm,' you know."

At the beginning of March 1862, afflated by his Esmeralda friends' optimism, Clemens bought 1,400 feet in sixteen different claims in Aurora, a kind of primitive mining stock mutual fund, to add to the Esmeralda feet he had purchased previously. None of these had yet produced marketable ore. Shareholders expected to win two ways simultaneously: share value would soar and the dividends from profitable strikes would flow. The thousand-dollar cost he pieced together from Orion's wages, credit from the seller, loans from friends, and his own savings. From early October to the end of November 1861, he had worked as Orion's clerk at a salary of eight dollars a day, and gambling winnings may have been a supplement. In Carson City, he cooled his heels for the winter. Life in the territorial capital had begun to seem too genteel, though he took frequent opportunities to sharpen his poker skills, practice his penchant for swearing, and cultivate a western swagger, including carrying a pistol, which he had no skill at using. One self-imposed task that kept him there was his search for a better office for Orion, whose lack of interest in symbols of power seemed, to Sam, destructive self-effacement and political stupidity. Much of his time he spent scheming. In the spring he expected the arrival of "old St. Louis chums" who would join him in showing the world what their brains and ini-

tiative could do. With his usual combination of condescension and protec-
tiveness, he cautioned mining partner Billy Clagett that Orion did not have
the mettle to take disappointments. He warned Clagett to always mention
such things "in such a way that Orion cannot understand them." "I don't
care a d—n for failures . . . but they nearly kill him, you know."

At last, in April 1862, Clemens hastened to Aurora, now a colorful exemplification of the mining boom. Eager to accelerate what he thought the
certain profitability of their investments, he even hoped to buy more feet
in promising ledges. In Aurora, the silence of wilderness was being transformed into the roar of quartz-crushing machinery, the clunk and crack of
innumerable picks breaking pathways through rock to build timbered
shafts. The Clemens brothers were minority owners in some mines that
were being worked. The nonworked claims in which they were partners
needed to be tested, what Sam had come to Aurora to do. Testing was simply digging manually into "croppings" or "outcroppings" in an effort to
determine whether or not to make a commitment to dig deeper for quartz-
bearing ledges with a silver or gold content that might warrant a full-scale
mine. For those without capital to pay day wages, the only recourse was to
do the digging oneself. Not used to hard physical labor, Sam was exhausted
by the middle of April. He also realized that "the firm" had more feet on its
hands than it could work. He instructed Orion not to buy any more
"ground, anywhere. The pick and the shovel are the only claims I have any
confidence in now. My back is sore and my hands blistered with handling
them today. But something must come, you know." Or not, but he resisted
admitting that. In fact, he asserted, "things are so gloomy that I begin to
feel really jolly and comfortable again. I enjoy myself hugely now."

Some of this was existential whistling in the dark. But some was genuine, a talent for rejuvenation through irony and self-mockery, undergirded
by a resiliency of spirit that kept him focused and at the same time restless. He was indeed capable of honesty, especially if the payment for illusion was hard physical labor. "As far as I can see," he told Clagett, "there
are not more than half a dozen leads here that will do to bet on—only two,
in fact, that a man would like to risk his whole pile on." Apparently, he did
not own feet in either. Or, if he did, they were still a chancy bet. But he
was determined to "hold on a little, and see if I can make anything out of
them." Three additional problems confronted him: if his claims were not
worked a minimum of two days a month, they could be claimed by others;

when he needed cash, there was no cash market for the resale of feet in his ledges; and the cost of crushing his ore always seemed greater than the value of the minerals extracted. Some men made a profession of jumping claims. Sellers seemed everywhere, buyers rare, no matter how attractive the terms. And sharp, sometimes desperate, minds kept trying to devise processes to increase gold and silver yield from ore.

In late April, Clemens thought he had found the man who had such a process and was willing to sell it for one fourth of their profits. "Keep this entirely to yourself," he warned Clagett. With one of his partners, he worked for a week at a quartz mill to learn the magical process. Nothing came of it but exhaustion and a bad cold. When Orion broke what Sam considered a promise to leave all mining business to him, he scorched his brother with angry words, exercising his talent for denunciation. "I shall never look upon Ma's face again, or Pamela's, or get married," or return to Missouri, "until I am a rich man—so you can easily see that when you stand between me and my fortune (the one which I shall make, as surely as Fate itself,) you stand between me & *home,* friends, and all that I care for—and by the Lord God! you must clear the track, you know!"

Working in snow, mud, and sweltering heat, often all on the same day, he dynamited, picked, shoveled, and cursed. At some moments all his claims seemed worthless. But his ability to subordinate disappointment to desire, as well as his stubborn faith that he was both lucky and smart, kept him at it for the next four months. "Two years' time will make us capitalists," he assured Orion. Six more months of privation would certainly suffice. "Perhaps 3 months 'will let us out.'" Riches "*will* come, there is no *shadow* of a doubt." With a fragile rationality, he combined bluff and faith, an approach to money and business problems that was to become characteristic. "I have got the thing sifted down to a dead moral certainty. I own *one-eighth* of the new 'Monitor Ledge, Clemens Company,' and money can't buy a foot of it; because I *know* it contains our fortune," the details of which he laid out with precise calculations that may have impressed the easily credulous Orion. In May, he consolidated his efforts. "I have struck my tent in Esmeralda, and I care for no mines but those I can superintend myself." Most of his faith was placed in "The Clemens Gold and Silver Mining Company," one of the partners of which was a new friend, Calvin Higbie, whom he liked and admired and to whom he later dedicated

Roughing It. A civil engineer who shared a cabin with Clemens, Higbie was "a large, strong man" with "the perseverance of the devil." Later, in *Roughing It,* Twain maintained that he and Higbie staked a claim to a "blind lead," a separate and distinct spur that ran across a rich mine called the "Pride of Utah." In Twain's later account, they thought they had reason to believe it contained ore rich enough to make them millionaires. When Higbie left town to pursue another possibility, he assumed that Clemens would make their "blind lead" claim official. Assuming that Higbie had already done that, Clemens left to assist an ill friend. When, "within ten days after the date of location," neither had fulfilled the requirement of doing "a fair and reasonable amount of work on their new property," eager claim jumpers pounced.

By the end of June 1862, the often sanguine Clemens had had enough. He was restless and miserable. He was also sick of backbreaking labor. In one place "as long, now," he told Orion, "as it is in my nature to stay in one place. . . . Christ! how sick I am of these same old humdrum scenes." And he was desperate for cash, for some reliable source of income, even if modest. But when his mother and sister suggested that he return to the river and resume piloting, under the jurisdiction of the Union navy, he adamantly declined, and not because of Southern patriotism or opposition to the Union. He had less and less of that. His western experiences were increasing his national perspective, his identification with the Union as a whole. Nothing, though, could overcome his injured pride and his sense of thwarted personal destiny. "I never have *once* thought of returning home to go on the river again, and I never expect to do any more piloting at any price." This was news to his family, who had assumed that he loved the river and would return to his former lucrative profession at the first practical moment. That he did not desire to and never would came as a shock. "My livelihood must be made in this country—and if I have to wait longer than expected, let it be so—I have no fear of failure." He intended to spend the winter in San Francisco, where the profits from whatever his leads produced would follow him. When he learned that there might be an opportunity to write travel letters for the *Sacramento Union,* he urged Orion to make a case for his employment via the *Union*'s reporter in Carson City. There was also the possibility of employment on the staff of a new newspaper in the planning stage. He had already published a number of additional letters in the *Gate City,* and in late April 1862 he began sending letters, using the pen name "Josh," to the *Virginia City Territorial Enterprise,* partly because he was bored in Aurora. Certainly, though, he needed the money.

William Bartsow, the managing editor of the *Enterprise,* whom Orion knew well and whom Sam had at least met when Barstow had served the previous year as assistant secretary of the territorial legislature, liked "Josh's" contributions. Orion was not likely to keep his brother's authorship a secret. By August, Barstow knew the Josh letters were by Clemens. When the *Enterprise* needed a replacement for a reporter leaving to visit his family in Iowa, Barstow persuaded the *Enterprise* editor, Joseph Goodman, to offer Clemens the job at twenty-five dollars a week. It might have helped that Orion had the power to provide newspapers of his choice with lucrative contracts for printing state documents. "I have written Barstow," Sam wrote to Orion, "that I will let him know next mail if possible, whether I can take it or not. If G. is not *sure* of starting his paper [in San Francisco] within a month, I think I had better close with Barstow's offer." He soon happily said good-bye to unprofitable, backbreaking work in Aurora.

By late September 1862, one year after his arrival in Nevada, he was at work in the office of the *Virginia City Territorial Enterprise,* never to raise pick and shovel again, though he still hoped to make his fortune from the value of his mining stocks and whatever future stocks he would own. And Clemens found that he could have both his regular salary and his speculative ventures. The next year he told *Enterprise* readers, who had begun to recognize his satirical humor, that he had made a grand mineral discovery and claimed several thousand feet in the heart of Virginia City. It was to be named after him, and it would include the entire Comstock. "The company shall be known as the Unreliable, Auriferous, Argentiferous, Metaliferous Mining Company." He had at last discovered a vein that was to prove valuable.

3.

That literary vein has one of its breathtaking and significant expressions in chapters 22 and 23 of *Roughing It,* dramatizing an incident that happened soon after Clemens' arrival in Nevada. In the middle of September 1861 he set out with a friend, John Kinney, a twenty-one-year-old realtor and mining claim speculator, to visit Lake Tahoe, twenty miles west of Carson City on the Nevada-California border, then called Lake Bigler after the pro-secessionist governor of California. They "had heard a world of talk about [its] marvelous beauty." Rumor reported that vast expanses of fine forest surrounded the lake, which had been revealed to the Anglo-American world only recently, the shores of which very few had visited. "We intended," he later wrote, "to take up a wood ranch or so ourselves and become wealthy." Though he had only just started his mining activities, he had quickly realized that the nearby Virginia City mines had a rapacious need for timber for shoring tunnel walls, which Mount Davidson's barren slopes could not provide. Hauling lumber from the eastern shore of Lake Tahoe to Virginia City might prove profitable.

Without a map, the two men trudged across valleys and over mountains for a distance that seemed much longer than the eleven miles they had been led to expect. Still no lake. At last, though, "the Lake burst upon us—a noble sheet of blue water lifted six thousand three hundred feet above the level of the sea, and walled in by a rim of snow-clad mountain peaks that towered aloft full three thousand feet higher still! . . . I thought it must surely be the fairest picture the whole earth affords." Forests of yellow pine surrounded the shoreline. Except for one sawmill and a few workmen, hardly another human being appeared in the pristine paradise, its pure air "bracing and delicious," the American west in its natural state of innocence. After a good night's sleep, "lulled . . . by the beating of the surf upon the shore," the first thing they did was to claim three hundred acres of timberland, sticking up "notices" on a tree. "We were land owners now, duly seized and possessed, and within the protection of the law," he later wrote. Legal niceties they decided to satisfy by creating a fence of trees cut to fall in a pattern that approximated their boundaries. After cutting down three trees each, they rested. It would be enough, they decided. To satisfy another nicety they began to build a "substantial log house." They soon decided that a "brush" house would suffice. Now, having legalized their claim, and with the satisfaction of ownership, they could loaf. Solitary, blissful days followed. At night they played cards "to strengthen the mind." Each morning they awoke at dawn, alert, vigorous, happy. During the days they drifted in a small boat on waters "so singularly clear" that, no matter how deep, "the bottom was so perfectly distinct that the boat seemed floating in the air!" They seldom talked, "the luxurious rest and indolence" uninterrupted as they "lolled on the sand in camp, and smoked pipes and read some old well-worn novels." They fished, bathed, and smoked, companions of the wilderness, liberated from anyone else's calendar or clock, with no one to tell them what to do; a separate, more congenial civilization.

One early evening, after returning from replenishing supplies, Clemens started a small fire to cook bacon and heat coffee. Suddenly he heard Kinney shouting. Looking up, he saw that his fire was "galloping all over the premises!" Kinney ran through the flames to join him on the lakeshore. The fire raced through acres of dry pine needles "as if they were gunpowder." Then the "dry manzanita chapparal six or eight feet high" were seized by the flame. The intense heat forced the two men into their small boat from which, spellbound, they watched the fire spread. All they could see was aflame, and, as they raised their eyes, they saw the fire surge up adjacent ridges. It disappeared "in the canyons beyond," then burst into view at a level higher on the further ridges, and then higher and higher, diving and rising again and again, until it suddenly flamed out on the lower mountainside. "Crimson spirals" appeared on the higher slopes and "as far as the eye could reach the lofty mountain-fronts were webbed as it were with a tangled network of red lava streams. Away across the water," on the other side of the lake behind them, "the crags and domes were lit with a ruddy glare, and the firmament above was a reflected hell!" They watched the compelling scene with terror and pleasure. They had set the whole world on fire. "Every feature of the spectacle was repeated in the glowing mirror of the lake! Both pictures were sublime, both were beautiful; but that in the lake had a bewildering richness about it that enchanted the eye and held it with the stronger fascination." For four hours they watched, riveted by the spectacle, oblivious to heat or hunger. That the wilderness had been destroyed by his carelessness was less significant than the deep impression nature's power made.

Embodied in words in *Roughing It,* the relationship between the mirroring lake—a nineteenth-century image of the creative process—and the actual event was heightened and made even more expressive. In *Roughing It* Twain dramatized his coming of age as an artist and the relationship between his art and the world. The fire at Lake Tahoe had been powerfully destructive. A paradise had been destroyed by carelessness, by human nature and its intersection with chance; as Henry had been killed by the *Pennsylvania* explosion, as this lofty forest had been by Sam Clemens' attraction to disaster, so the American wilderness would be destroyed in the interest of commerce and economic growth. "We were homeless wanderers again, without any property. Our fence was gone, our house burned down; no insurance." Eden could not last, and the expulsion was self-generated. The image of "homeless wanderer" always appealed to Twain, an anticipation of his frequent and warranted admission that often he himself had put the match to the flame. He did, though, always have an insurance policy of a kind: his ability to change some aspects of loss into gain by transforming the conflagrations of his life into literature.

4.

When in early September 1862 twenty-six-year-old Sam Clemens, dusty, in a woolen shirt, his pants tucked into his boots and his slouched hat pushed back, probably having walked all the way, entered the *Virginia City Territorial Enterprise* office to introduce himself as their new local reporter, he had some idea of what it meant to be a journalist, though no notion of what his exact duties were to be or how long the job would last. He did know that he badly needed the work. His model of what journalists did was derived from his adolescent years as a printer, editor, and writer for his brother's newspapers, as well as his observations as a printer and a reader in St. Louis, New York, Philadelphia, and Cincinnati. During his months in Carson City he had read the local newspapers, including Virginia City's *Territorial Enterprise*. To the extent that he was prone to be self-conscious about such matters, he could readily establish in his mind a model of the overall balance between information, entertainment, public service, editorials, and advertisements that characterized nineteenth-century American journalism.

In the early stages of the information age, newspapers proliferated and competed vigorously with one another. New towns in particular leaned heavily on them for civic and corporate identity. A town without a newspaper was almost no town at all. Though there were rivals, especially the *Union*, the *Enterprise* and the town of Virginia City were inextricably identified with each other. Founded in 1858, the *Territorial Enterprise* had been failing when bought in March 1861 for a thousand-dollar promissory note. The owners were twenty-three-year-old Joseph T. Goodman, a handsome, self-educated compositor who directed the editorial department, and Denis McCarthy, a twenty-one-year-old printer from San Francisco who managed the print shop. Goodman was sensible, amiable, and talented, with great energy and independence. A sharp writer and an outspoken editorialist, he encouraged good writing and professional esprit in others. In his year and a half of tenure he had made *Enterprise* editorials the most compelling and its reporting the best in Nevada. McCarthy was lively, ambitious, and eager to get rich, an obsessive speculator in mining stocks, in which he was to gain and lose two fortunes.

When Clemens walked through the door, his temperament and ambition found a nurturing home. William Wright, the thirty-two-year-old local reporter he was temporarily replacing, immediately liked the new hire. In the three months before his departure in December, Wright, who used the pseudonym Dan De Quille, broke in the younger man to the extent that he was breakable. Steve Gillis, a twenty-two-year-old Mississippian whose two brothers were later also to be Clemens' friends, was the newspaper's best compositor. Volatile, rambunctious, loyal, Gillis took a brotherly liking to Clemens; they became close friends in practical jokes and humorous adventures, including late-night drinking and occasional brawls. Rollin Daggett, four years older than Clemens, had set out from Ohio to California, alone and on foot, at the age of eighteen. An experienced newspaperman who had recently edited San Francisco's *Golden Era*, a weekly literary journal, he had quickly become a valued member of the inner circle. He competed with Goodman for the title of bard of the Comstock, and, as part owner of a brokerage house specializing in mining stocks, he was a capable businessman.

For his part, Clemens could drink and swear as well as the best of them, and smoke even more. Like the others, he was idiosyncratic but dependable; amiable but also engagingly cantankerous; stubborn and self-assertive but also generous and funny. Disheveled and roughly attired, he took what they all valued as western individualism and disregard for genteel appearances to a level appropriate to the group's self-image and the self-definition of the rugged mining town they served. Western American Victorians, they had a high regard in principle for propriety and especially for sentiment and morality in regard to "ladies." But manliness and masculinity, defined by frontier appearances and rhetoric, meant much to them. They all found it appropriate and quietly amusing that Clemens carried a pistol that he hadn't the slightest idea how to use.

When Clemens arrived in Virginia City in September 1862, the three main recreational activities were drinking, card-playing, and fighting. Although there was a small civic-minded middle and proprietary class and a number of churches, the town took its flavor from the mining community; from the three town newspapers; from the dozens of bars, restaurants, rooming houses, brothels, and laundries; from the daily traffic jams of heavily loaded wagons in the streets; from the barroom fights, music, dancing, vulgarity, and commercial sex available at a strip of seedy all-purpose entertainment emporiums; from the sense of isolation and self-sufficiency alleviated mainly by stagecoaches southwest to Carson City and west to San Francisco; from the irritability and paranoia of aggressive, disappointed men; from the ethos of competition, often settled by force, sometimes by the courts, where one lawyer or another always won; and from the widespread feeling that every man had the right to be rich. If he were not, someone else was to blame.

With more than 3,000 people in 1860, about 2,800 of whom were men, two thirds of whom were in the mining industry, Virginia City had a population in which one out of three citizens had been born in a foreign country. Most came from Ireland and Germany, drawn to the third largest city in the West (after San Francisco and Salt Lake City) by the hope of getting rich. All effort was concentrated on Mount Davidson's Comstock Load, a ledge of silver ore that ran through the mountain that towered over the city, which expanded up the slopes. Thousands of miners and dozens of companies competed for ore-bearing space on this main ledge, desperate for some piece of it to call their own. With the invention of the square-set timbering system in 1860, Mount Davidson had become a honeycomb of tunnels. Every day thousands of miners descended hundreds of feet into darkness and danger. The danger for everyone else was that, as they went about their ordinary business on town streets, what seemed solid ground suddenly might collapse into a tunnel. Every day people plunged into injury or death. In 1860, the Comstock produced a million dollars worth of bullion, the figure rising until in 1864 it was almost $16 million. By 1870, the population had risen to over 11,000, more than 60 percent of which were men.

Within a short while, Clemens learned what it meant to be the *Territorial Enterprise* "local," a combination desk editor–reporter in a raucous town anchored by sagebrush and swearing. His job was to report on local happenings in small squibs of mostly inconsequential news and in occasional articles about significant events, particularly those affecting the mining industry. From the start, local reporting in the conventional sense did not appeal to him. The daily round of the courthouse, the jail, and the commercial district offered little new after the tenth story. He was indeed grateful for the notorious criminals of the area, his "crimson discipleship"—Sam Brown, Farmer Pete, Six-Fingered Jake, and Bill Mayfield, among others—who provided the murders that tingled the palates of the jaded writer and his readers. He also took the opportunity nineteenth-century journalism offered for humor and satire. De Quille's sketches in the *Enterprise* had led the way. Clemens' first major piece for the paper, published in October 1862 and under his own name, was a tongue-in-cheek fictitious report of the discovery of a "Petrified Man." Despite its use of scientific detail and its seriousness of tone, it was easily identifiable as a hoax to a careful reader, one of whom, a Judge Sewell in Humboldt County, the article mentions derisively. Why Clemens had a grudge against him is unclear, but in April 1863 Sewell threatened to thrash the young writer. De Quille, by example or by comment, may have suggested using a pseudonym, which, for this kind of journalism, could provide some minor protection as well as a level of deniability that might be advantageous. It would also give Clemens a little more inventive freedom than he might otherwise have felt.

Early in February 1863, shortly after De Quille's departure, Clemens for the first time used the byline "Mark Twain." Writing from Carson City to the *Enterprise* about a party he had attended, he began with the phrase, "I feel very much as if I had just awakened out of a long sleep." He could have no idea that commentators in the future would make much of the phrase, as if he were self-consciously alluding to his transformation from Sam Clemens to Mark Twain. Actually, he had literally "just awakened," resting two days after a sleepless night prior to traveling from Virginia to Carson City and then attending a late-night party there.

Everyone who counted, including Goodman, with whom he traveled to Carson City, liked his *nom de plume*. Within a short time, Clemens' Nevada friends were calling Sam "Mark." Clemens himself also began to refer to himself sometimes as Mark, a practice he continued throughout his life, though he often maintained the distinction between the two for practical reasons. Once he took the name "Mark Twain" it stuck, an inseparable part of a unified public and private personality. Later, of course, it provided no cover, no deniability, at all, and part of Twain's growth as a writer that began during his years at the *Territorial Enterprise* was learning to control his aggressive humor in keeping with the transparency of his pseudonym. He would never experiment with any other, or publish again as Sam Clemens.

His Nevada friends were certain that he had taken his pen name from a Virginia City barroom practice: a customer's debt for two drinks was indicated by chalking up two parallel marks, one beneath and to the side of the other. Twain himself wrote to a correspondent in 1899, "As I remember it, two marks were used (mark twain), instead of two crosses [xx]." Beginning in 1877, he explained many times that he was indebted for the name to Isaiah Sellers. " 'Mark Twain,' " he wrote, "was the *nom de plume* of one Captain Isaiah Sellers who used to write river news over it for the New Orleans *Picayune*: he died in 1863, and as he could no longer need that signature, I laid violent hands upon it without asking permission of the proprietor's remains." And in 1881 he told an old acquaintance, "No; the *nom de plume* did not originate in that way," though what way "that" was is unclear. "Capt. Sellers used the signature, 'Mark Twain,' himself when he used to write up the antiquities in the way of river reminiscences for the New Orleans *Picayune*. He hated me for burlesquing them in an article in the *Delta;* so four years later, when he died, I robbed the corpse—that is, I confiscated the *nom de plume*. I have published this vital fact, 3,600 times now. But no matter, it is good practice; it is about the only fact that I can tell the same way every time." Apparently not. In fact, Sellers died in 1864. And scholars have examined his river reports without finding any signature but the captain's name. It is unlikely that the stories will ever be reconciled.

The "Petrified Man" article caused a considerable stir, especially since Nevada and California newspapers had reprinted it under the impression that it was a straight news story. A year later, Twain published another hoax, "A Bloody Massacre Near Carson." Intended as a satirical attack on speculators who created false dividends to attract unwary investors, similar to the practice of "salting" mines to profit from the news of a great strike, the article reported, with gory details, that a deceived investor had ax-murdered his family and then killed himself. Since there were no explicit signals from the author as there had been in "Petrified Man," most readers apparently did not readily determine that this was a work of fiction, though the moralistic final sentence might have alerted some. Still, readers were entitled to their expectation that, given its source, it would be fact; and the sensationalism of its details carried an emotional impact that made its fictional guise harder to see through. Editors and readers were outraged. Dan De Quille, who had just returned from Iowa and was sharing a room with Twain, later recalled that "there was a howl from Siskiyou to San Diego. Some papers demanded the immediate discharge of the author of the item by the *Enterprise* proprietors." Outraged readers felt victimized by dishonesty; angry editors felt professionally demeaned. The rival Virginia City newspapers sanctimoniously gloated. Some California newspapers that conducted exchanges with the *Enterprise,* permitting mutual at-will reprinting, ended the relationship.

Apparently, De Quille recalled, his roommate had second thoughts and painful regrets about undermining the *Enterprise's* credibility. Characteristically, he had not anticipated even the possibility of such a response to his piece. He tossed and turned sleeplessly, as if he were "being burned alive on both sides of the mountain." Later commentators provided the undocumented report that he had published an apology and offered to resign. Daggett provided comforting words, Goodman unflinching support. The *Enterprise* proprietors stood behind their local troublemaker, in part because they felt it their highest journalistic duty to stir things up. That Clemens had a sassy attitude was part of his attraction. Certainly Goodman and McCarthy had a keen sense of the value of publicity and of their talented, intemperate, independent, occasionally insecure and defensive local reporter who constantly dared them to fire him, boasting that he made fifty percent profit on his salary by being paid six dollars a day and "only doing three dollars' worth of work."

5.

Though Twain was to spend less than three years in Nevada and less than two in Virginia City, they were formative in his development as a writer and in the emergence of a distinctive personality. The *Territorial Enterprise* gave him the freedom and support that allowed him to experiment with the borderline between fact and fiction. The paper helped him develop a particular voice, though he was still to struggle for some years to find the appropriate genre to contain its expression. But in his letters to the *Enterprise* when he was away from Virginia City, his frequent, probably daily squibs and paragraphs, his humorous sketches of local activities, and his satirical hoaxes like "A Bloody Massacre," there had surfaced a "Mark Twain" whom his later readers could recognize on stylistic grounds alone. There had also materialized a Mark Twain persona, a combination of his Missouri drawl, his attraction to distinctive dress, and his characteristic mustache, which first appeared in late 1863. Not everyone appreciated this new local "character," however. He had enemies, those who thought him callow, a jokester who preferred a laugh to the truth and found amusement in someone else's pratfall, and much bluff and no substance, both in person and in print, especially in regard to his tough exterior and challenging words.

In Missouri, the Clemens family heard from him with infrequent regularity, his letters sanitized to avoid upsetting his mother. "It is misery to me to write letters," he told her. When he learned that she proudly passed them around to various St. Louis people, he complained, "Can't you let me tell a lie occasionally to keep my hand in for the public, without exposing me?" If he told his mother that he went to church, he was not entirely lying. He had become friendly with the local Episcopal priest, Franklin Rising, a friendship which probably required occasional Sunday mornings. "I used to try to teach him how he ought to preach in order to get at the better natures of the rough population about him, and he used to try hard to learn—for I knew them and he did not, for he was refined and sensitive and not intended for such a people as that."

Enjoying the bachelor life, Clemens abhorred the notion of exposing a wife to frontier discomfort and the labor it entailed. For the time being, chambermaids would do. "I don't mind sleeping with female servants as long as I am a bachelor," he wrote his sister-in-law, "—by *no* means—but *after* I marry, that sort of thing will be 'played out,' you know." His promise to live a pure life, untouched by tobacco or drink, he observed mainly in the breech. He smoked incessantly, and, while never a serious drinker, he enjoyed the fellowship of alcohol. Swearing came to him as naturally as talking, gambling less so, though he played cards to alleviate boredom or to be sociable. Billiards became a passion. "Once, when I was an underpaid reporter in Virginia City," he recalled in his old age, "whenever I wished to play billiards I went out to look for an easy mark. One day a stranger came to town and opened a billiard parlor. I looked him over casually. When he proposed a game, I answered, 'All right.' 'Just knock the balls around a little so that I can get your gait,' he said; and when I had done so, he remarked, 'I will be perfectly fair with you. I'll play you left-handed.' I felt hurt, for he was cross-eyed, freckled, and had red hair, and I determined to teach him a lesson. He won first shot, ran out, took my half dollar, and all I got was the opportunity to chalk my cue. 'If you can play like that with your left hand,' I said, 'I'd like to see you play with your right.' 'I can't,' he said, 'I'm left-handed.' "

He persisted in his conviction that if he continued to play the mining stock market, intelligence and luck eventually would make him wealthy. He was, he explained to his skeptical mother, like other reporters on the *Enterprise* staff, the frequent beneficiary of gifts of feet in promising ledges. He boasted, "If I had any business tact, the office of reporter . . . would be worth $30,000 a year—whereas if I get 4 or $5,000 out of it, it will be as much as I expect." Reports in the *Enterprise* of promising strikes or of likely dividends were worth huge sums to those with shares to sell or positions to take. *Enterprise* news and rumor columns were frequently "salted." In exchange for shares, reporters published "information" that enriched some speculators. "I pick up a foot or two occasionally for lying about somebody's mine," he told Jane Clemens, not in the least embarrassed to tell her that he had "raised the price of 'North Ophir' from $13 a foot to $45 a foot, to-day, and they gave me five feet." Just as his favorable word in print could increase share value, his unfavorable could decrease it. "If I don't know how to levy black-mail on the mining companies—who does, I should like to know?" Adding irresponsibility to dishonesty seemed redemptive. These stocks most likely would "go the way of all the rest," he explained. He would probably mislay the certificates or throw them in his trunk "and never get a dollar out of it." In fact, he would finance two high-living months in San Francisco with profits from gifts of wildcat mining shares.

Restless, often bored, after six months as the *Territorial Enterprise* local, he was eager for a vacation, a break from the bleak February weather and mining-town discomfort. Trips to Carson City, including a week in early February 1863, provided minor relief. He had friends there, among them Abe Curry, one of the city's founders, who gave the territorial legislature free use of his hotel in nearby Warm Springs; Sandy Baldwin and William Stewart, the best lawyers in Carson City, who frequently litigated mining disputes; Neely Johnson, another prominent Carson City lawyer and California's fourth governor; and John North, surveyor general of Nevada and associate justice of the territorial supreme court. Through Orion and by virtue of his own stint as legislative clerk, he had gotten to know most of the territory's prominent men. As a reporter, he now had the opportunity to make their deeds known in print. The *Territorial Enterprise* editors welcomed his letters from Carson City. His eyes were set, though, on California, to which he had never been. The Nevada world looked westward for prosperity and civilization, to Sacramento and especially San Francisco, home of the bank vaults and stock market into which Nevada's wealth flowed.

Balked in mid-February 1863 because there was no one to take his place, at last in early May he left for San Francisco with the loose understanding that he would return in about a month. "Mark Twain," the newspaper announced, "has abdicated the local column of the ENTERPRISE, where, by the grace of cheek, he so long reigned Monarch of Mining Items, Detailer of Events, Prince of Platitudes, Chief of Biographers, Expounder of Unwritten Law, Puffer of Wildcat, Profaner of Divinity, Detractor of Merit, Flatterer of Power, Recorder of Stage Arrivals . . . and things in general." He may himself have written the description. If Joe Goodman were not the author, which he might have been, he certainly seconded the sentiment. The column ended with the teasing claim that Clemens was leaving behind his "plighted sage-brush maid" for some city belle. With some savings and stock profits and a pocketful of certificates representing feet in various ledges, "he had gone," the *Enterprise* stated, "to display his ugly person and disgusting manners and wildcat on Montgomery street." Apparently he intended to support himself as a day trader.

With his closest friend in Virginia City, Clement T. Rice, a star reporter for the main opposition newspaper whom he had nicknamed "the Unreliable," he squeezed into a stagecoach, which bumped them across the high Sierras. Rice and Twain frequently used each other as humorous foils in their newspaper stories, firing at each other a day-by-day colloquy of humorous insults, including Twain "giving the Unreliable a column of advice about how to conduct himself in church." A New Yorker, Rice had come to Nevada in 1861. As a reporter, he had moved with the *Carson City Silver*

Age to Virginia City, where it changed its name to the *Union*. Like Clemens, after trying his hand at prospecting he found it more profitable and less work to line his pockets with gifts of shares in return for publishing falsehoods. Off to San Francisco to have fun, the two friends were not disappointed. They stayed first at the second best hotel in town, the Occidental, then, after two weeks, moved to the best and newest, the Lick House, where they dined luxuriously, the days filled with sightseeing, the nights with entertainment. Clemens found time to write only two letters to the *Enterprise,* humorously berating the Unreliable for his conduct and his dissipation, into which he led the innocent Mark Twain.

They ferried across the bay to Oakland, visited San Leandro, Alameda, Fort Point, and the Ocean House, near the Cliff House, "to see the seahorses, and also to listen to the roar of the surf." Splashing his feet in Pacific waters, he remembered doing the same thing on the Atlantic shore—"and then I had a proper appreciation of the vastness of the country." With a newspaper reputation to attend to, he met with the editor of the *San Francisco Call* for whom he contracted to write letters from Virginia City, a possibility he had apparently been encouraged to pursue by the *Territorial Enterprise* editors. It would be a valuable exposure of a *nom de plume* becoming increasingly well known on the West Coast. It also would be an opportunity to puff in the San Francisco market the value of mining stocks he and his friends owned. Each day he kept his eye on the stock market reports, especially those of the Echo Mining Company, which over the next months he was to do everything in his power to puff up. He bought another promising stock on margin, but lost it when Orion could not get him the funds quickly enough. San Francisco itself made him happy. At the end of a month, he told his Missouri family, "I do hate to go back to Washoe. . . . It seems like going back to prison . . . after living in this Paradise." So he extended his stay another month.

Clemens and Rice finally returned to Virginia City at the end of July 1863. With a persistent cold, at the end of August he went to Steamboat Springs to recuperate from the dissipation in San Francisco that he swore to his mother he had not indulged in. He made a brief visit to Lake Tahoe, the beauty of which continued to astound and delight him, though he was startled by the crowds of wealthy people from Virginia City at a newly built luxury hotel, a sign that the commercialization of Lake Tahoe was already well under way. Either because his cold really did not get better or because it was a handy excuse, he returned to San Francisco in early September, still on the *Enterprise* payroll. De Quille's return from Iowa provided local coverage when Clemens was gone. Staying at the Lick House, now a familiar figure whom the owner treated as a special guest and friend, he wrote letters for the *Enterprise,* including an account of his stagecoach trip from Nevada to California, and continued his columns for the *Call,* in which he published his humorous "How to Cure a Cold." In a sketch written in San Francisco, he concluded with a note to the editors ironically claiming that not only was he eager to go home but that "they all say it is healthier up there than it is here. . . . I don't eat enough, I expect." The Lick House banquet room staff would have found this amusing.

Soon after he returned to Virginia City, the building he had been living in burned down, providing him with copy for his first letter to the *San Francisco Call*, a humorous account of the fire. At the end of October he moved into an apartment that he shared with Dan De Quille in a building half owned by Rollin Daggett. When De Quille and Twain, perfect roommates, tried to get Goodman to pay for the furnishings, he refused. They tried to have the tradesman get the money from Goodman, and the tradesman sued. "Mark said we might have known better to try such a trick with 'a man whose front name was Moses and whose rear name was Goldman,'" De Quille later wrote. When the ladies of the Fitch family, residents in the same building, provided pie and milk for the two journalists, who usually got home at one in the morning, Clemens found out where the pies were kept and stole a few. When he hinted that De Quille was the culprit, the ladies were not fooled. His embarrassed stammer gave him away. When De Quille was not at home, Clemens stole wood from the Fitch pile, De Quille recalled. "As soon as he opened the door backing into our room he would call out: 'Damn it, Dan, you haven't been at Daggett's wood again, have you? It's too bad to take so much of his wood.' Then he would throw the wood on the floor and make a great racket, at the same time crying out: 'Damn it, Dan, don't make such a noise! Everybody in the house hears you!'"

At the end of October 1863 he returned to Carson City to cover Nevada Territory's first constitutional convention, which was abuzz with pre-statehood political activity, and published a burlesque account of the putative Third House of the convention, a mock legislative body composed of the attending journalists. At the end of December 1863, he was again in

Carson City, this time to attend the Union Party convention, a sequel to the constitutional convention, during which Orion became the party's nominee for secretary of state in the first state election, to be held in January 1864. Because of earlier irregularities, the state constitution proposed for approval at the election on January 19 was rejected, nullifying the election held for state offices. It voided an election that Orion had won. A new constitution was soon drawn up and approved, which, at the end of October 1864, resulted in Nevada becoming the thirty-sixth state. The nullification had been a great disappointment to Orion, but, in a characteristic spasm of self-destructive virtue, he declined to attend the October state Republican Party convention to nominate or renominate candidates. His presence, he believed, would put unfair pressure on delegates to vote for him. At the same time, he announced that he favored prohibition. When he did not appear at the convention, his colleagues took it as a slight. Besides, whiskey was a staff of life at the convention and in Nevada in general. The convention nominated someone else, who was elected. Orion would never hold government office again, and in two years he would leave Nevada. In February 1864, he and Mollie had buried Jennie Clemens, their eight-year-old only child, in Carson City, a victim of cerebrospinal meningitis. After their departure, they never saw her grave again.

In late November 1863, an editor and writer associated with the New York literary group the Bohemians had come west on assignment to recount his experiences for the *Atlantic Monthly*. He described Mark Twain in an article for the *San Francisco Golden Era* as "that Irresistible Washoe Giant" who as a humorist was "a school by himself." Less than a month later, a nationally famous humorist lectured at Maguire's Opera House, the all-purpose auditorium in Virginia City, and also had high praise for the "Washoe Giant." A year younger than Twain, Charles Farrar Browne, under the pseudonym "Artemus Ward," had made a great reputation as the author of letters and sketches in which the narrator was the butt: an illiterate Yankee who mangled English, his speech highlighted by malapropisms, misspellings, and puns. Like Clemens, Browne had been apprenticed to the printing trade and had become a journalist. While writing for the *Cleveland Plain-Dealer*, he had created "Artemus Ward." Taking to the lecture stage, he toured the country, his sense of timing transforming his primitive, intermittently funny essays into uproarious stage howlers. His lecture at McGuire's had his audience, including the entire *Enterprise* staff, doubled over with laughter. Clemens always remembered "Babes in the Woods" as one of the funniest things he had ever heard. Having already developed a reputation as a clever speaker himself, Clemens had his eyes opened by Ward's mastery, which he later described as "his inimitable way of pausing and hesitating, of gliding in a moment from seriousness to humor without appearing to be conscious of so doing. . . . There was more in his pauses than his words." He also took notice of Ward's financial success, later remarking that "his profits during that season amounted to something like $30,000 or $40,000."

During ten days in Virginia City, Ward used the *Enterprise* office as his headquarters. De Quille and Twain showed Ward around, an excursion that probably included silver mines and quartz mills but most certainly saloons and nightlife. On Christmas Eve, Goodman remembered, Ward appeared around midnight at the *Enterprise* office, where the next day's paper was being put to bed. He ordered "the editorial slaves to have done with their work, as his royal highness proposed to treat them to an oyster supper." By morning they were drunk enough to imagine that they had all been inexhaustibly witty. In a sober moment, Ward urged Twain to write a sketch for the *New York Sunday Mercury*, to the editors of which Ward would recommend him. After Ward left for Salt Lake City, Twain sent off, under the title "Doings in Nevada," an article detailing the illegal process that had produced the constitutional proposal at the territorial convention. He assumed, incorrectly, that Ward had already been in touch with the editors. The article was accepted anyway. In mid-January, he wrote and sent another essay, "Those Blasted Children," which the *Mercury* also published.

At the end of February 1864, the actress Adah Isaacs Menken, known as the "Great Unadorned," came to Virginia City to dazzle Nevada audiences with her role in a dramatic adaptation of Byron's *Mazeppa*. Six months earlier, in San Francisco, Twain had already reviewed—harshly—the erotic sensationalism of her performance, including her semi-transparent costumes. Soon after her arrival in Virginia City, Menken wrote Twain a note, asking him to publish a sketch of hers in the *Enterprise*. In a long, frosty, and, he thought, humorous response that has not survived, he declined. She tried again. "She is friendly, now," Twain commented. When Menken invited him to a literary dinner, with Dan De Quille and the poet Ada Clare, yet excluding her own husband, the humorist Orpheus V. Kerr,

Twain saw neither the humor nor the human interest of the situation. From first sight, he had felt uneasy about her challenge to Victorian moral standards. At dinner, he was unhappy to find himself assigned to sit next to her. In De Quille's account, the evening ended abruptly when, attempting to kick one of Menken's dogs, Twain kicked her instead on a tender corn, "causing her to bound from her seat, throw herself on a lounge and roll and roar in agony." He "soon imagined a pressing engagement and begged to be excused."

Twain was far more comfortable in the role of Victorian civic booster. In mid-May 1864, he got happily swept up in the local manifestation of a well-publicized national campaign to raise money for the Sanitary Fund, an early version of the Red Cross, which provided vital services for wounded Union soldiers. One of his schoolmates, Reuel Gridley, the young man who in 1848 had volunteered for an infantry company being raised in Hannibal and had marched out of town in his splendid uniform to Sam's immense envy, now lived in Nevada. A Unionist with Copperhead sympathies, Gridley had bet a Republican neighbor that, if a Republican were elected mayor, Gridley would give him a fifty-pound bag of flour which he would carry to him "with a brass band at his heels playing 'John Brown.' " If a Democrat were elected, his neighbor would do the same and the band would play "Dixie." Gridley lost the bet. With the whole town following him, he carried the sack to his neighbor, who gave it back to him. When he put the sack up for auction, prompted by a circular that had come from St. Louis to Virginia City, he took in more than five thousand dollars. When he brought his sack to Virginia City on his way to St. Louis, Twain suggested auctioning the sack again. When they got only about five hundred dollars, they were disgusted and took it to nearby Gold Hill, where Reuel Gridley told the story of the sack and raised almost seven thousand dollars. They went to Silver City, then Dayton. Suddenly the flour sack had turned into an ark of the covenant, followed by a caravan that Twain was credited with calling the "Army of the Lord." By now they had raised more than ten thousand dollars. When they returned to Virginia City, they found it charged with enthusiasm. Determined not to be outdone, in two and a half hours of meetings, speeches, and bidding, Virginia City raised thirteen thousand dollars. The provincial flour bag had turned into a money machine, which Gridley soon took to California, then to the East, raising, over the next year, several hundred thousand dollars for the Sanitary Fund. Pleased with his role in the enterprise, Twain was bursting with pride at Nevada's generosity. "I had rather die in Washoe than live in some countries," he wrote to his mother and sister.

Soon those words turned bitter in his mouth. Late on the night of May 16, when he and De Quille were closing the next day's edition of the *Enterprise,* both in high spirits, Twain wrote a brief squib for inclusion, apparently based on joking words he had overheard earlier in the day while the auction festivities were in full flourish. The reason that "the Flour Sack was not taken from Dayton to Carson," he wrote, "was because it was stated that the money raised at the Sanitary Dress Ball, recently held in Carson for the St. Louis Fair, had been diverted from its legitimate course, and was to be sent to aid a Miscegenation Society somewhere in the East; and it was feared the proceeds of the sack might be similarly disposed of." It was "a hoax," he also wrote, "but not all a hoax, for an effort is being made to divert those funds from their proper course." He intended it as a witty tease. According to De Quille's recollection, when De Quille counseled against publishing the paragraph, Twain agreed, putting aside the sheet of paper on which it was written. He and De Quille then went to the theater, forgetting that they had left the paragraph on the desk. The composing room foreman, who found it in the editorial office, assumed it was intended for publication and set it in type. When it appeared in the next morning's *Enterprise,* all hell broke lose. For whites of whatever political position, even abolitionists, any mention of racial intermarriage was taboo.

Those who found Twain's sarcasm neither funny nor fair had a reservoir of longstanding anger against him that much preceded his miscegenation gaffe. Often what seemed funny to him, others thought hurtful. What to him seemed sly wit, others thought hammerheaded bludgeoning. The *Virginia City Evening Bulletin,* early in April 1864, a month and a half before the miscegenation affair, had already counterattacked that "Sammy Clemens, or as he styles himself, Mark Twain, who scribbles the funny things . . . and is not a little addicted to saying hard things about others, as he pretends, in joke, appears to feel it intensely when the others turn the joke on him. . . . Merciless himself in perpetrating jokes on others, he winces like a cur with a flea in his ear when others retort." In this blunder he had a reasonable defense—the publication had been accidental. Still, he told his sister-in-law, "Whatever blame there is, rests with me alone."

But if she could not persuade her charity ball colleagues that he had "dealt honorably by them" when he had consented to have Dan "suppress that article," then "make them appoint a man to avenge the wrong done them, with weapons in fair and open field." Since dueling was illegal in Nevada (even offering a challenge carried a two-year penitentiary sentence) and he had no skill with any kind of weapon, including the pistol he regularly carried, it was a ludicrous proposal.

On May 18, adding fuel to the fire, he published an article attacking the *Virginia City Union* for allegedly reneging on its bid for the flour sack. In response, the *Union* accused the *Enterprise* of not yet having paid its own pledge. Charges of hypocrisy, dishonesty, and unmanliness volleyed back and forth. The best surviving sentence of stereotypical vilification came from the *Union,* which declaimed that Twain "conveyed in every word . . . such a groveling disregard for truth, decency and courtesy, as to court the distinction only of being understood as a vulgar liar."

On May 21, signing himself "Sam L. Clemens," Twain challenged the editor of the *Union* to a duel. His second, "Mr. Stephen Gillis—will receive any communication you may see fit to make." That evening, in receipt of a letter from the author of the *Union* letter, who was not the editor, James Laird, but J. W. Willington, a compositor, stating that he had "nothing to retract," Twain accused the editor of hiding behind one of his employees. He had issued the challenge to the editor alone. Since the *Union* had printed "undignified and abominably insulting slander" about him, he now issued a "peremptory challenge." Whereas the first challenge was an "alternative" challenge, which could be satisfied by an apology, this one could be satisfied only on the field of honor.

The *Enterprise* was abuzz with excitement, and, with every colleague offering advice about the code of dueling, Twain began to feel increasingly nervous. Aware that he owed the Sanitary Ball ladies an apology, he held off giving it, afraid that his *Union* enemies would take it as a sign of weakness. Then a challenge came from the husband of the president of the committee. How many more would follow from other outraged husbands? The main action, though, was in Virginia City, where he sent "another challenge" to the *Union* editor. And "another and another," he later wrote. "The more he did not want to fight, the bloodthirstier I became." He was, he hoped, scaring off his enemy. But if that strategy didn't succeed, he would need to sharpen his shooting skills. Accompanied by his second, he went out for an early-morning practice. Gillis, who was as good with a pistol as he was with his fists, shot the head off a sparrow. Laird's seconds saw that the head had been shot off but not who had done it. Gillis convinced them that Clemens was the marksman, and Laird withdrew from the duel. The *Enterprise* people were "exultant." But Twain soon had additional reason for concern. Rumor reached him that his enemies might have him charged with issuing a challenge, which could put him in jail for two years. It was reasonable to think that life in Virginia City would be more difficult for him now than it had been before, even if he should not be arrested. It seemed a good time to visit San Francisco.

By the middle of the last week in May 1864, Twain and Gillis had made their travel arrangements, though their intention was to spend no more than a month away. By then, they expected, the threat of arrest would have passed. Not all Twain's *Enterprise* colleagues expected him to return. Twain had done well in Nevada, but to some extent he had worn out his welcome. He was not the novelty he once had been. And there were those who did not find him funny as a writer or attractive as a human being. A wider sphere, an opportunity for additional and broader experience, seemed desirable, though he was too rushed and harried now to think this through. He could assume that the *San Francisco Call* would continue to publish his columns. Perhaps he might send letters to the *Enterprise* from San Francisco. The details could be worked out later. Right now, he needed to be quickly on his way.

"*If you can spare it comfortably,*" he wrote to Orion, "send me two hundred dollars." On second thought, send it to San Francisco. "We are not afraid of the grand jury, but Washoe has long since grown irksome to us, and we want to leave it anyhow." He had a pocket full of mining stocks, which he still hoped would make him rich, though the boom and bust of the market and ongoing heavy assessments had begun to disillusion him. He had lived luxuriously in San Francisco on mining stocks during his 1863 visits. Now it would be a different story. On the day before his scheduled departure, another aggrieved Carson City husband arrived with an "alternative" challenge. He declined to apologize. "Having made my arrangements—before I received your note—to leave for California, and having no time to fool away on a common bummer like you, I want an immediate answer to this." He sent his ace in the hole, the pugnacious Steve Gillis, to the man's hotel, either to bluff or to frighten him. He did one or the other successfully, and the challenge was retracted. The next day Gillis and Twain, the latter undoubtedly with a deep sigh of relief, left on the morning stage for California. Joe Goodman, intending to accompany them part of the way, found spirits so high and humor so keen that he continued with them all the way to San Francisco. It looked to be a holiday for them all. Soon the stagecoach, laboring up the Sierras, crossed the high pass, and left Nevada behind.

CHAPTER FIVE

A FAIR WIND

1864–1866

1.

Though he arrived in San Francisco at the end of May 1864 with the intention of staying a month or two, Twain was to remain in northern California for close to two years, much of the time attempting to earn his living as a journalist. Within six weeks of arrival he was working hard to suppress his restlessness. He had it in mind to go east, to the "states," after he had sold his and Orion's few shares in a once valuable Virginia City mine. But the stock fell even lower, to one tenth of its previous year's value. Twain's pockets were as good as empty, yet he could not get himself to sell at three hundred dollars a share what had once been worth three thousand. His thought of going to New York to sell his stock, he realized, was as unrealistic as his original expectation that it would make him rich in San Francisco. He soon sent the certificates to Orion and Mollie, made out in Orion's name so if he himself wanted to leave at anytime, there would be "no bother about it." "Put it in the safe," he instructed, "& if I get a chance to sell it well, endorse it & send it to me." That he had little cash and no certainty about how he would replenish his pocketbook did not prevent him going, with Steve Gillis, directly from the stagecoach to the expensive Occidental Hotel, which was, he told his *Territorial Enterprise* readers in

"Mark Twain in the Metropolis," "Heaven on the half shell." After the alkali dust of Washoe, San Francisco's breezes were heaven indeed.

Though he expected never to return to Nevada, he had no firm plans
about anything else. To friends and to his Missouri family he mentioned
that he intended to write a book about his experiences in Nevada, the text
to be taken substantially from his *Enterprise* articles. At the end of September 1864, he alerted Orion that he would soon send for the files "& begin on" the book. The thought, though, was far from fully formed, and the
gap between idea and realization immense. There was also little likelihood
that its publication would significantly improve his financial situation. For
the time being, his preference was for life on the "half shell," the sheer
pleasure of being at no one's beck and call, of nights out as late as he liked.
Laziness and restlessness, though, were always in precarious balance. "I
have got the 'gypsy' only in a mild form," he wrote to Dan De Quille. "It
will kill me yet, though."

In June, he joined the San Francisco Olympic Club, which held classes
in boxing and fencing. Though he mostly confined his exercise to devising
jokes "to play on his fellow members," he had not forgotten an incident at
a Virginia City gymnasium in which he had pranced around wearing a pair
of boxing gloves. "Working his right like the piston of a steam engine, at the
same time stretching out his neck and gyrating his curly pate in a very astonishing manner," he squared off in front of one of his *Enterprise* colleagues. An excellent, hard-hitting boxer, George Dawson took this as a
challenge and smashed Twain in the nose. Blood spurted. His nose
swelled. Embarrassed, he accepted "a reportorial assignment outside Virginia City," De Quille recalled, "just 'to get his nose out of town.' " Slim, of
medium height, he maintained a dancing, sporting walk that matched his
cocky, teasing attitude. Years later, the famous Mark Twain posed as a
boxer, his shirt off, his chest hairy, his quick eyes mischievous, a pose
he liked.

His current pose as a grandee at the Occidental was coming to an end.
With no money to pay the hotel bill, he and Gillis soon repaired to the first
of a series of nondescript, downscale lodgings. They were not good tenants. Their loud voices, practical jokes, erratic schedules, and noisy visitors
made them the scourge of five landladies within four months. Without income, they were always behind with the rent, yet Twain had no desire for
a regular, full-time job. Occasional letters to the *Call* and the *Enterprise*

were what he had in mind. But when he had moved from Virginia City to San Francisco, his letters to the *Daily Morning Call* had lost their reason for existence. In fact, his departure from Virginia City had undercut his main attraction to San Francisco newspapers, though he may not have realized it at first. In San Francisco he was just another reporter in a tight labor market. Apparently he had not tried to arrange a position as the *Territorial Enterprise* regular in San Francisco, which at least would have produced a monthly salary. Meanwhile, the occasional letters, which better suited him, and for which he would have been paid per item, were not getting written.

In early June Twain bit the acrid-tasting bullet and got a regular job. It helped pay the rent and other expenses, including some Virginia City debts. Though he fantasized about a voyage to Hawaii and even more distant places, for the time being he was not going anywhere except to the office of the *Daily Morning Call,* in a new brick building at 612 Commercial Street, not far from the center of civic life at Portland Square. He had been hired by its editor, George Barnes, as local editor-reporter, apparently the only one, at forty dollars a week. He was responsible for covering all local news. With a two A.M. closing, his day stretched from mid-morning to the wee hours of the next, far from a lazy man's idea of a good job. It was, however, the best one at hand. And straight journalism was what was required. Still, his conviviality, his engagement during his previous visit with the city's cultural life, and his amusing 1863 letters to the *Enterprise,* which had been reprinted in San Francisco, had made him many well-disposed San Francisco acquaintances and some friends. He was especially sought out when drollness and laughter were desired. On June 12, before a high-living audience at Maguire's Opera House, he gave a speech, which he read from a seven-foot-long illuminated parchment, in honor of Major Edward Perry, who had earned San Francisco's praises by raising a Union gunboat sunk in the harbor. "The entire audience was dissolved in tears" of laughter, the *San Francisco Alta California* reported. The humor was based on the claim that the speaker was a member of and represented a large number of Indian tribes, in whose name he praised the Major. When he raised his glass to remind everyone that they were all thirsty, they acknowledged that Mark Twain, the well-known humorist, was a presence, even if a minor one, in San Francisco.

Within days the editor-reporter job seemed drudgery to him, mainly because he had to produce daily a set amount of copy, whether or not he found events that engaged his interest. "By nine in the morning I had to be at the police court for an hour and make a brief history of the squabbles of the night before . . . usually between Irishmen and Irishmen, and Chinamen and Chinamen, with now and then a squabble between the two races for a change. Every day's evidence was substantially a duplicate of the evidence of the day before, therefore the daily performance was killingly monotonous and wearisome." Except, he noticed, to the court interpreter, who had the challenge of having to switch rapidly among "fifty-six Chinese dialects." Raking the town "from end to end," he spent the day scurrying around for news, to courts, offices, political events, and exhibitions, even on excursions to places of local interest, like the Cliff House, which gave him the opportunity to expand a report into a sketch. At night, he made short visits to each one of the theaters, either for a review comment or a squib. George Barnes required that he report, not invent, news. It was nothing like what he had been able to do in Virginia City.

His own ideas and sympathies glowed through every now and then, sometimes with a touch of irony or straight humor, mostly by general comments. His attendance at the courts and jails encouraged his sympathy for the unfortunate. Muted criticism of the authorities, when justice was not done, became his leitmotif. He was particularly interested in the Chinese. When, "with considerable warmth & holy indignation," he filed an account of a policeman standing idly by while "hoodlums" stoned "a Chinaman heavily laden with the weekly wash of his Christian customers," he was surprised, and then outraged, that it did not appear in the next day's paper. Barnes explained that they could not afford to offend their subscribers. Since he could not quit without having another job to go to, he could find no action to relieve his anger. But by the middle of September, he had altered his arrangement with Barnes. "I don't work after 6 in the evening, now," he wrote to De Quille. "I got disgusted with night work." To his mother he said, with lighthearted optimism, "I am taking life easy, now, & I mean to keep it up for a while."

The trade-off was a reduction in salary to twenty-five dollars a week, which required him to tighten his belt. But with a schedule that allowed him to get up "at 10 in the morning, and quit work at 5 or 6 in the afternoon," he now had time to supplement his income with occasional articles for the *Golden Era*, the literary journal that had published some of his sketches in 1863, particularly "Stories for Good Little Girls and Boys," "Curing a Cold," and, in October 1863, "The Great Prize Fight," a satire on California politics written as a parody of the language and style of contemporary sports writing. More suited to his interests and talents than the *Morning Call,* the *Era* had offices in the same building, which easily allowed him to renew his acquaintance with its editors and to make new friends there. One of its two founding editors, Twain's friend Rollin Daggett, had sold the paper in 1860 to Joseph E. Lawrence, an urbane editor who added a literary emphasis to Daggett's rough frontier material, catering to more sophisticated city readers with serial novels, short stories, poems, and a lively letters-to-the-editor column. When Twain had been in San Francisco in 1863, Lawrence had sought him out and hired him to write letters from Virginia City. Twain's recent literary acquaintance, Artemus Ward, was publishing in its pages, as was Bret Harte.

A year younger than the almost twenty-nine-year-old Twain, Francis Bret Harte had published numbers of well-received stories and poems in the *Era* and was, by late 1864, its most esteemed writer. Harte's father was an improvident literature teacher who had cut himself off from his well-to-do orthodox Jewish family in New York, and his mother was the daughter of an old New York family whose ancestors had been Revolutionary War heroes. Nine years old when his father died, he was raised amid genteel poverty and at seventeen followed his remarried mother to northern California, where he tried various jobs, including teaching, setting type, and mining in Tuolumne County, where he met Steve Gillis' two brothers. In 1860 he settled in San Francisco, working as a typesetter in the *Era*'s print shop. Like Twain, he rose from typesetter to author. Under the patronage of Jessie Benton Fremont, the wife of the 1856 Republican candidate for president, Harte began to come into his own as a writer. Shy, ambitious, uneconomical, he married in 1862, helped by his salary as secretary to the superintendent of the San Francisco mint, a patronage position arranged by influential friends. The mint's office was in the same building on Commercial Street in which Twain worked as a reporter for the *Morning Call*. George Barnes had introduced the two writers and, on his way up and down from the *Call* offices, Twain regularly stopped to chat. Soon they were more than friendly, bound together and kept apart by the awareness that they might be in competition. "His head was striking," Harte later recalled. With an aquiline nose and curly hair, with thick and bushy eyebrows, Twain had "an eye so eagle-like that a second lid would not have surprised me. . . . His dress was careless, and his general manner one of supreme indifference to surroundings and circumstances."

The *Golden Era* paid Twain twelve dollars an article or fifty dollars a month for the promise of four contributions each month, which soon included two delightful sketches, "The Evidence in the Case of Smith vs. Jones," an ironic mock report of a trial, stressing the unreliability of witnesses, and "Early Rising, As Regards Excursions to the Cliff House," a humorous sketch about, among other things, the undesirability of getting up early. When a new literary journal, the *Californian,* the editorship of which Bret Harte had assumed in September and shared alternately with former *New York Times* correspondent Charles Henry Webb, encouraged him to contribute and would pay as at the same rate the *Era,* he had an outlet that seemed a superior venue for his talents: one more "high-toned" than the *Era,* he wrote to his family. "The *Californian* circulates among the highest class of the community, & is the best weekly literary paper in the United States—& I suppose I ought to know." In October 1864 it published the first of more than twenty Mark Twain sketches and was soon to publish the best known San Francisco literary writers, including two poets, Ina Coolbrith and Charles Warren Stoddard. Stoddard would become Twain's friend.

In mid-October 1864, George Barnes fired him. It was an amicable axing, done graciously, though it had damaging consequences for Twain. After an energetic initial few weeks, he had treated his *Morning Call* responsibilities with less and less commitment, partly rationalized by his belief that the position was beneath him. The mid-September reduction in his schedule had not made him any happier. He remained as negligent as ever and soon let the half-time assistant hired to help with his overload take over most of his work. He spent even more time downstairs chatting with Harte. He depended, though, on the twenty-five-dollar-a-week salary. At last Barnes took him "privately aside and advised" him to resign. "It was like a father advising a son for his good, and I obeyed." Barnes and his partner were relieved. He was, Twain later wrote, "on the world, now, with nowhere to go." The fifty dollars a month provided by his *Californian* articles was insufficient to keep body and soul together, and he still refused to sell the few Hale and Norcross shares he and Orion owned, which would at best have produced about six hundred dollars for him. By September, he and Steve Gillis had changed their lodgings five times. At the end of October the new local reporter for the *Morning Call* published a paragraph about "a melancholy-looking Arab, known as Marque Twein," who by necessity, like an Arab folding his tent, moves often. "His hat is an old one, and comes too far down over his eyes, and his clothes don't fit as if they were made for him." When Twain and Gillis had no other recourse, they lodged on credit at Gillis' parents' rooming house.

Almost penniless, he took to "avoiding acquaintances," slinking through the streets with only ten cents in his pocket, so he later claimed, clinging to his dime in the fear that actual pennilessness "might suggest suicide." Pride kept him from trying to borrow from the family he had boasted he would make wealthy. When a poet friend who could not sell any poems asked for advice about whether or not he should kill himself, Twain responded that he should. It was, he later remarked, positive advice. "It was somewhat disinterested, but there were a few selfish motives behind it. As a reporter, I knew that a good 'scoop' would get me employment, and so I wanted him to kill himself without letting anybody but me know about the deed. Then I could sell the news and get a new start in life." Whatever grain of truth in the story, suicide was on his mind, if only in passing. Later, he referred to an actual attempt. Throughout November he kept his eye on the price of Hale and Norcross shares, his only reserve. "I was once dead broke for several months," he wrote to Will Bowen in 1882, "& sewed up bursted grain sacks on the San Francisco wharves for a starvation living (when I was already sufficiently famous to be welcome in the best society of the city and state) rather than borrow money." In his depressed mood, it was increasingly difficult for him to write sketches for the *Californian,* his only certain source of income.

In late November 1864, Steve Gillis got into one of his frequent barroom fights and badly beat up a bullying bartender. Twain signed a five-hundred-dollar bail bond note, somehow managing to create the impression he had the resources to cover it. When Gillis' arrest on charges of assault with intent to kill seemed imminent, he fled to Virginia City. Feeling responsible for Twain, whom the law now would require to pay the bond, Gillis urged his friend to get out of town also. The police, he warned, might take extra pleasure in arresting him because of the critical view of them he had expressed in print. For whatever reason, perhaps his desire to return soon to San Francisco, where he could earn money as a writer, or from which he could sail away to distant places, Twain preferred to hide out for a short while with Gillis' two brothers in their mining camp in Tuolumme County, a hundred miles east of San Francisco. On December 3 his story, "Lucretia Smith's Soldier," a parody of sentimental Civil War stories, appeared in the *Californian*. Twain prefaced it by remarking, "[The inspiration] which enabled me . . . to soar so happily into the realms of sentiment and soft emotion, was obtained from the excellent beer manufactured" at a local brewery. The next day, with three hundred dollars probably gained from selling one Hale and Norcross share, he left San Francisco for Jackass Hill, accompanied by Steve Gillis' brother Jim.

2.

Having, so he had thought, escaped mining camps forever, Mark Twain spent the next twelve weeks again immersed in mining culture. This time, though, he did not bring with him the expectation that he would get rich or the intensity with which, during his first year in Nevada, he had defined himself as a man who must grab the opportunity of a lifetime to extract the gold and silver that would transform his life. He was there only because he needed to lay low, and Jackass Hill's mostly played out pocket mines (shallow holes to avoid the expense of tunneling) had little gold to offer, anyway. Samuel Clemens had become Mark Twain in that he had redirected his interest from gold in the ground to what he could extract from literary work.

Twain may indeed have been keeping journals during his Nevada years and his months in San Francisco, but, if so, they have been lost. More likely, he had been too busy to keep any kind of record. Years later, when he began writing *Roughing It*, he relied for the Nevada period almost entirely on memory and on his file of *Territorial Enterprise* clippings. At Jackass Hill, though, he had the leisure to read and to make regular entries in a journal that from the start had the unmistakable features of a writer's notebook—observations, reflections, descriptions of selected items of literary interest, encapsulated reminders of ideas for later use. Still very much an author in the process of discovering his materials, he did not start the notebook until New Year's Day, 1865, four weeks after his arrival. For the first time, though, his observations were tempered by and mediated through a literary self-consciousness, a sense of self that he had not had before. For most of the rest of his life, he kept similar notebooks.

With Jim Gillis, a thirty-five-year-old Georgian who had earned a medical degree in Memphis and had come west in the gold rush, he climbed Jackass Hill for the first time. There he found a one-room wood-plank cabin at the edge of a ridge. In one direction, the earth fell away into a narrow valley. In another was a pockmarked hill in which miners had been making small holes and trenches for more than fifteen years. Scattered houses collapsed into the landscape; a few collected into the nearby tiny town of Jackass Gulch or Tuttleton.

More than three thousand men had attacked Jackass Hill and the area in 1849. Most had moved on, leaving Tuolume County's population reduced by half. Though Jackass Hill provided small strikes to persistent miners, those who remained, like Jim Gillis and his partner, Dick Stoker, had discovered something within themselves beyond acquisitive desire. It was a love for the special quality of life in the Sierra foothills: the isolation, the simplicity, the opportunity for self-sufficiency, the discovery of a stable interplay between fantasy and reality, a balance between mind and matter that elevated into spiritual importance the man who dug and the particular piece of earth in which he dug. Gillis had been living in the cabin for about ten years. Forty-five-year-old college-educated Jacob Richard Stoker, a quiet, good-natured, gray-bearded, pipe-smoking native of Kentucky who had fought in the Mexican War, had been making a bare living there since 1849. It was he who had built the cabin in 1850. He had no intention of ever leaving. In spring, flowers blazed with a brief dazzle of color. For the rest of the year the landscape was a study in browns. In the winter, storms brought torrents of mud and water, and there were occasional blue, crisp, sunny days. This was all the world Stoker wanted.

Gillis and Stoker, with Steve's other brother Bill, provided amiable hospitality in the cramped cabin. Hygiene and cuisine were minimal. If the weather were good, the brothers and Stoker would be out on the hill panning for gold, shaking a dirt-filled sieve, sifting the sediment, hoping that small gold particles would flicker. During his first weeks Twain helped them, apparently without expectation that he now at last would strike it rich. It was merely something to do. Since his lodging for so long had been rooming houses and hotels, he quickly felt at home. The company was congenial. A family in nearby French Flat had two attractive daughters, the subject of jokes, nicknames, and erotic reveries. His lost Missouri love was still on his mind, as she had been the previous September when he had asked his mother, "What has become of that girl of mine that got married?

I mean Laura Wright." At Jackass Hill he dreamt that he saw Laura driving in a carriage, "said good bye and shook hands." Each day one or more
of the trio walked to the general store for supplies. Jim Gillis and Stoker
generally had no cash. Twain's three hundred dollars paid for groceries. In
the saloon he played billiards on a battered table. In the cabin there were
some books; a small collection in Tuttleton, the remains of a literary society formed in more populated days, provided "first class Literature: Byron
Shakespeare, Bacon Dickens." He had time to read, and did.

At Jackass Hill, at night, in front of the fireplace, Jim Gillis loved to tell
rambling tall tales, as both entertainment and put-on, particularly in the
hope of getting the amiably skeptical Dick Stoker, whom he often made
the "hero," to believe the tale. A compulsive storyteller with a talent for invention, Gillis "always soberly pretended that what he was relating was
strictly history, veracious history, not romance. Dick Stoker . . . would sit
smoking his pipe and listen with a gentle serenity to these monstrous fab-
rications and never utter a protest." When Jim told an impromptu tall tale
about "a poor innocent and ignorant woodpecker" who "tried to fill up a
house with acorns," the story stuck in Twain's mind. Another memorably
surreal animal tale was about a remarkable cat named Tom Quartz; another
a raunchy story, "The Tragedy of the Burning Shame," "one of the most outrageously funny things" Twain had ever heard, a version of which Stoker
acted in while Twain was visiting. It became, in an expurgated version,
years later, "The King's Camelopard or the Royal Nonesuch" in *Huckleberry Finn*.

Late in January, Clemens went to the mountain town of Angels Camp
in Calaveras County, where Gillis had a claim he wanted to work. Endless
sifting at Jackass Hill had produced very little since his arrival. At Angels
Camp, heavy winter rains made work impossible. Muddy torrents made
the hillsides slippery; gullies and canyons became impromptu reservoirs.
With little to do, the men spent much of their time at the bar in the newly
renovated Angels Hotel, into which they moved at the end of the month.
One night, desperate for air and exercise, Twain walked into the rain and
fog. He stopped, thinking about whether he should go on. As he considered stepping forward, his eyes grew accustomed enough to the darkness
to allow him to see that he was at the edge of a precipice. "One of my feet
projected over the edge as I stood." A half a step more and he would have
been over.

The rest of the days and nights, as the rains fell, they talked with other miners, a community of people with nothing to do for two weeks but talk. A story he found particularly compelling was of "Coleman with his jumping frog—bet stranger $50—stranger had no frog, and C got him one—in the meantime stranger filled C's frog full of shot and he couldn't jump—the stranger's frog won." How funny, though, depended on the manner of telling, variations on which Gillis and Twain provided for mutual entertainment for themselves and Stoker as they refashioned stories that appealed to them. Twain later recalled that the man who told the jumping frog tale, along with his mining-town audience, saw nothing funny about it. They focused, seriously, on how knowledgeable the stranger was about frogs and how shrewd he was to outsmart Coleman. Gillis remembered Twain attempting to write it out when they returned to Jackass Hill, saying, "If I can write that story the way Ben Coon told it, that frog will jump round the world." Such memories are often unreliable, and Gillis may only have noticed Twain writing his summary into his notebook. Twain could not have known that a short version of the story had appeared in the *Sonora Herald* in 1853.

In early February 1865, there were "blazing hot days & cool nights. No more rain." With Stoker, also a Mason, he attended a meeting of the Bear Mountain Masonic Lodge. Two weeks later the three of them left Angels Camp, walking "over the mountains to Jackass in a snow storm—the first I ever saw in California." He had decided that his temporary exile was over, that it would be safe enough now to return to San Francisco. He had little to nothing left of the three hundred dollars, though he felt he had gotten good value in exchange: the pleasure of the company of two men for whom he had developed great affection and respect, and a notebook with dozens of ideas for stories, the precise usefulness of which he had little idea of at the time.

There is, though, reason to think that whatever concerns he had about himself and his future began to take on a brighter cast during his stay. The searching focus of the notebook on observation, description, and story testifies to that. Five years later he wrote to Jim Gillis, "[Though] it makes my heart ache yet to call to mind some of those days . . . it shouldn't, for there . . . lay the germ of my coming good-fortune. You remember the one gleam of jollity that shot across our dismal sojourn in the rain & mud of Angel's Camp—I mean that day we sat around the tavern stove & heard that chap tell about the frog & how they filled him with shot. And you remember how we quoted from the yarn & laughed over it, out there on the hillside while you & dear old Stoker panned & washed. I jotted the story down in my note-book that day, & would have been glad to get ten or fifteen dollars for it—I was just that blind. But then we were so hard up."

From Jackass Hill, on February 23, he went twelve miles on horseback to Copperopolis, where he descended three hundred feet into the Union Copper mine, then left by stage for Stockton. Three days later he was "home again," at the Occidental Hotel in San Francisco, a luxurious contrast to his life in the Sierras. With little to no money in his pocket, it was both the most absurd and the most characteristically appropriate place for him to go.

3.

Though he could count on credit from the proprietor, his friend Lewis Leland, Twain needed to secure a regular income quickly and find a home other than an expensive hotel. That was difficult to do. Apparently he did not want the schedule that employment with a morning newspaper required. "There were no vacancies on the evening journals," he stated years later in *Roughing It*. The *Californian* still desired his contributions. Webb printed Twain's humorous "Unbiased Criticism" in mid-March 1865, a sketch set in Angels Camp, satirizing art criticism, inflated political rhetoric, and political corruption. Its centerpiece is a fictitious political oration made by the author in the barroom of the Union Hotel at Angels Camp where he "had a very comfortable time . . . in spite of the rain," a sketch in which the real author creates a fictional alter ego called Mark Twain, who has the experiences of Samuel Clemens but who also participates in events the real author has made up. At the end, a fictional interlocutor named Brown, a friend of a friend from Nevada, and the Twain persona become friends so intimate that they tell each other everything.

In mid-April, when Webb resigned, Harte resumed his editorship and Twain began a series of sketches that appeared almost weekly in May and June. They took on increasing fictive, comic, and stylistic power. In one of his "Answers to Correspondents," he tells a "Moral Statistician," "I don't approve of dissipation, and I don't indulge in it either, but I haven't a particle of confidence in a man who has no redeeming petty vices whatever, and so I don't want to hear from you anymore." In dealing with an invented

"Literary Connoisseur," he provides a comic guide in which his descriptions of the great writers of English poetry reveal that he has not only read widely but can in brief phrases effectively epitomize their styles. "Bear these rules in mind, and you will pass muster as a connoisseur; as long as you can talk glibly about the 'styles' of authors, you well get as much credit as if you were really acquainted with their works." Humorously and self-consciously, he was himself moving back and forth across the boundary between glibness and art.

But even frequent freelance articles for the *Californian* did not provide a living. Debts needed to be paid, at a minimum those to Leland and Steve Gillis' parents for his board and lodging the previous fall. Finally, in response to Jane Clemens' pressure, Horace Bixby gave her the money he owed her son and, in March, Will Bowen gave her one of the two hundred dollars he owed Sam. Her son's pride, though, forbade asking his mother to send him money. On the contrary, he regretted that he had nothing to contribute to her support other than those repayments. To borrow from Orion was out of the question; with only a government salary, he was vainly trying to earn a living as a lawyer in Carson City, soon to return to Iowa penniless. Sam's financial position was no better than it had been the previous autumn. However, the danger that he might be imprisoned or asked to make good on the bond he had posted for Steve Gillis seems to have disappeared.

By late May 1865, Twain had gotten back into a writing routine. In early July "Advice for Good Little Boys" and "Advice for Good Little Girls" appeared in the San Francisco *Youth's Companion*. These are sardonically funny companion pieces whose rules for a successful gender-inflected childhood anticipate Twain's ability to enter into the morally mixed and strategically immoral minds of children—an ability with which he later triumphed in more sustained works. At the end of June, he reappeared in the *Territorial Enterprise* with a tongue-in-cheek satire of "vice" in San Francisco, an account of a young white woman who had been living a life of immorality and crime "with a strapping young nigger for six months" without any awareness of iniquity. Her lack of awareness that there was anything "unbecoming" about her sexual life indirectly raised the question, Was there? And the absence of an answer left open the possibility that the author, without committing himself either way, did not think there was. His *Territorial Enterprise* friends would have been delighted with it. In another letter to the *Enterprise,* he described the cleverness of a group of very happy blacks who had reluctantly been given the privilege to march in a white-led civic procession: "They did all it was in their power to do, poor devils, to modify the prominence of the contrast between black and white faces which seems so hateful to their white fellow-creatures, by putting their lightest colored darkies in the front rank, then glooming down by some unaggravating and nicely graduated shades of darkness to the fell and dismal blackness of undefiled and unalloyed niggerdom in the remote extremity of the procession. It was a fine stroke of strategy—the day was dusty and no man could tell where the white folks left off and the niggers began."

At the end of the summer or in the early fall his *Territorial Enterprise* friends resolved his financial problems by contracting for a regular letter from San Francisco at a salary of a hundred dollars a month. That, in addition to his sketches for the *Californian* and a few brief articles he wrote for the *San Francisco Dramatic Chronicle,* would make him financially viable again. "I have gone to work in dead earnest" to get out of debt, he wrote to Orion in October. For the first time since he had been fired from the *Morning Chronicle,* he did not have to worry about money, as long as he kept writing.

When he returned in February 1865 from Jackass Hill, he had found in his mail a November letter from Artemus Ward, asking him to contribute a sketch to a "new book of Nevada Territory travel." Twain wrote to Ward that he wished he had received this invitation when it had been extended. He mentioned the story of the jumping frog. It was not too late, Ward responded, urging him to write and send the sketch directly to George W. Carleton, Ward's New York publisher. Soon after returning from the Sierras, Twain had told Harte and others a version of the jumping frog story, his voice communicating the humorous absurdity of the seriousness with which the unselfconscious narrator narrates it. In mid-March, he published "An Unbiased Criticism" in the *Californian,* mostly set in Angels Camp. It contains a character named Coon, based on Ben Coon, an ex–riverboat pilot he had met in Angels Camp and mentioned in his notebook. Much later he implied that Coon had told him the jumping frog story. In the middle of June, in his "Answer to Correspondents" in the *Californian,* he had introduced as partial narrator a character named Simon Wheeler, apparently based on Coon. Between early September and mid-

October 1865, with Ward's renewed invitation in mind, he wrote two unfinished sketches, "The Only Reliable Account of the Celebrated Jumping Frog of Calaveras County" and "Angel's Camp Constable," both of which are unsuccessful attempts to tell the jumping frog story. In mid-November, trying for a third time, he at last found an effective way to tell it. Retaining from the earlier efforts the opening paragraph addressed by Mark Twain to "Mr. A. Ward," mixing fact and fiction in regard to Ward's solicitation of the story, the narrator introduces Simon Wheeler, a garrulous mining camp veteran eager to tell him about Jim Smiley and the jumping frog. Wheeler has no idea that the story he relates in language that reflects his class and education is humorous, especially because he takes the events so seriously. He is not telling a funny story but the telling is very funny indeed.

With no sense that this was a breakthrough, let alone an important literary accomplishment, Twain sent the sketch to New York, hoping it would arrive in time for inclusion in *Artemus Ward: His Travels*. In mid-October, while writing the last version of the frog story, he was shown an article from the *New York Round Table*, reprinted in the *San Francisco Dramatic Chronicle,* in which Charles Henry Webb praised Twain as one of the "foremost" of the "merry gentlemen of the California press." With unintended inconsistency, Webb compared him to Shakespeare and simultaneously extolled him as one of the "Wild Humorists of the Pacific." A few days later, in an exchange of letters with Orion about vocation, Twain took the opportunity to respond to Orion seeing in him "a talent for humorous writing," to urge his brother to become a minister, a career that he had long thought Orion well suited for. "Go forth," he exhorted him, "and preach."

He himself, he maintained, had had only "two powerful ambitions" in his life, to be a pilot and to be a preacher. He had accomplished the first. But he had never even attempted the second because he "could not supply" himself "with the necessary stock in trade—i.e. religion." From childhood on, Christianity had fascinated him as a powerful human phenomenon but not as a belief system to which he could give credence. His piloting career was over, not because the river, soon to be reopened, was closed to him, but because it was a closed book that he would have to open and relearn. He had no desire to do that. But he did, he recognized, have "a 'call' to literature of a low order—i.e. humorous. . . . It is nothing to be proud of, but it is my strongest suit." In his assumption that a humorist made literature of a "low order" he accepted the premise from Aristotle to Emerson that literary works defined in the main as humorous were inherently inferior. But even about this talent for humor he had felt tentative. Orion's praise had always seemed "brotherly partiality. . . . It is only now, when editors of standard literary papers in the distant east give me high praise, & who do not know me & cannot . . . be blinded by the glamour of partiality, that I really begin to believe there must be something in it." He would give up his sighing after "vain impossibilities." He would, if he could, be another Artemus Ward.

In early December 1865, he received the surprising news that "Jim Smiley and His Jumping Frog" had been published not in Ward's book but in the *New York Saturday Press,* which Twain had believed was about to go out of existence. In fact, it was temporarily healthy, under the editorship of the New York journalist and humorist Henry Clapp, a friend and champion of Walt Whitman, who had founded the *Saturday Press* in 1858. When "Jumping Frog" had come into Carleton's hands too late for inclusion, he had turned it over to Clapp, on the assumption that the author would be grateful for this helpful initiative. Clapp liked it, and he would soon put himself on record as wanting more contributions from Twain. What surprised Twain even more was the report from the New York correspondent for the *San Francisco Alta California* that the sketch had "set all New York in a roar. . . . I have been asked fifty times about it & its author, & the papers are copying it far and near. It is voted the best thing of the day." Suddenly the name Mark Twain had currency on the East Coast. And, since the prestigious East Coast newspaper standard-setters had given the author of "Jim Smiley and His Jumping Frog" their stamp of approval, his West Coast literary stock went up as well. He was now potentially marketable in a way that he had not been before.

Still, in a move that was characteristically imperceptive, he expressed annoyance: "After writing many an article a man might be excused for thinking tolerably good, those New York people should single out a villainous backwoods sketch to compliment me on!" In his moody myopia, Twain himself failed to see that the narative strategy of "Jumping Frog" had an artfulness far beyond anything he had written before. The strategy of a narrative within a narrative had allowed him to transform what otherwise would have been a sketch into an ironic short story in which the narrator is a fictional character as important to the story as the story he tells. It was to take him many years more to establish a self-aware working relationship between the journalistic and the novelistic aspects of his art. Certainly, he was thrown off stride by the success of "Jumping Frog." Not only did he lack a clear grasp of the qualitative difference between this "sketch" and others he had written previously, but, as he searched for a suitable follow-up, he was uneasily aware that he did not readily invent subject matter. His impulse was less toward fiction made out of whole cloth than toward arrangements and rearrangements of cloth that the world provided. "I don't know what to write—my life is so uneventful," he complained to his mother. "I wish I was back there piloting up & down the river again." Nevada and California had provided him with material heretofore. But what now? Both subjects seemed a touch stale, and the issue of what form to write in perplexed him; though he needed to make a living, the kind of journalistic sketch he had been writing no longer seemed as attractive as it once had.

Early in 1866, he canceled his arrangement with the *Californian*. The burden of writing for it weekly in addition to his letters to the *Territorial Enterprise* seemed too heavy; he was having trouble manufacturing subjects to write about for the *Enterprise* alone. The best he could do to stimulate his pen was to instigate, in November 1865, a minor journalistic feud with an editor and writer for the *Alta California*, the highlight of which was his severe criticism of the San Francisco police, whom his antagonist defended. "Mark Twain is still on the war-path," the *Examiner* commented in February 1866. "He is after the San Francisco Policemen with a sharp stick." Twain's attacks on the incompetence and corruption of the police, who selectively enforced the law, added some titillation, even danger, to his daily life, and they were based on his continuing concern for justice. But this subject still did not provide him with material to write about other than the stuff of ephemeral local journalism. "Verily, all is vanity & little worth—save piloting," he again complained to his mother. Though he himself was "generally placed at the head of [his] breed of scribblers in this part of the country, the place properly belongs," he confessed, to Bret Harte. An idea that he had had in back of his mind for some years now came strongly to the fore, perhaps catalyzed by Harte's suggestion that they publish a joint volume of sketches. "I will only have to take the scissors & slash my old sketches out of the *Enterprise* & the *Californian*," he wrote to his mother. That would be enough for a book of his own. "I burned up a small cart-load of them lately—so they are forever ruled out of any book—but they were not worth republishing." At the same time, he announced to the *San Francisco Examiner,* which promptly published the news, that he had started writing "a book . . . on an entirely new subject, one that has not been written about heretofore." "It will be a very popular book," the *Examiner* predicted, and "make fame and fortune for its gifted author." The first three hundred pages would take him a year to write, he told his mother, and the remaining three hundred "will have to be written in St. Louis, because the materials for them can only be got there." Apparently this book was to be about the Mississippi, not about his life as a miner in Nevada. His friends and enemies at the *Virginia City Union* surmised that "the subject will be 'Adultery, more and more of it,' and the conclusion, 'The Incest case.' We know of no one capable of writing such a book than Mark Twain." It was the kind of western humor he was becoming eager to escape.

He was tired, he wrote to Orion, of "being chained to this accursed homeless desert,—I want to go back to a Christian land once more." Even if overstating his antipathy for rhetorical purposes, he was, in a mood shared by other immigrants to California, speaking from the heart. For Twain, its novelty had worn off; its promise had not been realized. "Tired being a beggar," he brokered an arrangement to sell the family's Tennessee land, "valuable now that there is peace & no slavery," for $200,000 to a Nevada friend who had had great success in selling mining stock in New York. But, because the buyer planned to grow wine grapes to be harvested by immigrants from wine-producing regions of Europe, Orion's temperance scruple vetoed the transaction. Disappointed, Twain cursed what seemed to him his brother's impractical scrupulosity about matters for which he himself didn't care a damn. "That worthless brother of mine, with his eternal cant about law & religion. . . . He sends me some prayers, as usual." Soon, on his own authority and for himself, he made a sale of a different kind.

In mid-January 1866, Twain declined an invitation, extended to him as a journalist, to accompany a group of distinguished people, including his friend Lewis Leland, on the maiden voyage of the steamship *Ajax* to the Sandwich Islands, later to be renamed Hawaii. It was a public relations venture, initiating the California Steam Navigation Company's Pacific route, the ultimate destination of which was China. Twain had been eager to go; his restless thoughts had been drifting for years to exotic Asian distances. At the same time, San Francisco's business elite had begun to conceptualize its future greatness in trans-Pacific terms. The Bay City would be America's gateway to the Orient, especially now that the transcontinental railroad was about to reduce the time it took to cross the continent from a month to little more than a week. The San Francisco–Honolulu route would be the first stage in the larger scheme. Twain could not, though, accept the invitation, he told his mother, "because there would be no one to write my correspondence while I was gone." When the *Ajax,* after being away a little more than a month, returned in late February, he interviewed the passengers for the *Enterprise,* further whetting his appetite for experiencing the adventure himself. Twain made up his mind to leave California, and Hawaii suddenly seemed irresistible.

Two days later, he went to Sacramento. At the offices of the *Daily Union,* he finalized a deal probably initiated soon after the *Ajax* had left on its maiden voyage. One of the West Coast's most prosperous and its most prestigious newspaper, the *Union* had declined to be Twain's employer in 1862. It was now eager to send the highly praised journalist and humorist to Hawaii to write informative and entertaining travel letters. Hawaiian breezes were in the American air, entrepreneurs sniffing the scent of profits. Twain had an easy time selling the proposal. The *Union* agreed to pay Twain's fare and a set sum for each letter, though memories differ as to the exact amount, perhaps as much as fifty dollars, perhaps as little as twenty. With "letters of introduction to everyone down there worth knowing," he was "to remain there a month and ransack the islands, the great cataracts and volcanoes completely, and write twenty or thirty letters to the *Sacramento Union.*" That one month would be enough in which to write so many letters as well as do the requisite travel is inconceivable. On another day he told the San Francisco reporter for the *Humboldt Register* that he would be gone two months. He was, of course, in an effervescent mood in which excitement outweighed sense and consistency. No matter, for he had all the time in the world for Hawaii. "If I come back here," he told his family, "I expect to start straight across the continent by way of the Columbia river . . . through Montana & down the Mississippi river—only 200 miles of land travel from San Francisco to New Orleans." Presumably, at the end of that voyage, he would write the Mississippi book. "Good bye for the present," he told his mother. The next day, with Mark Twain and an odd acquaintance named Brown also on board, the *Ajax* steamed westward through the Golden Gate.

4.

Land was in sight twelve days later, on March 18, 1866, looking "like a couple of vague whales lying in blue mist under the distant horizon." Even before the California coast had disappeared, many of the sixty or so passengers were depositing their guts into stormy seas that persisted for more than half the voyage. A stalwart ship built by the Union for military service, the *Ajax* took the battering easily. And apparently Twain was not seasick at all, though the most volatile body of water he had ever sailed before was the placid Mississippi. As the captain swayed to the movements of the "fearfully rolling" ship, Twain tried to imitate him, and he fell down, embarrassed. He was delighted by the captain's nautical language, so different from Mississippi River jargon.

From the start of the voyage, the young writer had his wits about him, his enthusiasm heightening his excitement, his sense of adventure searching for a language both sensitive and solid that expressed itself in the notebook he soon began to keep. When he misplaced that journal, he started afresh in a new one, summarizing what he recalled he had written. In preparation for arrival, anticipating his tight schedule, he had books about the Sandwich Islands with him, including a Hawaiian language dictionary and phrase book. He needed to bone up quickly on a world about which he knew almost nothing. After all, he was expected to entertain and instruct his *Sacramento Union* readers. When, mid-voyage, he came down with "something like mumps," he had more time for reading than he had expected. He could hardly believe that he had "a d——d disease that children have—I suppose I am to take a new disease to the Islands and depopulate them, as all white men have done before."

When his fellow passengers began to appear in the dining room, Twain got to know some of them, particularly the old salts, nautical characters who played cards and told stories. Some passengers were genteel, some businessmen, some connected to the longstanding American mission to Christianize the natives. To pass time they invented games, poked into one another's business, endlessly discussed the weather. A week out of San Francisco that weather changed favorably, and the deck became their stage. Standing by the rails, the passengers began to sniff South Pacific breezes. The cold sting gave way to balmy warmth.

A businessman named Brown, a name Twain had used for his interlocutor in "An Unbiased Criticism," was a passenger. Twain began to subsume this real Brown into his fictional character. Having discovered the advantages of "Brown" a year before, he now developed him for use in Hawaii, part comic foil, part alter ego. "Brown" could say things Twain wanted to say that would be awkward, even embarrassing, to attribute to himself. When he found "twenty-two passengers leaning over the bulwarks and vomiting and remarking, 'Oh, my God!' and then vomiting again," it was "Brown," not Mark Twain, he told his *Union* readers, who, "ever kind and thoughtful," passed from one to another, saying, "That's all right—that's all right—you know—it'll clean you out like a jug, and then you won't feel so onery and smell so ridiculous." When the garrulous Brown realizes he has been tricked by mischievous fellow passengers into drinking many glasses of water before starting his dinner, he explodes to the waiter: "Take that water and go to blazes with it! Beefsteak! no! I've drank eleven gallons of water in fifteen minutes, and there ain't room enough in me for a sirloin steak off'm a sand-fly."

With the stars and stripes flying higher than the Hawaiian flag, the *Ajax* steamed past Diamond Head on the island of Oahu, the most politically important of the seven Sandwich Islands. Looking down, Twain marveled that he could sometimes see the shadow of the ship's bottom through one hundred feet of water so transparent that it "shamed the pale heavens with the splendor of its brilliant blue." In front of him was Honolulu, a city of fifteen thousand, Hawaii's largest, built on level land at the ocean end of a long valley rising into mountains.

A quick study, assisted by borrowed books and persistent inquiry, Twain soon had the basic geopolitical facts in mind, particularly that the current king of this legislative monarchy was the fifth in the Kamehameha dynasty, which had united the islands into a single kingdom in the early eighteenth century; that Kamehameha II had rejected the ancient polytheistic religion of the islands, defying a system of powerful taboos and destroying idols and temples; that Europeans and Americans had made Honolulu a refueling port for the whaling industry in the 1840s; that American Protestant missionaries then targeted the islands as fertile ground for saving heathen souls; and that when British Anglicans and French Catholics competed for Christian honors, religious missionary fervor had become inseparable from competition for political and economic control. To Twain's amusement, even modern Hawaiian law had originated with the missionaries, including Sunday closings and penalties for selling liquor to the natives. With Hawaii dependent on Western expertise, some Americans even held high official positions. Actually, the American Board of Commissioners for Foreign Missions performed like a shadow government. He wrote in his notebook that this was "how firm a hold & how powerful a supremacy these people have gained by their 46 years of breeding and training voters."

When Twain arrived in Hawaii in 1866, the sugar cane industry had become predominant: agriculture was more important than whaling, and the political future of the islands was uncertain. Should Hawaii remain independent? Should it be annexed by one of the Western countries? Having been insulted in the United States by being treated like a black man, Kamehameha V favored the British. "This King has never forgotten or forgiven that trifling stab at his little vanity," Twain wrote in his notebook. American businessmen and politicians were fighting for dominance. "I am now personally acquainted," Twain remarked after a few days in Honolulu, "with seventy-two captains and ninety-six missionaries." The largest number of foreign nationals in Hawaii were American, and Americans were in the process of creating regular service between the West Coast, Hawaii, and China, one purpose of which was to bring American immigrants in large numbers to the balmy Hawaiian paradise. Thus California would not be the last frontier. The crucial issue was whether to establish control by trade reciprocity or annexation. Wily strategists believed that a reciprocal trade treaty would result in such close ties that, in the end, annexation would be likely. Twain had, in the larger view, been sent by the *Sacramento Union* to work in his way to help fulfill long-term American aspirations. By training and self-interest, he readily accepted the geopolitical frame. A reciprocal trade treaty lowering or diminishing import-export duties between Hawaii and the United States and a federal subsidy to initiate regular trans-Pacific service for goods and people, he soon concluded, seemed reasonable and desirable. "It is a matter of the utmost importance to the United States," he told his *Union* readers, "that her trade with these islands should be carefully fostered and augmented."

From the moment Twain stepped ashore, he liked Hawaii and its capital. With a strong attraction to the tactile, and responsive to unfamiliar shapes, colors, and customs, he wandered "alone about this odd-looking city of the tropics." Brown—the real and fictional indistinguishable in Twain's *Union* letters—had gone "off to bed." The air was warm, almost hot. Bright fruits and flowers excited his eyes. One- and two-story cream-colored wooden houses lined the wide streets. The breadth of the avenues and the green-carpeted depths contrasted pleasurably with cramped, comparatively color-less San Francisco. Dusky-skinned, long-haired native women sat cross-legged. Occasionally one rode swiftly by on horseback, streamers drap-ing out behind in the wind. Their comparative undress appealed to him, their unselfconscious sensuality an image of escape from, rather than an ex-ploitation of, European and American puritanism. In contrast to the "hurry and bustle & noisy confusion of San Francisco," no one seemed to be in a hurry, or even at work. Cats, his mother's passion, were everywhere, "Tom cats, Mary Ann cats, long-tailed cats, bob-tail cats, blind cats, one-eyed cats, wall-eyed cats, cross-eyed cats, gray cats, black cats, white cats, yellow cats, striped cats, spotted cats, tame cats, wild cats, singed cats, individual cats, groups of cats, platoons of cats, companies of cats, armies of cats, multi-tudes of cats, millions of cats, and all of them sleek, fat, lazy and sound asleep." Other observers of those Honolulu days have remarked that there was not a noticeably larger cat population than anyplace else. Twain's obser-vations, though, were never to be limited by mere fact. The impression Hon-olulu made was on his senses and his imagination. Walking on a "firm foundation of coral," he was transported into a reality so different from any-thing he had experienced before that he felt giddy. On the whole Hawaii was one of the few places in the world that did not disappoint him, a haven "in the midst of a Summer calm, as tranquil as dawn in the Garden of Eden."

"If I were not so fond of looking into the rich masses of green leaves that swathe the stately tamarind right before my door, I would be less idle and write more," he told his *Union* readers. But his penchant for dawdling, for seemingly idle excursions and impromptu explorations with little regard to the clock, was a trait of service to the journalist, and even more service-able to the writer on human affairs in general. His letters to the *Union* now gave him an opportunity to be that observer of the human condition, in a sustained way, for the first time. Almost anything might be appropriate subject matter for his assignment. "Brown" was useful. So too was Twain's ear for dialect and dialogue. And his own voice was essential to these letters. It provided the tonal glue of personality, the references to an authorial self, often charming, sometimes mildly ironic, usually a riveting combination of self-effacement and egomania, a distinctive personality that was both humorous and serious, independent and accommodating, someone whose company was compellingly pleasant.

He quickly made friends in Honolulu. To his delight one old friend from Virginia City was there, Franklin Rising, who had come for his health, though his health did not seem "much improved." The United States Minister invited Twain to dinner, where he met the king's grand chamberlain. Some sea captains, restocking in Honolulu for voyages to Australia and beyond, invited him along, invitations that he had to refuse, with regret. A popular guest at local functions, he was warmly welcomed, a homegrown exotic to add spice to the blandness of the American community. As he walked or rode on horseback, in a canvas coat down to his ankles, in shabby, irregular clothes, a pipe or cigar always in his mouth, he attracted comment. "All small villages are gossipy," as was his childhood town, he noted, "but Honolulu heads them a little." The pastor of the Oahu Bethel Church and the chaplain of the Honolulu American Seaman's Friend Society, Samuel Damon became a friend and admirer. "Beloved by all" and "always collecting and caring for the poor," Damon put his large collection of books about Hawaii at the visitor's disposal. One of them, James Jarves' *History of the Hawaiian Islands,* Twain relied on heavily as he articulated for his *Union* readers Hawaii present with Hawaii past.

Hawaii present was the excellent water system; the prison, the "hideous" leprosy hospital, and other official institutions; the marketplace, with cigars, fruit, wine, liquor, strange foods like poi; and of course etiquette and manners, the life of the Kanakas, the word used for the natives, whose customs Twain found fascinating. "Kanakas will have horses and saddles, & the women *will* fornicate," he wrote in his notebook, "2 strong characteristics of the people." The present was also commerce: the reason that San Francisco had lost out to Honolulu as a port, and the kinds of changes that needed to be made. Hawaii past was embodied in its ancient legends and in the history of the Kamehameha dynasty. With only minor qualification, Twain had no doubt that the missionaries had done a good thing. "The king and the chiefs [had] ruled the common herd with a rod of iron." They suffered "death for trifling offenses," or yielded "their lives on the sacrificial altars to purchase favors from the gods for their hard rulers. The missionaries have clothed them, educated them, broken up the tyrannous authority of their chiefs, and given them freedom and the right to enjoy whatever the labor of their hand and brains produces, with equal laws for all." Though he had no belief in Christian theological claims and abhorred clerical intrusion in secular life, he still commended the changes in the value placed on each human life that had been effected by Christian missionaries. He scathingly commented in his notebook, "More missionaries & more row made about saving these 60,000 people than would take to convert hell itself." This part of his Hawaiian experience was an early stage in what became an increasingly compelling concern. Years later, in *A Connecticut Yankee in King Arthur's Court,* one of his fictional engagements with the Western past versus the Western present, he aggressively condemned Europe's feudal past and the clergy who controlled it as he now did Hawaii's.

From the moment of his arrival, he found Hawaiian culture engaging. There seemed to him "no care-worn or eager, anxious faces in the land of happy contentment—God! what a contrast with California & Washoe." He liked some of the native foods that most Westerners disliked; he found Kanaka women attractive—their custom of disrobing in public to bathe amused, riveted, and on one occasion clearly excited him; and he was good-humoredly fascinated by the natives' bargaining powers and their casually accepted duplicities in trade. A poor horseman and perhaps an even worse bargainer, when he bought a horse for excursions he was tricked into getting either an animal who wouldn't go or one who would go much too fast and decline to stop. He preferred mules, as he had in Missouri and Nevada. With his behind painful from saddle sores, he stumbled down from his horse after one hectic trip to distant ruins, one among many in which he traversed Oahu, visiting palaces, mausoleums, and ancient battlefields. With his keen eye for the absurd, he made serious fun of both some Kanakan and some Christian practices.

Prompted partly by his reading, and probably also by handling bones at these sites, he wrote an invented account of the whereabouts of the remains of Kamehameha I, which he called "A Strange Dream." This took the form of a letter to Henry Clapp's *New York Saturday Press,* in which he had published "Jumping Frog." Though he had not yet set foot out of

Oahu, and as if he were providing an on-location factual report of real events, he dated the letter with a location of "Volcano House," a well-known hotel at the base of the "Crater of 'Kilauea,' " a 4,090-foot-high active volcano on the island of Hawaii. In the dream the narrator descends into the bowels of the volcano, through intense heat and fumes, guided by a specter to a concealed chamber, where he discovers the "crumbling skeleton" of the great king. Then, with an appropriate Gothic and ghost-story effect, "a hollow human groan issued out of . . ." The sentence ends with the ellipsis. And the account concludes, "I woke up." He soon dreams the same dream again. Sleepless, defying superstition and the irrational, he descends into the crater to test the recurrent dream. Everything is as it had been in the dream. But when, after great effort, he pushes aside the boulder that reveals the hidden chamber, "after a solemn pause to prepare," he discovers that "there wasn't any bones there." "You can't bet anything on dreams," he concludes. Later, dreams were to be central to some of his fictional explorations of the complicated interplay between the real and the imaginary.

After four weeks and seven letters to the *Union,* he left Honolulu in mid-April for the island of Maui, where he spent a month sightseeing. He wrote no letters for publication during this time, for which he later apologized to his *Sacramento Union* readers. The more relevant audience, the editors who had hired him, must have been puzzled, even irritated. "I never spent so pleasant a month before, or bade any place good-bye so regretfully," he wrote, a charming but odd rationale for his silence. He could not and would not be held to a regular delivery schedule. He had taken on the work obligation to make the adventure possible, and pleasure and convenience would come first.

The three plantations he visited, to whose owners he probably had letters of introduction, seemed almost idyllic. At one, he enjoyed the company of "two pretty and attractive girls in the family and the plantation yields an income of $60,000 a year—chance for some enterprising scrub." One of his companions, with whom he boarded at Maui, recalled, "Sam liked to ride, and used to go a great deal with my wife's sister," who was beautiful. He was "inclined to be soft, and I think that on one occasion he came near to proposing. . . . Sam probably didn't know himself just how far he could trust himself with a pretty girl. For he hadn't a red cent, not even decent clothes." At the Rose plantation, famous for its lavishness, he had a delightful visit, probably at the recommendation of his San Francisco friend the poet Charles Warren Stoddard, whose sister was married to a son of the Rose family. At the Kualoa plantation, he witnessed a native burial. After "clattering around" for three weeks and climbing the volcano, he wrote to his old Hannibal and steamboating friend Will Bowen, "I wish you . . . were here. We would sail from Island to island for a year & have a merry hell of a time."

If there were poison for him in this paradise, it had to be imported. When, in late May 1866, he returned to Honolulu from Maui's "splendid scenery," eager to depart for Hawaii, the largest of the islands, he found a letter from his sister-in-law that made him furious, "opening the old sore afresh that cankers within me." Mollie and Orion were in California, attempting to raise money to return to Iowa by selling their few shares of mining stock and their Carson City home. Apparently Mollie suggested that, since Sam might return to St. Louis or even the East Coast before they did, he take responsibility for selling the Tennessee land. "It is Orion's duty," he angrily responded, "to attend to that land & after shutting me out of my attempt to sell it (for which I shall never forgive him,) if he lets it be sold for taxes, all his religion will not wipe out the sin." Both Orion's and Mollie's Christian piety irritated him into volatile fury. If Orion's religion kept him from performing a solemn duty he owed to his mother, sister, and brother, then Sam Clemens wanted no part of such a religion. Orion will save himself, he wrote to Mollie, "but in doing so will damn the rest of the family." With almost effortless irrationality, he widened his charges. Not only had they all suffered in general from Orion's narrow-mindedness, but he himself was "in poverty and exile now because of Orion's religious scruples." Orion, he implied, was responsible for all the years of his "exile" from the Missouri home in which he would have preferred to have remained. As if this were not melodramatically and self-servingly inaccurate enough, he had more. Think of "Ma and Pamela grieving at our absence," he wrote, "and the land going to the dogs when I could have sold it and been at home now, instead of drifting about the outskirts of the world, battling for bread."

Within a week of his return from Maui, he sailed for the big island of Hawaii. He had heard much about its wonders, particularly its two highest mountains, Mauna Loa and Hualalai. Before leaving, he mailed two letters to the *Union,* the first in more than six weeks, both focusing on the Hawaiian legislature, describing its organization, episodes from its history, and its current activities. Its composition he described as "half a dozen white men and some thirty or forty natives," a "dark assemblage." Most impressive in his eyes was Bill Ragsdale, half white, half Kanakan, who rapidly translated every statement in English into Kanakan, every Kanakan statement into English. One "startling peculiarity" of the legislators was that "they do not accuse" one another "of being stained with bribery and corruption. It is a new and pleasant sensation to me." He was aware, though, that one theory attributed the civility to innate virtue, but another to their not being offered bribes because "they are such leaky vessels that they would be sure to let it out." Mark Twain's fictitious "Brown," visiting the legislature with him and about to accompany him to Hawaii, was disappointed that the king, whom he had "been keeping a sharp lookout for," was not there. " 'Blame that King, ain't I ever'—'Peace, son!' said I; 'respect the sacred name of royalty.' " For publication, Twain pretended to have only mild criticism of Hawaii's government, including the king. In private notes, he was acerbic. He gets "loved and cherished compliments from the English & his revenues from the Americans . . . & with characteristic consistency he worships the men who have degraded his country & hates the strong & steadfast [American] hands that have lifted her up. . . . Royalty! I don't think much of Hawaiian Royalty!" Americans "have given religion, freedom, education, written language & Bible—England & France have given insults."

Since the only steamer to the big island was laid up for repairs, he sailed on a dirty, crowded schooner, a rough voyage against "baffling winds & dreadful calms." Brown (in this instance a substitute name for a fellow passenger: anyone Twain chose could now be "Brown") became wretchedly seasick. The next day fourteen-thousand-foot-high Mauna Loa appeared in the distance. Landing at Kailua, Twain was soon on horseback, eager to see the island's attractions. Traveling southward on the coast, he noted sugar and coffee plantations, fine orange groves, and the many varieties of trees, especially the huge koa, the beautiful wood of which he admired. His destination was Kilauea, accessible from the western side of the island, the four-thousand-foot-high volcano that had erupted in late May and continued to provide awesome fireworks. At the site where Captain Cook had been murdered, Twain meditated on the event and concluded for his *Union* readers that "small blame should attach to the natives. . . . They treated him well. In return, he abused them. He and his men inflicted bodily injury upon many of them at different times, and killed at least three of them before they offered any proportionate retaliation." Though he had earlier concluded that on balance the missionaries had done more good than harm, he had also begun to weigh colonial incursions on a morally sensitive scale, on which he sometimes found the victims' case the stronger.

"Brown" continued to be the foil for Twain's observations. As they traveled, he could be rebuked for looking over Twain's shoulder while the author was writing, could be made to do silly and selfish things, could stand in for the tourist as vandal and shamed into putting back a log sheathed with "copper memorials" to Captain Cook, which he was taking home for "a specimen." When Twain arrived at Volcano House near Kilauea, he amused himself by addressing an immaculately dressed Englishman, who had joined him on route, as Mr. Brown. "My name is not Brown. It is Howard," the irritated Englishman protested. Twain continued to introduce him as "Brown," and Howard continued to protest, to no avail. "He talks all the time," Howard complained, "telling no end of silly stories." The Volcano House and its proprietors, delighted to have Twain and eager for the publicity his letters would provide, were charming and hospitable. "They didn't charge me anything," Twain later wrote to his mother.

From the lookout half a mile above, he viewed the two-mile-wide and mile-high crater "illuminated by the glare from the fires below." The next morning, as they ascended, Twain threw away their lunch basket, certain they'd reach "the Half-Way House before noon." When darkness fell, Howard realized that they were lost. Twain, who seemed to agree, bedded down on the ground for the night. "Even then the man wanted to tell me a story that he was reminded of," Howard recalled, "hungry as we were." In the morning a native guided them to the Half-Way House. From there they went to the volcano's edge. Below them, molten fires and lava streams, with "circles and serpents and streaks of lightning," boiled and flared. Fountains of fire were being flung into the air. He had witnessed, he later wrote to his family, "the greatest eruption that had occurred for years."

On horseback again, needing rest but eager to return to Honolulu, he continued his circumnavigation of the island. At Hilo, north of Kilauea, he rested comfortably for three days, then resumed his "mighty hard trip," whose alternations between luxury and deprivation seemed to him extreme.

When he arrived back on Oahu in mid-June, his discomfort from raw saddle sores had become serious pain. He went right to bed, not by preference but by necessity: he could hardly walk. Since his hotel had only one book, a volume of Oliver Wendell Holmes' poems, he read it repeatedly from cover to cover. A few days later, he dragged himself out to visit prominent new arrivals who had threatened to do him the honor of visiting his disheveled quarters. The better part of wisdom was to go to them at the residence of the American minister.

On the same day that Twain had returned from Hawaii, Anson Burlingame, the forty-six-year-old former Republican congressman from Massachusetts, America's minister to China, had landed in Honolulu en route to resume his duties. He traveled with his son, Edward, and with General Robert B. Van Valkenburgh, the commander of a New York regiment at the battle of Antietam and also a former Republican congressman, on his way to Japan to assume ministerial responsibilities. How much Burlingame knew of Twain before arriving in Hawaii is unclear. Perhaps Twain's letters to the *Union* advocating trade policies that Burlingame himself strongly advocated had been brought to his attention before leaving San Francisco. Twain's reputation as a serious humorist might have come to his notice since his son Edward knew and admired "Jumping Frog." In fact, Twain told Edward, he was glad to hear him tell it so well, since he himself "never tried to tell it without making a botch of it." General Van Valkenburgh, Twain wrote home, said "California is proud of Mr. Mark Twain, & that some day America will be too, no doubt." It may be that Burlingame, who got from Twain "pretty much everything" he ever wrote, copies of which Twain must have brought with him from the mainland, initiated the meeting with an agenda in mind: an interest in a writer writing about American interests in the Pacific.

With sharp eyes "that could beam and persuade like a lover's" or "blast when his temper was up" set in a mature face bearded with full side whiskers, anchored by a stout stentorian body, Burlingame was a formidable figure, the most imposing embodiment of America's political and financial elite Twain had met. Burlingame, who liked the young writer immediately, was solicitous and avuncular, expressing a paternal interest that no one, including Twain's father, had ever expressed before. Soon they were indulging in a happy exchange of puns, the more horrible the better. Twain likewise took to Anson Burlingame from the start. He admired his accomplishments and respected his position, though Twain was later to disagree with Burlingame's imperial view of America's role in the Pacific. Burlingame advocated annexation. Twain, who preferred that Hawaii remain under native rule, acknowledged that that "won't suit those planters. Mr. Burlingame told me privately that if he were minister . . . he would have the American flag flying on the roof of the king's palace in less than two weeks. And he is in earnest, too. He hungered for those rich islands."

Well enough to resume his letters to the *Union,* Twain sent off his first in almost four weeks, the fourteenth in the series, with two postscripts. One stated that Burlingame and Van Valkenburgh were to be feted by Honolulu's American citizens, the other summarized a letter that had just arrived from Hilo, with a brief account of the arrival on June 15 "of nineteen poor starving wretches," the remnants of the crew of the *Hornet,* a clipper shipwrecked in the Pacific en route from New York to China, "who had been buffeting a stormy sea in an open boat for forty-three days." When eleven members of the crew arrived in Honolulu, Twain had an opportunity for a scoop. Previously, in Nevada and California, he had had little interest in that kind of journalism, and there were other journalists who could more readily fulfill that mission. But if he could get an account of the shipwreck from the survivors quickly enough to get it off on the next boat, leaving on June 26, the *Union* would certainly be the first mainland newspaper to have the story in detail. Burlingame, a man who made initiative a philosophy of life, strongly encouraged him. When it was clear that Twain could not walk or ride to the hospital, Burlingame had the writer put on a cot and carried there. To facilitate the interviews, Burlingame asked the questions while Twain wrote down the responses. By six that evening they had finished soliciting the details, a harrowing tale of courage, deprivation, suffering, near starvation, incipient cannibalism, and extraordinary leadership that allowed the survivors, shipwrecked off the coast of Chile, to survive for forty-three days.

Working through the night, Twain wrote a detailed account, dated June 25, 1866, which he just managed to get on the schooner moments before it left for San Francisco. Four weeks later his was the highlighted story on the *Union* front page. A grateful Twain wrote to his mother, "[Burlingame] hunted me up as soon as he came here, & has done me a hundred favors since, & says if I will come to China in the first trip of the great mail steamer next January & make his house in Peking my home, he will afford me facilities that few men can have there for seeing & learning." Twain loved the idea. "I expect to do all this," he wrote home, "but I expect to go to the States first,—& from China to the Paris World's Fair." Burlingame gave Twain advice that he believed applied to every profession: "Avoid inferiors. Seek your comradeships among your superiors in intellect and character; always climb." The young author had already figured that out for himself, though he had not and never would entirely apply that as his standard for companionship. But he quickly perceived the advantage of being in the company of men like Burlingame, the start of a lifelong attraction to successful, powerful people, especially when there existed mutual warmth and respect. On July 4, recovered from his saddle boils, he danced much of the night at a party hosted by his American friends. When within the week Burlingame sailed from Honolulu, Twain expected to see the minister in the not too distant future, probably in Peking.

Twain himself, departure on his mind, remained in Honolulu, where he paid close attention to the activities of a month-long mourning period for the death of the heir presumptive to the Hawaiian throne, Princess Victoria Kaahumanu Kamamalu, whose impressive funeral he attended on June 30 and described in detail to his *Union* readers. Fascinated by the colorful procession and the hierarchical arrangement of royalty, clergymen, and government officials, he at last saw the king himself. The monarch seemed to Twain much better-looking than in his widely displayed photographs. "I speak feelingly of this matter," he wrote, "because by turns the [camera] has represented me to be a lunatic, a Solomon, a missionary, a burglar and an abject idiot, and I am neither." What he told only to his notebook is that the princess, who "kept half a dozen bucks to do her washing, & has suffered 7 abortions," had died "in forcing abortion."

If in Nevada and California scruples or anxieties had made Twain abstinent, which is unlikely, his respect for Victorian decorum was genuine. In Hawaii, though, he gazed with open eroticism at the native women. They were "more immoral" than American women, he noted. And the "young girls" were "innocent & natural—I love 'em same as others love infants," that is, not as erotic objects. The comparison suggests some self-conscious defensiveness, as if aware that others might read more into it. In one of his last letters to the *Union* about Hawaii, written after he had returned to California, he told his readers, with careful precision and humor, that on one of their excursions Brown, tired, perspiring, and thirsty, had jumped unawares into "the midst of a party of native girls who were bathing." Hawaiian ladies, he noted, tended to be modest only in the act of actually undressing, which they do in a particular way. Once undressed, they feel quite natural and at ease. "Many of the native women are prettily formed, but they have a noticeable peculiarity as to shape—they are almost as narrow through the hips as men are." When the bathing women saw Brown among them, they "scampered out," as Twain watched. Brown said, "They were very handsomely formed girls. I did not notice particularly."

5.

After almost precisely four months in Hawaii, Twain left on the clipper ship *Smyrniote,* on July 19, 1866, a few hours after the *Comet,* another clipper, had gone out "with a great firing of cannon." Everyone looked forward to an impromptu race to see which would get to San Francisco first. Under experienced captains, both took the northward route to catch favorable winds. With "a devilish saddle-boil to sit on for the first two weeks at sea," Twain was delighted to have familiar company, including Franklin Rising, his minister friend from Virginia City, and Captain Josiah Mitchell and some of the other *Hornet* survivors, whom he now had the opportunity to interview more fully, with the idea that he would write an extended account of the disaster for publication in a prestigious eastern journal like the *Atlantic.* The *Hornet* survivors' willingness to eat human flesh came up in their discussions. "Horrible! God give us all full use of our reason & spare us from such things!"

He also had the task of adding to his notebook observations and recollections about Hawaiian people and customs (he had with him Samuel Damon's copy of Jarves' *History,* which he had "stolen," so he and the Hawaiian press soon joked), some of which might be useful in writing his remaining letters to the *Union.* He was to date the last eight letters of a total of twenty-five as if written from the places in Hawaii they described, a flexibility of exactitude characteristic of his attitude in such matters. In his imagination, he was in Hawaii, so to speak, when he wrote them. His visit to Volcano House and Kilauea in eruption concluded the series, a dramatic finale, though the visit had occurred weeks before events described in preceding letters. Perhaps he already had in mind transforming his *Union* letters into a book in which, as when he did draw on them in *Roughing It,* he would freely rearrange chronology for dramatic effect.

Under full sail, the *Smyrniote* sprinted for four days, then slackened when the trade winds fell. The eagerly anticipated China winds did not appear. As the captain maneuvered, Twain wrote in his notebook, "We are abreast of San Francisco, but seventeen hundred miles at sea!—*when* will the wind change?" The continuous calm soon frayed everyone's nerves, the miles ahead seemed interminable. He was, though, pleased to experience "the first *twilight*" he had seen in six years, for there are "no twilight[s] in the S. Islands, California or Washoe." His standard was Missouri and the Mississippi River, Keokuk sunsets remaining in his memory as the most superlative of all. The calm Pacific seemed "fully as level as the Mississippi, at least as smooth as the river is when ruffled by a very light breeze." The emptiness and monotony began to distress him. Though he had work to do and companions aboard, he felt eerily alone, an existential sense of isolation.

"Pacing the deck night and day," he and Franklin Rising talked endlessly. Rising "tried earnestly to bring me to a knowledge of the true God," he later recalled. "In return, I read his manuscripts and made suggestions for their emendation." Neither Rising nor God, whom Twain did not find available despite the minister's efforts, relieved his loneliness. "We see *nothing* on this wide, wide, lonely ocean—nothing but . . . sometimes a dolphin." When a land bird "hovered over the ship a while," the bird's distance from home made Twain's distance seem even greater. Painful memories surfaced, such as "the stabbed dead man in my father's law office." A more recent death came to mind, in reference to issues of literary style with which he identified: "Eloquence Simplicity—Lincoln's 'With malice toward none, with charity for all, & doing the right as God gives us to see the right, all may yet be well.'—Very simple and beautiful." On the first of five Sundays at sea, Rising held services on deck. The passengers formed a choir. "But of the 15 passengers, none even pretended to sing." The shy Rising couldn't conduct the service without a choir. "I said, 'Go ahead—I'll stand by you—*I'll* be your choir.' And he *did* go ahead—and I was his choir." The only hymn Twain knew was "Oh, Refresh Us." "So for five Sundays in succession [Rising] stood in the midst of the assembled people on the quarter-deck and gave out that same hymn twice a day, and I stood up solitary and alone and sang it!"

Hawaii was still much on his mind, especially its colorful, dreamlike sensuality and relief from puritanical travail. Decades later, the smell and taste remained fresh in his senses, all the more so because he was never to return. That element of him that was Victorian and conventional controlled but never silenced his periodic longing for a restful alternative to a busy, entrepreneurial life in America and Europe. For an after-dinner audience in 1889 he invoked, with words carefully written and memorized in advance, the personal Hawaii he carried in his feelings. "No alien land in all the world has any deep, strong charm for me but that one, no other land could so longingly and so beseechingly haunt me, sleeping and waking, through half a lifetime, as that one has done. Other things leave me, but it abides; other things change, but it remains the same. For me its balmy airs are always blowing, its summer seas flashing in the sun, the pulsing of its surf beat is in my ear; I can see its garlanded crags, its leaping cascades, its plumy palms drowsing by the shore; its remote summits floating like islands above the cloud rack. . . . I can hear the plash of its brooks, in my nostrils still lives the breath of flowers that perished twenty years ago." It is a bravura invocation that perhaps first gathered force as he felt increasing anxiety when the *Smyrniote*'s sails at last had wind to gather and, more than three weeks out from Honolulu, began to speed Twain toward a world to which he did not want to return.

For the time being, though, he had no choice. He needed to finish his *Sacramento Union* letters. Unless he undertook a regular journalistic job, his income would be erratic. Foreign correspondence also had limitations. The pay would not be sufficient to liberate him from a vagabondage that would condemn him to visiting places to which other people wanted him to go. And it would not relieve him of financial uncertainty, let alone allow him to pursue the attractions of domestic stability. "Marry be d——d," he soon wrote to Will Bowen, since it seemed out of the question anyway. "I am too old to marry. I am nearly 31. Women appear to like me, but d——n them, they don't *love* me." For the moment, the best he could do was to go to California, then Missouri, then China, returning via the Paris world's fair; or perhaps to China directly from San Francisco; or to New York and then Missouri and then . . . All was indeed a variable uncertainty, even a muddle, though it was clear to him that he would remain in California only as long as practicality required. To some considerable extent, he was "floating at random," a phrase he was soon to use about this stage of his life.

Eight hundred miles west of San Francisco, a strong breeze arose. "Every rag about the ship is spread . . . she is speeding over the sea like a bird." Within a day of San Francisco, they suddenly made out in the distance another clipper ship racing eastward. Eager to overtake her, the *Smyrniote* strained to increase its speed. "The race is very exciting," he wrote in his notebook, apparently with one eye on the horizon. As they closed the gap, the *Comet* was framed by "the setting sun," looking as "sharply black as coal against a background of fire & floating on a sea of blood." With a gale wind filling every stitch of canvas, both ships paraded proudly through the Golden Gate, "*side by side,* & 300 yards apart." It was both the happiest and unhappiest moment of the voyage. As soon as he stepped ashore, the wind again went out of Twain's sails. "Home again, No—*not* home again—in prison again," he wrote in his notebook, "and all the wild sense of freedom gone. The city seems so cramped, & so dreary with toil and care & business anxiety. God help me, I wish I were at sea again!"

A reverse daguerreotype of Sam
Clemens as a printer's apprentice at
about the age of fifteen

Jane Lampton Clemens,
in the late 1850s

Samuel Clemens, c. 1851–52

Orion Clemens,
early 1860s

Mark Twain, Constantinople,
October 1867

Bret Harte, c.1868

Artemus Ward as a public lecturer
(*Vanity Fair*, 1862)

Olivia Lewis Langdon,
about sixteen years old

The Buffalo house Jervis Langdon
gave as a wedding present to his
daughter and son-in-law

Olivia Langdon Clemens,
c. 1872

Mark Twain, in his sealskin coat, c. 1870

Clara Spaulding holding Susy Clemens, Livy, Sam, and Dr. John Brown, Edinburgh, 1873

Quarry Farm, Elmira, New York

Twain's publisher, Elisha Bliss, Hartford, 1870s

The Mark Twain house, Hartford, late 1870s

Mark Twain in his octagonal studio
at Quarry Farm, Elmira, c. 1875

The view of and beyond the octagonal study,
Quarry Farm

CHAPTER SIX

STRAIGHT GATE
1866–1867

1.

Within six months of returning from Hawaii, Twain sailed from San Francisco, crossed Nicaragua, and then voyaged northward from Key West. In the middle of January 1867, he stepped off the steamer and descended onto a New York City dock. He would not have been overdramatic if he had kissed the ground. There were moments when the ship from Nicaragua to New York seemed likely to be his coffin. Cholera had broken out, and many passengers had died.

His six months in San Francisco after returning from Hawaii had been a difficult and a defining time. He was greeted with a joke that was also perhaps a threat. " '*Mark Twain,*' the intimate friend of the San Francisco Police Department, returned yesterday from the Sandwich Islands. It is said they are planning to give him a champagne blowout," the *San Francisco American Flag* wrote. The city did not prove to be the "prison" he feared as the *Smyrniote* approached the Golden Gate. Nor did he again ruffle police feathers. But he had returned in a glum mood, unhappy at the necessity to bear down and write his remaining Hawaii letters when no longer there, and ill at ease if not anxious about his personal and professional prospects. Almost immediately he went to the *Sacramento Union* office, mostly because he needed the money owed him, partly to find out what the editors thought of his contributions. That he was greeted with bouquets pleased him. When he requested payment for his letters, the cashier happily obliged. When he then "presented a bill for 'special' service on the *Hornet* matter of three columns of solid nonpareil at a *hundred dollars a column*," the cashier came close to fainting. "He sent for the proprietors, and they came and never uttered a protest. They only laughed in their jolly fashion, and said it was robbery, but no matter; it was a grand 'scoop.'" They were "the best men that ever owned a newspaper."

Soon he was at work on the final eight letters, fulfilling his obligation with workmanlike determination. The letters hardly reveal that he felt them a tedious addendum to an experience already behind him. As he wrote, the sulfur fumes and fires of his visit to Volcano House were still sharp in his memory. But his restlessness had barely slackened, his desire to leave San Francisco and get on with it ever present. But to get on with what? At the core of this question was an uncertainty about himself, a compelling inclination to question his personal self-worth and his vocational future as a humorist. "I have got a spirit that is angry with me & gives me freely its contempt," he soon wrote to his mother.

On the one hand, he felt lucky, the darling of fortune. On the other, he felt that he had blighted much that he touched. In addition, he had a talent for bungling, especially for saying and doing the wrong thing, a clumsiness dangerous to others, damaging to him. Henry's death was always the touchstone. Memories of childhood humiliations, blunders, and lucky escapes contributed. Perhaps his father's death played some role, though the only evidence is his avoidance of and seeming lack of interest in the subject. The roots of his compulsion to be hard on himself are difficult to disentangle. Often there was nothing visible at hand to trigger his self-criticism. Sometimes the impulse was transformed into lassitude, sometimes into indecision. Extended indecision occasionally led to precipitate choices. At the moment, he felt he was spinning his wheels, dissatisfied and unable to come to terms with the alternatives available to him. He projected various scenarios, including departing on the inaugural run of the new China steamer, to continue around the world and visit the Paris world's fair. For the moment he favored that scenario, though the China Mail Steamer was not to depart till December. In the meantime he clearly had no desire to resume reporting for the *Territorial Enterprise* or for any San Francisco newspaper.

Meanwhile he slept each morning until eleven, he wrote Will Bowen, because he was "naturally lazy" and because the "pleasantest of [his] acquaintances [were] at the hotel breakfast at that hour." But laziness, always a relative matter, was, in his case, far from sloth. Within eight weeks he composed the eight remaining Hawaii letters and drafted "Forty-three Days in an Open Boat," his extended account of the *Hornet* catastrophe based on the interviews aboard the *Smyrniote* with the *Hornet* captain and crew. He soon sent it to *Harper's Monthly,* which published it in December 1866, mangling the author's name into "Mark Swain." Regardless of the accidental disguise, it was his first appearance in an elite eastern magazine with a reputation superior to all but that of the *Atlantic Monthly*. Sleeping late did not prevent him also publishing a brief essay in the *New York Weekly Review* and reporting for the *Union* on the California State Agricultural Society annual fair. He was "the best reporter of a horse-race that ever was made," one of the *Union* owners later remarked.

With the money from his Hawaii letters, he was not in the least pinched for cash. He was uncertain, though, about what to do next, except that he did not want to continue his San Francisco life. At the end of September he published a brief comic essay in the *Californian,* his last contribution to that journal. When Bowen raised the possibility that he might want to return to the river, he responded, "You bet your life I do. It is about the only thing I *do* feel any interest in & yet I can hear least about it. If I were two years younger, I would come back & learn the river over again. But it is too late now. I am too lazy for 14-day trips—too fond of running all night & sleeping all day—too fond of sloshing around, talking with people." He did not want to do the hard work necessary to qualify again. And, as a matter of emotional preference, he simply was not inclined toward it. The river was best reserved for memory.

Since he backdated the Hawaiian letters, with the exception of the third from the last, it is uncertain precisely when he finished them. The final letter appeared in the *Union* on November 16. From August on, he and others had it in mind that he would turn the letters into a book. In late August his *Californian* friends reported, "There seems to be a very general impression that Mark Twain's Sandwich Island letters . . . possess sufficient intrinsic interest . . . to justify their publication in book form. If the writer could be persuaded to collect and revise them, he would have no difficulty in finding a publisher . . . the book would prove both a literary and a pecuniary success." He needed little persuading, and probably he himself more or less planted the notice. His intention was so far advanced that sometime in mid-September he composed a dedication for the volume. It was to his mother, whom he had not seen since 1861, and whom, if he went west on the China Mail Steamer, he might not see for at least another year. If the dedication was in lieu of a visit, its praise of her "exquisite appreciation of the Good & the Beautiful" was oddly compromised by its claim that to Jane Clemens' "darkened understanding . . . even the mildest joke hath ever been a dark & bloody mystery." She marches "over the most elaborately humorous . . . jokes with the tranquil indifference of a blind man treading among flowers." In fact, so blind is she to humor that "she will not discover the irreverent levity that is hidden in this ded[ication]." Fortunately, he never published it. That he believed his mother totally deaf to what his contemporaries thought his strength as a writer must have further chilled his already dubious pleasure in being defined as "the wild humorist of the West," or as a humorist at all.

As he resumed his San Francisco life, he had the opportunity to see the one member of the family who had encouraged his career as a humorist—his brother Orion, who had arrived in San Francisco in late July 1866, not to sail to New York via Panama until the end of August. Orion had probably sold his few remaining mining shares and his Carson City house to pay for passage, his mind set on attending "to the family's Tennessee land." Sam, with his pay for his Hawaii letters in his pocket, may have lent some of it to Orion, his impatience with his brother's impracticalities never outweighing his loyalty. A few months later he was still steaming at Orion's refusal to pursue the one thing he had talent for, the ministry. "I am utterly & completely disgusted with a member of the family who *could* carry out my old ambition & won't. If I only had his chance, I would make the abandoned sinner get up & howl." In San Francisco, Twain had gotten to know some of the leading clergymen. Before leaving for Hawaii, he had jokingly claimed in his column in the *Californian* that he had great influence with the San Francisco clergy: "I write their sermons for them." Some of the best talent of nineteenth-century America went into the Protestant clergy. Like Twain, many of them tended to be amiable, gregarious, morally resolute but not priggish, eager to argue and persuade, with a sense of proportion, and especially a sense of humor. Such clergymen could take either solace or pleasure in Twain's moral seriousness. If neither belief nor theology were relevant, he could easily have been taken for a Christian.

The literary San Francisco that Twain returned to still flourished, particularly marked by Bret Harte's increasing national reputation. Harte had begun writing regularly for the *Christian Register* in Boston and the *Springfield Republican,* one of the country's most influential newspapers, and less for the *Californian,* which was to end its life in 1868. To the extent that, in the summer and fall of 1866, Twain participated in literary camaraderie it was with Harte and Charles Warren Stoddard, whose homosexuality did not make him at all less endearing to his heterosexual friends.

In late September 1866, Twain persuaded himself or allowed himself to be persuaded to give a public lecture about Hawaii. His later claim that he thought to join the ranks of public lecturers because he was broke and desperate is untrue. Whether his literary focus flagged or his usual restlessness sought another outlet, his interest in entertaining paying audiences had a more complicated genesis and a partly different motivation. From early adolescence, he had indeed imagined himself a charismatic preacher entrancing rapt audiences who would admire his hortatory skills. How he would "make them howl" with a combination of moral insight and rhetorical passion. Alas, as he had readily admitted, the necessary element egregiously absent was religious belief. But the desire to have an audience in the palm of his hand was there from almost the start. Opportunities to address audiences had arisen over the years, but, when Artemus Ward lectured in Virginia City in late 1863, Twain saw how a professional humorist entertained an audience. Which was not in an impromptu manner.

In Ward's case the success of his performance depended partly on the audience seeing unmistakably that he was reading. Twain observed Ward closely, as he had watched other speakers, particularly ministers and politicians, with a semi-professional curiosity. Ward's command of rhythm, pace, and pauses, and his deadpan delivery of absurdities in which the audience's laughter would be amplified by the fact that the speaker did not break into a smile, impressed him. In "Jim Smiley and His Jumping Frog," Twain had made effective use of the latter effect. Now he was prepared, in September 1866, to try his hand at that device and others in a public entertainment.

About mid-September he consulted with a friend, John McComb, the editor of the *Alta California,* who thought well of Twain going on the platform. Apparently he had two pieces of advice: take the largest hall in town and charge a dollar a ticket. Tom Maguire, San Francisco's reigning theatrical impresario, with whom Twain had been on convivial terms since his visits from Virginia City, owned the largest hall, the newly built Maguire's Academy of Music, which Twain rented for fifty dollars, half the usual price, for the night of Tuesday, October 2. Posters immediately went onto walls and billboards. Newspaper ads soon appeared. On the day of performance, the morning edition of the *Alta California* concluded its humorous account of what to expect with Twain's thereafter famous variant on the ordinary announcement, "DOORS OPEN AT 7 O'CLOCK. THE TROUBLE BEGINS AT 8 O'CLOCK."

Local San Francisco buzz elevated it into a highly anticipated event. Twain's friends in journalism and among the San Francisco elite expected fun, though they were not exactly sure what form it would take. In fact, Twain had carefully prepared a lecture based on his Sandwich Island letters. Extracting humorous and serious highlights, he had revised them into a ninety-minute presentation, with movable and removable parts that could be added or dropped as his sense of the audience and his observation of the clock would suggest. The key issue of persona he apparently resolved quickly; he would create the impression that he was talking his lecture, speaking directly and spontaneously to his audience, without the benefit of a manuscript. To make that possible and still have the security and control of a text, he memorized his presentation, with large blocks to be triggered by particular phrases and references. Additional material would be available in variable units, to be used or not as the occasion called for. His Missouri drawl and his attraction to pregnant pauses, of the sort that Ward had mastered, would heighten the effect of spontaneity, of colloquial off-the-cuff storytelling. If he forgot something or lost his way, he would be able to find it by manipulating his blocks of material. Anyway, how would anyone know he had lost his way when he had incorporated into his presentation the rhetorical ploy of claiming that he had when he might or might not have?

Since the structure and rhetoric of the illusion of improvisation encouraged rambling, the impression of informally talking to his audience was a reality as well as an artifice. And his absolute rule, like Ward's, was never to laugh at any of the funny things he said, and never to say them in a funny way. The preparatory work would be memorization and practice. Each phrase had to be shaped in advance. Every pause had to be scripted and mastered. And, if he failed to get it right this first time, he had already committed himself to additional opportunities to perfect the presentation. After the San Francisco performance, he would go on tour to a number of Bay Area cities, and to Nevada also, where his reputation as the *Territorial Enterprise*'s best-known ex-reporter would produce audiences for him if the San Francisco response was favorable.

2.

Anticipating failure, worried that, despite all the talk and advertisements, few people would show up at the Academy of Music, he kept an anxious eye on the box office and arranged with some friends to lead the audience by laughing heartily at his jokes. The newspapers beat the drums and blew the trumpets. The *Californian,* which sold tickets at its office, headlined a squib, "Mark Twain in Trouble," but the trouble, it noted, "has already commenced—in the shape of an overwhelming rush for tickets, the demand for which was yesterday so pressing, as to interfere seriously with the regular routine of our office duties. Those wishing to secure seats for the occasion, can apply at the Academy of Music at any time after nine o'clock on Monday morning." He persuaded a well-known couple who were his friends to take prominent seats to the left of the stage. When he turned to them with a smile, that would be their signal to laugh and applaud.

Late in the afternoon of the performance day he went to the theater box office. It was closed and locked, no one in sight. He assumed it had closed because no one had come to buy tickets. At six o'clock he entered the dark theater. Stumbling against props and scenery, he made his way onto the stage. "The house was gloomy and silent, and its emphasis depressing. I went down among the scenes again, and for an hour and a half gave myself up to the horrors, wholly unconscious of anything else." Stage fright overwhelmed him. To his shock, by eight o'clock every seat was filled, the house sold out. Patrons began stamping their feet in anticipation. When he tentatively appeared in the wings, those who could see him applauded vigorously. Slowly, hesitantly, he came onto the stage, into the bright lights. Within minutes, at the sight of so many familiar, friendly faces, his stage fright was gone, "never to return."

With his eye on the box office, his actual stage fright was preceded by a publicity ploy, invented sufficiently prior to the performance to allow the *San Francisco Dramatic Chronicle* to print a humorous account of it for the October 2 morning edition, headlined "Sensational Rumor."

It is reported about town, we know not upon how reliable authority— that last night "Mark Twain" had an attack of stage fright in advance. [He] was so overcome at the near prospect of having to make a first appearance before a metropolitan audience that his courage broke down, and he secreted himself in the baggage room of the Occidental, with the intention of taking the 4 o'clock boat to-day, and making his escape to Sacramento. The panic was produced, it is said, by the contemplation of his own huge posters ornamenting the dead walls and bulletin boards throughout the city. P. S. We learn just as we are going to press that the holders of tickets for the lecture this evening have engaged a police force to be on hand at the departure of the Sacramento boat, in order to apprehend the fugacious lecturer and prevent the contemplated swindle. Owing to these precautionary measures, "Mark's" attempt at evasion will probably be frustrated, and the lecture will, we hope, come off according to announcement. P. P. S. We stop the press to inform our readers that "Mark" has been secured, and has, after the administration of one dozen bottles of Mrs. Winslow's soothing syrup, become reconciled to the situation. He will *positively appear, but holds the public responsible.*

Undoubtedly, Twain instigated and may even have written the article.

Reviews were mostly glowing, though some expressed scruples about the suitability of some of the jokes for ladies. "True," the *Californian* remarked, "he displayed not the polish of the finished lecturer—nor did he need it; the crude, quaint delivery was infinitely preferable." It was also a purposeful part of the effect. A week later the *Dramatic Chronicle* headed a squib, "Mark Twain's Consolation." "They have the consolation of abusing me, and I have the consolation of snapping my wallet and hearing the money jingle. They have their *opinions,* and I have their *dollars.* I'm satisfied." Bret Harte gave it the most perceptive praise. Twain's brilliant performance had "the Western Character of ludicrous exaggeration and audacious statement," he wrote. It was indigenous art, both regional and national, superior to Artemus Ward and even to James Russell Lowell, the high-caste Bostonian who had created a literary voice that epitomized the New England Yankee. Harte's praise provided a western imprimatur. It also paved the road eastward that both would soon take.

Before any such departure, though, Twain took his highly praised act on the road to nearby California towns and across the Sierras. Dennis McCarthy, the former co-owner of the *Territorial Enterprise,* arranged a schedule that had him performing in nine different cities in four weeks. Word of his successful San Francisco performance paved the way. In Red Dog, where Twain was booked into a log cabin schoolhouse before an audience of rough miners, a reluctant miner was persuaded to provide the introduction. "He said he had never appeared in public," Twain later recalled, "and had never done any work of this kind; but they said it didn't matter. And so he came on the stage with me and introduced me in this way. He said: 'I only know two things about . . . this man. . . . One is, he has never been in jail; and the other is, I don't know why.'" In response to an invitation signed by many Carson City notables, he responded that he felt "a natural pride in being welcomed home again by so long a list of old personal friends."

By late October he was in Nevada. Virginia City friends greeted him as a conquering hero, his reputation so high that they felt it desirable to bring him down a notch and also to remind him of their joke-filled days together. An overflow audience of more than eight hundred crowded the Opera House. Joe Goodman and Dan De Quille, both in the audience, also knew how to puff a friend. The lecture, the *Territorial Enterprise* remarked, combined "the most valuable statistical and general information, with passages of drollest humor—all delivered in the peculiar and inimitable style of the author—and rising occasionally to lofty flights of descriptive eloquence." On November 10 he spoke at nearby Gold Hill, where a large audience put a handsome profit into his pocket. As he and McCarthy walked up the hill back to their Virginia City hotel, they were challenged in the darkness by a group of armed masked men who demanded money and valuables. Frightened, Twain gave them all he had, including his gold watch, the gift he had received as a remembrance of his presiding over the meeting of the Third Estate at the territorial legislature in 1864. He spent an angry night. The next day he discovered that the robbery had been committed, with McCarthy in on the plot, by his Virginia City friends as a practical joke at his expense, in the expectation of exposing what they assumed would be Twain's elaborate, self-serving embellishments. Steve Gillis later claimed that they had done it to give Twain material for another Virginia City lecture, which he had declined on the grounds that he would not repeat himself in the same town and did not have another lecture prepared. Furious, Twain fired McCarthy and left the next day for San Francisco. His watch and other possessions had been returned to him. When the newspapers took up the story, a reporter for the *San Francisco Golden Era* claimed that Twain himself had been in on the plot, gotten up to generate publicity for a second lecture in San Francisco. It seems unlikely.

With little other advance publicity, he did give his Hawaiian lecture again to a full house, at San Francisco's Platt's Hall. His Californian friends thought it informative and amusing, "full of genuine flashes of humor," though the *Dramatic Chronicle* deplored its occasional impropriety, even crudeness. It was not something the novice lecturer would have liked to hear. The accusation touched a sore spot. He needed to be himself, with the attractions of his down-to-earth middle-American stage manner, and at the same time in no way offend elite standards of propriety.

His planned departure at the beginning of December was postponed long enough for him to regret, when the mail steamer left for China, that he was not on it. "Everybody says I am throwing away a fortune in not going in her. I firmly believe it myself." But he had changed directions. He had determined to go west by first going east, by steamer via the Central American crossing to New York, then westward to visit his mother and sister in St. Louis, and to then sail eastward from New York to the Paris world's fair. From Europe, he would continue eastward around the world to China and Japan, then return across the Pacific to California. Urged by friends and by success, he had it in mind to look into giving his Hawaiian lecture on the East Coast. John McComb had decided that the *Alta California* would sponsor Twain's round-the-world voyage at twenty dollars a travel letter and transportation costs. He would provide the *Alta* with about fifty letters of about two thousand words, similar to his letters from Hawaii, which McComb admired. Whether or not Twain gave the *Sacramento Union* editors the chance to compete for his services is unknown. Probably, after McComb's help in arranging for Twain's San Francisco lectures, the arrangement simply fell into place.

To take advantage of the time before sailing, he lectured in San Jose and then in Oakland at the College of California, later to be transformed into the University of California. "Use the pruning knife freely, and lop off, not a branch of humor or a twig of wit, but all of the buffoonery and not a little of the vulgarity," the *San Jose Mercury* advised. At the request of friends and sponsors, in response to the usual name-studded petition for an encore, probably part of a pro forma conspiracy in which he participated, he repeated the lecture for another large San Francisco audience at Congress Hall on December 10. Adding some farewell remarks, beating the drum for California's great future, he bid "the old city and [his] old friends a kind, but not a sad farewell." The overdose of sentiment was not without genuine feeling, but he was happy to be leaving. The day before departure he wrote to his mother that he was "leaving more friends behind . . . than any newspaper man that ever sailed out of the Golden Gate." Some of them came to see him off. An irate father came aboard with a policeman to rescue his fifteen-year-old runaway daughter from the clutches of the young man she claimed she had just married. Twain and the other passengers sided with the couple, and the father was beaten off. Amid clatter, excitement, and hurrahs, in the middle of December 1866, the *America,* with four hundred passengers, steamed out of San Francisco, heading southward down the California coast.

3.

The first night out, a storm battered the passengers until most were seasick and all severely frightened. High seas broke over the bulwarks, drenching the forward cabin and flooding the steerage. A case of claret floated in six inches of water. "A man's boots were washed" to the far end of the room as the overheavy ship "fought the seas, instead of climbing over them." Afraid of drowning, many of the passengers below dressed and went to the highest places aboard. While the crew prepared small boats for possible evacuation, passengers in the main cabin fell to their knees, praying. In the comparative safety of an outside upper-deck berth, Twain at first did not realize how precarious the situation was. And though he was not seasick, he was ill with "something worse," probably diarrhea. Soon the commotion and the accounts of frightened passengers made the situation clear to him.

Much faith was placed in the expertise and experience of the captain. "If anybody can save [us] its old Wakeman," one of the passengers said. To Twain, the danger seemed exaggerated. The *Ajax* on route to Hawaii had been, he thought, in more peril. Edgar Wakeman, though, was a delight, an old salt whose sailor's vocabulary and vulgar language embodied an authenticity that made him a compelling figure to Twain, who could not get enough of his fascinating talk. "A great burley, handsome, weather-beaten, symmetrically built and powerful creature, with cola-black hair and whiskers . . . he was full of . . . the best kind of human nature." A one-of-a-kind verbal autocrat, a nonstop talker, he had memorized the Bible, his favorite book, and used it as his trump card. Wakeman loved to argue. Disputes about what the Bible meant were for him the best disputes of all. "He believed that he was the only man on the globe that really knew the secret of the Biblical miracles. He had what he believed was a sane and rational explanation of every one of them, and he loved to teach his learning to the less fortunate." An eccentric moralist, he upheld his version of biblical law with an iron hand. When it became known that the runaway couple were, after all, not married, or at least could not produce a marriage certificate to the captain's satisfaction, he ordered them to his cabin, where he peremptorily married them in front of five witnesses. When it was discovered that the groom had given the captain a false name for the ceremony, he "got off some more complicated and appalling blasphemy, and hauled up the young man and married him over again!" Whether or not his authority had anything to do with it, after two days the storm subsided.

Gradually, the *America* got down to the normal activities of life at sea. Two passengers conveniently named Brown reminded Twain, if he needed reminding, that he would do well to have his "Brown" aboard. With "Brown" and a new notebook, he made frequent entries, observations, descriptions, memorable comments by passengers, personal notes and reminders, much of it written to the moment, occasional remarks directed toward use even beyond his letters to the *Alta*. Five days out of San Francisco, as the *America* tacked southward along the California coast, the weather turned pleasantly warm. Awnings were raised on deck to provide comfortable shade. They passed two anchored whalers, one of them hoisting a "vast mass of blubber aboard." On the sixth day they crossed the tropic of Capricorn, abreast of the Gulf of California. Groups of passengers sang songs and played leapfrog on deck. On Sunday a choir with an actual organ celebrated Sabbath services. Twain got his exercise swinging gently for hours in a large hammock and moving his pencil across his notebook pages. "Brown" continued to perform his usual function as the same character who had been Twain's Hawaii foil, an epitome of boorishness and ignorance, the all-knowing traveler, the unselfconscious blunderer. In a notebook entry Twain focused on the notion of poetic "genius," a serious one for Twain, who puzzled about the level of his own talents. His defense was to treat it satirically. "But above all things," he concluded, "to deftly throw the incoherent ravings of insanity into verse & then rush off to get booming drunk, is the surest sign of genius."

The captain continued to fascinate. Twain could not get enough of his blustery, outspoken, extravagant stories and his comments on people. He wrote that he would "rather travel with that old portly, hearty, jolly, boisterous, good-natured old sailor" than with anyone else alive. "His feats of blasphemy are calculated to fill the hearer with awe & admiration." Aware of his own capacity for obscenity, he admired and envied Wakeman's superior talent. Obscenity was a way of both damning and celebrating the world simultaneously, of dramatizing the claim that forbidden language in the hands of genius elevated rather than degraded language and life. For Twain, it was inseparable from his definition of sympathetic manhood, of the relation between language and anger, of an expressiveness that provided release, relief, and pleasure. And part of the pleasure was the descent into the natural man that religion and polite society deplored and repressed. Twain respected and admired Wakeman, a master of irrepressible profanity, and immediately began imagining ways in which he could make him the center of something literary. He was to try over much of the rest of his life to find ways to capture this character in prose. Wakeman would be the model for Ned Blakely in *Roughing It*, Captain Eli Stormfield in "Captain Stormfield's Visit to Heaven," Captain Saltmarsh in *The American Claimant,* Captain Davis in "The Great Dark," Admiral Abner Stormfield in "The Refuge of the Derelicts," and Judge Sim Robinson in *Those Extraordinary Twins*. Wakeman's actual language, though, would be impossible to make literary use of; Victorian standards in such matters forbade it. And even in his private notebook Twain wrote "damn" as "d——n." He could curse himself hoarse, but not in writing.

On December 27 the *America* docked in San Juan Bay, Nicaragua. Unhappy news awaited. The *San Francisco,* the ship scheduled to take the passengers from the eastern side of the Isthmus to New York, had broken down off the Virginia coast. The news was doubly bad. Cholera had broken out among six hundred travelers from New York who had been waiting in San Juan for the *America* to take them to California. In San Juan alone there had been almost seventy deaths in the past week. For the time being, though, the path ahead was obvious and hampered only by anxiety. On December 28 the *America*'s disembarked passengers, on horses and mules and in carriages, left on the twelve-mile journey to Lake Nicaragua, where they boarded a small boat. Twenty-four hours later, on the San Juan River, they boarded a large, open, double-decked, stern-wheel steamer. At Castillo they went ashore to skirt impassible rapids and embarked on another stern-wheel steamer, which at last brought them to Greytown, on the Atlantic side. Unexpectedly, the *San Francisco* was waiting. On New Year's Day 1867, in a driving rain, Twain boarded the ship that would take him on the last part of his long voyage.

As the travelers had made their way from San Juan to Lake Nicaragua, the native women by the roadside, like the women of Hawaii, seemed to him happy embodiments of natural eroticism, of unselfconscious and unembarrassed sensuality. Aroused both erotically and imaginatively, he put to the test, in his fourth letter, the *Alta*'s sense of propriety. "Such liquid, languishing eyes!" he wrote. "Such pouting lips! such glossy, luxuriant hair! such ravishing, incendiary expression! such grace! such voluptuous forms, and such precious little drapery about them." Twain valued intellect but, as a writer, feeling was the fountainhead from which everything flowed: the tingling sense of responsiveness, which, in combination with intuition, placing trust in what came unbidden by the conscious mind, drove his memory, his reactions, and especially his pen. Dazzled by sensual lushness, his descriptive powers responded to the tropical landscape: oranges, bananas, coffee beans, tobacco, cattle, "hot corn, carved cups," a "snake cactus clasping trees," mountains abruptly rising from water, "great alligators lying on [a] bank sleeping in the sun," a fairyland grotto with an "endless confusion of vine-work" in which "no shape known to architecture [was] unimitated," "waterfalls of glittering leaves" through which could be seen glimpses of wild monkeys, "birds warbling—gorgeous plumed birds on the wing—Paradise itself—the imperial realm of beauty—nothing to wish for to make it perfect."

In Atlantic waters, as the ship beat northward in heavy seas, Twain went to bed, "the same old thing" incapacitating him. A monkey, who had been given swigs of straight brandy, scampered from rope to rope on the top mast, providing deckside entertainment. "The dizzy heights, the blowing of the gale & the plunging of the ship have no terrors for him." A report of smallpox at Greytown and the threat of cholera made every passenger uneasy. Twain believed (more hope than knowledge) that there was neither cholera nor smallpox aboard, that the so-called cases were drunken men sick to the stomach from eating unripe tropical fruit. But on January 2, two cases of cholera appeared in steerage. That night one passenger died; a second soon followed. Then a third. The coast of Cuba came in sight on January 4 as the ship headed for Key West, where they were to put in for supplies and medicine. Another passenger died that morning, "& was shoved overboard half an hour afterward sowed up in a blanket with 60 pounds of iron." The terrified passengers wondered who would die next. And how long would those who survived be quarantined, either aboard ship or in some other unattractive place? Afraid of doctor bills they could not pay, the steerage passengers concealed their illnesses to the last moment. The disease rose from steerage to the second cabin, then the first. There were dozens of cases of serious diarrhea. The ship's doctor was helpless. "Verily, the ship is fast becoming a floating hospital," Twain wrote in his notebook. "I myself may be dead to-morrow."

On January 5 he started to keep a list of names and brief biographies of the dead. Also, with some desperation, he kept writing into his notebook ideas and sketches for stories, including a burlesque of a Victor Hugo novel, as if work could help control anxiety. A passenger, who most of all feared being buried at sea, asked the captain "to promise not to throw him overboard in case he died. . . . as if his dead carcass would be more comfortable being eaten by grub-worms than sharks." At Key West, to great relief, they were allowed to disembark. "This Key West *looks*," he wrote in his notebook, "like a mere open roadstead, but they call it one of the best *harbors* in the world . . . a very pretty tropical looking town, with plenty of shade trees. It is very cool & pleasant." They were mercilessly gouged, though, by local tradesmen. They had not been quarantined, he thought, because the Key West people desired their money more than they feared their illness. "We don't calculate to find any Key West folks in Heaven." The ship's doctor told him that "it was Asiatic Cholera, but they must have deceived the port surgeon else they wouldn't have let [them] land." With many of the passengers, he attended an Episcopal service, observing how well people were dressed, bought four hundred Cuban cigars at a cheap price, and arranged a hearty dinner for a group of his fellow survivors. In church, "they put me in the aftermost seat . . . with the niggers d———n them. They always gauge me, somehow or other." What he remembered best about Key West were the "noblest cigars in the world," smuggled from Havana.

Soon the *San Francisco* was under way again, with a sharply reduced passenger list. Twelve had died. A larger number decided to take a different boat, to New Orleans if that were possible or to New York at a later time. On January 10, 1867, as they left the Gulf Stream at Cape Hatteras, twenty-six days out from San Francisco, "less than 400 miles south of New York," the weather began to turn cold. Feather mattresses and warm blankets appeared on the bunks. Rain fell hard. Twain stayed mostly in bed, trying to keep warm. Standing on deck in the dark, he felt something blow in his face "like snow." It was too dark to tell. During the day most of the passengers huddled in the salon and drank and sang. Whenever anyone was sick, they all felt certain cholera was breaking out again. With only one day of the voyage remaining, an infant died. The ship could not steam fast enough to outpace their fears. On January 12 the lights of New York Harbor guided them toward the city. It was a sight many of them thought they would never see. For Twain, the voyage had been his closest brush with death since the explosion of the *Pennsylvania*. He descended onto the dock with an immense sense of relief, accompanied by his "Mr. Brown" in his notebook and in his mind. The cold winter chilled his body. Snow lay on the ground that he would otherwise, at least metaphorically, have kissed.

4.

His mind filled with business, his feet aching and cold from snow and frost, he spent most of the next month running from appointment to appointment. The New York he had known in 1853 hardly existed anymore. Big as the city had seemed then, it was huge now. Crowded, horse-drawn passenger trolleys steamed and stamped through streets narrowed by too many vehicles, too many people, and too many piles of snow. Skidding, unhappy horses and broken-down wagons made riding slow and insufferable. So he walked everyplace, as quickly as he could, both to keep warm and to traverse the distances that always seemed much too great for pedestrian comfort. "Time presses me mighty hard here," he wrote to his sister-in-law, "& . . . it destroys a whole day to make only a single visit in New York," partly because "many business men only give audience from eleven to one." The freezing weather in January and February sent a shock through his thin California blood. A New York reporter for the *San Francisco Evening Bulletin* told the warmer folk back home that he had met Twain "a few days after his arrival and found him shivering and chattering his teeth at the 'damnation cold weather,' and complaining of the 'infernal long distances.'"

Fortunately, Charles Henry Webb's office on Broadway was just a few streets north of his hotel, the Metropolitan, a large post–Civil War hostelry boasting luxuries such as gas lighting throughout. New York seemed to Twain bursting with energy and money, the result of a brief postwar boom prior to an impending recession, the earliest days of the Gilded Age. Despite the city's frenetic pace, its citizens seemed "the most liberal, pleasant and companionable people you can find." The cracks in the economy, though, were widening. Unemployed veterans scraped to make a living; ragpickers starved and froze in the streets; inflation had driven prices so high that old New York fortunes were suddenly deflated. Webb, who had coedited the *Californian* with Bret Harte and thought highly of Twain, was eager to help his talented friend. He suggested that he and Twain gather the best of Twain's sketches for book publication and volunteered to collate the sketches and handle the business end.

Twain, in fact, did most of the work, cutting and pasting from his *Territorial Enterprise* and *Californian* scrapbooks, which he had brought with him and which served as printer's copy. Evenings, he shared stories and had drinks with Webb and his friends, with one of whom, Edward House, music critic for the *New York Tribune*, he struck up a friendship. In order to pay his bills he needed to continue writing letters for the *Alta California*. Seven had been written en route, but now he had to churn them out. Having prepared a book-length manuscript from his Sandwich Island lectures, he hoped to find a publisher. And there was also reason to hope that he could serve himself well by giving his Hawaii lecture in New York. At the same time, he had his eye on fulfilling his commitment, sometime in the not too distant future, to provide *Alta California* readers with humorous letters from foreign lands. He was, so to speak, in transit. Even when he rested, having all this on his mind made him feel he was working.

Fortunately, New York readily provided much of the subject matter for the nineteen letters he wrote for the *Alta* between February and June 1867. His first, early in February, began with the good-humored complaint that "the only trouble about this town is, that it is too large," immediately followed by a description of erotic performances, focusing on stage shows that highlighted nudity. His tired feet, apparently, had no trouble taking him to the theaters showing plays that existed for the advantage of displaying female bodies. "The scenery and the legs are everything," he said of one. In his account of his visit to the "Model Artists" exhibition at Niblo's Garden, "the wickedest show you can think of," he pointed out that in the New York he had visited in 1853 the police would have closed down such a display. Now it was one among many such, packed every night with audiences of enthusiastic men. Whatever might interest his readers was worth a few paragraphs, and over the next month he covered topics from women's fashions to Sunday amusements, from "my Ancient Friends, The Police," to various fashionable preachers, famous actresses and actors, the latest scandals, the peculiarities of New York laws and customs—a potpourri of paragraphs on anything that struck him as good copy. At Cooper Institute, he heard Anna Dickinson, one of the best-paid lecturers of the day, introduced by Horace Greeley, the editor-owner of the *New York Tribune,* urge equal employment rights for women to an audience of 2,500 people. "She did her work well," he wrote. "She made a speech worth listening to." With so much to describe, there was little to no room for "Mr. Brown." Apparently, a plethora of fascinating fact made fiction unnecessary.

Always attracted to new ways of managing time and materials, Twain had a mind that quickly grasped general possibilities, though less of a sense of the fine print, the impediments, and the risks. Like most entrepreneurial Victorians, he shared the culture's faith in the wonders that technological progress would bring, some of which would make fortunes for those of vision and initiative. As a journalist and a former printer, he was particularly fascinated by a stereotyping machine. Watching this new invention preparing "Webster's Unabridged for the press in a space not larger than a common bath-room" and which allowed a man to "set up . . . on a large scale, on a capital of $200," his mind zeroed in on both the wonder of it and "the patent rights," which, he remarked, "have been sold for a fabulous sum." He was making mental calculations about how rich the holder of that patent would become.

Another booming nineteenth-century industry also caught his attention. He went to Brooklyn Heights' Plymouth Congregational Church, home of America's most famous Protestant clergyman, Henry Ward Beecher, whose brilliance was helping to adapt American puritanism to nineteenth-century middle-class needs. The son of a well-known clerical father among whose prominent children was Henry's half sister Harriet Beecher Stowe, Beecher exemplified to American Protestants the high level of leadership God had provided as a sign that he was on their side. Beecher's Sunday sermons were the hottest ticket in town. A post–Civil War religious revival, led by Beecher and a national cadre determined to bring America back to the straight and narrow, eager to wipe out private and public sins, particularly alcoholism, felt it had a winning hand. Beecher believed that puritan righteousness and Victorian materialism could be reconciled. Congregational Calvinism promised much to those who would follow its version of Christ, to those who would accept Church discipline and religious direction. Abolitionist, idealistic, and at the same time practical, the Plymouth Congregation had come out of the war strengthened and even more intent on playing a major role in American life. Henry Ward Beecher would lead the way, and every Sunday he was on show.

Promised a seat by a prominent congregant, who had advised him to come early, Twain also had a letter of introduction from one of his San Francisco clerical friends. Arriving at ten A.M., "earlier than any Christian ought to be out of his bed on such a morning," he found the street lined with people eager to get in. When he presented his reservation number he was chastised for his lateness by a haughty usher who directed him to the upstairs galleries. That's where he remained, "the last individual," he was sure, "to get a seat in Mr. Beecher's church that day. . . . Every pew above & below was filled with elegantly-dressed people, & the aisles and odd spaces in both places occupied with stools like mine." The choir sang beautifully. Beecher got up and began to preach "one of the liveliest & most sensible sermons" he had ever heard. His voice was rich and resonant. "His discourse sparkled with felicitous similes & metaphors." Sometimes he walked away from his notes, "sawing his arms in the air, hurling sarcasms this way & that, discharging rockets of poetry, exploding mines of eloquence." He knew how to make the congregation hang expectant on his every word, to be so silent that Twain had the desire to startle them with a single clap of the hand. He even knew how to make his audience laugh as he tore satirically into the corruption of American political life. Twain marveled not only at the performance but at how "remarkably handsome" Beecher was "when he is in the full tide of sermonizing, & his face is lit up with animation." He was, though, "as homely as a singed cat" when he wasn't speaking. It was a performance of the sort that epitomized his own longstanding fantasy of Samuel Clemens the powerful preacher holding an audience in the palm of his hands.

In early March 1867, the *Alta* editors received a brief, unexpected telegram from Twain: "Send me $1,200 at once. I want to go abroad." They were taken aback. Undoubtedly they had expected to provide their correspondent with travel funds for his trip eastward, eventually to the Orient. But a request for such a large sum of money in advance, rather than smaller sums as reimbursement, was highly unusual, even for their eccentric young star. Twain's *Alta* letter, written March 2 and received in California by mid-month, explained the request. The Plymouth congregation had become the informal sponsors of an innovative venture that Twain called a "Grand European Pleasure Trip." He wanted to join the party. Newspapers across the country announced that "members of Beecher's congregation were organizing an excursion to the Holy Land, Crimea and Greece." Among the passengers would be Beecher and other dignitaries. The venerable patriarchs, sacred sights, and salvatory biblical associations, elevated by American Protestantism into its daily texts, would be the justification for the excursion. Everything else would be, so to speak, along the way; though inherent in the conception of the venture was the assumption that a sacred pilgrimage to the Holy Land and a European grand tour were compatible, or at least that the pilgrims could find some harmonious balance between piety and pleasure.

Whether or not Twain had read the newspaper squibs or, if he had, paid any attention to them before going to Brooklyn is unclear. But the visit to the Plymouth Congregational Church obviously captured his attention. Moses Beach, the owner-editor of the *New York Sun,* who had given him his pew ticket and was one of the prominent Brooklynites committed, with his daughter, to take the trip, may have dangled it before him. So too perhaps did the *New York Times,* which in late January blew its self-congratulatory patriotic bugle: "We doubt if any other people on the face of the globe would think of chartering a first-class steamer and starting, one hundred and fifty strong, on a voyage of observation and entertainment."

With Ned House, Twain went to the Wall Street office of Captain

Charles Duncan, a Beecher parishioner and the energizing force behind the expedition. A marine businessman, Duncan had taken up what was probably his pastor's idea, conceived as preparation for the life of Christ that Beecher had contracted to write. Duncan expected the profits from the expedition to help him overcome a recent bankruptcy. The organizer and manager of the enterprise, he was keen to have well-known people sign on for the voyage in order to help attract a full complement of passengers, all of whom, he initially assumed, would be members of the Plymouth Congregation, except for a few celebrities. There were three selling themes: piety, education, and exclusivity. The pilgrims would elevate and refine their spiritual essences at the fountainhead of Christianity itself; they would learn from the cultural attractions of the European cities they would visit; only select people would be aboard. The Paris Exhibition, long on Twain's mind, was to be one of the destinations. With lots of good press, capitalizing on the interest in European travel that had been repressed during the war years, this was to be the first instance in which a management firm had hired an entire steamship for a customized European excursion. The Civil War had made many Northerners well-to-do, and some rich. When the end of the war reopened Europe to American curiosity and exploration, the middle class surged eastward. Demand for passenger ship reservations for spring and summer 1867 far exceeded available capacity, and Americans were expected to spend $75 million in Paris alone that summer, so the United States secretary of the treasury estimated.

Duncan had leased the *Quaker City*, an oceangoing 1,428-ton steamship with side paddles and auxiliary sails, named after Philadelphia, where it had been built in 1854. A Union supply ship during the war, it had been converted by new owners eager to sell it as a vessel designed to carry 110 passengers in luxury and high style. It was now being even more handsomely refitted to meet the expectations of those who could afford the $1,250 fare (at a time when first-class round-trip tickets to Paris cost $200) and $750 in gold for onshore expenses for this five-month voyage. *Quaker City* passengers, though, would be getting not only Paris but spiritual enrichment; not only an experienced captain but a nationally famous clergyman; not only passage to Europe but a place among the exclusive and famous. Strangers needed to submit an application to determine whether or not they were worthy to be elected to this community of saints.

When House and Twain walked into Duncan's office, the music critic of the *New York Tribune* introduced his friend as the Reverend Mark Twain, "a clergyman of some distinction, lately arrived from California," or at least so Twain described the exchange in a letter to the *Alta California*. House allegedly told Duncan that Twain was a missionary recently returned from the Sandwich Islands, eager to continue traveling for his health and to assist Beecher in conducting services on the *Quaker City*, even though he was a Baptist and Beecher a Congregationalist. Would that be permitted? Was it certain Mr. Beecher would be going? Yes and yes were the answers. The next day Twain returned, acknowledged his "true occupation," and paid the ten percent deposit, the remainder due on April 15. In Captain Duncan and his daughter's probably more accurate recollection, Duncan responded, "You don't look like a Baptist minister and really, Mr. Clemens, you don't smell like one either."

Apparently the captain and the committee nevertheless decided that it would be advantageous to have aboard a well-known journalist whose letters would be widely reprinted. Probably they did not bother to consult the people whose names Twain gave them as guarantors of his "high moral character," one of whom was Reverend Damon in far-off Hawaii. "For my other references I chose men of bad character, in order that my mild virtues might shine luminously by contrast with their depravity." He did not name names. That he did not share the religious beliefs, let alone possess the pious sincerity, of the other passengers does not seem to have been a hindrance or even a consideration. Superficial reputation was all. Apparently it did not occur to the membership committee that a humorist whose métier was irony might provide exposure of an undesirable sort.

Presumably McComb made the case for Twain to the other three *Alta* owners, though much of the justification was already in place. There was in fact little difference in cost between sponsoring letters from an around-the-world trip and sponsoring Twain's going partway around the world on the *Quaker City*, except, apparently, additional cash up front. Sometime between March 2 and the publication of his letter on April 9, the *Alta* requested that its New York agent provide Twain with the balance. "No veto," the editors printed in parentheses next to Twain's statement of expectation. "He has been telegraphed to 'go ahead.'" By April 15 Twain paid the balance. His temporary and uncertain residence in New York was to end with the scheduled departure of the *Quaker City* on June 8, 1867.

Soon Duncan threw some additional light on why Twain had been so readily accepted by the committee. Rumors that Beecher would not, after all, be taking the excursion proved to be true. Either Duncan had misread a maybe as a yes or Beecher had changed his mind. With Beecher's declination, many of his followers also decided to withdraw. Duncan, now nowhere near the 110 that he had expected, needed more passengers. "Will you allow me, through your columns," he wrote to the *New York Evening Post*, "to state in reply to questions that are coming in from all parts of the country" that the "limited amount of room we have is open to any," provided that the applicants "have good moral character, good health, and a fair share of good humor." Twain now qualified on at least two of three counts. On April 1 Duncan shared with the *Evening Post* the good news that General William Tecumseh Sherman, the hero of the Army of the Tennessee, would be among the passengers. Duncan hoped Sherman's inclusion would help sell the remaining berths.

5.

A squib in the *New York Dispatch* in January 1867 announced that "Mark Twain, of literary and lecture renown on the Pacific, intends trying his fortunes this side of the Rocky Mountains." It was probably alluding to the expectation that he would give his Sandwich Islands lecture in New York and perhaps go on the East Coast lecture circuit. Twain himself had assumed that he would, and the high cost of living in New York catalyzed him into action. He needed to supplement his *Alta California* income. Some New York newspapers and magazines that had published a few of his western sketches seemed possible prospects. Though he had nothing new to show, he saw no reason why he couldn't have his *Alta* letters do double service or why he could not make an arrangement for new material with a newspaper that would give him a free hand to write whatever he pleased. He soon found takers for new sketches, particularly the *Sunday Mercury* and the *Evening Express;* the *New York Weekly Review* took some Sandwich Island letters, though published without acknowledgment that they had already appeared in the *Union*. By June, before the *Quaker City's* departure, he was to make agreements with the *New York Tribune* and the *New York Herald* for occasional letters from abroad. The Sandwich Islands book he now put on the back burner, probably because his attempts to find a publisher had not been successful, but also because Webb had aroused their mutual enthusiasm for a volume of sketches, an idea that Bret Harte had originated the previous year. Twain prepared copy from his clippings files, selecting what he thought his best work, editing the material to make it less offensive to refined readers by omitting the mild profanity and toning down references to subjects like drink and death.

However, they needed a publisher. Webb sent Twain to Carleton, who had brought out Artemus Ward's sketches for which "Jumping Frog," with an altered title, had arrived too late for inclusion. According to Twain's recollection, the publisher's clerk turned from amiable to cold when he realized that the stranger had come not to buy but to sell. Nevertheless, since Webb had secured Twain an appointment, the clerk reluctantly let him into the inner sanctum, where the tone turned from chill to heat. Carleton "began to swell, and went on swelling and swelling and swelling until he had reached the dimension of a god of about the second or third degree." Then his words "fell so densely they darkened the atmosphere. Finally he made an imposing sweep with his right hand which comprehended the whole room and said, 'Books—look at those shelves. Every one of them is loaded with books that are waiting for publication. Do I want any more? Excuse me, I don't. Good morning.' " Humiliated, furious, Twain was soon to call Carleton a "Son of a Bitch" and a swindler. It was "only the frog that was celebrated," Twain realized. "It wasn't I. I was still an obscurity." Webb decided to make matters right. He himself would publish the book, his debut as a publisher.

Despite his desire to lecture in New York, Twain continued not to have success finding a professional manager to make the arrangements. Soon after his arrival, his California friends in New York had organized a sponsoring committee and sent out public relations releases in an effort to drum up support. Twain urged the manager of Artemus Ward's English tour, "Come & engineer me. Ward is so well established in London now that he can easily spare you. . . . If you will come & get the audiences for me, I will engage to send them home d——d well satisfied." By return mail he learned that Ward, desperately ill, had collapsed. His death in England, early in March, was a shock, but Twain, busy and ambitious, a friend but not an intimate of Ward's, took the news well.

Also, in March, Twain traveled to St. Louis to visit his mother and his sister, Pamela, now a widow with two children. His stay of almost a month was not entirely a pleasure trip. He had his *Alta California* letters to write, and he delivered his Sandwich Islands lecture in St. Louis and in Keokuk, where he visited Orion and Mollie, who had just returned from Tennessee, still pursuing John Marshall Clemens' dream. When he left New York for Missouri he still did not have a New York engagement. He self-protectively remarked to his sister-in-law that, though "the Californians in town" had almost persuaded him to lecture, "it is too hazardous a business for a stranger." He wouldn't rush into it until he had gotten his "cards stacked to suit [him]." The returning prodigal gave a charity performance at St. Louis Mercantile Hall, which he repeated a few days later before a large audience. St. Louis audiences were among the best he had ever had, he boasted to his *Alta* readers. They "snap up a joke before you can fairly get it out of your mouth." The *Missouri Democrat* reviewer gave high praise to his performance. "Everybody retired highly delighted with the irrepressible Californian," as if he were now defined by his California years. Though the review must have pleased him, he was unhappy when the *Democrat* printed a transcript of his entire lecture. Future audiences, he feared, would be less eager to pay to hear him.

In St. Louis, he was "busy visiting old friends," he told his *Alta* readers to whom he sent three letters. With his mother and sister, he attended prayer meetings and church "sociables." "I don't think I can stand it much longer. I never could bear to be respectable long at a stretch." One Sunday afternoon a church Sunday school superintendent asked if he "had ever had an experience in instructing the young." "I said, 'My son, it is my strong suit.' . . . He said he would be glad if I would get up in the altar and make a few remarks. . . . So I got up there and told that admiring multitude all about Jim Smiley's Jumping Frog. . . . I suppose those children will cipher a moral out of it somehow, because they are so used to that sort of thing. I gained my main point, anyhow, which was to make myself respected in California, because you know you cannot help but respect a man who makes speeches to Sunday Schools and devotes his time to instructing youth." Another *Alta* letter included a lightly mocking response to a suffragette campaign, a topic on which he created an expanded riff in four letters to the *Missouri Democrat,* the second of which claimed that the first letter had been written by an imposter who had signed his name, a comic ploy that helped him navigate between his desire to amuse satirically and a subtext that took the women's claims seriously. The Mark Twain voice representing common male opinion comically emphasizes the difficulties that might result if women had the vote. The Mark Twain countervoice remarks, "I could write a pretty strong argument in favor of female suffrage, but I do not want to do it." One important argument in favor was his mother. It seemed to Twain that she was as qualified to vote as any man, and a lot more so than most.

To his *Alta* readers he provided effective descriptions of St. Louis life and customs, and particularly remarked "on those old-fashioned twilights," enriching "all the landscape with a dreamy vagueness for two hours after the sun has gone down," which "they forgot to put in . . . when they made the Pacific Coast." From St. Louis, he went upriver to Hannibal, which, he remarked, "had a hard time of it ever since I can recollect. . . . First, it had me for a citizen." He kept the letter chatty and informally distant, as if this horseman had passed by. Probably he saw old friends, as he had in St. Louis. Soon he was on his way to Quincy and then Keokuk, telling his *Alta* readers much about his impressions of the local economies and little about himself. In Keokuk, where he lectured to the Library Association, he was acclaimed by the *Keokuk Gate City* as a native semi-son. The "Mark Twain that is now, was S. L. Clemens, one of the cleverest, and most popular of 'printer boys' in Keokuk. He returns to us now, a famous man, and proverbs or scripture to the contrary, we trust that our citizens will honor him with a rousing house." He continued to keep his distance in print, however, choosing to limit his discussion of Keokuk almost entirely to a humorous episode at his hotel and, in another letter, a friendly account of a Mormon splinter group holding its convention there. Apparently he was not yet ready for autobiography. And the visit to St. Louis in particular had caused him some emotional turmoil.

Before he left to return to New York a little before mid-April, he felt a keen, painful sense that his visits to his Hannibal "home" and his St. Louis "home" had been to homes from which the years had permanently separated him. His mother's house was no longer his. "You shall never know the chill that comes upon me sometimes when I feel that long absence has made me a stranger in my own home," he wrote a few years later in a private letter designed to play a role in his search for a replacement hearth. "I can only look in upon their world without entering; & I turn away with a dull aching consciousness that long exile has lost to me that haven of rest . . . HOME." But when he was to need the Hannibal of his memories and his imagination, it would be there to do good service.

When *The Celebrated Jumping Frog of Calaveras County, And other Sketches* appeared late in April, both author and publisher were delighted by its reception, its "damnable errors of grammar & deadly inconsistencies of spelling" less important to Twain than its handsome appearance. The author was widely praised on both coasts as "a genuine humorist," infinitely superior to Artemus Ward. "Beneath the surface of his pleasantry lies a rich vein of serious thought," the *San Francisco Evening Bulletin* remarked. "There is a great deal of quaint humor and much pithy wisdom in his writings," the *New York Times* declared, "and their own merit, as well as the attractive style in which they are produced, must secure them a popularity which will bring its own profit." Twain's profits were, in fact, to be minuscule, and years later he was to conclude bitterly that Webb's accounting had been fraudulent. "I hate both the name and memory of Charles Henry Webb," he wrote in 1905.

Publication, though, did not insulate him from the combination of ennui and restlessness he had again begun to feel. Comfortably ensconced at the elegant Westminster Hotel, to which he had moved, Twain kept a hectic schedule, but he found New York increasingly distracting, a "splendid desert" with a variety that bewildered as much as entertained, and though he had many acquaintances he had no intimate friends. "This fidgetty, feverish restlessness will drive a man crazy after a while," he told his *Alta* readers, "or kill him. It kills a good many dozens now—by suicide. I have got to get out of it." Gray, wet winter weather continued through the early spring months. He now had in hand the $1,250 *Alta* check to pay for his passage on the *Quaker City*. At Duncan's office, handing over the check, he had the disconcerting experience of hearing the clerk answer a newspaperman's question about "what notabilities were going . . . Lt. Gen. Sherman, Henry Ward Beecher & Mark Twain are going. . . . I thought this was very good," he wrote to his mother—"an exceedingly good joke." Counting the days until departure, he was excruciatingly eager to leave.

Finally, in May, the long-contemplated New York City lecture was in the nerve-wracking process of becoming a reality. While he had been away, the New York–California contingent had been catalyzed into action by

Frank Fuller, who had agreed to become Twain's lecture manager. Originally trained in Boston as a dentist, and a prominent newspaperman in the late 1850s, Fuller was now an energetic and successful New York businessman. Appointed secretary of Utah Territory by the Lincoln administration, he had arrived in Salt Lake City in 1861 and soon become acting governor. From there he moved to Virginia City, where he and Twain met in 1862, and then on to San Francisco, where they had ample opportunity in 1863–64 to get to know each other. Having arrived in New York in 1865, Fuller was solidly in place when Twain searched him out in January 1867. He probably was among the group of distinguished Californians that met, as the *San Francisco Evening Bulletin* reported, with Twain at the Metropolitan Hotel in January, urging him to rise to the platform. Soon after his return from the West, Twain came to Fuller's office on Broadway and drawled out, so Fuller later reported, "Frank, I want to preach right here in New York, and it must be in the biggest hall to be found. I find it is the Cooper Institute, and that it costs $70 for one evening, and I have got just $7." More likely, Twain, nervous and tentative, enlisted the willing Fuller as his manager in less peremptory terms. Fuller soon put his excellent managerial skills to work.

Two weeks later, on May 6, Mark Twain, in a tuxedo newly purchased for the occasion, his first ever, walked out on the stage of the Cooper Institute auditorium before an audience of three thousand people, the same stage on which, seven years before, Abraham Lincoln had given the speech that was instrumental in his gaining the Republican presidential nomination. The week before, Twain had discovered that he would be going up against formidable theatrical and political entertainment that night. "With all this against me I have taken the largest house in New York & cannot back water," he wrote to his mother. This time the advertisements promised, "Doors open at 7 o'clock. The wisdom will begin to flow at 8." Nevada's former governor Senator James Nye agreed to introduce him to the audience. Fuller actually had gone down to Washington to get his consent. A potpourri of the great names of the land—Emerson, Whittier, Grant, Peter Cooper, Horace Greeley, Anna Dickinson, Josh Billings, Petroleum V. Nasby, Whitelaw Reid, William Dean Howells, and John Hay, among others—were invited. Regrets came "from everybody except Boss Tweed," Twain later joked, "and a few Sing-Sing people." Terrified that there would be acres of empty seats, he persuaded Fuller to paper the house. Free tickets went to thousands of New York City schoolteachers. On the evening of the performance, many who came to the box office to buy tickets were disappointed. The house had been "sold" out.

When by seven-thirty P.M. Senator Nye had not shown up, Twain was in a cursing frenzy, but he did not disappoint the audience. Resorting to a standard ploy, he wandered out on the stage at eight P.M., his face to the floor, as if looking for a lost penny. Looking up, he remarked bemusedly, "I was looking for General Nye who had promised to introduce me, but I see nothing of him and as there are no other generals in town just now we will have to worry along without him." "And so he went on," Fuller recalled, "and the shouts of laughter and the bursts of applause were far beyond anything I have ever witnessed." Every word of the lecture had been memorized (and rehearsed in Fuller's office during the previous ten days), with appropriate laugh-line pauses and seeming attempts to think of what to say next. And he had already given it about twenty times. It followed the outline the advertisements set out.

1. Horace Greeley and Hank Monk—a topic which is new to California—maybe (sarcasm). 2. Where Kanakadom is situated. 3. What it was situated there for. 4. Its dimensions. 5. What it is made of—and why. 6. Its population, and who killed it. 7. How the natives dress, and, more particularly, how they don't dress. 8. The King. 9. The other natives. 10. The Tabu. 11. The Missionaries. 12. Native hospitality. 13. Native rascality. 14. Their multiplicity of mothers. 15. Their talent for dying when they have got ready to die. 16. A singular custom. 17. How they dispose of their dogs. 18. Another singular custom. 19. A wicked slander refuted. 20. Why the natives don't walk much, as a general thing. 21. What becomes of the surplus children. 22. The cheerful spirit of Kanakadom, under any and all circumstances. 23. How they do everything wrong-end foremost; however, no attempt will be made to explain this peculiarity. 24. A powerful description of a volcanic eruption. The lecturer knows it is powerful because it has got so many long words in it. 25. The Boo-hoo fever. 26. A word about the religious aspect of Kanakadom. 27. The white people, and their peculiarities. 28. Terrific drinkers. 29. An unpalatable subject.

The next day the New York newspapers were laudatory. Though he had cleared only about thirty-five dollars, he would never again have to paper a house.

6.

With the publication of his first book and the success in May of the Hawaii lecture at Cooper Union, the Mark Twain who was about to depart on one of the supreme voyages of his life was not the relatively unknown journalist and lecturer of just a short time before. He had risen to the stature of a minor national figure. He had become a presence on the East Coast, and most of those who had declined invitations to the Cooper Union lecture now at least recognized his name. Soon he was to know many of them, a few very well, and he was to make a number of new friends, some of them lifelong, on the *Quaker City* voyage. In honor of General Sherman's presence, "the government has issued a circular letter instructing ministers and consuls of the United States, in the various countries to be visited to show every attention to General Sherman and the party on board the *Quaker City*," the *New York Evening Post* reported. And "the commandant of the New York Navy Yard has received orders to place the necessary arms and flags on the ship, that she may properly acknowledge salutes in foreign ports."

Busy tying up loose ends, Twain kept to the journalistic grindstone, doing eleven letters for the *Alta California* between April 30 and June 6. Three weeks before sailing he was still "one magazine article & eighteen letters behindhand." For some time he had been bored with the task. On May 10 he gave the Sandwich Islands lecture at the Athenaeum in Brooklyn to a prominent audience, some of whom would be his traveling companions. Unfortunately, he had to give up an invitation for a second Brooklyn lecture under the press of his *Alta* responsibilities.

On May 27 the *Brooklyn Eagle* asked, "Is General Sherman Going to Palestine?" It was being rumored that he had withdrawn. Captain Duncan, who probably knew for a certainty that the famous general and his daughter would not be among the passengers, did his best to hold back the news. But attempts to lure replacement celebrities with the offer of free passage were unsuccessful. In the end, absurdly and ironically, the best-known passenger turned out to be Mark Twain. Apparently, despite the show of rigorous vetting, no paying applicant was refused. Of the 110 berths, only

77 had been filled. It had been expected initially that most passengers would come from Beecher's urbane congregation. When forty or so followed their leader into withdrawal, their places were filled in part by a contingent of a more fundamentalist disposition from upstate New York, Pennsylvania, Ohio, and Missouri. Some prospective customers may have been put off by the most rigid of these pilgrims, one of whom, at a meeting at Beecher's house, urged the captain to bring the excursion to a halt on Sundays. Twain described him to his *Alta* readers as "a solemn, unsmiling, sanctimonious old iceberg that looked like he was waiting for a vacancy in the Trinity." The captain replied that, regretfully, he could not be expected "to anchor the ship in the middle of the Atlantic." In all other ways, though, the Sabbath would be observed, which was humorous news to Twain's ears. With other passengers, he responded to a list of books suggested as useful to bring, including William Cowper Prime's *Tent Life in the Holy Land*, John Bunyan's *The Pilgrim's Progress and Other Travels from This World to That Which Is to Come*, Hannah Moore's *The Shepherd of Salisbury Plain*, and *The Whole Duty of Man, Laid Down in a Plain Familiar Way for the Use of All*, a heavy dose of sanctimonious reading certain to put Twain to sleep, though of the recommended books, William McClure Thomson's *The Land and the Book* became his prime source for information about the Holy Land. He recognized that he was to be under the eye of pietistic supervision but was resigned to that annoyance.

"I am wild with impatience to move," he wrote to his mother—"move—*Move!* . . . Curse the endless delays. . . . I do more mean things, the moment I get a chance to fold my hands & sit down than ever I can get forgiveness for." Whatever the longstanding sources of his self-criticism, there was no obvious, let alone recent, list of specific transgressions to explain his self-flagellation. Apparently, though, he felt guilt at having neglected his mother and having behaved unworthily toward her and Orion. "An accusing conscience gives me peace only in excitement & restless moving from place to place," he wrote to Jane Clemens on June 7. He could not "say that he had done one good thing" for his family that entitled him to their "good opinions," though he felt certain of their love. If he had, he felt he could "go home & stay there": "I *know* I would care little for the world's praise or blame." He was, in fact, not yet ready to settle anyplace, especially in a "home" circumscribed by his mother, from whose company he had long before separated himself.

On June 8, after delays that caused him to worry that the ship might not sail at all now that General Sherman had withdrawn, the *Quaker City* steamed out of its New York City pier accompanied by two local excursion boats hired to make celebratory noise. An immense storm was creating rough seas. Prudently, Captain Duncan anchored in Gravesend Bay. With Brooklyn barely in sight through the storm, they waited for the weather to clear. On Sunday one of the three ministers aboard "preached from II Cor. 7 & 8th about something," Twain wrote in his notebook. From the boat he sent a last-minute note to Fuller, deputizing him to handle his business affairs, particularly to collect his royalty remittances from Webb and send "all such moneys to my mother," though he self-protectively soon told Jane Clemens that he didn't believe it would "ever pay anything worth a cent." In fact, he hoped, even expected, that it would sell fifty thousand copies and bring him a huge royalty. On June 10, 1867, the *Quaker City* was finally under way. "I say good bye & God bless you all," Twain wrote home, "& welcome the wind that wafts a weary soul to the sunny lands of the Mediterranean!"

CHAPTER SEVEN

AND NARROW WAY

1867

1.

The coal-burning *Quaker City,* driven by side paddle wheels, a hybrid powered by both steam and sail with a cruising speed of ten knots, had two saloons, a large dining room, comfortable lower and upper deck cabins, and a promenade deck extending the length of the ship. It had the additional ballast of some very grave people aboard. They had dark, sepulchral Sunday-school souls and dressed in black for whatever party they attended. "I am going on this trip for fun only," Twain wrote to Bill Bowen a few days before departure. And it had been fun, two days before sailing, to attend a reception at which Twain was introduced to numbers of his fellow voyagers, mostly serious pilgrims traveling for cultural and spiritual enlightenment, including a strong coterie of single-minded Christians aggressively yearning for tombs in Palestine. Many were considerably older than Twain, stolid citizens and church elders, representative of the Christian straight and narrow. Tobacco and alcohol were frowned on. Sunday pieties were to be observed. When worshipers gathered around the *Quaker City's* organ, they did not need to look down at their copies of *The Pilgrim Collection of Hymns*—with one exception. Twain always had to look at the words.

Inevitably, his reaction to the Calvinism of his colleagues would be in constant counterpoise to his happily fallen state; he had considerably greater tolerance for sinners than for the sanctimonious. He did not in the least believe that God had elected some to be saved, others to be damned. In fact, he hardly believed in God at all, except as a convenient rhetorical locution, especially as in "God damn it!" People who smoked, drank, and cursed were those whose company he generally preferred. Of course no one aboard the *Quaker City* or, with a rare exception, in Twain's mainland world was not a Christian. Gradations in Christian belief and practice were many, Twain well knew. But he had not been so fully exposed for so long a period to Calvinistic fundamentalism since his Hannibal childhood.

A week before sailing he happily discovered that his cabin-mate-to-be, a New Yorker named Dan Slote in his late thirties, co-owner of a stationery manufacturing business, belonged to his portion of the happy minority. "I am *fixed,*" he wrote to his family. "I have got a splendid, immoral, tobacco-smoking, wine-drinking, godless room-mate who is as good & true & right-minded a man as ever lived." Round-faced, balding, and with a mustache and a dry sense of humor, Slote brought aboard so many cigars and other good things, Twain told his *Alta* readers, that he himself would not have to bring any baggage. Just before sailing, Twain was delighted to learn that he had been bumped up to a handsome upper-deck portside cabin that had originally been assigned to General Sherman. Sinners of like habit were to make Twain's cabin number 10 their smoke-filled retreat. One of them, Daniel Leary, co-owner of the *Quaker City,* felt dread-stricken when the organ and hymn-singing had started up. "I hope they will not overdo this kind of thing," he wrote home, "because if they do I shall feel as if an accident should happen to that organ." Julius Moulton, whose father owned the North Missouri Railroad, joined the festivities in number 10. So too did Abraham Reeves Jackson, a Chicago gynecologist with a deadpan sense of humor, and John Van Nostrand, a good-hearted New Yorker barely out of his teens whose witless good humor endeared him to Twain. Charles Langdon, the seventeen-year-old son of a coal and lumber merchant in Elmira, New York, whose parents hoped he would become more soberly mature in the company of such pious pilgrims, gravitated to Twain and Slote. They were not the role models the Langdons had hoped for.

Solon Long Severance, a banker, and his attractive wife, Emily, became conversational companions, though not habitues of number 10. A fervent evangelical Christian, like the others from Cleveland, Severance, with his wife, was a member of that city's First Presbyterian Church. When the ship was still at anchor in New York Harbor, Mary Mason Fairbanks, married to the co-owner of the *Cleveland Herald,* composed the first of her travel letters. She noted that from one table in particular came regular peals of laughter, "and all eyes are turned toward 'Mark Twain,' whose face is perfectly mirth-provoking. Sitting lazily at the table, scarcely genteel in his appearance, there is nevertheless a something . . . that interests and attracts. I saw today at dinner, venerable divines and sage looking men, convulsed with laughter at his drolleries and quaint original manners." She was soon to change her view that he would "never win the laurels destined to deck the brow of our poor friend" Artemus Ward. Educated and literary, Fairbanks was one of the catalysts of cultural life in Cleveland, where Ward had lived. At forty years of age, with two children and a husband at home, a lively, intelligent matriarch, she was to take her place as the central figure in this heterodox *Quaker City* group, and she and Twain would become lifelong friends.

As the *Quaker City* steamed eastward, daily routine established itself. Sunday morning service was conducted in the dining room. With Duncan's bullying encouragement, a "prayer meeting" between eight and nine P.M. every night seemed inescapable, the bellowing organ and the choral voices accompanying the order of the Plymouth Church service as regularly as daily meals. Male passengers took turns leading the congregation. Twain did his duty, amused at the spectacle of himself as the chief hypocrite in what he called the "synagogue." Though he resented it, he did not make the pressure to attend prayer meetings an issue, partly because in his role as journalist–cum–cultural anthropologist he needed to observe, not create, events.

On the longest leg of the voyage, from New York to the Azores, the passengers looked for entertainment to help them through the tedium. There were birthday parties, a magic lantern show, and lectures about their itinerary. The ship's library turned out to have only a few books, all on religious and travel subjects. Twain played his part, amusing people with comments and stories. He was the "ruling spirit," Emily Severance noted, in a mock trial in which a purser was charged with stealing Twain's overcoat. After the purser was declared guilty, the sentence was "inflicted on junior counsel" for the state, one Samuel Clemens, "in absence of the criminal— solitary confinement on straight whiskey in room 10 for one hour and may

God have mercy on your soul." The "whiskey" punishment was both a joke and a serious comment. Gossip among the straightlaced declared that Twain drank considerably.

To most of the passengers, apart from the issue of his comparative impiety, the amusing Mark Twain was a vulgar plebian without education, manners, or taste. He himself had only a minor argument with that view. Though he had little to say to Moses Beach, Twain spent hours poised over a chessboard with his seventeen-year-old daughter, Emmeline, an adequate player whom he found enticingly attractive. At half his age, she may have reminded him of Laura Wright. Always attracted to small-figured adolescent cynosures of Victorian purity, Twain, under other circumstances, might have tried to court her. Instead, they only played chess. Later, during the final leg of the excursion, his friendship with Mary Mason Fairbanks, a completely ineligible woman, was to flourish. Mrs. Fairbanks, unlike the others, liked Twain, and she succumbed to the fantasy that she could help raise him to acceptable social standards. Twain, her superior in every other way, liked the idea that she would teach him manners, partly because he liked Mary Fairbanks, mostly because he realized that he might benefit from some upper-middle-class polish. He was soon, to their mutual amusement and pleasure, calling this forty-year-old matriarch "mother."

In rough weather, tired of being at sea, the *Quaker City* passengers sighted the Azores on June 19, 1867. Twain got up at four A.M. to see the first land since leaving New York. With heavy gales tossing the ship, the impatient passengers amused themselves with a meeting of their newly formed debating society. Twain jotted in his notebook possible debate topics, such as "Is Captain Duncan responsible for the head winds?" "Is a tail absolutely necessary to the comfort and convenience of a dog?" and "Which is most desirable—the single or the married state?" With the *Quaker City* anchored off Fayal, its passengers enjoyed the lush volcanic island. Its Catholic cathedral was the first of many with which the anti-Catholic pilgrims would need to come to terms. Twain, too, associated Catholicism with papal autocracy, priests with poverty. As he was to do throughout the voyage, he made extensive notes, brief descriptions of impressions, perceptions, and conversations, compact source material to be expanded into letters for the *Alta California*. The attractive symmetry of architecture and landscape impressed him. So too did the jackasses that the travelers rode on a ten-mile excursion through the hills. When, instigated by one of his companions, a toothless old beggar woman persistently followed Twain, he responded, "Madame, these attentions are very flattering to me . . . but it is impossible for me to return your affections, for I am engaged—but for that it might be otherwise."

Two days later the *Quaker City,* heading toward Gibraltar, steamed into calm weather. South of Cape Vincent, with Morocco and the Pillars of Hercules visible, the water turned "a deep, splendid, lustrous purple-blue." One calm night they danced in the moonlight on the upper deck; the swaying boat and the water-slippery deck sent the dancers sprawling. Twain now finished the first of many letters to the *Alta* that attempted to meet the difficult challenge of having at the same time to travel, sightsee, take notes, and write extensively. His notebook, filled with on-the-spot observations, helped, though sometimes a particular note meant to remind him of something to write about lost its meaning by the time he was ready to make use of it. The loss was compounded since the letters were to be the basis for a book that he had from the start assumed he would write. He soon realized that writing frequent, effective travel letters under these conditions took all his commitment and resources. The fun-filled escape from daily tedium that he had blithely anticipated was turning into a great deal of hard work.

Sailing through the Strait of Gibraltar in a splendid breeze, everyone gazed on the impressive Rock. When "a lordly ship with every rag of canvas set and swooping down upon us like a bird . . . flung the stars and stripes to the breeze . . . a thrill went through the whole ship." Gibraltar itself seemed tame and uninteresting, notwithstanding its monkeys. The excursionists soon had a choice to make: to stay in Gibraltar while the boat refueled, then to sail on to Marseilles and from there take the train to Paris, or to travel northward by railroad to Madrid and then Paris. At that point there would be another decision to make: to return to the *Quaker City* and sail to Genoa, or to go by land from Paris.

Moses Beach persuaded Twain to join the Spanish excursionists, but, as he was getting into a small boat about to take him to the Cadiz steamer, the steamer inexplicably weighed anchor and sailed off. Instead, Twain organized a thirty-six-hour trip to Morocco, accompanied by Dan Slote, Jack Van Nostrand, and Dr. Jackson. "I would not [exchange] this experience," he wrote his Missouri family from Tangier, "for all the balance of the trip combined. This is the infernalest hive of infernally costumed barbarians I

have ever yet come across." Wandering through the marketplace surrounded by importunate salespeople and beggars, hearing calls to prayer
and the braying of donkeys, trying to make sense out of the exchanges of
sound and goods, seeing people dressed in a way he had never seen before,
observing the poverty and filth, the strangeness of the food, the absence of
alcohol except among visitors like himself—this was his first exposure to a
non-Christian world. In Hawaii, American Protestant power had dominated. In Tangier, Americans were just another variety of infidel. If to Twain
the Arabs were "costumed barbarians," to the Arabs the visiting Americans
were "Christian dogs," as he wrote in his notebook. His purchase of an
ankle-length Moorish costume, while partly a venture in costume drama,
was also an acknowledgment that he was not blind to the power of cultural
differentness. A Moorish wedding caught his attention, as did a Jewish one:
Jews were everywhere in Tangier. To his astonishment, though, they were
not like the Westernized German Jews of New York or San Francisco. These
were Sephardim, Oriental Jews, their dress, habits, and customs noticeably
alien; they were his first hint of what he and his fellow pilgrims would find,
to their shock, in Palestine. They dressed like Arabs, they did not know that
cleanliness was next to godliness, and their manners were those of the Near
Eastern bazaar, not the New York stock exchange. "Tangier Jew won't touch
fire on Saturday—steal though," he wrote in his notebook. "Curious the
lord made *these* his chosen people," he noted. Eventually this was a puzzle
of dramatic proportion more for the Christian puritans among the *Quaker
City*'s passengers than for Twain. He made frantic notes for letters to be
written about Islamic rituals, government practices, Moroccan history, and
the rich but strange details of everyday life.

"After all this racing and bustling and rollicking excitement in Africa,"
he wrote, "it seems good to get back to the old ship once more. It is so like
home." They celebrated the Fourth of July at sea, with cannon blasts and
speeches, prayers and amusements, a gala lunch, and verses created for
the day by an eccentric and absurd Long Islander who had established
himself as the ship's poet, churning out ludicrous rhymes for every occasion. Twain nicknamed him the "poet lariat." Another passenger, given to
frequent predictions, he called "The Oracle." Some of the passengers
brought to mind "Mr. Brown," to whose imaginary presence Twain added
"Mr. Blucher," who now played the same role that "Brown" had played in
the Hawaii letters. Confining himself to his cabin, Twain wrote accounts

of their visits to Gibraltar and Tangier, transforming raw material into smooth presentations, editing out any directness or harshness that would perhaps be too strong for the tastes of his readers. A mixture of statistics and facts, of personal observation and perception, of humorous opportunities almost always taken, sometimes with irony, often with a heightening of the ridiculous, held together by a narrative of travel and the tone of the engaged and funny skeptic, the letters had much in common with those he had written from Hawaii. Hawaii, though, had been inconsequential fun. In contrast, this voyage was, for Twain, a pilgrimage that touched on core issues of identity and belief.

From Marseilles, following two days of frantic sightseeing, he took the train northward. His six days in Paris were a whirl in which the Exhibition that he had for so long been eager to see was a disappointment. Paris itself was not. After an uncomfortable railroad trip, he delighted in the luxury of the Grand Hotel du Louvre. He was indeed tired, not just from the constant need to take notes in order to recall at least something of what he had seen and his obligation to write frequent letters to the *Alta,* but from the drain of an ambitious schedule that left the *Quaker City* travelers too little time to visit major cities, so hectic that sometimes they couldn't be sure exactly where they were. Like other American travelers, he could not avoid being a consumer of the grand European emporium: the museums, the architecture, the sights, the shops, a long-awaited, perhaps once-in-a-lifetime opportunity requiring one to move through it all as quickly as possible in the time available. And, as if these demands were not by themselves enough, he needed to devote mental energy to positioning himself culturally in reaction to this confrontation with the European experience.

Like many nineteenth-century Americans, he brought with him to Europe a fragile barometer of cultural and personal worth. Were Europeans superior to Americans? Was European culture superior to American culture? Were Europe's highly revered works of art as good as they were touted to be? Should Americans feel humble, exalted, skeptical, selective, intimidated, or hostile (or any combination of these) in the presence of European high culture? And was it permissible to feel bored? Or indifferent? Some Americans went boastfully on the offensive. Nothing in Europe was as good as at "home." Others plunged into defensive capitulation. Nothing American could measure up to anything European. In his letters to the *Alta,* Twain needed to stake out his position, which he did, but in a direction that strengthened what he already was and was still becoming. Europe did not change him; it confirmed him in his particular way of being an American. Old master artworks were the most obvious and available test. Mostly he did not like them. Partly, he granted, his lack of education was the cause. But he also did not like them for aesthetic and cultural reasons. If they were not realistic, they could not evoke the real emotions of ordinary people. If they were religious, they represented Catholic absurdities. If they were true to European history, they memorialized political and social barbarism, a world before democracy gave dignity to human life. He could, and did, in his *Alta* letters, make fun of European art and history, and also make fun of himself, in his role as self-conscious American primitive, for making fun of them.

In Paris for four days instead of the ten he had originally planned, he crowded in visits to all the usual sights: Notre Dame, the Pantheon, the Louvre, the Tuilleries, the Madeleine, parks, boulevards, boutiques. Whether or not he had time to take detailed notes, he soon lost his notebook. When he discovered that a well-to-do San Francisco friend, twenty-five-year-old Lily Hitchcock, a lively, outgoing socialite who had written for the *Alta California,* was now a Parisian and actually resided at his own hotel, he made sure that he had her welcome company on his Paris excursions, especially to two of the famous pleasure gardens and dance halls, the Jardin Mabille and the Jardin Asniere. On the Asniere's brightly lit stage, long cancan legs kicked high, and, whatever slight embarrassment he may have felt at the sight of erotic embraces in Asniere's dimly lit public pathways, he had no reservations about his own attraction to lovely ladies and erotic possibilities, though he apparently never developed other than a friendly relationship with Hitchcock. Like most Americans in Paris, he watched enthusiastically a two-hour-long military parade of twenty thousand soldiers on the Champs Élysées, resplendent in their glittering uniforms of empire, led by Napoleon III, whose capable reformation of France into a disciplined, well-run nation Twain admired. Like many Victorians, his liberal values stopped short of the rule of the lowest common denominator, and characters like Colonel Sherburn in *Huckleberry Finn* and Hank Morgan in *A Connecticut Yankee* were to exemplify the paradox. "There is no element of true greatness which [Louis] Napoleon does not possess," he was to write to his *Alta* readers, a misjudgment far greater than even his prejudice for strong leaders would seem to warrant.

From Paris he took the overnight train to Marseilles, where he caught up on his letters to the *Alta*, took an excursion in the harbor, and impatiently tramped through the city streets. Finally, on July 13, the *Quaker City* left for Genoa. He awakened the next morning with a sudden and thorough sense of delight. Bright, sharp sunlight outlined the bay and the rising hills above the ascending city. That night, as he "sat in a great gas-lit public grove or garden" in which men and women "were crowded together drinking wine & eating ices," he thought that "it would be good to die" and go to Genoa. The rest of Italy seemed less heavenly, partly because of a schedule in which he traveled more than six hundred miles and visited four historic cities in three weeks, but also because, like all travelers, he was forced to undergo constant "purification, suffocation and fumigation through the medium of a combination of miraculous stinks and stenches such as only Italian ingenuity could contrive." A cholera epidemic was spreading rapidly. The *Quaker City* travelers got their first taste of Europe's two favorite (and futile) measures to stop its spread: drenching travelers and their clothes for thirty minutes in sealed rooms with noxious fumes of burning lime and sulphur, and quarantining any vessel arriving from a port where cholera had been so much as rumored. An ongoing but momentarily quiescent civil war between republicans and monarchists, with the disposition of the Papal States a key issue, also produced some inconveniences.

At Milan, visiting the Duomo as soon as he could get out of his hotel, he found the view at night from the highest ramparts breathtaking, though the city's churches and Da Vinci's *Last Supper* evoked his skeptical antagonism. They represented to him the absurdity of the Catholic Church's veneration of relics and his sense of the herd mentality's glorification of artworks because of their fame. With the help of "Mr. Brown," he took his stand on the side of Protestant superiority to Catholicism and on the side of "the great uncultivated. . . . Now forever more I am down on the old masters," he told his *Alta* readers, though, later in life, when Europe had become his second home, he was to have another, more thoughtful try at attempting to see what all the fuss was about. But in 1867, like many thinly educated, positivistic Americans, he could find in the fine arts only what he brought, and his strong bias in favor of realistic representation anchored in everyday life made Renaissance religious imagery unpalatable. "I was not able to find in the old masters the joys which other people found there," he told an audience more than thirty years later. "I could not find beauty of anything to enthuse me in a Saint Sebastian stuck fill of arrows. Moreover, I objected to every Saint Sebastian that I ever saw, because they all seemed to be enjoying it. And I said, 'That old master that considers that saint or sinner can be a pincushion of arrows, and smile, does not know human nature.'"

Fortunately, Milan had much else to offer, particularly European social relaxation of the sort that he had already recognized as alien to the structure and psychology of American life. But, with a commitment to write frequent letters to the *Alta* and occasional letters to two other newspapers, he had little time to lounge in coffeehouses and piazzas anyway, and he had already been on the go for so many years that European leisure could hardly slow him down. From Milan they went to Como, where they took the ferry. The still fullness of the lake, the colorful gardens and hillsides, the waterfront villas and steep cultivated ascents, delighted him. From the Hotel Bellagio, with its peaceful lakeside view, he ascended to the Villa Serbelloni for panoramic views in three directions, where Lake Como and Lake Lecco meet. After a quick trip further up the lake to put his feet briefly, for the first time, on Swiss soil, he took the train to Bergamo, the high Alps visible in the distance, and then to Venice. Arriving at dusk, he had his first sight of the city from a gondola on the Grand Canal. Behind with his letters, he had little time to sightsee. Apparently Venice, except for the gondolas, did not stimulate his fancy or his intellect. To the antisentimental Twain, its fairyland appearance may not have seemed gritty and real enough, too much a Renaissance theme park with aesthetically and morally distasteful motifs. After three days in the city of illusions, they were off to Florence. He flogged himself through the usual attractions, as many as he could see in less than two days. Utterly exhausted now, he took the train to Livorno, via Pisa and its leaning tower, to take refuge on the *Quaker City*. It waited in the harbor for its tired, straggling travelers.

Rome and Naples still remained on the itinerary. Rumor, though, threatened quarantine at Rome's port, Civita Vecchia. Aboard ship at Leghorn, Twain was annoyed to learn that Captain Duncan and those who had remained aboard at Genoa had had an audience with Garibaldi, whose republican principles Americans admired, so much so that the pilgrims even overcame their reluctance to travel on a Sunday. Regretting having missed that opportunity, Twain had no intention of being prevented from seeing Rome. Since he had had enough of train travel, he and Dan Slote took passage on an uncomfortable French steamer to Civita Vecchia, where they were put through a particularly detestable customs procedure, their luggage ransacked, themselves detained for hours. The Papal State authorities assumed all Americans were republican sympathizers and Garibaldi supporters. Apparently, though, politics was more important than health and they were spared another fumigation, though Twain and the *Quaker City* pilgrims, who arrived the next day in Rome by train, had their antipapal feelings reinforced simply by entering the territory of the Antichrist.

If Rome was blessed, to these bristling Protestants it was at best a mixed blessing. St. Peter's splendors highlighted the worldliness of Catholicism, its misuse of wealth for institutional glorification rather than for good works, and its manipulation of superstition to augment its power. Classical Rome, though, had its presence and attractions, and Twain toured the Pantheon, the Coliseum, the Forum, the Catacombs, and all the usual imperial monuments. But Rome's poverty, disarray, and degradation of the common people dominated his impressions. Catholic Rome and its history he could mock, as he did in his letter about Rome to the *Alta*. But the city's filthy water, its disease-ridden streets, its pervasive air of poverty and backwardness, had a weight beyond humor. Having soon seen enough, he was happy to leave by train for Naples.

As the Bay of Naples came into sight, he saw the yellow quarantine flag flying from the *Quaker City*'s mast. The ship had been held in port for four days, with three more to go. Irritably, Twain settled into a hotel with a magnificent view of the bay, but he was relieved, at least, not to be on board. After some urban sightseeing, he took a ferry to Ischia, partly to find quiet privacy for a few days of writing, mostly to escape the city's depressing dirt and poverty. With an all-night letter-writing stint, he managed to catch up. Returning from Ischia, he was delighted to see that the quarantine had been lifted. Some of his fellow pilgrims were organizing a trip to Vesuvius, but, rather than travel with these less than favorable companions, he decamped immediately with Slote, Jackson, and four or five others. The men took a train to the base of the mountain and, in the early-morning darkness, ascended on mules. On the way back, they stopped at Pompeii, where the remnants of artifacts of everyday life spoke to Twain more cogently than any of the thousands of paintings he had gazed at. Later, on that same long summer day, he went, seemingly tireless, with a large *Quaker City* group on a steamboat Solon Serverence had hired, to Capri. The "blue theatrical fires" of its famous grotto glittered in his memory thereafter. Returning that night to Naples, he had good reason to sleep soundly. Italy had done its best for him, and he and the other pilgrims were ready to move on. The morning after, at eight A.M., the *Quaker City* steamed southward into the Mediterranean.

2.

Sailing into a stiff breeze, "the western horizon all golden from the sunken sun," the *Quaker City* steamed through the Gulf of Messina into the Ionian Sea, where the pilgrims felt the highest quickening of expectation. Classical culture was a sanctified secondary preoccupation, especially for those passengers with more formal education than Twain. Even he, who hardly knew a word of Greek or Latin, had absorbed in his Hannibal childhood and his reading thereafter a wide variety of classical authors in translation. On August 14, 1867, the port of Athens came into view. Entering through a narrow canal, the pilgrims suddenly found themselves trapped by the immediate imposition of quarantine—eleven days. Remembering the disastrous results of not having quarantined a British ship ten years before, the authorities were taking no chances. Incredulous and furious, the *Quaker City* travelers, for whom cleanliness equated with godliness, could not believe they were being treated as contagious. Bitterly disappointed, they gazed at the shoreline. They could see the hazy outline of Athens in the distance. Some even thought they could make out the Parthenon and the Areopagus, a site combining the epitome of classical architecture and the first place of Christian significance they had expected to visit. It was almost as if they could hear the voice of Paul calling to them.

The American vice consul came alongside to commiserate, but pleas to the authorities were unavailing. Surprisingly, though, no one interfered when Moses Beach, with a few others, took a small boat to a nearby beach to swim in the quiet surf. Beach and one companion, hiding behind some rocks, stayed ashore. Undetected, they casually walked into Piraeus and hired a cab to take them to the Acropolis. No one stopped them. They returned to the *Quaker City* the envy of their fellow passengers. Later, when the military commandant, who had been unavailingly representing their pleas to the port authorities, remarked that he himself would not be able to detect any small boats that might come into the port at night, Twain decided to take the hint.

An hour before midnight, with Jackson and two others, he rowed to shore at a point just beyond the quarantine boundary. Since they could not find a road, they climbed over rocky hills, through fields and vineyards, eager to get there and back before dawn. After two hours of tramping they stood "under the towering massive walls of the ancient citadel of Athens, walls," Twain wrote, "that had loomed above the heads of better men than we, a thousand years before the Son of God was born." Some small coins bribed the guard they awakened to let them in. As Twain ascended the Areopagus, Demosthenes and Themistocles were as much a presence for him as St. Paul. The stunning beauty of the temples of Minerva and Hercules and the exhilarating symmetry of the Parthenon, silver-bright in the moonlight, with no other human beings there but themselves, gave him the chills. There was nothing tawdry, nothing degraded, about this miraculous gift from the past, no encrustations of human superstition or sentimentality. He put into his pocket a shard from the fragments of ancient statuary that were everywhere, a practice shared by his fellow travelers, whom he later humorously criticized for their vandalism. From the bastions, with the ruins towering over his head, he looked down at the city "by moonlight! When I forget it I shall be dead—not before."

Returning to the ship at four-thirty A.M., they fell asleep. When Twain awakened, the *Quaker City* was heading toward Troy and Asia Minor. Constantinople, their next destination, proved an unhappy visit. What they had anticipated as a Turkish delight tasted bitter in reality: their first encounter with filth, poverty, and disease on a scale so huge that even Naples paled in comparison. It was their first exposure to the gap between the ideas they had gotten from studying the Bible and reading fairy tales like *The Arabian Nights* and the modern reality of the Middle East. Twain thought Islam deplorable, a religion that had produced an inefficient, autocratic, and barbaric culture in which the common people were treated miserably. At best, Constantinople was "an eternal circus" filled with heathen clowns, as Twain told his *Alta* readers, though he generally toned down the strength of his critical responses for them, usually with humor.

On August 19 they left the city, and two days later they arrived at Sebastopol. Having allotted two days to the city, where the Russian authorities were unexpectedly cooperative, even friendly, they found one day more

202 ⮜   *The Singular Mark Twain*

than enough. After a visit to the melancholy battlefield ruins, they sailed to Odessa, a substantial seaport and center of Russian commerce on the Black Sea. At nearby Yalta, the Russian royal family summered. Greeted by the American consul, some of the passengers thought that the czar, Emperor Alexander II, ought, in the interest of Russian-American relations, to hold an audience for the distinguished American visitors. The consul thought it an unlikely request. The emperor had, in fact, recently turned down a similar request from British travelers. Since Odessa, distinguished primarily as one of the largest grain-shipping centers in the world, had little to interest Twain, he remained aboard writing; then, later in the day, went ashore alone. In a Greek church, he gave an aged beggar a coin. By mistake, he gave her "a French gold piece worth about four dollars" instead of "a Turkish coin worth two cents and a half." Later, realizing his mistake, he hurried back to the church. "I got my Turkish penny ready, and was extending a trembling hand to make the nefarious exchange, when I heard a cough behind me. I jumped back as if I had been accused and stood quaking while a worshiper entered and passed up the aisle. . . . At last my opportunity came. . . . I whipped the gold piece out of the poor old pauper's palm and dropped my Turkish penny in its place. Poor old thing, she murmured her thanks—they smote me to the heart. Then I sped away in a guilty hurry."

That there had been no response from the emperor made it likely that they would sail without experiencing the magic presence of royalty. Though the desire had started as an afterthought, it had grown into an obsession, the paradox of American republicans, especially of the middle class, becoming as entranced and self-inflated by the royal touch as the most abject royalists. When the now unexpected news came that the emperor would indeed receive them, Twain, appointed chairman of a committee of response, wrote the formal acceptance: "We are a handful of private citizens of America, traveling simply for recreation—and unostentatiously, as becomes our unofficial state—and, there, we have no excuse to tender for presenting ourselves before your Majesty, save the desire of offering our grateful acknowledgments to the lord of a realm, which through good and through evil report, has been the steadfast friend of the land we love so well." He felt enough ill at ease with the sycophantic rhetoric to confide to his notebook, "Writing addresses to Emperors is not my strong suit." Though a liberal autocrat compared to his father Nicholas I, Alexander II had brutally repressed further efforts at liberalization. Russia, still a police state, was a miserable, primitive prison. And other than the unintentional benefaction of having sold Alaska to the United States in April 1867, it was hardly a friend of America.

When the fawning pilgrims, dressed in their formal best, arrived at the summer palace, a condescending, genial monarch treated them kindly during an audience of fifteen minutes. The consul read the speech Twain had written, adding further nonsense of his own. The "poet lariat" unsuccessfully tried to recite his recently penned verse in honor of the occasion. Daniel Leary, thinking the czar might be a prospective buyer, attempted to persuade him to visit the *Quaker City*. When the exhilarated Americans left, they were hopeful that their hosts, particularly the emperor and grand duke, would visit the ship. In the late afternoon, the governor general brought news that the emperor was ill. Eager to entertain the governor general's party, the ship hosted a ball at which Twain danced an "impossible Russian dance" with a "beautiful little devil" whose attractions he could not quickly forget. "It was splendid. . . . Her dear name still haunts me in my dreams," he wrote in a letter to the *Alta*, though he reserved for his notebook the comment that "all day the ladies bathed naked in full view of the ship."

The next evening, with the *Quaker City* under way again, the passengers were floating with a newfound sense of self-importance derived from their royal experience, the highlight of the voyage so far. Some passengers signed a letter of appreciation to Leary, probably written by Twain, for his "kindness in affording . . . an opportunity to visit the Emperor of Russia at Yalta." They had no idea that Leary had been trying to sell the boat out from under them, though undoubtedly if the sale had occurred Leary would have had the *Quaker City* return first to New York. "The sun is setting on our Russian greatness," Mrs. Fairbanks wrote in her next letter to the *Cleveland Herald*. Back at Constantinople, refueling seemed to take forever, partly because of local inefficiency. The pilgrims amused themselves buying local trinkets; they were gradually to turn the ship's hold into a vast storeroom of accumulated trivia. To kill time, they took side excursions. When they sailed at last, Captain Duncan, either so eager to get under way that he was careless or simply manifesting what Twain thought his incompetence, drove the *Quaker City* across the bow of another steamer. Fortunately, the damage was slight. Two days later, on September 5, 1867, they were in sight of Smyrna. At last the Holy Land was about to be theirs.

3.

Like most dreams deferred, the realization proved, to some of the pilgrims, and particularly to Twain, more complicated and less satisfactory than the anticipation. Unlike a large number of his fellow voyagers, he had not spent Sunday mornings dreaming about walking the ground where Jesus had trod. But he did come to Palestine with the expectation that it would be pleasurable and elevating to bring together the sacred places of Holy Scripture with the actual sites in which the word had become incarnate. Indeed, he was being paid by the *Alta* and the *Tribune* to provide an account that would conjoin biblical and geographical coordinates for the education and enlightenment of his Christian readers. Facts and statistics were important. Humor might be appropriate; skepticism and irony were his tools in trade. But this was mainly serious business, which he prepared for, as the *Quaker City* steamed toward Smyrna, with an intense reading of guidebooks such as David A. Randall's *The Handwriting of God in Egypt, Sinai, and the Holy Land* (1862), which he drew upon heavily, preparing to make his travel time more efficient by creating reference lists of the biblical citations that correlated with each destination on his Holy Land itinerary.

After sightseeing in Smyrna, where Twain found his first sight of a camel caravan at least as interesting as the city's churches, the *Quaker City* pilgrims went by train and then donkey to nearby Ephesus, where "Apollo and Diana were born" and "Paul and John preached." Many of the pious souls were deeply moved; at last they were standing on the very earth on which Christ's disciples had trod. On this rich archaeological ground, Twain had a keen eye for historical and ideological layering. That the Christian, Classical, Jewish, and Arab pasts shared the same sites, that what was sacred to one could not readily be disentangled from what was sacred to another, came as a surprise to all the pilgrims, even to the comparatively secular Twain. The extent to which one culture had cannibalized another, that the "noble ruins" of Classical Ephesus had supplied "many a church in Christendom & many a mosque . . . with its grandest, its costliest, its most enduring columns," became the leitmotif of that aspect of his experience of Palestine. The Protestant's belief in the Christian particularity of the Holy Land was difficult to sustain when actually there, and the noble, handsome biblical ancients, instilled in the mind's eye by centuries of idealistic Western art, were nowhere to be seen. The pilgrims looked for what they expected the descendants of Abraham, Isaac, Jacob, and Jesus to look like; they saw instead mostly small, swarthy Arabs and impoverished communities of Jews. And, having given no thought to the conditions in which modern Palestinians lived, they were shocked to discover that this was not a land of milk and honey. Public sanitation was nonexistent. Disease and disfigurement were rampant. "The inhuman tyranny of the Ottoman Empire," Twain told his *Alta* readers, was to blame for much of the misery. Soon they discovered that the heat and dust were hardly bearable, the terrain barren and rocky, roads mostly absent.

From Ephesus, they returned to the *Quaker City* in Smyrna's harbor. Years later Twain recalled that before weighing anchor at Smyrna, Charley Langdon had shown him a miniature portrait of his sister, whose image he fell in love with immediately. If so, Twain kept it entirely to himself; not a word about Olivia Langdon appears in his notebooks or letters, and he was to continue with the activities of his life as if this seminal moment had not occurred or had been quickly pushed to the back of his mind. The belated account, perhaps a revisionist narrative to serve new purposes, may say more about Twain's much later feelings than about his likely reaction to a small, insensate photograph of a thin, moderately good-looking young Victorian lady. And other exciting interests were immediately at hand, including preparations for the land journey through Palestine, which required the travelers to bring up from the storerooms the saddles, revolvers, and clothes they had packed.

At Beirut, where they learned to their disappointment that only a small number of them could go on the one-trip a day to Damascus, they divided into three groups with separate itineraries. Suddenly the elaborate lists and diagrams that Twain had written in his notebook for the travel schedule he had expected were relatively useless. With Dan Slote, Jack Van Nostrand, Julius Moulton, and four others, he hired a guide to make arrangements, including tents, horses, and servants, at the cost of five dollars in gold each per day, for a difficult three-week journey from Beirut to Damascus, then to Lake Galilee, "then south through all the celebrated Scriptural localities to Jerusalem," he wrote to his mother, and then to the Dead Sea. It was a more ambitious plan than the original. Everyone's final destination would be Jaffa, where the *Quaker City* would be waiting. "Brown," of course, was the ninth traveling companion in Twain's group, a desert phantom but an epistolary reality.

Mounted this time on a mare named Jericho that "looked like she wanted to lean up against something and think," Twain was at last off to the Jerusalem he used to sing about in his favorite ditty. At the "magnificent ruins" of Balbec they met Mrs. Fairbanks' group, then ran across the Leary party, a beginning of the crisscrossing of paths that would continue throughout. On September 11 they left Beirut, camping that night in the mountains of Lebanon. Four of his companions were invited so that the "happy sinners" could meet the minimum of eight necessary to make the trip economically feasible. Two of them he disliked; the other two he soon despised. They demanded that the caravan come to a halt on the Sabbath, no matter at what inconvenience or loss. So they insisted on hurrying to Damascus before Saturday night fell rather than take the time to see sights they would never have the opportunity to see again.

At Damascus in mid-September, Twain came down, he thought, with cholera. More likely it was a less lethal viral infection. Dr. George Birch, a *Quaker City* passenger and coincidentally a resident of Hannibal, faithfully attended to him. Feverish, shaking, unable to hold food, he felt awful, though the next day he was so determined not to miss anything that he sat uneasily on a jackass whose driver showed him the sights. "Got enough of Damascus. Don't want to see any more," he wrote in his notebook. On September 16 the entourage left for Nimrod's tomb. Apparently Twain had partly recovered, but the conditions of Syrian life appalled him. "A Syrian village is the sorriest sight in the world," he wrote to his *Alta* readers.

Soon the caravan edged into the Holy Land. From a height they gazed down on the great plain, the streams of which created the River Jordan. At Casarea Phillipi they first walked on pavement "trodden by Jesus Christ." They bathed in the Sea of Galilee, then passed near Safed to Bethsaida. "I can go as far as the next man in genuine reverence of holy things," he wrote inaccurately, since he could not go nearly as far as most of his fellow pilgrims. "But this thing of stretching the narrow garment of belief till it fits the broad shoulders of a wish, is too much for my stomach." At night, sleeping in a tent, he admired the "splendid stars—when blue waves roll nightly on Galilee," paraphrasing Byron's "Destruction of Sennacherib," one of the two poems he claimed he had memorized as a schoolchild. Most days the caravan of twenty-four mules and horses, fourteen servants, and twenty-eight men set off in the darkness or at the break of dawn. Unfortunately their route directed them through Palestine's hottest, most rugged terrain, mostly desert, rocks, and steep hills, rather than the higher, cooler route that would have taken them through Safed. Neither biblical sites nor occasional natural beauty outweighed Twain's interest in people: "The people of this region in the Bible were just as they are now—ignorant, depraved, superstitious, thieving *vagabonds*." Desert Arabs twice attempted to raid their campsites and, with "no glamour of Sabbath-school glory to beautify them," the Jews he saw were "like any other savages."

From the top of Mount Tabor he looked across the Plain of Ezdraelon, then proceeded to the "slow village of Nazareth." It staggered his imagination that Jesus had spent thirty years of his life in this desolate, ugly place. Constantly mediating in his own mind between dream and reality, between past and present, he did his best not to attack flagrantly the literalism and ahistoricism of the pious pilgrims, just as later, when creating *Innocents Abroad*, he avoided as much as he could offending reasonable and temperate Christians. His satire was directed not at Christianity but at human folly, hypocrisy, and selfishness. Over dusty roads and craggy rocks, his tired horse, no more eager for the jolts than he, carried him to Jezrell, El Genin, and Samaria, to Joseph's tomb and Jacob's tomb, to Shiloh and Bethel, over "rocks—rocks—rock . . . roads infernal," and finally to Jerusalem, which they entered through the Damascus Gate on September 23. "Thought we *never would* get there," he wrote in his notebook.

Most of the biblical sites had been disappointing, ruins identifiable only by signs and guidebook claims. Few if any were historically verifiable, their designations the result of ignorance and clerical cupidity. Jerusalem, though, was a different matter. Having gone ahead of his party, Twain immediately went to a comfortable hotel, which became his Jerusalem residence. As they straggled in, the three *Quaker City* groups camped outside the city walls, between the Joppa and Damascus Gates. Twain had clearly experienced enough of sleeping in a tent. Visiting the Western Wall and the Temple Mount, he took some ancient shards as souvenirs, then went to the Mosques of Omar and Al Aksa, the Garden of Gethsemane, Mount of Olives, Calvary, and the Via Dolorosa, where he walked the stations of the cross and found time to select a small King James Bible to be decorated and inscribed, "Mrs. Jane Clemens—from her son—Mount Calvary, Sept 24, 1867."

At Jerusalem's Pool of Bethesda, which he described as "a slimy cesspool" but which supposedly had curative powers, he and Dr. Birch filled a bottle with water "when the angel wasn't around," a bacteria-laden souvenir. Giving more credence to Masonic than Christian claims, he had a branch cut from a cedar tree supposedly planted by a Mason in the eleventh century. He soon had it made into a gavel, which he gave as a gift to his St. Louis lodge. Much of what he saw, though, seemed to him grounded in either superstition or historical falsification. Still, he was sometimes moved and often fascinated, not as a believer but as a passionate observer of all things human. The Church of the Holy Sepulchre particularly captured his interest, though he exaggerated later in *Innocents Abroad* the frequency of his visits. At the Dead Sea, after taking a long bath, his face blistered, his hair filled with salt, he "took a horse in and he upset." His tiredness was burdensome now, the heat oppressive, and much of what he had seen, as well as what he soon saw at Bethlehem and Jericho, had no more status for him than any other representation of an unreliable historical record. "No second Advent," he wrote in his notebook—"Christ been here once—will never come again."

On September 29 he left Jerusalem with no desire ever to see it or Palestine again. Arriving in Alexandria after a difficult, wind-buffed voyage, most of the pilgrims were relieved to have left the Holy Land behind. Many had expected something other than what they got. Egypt, fortunately, was uncomplicated, its impressive remnants of a great civilization creating few religious considerations requiring adjustment to reality. Rested by the voyage, Twain immediately took the seven-hour express train to Cairo, where he and his usual companions stayed at Shepheard's Hotel, the favorite residence of English colonials. On donkey-back they went to the Ghiza monuments. From the platform on top of the great pyramid of Cheops, Twain had a dramatic view of the Nile valley. Memphis he saw in the distance from the Mosque of Mehemet Ali high above Cairo. Ironically, when he rushed to the Egyptian Museum he discovered that the best of the collection was at the Paris Exhibition, where he had skipped the Egyptian hall, assuming it inferior to what he would see in Cairo. From Cairo, he made a quick visit to Suez and the Red Sea, and then returned to Alexandria.

When, at the end of the first week in October 1867, the *Quaker City* steamed westward into the teeth of a storm, Twain regretted that Dan Slote, his most companionable friend of the last four months, was extending his European tour and not on board. Twain felt fortunate, though, that at least he would not have to bear the company of the pious pilgrims for more than another month. The mutual antipathy had intensified. At Alexandria he may have received disconcerting news—some of his letters to the *Alta California,* for which he had already been paid, seemed to have been lost, though how many if any at all had actually been lost or simply had never been written remains unclear. In any case, he would have to spend much of his time on the return voyage writing letters, relying on his patchy notes and fading memory. He also would not have time to do any more of the well-paying letters he had promised the *Tribune*. Mrs. Fairbanks provided consolation and support, an amiable relationship now becoming an intensely friendly one. He read his new letters to her as he finished each. Many of her suggestions he took as useful correctives to his playful attraction to impropriety. Solon Severance recalled that Twain, whom he observed throwing torn-up paper overboard, explained to him, "Mrs. Fairbanks thinks it oughtn't to be printed, and, like as not, she is right."

Since most of the passengers had seen little of Spain three months before, the *Quaker City* cancelled its scheduled visit to Malta in the interest of a much-desired Spanish tour. After antagonistic discussions between competing factions, the pilgrims agreed to stop at Sardinia, then Algiers, and finally Malaga, where, to their relief, the local authorities granted them a clean bill of health to enter Spain. Most, however, steamed to Gibraltar for local sightseeing. In the less than six days available, Twain, Van Nostrand, and Jackson, with Jackson's fiancée, made an exciting excursion through Andalusia, where they visited Seville, Cordoba, Jerez, and Cadiz. "The country is precisely as it was when Don Quixotte & Sancho Panza were possible characters," he wrote to his family. At Cadiz, on October 24, they rejoined the waiting *Quaker City*. Many of the travelers wanted to stop at Lisbon, but Captain Duncan, irritable and overburdened with shipboard problems, refused. At Madeira a cautious official forced them to wait out a three-day quarantine before disembarking. They voted not to do so, apparently because Duncan wanted to stay, greatly disappointing the Funchal merchants.

Civility was wearing thin, tempers fraying. At Gibraltar, where mail had caught up to them, some of the travelers had read one of Twain's *Tribune* letters in which his high praise for Mrs. Fairbanks' amiability with the Russian visitors to the ship seemed an implied insult to the other *Quaker City* ladies. As they sailed westward, complaints and arguments broke out. Some of the long-simmering outrage at Twain and his friends constantly playing poker and smoking in his cabin boiled over. "This pleasure party of ours," he had written to Joe Goodman from Cadiz, "is composed of the d— dest, rustiest, ignorant, vulgar, slimy, psalm-singing cattle that could be scraped up in seventeen States. They wanted Holy Land, & they got it. It was a stunner. It is an awful trial to a man's religion to waltz it through the Holy Land."

If the *Quaker City* captain and passengers, with a dozen exceptions, had been forewarned how Twain would represent them to the world in *Innocents Abroad,* many might have forfeited their tickets. Later, they might have thrown him overboard. Their ire would not have been so roused by the letters he wrote to the *Alta California,* since those were designed to emphasize informative descriptions of exotic places. But in the notebooks he kept it would have been unmistakable to this community of saints that they had taken a mischievous devil into their bosom. It was not until *Innocents Abroad* appeared in July 1869 that the full force of Twain's mockery of many passengers and of the captain became reading entertainment for the entire country. Much happened during the voyage and especially afterward that increased Twain's desire to express his hostility. But, during the voyage itself, as Fairbanks noticed, he mostly appeared in the public clothes and manner he generally wore—genial, humorous, and cooperative, even when inwardly begrudging and resentful. As always, he respected peer pressure, at least to a point, and preferred passive resistance and flight to direct defiance. He admired Satan's energy. He also admired his cunning and prudence.

4.

If indeed the waltz through the Holy Land was a trial, it was a profitable one for Twain, perhaps the most significant voyage of his lifetime. With the twenty-two letters that had reached San Francisco, the twenty-one or so he had frantically written on the return voyage, and the additional letters he composed after the *Quaker City* docked in New York on November 19,

1867, he had enough material for a book. That prospect would have been foremost on his mind if he had not had to scurry to earn a living as soon as he stepped off the boat. It infuriated him to learn that the *Alta* had copyrighted the letters to discourage other newspapers reprinting extensive excerpts, a reversal of the usual practice of encouraging it. He knew it would have been to his advantage to have his name broadcast extensively by widespread newspaper republication, preparing the way for a Holy Land lecture tour. Still, he was optimistic that, under Frank Fuller's management, he could earn "$2,000 to $3,000 in gold" lecturing in San Francisco and Sacramento. But, in fact, he dreaded "the idea of appearing before those miners of Montana, or those Mormons of Salt Lake." Expressing his lifelong attitude toward lecturing, he would do it only under the pressure of necessity.

Within a day of stepping off the *Quaker City,* he wrote a scathingly humorous letter that the *New York Herald* published, lambasting the Holy Land pilgrims as pious frauds, their pleasure excursion a "funeral without a corpse." He first attempted to have the more prestigious, better-established *Tribune* print it. But since his contact at the *Tribune,* John Russell Young, the distinguished managing editor, was out of the office, he went, feeling pressed by time and need, to his second choice, which took it immediately. That the *Herald* accidentally omitted his byline angered him, though his authorship was widely recognized. The publicity seemed to him as desirable as the payment. It also made him feel good to be satirically savage toward people he had come to detest but with whom he had been forced to maintain some semblance of cordiality. When, from Cleveland, Mary Fairbanks chastised him, he assured his "Dear Forgiving Mother" that he had done it on purpose and wasn't in the least bit sorry. Even two weeks later he strongly desired to "print the savagest kind of a history of the excursion. I have promised you that I wouldn't do, & I haven't the slightest doubt in the world *but that* I *will*. I can't keep a promise." Especially when he did not want to. "I don't want their good opinions, I wouldn't have their good offices. I don't want any commerce with people I don't like. They can hurt me. Let them. I would rather they should hurt me than help me."

"I have some hope," Twain remarked, "that the harmless squib in the *Herald* will bring out bitter replies from some of the *Quaker City*'s strange managerie of ignorance, imbecility, bigotry & dotage, & so give me an excuse to go into the secret history of the excursion & tell truthfully how that curious company conducted themselves in foreign lands and on board ship." Captain Duncan slashed back immediately, accusing Twain of immoral behavior, including drunkenness. It was a charge to which the writer was sensitive. In Nevada and California he had enjoyed the widespread drinking characteristic of mining life and newspaper circles. But occasional binging nights never rose to the level of alcoholism. Drinking was a preference, not a compulsion, unlike his addiction to smoking. The *Herald* editorialist saw Twain as the fitting vehicle to smite hypocrisy and smugness. "It was scarcely wise on the part of the pilgrims, although it was well for the public, that so strange a genius as Mr. Mark Twain should have found admission into the sacred circle." By "strange," the *Herald* apparently meant distinctive, Twain's unusual combination of sly humor and sharp satire, the mild irony of Horatian satire in which it takes a while to realize that the genial humorist has slipped a knife between the ribs. However the *Herald*'s readers understood the word "strange," there was no mistaking the meaning of "genius." It was a level of recognition, even if only in an uncultivated New York newspaper, that elevated Mark Twain to a new level of public prominence.

Within days of stepping off the *Quaker City,* he attempted to supplement his *Herald* attack with two abbreviated acts of a burlesque drama about "the Grand Holy Land Funeral Excursion," which he hoped Charles Henry Webb would sponsor as a full-length New York stage production. Webb immediately recognized a nonstarter, and Twain put the fragment aside, though his need to find income additional to what he would be paid for letters to the *Herald* was even stronger than he had anticipated. He was shocked to learn from Webb that no royalty money was due him from sales of *The Celebrated Jumping Frog of Calaveras County, And other Sketches.* Webb told him that "The Jumping Frog book had been favorably received by the press and that he believed it had sold fairly well, but that he had found it impossible to get a statement from the American News Company. Webb said that the book had been something of a disaster to him, since he had manufactured it with his own private funds and was not able to get any of the money back because of the dishonest and dodging ways of the News Company." Twain received nothing. Years later he claimed that he ran into the owner of the American News Company, who told him that Webb had received regular statements and had been paid promptly. The book certainly had sold well enough for some royalty to have been due the author.

Fortunately, Twain had already accepted an offer from his Nevada friend Senator William Stewart to serve as a combination private secretary and legislative assistant. An influential pro-Reconstruction Republican, Stewart was to help write the Fifteenth Amendment, extending suffrage to former slaves. On the morning of November 22, 1867, two days after arriving back in the United States, Twain walked into the F Street rooms of his new employer, the second time in his life that he was in the nation's capital. In 1853, Washington's combination of muddy provinciality and historical resonance had seemed tolerable for a few days, its monuments and grand political figures interesting, the presence of power even riveting to the seventeen-year-old. Post–Civil War Washington was larger, more bustling, and wealthier. It was also egregiously corrupt and still deeply divided on major issues, particularly Reconstruction.

Stewart's later estrangement from Twain may have influenced his recollection of what Twain looked like when he entered the senator's apartment, where Twain also was to room. "I was seated at my window," Stewart recalled, "when a very disreputable-looking person slouched into the room. He was arrayed in a seedy suit, which hung upon his lean frame in bunches. . . . A sheaf of scraggy black hair leaked out of a battered old slouch hat . . . and an evil-smelling cigar butt, very much frazzled, protruded from the corner of his mouth. He had a very sinister appearance." Twain, who had been sitting up awake or slouching into naps on the night train, would have had little time to clean his clothes or get new ones since landing in New York. Stewart recalled that Twain immediately proposed the senator lend him money. "All I need is a little cash stake. I have been to the Holy Land with a party of innocent and estimable people who are fairly aching to be written up, and I think I could do the job neatly and with dispatch if I were not troubled with other—more pressing—considerations. I've started the book already, and it is a wonder. I can vouch for it." Apparently Stewart thought that giving Twain employment was sponsorship enough.

In the next few days Twain learned that both the *Herald* and the *Tribune* wanted him to write letters from Washington. His old friends at the *Territorial Enterprise* asked him to send occasional letters, and he still had obligations to the *Alta*. By late January 1868, his journalistic cup over-flowed. James Gordon Bennett, Jr., the *Herald*'s managing editor, took the opportunity of Twain's stopping by the New York office to propose that he write for the *Herald* twice a week. Bennett said that he would have "full swing, & abuse anybody & everybody" he wanted, so he told his mother. Soon he was, in practice, the *Herald*'s Washington news bureau. Watching Congress in session, he wrote into his notebook sharp descriptions of a number of the legislators, from Thaddeus Stevens to James Garfield, con-trasting the older generation with the new, observations he was to draw on five years later when writing *The Gilded Age*. Although there were no out-ward signs of antagonism, he was soon no longer working for Stewart or liv-ing at his apartment.

With another journalist, the hard-drinking William Swinton, now his roommate, Twain concocted a scheme whereby they each wrote one letter a week, made twelve copies by hand, and sent them to newspapers around the country at a dollar a letter, a primitive version of syndication. "Although we didn't get rich, it kept the jug going and partly fed the two of us," Twain later recalled. "But there was a day when we felt that we must have three dollars right away," Twain told an audience fifty years later.

> The Scot sent me out . . . to get it. He had a great belief in Provi-dence. . . . He said: "The Lord will provide." I had given up trying to find the money lying about, and was in a hotel lobby in despair, when I saw a beautiful unfriended dog. The dog saw me, too, and at once we became acquainted. Then General Miles came in, admired the dog, and asked me to price it. I priced it at three dollars. . . . The general carried the dog to his room. Then came in a sweet little middle-aged man, who at once began looking around the lobby. "Did you lose a dog?" I asked. He said he had. "I think I could find it," I volunteered, "for a small sum." "How much?" he asked. And I told him three dollars. He urged me to accept more, but I did not wish to outdo Providence. Then I went to the gen-eral's room and asked for the dog back. He was very angry, and wanted to know why I had sold him a dog that did not belong to me. "That's a sin-gular question to ask me, sir," I replied. "Didn't you ask me to sell him? You started it." And he let me have him. I gave him back his three dollars and returned the dog, collect, to his owner. That second three dollars I carried home to the Scot, and we enjoyed it.

Delighted to find that a friend, John Henry Riley, was the *Alta California* Washington correspondent, Twain found opportunities to admire Riley's capacity for drink and wit. One night Riley, accosted by an eager office seeker who seemed confident of success, told a long story about a man who impoverished himself by waiting indefinitely at an expensive Washington hotel. "He never got that post-office." Riley, who advised this man to stay at the same hotel, seemed to the admiring Twain, who used the incident as the basis for a sketch, "The Man Who Put Up at Gadsby's," "the most self-possessed and solemnly deliberate person in the world." Back home in Missouri, Orion also waited for a patronage job, which his brother had high hopes of getting for him.

Late in December, Stewart introduced Twain to Ulysses S. Grant, the secretary of war under President Andrew Johnson. Grant, notoriously shy, and Twain, for once tongue-tied with awe, experienced moments of mutual embarrassment when neither could find anything to say. Supposedly, Twain at last said to the then Secretary of War, "I am embarrassed. Are you?" That broke the ice, though he undoubtedly did not ask the general to do anything for Orion. All Twain got for his troubles on Orion's behalf were a few offers of such jobs for himself, none of which he thought suitable. Only his *Quaker City* excursion book had the potential to get him off the journalistic treadmill.

In December he received a letter from Elisha Bliss, a forty-six-year-old former dry goods and lumber merchant who now headed the recently founded American Publishing Company. Located in Hartford, Connecticut, the firm specialized in publishing subscription books with print runs that were determined by advance sales obtained by salesmen traveling door to door in assigned territories. Only as many books as had been presold were printed. Directed at popular taste, subscription volumes needed to appeal to nonliterary readers, to provide value, and to attract a market often beyond the reach, both physically and intellectually, of the nation's bookstores. One of the American Publishing Company's recent subscription books had sold 100,000 copies, a huge number rarely achieved in conventional trade publishing. Twain's *Alta* letters, Bliss thought, would almost certainly make a successful subscription book. Twain requested that, if such a book would suit his purpose Bliss provide the particulars about length, style, and schedule, "& particularly . . . what amount of money [he] might possibly make out of it." Soon he was convinced that he might profit more from subscription publication than from conventional publication with a trade press. "Their house is a very live concern," he told Fuller. But he still needed money to buy time to transform the letters into a book. Paying advances against royalties was almost unheard of.

As all this was in progress, Twain regularly went from Washington to New York, partly as an expression of the restlessness he quickly began to feel again, and partly to see friends, including some from the *Quaker City* voyage. At Dan Slote's parents' comfortable house in Manhattan he always had a warm welcome, though Dan himself had not returned yet from Europe. "I am already dead tired," he wrote to Fuller in mid-December, "of being in one place so long." It had been a mistake, he now thought, not to have done a lecture tour. He had in mind a "half-formed notion of sailing for California." The *Quaker City* intemperance accusations still continued, and on December 30 the *Brooklyn Eagle* published a letter from Twain attempting to put to rest the charge that he had been the center of "a vast deal of drunkenness." In the interest of comity and finality, he ameliorated his charges against Duncan. "Let us pour [no more than] ink upon the troubled waters," he counseled.

Two days after Christmas 1867, while visiting New York, Twain was the dinner guest of the family of Charley Langdon, his *Quaker City* "cub," at the luxurious St. Nicholas Hotel on Broadway. Young Langdon desired to introduce his well-known *Quaker City* companion to his parents and sister. In Charley's eyes, Twain was the epitome of wit and worldly sophistication. Whether or not Twain had actually been compelled to attention by Olivia Langdon's miniature portrait in Smyrna remains unclear. But Charley, let alone his parents, might not have arranged the dinner if he had suspected that Twain had an interest in the girl, let alone a presentiment of how strong that interest was to become. Churchgoing pillars of their Elmira, New York, community, the wealthy Langdons were intelligent, honest, and serious Congregationalists who cherished their daughter.

Apparently, though, the evening went well enough for the Langdons to invite Twain, as their son's friend, to join them on December 31 to hear Charles Dickens read at Steinway Hall. Early in the month, Webb had taken the opportunity of Dickens' visit to place a newspaper advertisement for *The Celebrated Jumping Frog* as a suitable Christmas book, linking Twain with Dickens. The most famous living English novelist, on his second and last reading tour of America, read from *David Copperfield*. Twain was on his best behavior, perhaps hoping that the novelist's rags to riches story of a writer's success might reflect favorably on the Langdons' image of his own prospects. On New Year's Day 1868 he went out, as was the New York custom, to make a long list of courtesy calls. He did not, though, get beyond the first. "Charley Langdon's sister was there (beautiful girl)," he wrote to his mother. Apparently he stayed the entire day in happy conversation with her and her friend Alice Hooker, Henry Ward Beecher's niece from Hartford, a family friend of the Langdons. "We sent the old folks" (probably the Langdons, perhaps also Alice's mother, Isabella Hooker) "home early, with instructions not to send the carriage till midnight, and then I just staid and deviled the life out of those girls." Apparently the girls did not particularly mind.

When at Charley's instigation the Langdons invited Twain to visit them in Elmira, the family still had no idea they were offering hospitality to a man who saw their daughter as a special version of the holy grail, simultaneously erotic and pure, and tantalizingly out of reach. It was immediately clear to him, even in his most sanguine imaginings, that he would have to pass through a straight and narrow gate even more formidable than that of the pious pilgrims if there was to be any future for him with this young lady. He found her compellingly irresistible. Every inch the Victorian idealized woman, she seemed to glow with an inner feminine intensity, a slim, dark-haired, dark-eyed, creamy-complexioned exemplar of shyness, modesty, virtue, and youthful beauty. If Twain were to win her, it would take reformation and strategy.

CHAPTER EIGHT

HOME AND ANCHORAGE

1868–1870

1.

Two years later, at the beginning of February 1870, what had seemed unimaginable happened. Standing in the Langdons' plush drawing room in Elmira, New York, astounded at his good fortune, Samuel L. Clemens married twenty-four-year-old Olivia Langdon. Two years earlier, it had seemed inconceivable that he could marry at all. "I want a good wife—I want a couple of them if they are particularly good," he responded to Mary Mason Fairbanks when she urged that "a good wife would be a perpetual incentive to progress." But how could he afford one? "I can't turn an inkstand into Aladdin's Lamp." Anyway, he seriously joked, "I wouldn't have a girl that I was worthy of. She wouldn't do. She wouldn't be respectable enough." Marriage seemed out of reach.

In December 1867, in Washington, attempting to earn a living at the journalistic grindstone, he was writing letters for the *Tribune*, the *Herald*, the *Enterprise*, the *Alta* (to fulfill his *Quaker City* assignment), and the *Chicago Republican*, and he would soon do some sketches for a New York monthly, the *Galaxy*. In addition, he had "to get up that confounded book," he told his mother, and asked her to send her scrapbook of *Alta* clippings. Elisha Bliss's proposal seemed too good not to accept, and no other publisher had made an offer. In late December Bliss wrote again, perhaps prompted by the *Hartford Courant*'s announcement that the American Publishing Company would bring out an account of the Holy Land excursion by Mark Twain, "one of the funniest writers of the day," a story Bliss may have planted. He urged Twain to sign. A five percent royalty on each volume sold or ten thousand dollars cash for outright purchase seemed to Twain handsome, especially in the light of Bliss's claim that he paid his best-selling author, with whom he assumed Twain was consulting, a four percent royalty. And even if five percent was less than what a trade press might offer, subscription, Bliss maintained, would sell more copies. Twain readily bought the argument. He accepted the five percent offer, gambling that his share of sales would exceed ten thousand dollars. It was indeed a gamble. The book would have to sell thirty-five thousand copies at $3.50 each and ten thousand at $8.00 to produce ten-thousand dollars for the author. "But I had my mind made up to *one* thing," he boasted to his family. "I wasn't going to touch a book unless there was *money* in it, & a good deal of it."

Working frantically at journalism, he was, he told his mother, "gradually getting out of debt," though she might well have advised him to take the ten-thousand up front and forgo the gamble. "These trips to New York do cost like Sin," he complained. Right after Christmas "the unholiest gang that ever cavorted through Palestine," he wrote to his mother, had a "blow-out," drinking copiously to the reunion and the season. Van Nostrand was there. Charley Langdon attended, now part of the inner circle at least as much for his sister's sake as his own. Soon Twain was to send him an inscribed copy of *The Celebrated Jumping Frog*. He was not on terms with anyone else in the Langdon family that would permit him to send them gifts directly without appearing presumptuous. Olivia had given him no encouragement other than as Charley's friend.

His partying spirit was considerably less in evidence in early January 1868 when he was Henry Ward Beecher's dinner guest in Brooklyn Heights. There he met Harriet Beecher Stowe, Henry's sister, the fifty-seven-year-old author of the novel that Lincoln had said started the war. The mother of Olivia's friend Alice, whom Twain had recently met, was also there: Isabella Beecher Hooker, Henry Ward Beecher's half sister. Like Stowe, she lived in Hartford. At dinner, Beecher preached a practical sermon about book contract negotiations, having received a ten-thousand-dollar advance for his proposed life of Jesus. " 'In matters of business,' "

Twain quoted Beecher as saying, " 'I don't suppose you know more than enough to come in when it rains; I'll tell you what to do and how to do it.' And he did." After evening services at Plymouth Church, they returned to Beecher's, where they "had a very gay time," even "if it *was* Sunday" and even though we had "nothing to drink but cider," he wrote to his mother. Twain, perhaps mischievously, "told Mr. Beecher that no dinner could be perfect without champagne, or at least some kind of Burgundy." Beecher "said that privately he was a good deal of the same opinion, but it wouldn't do to say it loud," a sly admission from the high priest of temperance. "Henry Ward is a brick," Twain concluded, a view he would hold on to as long as he could.

With Beecher's advice and an invitation from the Hookers, Twain went to Hartford soon after mid-January to settle the details of the contract for what had been tentatively named "The New Pilgrim's Progress." Bliss thought that "Twain would cut the matter short by coming up for a *talk*," he told his mother, triumphantly. "They pay me more than they have ever paid any author, except Horace Greeley," Twain boasted inaccurately, since Greeley had not been published by the American Publishing Company at all. Bliss stood to benefit from Twain's confusion, and probably provided selective figures to elicit the most favorable contract for himself, then happily encouraged Twain's self-congratulatory boasting. The deal was "for a Quaker City book of 5 or 600 large pages, with illustrations," the manuscript due by summer 1868, the book to be set in type within four months of receipt and to be sold by the publisher's agents in spring 1869, an agreement soon put into an informal exchange of letters.

Hartford, an attractive city of thirty-five thousand people, was a flourishing center of small skilled enterprises such as the Colt Arms Factory, the center of the growing insurance industry, and the home of the best-known subscription publishing company in the country. It had an influential clerical community in which Presbyterianism and Congregationalism flourished, with easy railroad access to Boston to the north and New York to the south. It also had a serious Republican newspaper, the *Hartford Courant*. Its compact downtown business area was anchored by the state capital building and the Connecticut River to the east; to the west, Farmington Avenue stretched into farmland and woods.

Isabella Beecher Hooker, who was hosting Twain, lived with her lawyer husband, John Hooker, about two miles from the center in a residential area of 140 acres called Nook Farm, situated by the left bank of the North Park River. Purchased and subdivided in 1853 by Hooker and his brother-in-law, Francis Gillette, a wealthy insurance executive who had been a senator, it became the home of many of the Hookers' friends, including Isabella's half sister Harriet. Nook Farm was also home to Joseph Hawley, the former governor of Connecticut who edited and owned the *Courant,* his friend and coeditor, the essay and travel writer Charles Dudley Warner, and the lawyer Thomas Perkins, married to another of Isabella's sisters. The reigning comatriarchs were Isabella, an avid pioneering feminist and later an idiosyncratic spiritualist, and Harriet, whose novels dramatized human love as the key to heavenly salvation.

At Nook Farm, and in Hartford in general, the spirit of Calvinistic Congregationalism had been transformed into an Emerson-like religion of the heart. Nook Farm residents attended the Fourth Congregational Church, led by one of their neighbors, Nathaniel Burton, or Edwin Parker's Second Congregational Church, or the newly built Asylum Hill Congregational Church, whose young pastor, Joseph Hopkins Twichell, was a disciple of Horace Bushnell, the most distinguished liberal American theologian of the period. In this first visit of a few days, the Hookers introduced Twain to some of their friends. Mostly they were Beechers or were related to Beechers and Hookers. The Langdons, too, had a connection to the Nook Farm community—the pastor of their church in Elmira was Thomas Kinnicut Beecher, Isabella's brother and the half brother of Harriet Beecher Stowe and Henry Ward Beecher.

"Puritans are mighty straight-laced," Twain wrote to his mother, "& they won't let me smoke in the parlor, but the Almighty don't make any better people." He soon amused his *Alta* readers with an account of Hartford's high moral practices. "I have to smoke surreptitiously when all are in bed, to save my reputation, & then draw suspicion upon the cat when the family detect an unfamiliar odor. I never was so absurdly proper in the broad light of day. . . . So far I am safe; but I am sorry to say that the cat has lost caste." Apparently he very much wanted to please his hosts, perhaps with the Langdons in not so far-off Elmira in mind. But he also knew that these people were well-connected movers and shakers, a community combining cultural and intellectual accomplishment with material prosperity. "I desire to have the respect of this sterling old Puritan community, for their respect is well worth having," he wrote to Mary Fairbanks.

The problem was his own mischievous nature, particularly his deeply in-grained colloquial language and ironic humor. "I can," he assured Fairbanks, "be most laceratingly 'funny without being vulgar,'" though he acknowl-edged that he himself could not easily distinguish between what the Fair-bankes' ilk considered vulgar and what not. Thus "I am bound to wander off the straight path & do outrageous things, occasionally, & I believe I have got a genuinely bad heart, anyway." Still, he was not incorrigible. "In the course of time I will get some of the badness out of it or break it," a challenge of selective reformation that he was soon to have even greater motivation to achieve. His overriding aesthetic principle applied a test that transcended language and genre. "I don't care anything about being humorous, or poeti-cal, or eloquent, or anything of that kind—the end & aim of my ambition is to be authentic."

Back in Washington again, he confessed to Fairbanks how hard it had been "to lead such a sinless life" in Hartford. But in Washington he was too exhaustingly busy with writing commitments to have time for any transgression but smoking. He "*could* make eight hundred a month . . . if [he] didn't have the book to write." As it stood, though, he was probably making about three hundred dollars, though not even his facility made writing so many letters for different venues less than dizzying, especially when, by February 1868, he had begun to rewrite the *Alta* letters into a book, while at the same time still writing some of the letters themselves, which the *Alta* continued to publish until May. The letters were backdated as if they had been written in the Holy Land. In order to create the book, he needed to write fewer articles.

When offered a patronage position as San Francisco postmaster, he turned it down when he discovered it actually required considerable work. Instead he wrote to Bliss requesting an advance of a thousand dollars. Ap-parently Bliss complied, though that sum would not buy Twain much time, especially as he began to realize that the *Quaker City* letters would com-prise only about half the length he had promised for the subscription book. Not only would he have to rewrite some existing letters to bring them into conformity with the scheme, but he would need 250 pages of new mate-rial, a daunting task. To refresh his memory, he got Fairbanks' *Cleveland Herald* letters and Emmeline Beach's diary entries. "If you can't recollect accurately, *invent—invent*" he told Emma. "Let the sin be upon my head. I think that book of mine will be full of inventions anyhow."

Sequestered in a cheap "little back-room" on Indiana Avenue, from which the cleaning lady was banned, stripped down to his suspenders, cursing as he walked the floor in slippers, breaking stride for quick dashes to his writing paper, he "was like a steam engine at full head," one of his journalist friends observed. Newspapers were piled high everywhere, pipes strewn about in unlikely places, the one in his mouth helping to make the smoky air so thick, he joked, that the usually hardy Washington flies immediately fell down dead if they dared to enter. He had changed lodgings five times since he had left Stewart's, and thought he would "move again, shortly." "Shabby furniture & shabby food—*that* is Wash—I mean to keep moving."

Washington now bored and bothered him. Congress seemed a den of mostly thieves and the untalented. "To be *busy* is a man's only happiness,— & I *am*—otherwise I should die," he wrote to Orion, who alternated between being unemployed and doing low-paying typesetting. "We chase phantoms half the days of our lives," he preached to his brother, callow solace for his failure to find him a patronage position. He, too, he assured Orion, was chasing phantoms: "[I] must go on chasing them—until I marry—*then* I am done with literature & all other bosh,—that is, literature wherewith to please the general public." Why marrying should allow that difference he did not explain. Perhaps he had marrying well in mind, possibly even Olivia Langdon's parents' wealth. Perhaps he meant only that he would find some way to devote himself to serious literature rather than to ephemeral journalism and low-caste humor.

Orion's life in St. Louis as a poorly paid substitute printer was going from bad to worse. The unsold Tennessee family land, though, still seemed to him a lifeline that he might grab, and he made visits to Tennessee that his brother thought absurd. "I hope you *have* sold, even though it be for a mere song," Twain told his family. With his contract from the American Publishing Company, his own life was going from good to better. There was, though, one new fly in the ointment. The *Alta California* owners responded to the news that he was under contract for a book based on his letters with the claim that they in fact owned the copyright: each published letter had been prefaced with a copyright statement. In fact, they told him, they were planning to bring out the letters as a book themselves. Apparently the issue had arisen in Twain's discussion with Bliss. He had declined, though, to ask the *Alta* to do him the favor of permitting him to reuse the letters, as if he were unaware (more likely he was not willing to admit awareness) of the copyright statement preceding each published letter. When the *Alta* learned of Twain's intention, it made it known that it would not accept Twain's hijacking its rights without so much as a by-your-leave.

Now, reconsidering his strategy, Twain telegraphed the *Alta,* requesting permission, a request that he still believed he should not have to make. In fact, the *Alta* people, he wrote to his sister-in-law, were thieves, as he usually described anyone who opposed what he considered his business interests. He had made a "superb contract for a book . . . but I will bet it never sees the light."

Angry and frightened, he decided that his best recourse was to go to San Francisco immediately, a destination that had been in his mind since the previous fall anyway, to attempt to persuade the *Alta* not to publish its edition and to grant him his request. He could also make up for the loss of journalistic income by lecturing in San Francisco and environs. If the *Alta* problem could be resolved favorably, he would stay and work at the book in San Francisco, hoping to have a manuscript for Bliss by the August target date. Though Bliss urged him to do the book without reliance on the letters "and not mind what the *Alta* does," Twain refused. "If the *Alta's* book were to come out," he told Fairbanks, "with those wretched, slangy letters unrevised, I should be utterly ruined." His new Hartford friends would not approve, and neither would the Langdons. From New York, toward mid-March 1868, he sailed on the SS *Henry Chauncey,* via Panama, happy to have "an excuse to go to sea again."

2.

As for the *Alta* situation, ludicrous as his distortions were, he easily convinced himself that his view contained the entire truth. That the *Alta* had paid him $1,200 in cash for the letters as well $1,250 for his *Quaker City* passage and that each letter had been prefaced with a copyright statement to which he had not previously objected had no relevance for him. These were, in fact, his letters, and the *Alta* had damaged him to the tune of ten thousand dollars, a figure invented to serve his argument, by having forbidden their being reprinted in eastern newspapers.

The *Alta* owners must have seen quickly what a cast of mind they were up against in a man who had done them some service and whom they genuinely liked. They first proposed a compromise in which the *Alta* would pay Twain a ten percent royalty on their book version of the letters. "I was now quite unknown outside of San Francisco," Twain recalled responding. "The book sale would be confined to San Francisco, and my royalty would not pay me enough to board me three months." But an East Coast publication, by a subscription publisher, could be very profitable.

Fortunately, his *Alta* employers were still his friends, and it may have been the case from the start that they felt more aggrieved at Twain's assumption of ownership than determined to enforce their legal rights. And the idea of using the letters as a basis for a book had occurred to the *Alta* owners only after they had learned about Twain's intention. If he had asked before he had made his agreement with Bliss, perhaps the release would have been granted. He did not ask once Bliss had raised the issue because he resented that someone might think he had an obligation to do so. That he was forced to ask left him feeling resentful, as if he needed to believe that the *Alta* people had mistreated him and he owed them nothing, even thanks. In the end, they gradually and graciously acceded to Twain's urgent arguments and returned the copyright to him on the easiest of terms. The *Alta* agreed not to publish its collection of the letters on certain conditions: "In my preface I must thank the Alta for waiving its 'rights' and granting me permission. I objected to the thanks. I could not with any large degree of sincerity thank the *Alta* for bankrupting my lecture-raid. After considerable debate my point was conceded and the thanks left out."

Since, as always, Twain's general approach to a financial balance sheet was to ensure that his expenses rose to the level of his income, he took up residence at the Occidental Hotel, then at the even more expensive Lick House. Only moderately well known in the northeast, in San Francisco he was a celebrity. Its newspapers took happy note of his arrival. His daily doings were of public interest, especially if something funny could be made of them. Whatever restaurant or bar he entered, he was likely to be recognized. His thick, droopy mustache and curly hair, sharp nose and steely eyes, square-jawed chin and face, were captured in *two carte de visite* photos taken by a San Francisco photographer. Though he generally slept until close to midday, he went to church one Sunday only to discover that his presence in San Francisco was providing fodder for occasional pulpit denunciations. Some literal-minded clergymen had taken his *Alta* letters as an assault on the clergy in general. Irked when a minister lambasted him twice on one Sunday, he attempted to respond, though that and two other written defenses remained unpublished. "It is only the small-fry ministers who assail me," he wrote Mary Fairbanks. "All those of high rank & real influence I visit, dine & swap lies with, just the same as ever."

In mid-April 1868, having enlisted his contacts to line up a series of Bay area lectures, he slouched onto the stage, drawling out to a full house of sixteen hundred, with most of the $1,600 ticket sales going into his pocket. The offering was a revised version of "The Frozen Truth," a lecture he had presented in Washington in January. It highlighted the dour pietism of the *Quaker City* zealots and got most praise for its descriptive evocations of the Holy Land and of the Sphinx. So many people had to be turned away that he repeated the lecture the next night. Eager to keep it fresh, he asked his audiences not to give "any of [his] good sayings in the morning papers" and his newspaper friends to see that no reports or synopses of the lecture were printed. Apparently they complied. He was soon on the road to the usual places, first by riverboat to Sacramento, then over the snow-heavy Sierras to Carson City, where he lectured twice, and to Virginia City, where he reveled for a few days in the embrace of his former home and in the hospitable presence of the *Territorial Enterprise* crowd. The tour went so well that he wrote to Frank Fuller in New York that he wanted "to preach in the States all winter. I mean to get up a lecture on California, another on 'Paris and Pompeii,' & revamp my Sandwich Island talk." To refill his pockets, to help the sales of what would soon be named *Innocents Abroad,* and no doubt to further his marital hopes, he repressed how much he disliked lecturing.

With ten chapters of his book already completed, he spent the first two weeks of April reorienting himself to San Francisco and negotiating for the *Alta*'s permission to reuse the letters. The next two weeks he devoted mostly to lecturing. Then, with the *Alta* matter resolved, he settled down to two months of intensive writing, about three thousand words a day, as he later recalled, working "every night from eleven or twelve until broad day in the morning," tightening, restructuring, providing a developmental narrative and thematic pattern, and drawing less on the original letters than he had anticipated. Though the themes were essentially the same, he embodied them in a structure that provided greater narrative and tonal coherence. He later exaggerated the extent to which the material was new, but there was some truth to his later comment that he could have gone ahead without the *Alta*'s permission. By mid-June he had done 2,343 of his longhand pages, he wrote to Fairbanks, and was *"homeward bound.* . . .

There will be a great deal more than enough for the book . . . & I am glad. I can cut out a great deal that *ought* to perish." He finished the manuscript in mid-to-late June.

With Fairbanks' editorial hand more than half a continent away, he turned to Bret Harte, who agreed to read with a critical eye. Having made fun of both the pilgrims and the Holy Land, Twain wanted to be certain that he had done it stylishly and without vulgarity. Harte, despite his busy schedule, which included editing the *Overland Monthly,* a new literary magazine, made careful marginal annotations in the manuscript. In response, Twain cut about sixty-five pages. To return the favor, Twain gave Harte for the *Overland*'s first issue an extract of Harte's choosing from the manuscript, the first of four the *Overland* published. Considerably better known than Twain and better paid for his literary work, Harte had done the generous thing. The two men found ample time for dinner and drinks together, including a Lick House "State Banquet" for which Twain created a burlesque menu. With his large manuscript in hand, intending to "reduce it at sea," he booked passage for his return to New York. Hartford and Elmira were prominently on his mind. Instead of sailing at the end of June, though, he postponed departure to present a new lecture, this one based almost literally on his description of Venice in *Modern Pilgrim's Progress and Cruise of the* Quaker City. He did not want to forgo an opportunity to make some easy money.

On July 6, 1868, Twain sailed on the SS *Montana,* to take the *Henry Chauncey* again on the eastern side of the Isthmus for the return to New York. He experienced for the first time a celebrity courtesy. The steamship line would not take his money, an indication of how high he had risen in San Franciscan esteem. Crossing the Isthmus by train now took only six hours. As he sailed northward, he added ideas and observations to his notebook. They reinforced his preoccupation with the account of a dream told to him by Ned Wakeman, the loquacious captain whose blustery nautical obscenities had delighted him in late 1867 and whom he had seen again on his voyage to San Francisco in April. Twain soon began the first of many attempts to transform the story into "Captain Stormfield's Visit to Heaven." On the voyage back, as on the voyage to San Francisco, he experimented with two other long, never-to-be-finished narratives. He felt "in splendid condition," and by the start of August he was in the familiar comfort of New York's Westminster Hotel.

He did not rest long, though. At the end of the first week in August he went to Hartford to be close to his publisher for the final edit. He still expected *Modern Pilgrim's Progress and Cruise of the Quaker City* to be published in December. On August 21 he at last went, by slow train which he had mistaken for an express, to spend the weekend in Elmira as Charley Langdon's guest. Charley and Jervis Langdon greeted him, the former with his fingers crossed, worried that Twain might not know how to conduct himself in proper society. After all, his sister Olivia would be at home.

3.

The Samuel Clemens/Mark Twain who arrived in Elmira in late August 1868 was preceded by a growing national reputation for wit and irreverence. He was a minor celebrity of the sort to which Americans in general had a great attraction, a writer whose work could be counted on to provide a high quotient of entertainment in relation to the amount of intellectual concentration required. Humor eased his entry into the consciousness of a generally non-self-critical public, which appreciated satirical criticism mainly at someone else's expense. Generally, his was a winning formula, but not in all households. It did not, for example, necessarily sit well with the Nook Farm puritans. The Langdons were equally sober Christians, devoted to good works and walking in the path of the Lord. This was a visit and a visitor about whom they at best would have had mixed feelings.

Outside the Langdon family, Elmira, as a social and corporate community, was happy to receive Mark Twain. Within twenty-four hours of his arrival, the *Elmira Advertiser* reported that it was hoped that the Langdons' guest, who had "already attained a great notoriety in California as a writer and editor," would be induced to give a lecture at the Opera House during his stay." The newspaper was unaware that Twain's schedule required that he leave early the next week, accompanied by Charley, to pay a visit to Mary Fairbanks in Cleveland, whence he would finally go on to St. Louis to visit his mother. During the *Quaker City* voyage he "had established a close fellowship with CHARLES LANGDON of this city," the *Advertiser* reported. In fact, he had not. At most he had gradually tolerated the cub's occasional presence and grown moderately fond of him.

The impending visit was made additionally nerve-wracking for Charley by a telegram Twain had sent: "Train stops every fifteen minutes and stays three quarters of an hour, figure out when it will arrive and meet me." When

Charley did, at a point fifteen miles from the city, he found a disheveled, badly dressed, heavily smoking Twain, who cursed the train's slowness and himself for having been misled into thinking it was an express that would get him to Elmira at dinnertime rather than midnight. Seeing Charley's reaction to his clothes, Twain assured his host that he had in his bag a "brand-new outfit" and planned to buy a hat in Elmira early the next morning. No matter Twain's level of confidence, often as much self-defensive anger as self-assurance, he knew that in the Langdon world appearances were important. In the Langdons' eyes, he was an uneducated westerner who had little to no money, a precarious future as a freelance writer, and, as a self-defined, hard-living, rough-talking iconoclast, had made his reputation, such as it was, satirizing biblical literalism and pious people.

Heretofore, travel and dislocation had been essential to Twain's livelihood. The publication of *Innocents Abroad* might alter that. From as early as 1858, the period of his passion for Laura Wright, he had held in dialectical tension the side of him that desired a domestic bed and the side deeply attracted to ships' bunks and hotel rooms. That Twain found himself convinced, perhaps by the end of the weekend, that he was totally in love with Olivia Langdon, probably came as only a minor surprise to him. She had been on his mind since at least their two or three meetings in New York during the last Christmas–New Year season. For the Langdons, though, the quick transformation of Twain from Charley's friend to Olivia's suitor came as a shock. It also came as a shock to Olivia. She was almost exactly ten years younger than Twain, and, unlike most Victorian young women, she did not have marriage particularly in mind, though she had a local suitor, a hardware store employee.

When Livy and her cousin Harriet Lewis welcomed their guest, they felt relieved that he was neither awesomely impressive nor offensively boorish. Attractive, lively, quick to see and enjoy a joke, Twain had, Harriet thought, potential as a companion for herself. In the next few days, the writer and the two cousins did sightseeing in Elmira, talked engagingly, and sang at the piano. "Mr. C. had a very sweet tenor voice," Harriet observed. Twain either did not notice or did not care that, like his mother, Olivia did not get his jokes. She seemed, in fact, to have no sense of humor at all. Aware that Twain only had eyes for Livy—"But alas—I soon discovered . . . that . . . Mr. C evidently greatly preferred her sense to my nonsense"— Harriet hinted that their guest might very well propose, and soon left the field to her cousin. That Livy would be an appropriate wife for Mark Twain would have seemed questionable to her parents. And much of the emotional focus of the family had for a long time been on Livy's health.

Born on November 27, 1845, Livy was the first natural child of Olivia Lewis Langdon and Jervis Langdon, both native New Yorkers. Married in 1832, the couple had adopted a four-year-old orphan, Susan Dean, in 1840. Five years later, Livy was born; four years after that, Charles. With a sharp mind for business and a firm but considerate manner in negotiation, Jervis Langdon, born in 1809, had prospered as a storekeeper and a lumber merchant in Ithaca, New York. After moving in 1845 to Elmira, a growing railroad hub and county seat in south central New York that was also a prospering agricultural and small industrial center, Langdon had given up shopkeeping and added a coal company to his lumber interests, two businesses that went well together. Elmira had cultural and educational aspirations. A city of about sixteen thousand in 1868, it had an active Protestant elite, much of it tempered Republican by the fires of national division, with sufficient intellectual curiosity to welcome new ideas brought by magazines, books, and lecturers. All in all, it was an attractive city beginning to absorb the changes of the industrial revolution at the cusp of the Gilded Age.

Jervis Langdon was one of Elmira's richest residents, with a fortune far from immense in comparison to those of New York's barons but which provided a handsome level of comfort and security. A stout, good-looking man of medium height, he carried his achievements lightly. Unlike his daughter, he had a sense of humor. As a host, he was generous and hospitable. As a father, he provided a stable home and opportunities for his children, a man with the means and desire to support handsomely those he loved, an exemplary Victorian patriarch who taught by example. Olivia Lewis Langdon, small, thin, with a serious, pretty look that her daughter inherited, ran her husband's domestic life, and with his prosperity came a household of servants to manage as well as children. Between 1862 and 1865 the Langdons established themselves in a well-located but small mansion on land that occupied a square city block at the corner of Church and Main Streets, close to downtown.

Before and during the war, the Langdons had combined their Christian beliefs and political views by supporting abolitionist causes. On a straight railroad run from southern Pennsylvania to the Canadian border, Elmira's citizens helped funnel runaway slaves out of the reach of federal law. Active in charitable causes from education to support of the poor, the Langdons made sizable contributions to the Independent Congregational Church, a center of abolitionist sentiment, which had been founded in 1846 when the Langdons and others left the Presbyterian Church because of its refusal to condemn slavery. Their church's independent-minded pastor, Thomas Beecher, had become a close friend, and well-known abolitionist leaders, including Frederick Douglass, had been guests in the Langdon home at a time when it would have been rare for a prominent white family to host a black visitor. Like the Hartford Nook Farm residents, the Langdons also supported the temperance movement, prison reform, and rights for women, particularly suffrage.

Cosseted by a loving, principled family, Olivia, nicknamed Livy to distinguish her from her mother, was from childhood the beneficiary of her parents' enlightened ideas and of Elmira's cultural resources. In 1850, at age five, she was enrolled in Miss Thurston's Seminary, which her adopted sister Susan attended and where she remained until 1858. A serious girls' school, it taught the usual range of subjects but also mathematics and science. The Bible had an honored place in the curriculum, science and religion happily aligned for liberal Protestants attempting to be both sincere believers and scientifically literate. At home, the Langdons hosted Elmira Academy of Science meetings, at which experts reported the latest findings to gatherings of a hundred or so. With a strong commitment to education and equity for women, they transferred Livy, at thirteen, to the preparatory division of Elmira Female College, of which Jervis Langdon was a patron, apparently the first college in the United States chartered to grant bachelor's degrees to women. A serious student, she was excited by her favorite authors and eager for information and learning. Like her parents, she had no interest in heterodox lessons; her education existed to reinforce the values of her Victorian Protestant world. Female minds and talents were to be developed for the home and its communal extensions. Thinking beyond or outside the conventional boundaries was not part of the curriculum. What the Langdons hoped for their daughter was a useful education, a marriage with the virtues of their own, and a happy life as a wife and mother.

In 1861, sixteen-year-old Livy became ill with a disease that sapped her strength, kept her in bed for long periods, and required that she withdraw from school. It sent her and her parents in search of a cure to various restorative establishments, including the highly regarded Elmira Water Cure, run by two friends of the family, and then, over a six-year period, to sanitariums in Washington, D.C., and New York City. What exactly Livy's illness was is unclear. According to an account Twain developed years later, the sixteen-year-old had taken a fall while ice-skating that resulted in partial paralysis, from which she was cured by a faith healer six years later. A skeptic about many things, he was led by his skepticism about the medical profession to alternative forms of healing, and he needed a narrative to give shape and significance to Livy's medical history. He preferred one that implied that she had ultimately risen, by some destiny that guided both of them, from her sickbed into his arms. The only verifiable element in his account is that she was, at a point late in her illness, attended by a faith healer. It may be that her condition was psychosomatic, an instance of the widespread phenomenon of Victorian young women withdrawing from the world for unspecified emotional reasons with serious physical symptoms, often referred to as neurasthenia. It may be that her illness was organic. Perhaps she indeed had a disease of the spine, such as Pott's disease, which has recently been suggested: an illness in which chronic back pain and stiffness lead to partial paralysis. Perhaps she had in fact injured her spine in a fall. Without magnetic resonance imaging and CAT scans, the Victorians were even more helpless than later generations to diagnose or cure back pain.

In May 1860, Hartford's Isabella Hooker had Livy for a roommate at Dr. Silas Gleason and Dr. Rachel Brooks Gleason's well-known Elmira Water Cure establishment. Livy, she noted, was "in very delicate health . . . living on her nerves instead of her muscle." In 1862 Livy was again a patient at the Gleasons', at a sanitarium in Washington, D.C., and at the Institute of Swedish Movement Cure in New York, which emphasized specific muscle and bone exercises with aggressive hand manipulations of muscle and especially bone, later to be thought of as chiropractic. The institute also favored the immobilization of patients by traction and braces as potential cure for diseases associated with the spine. It was a movement that Livy, her husband, and their children would again turn to more than thirty years later.

Thin, almost emaciated, seventeen-year-old Livy, who could hardly walk, kept a commonplace book and read as much as she could. In June

1864 she returned to Elmira, slightly better but still mostly confined to bed. In November, the faith healer of Twain's account, Dr. James Rogers Newton, came to the house. Apparently he played some role in getting her out of bed, probably with emotional support and persuasion. Over the next fifteen months she gradually began to walk again. In January 1865 her mother remarked that for the first time Livy "bore her weight alone on her crutches." One morning in February "Livy breakfasted with the family. The first time she has done so in *three years*." Soon she was spending time in the sitting room. In April 1866, she went to church *"for the first time in more than 5 years."* In October, she returned to the institute for additional but brief treatment. A year later, still frail and never again to be without an aura of fragility, she was moderately active though widely perceived, especially by her family, as having delicate health. Even they recognized, though, that she was amazingly strong and resilient as a personality, with a character both saddened and strengthened by her ordeal.

Jervis Langdon and his wife loved their daughter with an intensity increased by her six years of misery. But as long as Livy did everything moderately, all would be well, the doctors assured them. The young girl had friends nearby, particularly Emily Nye, her cousin Harriet Lewis, her closest friend from childhood, Clara Spaulding, and Alice Hooker, who came from Hartford for long visits. Livy soon resumed her education informally, at home, with tutors such as the handsome Darius Ford, professor of physical science and astronomy at Elmira College, whom Alice and Livy delighted in and tittered over. She also studied French, read constantly, and participated in a Shakespeare study group. On Sundays she joined her family in church attendance, sometimes twice, and every day in prayers at home. Livy's recovery, along with their continued prosperity, confirmed the family's strong religious faith.

After just a weekend, dazzled by his hosts' hospitality and their daughter's attractions, Twain wrote his mother that the Langdons were "the pleasantest family" he had ever known. His brief visit extended into an almost two-week stay. Twain used the additional time in Elmira to propose marriage, to which Livy's answer was an unequivocal no. However, she did not demand either her suitor's departure or his silence. Whatever her reasons for rejecting his proposal, he accepted her terms without argument. But he needed a courtship strategy, and she provided a conventional one that was often the platonic prelude to a romantic involvement. She suggested that he think of her as his sister. He soon addressed her, in a long letter, as "My Honored 'Sister,' " the uncomplaining and undeserving suppliant eager to be taught to be more worthy if only she would do the teaching. "I do not regret that I have loved you, still love & shall always love you," he began. "I accept the situation, uncomplainingly, hard as it is, [for] it is better to have loved & lost you than that my life should have remained forever the blank it was before. . . . I worship you. . . . But no more of this." In obedience to her injunction, his tongue and pen would now be silent on this subject. If only she would agree to write to him "from time to time— texts from the New Testament, if nothing else occurs to you . . . or extracts from your Book of Sermons—*anything,* whatever," even, if she desired, "dissertations on the sin of smoking." Whatever she suggested, he would consider; whatever she ordered, he would obey. He was available to be reclaimed. What more fertile ground for reclamation than a man who had so many bad habits that undoubtedly one or more could be removed by a reformative angel? Who could be a more worthy subject for spiritual revival than a man who wanted to be saved?

4.

When he left with Charley for Cleveland on the morning of September 8, 1868, Twain's greatest concern was whether Livy would respond to his letter at all. The issues, the strategies, had been laid out, the bait, the hook, the hopes, dangled. He felt it likely that if she came to love him she would accept some combination of who he was and what she could help him to be. His bad habits he was willing to eliminate, or at least alter, even his addiction to smoking. He was prepared, once again, to give up drinking entirely. His character he could not change, though he believed that deep down it was anchored by a good heart. Friends, he was sure, would testify to this. Despite his adventuresome western life, he was not so far outside the pale of respectable Christian orthodoxy that he could not be brought back in, even if just barely, with Livy's help. That was the key. Her Christian faith almost required, if approached the right way, that she help him become a better Christian, and the rhetoric of a dialectic between them in which she would be the teacher, he the student, had the potential to shape a rope that would bind them together. Once Livy loved him, he surmised, she would commit herself to him, whatever the practical impediments, providing that she took him for sincere both in his spiritual striving and in his efforts to earn the income to support a home. And if Livy committed herself to him, her parents would not be far behind.

In Cleveland, Fairbanks offered encouragement, which in his anxious state he needed desperately. To have status as Livy's suitor he required additional literary success, which his book might provide. He also needed a larger, more reliable income, the most obvious source of which would be lecturing. The American Literary Bureau in New York and a midwestern agent had arranged a series of more than twenty speaking engagements, to start in Cleveland in November, the subject "Americans in the Old World." Under the Fairbanks roof he tinkered with his lecture manuscript, happy to have his host's suggestions for revision. On the defensive about the lecture's comic tone and sardonic anecdotes, he explained to Fairbanks, who preferred that he be more serious, that he was indeed being paid to entertain. "I *must* not preach to a select few in my audience." What the people who invited him to lecture asked of him was "to *relieve* the heaviness of their didactic courses." "In accepting the contract I am just the same as *giving my word* that I will do as they ask." His livelihood was based on humor, no matter how much he and others, like Fairbanks and soon Livy, desired him to be a serious writer for the literary elite.

After two weeks with Twain in Cleveland, Charley returned to Elmira. Twain said good-bye to him with a more secure sense of connection than he had had before. A letter from Livy had come, responding to one of his, and it gave him hope. It contained not only gentle words but also a photograph, for which he had not even dared to ask. That it had come unbidden meant much, and Livy, inexperienced though she was, undoubtedly knew that when a young woman voluntarily sends a photograph to a man who has proposed to her she is signaling that she wishes him to continue his pursuit. Thrilled "with the happy surprise the picture brought," he thanked her for the kindness of her words. To her offer to pray for him daily, he responded that he would now say "these grave words, which, once said, cannot be recalled . . . I *will* 'pray with you,' as you ask, [for] you must surely have some faith that it will not necessarily be useless, else you would not have suggested it." The sinner could be saved, which meant, for Twain, that the suitor could be made eligible.

Having been declined by Livy, he was melancholy and irritable, especially on arriving in St. Louis. With his feelings so strongly located in Elmira, St. Louis seemed both meaningless and troublesome. Apparently he confided to friends of the family that he wanted advice. "I am desperately in love with the most beautiful girl. So beautiful. Unfortunately very rich. She is quite an invalid. I have proposed & been refused a dozen times. . . . I know I'm too rough—knocking around the world. . . . I never had wish or time to bother with women, & I can give that girl the purest, best love any man can ever give her. I can make her well and happy." St. Louis he abhorred. "There is something in my deep hatred of St. Louis that will hardly let me appear cheery even at my mother's own fireside. Nobody knows what a ghastly infliction it is on me to visit St. Louis. I am afraid I do not always disguise it, either."

That St. Louis was his mother's and sister's home seemed to make no difference. In fact, that was part of the problem, especially since he had found a new family that he was eager to join. Just as Anson Burlingame had proved an attractive father figure, which John Marshall Clemens had never been, so now the Langdon family had the potential to provide a wife and a father simultaneously. Wherever she resided, his mother had no important place in his present and future life. Sam Clemens had weaned himself of his dependency on her when he had gone west. By 1868 his visits were few and far between, and she would come alive to him again only as the mother of his Hannibal childhood. The previous January, Hannibal had been on his mind. "I have been thinking of school-days at Dawson's, & trying to recall the old faces of that ancient time," he wrote to Will Bowen. "But I cannot place them very well—they have faded out from my treacherous memory, for the most part, & passed away." The Hannibal that became so available to him seven years later, when his circumstances had changed, he could not recall in any detail now. He began a short story set in his childhood about a lovesick young Tom Sawyer–like boy who loses his eight-year-old sweetheart in his attempt to impress her. At a point soon after, when he falls in love with an older girl, the story stops.

In late September, on his way back to New York from the Midwest, he returned to Elmira for a twenty-four-hour visit. Welcomed by the Langdons, he either calculatedly or impulsively confided to Charley that he was in love with his sister. Shocked and angry, Charley asked Twain to leave, though he soon relented. He was concerned about how his parents might react, especially his father, whose poor health was an increasing family concern. Jervis Langdon was ill enough for Twain soon to write, "I could not be blind to the truth that he needed quiet & repose more than anything else, & I don't carry much quiet among my baggage." Actually, Langdon liked Twain, perhaps, among other reasons, for the noisy amusements he did carry in his baggage. He also may have begun to sense that the visitor had a special relationship with his daughter, whose happiness had the highest priority for him. His case with Livy, Twain soon wrote to Fairbanks, bore "just a *little* pleasanter aspect" than it did when he had been in Cleveland. "*I am just about* that much more cheerful over it, you know."

Still suffering from a bad cold and warned by Livy of a relapse if he should travel prematurely, he nevertheless honored his agreement to visit for only twenty-four hours. However, when he and Charley were getting into the backseat of the wagon taking them to the station, the horse bolted. Since the seat had not been locked securely in place, they both fell over backward onto the cobblestones. "Charley [fell] in all sorts of ways and I [lighted] exactly on my head in the gutter and [broke] my neck in eleven different places." He "lay there about four or five minutes, completely insensible." The alarmed family immediately brought them into the house. Obviously, he could not leave now, he happily discovered, and he stayed another day. "Charley's head was quite badly cut," Livy wrote to Alice Hooker. "Mr Clemens was stunned—It did not prove to be serious in either case—We all enjoyed Mr Clemens stay with us very much indeed."

5.

For much of October 1868 Twain stayed in Hartford, working with Bliss on *Innocents Abroad*, extending and expanding his Hartford acquaintanceships, and preparing his lecture, "The American Vandal Abroad," for the start of his lecture tour in mid-November. "I am here, getting out a book," he wrote to Burlingame. When Bliss made the case that *Innocents Abroad* could not "be illustrated profusely enough" in time for December publication, Twain agreed that lavish illustration "sandwiched in with the text" would make the book more marketable. But his income since midsummer had been only the small sums paid for occasional letters to the *Alta* and other newspapers. Fortunately, since late August, his hotel bills had been minimal. In Hartford, he stayed with Bliss; in Elmira, Cleveland, and St. Louis, he was a guest at private homes. In New York he mostly stayed with the Slotes. If he had gotten one thousand dollars from Bliss before sailing for San Francisco, it was long gone. So, too, it seems, were his California lecture fees. Though he expected lecturing income in the near future, the postponement of his book's publication also postponed royalties. Yet it seemed in a good cause, and his Hartford stay had value not only because of Nook Farm conviviality but because he at last met Joe Twichell, a Congregational minister three years his junior, a slim, tall, athletic man, an enthusiastic hiker and an excellent orator, whose parsonage, a short distance from Nook Farm, was across the street from Bliss's house.

Within a week of meeting, a bond of friendship developed, with a respect and warmth that delighted both. It included Twichell's wife, Harmony, who was two years older than Livy. The two couples were to have a long, interesting, and parallel history, Twain and Twichell almost doubles, Livy and Harmony almost sisters. Suddenly Twain was spending a great deal of time with his new friends at teas, at dinners, at parties, on rides in the country, at church events, on visits to the American Asylum for the Deaf, and in Twichell's study, where the sensitive, liberal Twichell provided the model of a flexible minister more interested in human fellowship than in mechanical duties. If Twain had been able to fulfill his youthful desire to be a minister, Twichell seemed the sort of minister he would have liked to have been. "[He] apologized to me for talking so much about religion," Twain wrote to Livy, calculatingly. "He would not have done me that wrong if he had known how much I respect him for it & how beautiful his strong love for his subject made his words seem." Twain was now at the most Christian moment in his life, eager to demonstrate to Livy that the sinner could be saved by her ministrations. The minister had said to him, so he told her, "You do not know what it is to have a pure, sinless, noble Christian woman pray daily for you." Yes, Twain swore, he had used exactly those words. "I said, 'I *do* know it—my sister.' " Not good enough, Twichell answered, assuming he meant Pamela. Only a wife would do.

It could not have escaped Twain's notice that having a friendship with a respectable Presbyterian minister might help him with the Langdon family. "Twichell is splendid," he wrote to Livy. "[He puts] other people's comfort before his own—& thus reminds me of you." Gradually in his letters it became safe to reveal other aspects of himself, even to include an occasional joke, though he still recognized the importance of caution. "I never put a joke in a letter to her without feeling a pang," he confessed. Livy adored Elizabeth Barrett Browning's poetry, particularly "Aurora Leigh."

Twain found it turgid and obscure. "Get your Browning ready," he wrote to her, "for lo, I come like a lamb to the slaughter!" And to explain indirectly how he desired her to understand his teasing, he remarked that he had gotten "mother Fairbanks in a stew again." . . . "I like to tease her because I [he next wrote "love" and then crossed it out] like her so."

By the end of October 1868, *Innocents Abroad* was ready for "the engravers and electrotypers, at last," he told his *Alta* readers, and on target for March publication. At the end of the month, he accompanied Twichell to a Yale College reunion in New Haven, where Twichell arranged to have him made an honorary member of the Scroll and Key society. At the end of the first week in November he returned to Cleveland, where he stayed with the Fairbankses, and on November 17 he gave his lecture "American Vandal Abroad," the message of which was that even American vandals should travel since the experience had the potential to rub out their prejudices and broaden their views. Speaking, as he was always to do, from a memorized script, an early departure of someone in the audience dislocated him and he could not remember his place. The audience began to titter, then laugh. When he told them he had lost his place and would someone please help him, the audience laughed even more, as if the incident were part of the performance. They did not believe he had any place to lose. Solon Severance, his *Quaker City* friend, rose and reminded him of where he had stopped. Even his missteps, Twain realized, could be transformed into purposeful jokes. "Made a *splendid* hit last night & am the 'lion' to-day. Awful rainy, sloppy night," he wrote to his mother, "but there were 1,200 people present . . . house *full*. I *captured* them, if I *do* say it myself."

For the next five months, and then from November 1869 through January 1870, "simply lecturing for societies," as he described it to his mother, "at $100 a pop"—though better-known lecturers received up to twice that amount—would dominate Twain's professional life. He could give the same lecture night after night in different cities to audiences more or less happy to have his company for the evening, a rate of performance return that writing could not match unless he had a best-selling book. He was soon to know the eastern and midwestern lecture circuit all too well, from Pittsburgh, Cleveland, Indianapolis, Detroit, and Davenport to New York, Ohio, and Illinois, among the stops in the tour of more than forty lectures in the winter of 1868–69, and from Providence, Boston, Brooklyn,

Philadelphia, and Washington, D.C., to Portland, Maine, in the East Coast tour of more than fifty lectures in 1869–70. When he did not stay with private hosts, he attempted to rest at the best hotel available, often enough one not sufficiently comfortable to allow him to sleep, especially since eager fans assumed that he was at their disposal night and day. Exhaustion, tedium, and irritability were inevitable, and avoiding staleness was a challenge. Though he did not always satisfy critics, on the whole reviewers praised and audiences crowded his appearances. But even more than before, lecturing seemed an insufferable way to make a living. The income was handsome, but, he complained, the expenses were "something frightful," even when he stayed at private homes. It took about half his fees to cover his travel and other costs.

In winter 1868–69 two things kept him going: the expectation that *The Innocents Abroad,* still titled "The New Pilgrim's Progress," would be published in March, and the hope that Livy would accept his proposal. The former, which had seemed a certainty, gradually became less so. Bliss constantly offered grounds for delay—to avoid competing with another of his books, to catch the market at the right time, to make certain a full subscription sales staff was in place. In February 1869 he suggested that, since Twain was considering visiting California, the American Publishing Company take responsibility for proofreading. Twain declined, remembering how badly Webb had proofread *The Celebrated Jumping Frog.* It took him some time, though, to realize that the same letter stated between the lines that the book would not be ready for March publication despite the contractual requirement. And there were too many engravings that still needed to be prepared for electrotyping for proofs to be available for some months yet.

When Twain visited Hartford for ten days in March 1869, he discovered that the book had now been put on indefinite delay: some of the directors of the American Publishing Company had raised moral scruples. As Bliss explained to him, or so Twain recollected almost forty years later, "The majority of them were of the opinion that there were places in it of a humorous character." The real issue, however, seemed to be humor directed at Christian superstition and hypocrisy. Twain was exasperated and furious. Apparently one director begged that the company be released from its contract. "I said I wouldn't. . . . Then I warned Bliss that he must get to work or I should make trouble." Eager for anticipated profits, Bliss told the directors that if they decided against publication he would, at his own expense, bring out the book as an independent publisher. The directors caved. In April, while working on proofs, Twain proposed three possible titles, "Crusade of the Innocents," "The Innocents Abroad," and "The Exodus of the Innocents." "It is a *readable* book, I know—because I wrote it myself. And it is going to be a mighty handsome book—as your letter-press & pictures show, plainly enough."

When in July Bliss raised the possibility of another snag, Twain angrily responded, "Every one of [these delays] has had for its object the furthering of the Am. Pub. Company's interest, & to compass this, *my* interests have been entirely disregarded." His patience at an end, he threatened legal action. At last, at the end of July 1869, the American Publishing Company brought out *Innocents Abroad; or, The New Pilgrims' Progress,* seven months later than the initial target date. Twain immediately and for the rest of his life insisted that it had been thirteen months late. A little before mid-August, with a copy finally in hand, he was proud and happy. "It is the very handsomest book of the season," he told Bliss. "You ought to be proud of your work. It will sell." A well-known minor writer was about to become a national celebrity.

Not coincidentally, he was also about to become formally engaged. It had taken him only three months, from late August to late November 1868, to persuade Livy to commit to him. How great an asset Twichell's friendship was soon became clear. Whether or not Twain believed anyone's prayers but Livy's made a difference, it helped that he could write from Hartford, "In the midst of the solemn night . . . [Twichell] prayed fervently for my conversion, & that your love & mine might grow until it was made *perfect* love by the approving spirit of God." That a Hartford minister of sterling Christian character bestowed his admiring friendship on Twain testified to Twain's good heart and redeemable soul.

In Elmira, Harriet Lewis provided a confidential ear into which Livy could whisper. When Twain visited, she even conspired to create the impression that she was Twain's romantic interest in order to take the pressure off Livy. Shy and anxious, Livy feared that if local newspapers connected her with Twain, it would cause her and her parents embarrassment. A "well-balanced, pleasant, spirited, excellent girl," Harriet facilitated their privacy, and once Livy committed herself to frequent letters, Twain had reason to think she was on his hook. At the start, he later told

Pamela, "She said she never could or would love me—but she set herself the task of making a Christian of me. I said"—though indeed it is unlikely he said it to Livy—"she would succeed, but that in the meantime she would unwittingly dig a matrimonial pit & end by tumbling into it." His own courtship letters were brilliant performances, encompassing a full range of tones and tactics, from passionate joy to humble supplication, from self-deprecation to overwrought praise, from heartfelt moral and religious seriousness to chatty information and occasional jokes. Hers, to his initial surprise and then total acceptance, were boringly serious mini-sermons without the semblance of a joke or a touch of literary talent.

"She thinks about me all the time, & informs me of it with Miltonic ponderosity," he wrote to Twichell. "She has a most engaging commercial reliability & promptness allied to her stately commercial style of correspondence. . . . Never any whining in it, or any nonsense, but wisdom till you can't rest. . . . In her sermons she excels. They are full of a simple trust & confidence, & touched with a natural pathos, that would win a savage. Ours is a funny correspondence. . . . My letters are an ocean of love in a storm—hers an ocean of love in the majestic repose of a great calm." To his amusement, she spelled abominably. It was, he saw, to his advantage that she was a mono-quilled correspondent, concerned entirely about his soul, deeply troubled by whether or not she could commit herself to a man who was not intent on personal salvation through Jesus, who had not been elevated by religious experience into transcendent belief.

When, before Thanksgiving 1868, he gave a charity lecture for the benefit of an Elmira volunteer fire company of which Charley was a member, he thought he saw "the first faint symptom" of Livy's commitment. With the Langdons in the audience, he performed poorly, his mind on his chances rather than his lecture. That Livy did not approve of what she considered his low literary level probably added to his nervousness as well. "Anybody who could convince her," he told Fairbanks, "that I was not a humorist would secure her eternal gratitude! She thinks a humorist is something perfectly awful."

Alone with Livy in the Langdon sitting room, her beauty and moral earnestness accented by her blue dress, which seemed to him always afterward the color of purity, he proposed again. She did not refuse. His heart in his mouth, he went to the Langdons to request her hand in marriage. Apparently they were stunned, though they likely knew of his interest from the time of his first visit in August. Mrs. Langdon had made it a point that Livy not accept her son and his friend's invitation for Livy to visit Cleveland with them. She seemed to Twain the more formidable of the parents, and her aura of emotional self-sufficiency he experienced as aloofness. Jervis Langdon, though, had given him discreet signs of personal goodwill and even amiability from the start. "I *do* wish you were here," he wrote to Fairbanks. "I have so suddenly sprung upon them, & they are bewildered. And yet they are (sensibly) more concerned about what I am likely to be in the future than what I have been in the past." Mother to mother, Mrs. Langdon wrote to Mrs. Fairbanks for her opinion "of him as a *man;* what kind of man he *has been,* and what the man he now is, or is to become." They did not doubt that he had a good heart and a great literary gift. And he had been undergoing a moral renovation. But "does this change, so desirably commenced make of an immoral man a moral one, as the *world* looks at men?—or—does this change make of one, who has been entirely a man of the world, different in this regard, that he resolutely aims to enter upon a new, because a Christian life?"

Eager to promote the marriage, Mary Fairbanks and others provided the anxious mother with a range of answers to her questions. The vetting process of course caused him anguish, and her parents' permission was essential. Langdon pointed out to him, accurately, that he was "an almost entirely unknown person" on the East Coast. He would have to provide third-party assurances, at least for the record, testimonials about his character from those who had known him in his six years in Nevada and California. Soon Twain provided a list of referees, and Langdon directly queried some of his own San Francisco contacts. "I never yet made an individual a friend, *called* him my friend, & lost him," Twain assured Livy. If accurate, it was not quite relevant. All the while, he knew that he had two great assets: "They all like me, & they can't help it." And Livy had already revealed that she loved him.

He hoped all the responses would be favorable, but he had reason to suspect otherwise: "Much of my conduct on the Pacific Coast," he wrote to Langdon, "was not of a character to recommend me to the respectful regard of a high eastern civilization, but it was not considered blameworthy there, perhaps. We go according to our lights. . . . I never did anything mean, false or criminal." He provided the names of six people he thought would be impartial, including two of his San Francisco minister acquaintances. Nervous, he then submitted an additional ten, this time only of people he thought he could count on for favorable responses. By mid-January 1869 the replies were trickling in, among them "I would rather bury a daughter of mine than have her marry such a fellow" and "Oh, Mark is rather erratic, but I consider him harmless." Letters from loyalists like Joe Goodman were helpful. "The friends that I had referred to in California said with one accord," Twain wrote six months later to Charles Warren Stoddard, "that I got drunk oftener than was necessary & that I was wild & Godless, idle, lecherous & a discontented & unsettled rover & they could not recommend any girl of high character & social position to marry me—but as I had already said all that about myself beforehand there was nothing shocking or surprising about it to the family." Of course he had not quite said that at all. In the end, Langdon tossed aside the negative letters. He liked and trusted Twain, and his daughter loved him. "I can state as an absolute *truth*," Twain wrote to Mrs. Langdon, "that only one person in all the world really *knows* me, & that is Miss Langdon. To her I must refer you."

Testimonials from people like Mary Fairbanks, as well as their own experience, convinced the Langdons that Twain had in essence a good heart and was consequently susceptible to Christian renovation. They hesitantly assumed that his love for Livy and his evident sincerity in desiring to please her was not for the sake of the relationship but for the sake of his own soul. This would create a Christian life. Over and over again in their letters Livy provided the sermon, Twain the appropriate response. "I am upon the right path—I shall succeed, I hope. Men as lost as I have found a Savior, & why not I?" But he would not succeed, he argued, without her help. She also was, so to speak, his savior. "I *can* be a Christian—I *shall* be a Christian." His focus was on what he was "*likely* to be" rather than on what he had been. Like an actor becoming, temporarily, the character he is acting, sincerity and performance became indistinguishable.

When practical issues arose, he assured the anxious parents that he would provide for Livy as well as love her, though the principals were well aware that a class and economic gap, as well as a religious one, separated Livy and her suitor. The Langdons were remarkably calm, even indifferent, about the class issue, perhaps because they believed Twain's genius transcended such distinctions. Two brilliant women the young couple admired, one of them Mrs. Fairbanks, had "married away down below them," Twain pointed out to Livy, "& it would be hard to convince me that they did not love first & *think* afterward." The money issue was more sensitive. "I do not wish to marry Miss Langdon for her wealth, & she knows that perfectly well," he wrote to Mrs. Langdon. It would be all right with him if her parents cut her off without a penny, a bravado at least partly sustained by his certainty that they would never do so. The two of them, he assured the Langdons, could live on a modest annual income, for neither of them was "much afflicted with a mania for money-getting." It was an odd claim, more tactical than true. Livy had not the slightest concern about money because her generous father was wealthy. And Twain, of course, had spent a good part of his western years preoccupied with getting rich.

On the last day of 1868, his confidence high, he felt the coming year "the gladdest that ever dawned" on him. The old year had done him good service. "It found me a waif, floating at random upon the sea of life, & it leaves me freighted with a good purpose, & blessed with a fair wind, a chart to follow, a port to reach," he reassured Livy. "It found me well-nigh a skeptic—it leaves me a believer. . . . If I forget all else [the old year] has done for me I shall still remember that it gave me your love, Livy, & turned my wandering feet toward the straight gate & the narrow way."

On February 4, 1869, the couple was officially engaged, and Twain could tell the world of his good fortune. Almost exactly one year later, in early February 1870, they were married in the Langdons' house in Elmira. Joe Twichell came from Hartford to co-officiate with Thomas Beecher. Two days later, in his own home, the bridegroom joyfully wrote to Will Bowen that his blocked memories of his Hannibal childhood had suddenly become accessible. "The fountains of my great deep are broken up & I have rained reminiscences for four and twenty hours." Livy, of course, was his audience. "The old life has swept before me like a panorama; the old days have trooped by in their old glory, again; the old faces have looked out of the mists of the past."

CHAPTER NINE

COMFORT

1 8 7 0 – 1 8 7 2

1.

The year between his formal engagement and his marriage in February 1870 was one of the busiest of his life. Almost ceaseless public appearances during the four-month winter lecture season were imperative. And something more, perhaps a year-round job with a title and salary, preferably with an ownership interest that would liberate him from being under an employer's thumb and would provide opportunity for profits. Neither Twain nor anyone in his circle had reason to think that he could earn his living exclusively as a writer, let alone the level of income necessary to support Livy in the style to which she was accustomed. Even if *Innocents Abroad* should be a financial success, his royalties could support them for a year or two at most unless he followed that success with another and then with more, which not even a self-confident writer could predict with certainty. Though they determined that they would live penuriously, Livy had no idea what that meant or what it would be like. Twain indeed knew from personal experience the discomfort of poverty, to which he had no intention of subjecting a wife. The Langdons made it clear he would have their support. He would not have to provide a stable home for her entirely on his own.

From November 1868 to March 1869 he rode the lecture circuit rails, climbing onto more than forty platforms to recite "The American Vandal Abroad." He repeated the experience in the 1869–70 lecture season, though he changed the lecture, for his sake more than for his audience's. When *Innocents Abroad* was published in July 1869, he felt he needed a presentation that did not draw heavily on the materials in the book. After a few trials, he returned to a revised version of his May 1868 Cooper Union lecture, "Our Fellow Savages of the Sandwich Islands." That seemed desirable, especially to James Redpath, founder and co-owner of the Boston Lyceum Bureau, the best-known central booking agency for lecture tours, who was eager to have his newest and now well-known lecturer take a fresh performance out onto the hustings. Twain and Redpath hit it off: Twain was impressed with Redpath's competence and honesty, Redpath with Twain's talent. In early spring 1869, the writer agreed to sign on with Redpath for the next lecture season, which associated him with Redpath's prestigious list and Boston's primacy. A clever impresario, Redpath usually had his full stable do tryout lectures in the Boston area. Then those in the "Star Course" appeared before audiences of 2,500 in Boston's Music Hall, which gave a verdict by which the lyceums around the country determined the lecture's commercial value. "This system," Twain later recalled, "gathered the whole tribe together in the city early in October, and we had a lazy and sociable time there for several weeks."

He had already met one of Redpath's stars, David Ross Locke, who lectured under the pseudonym "Petroleum Vesuvius Nasby." "His lecture was a volleying and sustained discharge of bull's eye hits, with the slave power and its Northern apologists for target, and his success was due to his matter, not his delivery," a lesson in opposites for Twain, who had begun to realize that he could have an audience in the palm of his hand by the effectiveness of his delivery, regardless of subject matter. In a series of newspaper articles for the *Toledo Blade*, Locke had created Nasby as a bigoted, ignorant clergyman, and refined his characterization into a satirically hilarious lecture, "Cussed be Canaan," attacking injustice and racial prejudice. A great hit in post–Civil War northeastern and midwestern America, he received three to four times per engagement what Twain earned. "He was a great, burly figure, uncouthly and provincially clothed, and he looked like a simple old farmer. . . . *'We are all descended from grandfathers!'* Then he went right on roaring to the end, tearing his ruthless way through the continuous applause and laughter."

To reach Hartford in time for a lecture in March 1869, Nasby traveled "two-thirds of a night and a whole day in a *cattle car.*" He went, Twain marveled, directly from his train to his performance. Afterward the two men talked "until after midnight," reminiscing about their experiences lecturing in the West. Then Twain, not Nasby, collapsed with fatigue. Nasby's energy seemed inexhaustible. Twain's own was not. It seemed to him that during four torturous months his bedroom was a noisy railway car in which he drifted "over the slowest railways" in America, "inexpressibly . . . drowsy . . . & dreary." His refrain to Livy in more than fifty letters composed in bouncing trains and badly lit hotel rooms was "How I long to have a home & never leave it!" A price he had to pay for his decade of wandering was to have to wander for a while more, though he had the sustaining consolation of a well-defined itinerary and purpose. Half his lecture fees still went to cover his expenses, but at least he was demonstrating to the Langdons that he was capable of hard, steady, and remunerative work.

And it was not all among strangers. In Cleveland, the Fairbankses and the Severances, among other *Quaker City* friends, provided affectionate hospitality. Mary Fairbanks was delighted with her protégé's progress, especially his impending marriage, though she still worried about his unrefined manners and inclination to say the wrong thing. In late 1868, the Cleveland connection took on new prominence when Mary's husband, Abel Fairbanks, co-owner of the *Herald,* seemed attracted to the possibility of Twain's buying an interest in the newspaper. Having for years observed editors at work, Twain, who did not want to be anybody's employee, thought that he was well suited to be an editor-writer-owner of a prominent newspaper. Journalism had been one of his trades. Writing was his profession; if he were a proprietor, he would be working for himself. Jervis Langdon agreed to supply the down payment for an ownership share, the remainder to be Twain's obligation, probably a loan from the seller as a condition of purchase. Langdon's would be a long-term loan, the terms of repayment to be determined at a later date and adjusted to whatever circumstances developed. To Twain's disappointment, Fairbanks' co-owner declined to sell any part of his share. Twain gave up the idea only to have it revived in April 1869 when it seemed possible Fairbanks might sell a piece of his own interest.

In the meantime, Twain had asked Joseph Hawley, the principal owner of the *Hartford Courant,* if Hawley would sell him an interest in that reputable newspaper. He and Livy would have been delighted to make Hartford their home. Neither possibility materialized, in the Cleveland case because of Fairbanks' dilatoriness, then because he raised the price; in Hartford because Hawley had no real interest in diluting his control, especially to a lightweight humorist. In the end, all Fairbanks had to offer was a job as the *Herald* political correspondent, which was of no interest to Twain. Hawley had no interest in Twain at all, treating him with what Twain thought "insultingly contemptuous indifference." But his new friend Nasby, soon after their all-night talk, weighed in with an offer for Twain to join him in editing the *Toledo Blade,* the weekly edition of which had a circulation of seventy-five thousand and a huge readership, though the discussion apparently never got to the detail of whether or not Twain, like Nasby, would be a part owner. When Twain went up to Boston with Nasby in mid-March 1869, and for much of the next month, he had the offer under consideration. In Boston he met Oliver Wendell Holmes. At the home of James Fields, the owner-editor of *Atlantic Monthly,* he was introduced to Henry James, Sr. When Annie Fields asked Twain where he lived, he answered, "I don't know where I live but I find letters directed to Elimir-y (*sic*) always reach me; if they are sent anywhere else, they don't."

Much of his time was divided between Hartford and Elmira. In Hartford, he and Bliss worked through delays in publication of *Innocents Abroad*. When in July it at last appeared, even the recalcitrant American Publishing Company board members began to appreciate the financial benefit of publishing a "mere" humorist. Well-trained subscription salesmen fanned out around the country with their multipaneled packets containing selected illustrations, brief samples from the text, and examples of the various bindings available, from cloth to deluxe leather. Circulars were widely distributed, and orders came thicker and faster than even Bliss had expected. Superlatives for the book and its author dominated the reviews, not only in New York, Hartford, Elmira, Cleveland, and San Francisco, not only from the pens of friends like Bret Harte, but in places with no home-town interest in vaunting a writer associated with their city and from newspapers with which Twain had no connection. Suddenly he was genuinely famous, "the prince of American humorists." The *Atlantic Monthly*'s young assistant editor, William Dean Howells, gave *Innocents Abroad* its imprimatur in the December issue. Under the impression that Fields had written the review, Twain stopped by to thank him, and he met Howells, the start of a lifelong friendship.

In December 1869, his first sales report indicated a cumulative five month's sale of 15,500 volumes, with another 6,000 books on order, producing gross receipts of $50,000 and $2,500 in royalties. It was a spectacular bestseller, though his boast to Livy that there had been "nothing like it since *Uncle Tom's Cabin*" was inaccurate. His Nook Farm friend's novel had sold 100,000 in five months, and he needed a sale equal to three times what had already been sold or ordered to equal the $10,000 flat fee he had turned down. "I like the circulars, I like the book, I like you & your style & your business vim," he wrote to Bliss when he received his first copy, "& believe the shebang will be a success." When, at the end of the year, his Hartford friends publicly assailed Hawley for having declined Twain's offer to buy an ownership interest, he felt "a malicious satisfaction to hear all this." Though revenge "is wicked, & unchristian & in every way unbecoming . . . it is powerful sweet, anyway," he wrote to Livy. He had long ago discovered and accepted that one of his greatest pleasures was to get revenge, preferably through the agencies of fact and fate, on people he believed had done him harm, even if he was mistaken.

In Elmira, he found that Livy also warmly anticipated the home that was now within reach. Her parents treated him graciously; Charley seemed reconciled; Mrs. Langdon continued to be calm and courtly. He also looked forward to Livy curbing his "little peevish spirit" and bridling his "irreverent tongue." Jokes got him into trouble, and if he sometimes could not resist levity, he needed to restrain himself. The more serious the subject, the more likely he was to find humor in it. It became an even greater challenge than before to be both funny and respectable. Jervis Langdon's acceptance of his future son-in-law seemed almost without qualification, and not just for his daughter's sake. Increasingly, as a self-made man himself, he could appreciate, even identify with, Twain's accomplishment. Beneath his portly Victorian propriety existed a vigorous, rough-and-tumble man of business, a glimpse of which Twain got when he spent some time with Langdon and his coal company associates. With a sense of humor of his own, Langdon, unlike anyone else in his family, took a bubbly, even mischievous delight in joking and teasing about the engagement and imminent marriage, his good humor the expression of genuine fondness for his son-in-law-to-be. His love for his daughter embraced the reality of her current happiness and the expectation of her happy future. Unfortunately, his ongoing illness was gradually resolving itself into disaster. In January 1869 he seemed much better, but he faltered again. He repaired to various spas and resorts, but his failure to recover seemed ominous; the doctors could not even agree on a diagnosis. Despite his poor health and his partial withdrawal from business responsibilities, he tried to play a helpful role in Orion's attempt to sell the Tennessee land. By midsummer he was playing a key role in determining where the newly wedded couple would live.

Jervis Langdon was instrumental in the arrival of a proposal that Twain purchase for $25,000 Thomas Kennett's one-third interest in the *Buffalo Express*. "I am grateful to Mr. Langdon," Twain wrote to his bride-to-be, "for thinking of Buffalo with his cool head when we couldn't think of any place but Cleveland with our hot ones." Langdon was well connected in Buffalo, a principal in the Buffalo-headquartered cartel controlling coal prices for western New York and Pennsylvania. His desire to situate his son-in-law favorably and close by would have motivated him to encourage his Buffalo-based partner and sales manager, John Slee, to approach the *Express*. When, at the end of July 1869, the Langdons took a Niagara Falls holiday with Livy and Twain, Jervis Langdon spent time at the nearby *Express* office, going through the firm's books—probably why the Niagara destination had been chosen in the first place. Apparently he was satisfied. Two weeks later Twain walked into the *Express* office and introduced himself as the new managing editor. His father-in-law had lent him $12,500. He himself had provided $2,500, almost every cent he had. Kennett took a personal note for the remaining $10,000, guaranteed by Langdon, payment to be spread out over a reasonable period. Langdon's $12,500 loan had no precise repayment requirements. "I wrote & asked whether I had better send him my note, or a due bill, or how he would prefer the indebtedness made of record," Twain wrote to his sister, "& he answered every other topic in the letter pleasantly but never replied to that at all."

It was a generous wedding present, an advance against Livy's inheritance, so to speak, though formally conceived and always described as a business arrangement. Twain of course took it as his debt, though in the event of default Langdon was responsible for all but $2,500. There would be a weekly salary for his editorial duties paid against his share of the profits and separate payment for specific articles he would write. "I have just purchased one-third of the Buffalo Express & gone pretty largely in debt to accomplish it," he wrote to Redpath in August, explaining why he would not be available to lecture that next season. However, when it developed that his November 1869 to January 1870 lecture series could not be cancelled without embarrassment—including a financial penalty—he changed his mind. He would have to labor at his *Buffalo Express* responsibilities and fulfill a lecture series at the same time, while, from a distance, keeping his eye on wedding preparations in Elmira. "The Express proposition arrived just in time to stop me from going to Cleveland to be a politician," he wrote to the Fairbankses, mending that broken fence for the sake of his relationship with Mary. At the same time, he expressed an edge of bitterness about Abel Fairbanks' slipperiness in blocking Twain's part ownership of the *Herald*. "I shall have to work hard in this Express office, & do a little of everything." But, he boasted, he was capable and willing to slave "over an editorial desk without rest from noon till Midnight, & keep it up without losing a day for 3 years on a stretch," since it would be agreeable work and he would be his own boss.

2.

At the *Express,* he had immediately set to work to shape the newsroom to his standards, including the typesetting, about which, as an experienced practitioner, he had strong feelings. With its new format, the paper was "vastly improved in appearance," he boasted. With Josephus Larned, his coeditor and a co-owner, he quickly developed a happy working relationship, sitting at opposite sides of a large table, occasionally swapping manuscripts in the middle of an editorial-in-progress when one or the other felt blocked. "Then we scribble away without the least trouble, he finishing my article & I his."

Twain also immediately altered one aspect of the *Express*'s editorial sympathies. Whereas it had heretofore aligned itself with the citizens' co-operative formed to challenge the high price of coal set by the cartel, it now announced, in an editorial probably composed by Twain, that the other side of the story needed to be heard. The *Express* ran a letter from John Slee, Jervis Langdon's sales manager, along with a pro-cartel editorial reprinted from the *New York Evening Post*. They both argued that the high cost of coal resulted from the "unreasonable demands" and actions of the striking miners. That Langdon was the editor's father-in-law-to-be and his partner one of Twain's Buffalo friends was not mentioned. The editorial vigorously exonerated Langdon, who had come under direct attack. A week later the *Express* trumpeted that Langdon had donated fifty tons of coal to the Buffalo General Hospital. "Although he is wealthy and a member of a corporation, he has a soul of *his own* and his liberality is not confined to the city in which he resides." There is no evidence that the young writer hesitated in the least in coming down on the side of his Langdon alliance.

Residing in a boardinghouse near the *Express* office, keeping his nose to the grindstone except for weekend visits to Elmira, he worried about where he and Livy would live. "We must board one year," he concluded, "& *then* we'll *both* be consumingly anxious to keep house." The strain of housekeeping on Livy was a concern, but the overwhelming issue was financial. The wedding, initially scheduled for December 1869, was postponed to February when he realized that the consequences of renouncing the lecture tour were more onerous than going through with it. The reviews of *Innocents Abroad,* though, raised his spirits, as did anticipation of handsome royalties. "The book is selling furiously," he wrote to his friend Whitelaw Reid, the publisher of the *New York Tribune*, soliciting a sympathetic review, "& the publisher says he is driving ahead night & day trying to keep up." The light, good-humored pieces that he published regularly in the *Express* ranged across a variety of subjects from Harriet Beecher Stowe's revelations about Byron's incest, to sycophantic praise of Henry Ward Beecher, to travel letters that Twain had solicited from Professor Darius Ford, traveling (with Charley) around the world, which he expected he would rewrite into pieces like those he had done for the *Alta*.

In New York, in late November, the Langdon family did wedding shopping. In Rhode Island, in mid-December, Twain met Jervis Langdon's friend Frederick Douglass, who impressed him with the story of his child's expulsion from Rochester's oldest female academy because the headmistress said "the pupils did not want a colored child among them." When Douglass challenged her, Twain wrote, "she put it at once to a vote of the school, & asked, 'How many of you are willing to have this colored child be with you?' And they all held up their hands! Douglass added: 'The children's hearts were right.' There was pathos in the way he said it. I would like to hear him make a speech. Has a grand face."

From Cambridge in mid-January 1870, he promised Livy that he would give up smoking, if she desired him to, just as he had given up drinking. At the end of the month he was back in Elmira. A few days before the wedding on Wednesday, February 2, he went to Buffalo to make sure that Slee had found an appropriate boardinghouse, which he had agreed to do. After taking care of some *Express* business, Twain could not locate Slee, but he uneasily assumed that he had made the arrangements they had agreed on. Guests began to arrive in Elmira, including Pamela and her daughter, Annie Moffett. Orion and Jane Clemens remained in Missouri, though Twain's mother promised that she would be one of their first visitors in Buffalo in the spring. The house was crowded with Langdon family and friends, many of whom, during the years of Livy's illness, had come to believe that she would never marry. Tears were shed, congratulations pronounced. The newlyweds spent the first night of their marriage in the bride's parents' home.

The next day, in the snow, they left for Buffalo, with the Langdons, Pamela, and some friends, Twain complaining about Slee and hoping nervously that whatever boardinghouse he had selected would be satisfactory. When they arrived in Buffalo, everyone but the married couple went to 472 Delaware Avenue in one of Buffalo's best residential areas. The newlyweds were purposely delayed until all the others were there. When they arrived, Twain was bewildered. This was not the cheap boardinghouse he had instructed Slee to secure. And why were all these people he knew assembled there, and how could this imposing, luxurious-looking establishment be a boardinghouse, let alone one he could afford to live in? To his amazement, Jervis Langdon handed the groom the keys to the fully furnished house, a wedding gift from his in-laws. Twain would never have to live in a boardinghouse again.

3.

From his first telling the Twichells, who visited the newlyweds in early February 1870, "what happened to Little Sammy in Fairyland when . . . hunting for a Boarding House," he grew, over the years, increasingly fond of this paradigmatic story. The moment he took possession (house and furnishings had cost $40,000—equal to about 800,000 early-twenty-first-century dollars; maid, housekeeper, cook, and coachman came with the premises) marked a momentous change in his life. He told the story as a vivid exemplification of his magical good fortune, of his having been chosen by a family with the power to grant him great gifts. In the larger perspective, though, he was being woven into a domestic, economic, and cultural web of support from which he would never be able, or want, to free himself. His entrepreneurial dreams, from riverboat business days to Nevada gold and silver mines, had been reformed into a literary living and a hugely profitable marital arrangement. He had married not only Livy but the Langdons, whose gift assured that their daughter would from the start not have to settle for a living standard lower than her parents'. It was a mutually satisfactory match. Jervis Langdon was a handsome replacement for the failed father of "Little Sammy's" Hannibal childhood. Sam Clemens had triumphed over external adversity and internal flaws, partly through his own efforts but mostly because great good fortune had been bestowed on him. That reality made all the difference. Hardscrabble days in Hannibal and in the West were behind and now beneath him, and though he frequently remarked, as he was to tell Horace Bixby in February 1870, that he "would rather be a pilot than anything" he had ever tried, his new life required that he conduct himself socially and economically as a member of the upper-middle class into which he had married. Livy and the house were gifts he would have to support. The maid, cook, and coachman had to be paid salaries. And what was the point having a coachman unless one also had a coach? A long series of economic necessities that defined the class status to which he had now risen inevitably proceeded from the tip of the coachman's whip. It was to be, in the end, a whip that sometimes turned on its master's hand.

The Buffalo house at first contained unalloyed domestic joy. Certainly Livy had little to no sexual experience. Twain himself, soon dubbed by his wife "Youth"—encapsulating her view of her husband's boyish delight in teasing jokes and humorous enthusiasms—clearly knew something about sexual relations from his Virginia City and San Francisco days. His sexual relationship with Livy was, for him, a success from the start. Clearly for her also. During their first months in their Buffalo nest, the married couple chirped morning and night from bedroom to parlor and back to the bedroom of their new home. "I have at this moment," he confided to one of his oldest friends, "the only sweetheart I ever loved, & bless her old heart she is lying asleep upstairs in a bed that I sleep in every night, & for four whole days she has been *Mrs. Samuel L. Clemens!*" When Livy wrote home that Ellen, the housemaid borrowed from Elmira, "asked me last night if I was not homesick, I said 'no, that I was as happy as a queen.'"

The king and queen were comfortable together, and playfully erotic. Some-time in February Livy became pregnant. "[She] has undergone the most astounding change," Twain reported to her parents. "She pulls & hauls me around, & claws my hair, & bites my fingers, & laughs so that you might hear her across the street; & it does appear to me that I never saw anybody so happy as she is in all my life—except myself."

During these first days an excess of happiness kept Twain from focusing on work. Taking full advantage of his ownership prerogatives, he began to stay away from the *Express* office. He had never felt and would never feel comfortable with regular office hours. He did take *Express* editorial work home, though most of his focus was on his own occasional contributions, more than fifty of which he had published from October 1869 to January 1870. From February to May 1870, though, he managed only fifteen, and, during the same period, a few contributions to the *Galaxy,* for which he had agreed to write "a department." Regular newspaper work was not turning out to be as congenial as he had anticipated. He much preferred domestic amusements and romantic hours to working on newspaper squibs.

"Every day I nerve myself, & seize my pen, & dispose my paper, & prepare to buckle on the harness and *work!* And then I pace the floor—back & forth, back & forth, with vacuous mind," he wrote to Mary Fairbanks, thanking her for a marriage announcement in the *Cleveland Herald,* one of many appearing nationwide. "[Finally] I lay down the pen & confess my time is not come—that I am utterly empty. But I must work, & I *will* work. I will go straight at it & *force* it." Livy, he admiringly noticed, kept the household books in a commendably workmanlike manner. Much of his own time, though, was taken up by the challenge of adjustment. A major worry was the proper dress for the coachman, Patrick McAleer. "I went & tricked him out in a livery coat . . . with enormous brass buttons . . . But I couldn't stand those buttons." In the end, "that coat of Patrick's cost me more than did any ever *I* wore." He had begun to learn that it wasn't going to be easy to be middle class or to appear to himself and to the public as if he was. And though he had ready money from his *Express* disbursements and could count on the Langdons for cash gifts, he owed $12,500. Fortunately, there was no pressure to repay his father-in-law.

Laudatory reviews of *Innocents Abroad* continued through winter and spring, including a review in the *Buffalo Courier* by its editor David Gray, a Scotland-born contemporary of Twain's who soon became a close friend.

Though, Twain wrote to Bliss, "it takes all my time to carry on the honey-moon," his mind soon was more on Hartford than Buffalo, more on the success of *Innocents* than on journalism. His Hartford friends had been urging him since the previous December to move there. Isabella Hooker and Joe Twichell thought he deserved to be among them and they deserved to have him. When Hartford circles began to report desire as fact, the *Buffalo Commercial Advertiser* announced that his departure was imminent. Twain began to think that Buffalo's attractions were too limited, its culture too provincial, its winters too cold. Hartford had the additional attraction of the American Publishing Company, which sent quarterly checks with wondrous regularity. The first of these he sent to Jervis Langdon, who had offered to put it to work to pay interest while Twain decided whether or not to use it as a first repayment to Kennett. In response to widely published announcements that he was planning to leave Buffalo, he printed a denial in the *Express*. "I am a permanency here. I am prospering well enough to please my friends & distress my enemies." As to lecturing, he was "out of the lecture field permanently," he told Frank Fuller. "I am not going to lecture any more forever," he declared to Redpath. He had done the calculations, knew what it cost him to live, and could earn it without submitting himself to endless train rides and painful separations.

What kept him especially buoyant was the $1,200 a month pouring in from *Innocents Abroad* royalties, a total of $11,250 by the end of April 1870, a sum now in excess of what he would have earned if he had accepted Bliss's offer of $10,000 for his rights in the book. By the end of the fourth quarter the total sale amounted to 69,500 copies. Over the next year he was to earn another $10,000 from *Innocents,* which, in the end, would sell more in his lifetime than any other book he published. His gamble had paid off. In the middle of July he agreed to write a new book for the American Publishing Company, for delivery as soon as possible but with a target date of January 1, 1871. This was to be an account of his time in Nevada and California that had been on his mind for close to five years and that he had been preparing for since moving to Buffalo. He urged the few people to whom he confided not to reveal the subject. Bliss urged him to write a sequel to *Innocents* and he had in mind the possibility of revisiting Europe for six months or so. But the western material seemed nearer at hand, even if he should need to revisit Nevada. Some of it was in his memory, much of it in the newspaper files of the *Territorial Enterprise*. It would be another six-hundred-page, heavily illustrated subscription book. Author and publisher happily anticipated a success at least equal to that of *Innocents*.

"I suppose I am to get the biggest copyright, this time, ever paid on a subscription book in this country," he boasted to Orion. He was already receiving a five percent royalty for each copy of *Innocents* sold, and there was no option clause in his contract. When Bliss offered seven and a half percent, Twain counter-offered. He wanted "half-profits," a widespread arrangement wherein the publisher shared with the author all revenues after expenses. When Bliss "drew the contract and brought it to the house in the afternoon, I found a difficulty in it," Twain recalled fifty years later. "It did not name 'half profits,' but named a seven and a half percent royalty instead. I asked him to explain that. I said that that was not the understanding. He said, 'No, it wasn't,' but that he had put in a royalty to simplify the matter—that seven and a half percent royalty represented fully half the profit and a little more, up to a sale of a hundred thousand copies, that after that the publishing company's half would be a shade superior to mine. I was a little doubtful, a little suspicious, and asked him if he could swear to that. He promptly put up his hand and made oath to it, exactly repeating the words he had just used."

Twain did not attempt to test Bliss's claim that a seven and a half percent royalty equaled half profits. Instead he assured him, "I never had the slightest idea of publishing with anybody but you," though he had, without solicitation, received feelers from publishers offering ten percent. Determined to disprove his publisher's inference that he might prove rascal enough to leave him, he assured Bliss that he was no rascal at all. He felt he was the cat who had swallowed the canary. He would have his seven and a half percent and his moral self-esteem. A clever businessman, anticipating profits on the new book to equal those of the old, Bliss stroked Twain's moral vanity. Actually, a true picture of Bliss's profits on *Innocents* would have been difficult to obtain. What five percent or seven and a half percent royalties or half profits in fact meant could be determined only if one accurately knew total costs and sales. Like most publishers, Bliss kept these figures close to the vest. When forced to reveal them, he would do so partially and misleadingly. No businessman at all, or at least an inconsistent one, Twain never thought even to try to get those figures.

Always concerned that Twain would turn to another firm, Bliss was angry when Twain succumbed to the blandishments of a small New York publisher who in 1871 brought out *Mark Twain's (Burlesque) Autobiography and First Romance,* a pamphlet parody of little consequence and modest sales. Bliss, though, was pleased when, late in the year, Twain offered him at a seven and half percent royalty his collected sketches, eventually published as *Mark Twain's Sketches, New and Old.* Without consulting with Bliss, who might have given him good advice, he negotiated with Henry Webb to have the rights for *The Celebrated Jumping Frog of Calaveras County, And other Sketches* returned to him. Webb demonstrated to Twain's satisfaction that he owed the writer $600 in royalties. Twain purchased the rights for that $600, plus another $800, paid an additional $128 for some unbound copies, and agreed that Webb would keep the remaining three hundred copies on hand. Bliss responded with gentle frankness to Twain's matter-of-fact summary of the negotiation. "Glad you have the Jumping Frog, in your own hands, but think he got the *big end of a loaf.* He ought to have sold you the plates for what he owed you." And probably would have if Twain had thought to ask some qualified person to negotiate on his behalf.

Domestic matters went far better, though Twain had become nervous, even hesitant, at the prospect of becoming a father. When, during his rootless years, he had fantasied about the attractions of a home, his focus had been on a wife, not on children. Babies had no special appeal to him. Used to his world revolving around himself, Twain might not have felt ready for a competitor for attention or for a heavier anchor than he already had. And both parents- and grandparents-to-be had to be concerned about the pregnancy's possible effect on Livy's health. Her fragility concerned them all, as did, increasingly, Jervis Langdon's. With his wife and personal physician, he had spent a month traveling in the South. On the one hand, it seemed to do him no good. "All my organs seemed to have suspended their functions," he wrote to his daughter and son-in-law. On the other, he still remained optimistic. In late June, when the doctors thought Langdon's death imminent, Sam and Livy were "summoned" to Elmira. In early July, when there seemed reason to think he would recover, his daughter and son-in-law decided to spend the summer by his bedside.

On July Fourth 1870 Twain went to Washington, D.C., to lobby Senate and House members on behalf of a bill to reorganize the Tennessee judicial system. The legislation might considerably improve chances of collecting a $500,000 debt owed by Memphis to a company in which Jervis

Langdon had a large interest. Twain again met President Grant, sat for a photographic portrait by Mathew Brady, did his best for the bank reform bill, and hobnobbed with some of his 1867–68 journalistic comrades. Corruption and self-interest seemed the common coin (often pocketed) of Washington politics. He had already written a number of Washington-based satirical sketches. Now he saw "material enough for a whole book! This is a perfect gold mine," he wrote to Livy. Its literary lode was to become the basis of his first novel, *The Gilded Age*.

Throughout July, Livy, with her sister, her mother, and her husband, tended the sick man around the clock. To the exhausted Twain, who battled sleepiness during his midnight-to-four A.M. watches, the sisters seemed inexhaustible. Soon the doctors realized or confessed that Langdon had inoperable stomach cancer, and on August 5 the family received the grievous news. The case was "utterly hopeless . . . the family . . . shrouded in gloom, awaiting the end," Twain wrote to Bliss. Exhausted, miserable, Livy prepared herself for life without the man who had always provided her with guidance and strength and prosperity. On August 6 Twain telegraphed to his sister and mother, "Father died this afternoon." The choice of words was indicative of how much he had identified with Langdon's paternal generosity, revealing how much of a father, especially in comparison to his own, the coal magnate had become. "This is a house of mourning, now," he noted five days later. "My wife is nearly broken down with grief & watching." Whatever his own pain in the loss of a newly adopted father, there was the ambiguous compensation that Langdon's death would remove a watchful eye, even though beneficent, as well as an example difficult to live up to.

In death, Jervis Langdon's generosity continued, in the form of an estate of about a million dollars to be divided equally among his wife and two biological children. Susan Dean, his adopted daughter, who had become Susan Crane, the wife of Theodore Crane, Langdon's office manager and head clerk, was bequeathed an attractive but modest country-style residence in the hills overlooking Elmira: Quarry Farm, which Langdon had recently purchased. The coal business he bequeathed to his son Charley, who hurried back from his around-the-world trip, returning too late for the funeral, and his two business associates, Crane and John Slee. The latter two had enjoyed Jervis' full confidence, whereas Charley's ability to carry on the firm successfully had always been in doubt. Her father's death made Livy a rich woman, though not as rich as she and sometimes her husband were to assume. Twain had reason to think that he did not have to hurry to repay the remainder of his debt to Langdon (he had already repaid five thousand dollars), but he chose to repay it in late 1871. His supportive father-in-law had even made him one of the executors. When Langdon was buried on August 8, Elmira mourned the loss of its premier citizen. Local businesses closed their doors during the funeral, and area newspapers published laudatory obituaries. Twain's appeared in the *Buffalo Express.* "All the impulses of Mr. Langdon's heart were good & generous. . . . He was a very pure, & good, & noble Christian gentleman. All that knew him will grieve for his loss." A huge assemblage gathered at the Opera House on Sunday, August 21, to hear a memorial tribute delivered by Thomas Beecher, who praised Langdon's charitable heart and the work he had done on behalf of fugitive slaves to affirm his belief that "all men are created equal."

Late in the same month, in Buffalo, Twain started writing *Roughing It.* At first he had little success, only six short chapters in three weeks, none of which he liked. He was "seriously obstructed," he believed, by his abstention from smoking, a voluntary forbearance since his wedding to show his devotion to Livy. He had always smoked incessantly while writing, the connection of nicotine and creativity wired into his nervous system. He soon "gave up the fight, resumed [his] three hundred cigars, burned the six chapters, and wrote the book in three months, without any bother or difficulty," so he later recalled, accurately about the smoking but not about how long it took him to write the book. To help his unresponsive memory, he asked his brother Orion to send him the journal he had kept while traveling from Missouri to Nevada in 1861. When it proved useful, he promised Orion a thousand dollars from his first royalty payment, not a mean consideration for the older brother still working night shifts as a printer and unsuccessful at everything else he tried, including a series of inventions.

By late October 1870, Twain was touting Orion to Bliss as an excellent editor whom Bliss might do well to hire. "Have you got a place for him at $100 or $150 a month in your office? . . . He will make a tip-top editor— a better than I, because he is full of talent & besides is perfectly faithful, honest, straightforward & reliable. There isn't money enough in America to get him to do a dishonest act—whereas I am different." When, in November, eager to keep his cash cow of an author happy, Bliss offered Orion the editorship of a monthly magazine he was initiating as an advertising vehicle for his books, Sam was delighted, proposing to pay Bliss the small difference between what Orion was being paid in St. Louis and what Bliss would pay him. "I have told Bliss *positively* that you are *an able editor* & I don't want you by word or gesture to show any lack of confidence about assuming responsibility." As always, he had much advice for Orion, in the barely restrained tone of a successful younger brother to an unsuccessful elder whose self-doubt, incapacity, and business stupidity got on the younger's nerves.

The Tennessee land was still a sore point, and Sam had angrily helped Orion pay the taxes as one scheme after another to dispose of it failed because of what he considered Orion's ineptitude. "The family have been bled for 40 years to keep that cursed land on their hands," he had written to his brother in August, "& perpetuate our father's well-intended folly in buying it. . . . If any stupid fool will give 2,000 for it, do let him have it— shift the curse to his shoulders. . . . I hate that vile subject." He soon had occasion to lecture Orion again, this time on Orion's effort to negotiate, as a condition of accepting the job, that Bliss raise his pay if he was a successful editor. "I do *resent* that idea of stipulating for advance of wages IN CASE a man is worth it. I haven't had anything incense me so in six months." He could not resist reminding Orion that the only reason he had been offered the job at all was because of what Bliss had been led to believe he was worth.

Suddenly the entire Clemens family was to be on or near the East Coast. Jane Clemens and her daughter Pamela, since 1865 a widow with two children, had decided in late 1869 to leave St. Louis. Just as Sam had been sending Orion small sums when he returned from the *Quaker City* voyage, he had resumed sending regular checks to his mother. She had urged her much traveling son to keep an eye out for the right kind of small town. Perhaps she too had become disenchanted with St. Louis. Apparently there was no thought of returning to Hannibal. She had lived in Missouri for thirty-five years; maybe, at sixty-seven years of age, she wanted a change. The idea had been initiated much before the prospect of Orion's being employed by Bliss had arisen. At the time it meant leaving Orion behind in St. Louis. If their mother's desire to move had anything to do with being closer to Sam, no one seems to have said that. Her son certainly did not encourage the change, though he did not oppose it. In April 1870, Pamela and Jane Clemens moved into "a beautiful home" Jane had rented and hoped to buy in the small town of Fredonia, New York, forty miles southwest of Buffalo, near Lake Erie. Sam had advised Pamela to "try to select a place where a good many funerals pass. Ma likes funerals. If you can pick a good funeral corner she will be happy." Though she was now only forty miles from her successful son, he knew that the rationale for his own residence in Buffalo was quickly disappearing. Mollie and Orion would move to Hartford by mid-December.

The Buffalo home to which the young couple returned in late August 1870 had lost its honeymoon glow. It also reminded Livy of what a father she had lost. Exhausted by his death and her pregnancy, Livy grieved painfully. "I give her a narcotic every night & *make* her [sleep]," Sam wrote to Pamela. They had two visitors, Mrs. Langdon and Livy's childhood friend Emma Nye, now on her way from South Carolina, where she lived with her parents, to assume a teaching position in Detroit. Both helped the semi-incapacitated Livy run the house and kept her company, especially when her husband was trying to write. He was happy to tell Mary Fairbanks on September 2 that Livy was "getting along tolerably well, now," helped by the "sleeping potion," but that Emma was "right sick." It turned out to be typhoid fever, which was virulently contagious. Suddenly the Clemenses had another seriously ill person on their hands and minds, this time in their own house, in fact in their own marriage bed. By the end of the first week in September "poor little Emma Nye [lay] . . . fighting wordy battles with the phantoms of delirium." With the help of a hired nurse, Livy attended her ceaselessly, her own grief and exhaustion pushed aside. Doctors came and went. Toward the end of September it looked hopeless. "During the last two or three days of it, Mrs. Clemens seldom took her clothes off but stood a continuous watch," Twain remembered years later. "Those two or three days are among the blackest, the gloomiest, the most wretched of my long life." His mood swung from depression to "half-insane tempests & cyclones of humor."

At the end of September, Emma Nye died. Now Livy could barely hang on herself. Twain kept "driveling along tolerably fairly on the book," he wrote to Bliss, "but it is *very* slow work." Ill at ease, impatient, he decided not to write for the *Galaxy* after the end of the year, partly because he blamed his occasional contribution for keeping him from other work. *Roughing It* was not coming easily, the effort against the grain of his recalcitrant memory and slow pen. Expenses, though, were high—"$600 to

$700 a month, latterly, because of sickness & funerals"—though he emphasized to Bliss (and indirectly to his Hartford friends), "I don't allow my wife to pay my bills." Livy's money they intended to reserve for special opportunities and expenses. The hated word "lecture" came to mind, which he "half expected" to do "a little next year," though at the moment his mind was awhirl with any and all alternatives to focusing exclusively on his book-in-progress. A little after mid-October, the focus necessary for writing became even more difficult. Livy got into their carriage with Mary Fairbanks, who had been visiting for a few days, to accompany her to the railroad station. Since they needed to hurry in order to catch the train, Patrick encouraged the horse into a gallop, which so severely jarred Livy that she seemed about to miscarry. Her doctor put her to bed for the duration. "I have moved her," Sam wrote to Orion "—bed & all—down stairs into the library, & there I mean she shall stay till her confinement in December."

Soon she appeared better, but Twain felt apprehensive. Visitors helped keep up her spirits, especially Susan Crane, whom Twain, since the summer stay in Elmira, had begun to know and like. A capable, diffident, kind person, she spent much of her time and apparently endless patience helping other people. Gradually she was to become as much an intimate of Livy's husband as she had always been of her sister. Childless, she would also become a second mother to their family. With Pamela visiting from Fredonia, both sisters were there when Livy unexpectedly went into labor. She gave birth on November 7, 1870, a month early, to a four-and-a-half-pound boy, to be named Langdon, who seemed likely to join his namesake soon. "Born to us this day, a *boy*," Twain wrote to Bliss. "Mother & child doing only tolerably well but we hope for the best. *Tell the Twichells.*"

Actually, mother and child were having a bad time. Within a few days of his birth, Langdon's condition became critical. The howling baby, too tiny to wear even the smallest clothes, unable to hold down Livy's milk and any substitutes they tried, seemed, as had Twain himself during his first six months, on borrowed time. After a few days, though, he actually gained an ounce or two. Exhausted, her spirits low, Livy kept to her bed, and a wet nurse was hired. But her strength hardly returned. Lonely, with her room kept darkened since light bothered her, she spent much of December and January barely managing. She had no energy, she wrote to her friend Alice, and she missed her father. "I often feel since Father left us, that he was my back bone, that what energy I had came from him, that he was the moving spring."

With the help of family and hired assistance, Twain did his best to keep the household running, including a minimal amount of professional work, mainly important business letters and effort on *Roughing It*. Lecturing was out of the question. When Livy's milk failed entirely, they needed a second wet nurse. The new mother became increasingly depressed. Soon after Twain, attempting to revive the banking legislation central to settling Jervis Langdon's estate, arrived in Washington at the end of January, he was urged to return home immediately. He found Livy "dangerously ill" with typhoid fever. It seemed that she would follow Emma Nye to the grave. "Sometimes I have hope for my wife . . . but most of the time it seems to me impossible that she can get well. . . . The subject is too dreadful." She could not sleep. Her mind drifted, her fever burned. Like Emma, she too began to babble deliriously. Heavy doses of an opiate finally gave her some rest. After "2 nights rest & sleep . . . she seems better, but still is very low & very weak." At least she was in her "right mind" one morning, Twain wrote to his mother and sister. But she was still "very seriously ill . . . & we watch with her night & day hardly daring to prophecy what the result will be." Afraid that she would relapse, a common occurrence in cases of typhoid fever, and with little confidence in their local physician, Twain asked Dr. Rachel Gleason, whom Livy had known since childhood, to come from Elmira. "In my belief there was but one physician who could save her," he recalled years later. Dr. Gleason agreed, though she expected to stay a few days or at most a week. "Her ministrations were prosperous but at the end of a week she said she was obliged to return. . . . I felt *sure* that if she could stay with us three days more Livy would be out of all danger. But Mrs. Gleason's engagements were of such a nature that she could not consent to stay. . . . I placed a private policeman at the door with instructions to let no one pass. . . . In these circumstances, poor Mrs. Gleason had no choice—therefore she stayed." By the end of the first week of March, Livy seemed at last out of danger. Mother and child had just barely come through.

4.

Sickness had helped make Twain sick of Buffalo. So too had the freezing winter weather. It seemed in March 1871 that spring would never come. Though out of danger, Livy was still feeble, hardly able to walk. The baby cried ceaselessly, so it seemed. "I believe," he wrote to Bliss, who was urging him to make quicker progress on *Roughing It*, "if that baby goes on crying 3 more hours this way I will butt my frantic brains out & try to get some peace." Doctors and nursemaids regularly trafficked through what had once been a bower of marital bliss and a peaceful domestic hearth. Time and quiet in which to write seemed unavailable. When Bliss pressed him to contribute to his company's new magazine, *American Publisher,* Twain was irritably resentful. When his name appeared as one of the writers engaged to publish there, he was furious and lashed out at Bliss's presumptuousness. Bliss had urged him to terminate his arrangement with the *Galaxy* and not waste his time publishing short pieces. Now, when it served Bliss's own interest, he wanted Twain to contribute to his magazine while still making steady progress with *Roughing It*. Actually, Bliss wanted Twain's name on the contributors' list for status as much if not more than he wanted a contribution.

His star author, though, was not in a compromising mood. It seemed to him that Bliss was making the magazine into one "which the people are to understand is Mark Twain's . . . and to sink or swim on his reputation." Orion's position as editor of *American Publisher* complicated the situation. When, still hoping to have success as a writer himself, Orion sent his brother a children's story for his opinion, Twain made it even more difficult by responding that he thought children's articles "wholly worthless." "I never saw one that I thought was worth the ink it was written with" was the resonant response from a writer who in five years was to publish a successful novel in that genre. Anyway, "the Great Public's is the only opinion worth having." Bliss, of course, hoped for Twain's cooperation at least as an expression of appreciation for having employed his brother. Distressed by his household misery and his inability to write, Twain wanted his name off the masthead. In the end, though, he did allow Bliss to keep his name on the contributors' list, and *American Publisher* did print small selections from the manuscript of *Roughing It*.

"I have come at last to loathe Buffalo so bitterly (always hated it)," he wrote, the latter a characteristic subordination of past fact to present feeling, to his old newspaper friend from San Francisco and Washington, John Henry Riley. Twain had hired Riley to provide firsthand observation of the diamond fields of South Africa, which Twain intended to make the basis of a subscription book for which Bliss had advanced $1,500. If he could have gone to South Africa himself, it would have been a welcome liberation. But the once footloose journalist was now heavily anchored, though not necessarily in Buffalo. In early March 1871 he put the house up for sale for $25,000. His interest in the *Express* he offered for sale also: "The man that will pay me $10,000 less than I gave can take *that*." The price for the house did not include the furniture, horse, carriage, or sleigh, valued at about $15,000. Much of what Langdon had loaned him had been repaid. There was, however, an automatic discount: the money went into an estate of which his wife was to receive a one-third share. Still, that and other expenses had been expending his cash as quickly as it came in, including *Innocents Abroad* royalties. When no outside buyer for his *Express* interest emerged, he sold it to one of his partners for $1,000 down, the remainder to be paid over five years. Twain would retain responsibility for his remaining debt of $7,500 to Kennett. Clearly, it was not as easy to get out of Buffalo as to get in. But, he wrote to Orion, he was willing to take the loss. "We . . . are going to spend the summer in Elmira while we build a house in Hartford. Eight months' sickness & death in one place is *enough* for Yrs Truly."

Eager to move to where they would have been all this time if Hawley had allowed him to buy into the *Courant,* he had no intention of ever roughing it again, especially now that he had a family. The move to Hartford, where they had friends, would correct the mistake of having chosen Buffalo. He had wanted regular work to impress the Langdons and to obviate the necessity for lecturing. Now, with three books under contract, two of which he expected would earn substantial royalties, and with the security of his wife's $300,000 inheritance, much of it invested in stocks and bonds managed by Langdon's business heirs, his circumstances were radically changed.

Whether it was husband or wife who originated the idea of building rather than buying is unclear. In order to purchase land and pay for house construction, Twain needed at least the twenty-five-thousand dollars he hoped to realize from the sale of the Buffalo house, and no buyer had yet emerged. When in June 1871 he was offered twenty-thousand he determined to take it if no better offer came within three months. He wrote Redpath, offering to take to the lecture platform for the next season provided that he receive higher fees than before, a minimum of $150 a performance and at least $250 in Boston. Since Livy was recovering and little

Langdon stable for the moment, Twain was eager to leave for Elmira, where they would stay with Mrs. Langdon at the downtown mansion, and occasionally as guests of the Cranes at Quarry Farm, which had recently been enlarged. Then, so he planned, they would rent a furnished Hartford house for occupancy in the fall, preferably as close to Nook Farm and the Twichells as possible. Bliss had arranged for storage of their furniture until they should need it again. That Sam would be leaving his mother behind in Fredonia does not appear to have been a consideration. What mattered was to leave Buffalo. Hartford glittered in their imaginations as a shining citadel of friendship and culture.

As soon as Livy could travel, transported on a mattress, the family moved to Elmira. In the still wintry March weather, weak and unable to eat, she stayed mostly in bed. "I find myself daily regarding her substantial recovery as farther & farther away," he told Mary Fairbanks. "She is hopeful & confident—but what does she found it on?" For a while the baby was "in splendid condition," he wrote to Orion in April, and, after a relapse, Livy's health slowly improved. In mid-June she became pregnant again, though the record is silent on whether it was intentional. Inversely, as Livy got better, little Langdon's health declined and seemed increasingly precarious. Still underweight, regularly suffering colds and infections, his hold on life seemed weak. Livy worried about her husband and baby, especially if she herself should die, an anxiety partly exacerbated by the pain she felt at the one-year anniversary of her father's death.

"Don't fear for us darling," Twain wrote from Hartford. "If you are taken away I will love the baby & have a jealous care over him. But let us hope & trust that both you & I shall tend him & watch over him till we are helped from our easy-chairs to the parlor to see his children married." At the end of August, it seemed likely that little Langdon, not his mother, was about to die. Twain immediately returned from Hartford, where he had been working with Bliss on preparing for the press the almost finished manuscript of *Roughing It*. He had also been searching for a house to rent, and both activities had gone well.

In April 1871 he kept "pegging away" at the manuscript, sometimes at the Langdon home downtown, often at Quarry Farm, to which he walked, where the Cranes encouraged him to come for the quiet he needed. Worried that the public might be getting tired of him at a moment when he was especially dependent on his new book's success, he was rattled by a few moderately critical words in a newspaper. Then, too, Bliss was pressing him to cooperate in getting out the prospectus for *Roughing It*. Bliss shrewdly kept Twain on the defensive, casually writing, "I do not think there is as much of a desire to see another book from you as there was 3 months ago. Then anything offered would sell. . . . Now they will inspect a Prospectus closer." This was hardly soothing to an irritable, insecure author, especially one under contract for two more books. He also had it in mind to coauthor with Joe Goodman a satirical novel about Washington, D.C. In Elmira, Twain was pleased to have Joe Goodman with him. "[He] writes by my side every day up at the farm. Joe & I have a 600-page book in contemplation which will wake up the nation."

Another old literary friend, Bret Harte, was on his mind. After Harte had helped Twain revise the manuscript of *Innocents Abroad* in spring 1868, they had had a falling out. Apparently Twain's attempt to have Bliss send Harte two complimentary copies left Harte with the impression that he was being billed for the books. He wrote Twain a *"contemptuous & insulting letter . . .* & what *I* want to know, is, where was *I* to blame?" Harte's immense success since 1868 made Twain nervous, if not envious. He himself needed to follow a first successful book with a second. When a comic poem that imitated Harte's sensational hit of the previous year, "The Heathen Chinee," was widely believed to have been written by Twain, he was livid. "I . . . hate to be accused of plagiarizing Bret Harte," he wrote, which was especially true because he gratefully acknowledged how much Harte had helped him with *Innocents Abroad* and because Harte had broken off their friendship a year before "without any cause or provocation" that he was aware of.

By mid-May 1871, totally absorbed in his work, eager not to lose "a single moment of the inspiration," writing about two hundred manuscript pages a week, he had two thirds of the book done, enough for the engraver to start work on the illustrations. With offers to write books and lectures flooding in, things were looking up considerably. In early June, with a batch of manuscript, he went to Hartford, visiting briefly with Orion and the Twichells, and returned to Elmira, where his sister Pamela and her son were taking the Gleasons' water cure. With lecturing on his mind, he began to sketch out a new presentation. To Redpath he outlined his terms and his schedule preferences for the 1871–72 season. He began to consider that it would benefit him to go to London sometime in the fall or

winter to protect his British rights in *Roughing It,* which required simulta-
neous publication in both countries. A British publisher, perhaps George
Routledge and Sons, whom he had contacted about *Innocents Abroad* too
late and after the fact, would be necessary. By early July he was three
fourths finished, "*so* sick & tired of it. If I were to chance another break . . .
before I finish it I fear I never *should* get it done."

In Hartford for most of August, he edited, rewrote, and kept creating
additional chapters, straining to reach the goal of a manuscript of six hundred printed pages. "I admire the book more & more, the more I cut &
slash & trim & revamp it." Livy, though, would be getting impatient for his
return: "I am going to begin tonight & work day & night both till I get
through. It is a tedious, arduous job." By the end of August, when the call
came from Elmira to hasten back because of the baby's deteriorating
health, he had finished *Roughing It.* He was still short about five chapters
of the advertised length, however, so he mined his "old Sandwich Island
notes" and used them to reach six hundred pages. The title that he had
proposed in July, *Flush Times in the Silver Mines, & other Matters,* had been
replaced with a better one. He had also rented a house. It was, coincidentally, the same Nook Farm Victorian Gothic owned by Isabella and John
Hooker where, three years before, he had blamed the smell of his cigar
smoke on the cat and had concluded that he desired the respect of these
Hartford puritans.

Langdon survived this August–September 1871 crisis, though at first
they had "scarcely any hope of the baby's recovery. . . . Three months of
overfeeding & surreptitious poisoning with laudanum & other sleeping po-
tions is what the child is dying of," Twain inaccurately concluded. When,
in September, a few newspapers reported that the Twains had bought a
house in Hartford, he had denials printed, though he failed to mention that
the reports were partly true. It was in his best interest, he believed, to keep
that news as quiet as possible until the move had been accomplished,
probably because of Buffalo sensitivities and negotiations. In late September, they packed everything for shipment: "We must take possession of our
house in Hartford Oct. 1." Though the baby was fine, Livy was ill, probably with morning sickness. With *Roughing It* finished and scheduled for
early 1872 publication, Twain's mind was mostly on his imminent
nineteen-week lecture tour.

There was room for one distraction, however—an invention, "Mark

Twain's Elastic Strap," a version of a vest strap, somewhat like suspenders, to attach a man's pants to his vest in order to keep the trousers in place in an age before zippers, belts, and modern suspenders. So optimistic was he about its likely success that he himself went to Washington in early September to apply for a patent. In his visits to Hartford he had gotten to see a number of the inventions that Orion had been working on for years, among them a paddleboat operated by chains and pulleys. To a great extent, inventing his vest strap had been fun, a diversion from his main business, with nothing at stake except the time he had put into it. Most men needed to keep their pants up, and there was indeed a rival inventor who filed a similar patent at about the same time and with whom he did battle, a harbinger of things to come. Orion dreamed that one of his inventions would release him from the bondage of lifelong failure. His brother also took pleasure in inventiveness, combining his belief in progress through technology and his eagerness to be rich. In Nevada, Twain had searched for better ways to mine and process precious metals. Now he shared the conviction that the world would beat a path to the door of whoever could make a better mousetrap and would pay for the invention through royalties on each use or sale.

Within two weeks of moving to Hartford, he was on the road lecturing. At first he prepared a lecture called "An Appeal in behalf of Extending the Suffrage to Boys," a parody of lectures on women's suffrage. When Redpath, who may have found the topic unsettling, given that he acted as an agent for numbers of prominent suffragettes, suggested that he prepare a second lecture as a backup, he was reluctant. Since he used "no notes in lecturing," he did not want to have to "use more than one lecture during the season," for he would have to memorize both. "If I write fifty lectures I shall choose one & talk that one," he wrote Redpath. Still, he wrote a second, which he thought unsatisfactory and put aside. Then in late June he wrote a third, "Reminiscences of Some un-Commonplace Characters I have Chanced to Meet," with which he was delighted. He also wanted "Nasby prices" and a manageable travel schedule. "Get me rid of Buffalo," he demanded. If not, he would be sure to have to cancel because of illness. Riley, who had returned from South Africa, had to be put off. "I can't talk diamonds this season," Twain told him. He proposed they start work in May, probably calculating that he would need to be an attentive husband and father of a new baby in the early spring. South Africa would remain alive and, he hoped, grow even more pertinent after his lecture tour. In mid-October 1871 he was in Bethlehem, Pennsylvania, for his first lecture, registering under a false name to avoid the elaborate reception that had been organized for Mark Twain. In the morning he went alone to the Moravian cemetery where, looking at acres of precisely identical graves, he was moved by this *"absolute simplicity,"* the acceptance of "Death as a great *Leveler."*

That night he began the first of more than seventy lectures. Letters to and from Livy sustained them both. "It is Saturday night," she wrote from Hartford, "and I am homesick for you, not hearing from you makes me feel still more homesick." On the last day of the year, writing from rural Illinois, he urged her, in response to her despair, "Be bright & happy—accept the inevitable with a brave heart, since grieving cannot mend it but only makes it the harder to bear, for both of us. All in good time we shall be together again—and *then*—!" As always, the emphasis on what they would do together *then* gave additional erotic spark to their romantic attachment. Early in the new year Livy had "a vivid dream" of his return. "In my sleep," she wrote to him, "I did all the things that I should have done waking if you had returned to me, put my hand in yours, stroked your hair, did everything that should make me really conscious of your presence—Youth don't you think it is very sweet to love as we love?" At the same time, his lecturing misery was intensified by his decision to change his subject. "Reminiscences of Some un-Commonplace Characters" proved unsuccessful. Late in October 1871 he pulled out the section on Artemus Ward and in two days in Washington expanded it into a full ninety minutes, which, since he had no time to memorize it, he read to a large audience. "It suits *me,*" he told Redpath. "I'll never deliver the nasty, nauseous 'reminiscences' any more."

The audience, though, and especially the all-important reviewers, liked it considerably less than he did. In early November he began to substitute a lecture based on selections from *Roughing It*. Audiences and the press responded more enthusiastically. By mid-December he had mastered his "tip-top lecture about California & Nevada. . . . Notify all hands from this date I shall talk nothing but selections from my forth-coming book." He and Redpath apparently breathed a sigh of relief, though Twain had very little free breath available as he toured the East and Midwest, night after night, with occasional short breaks that allowed him to go home only briefly. "With this new lecture," he told Redpath, "I'm not afraid of N.Y. or

London or *any* place." Or of the winter. He kept as warm as he could, wrapped in a dramatic sealskin coat he had purchased the previous September to ward off the Buffalo winters. On "a crisp, bitter day" in Chicago, which had been mostly destroyed by fire in October, he could only tell it was cold "by my nose & by seeing other people's actions." "There is literally no Chicago *here*. I recognize *nothing* here, that ever I saw before."

Boredom and loneliness were constant companions. And no matter how much he spent in order to be comfortable, his existence in hotels and trains seemed almost always comfortless. The Boston Lyceum commission he paid directly to Redpath. Expenses on the tour ate up a large portion of his earnings, and another large part went to pay off debts, including the remainder of what he owed Kennett and the Langdon estate. Though his net worth increased as he eliminated the obligation, it did not feel to him that he was getting any richer. "I haven't a cent to show for all this long campaign," he complained to Redpath. "Squandered it thoughtlessly paying debts."

Worse, traveling kept him away from family and home, especially from a pregnant wife due in March 1872. Though Livy had frequent visitors from Elmira and Buffalo, as well as a supportive community at Nook Farm, she missed her husband terribly. "I would like to have you or Sue here, I get a little homesick to see you once in a while, tonight I should like to put my head in your lap and cry just a little bit. I want to be somebody's baby— I have . . . four servants to manage, I have a glorious husband to try and be a woman for, but sometimes I would like to lie down and give it all up—I feel so incompetent for everything, I come so very far short, yet I think I do try earnestly every day." Servants helped, though at an expense that worried her. Little Langdon was the greatest concern. His health seemed stable for the moment, but he seemed disturbingly slow, even remedial, in some of his motor and mental functions. In the spring, at almost one and a half years old, "his teeth [had not] come—& neither [had] his language."

Another, more existential consideration bothered Livy. Though one of the major motifs of their courtship had been his commitment to do all in his power to become a believer in Christ and to lead a Christian life, a staggering change had developed since their marriage. Rather than his religious faith increasing, hers had declined. When her mother visited, she went to Sunday services for the first time in months. Twichell's prayer, as he prayed for those who had fallen away, touched her and made her cry.

But, apparently, the more she loved her husband, the less she loved God. When her neighbor and new friend, Susan Warner, Charles Dudley Warner's wife, remarked on the general problem of feeling "lukewarmness toward God," Livy told her, "If I felt toward God as I did toward my husband I should never be in the least troubled." She failed to tell Warner how "perfectly cold" she felt toward God. It was a soul-shaking change in her life, and one that brought the couple closer together. They were now bound to each other in the dangers of disbelief, or at least faltering belief, an ironic resolution of their previous struggle to find common ground. She had assumed their common ground would be a religious one. He may have known better all along.

5.

Gathered around the lunch table at a well-known Boston restaurant in November 1871 were old and new friends of Twain's: Bret Harte, James Fields, William Dean Howells, Thomas Aldrich, and Ralph Keeler, the latter a literary acquaintance of Twain's and Harte's from San Francisco days who accompanied Twain to his Boston-area lectures. Harte, who had recently signed a lucrative one-year contract with the *Atlantic Monthly,* was the darling of Boston: America's preeminent young writer at what would turn out to be the pinnacle of his success. He had contracted to provide the *Atlantic* with twelve stories for a guaranteed retainer of ten thousand dollars, an extraordinary venture by the normally prudent Fields, who hoped to vault his magazine above his New York competition, *Harper's Weekly* and *Harper's New Monthly Magazine.* The estrangement between Harte and Twain had already ended or now, at this festive lunch, soon disappeared. Howells later recalled Harte putting his hand on Twain's shoulder "and sputtering out, 'This is the dream of his life,' " and Twain's bright glance from under his "feathery eyebrows" revealing "his enjoyment of the fun."

Thomas Bailey Aldrich and Twain hit it off immediately. Another prominent *Atlantic* contributor, a year younger than Twain, well groomed and dressed, with a mustache that issued straight out horizontally, he was soon to become one of Twain's closest friends. Aldrich edited Fields's other magazine, *Every Saturday,* in which he had recently published his own successful book for boys, *The Story of a Bad Boy,* containing autobiographical elements from his childhood, which was to have a minor influence on

Tom Sawyer. With a penchant for refinement and sentimentality, a poet and a short-story writer who was also to try his hand at novels, Aldrich had become one of the prominent young men in the *Atlantic* literary circle.

William Dean Howells, recently appointed the *Atlantic*'s editor in chief, had retained a vivid memory of Twain's late-1869 visit to the magazine to express his gratitude for its good review of *Innocents Abroad.* A modest dresser, Howells found Twain's personal flamboyance, his idiosyncratic fearlessness, his natural instinct for self-advertisement, attractively impressive. Twain flared into bright flames; Howells was a steady, low-burning fire. From the start, they took to each other, flame to fire, fire to flame. Two years younger than Twain, a midwesterner, the son of a journalist who was a Swedenborgian and a militant abolitionist, the Ohio-born Howells was also eager to be accepted into the elite eastern world. A campaign biography of Lincoln had earned him a consulship in Venice, where he sat out the war years. His Venice sojourn became the basis of his second book, *Venetian Life,* and his next, *Italian Journeys.* In 1865, in New York, he had been appointed assistant editor of the fledging *Nation* magazine in which Henry James, also to become Howells' intimate friend, was publishing some of his first reviews. Fields soon enticed Howells to Boston as his subeditor. Modest and courtly but exquisitely frank, Howells loved and valued his new Boston world, his influential position, and his power to help shape American literature. He valued realism and admired humor, the difficulty of which he appreciated, and, as an editor, he had an eye for talent. Impressed by *Innocents Abroad,* he had Twain in mind for the *Atlantic.* From the start, Howells had a sense of Twain's genius and enough self-lessness to encourage it.

By mid-February 1872 "the most detestable lecture campaign that ever was" finally ended, Twain wrote to Mary Fairbanks, feeling both relief and disgust. "I lectured eleven or twelve thousand dollars worth . . . & came out of the campaign with less than $1,500 to show for all that work & misery. I ain't ever going to lecture any more—unless I get in debt again." The qualification was to become a haunting motif.

He now returned to a project that had been vividly in mind early in 1866 but which he had reserved for a more propitious moment: a book about the Mississippi River. In *Roughing It* he had touched on the subject in his description of the great river's mythical origin in the Rocky Mountains, an evocative linguistic journey from the fountainhead to the Gulf of

Mexico, an affirmation of national unity and the American landscape as panoramic drama. In 1871, that vision expressed his own identification with the country that the Civil War had unified, and with his own journey from southern sectionalist to nationalistic northeasterner. Apparently he had in mind from the start a book that would combine fact and autobiography, like *Innocents Abroad* and *Roughing It*. It would be, he hoped, the standard book on the Mississippi River, its past and present, its people, and the civilization that the river valley had created.

His putting it on the back burner may be explained two ways. He might not have been ready to deal with the most disturbing element of the pre–Civil War South, and he might not yet have reconnected himself sufficiently to his Hannibal childhood to find a way to balance impersonal fact with autobiography. To write his Mississippi River book, he had told his mother in 1866, would require retraveling his old river pilot route from St. Louis to New Orleans. In January 1872, on a lecture stopover on the Ohio River, the absence of river traffic on the "deserted stream" reminded him of the "starchy" pilots of his riverboat days. Letters to and from Will Bowen revivified his memory of Hannibal people and incidents.

In Paris, Illinois, in late December 1871, he spent enjoyable hours at a hotel listening to an eight-year-old boy, "Fat-Cholley," ramble on with unselfconscious enthusiasm in a black dialect with a lively authenticity that entranced him, resonant of the black voices of his Mississippi valley youth. Soon, attempting to capture this dialect and voice, he wrote up his recollections of the boy's account in a brief sketch, "Sociable Jimmy," which he eventually published in the *New York Times* in November 1874. The black voices that had been part of his linguistic consciousness since early childhood crystalized, though at the moment he had no plan to make literary use of them other than in this sketch and in his general desire to do for the Mississippi what he had done for Nevada and California. With no sense of himself as a novelist, he accepted that his bread was heavily buttered on the side of continuing to create books like those he had already done.

Though not as effusively praised as *Innocents Abroad*, *Roughing It* was mostly well received. Charles Dudley Warner, Twain's Nook Farm neighbor, was unstinting in the *Hartford Courant*; so too was Howells in the *Atlantic Monthly*, though even laudatory reviewers occasionally objected to a disjointed episodic quality more dominant in *Roughing It* than in *Innocents*, which had the advantage of being the account of a single voyage.

Hostile reviews judged Twain at best a vulgar humorist, subject to humor's limitations. The sales reports, however, indicated no falling off at all. By early February, twenty thousand advance orders had been received. By the end of the month the number had increased by five thousand. Newspaper accounts claimed that it was in the process of becoming the best-selling book of the year, perhaps of the century. Eager to have Twain sign a contract for his next project, Bliss happily reported in the first quarterly statement that *Roughing It* had now sold close to forty thousand copies, which at seven and a half percent royalty had earned the author $10,562.13. Orion, who had grown increasingly resentful of Bliss's unwillingness to give him more independence as editor of *American Publisher,* confronted Bliss on another issue: his conviction that the publisher had been cutting corners on production costs and calculating Twain's profit on the basis of the original sums. If Bliss saved money on the quality of the paper, binding, and engravings, the savings would not be reflected in Twain's royalties. Twain had taken Bliss's word that a seven and a half percent royalty equaled half profits. Even if that were true, the only way it could be verified would be to determine Bliss's actual costs. If his estimate was not accurate to begin with, then Twain had been deceived. If it had been true on the basis of the original projection of costs but economies had reduced them, then he still was not receiving the equivalent of half profits.

Having overstepped his bounds as Bliss's employee, Orion either resigned or was fired. He had also overstepped his bounds as a brother by confronting Bliss without first getting permission. The "*act* [was] indefensible," Twain wrote to Orion, but that "does not in the least blind me to the virtue of the *motive* underlying it, or leave me unthankful for it." Twain himself soon confronted his publisher. Was it or was it not the case that a seven and a half percent royalty equaled half profits? Was it or was it not true that Bliss had reduced the costs of production without sharing the savings with the author? At Bliss's home in Hartford, they examined the account books together. With no accounting skills or publishing expertise, Twain was no match for Bliss. "I am glad you convinced me," he told his publisher a few days later, "for I would be sorry indeed to have come away from your house feeling that I had put such entire trust & confidence in you to finally lose by it."

But he was, in fact, not in the least convinced. He responded as if he were, in order to make appear as unconfrontational as possible his request that the contract be altered to state "half-profits" rather than seven and a half percent royalty. A refusal, Twain silently considered, might be the basis for a lawsuit. By June, however, Twain had decided against suing Bliss. If Bliss were to deny that he had ever said that seven and a half percent equaled exactly half profits, it would be his word against Twain's. Also, the sales of *Roughing It* were going marvelously well. A legal suit against the American Publishing Company, which probably would require an injunction, would harm or even halt sales. And, since he was still tied by valid contract to Bliss for two more books, he could not readily change publishers. Pressure on Bliss now, short of legal proceedings, might encourage him to be more accommodating. But to go beyond that might do more damage than good, even if Twain won the suit. And the notion of his quarterly royalty payments being suspended was disconcerting. His expenses were high; he needed the money. From that time on, though, he never trusted Bliss again.

With the lecture tour over by mid-February 1872, and relieved to be home again in "Nook Barn," as they nicknamed the Hooker house, Twain held Livy's anxious hand as her pregnancy came to term. Plans for the house they would build were tentative. They had neither land nor architect, but they enjoyed fantasizing about how happy they would be, especially because lecturing would never force them apart again. Money was still an issue. By the summer Twain was to have about thirty thousand dollars in the bank, the amount they anticipated they needed to purchase land and build a house. Livy's inheritance, tied up in investments difficult to extricate from those of the other heirs, provided annual interest and dividends of about thirty thousand dollars. Livy did some budget calculations, something neither of them had much talent for, and, as usual, they underestimated expenses. She was quite certain, though, that in the event their estimates proved unrealistic they would "change entirely" their "mode of living" to fit their income. Gradually, regardless of budget, the notion of building a house became settled in their minds, as much a leap into the unknown and as inseparable from their domestic vision as sixteen-month-old Langdon and the baby about to be born. Close to mid-March they left Hartford for Elmira, for the springtime and summer pleasures of the Langdon mansion and the Cranes's hospitality at Quarry Farm. Apparently the baby's birth was still considered to be a month or two off.

Unexpectedly, Livy went into labor soon after arrival. Perhaps the train journey was responsible, but Langdon had also been premature. Early in the morning of March 19 was "born . . . to the wife of Saml. L. Clemens of Hartford, Conn., a daughter. Mother & child," the father wrote to his brother, "doing exceedingly well. Five pounder," though two months later he recalled that she had weighed four and a half pounds. By mid-May, the infant, named Olivia Susan after her mother and aunt, had about doubled her weight. "The new baby is as fat as butter, & wholly free from infelicities of any kind," her father happily reported. Langdon, though, declined, or at least was slow to gain health. "He is as white as alabaster & is weak; but he is pretty jolly about half the time." The parents worried about his wracking cough "& the suffering & irritation consequent upon developing six teeth in nine days." The rest of the time his crying wrung their nerves. The contrast between the children was stark. The father, so Twain remembered, perhaps accurately, took his son out for a ride in a carriage on a cold morning. "I soon dropped into a reverie and forgot all about my charge." The coachman noticed that the child's wraps had fallen away. "The child was almost frozen. I hurried home with him. I was aghast at what I had done."

The Clemenses' new daughter, who would be called Susy, was baptized on May 26, 1872. Two days later the family returned to Hartford, via New York. Livy was exhausted, at the edge of her endurance. Langdon's chest cold at first seemed slightly better, then got worse. Soon the doctor diagnosed diphtheria. On Sunday morning, June 2, their neighbor and friend Lily Warner, married to Charles Dudley Warner's brother George, reported that "the little Clemens boy at last finished his weary little life and died quietly in his mother's arms." Livy went into deep shock. The child she lost was now transformed into the child that could never be replaced. Twain steeled himself into consolation, and self-laceration. It seemed to him that the child had been almost a disaster from the start. "He kept thinking," Lily reported to her husband, "it wasn't death for him but the beginning of life. She will see it all by & by, but can't yet." She never could.

The Hookers and the Twichells did their best to comfort her. "Oh, how sweet & lovely the baby seemed & how my heart ached for those who must give up theirs," Lily wrote. Twain and his Nook Farm friends sat in the parlor with the corpse. Joe Twichell said a simple prayer and read from the Bible. Livy, though, did not have the strength to accompany the baby to Elmira for burial. Susan and Theodore Crane came to Hartford to comfort their sister and to escort the child. In Elmira, "in the same room where Mr Clemens & Livy were married," Susan wrote, "the beautiful child was laid, surrounded by all our best beloved friends—while Mr Beecher offered prayer." At sunset Langdon was put into the ground, close to his grandfather and namesake. There was never to be another male Clemens heir. For the rest of Twain's life he blamed himself for the child's death, just as he had felt responsible for Henry's, as if his neglect rather than diphtheria had killed him. Blaming himself was always his best comfort.

Twain's billiards
and writing room, Hartford

Susy, Livy, Clara, and Jean,
Hartford, 1884

The Clemens family, Hartford, 1884: Olivia, Clara,
Jean, Samuel, and Susy

Howells in Venice in
the early 1860s

Mark Twain and George W. Cable,
1884

PUCKOGRAPHS—NEW SERIES, NO. 1.

"MARK TWAIN,"
America's Best Humorist.

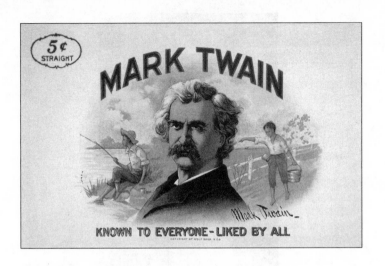

Jane Clemens's seventy-ninth birthday photo,
June 18, 1882

Clara at about twenty

Jean, 1898

MARK TWAIN'S TOUR

AROUND
THE WORLD,

BEGINNING IN CLEVELAND,

OHIO, JULY 15th, 1895,

CLOSING IN LONDON, MAY, 1896

ROUTE IN AMERICA.

JULY.

Mon	15.	Cleveland, Ohio	Stillman House
Tues	16.	" "	" "
Wed	17.	*Travel on Steamer.*	
Thur	18.	Sault Ste. Marie, Mich	Hotel Iroquois
Fri	19.	Mackinac.	Grand Hotel
Sat	20.	Petoskey, Mich	Arlington Hotel
SUN	21.	Mackinac..	Grand Hotel
Mon	22.	Duluth, Minn	Spalding Hotel
Tues	23.	Minneapolis, Minn	Hotel West
Wed	24.	St. Paul, Minn	Hotel Ryan
Thur	25.	*Travel.*	
Fri	26.	Winnipeg	The Manitoba
Sat	27.	"	" "
SUN	28.	"	" "
Mon	29.	Crookston, Minn	Crookston Hotel
Tues	30.	*Travel.*	
Wed	31.	"	

AUGUST.

Thur	1.	Butte, Montana	The Butte Hotel
Fri	2.	Anaconda, Mont	The Montana
Sat	3.	Helena, Mont	Hotel Helena
SUN	4.	" "	" "
Mon	5.	Great Falls, Mont	Park Hotel
Tues	6.	*Travel.*	
Wed	7.	Spokane, Wash	The Spokane
Thur	8.	*Travel.*	
Fri	9.	Olympia, Wash	The Olympia
Sat	10.	Tacoma, Wash	The Tacoma
SUN	11.	" "	" "
Mon	12.	Portland, Or	The Portland
Tues	13.	Seattle, Wash	The Rainier
Wed	14.	New Whatcom, Wash	
Thur	15.	Vancouver, B. C.	Hotel Vancouver
Fri	16.	*Sails from Vancouver for Australia.*	

ADDRESS ALL COMMUNICATIONS TO

MAJOR J. B. POND,

EN ROUTE.

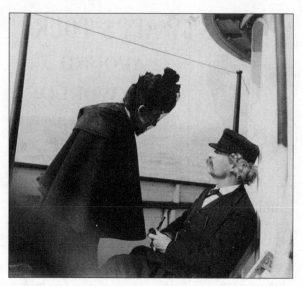

Livy urging her husband to put on his overcoat, July 1895

Twain, with local cat, dropping in on impoverished immigrants
at a Norwegian shantytown, Montana, July 1895

Twain relaxing in his Olympia, Washington, hotel room, August 1895

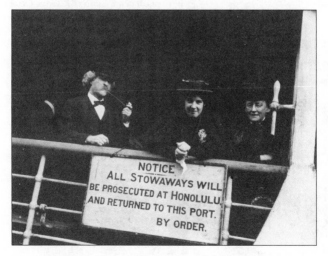
Twain, Clara, and Livy leaving on S.S. *Warrimoo*,
August 1895

Clara with her mournful parents,
Dollis Hill, near London, 1900

Anti-Semitic cartoon ("Mark Twain Seeks Material
in Vienna for New Stories," *Kikeriki!* October 10, 1897)
From Carl Dolmetsch, "Our Famous Guest": Mark Twain in Vienna *(1992*

The Hotel Metropole, Twain's Vienna residence,
where he worked on versions of his Satan stories
From Carl Dolmetsch, "Our Famous Guest": Mark Twain in Vienna *(1992)*

CHAPTER TEN

THE LION
1872–1874

1.

On "a splendid night" in late September 1872, Mark Twain discovered to his delight that he was a celebrity in, of all places, London. One among many invited to the annual Guildhall dinner celebrating the installation of the new lord mayor, he walked to his assigned seat next to Sir John Bennett, an enthusiastic reader of *Innocents Abroad*. Bennett had invited Twain to observe the ancient ceremony, one protocol of which was the requirement that each of the names of the 250 guests be ceremoniously intoned. The long roll call continued "in respectful silence—but when he came to my name along with the rest, there was such a storm of applause as you never heard," he wrote to Livy. "I was never so taken aback in my life. . . . I thought I was the humblest in that great titled assemblage—& behold, mine was the *only* name in the long list that called forth this splendid compliment. . . . I did not know I was a lion." In another account, he did not hear his name called out. Turning to Bennett, he inquired as to who was being so enthusiastically applauded. When Bennett asked if he would respond to the toast for literature, he could not say no. "I got up & said whatever came first," he told Livy, "& made a good deal of a success." Actually, it was a weak speech, the inevitable result of being caught off guard, an exception to his practice that his impromptu speeches be carefully prepared.

In the four weeks since he had arrived in Liverpool, Twain had met a number of prominent Englishmen, but he had gotten little sense of the size of his British readership. On the train from Liverpool to London at the beginning of the month he sat opposite a man reading *Innocents Abroad,* probably in the two-volume edition created by the London publisher John Hotten, who regularly published, without payment to authors, books not protected by British copyright. British law provided foreign authors the opportunity to attain copyright by being on British or commonwealth soil on the day before and on the day of British publication. Twain was pleased to see that his fellow passenger was reading the book, despite it being of no pecuniary advantage to the author, but he was not pleased to notice that this English reader never once changed the expression on his face. It was enough to make a humorist grim, even despondent.

In London, he went immediately to the office of George Routledge, whose offer of a contract to pay him for the English edition of *Roughing It* he would happily sign. Though it was a modest onetime fee, it allowed Twain to feel he wasn't being entirely cheated. It did mean, however, that on the actual date of London publication in mid-December 1873 he would have to be on British territory to insure copyright. Enthusiastically greeted by the Routledge firm, he soon was taken under their hospitable wing, which included sightseeing excursions and introductions to London literary and club society. British literary and aristocratic culture adored American celebrities, especially if they were talented and idiosyncratic: the more distinctively "Yankee" the better. To the English, Twain seemed like the second coming of Artemus Ward, though better. As long as his energy held out, Twain went to teas, dinners, banquets. He was the guest of honor at the Whitefriars club and the Savage Club, having the time of his life.

Though he missed Livy, he missed her less than he wanted her to know, not because he loved her the less but because, by contrast with the stresses of family and professional life during the spring and summer of 1872, his visit to England was a restorative holiday. It was partly justified by his claim that he needed to attend to his publishing interests in Britain and his intent to gather material for a new book. It was mainly, though, a flight from the aftermath of young Langdon's death, from the exhaustion arising from Livy's depression, from the excitement but also the partly compromised birth of little Susy, and from the hard work that had brought *Roughing It* through the press early in 1872. He had yearned for domestic life, and now he had it with a vengeance.

Fortunately, by late summer 1872 Livy was on her way to recovery, helped by the new baby's good health and quiet disposition. As soon as the June heat began to become oppressive, the family left Hartford for New Saybrook, Connecticut, a resort on Long Island Sound, two hours from Hartford. By the waterfront, Twain mainly kept his feet up on the porch rail, smoked cigars, and enjoyed convivial company, including refined parlor games with other vacationers. Livy and the nurse looked after Susy. With time on his hands, he devised another invention, *"a self-pasting scrapbook"* to consist of pages coated with a gluelike substance activated by a light application of moisture, page by page, as the need arose. His *Quaker City* friend Dan Slote, already in his family's stationery business, would handle manufacturing and selling what turned out to be the only invention Twain created or invested in that, over the years, made a profit, however modest. It was an appropriate invention for a writer who all his life kept and had others keep scrapbooks of his disparate publications and any mention of his name in print.

He also now had a chance to repay Bret Harte for his assistance with *Innocents Abroad,* though it was payment not in literary coin but in practical favors and real dollars. Harte's one-year, ten-thousand-dollar stint with the *Atlantic Monthly* had been a failure. Now, with a family but without a steady source of income, he borrowed widely, and Twain had generously doubled the $250 Harte had requested on a visit to Hartford in June 1872. To put himself financially on his feet, Harte agreed to a series of lectures for Redpath, though he had a morbid fear of speaking in public. No one was under the illusion that he was an outstanding lecturer, but he was serviceable enough, if he worked at it seriously, and his reputation was a magnetic draw. To Redpath's embarrassment, Harte treated his audiences contemptuously or, even worse, did not show up, the lecturer's cardinal sin. Soon Redpath canceled the remainder of the tour, to Harte's seeming indifference, as if he had been doing Redpath a favor and did not need the money. Redpath sued. To help Harte, Twain encouraged the American Publishing Company to offer him a contract for a subscription novel. Harte had never before written a novel, and his reputation for not fulfilling contracts may have hovered over Bliss's deliberations. But Twain soon had the satisfaction of brokering a deal. The promised novel, though, was to be long delayed, and neither author nor publisher was to profit from it.

At New Saybrook, Twain also worked on a revised edition of *Innocents* for Routledge, an attempt to reclaim his property from Hotten, though the revision consisted mostly of a new preface tailored to flatter the English audience. Its Anglophilia, though, was at least partly sincere, its emphasis on "our kindred blood & our common language, our kindred religion & political liberty." Twain took some minor pride in his ancestors having come from the British Isles. By early August he had decided to "leave for England in 10 or 12 days to be gone several months," his ostensible purpose to collect notes for a satiric book about the English. The diamond mine book was seeming less and less viable. Riley had become ill with cancer, and by June 1872 Twain "felt fully convinced that he would never get over it." The Mississippi River book had again been put on hold.

It was from the start assumed that Twain would go to England alone, but within weeks of his arrival he began to envision a more prolonged stay that would require his family to join him there. He was impressed by London's cosmopolitan charms, enchanted by England's graceful countryside, and happily gratified by how he was being received. London was for him a living textbook of history from the Renaissance to the nineteenth century. He tried, though, to "see as many *people*" as he could, rather than sights. "If I could take notes of all I hear *said,* I should make a most interesting book." Local customs, as always, intrigued him. The more he liked England and the English, though, the less sustainable seemed the kind of book he had intended to write.

An American in Britain, he kept his republican distance but, to his surprise, that was not as great as he might have expected. More and more, the English seemed to him to make sense, to cohere. And given their eagerness to welcome him, he found virtue in his upper-class hosts, at least in regard to their personal character and charm. That they were aristocrats was not entirely their fault. "But as Americans have *no* rank, it is proper to place us either *above* or *below* the nobles. Courtesy rather forbids the latter, & so we get good seats." Professional concerns demanded that he pay close attention. "About one thing there is no question whatever," he told Livy, "& that is, one mustn't tackle England in print with a mere superficial knowledge of it. I am by long odds the most widely known & popular American author among the English & the book will be read by pretty much every English-man—therefore for my own sake it must not be a poor book." More time in England was the answer, he wrote, promising to show wife and daugh-ter the beautiful English countryside, some of which he saw on an excur-sion to Warwickshire and Stratford-on-Avon in early September. "If you & Theodore will come over in the spring with Livy & me," he wrote to Susan Crane, "& spend the summer, you shall see a country that is so beautiful that you will be obliged to believe in fairy-land." He proposed to Livy that she come immediately and they stay for six months or that he return some-time late in fall or early winter and that they all return in spring 1873 for a long stay.

Invitations to lecture came thick and fast. "I am revamping, polishing & otherwise fixing up my lecture on *Roughing It* & think I will deliver it in London a couple of times about a month from now, just for fun," he wrote to Redpath, an odd comment to a man whose pleas for him to resume lec-turing in America he had resolutely turned down. Redpath may have sensed that this was another twist in Twain's love-hate relationship with the platform, though it probably also had a great deal to do with his desire to please his English hosts. His attitude about lecturing was still the same: "When I yell again for less than $500 I'll be pretty hungry. But I haven't any intention of yelling at any price." Obviously he did, or he would not have been revamping his *Roughing It* lecture. But he changed his mind again, and though he would stay into December he would not lecture on that visit but on the next one, a promise that he felt partial repayment for generous hospitality.

He went on a stag hunt just to see what the fuss was all about. "I hunted that stag in a wagon—but I didn't catch him. Neither did the red-coated, pigskin-breeched hunters—but it was fine to see the 250 scour over the hills & fields & sail over the hedges & fences like so many birds." When he arrived back in town, "nicely shaved & gotten up regardless of ex-pense" for the annual dinner at the Whitefriars Club, he discovered that it had been held the previous night. "I haven't done much but attend dinners & make speeches," he wrote to his mother. He attended the opening of the New Guildhall Library and Museum, where, to his surprise, he seemed to know almost everyone. At the lord mayor's annual state dinner, the lord high chancellor remarked to him "that when affairs of state oppress him . . . he always has my books at hand & forgets his perplexities in reading them!" He would, though, have had to do much rereading, since the entire Twain corpus consisted of two long travel books and an edition of sketches. And though there was unlikely to be any condescension in private comments, Twain probably gave little to no consideration to the likelihood that British readers found his humor attractive because it was idiosyncratically American, which partly meant unsophisticated and exotic. His bushy hair and mustache, his sharp nose and bright eyes, especially when perched on a giant frog in a caricature published in a widely distributed London magazine, were widely recognized throughout England. Twain himself had become a partial convert to what he felt to be a superior civilization. "I would a good deal rather live here," he wrote to Susan Crane, "if I could get the rest of you over." When he sailed from Liverpool in late November 1872, he and Livy had agreed that they would all return in the spring.

2.

At home in Hartford, he embraced eight-month-old Susy, who had flourished during his almost four-month absence. No one made a fuss about his being away, though Livy could not have been entirely happy. He had deflected potential criticism by downplaying how good a time he had been having, though his expressions of enthusiasm could not have escaped her notice. Separations like those that had wrenched his heart during their courtship and the first year of marriage were considerably less lacerating now. Still intent on writing his England book, partly to justify his long absence, he occasionally allowed his reservations to surface. Now, though, he had new tales to tell, among them the exciting rescue at sea he had witnessed on the return voyage. In a dangerously turbulent storm, the captain of the *Batavia* had orchestrated the rescue of ten surviving crew members of a wrecked ship. Watching intently, the passengers had applauded the heart-stopping heroics as the small rescue boat labored in high seas toward the men clinging to the mast of their sunken ship. Twain described the dramatic rescue in a letter to the Royal Humane Society, which the *Boston Advertiser* published. He had been deeply impressed during his stay in England by English benevolence, by silent acts of charity that seemed characteristic of the English upper class, even of English society as a whole, especially in comparison with tightfisted American sink-or-swim individualism or American charity as self-glorification. That the *Batavia*'s captain wanted neither praise nor publicity for fulfilling his humane duty to help others in distress, even at great risk, seemed characteristically English.

At Nook Farm, propriety was under assault. In September 1872, Isabella Hooker's ally and friend Victoria Woodhull accused Henry Ward Beecher of having committed adultery with Elizabeth Tilton, a member of his Pilgrim Church congregation. Hooker, Beecher's half sister, whose "Nook Barn" the Clemenses rented, was a prominent figure in the women's rights movement. She synthesized two mid-nineteenth-century preoccupations: spiritualism and suffragism. She envisioned a spiritual and utopian world that would exist if only women had the vote. In 1869 she had organized a convention in Hartford that helped pass a state law allowing women to own property. With allowance for his humor and satiric bite, Twain agreed with Hooker's platform. Despite his caustic deflation of Beecher's overly pious pilgrims, he knew and admired the minister, whose guest he had been and at whose dining table he had listened to words of advice. In November 1872, Woodhull, for whom marriage embodied patriarchal bondage, repeated the accusation, this time in print. She was soon imprisoned on the charge of having sent obscene materials through the mail. A three-year-long front-page scandal had begun. Was Beecher an adulterer? If so, was he not also a hypocrite, condemning in public what he practiced in private?

When Twain arrived home in late November 1872, the kettle of scandal was at a low boil, mostly at Nook Farm and in other small circles. Beecher refused to make public comment other than an indirect denial. Twain limited his criticism to Beecher's unwillingness to publish a document, alleged to be in his possession, signed by the Tiltons that purportedly denied any impropriety. Twain and Twichell believed Beecher innocent, though Twain, often the skeptic about human nature, entertained the possibility that he was not. It was "a filthy subject," and whoever had the means to obviate it had a moral responsibility to do so, including Beecher. Isabella Hooker sided with Woodhull. The rest of the Beechers believed Henry. Isabella's sisters refused to talk to her. Twain (with Livy's concurrence) chose to assume, until further evidence was forthcoming, that Beecher was being slandered. Totally separate from anything to do with the Hooker-Beecher estrangement, Twain expected to be out of "Nook Barn" by April 1873, when he and Livy would sail for England, to return, they expected, to a house of their own.

During her husband's absence, Livy had been scouting Hartford real estate. By January 1873, his royalties from *Roughing It* amounted to another $20,000, and they felt secure enough to move forward. Each had about $30,000 in separate accounts. Livy's cash was to be used for purchase, his for expenses. In mid-January 1873, to their excitement and delight, they bought a Nook Farm lot from a Hartford attorney for $10,600, "the loveliest building lot in Hartford," Twain declared, "544 feet front on [Farmington] Avenue & 300 feet deep—(paid for it with first six months of 'Roughing It'—how's that?) & the house will be built while we are absent in England." The George Warners would be their immediate neighbors. Harriet Beecher Stowe's house would be a few minutes' walk to the east. Senator Gillette and Joseph Hawley would be nearby, Twichell a few streets away.

Soon they put the design commission into the hands of George Warner's New York City architect, Edward Tuckerman Potter, a well-known practitioner of the High Victorian Gothic style. The front of the house would look eastward toward Forest Street; the westward view would be the glen descending to the border created by the north branch of the Park River. The entrance would be from Farmington Avenue. It would be a large turreted three-story building, 105 by 62 feet, with nineteen rooms, a combination manor house, steamboat, and castle, built in burnished brick and wood, with sloping roofs and overhangs for each segment, a large covered veranda curving around the south end and an octagonal tower on the west side. The interior, organized around a large three-story-high entrance hallway, richly ornamented in black walnut and oak, would have an elegant library, a glassed-in conservatory, ample bedrooms for family and servants, a billiards room on the top floor, the usual Victorian kitchen and pantry, the most modern toilet and water systems available, and Twain's own eccentrically imaginative contribution: a window through the fireplace that would bring wintry snows and red flames into the same gaze. The house was to be distinctive, stolid, and baronial, the residence of an imaginative Victorian man of means. Excavation would begin in April 1873, to be completed within a year. The estimated cost was between $55,000 and $60,000, including the land. Twain was later to say that it was "all bought with Livy's money."

Two other excitements filled the late winter and spring, both with a political cast. Just a few weeks before Twain stepped off the *Batavia* onto American soil, a bitter presidential election had been resolved. Twain had met the candidates, President Ulysses S. Grant, running for reelection, and his combined liberal Republican and Democratic Party opponent, Horace Greeley, founder of the *New York Tribune* and an originator of the Republican Party. Reconstruction divided the Republicans; opposition united the Democrats. The Civil War general's first term in office had not convinced many of his political and administrative abilities, and widespread rumors accused his supporters of enriching themselves dishonorably. Twain liked Grant and thought him an heroic figure. The irascible, temperamental Greeley he thought less well of. He deplored Greeley's defection, as a Republican, from support of the party's leader for a second term and his morally compromising decision to accept the Democratic nomination, as their platform took most of the teeth out of Reconstruction. He had humorously caricatured Greeley in *Roughing It* and had met him in 1871 when he had gone to the *New York Tribune* office in search of a staff member to whom he had been recently introduced, John Hay. Three years younger than Twain, Hay had already had a momentous political and diplomatic career. Also from the Mississippi River valley and a writer of a book of humorous verse, *Pike County Ballads,* he had had an inside view of the Lincoln White House as one of the president's two secretaries.

Hoping to continue as a *Tribune* contributor, Twain made certain to say nothing in print about the candidates during the 1872 election, but he strongly hoped Greeley would lose. He complimented Thomas Nast, the political cartoonist who had invented the donkey and the elephant as symbols of the parties, on his anti-Greeley drawings. Five years younger than Twain and the staff cartoonist for *Harper's Weekly,* Nast had in 1867 proposed that they become partners on a lecture tour. Nast's novel idea was to draw extemporaneous illustrations while Twain spoke humorously, creating the verbal captions, so to speak, on stage, in full view of the audience. Now Twain hoped to persuade Nast to come to England with him to create illustrations for the book he was planning to write. "More than any other man," he wrote to the cartoonist in late 1872, "you . . . have won a prodigious victory for Grant—I mean, rather, for Civilization & progress; those pictures were simply marvels; & if any man in the land has a right to hold his head up & be honestly proud of his share in this year's vast events that man is unquestionably yourself." When Greeley, who resumed his editorial duties immediately after his defeat, died suddenly at the end of November 1872, his potential successor for control of the *Tribune,* acting editor in chief Whitelaw Reid, entered into a vigorous struggle with the controlling stockholders, who had their own candidate.

Twain had an interest in the outcome. He knew Reid and believed he would keep the *Tribune* open to his contributions, especially letters to the editor, some of them long, for which he received payment, a favorite outlet of his for ad hoc comments on contemporary issues. When the stockholders triumphed, Reid resigned. So, in support, did many of his colleagues, including Hay. But when the stockholders' candidate unexpectedly withdrew, Reid borrowed enough money from the financier Jay Gould to buy a controlling interest. The weary stockholders thought it a sensible resolution. "I hope you will stand at its helm a hundred years," Twain wrote to Reid, now both editor and owner. Twain had Bliss send Reid a copy of *Roughing It,* hoping Reid would assign Hay to review it. Reid, though, gave it to someone else, who wrote an adequately favorable but uninspired review. Twain was disappointed and annoyed. He had expected better.

When the newly founded Lotos Club hosted a dinner for Twain in early February 1873, its president, Whitelaw Reid, welcomed him to membership and to the festivities. Twain grumbled a little about the *Tribune* review but restrained himself. In April, striving to keep sales interest in the book alive, he pressured Reid to "jam into . . . the Advertiser" the statement that "Mark Twain's new book, 'Roughing It' has sold 43,000 copies in two months & a half. Only 17,000 copies of 'The Innocents Abroad' were sold in the first two & a half months." This blurb was at best misleading but, Twain told Reid, "I hate to see our fine success wholly uncelebrated."

In early February he had *not* celebrated his and Livy's third anniversary with her. The Lotos Club dinner and other social activities kept him in New York for two weeks, and custom did not allow women, even as guests, at men's clubs. Both husband and wife, though, had been strongly touched by reformist ideas, especially Livy. Their political and social ideologies in general embraced liberal Republican post–Civil War views. Work for women was acceptable, but, if there were a conflict, motherhood and family came first. This married couple had no overall argument with the Victorian conventions governing women in the home and in society. Livy had indeed happily embraced her domestic role, which included total authority in her sphere and tremendous influence on her husband's decisions. Ultimately, though, her deference could be depended on. So too could her competence, both in regard to the household and as the first reader of her husband's work. He kept their anniversary, he wrote to her, "in the solitude of the hotel," recovering from the boisterous club dinner of the night before. His mind was at least partly on the changes that were occurring in the relationship, the gradual transformation of romantic passion into less turbulent feelings, the domestication of the erotic, for better and for worse. He put it in the most positive terms. If their "mutual satisfaction . . . continues to grow as it has grown since 1870, we shall by & by become not merely the lovingest couple in the land but the happiest. I think our gales of happiness, with lulls of depression between, are quieting down day by day, & will presently be resolved into a calm great deep of love & peace, untouched by any ruffling breeze, & unshadowed by any vagrant passing cloud." He was increasingly aware that he had made a thoroughly lucky marriage.

3.

When Twain returned to Hartford in November 1872, the presidential election had highlighted the Washington corruption that had been on his mind since his stay there three years before. A novel seemed the likely genre to explore this subject, since satiric fiction could more effectively highlight dramatic truth than the extended essay. The structures of *Innocents Abroad* and *Roughing It* were based on literal voyages. An attack on Washington corruption and American materialism did not come with a built-in story line; one would have to be invented. The previous summer he had tried his hand at fiction, though apparently he had not gotten far before putting the project aside. Written for boys, it was to be set in Hannibal, Missouri, based on characters and incidents from his childhood. He did not, though, consider himself a novelist of any kind.

It made him anxious to consider something he had never tried before, a radical departure from what he had been successful at. He could not afford a failure. One antidote to anxiety was to have two pairs of hands at work. A conversation with his friend Charles Dudley Warner quickly produced a literary partnership. Warner seemed a promising coauthor. A handsome New Englander with a gray-flecked beard and mustache, the forty-three-year-old Warner was a graduate of Hamilton College; he had worked as a railway surveyor, a lawyer, and a journalist. That he had been a surveyor in Missouri and knew Twain's childhood territory provided an unexpected link between them. As coeditor of the *Hartford Courant,* Warner was a man of standing. A writer of intelligent personal essays, he had had substantial critical success with his first collection, *My Summer in a Garden.* Widely traveled in Europe, he had just published a volume of travel sketches, *Saunterings,* which reminded critics of the work of Washington Irving.

About five months after Warner and Twain had decided to collaborate, Warner published, in June 1872, an essay in which lightly disguised versons of Twain, Twichell, Warner, and the latter's wife, Susan, discuss the failings of most recent women's novels. Twain and Warner apparently had been challenged by their wives to support their claim that they could do better than any of the popular novels published by women over the previous twenty years. Nook Farm critical tongues had harsh things to say about this aspect of the feminization of American culture. The vision that such novels idealized was anathema both to feminist reformers like Isabella Hooker and to exponents of aesthetic realism like Twain. Nook Farm readers, including Twain himself, read novelists such as Rebecca Harding Davis, who "drenches the whole field beforehand with a flood of lachrymose sentimentalism," with the same dry eyes as did the young Henry James. More sentimental than James in his attitude toward women, Twain was interested in fiction that would be realistic, morally serious, and also commercially successful.

Warner, like Twain, had also never written a novel, an indication of the degree to which their collaboration was the product of propinquity, not thoughtful deliberation. That *The Gilded Age* turned out as well as it did is mostly the consequence of Twain's satiric genius, his talent for revealing in broad strokes the best and worst of human nature. Actually, and surprisingly, in its totality the flaws in *The Gilded Age* arise only to a minor extent from the inexperience of the authors as novelists and the inherent problems of collaboration. Mainly, they are an exemplification of a major feature of Twain's work throughout: his difficulty in managing narrative structure.

Known best for the title that gave its name to an age in American history, *The Gilded Age, A Tale of Today,* published in late 1873, is arguably Twain's most autobiographical fiction. Some of its elements come with the barest of disguises from his family's history and his early life. Warner let Twain set the novel's agenda in every sense. No wonder Twain soon found himself so deeply engaged in his stint that he regretted, even resented, time away from his desk. The plan, which seemed sensible and obvious, was that Twain would do the first segment, to be followed by alternating stints. In the end, this resulted in his writing all of thirty-two and parts of three more of the sixty-three chapters. He wanted to be certain his aggressive imagination would determine the novel's initial setting, its major characters, and its likely development. The co-authors had already agreed on the novel's satiric targets. The narrative route was, at first, the one from Tennessee to Missouri that John Marshall Clemens and his young wife had followed in 1834. The autobiographical material, initially the engine that drives the novel, provides partly fictionalized portrayals of John Marshall Clemens, Jane Clemens, Henry, Pamela, Orion, and especially James Lampton, transformed into Colonel Beriah Sellers. Squire Hawkins and Colonel Sellers have a fatal genius for impractical ideas and inventions, an obsessive, unbalanced preoccupation with inevitably unsuccessful schemes to make themselves and their families rich, a failure of business sense and economic realism that make them both painfully pathetic. Hawkins has nothing comic about him. Sellers embodies the comedy of the grotesque, appropriate in a novel that unevenly combines satire, melodrama, and burlesque.

Two traumatic events in Clemens family history set the context, establish the themes, and initiate the major characters: the explosion that destroyed the steamship *Pennsylvania* in 1858, killing Henry Clemens, and John Marshall's obsession with his Tennessee land and the curse it inflicted on his family. On their journey westward, the Hawkinses witness the explosion of the steamboat *Amaranth,* and the details of misery, death, and the treatment of the wounded, including the hospital in a city like Memphis, are a minimally disguised account of the *Pennsylvania* explosion. Two important elements, though, are altered. The inquest concludes

"Nobody to Blame," an exculpation with a public irony that does not conceal that indeed the young Sam Clemens believed he knew exactly who was to blame for Henry's death. And, instead of the family losing one of its sons, it gains a daughter, whom it eventually will also lose, the troubled Laura, whose parents have died in the explosion and whom the Hawkins family adopts. The name of Twain's childhood sweetheart came to his mind both for his fictional family's last name and for the name of their adopted daughter, the beautiful, reckless, willful romantic who rises to the corridors of power as a Washington lobbyist, works to make the family's Tennessee land valuable, and eventually murders her faithless lover. On his deathbed, Squire Hawkins perpetuates the family curse: "I am leaving you in cruel poverty. I have been—so foolish—so short-sighted. But courage! A better day is coming—is coming. Never lose sight of the Tennessee Land. Be wary. There is wealth stored up for you there—wealth that is boundless! The children shall hold up their heads with the best in the land, yet." His son, Washington Hawkins, like Orion, embraces his father's legacy. It is a brilliant use of autobiographical material, family myth, and direct experience.

In minor but significant ways the novel reveals Twain's liberation from the view of blacks that his Missouri childhood had promoted, not only his rejection of the normalcy of the "peculiar institution" but his awareness of the morally damaging dehumanization that racial prejudice inflicted on masters and slaves. Part of the novel is set in pre–Civil War Missouri, from approximately 1845 to 1860, though a gap of eight years between chapters 17 and 18 moves the action to 1868, bringing the section of the novel dealing with political corruption into the early 1870s. Like all Twain's fictional returns to his childhood, the issues and complications of Reconstruction in the light of his later humanistic Republicanism permeate his historical depictions, forcing their way into a novel that has little to do with black-white relationships. When, before the war, the Hawkins family home in Missouri is put up for forced sale, the household servant, Uncle Dan'l, and his wife "pass from the auction-block into the hands of a negro trader and depart for the remote South to be seen no more by the family. It had seemed like seeing their own flesh and blood sold into banishment." When, after the war, a visiting Washington politician, a pro-Reconstruction Republican, remarks to Colonel Sellers, " 'Providence . . . has placed [the negro] in our hands, and although you and I . . . might have chosen a different destiny for them, under the Constitution, yet Providence knows best.' " Colonel Sellers interrupts, " 'You can't do much with em.' " The Senator continues: " 'They are a speculative race, sir, disinclined to work. . . . Still . . . we must fulfil our duty by this being.' 'I'd elevate his soul,' promptly responded the Colonel; 'that's just it; you can't make his soul too immortal, but I wouldn't touch him, himself. Yes, sir! make his soul immortal, but don't touch the niggro as he is.' "

Though the curse of the Tennessee land helps destroy the younger generation of Squire Hawkins' family, the curse of the novel is that the collaboration encouraged two plots, both of which had promising materials, neither of which was sufficiently compatible with the other. The inexperienced novelists could not, at least initially, see this; and in the division of labor each had some responsibility for the other's plot, which vitiated what each separately could do best. And each plot needed to coalesce and become part of the satiric exposure and condemnation of political corruption in Washington. Twain managed that by directing the Hawkinses' Tennessee land toward a Washington political redemption, just as he had himself lobbied for a political solution to Jervis Langdon's desire to be repaid for his investments in Nashville. At the end, Washington Hawkins, his youth mostly wasted, claims that he has broken the curse of the Tennessee land, which he voluntarily forfeits for a small amount of unpaid taxes.

Post–Civil War America was becoming the Gilded Age. The railroad construction boom had made the economy white hot. Investment capital would turn small sums into immense wealth. The power of positive thinking and investment would make the smart man rich. "I can put this money into operations here," Twain has Washington Hawkins confidently exclaim in a tone resembling that of his own letters from Nevada and California in the 1860s, "that will increase it a hundredfold, yes, a thousandfold, in a few months. The air is full of such chances." And if cash was unavailable for investment, there remained credit, "Beautiful credit! The foundation of modern society," Warner wrote. "That is a peculiar condition of society which enables a whole nation to instantly recognize point and meaning in the familiar newspaper anecdote, which puts into the mouth of a distinguished speculator in lands and mines this remark: 'I wasn't worth a cent two years ago, and now I owe two millions of dollars.' " One of the few levelheaded characters in the novel worries (and believes) that the day of reckoning will come, though, in Twain's words, her "household had no idea of the number of perils that hovered over them, any more than thousands of families in America have of the business risks and contingencies upon which their prosperity and luxury hang."

As he worked on *The Gilded Age,* Twain agreed to deliver in February 1873 a series of four lectures, a revised version of his now venerable Sandwich Island talk, in Manhattan, Brooklyn, and Jersey City. With no pressing need for lecturing fees, he lectured partly for publicity to help sales of *Roughing It* and, though still half a year or so off, *The Gilded Age.* He also may have seen it as a warmup for his British lectures, which he felt he would do, though arrangements were not yet in place. Resoundingly successful, the four lectures were applauded by audiences and reviewers, one of whom, in Reid's *Tribune,* wrote, "It must never be forgotten that Mr. Clemens is not only a great humorist, but a great observer and a deep philosophical thinker."

Eager to have *The Gilded Age,* a title settled on a little after mid-April, finished before he sailed, he and Warner pressed ahead through March and April. In his study at Nook Barn, each night they read the day's work to Livy and Susan Warner. "They have done a power of criticising," he wrote to Mary Fairbanks, "but have always been anxious to be on hand at the reading & find out what has been happening . . . since the previous evening. They both pleaded so long & vigorously for Warner's heroine, that yesterday Warner agreed to spare her life & let her marry. I killed my heroine as dead as a mackerel yesterday (but Livy don't know it yet)." To his perturbation, the world soon knew that *The Gilded Age* was a novel, a fact that Twain still wished to down play if not conceal. The public, he assumed, as did Bliss, wanted from Mark Twain another humorous book like those that had made him famous. By mid-April he began to describe the book to certain editors, emphasizing, "[Warner] has worked up the fiction & I have hurled in the facts. I consider it one of the most astonishing novels that ever was written." What he wanted was free publicity in advance of publication and, later, newspaper reviews, a reversal of his policy with *Roughing It.*

On the assumption that the *Tribune* would set the tone, he sent Whitelaw Reid suggested wording for a publication announcement. John Hay used it, along with a letter Warner had sent, to write a lighthearted notice that the *Tribune* published in small type in the bottom-right corner of its editorial page. Misreading the goodwill of the notice, Twain was infuriated, and frightened. "You give us a notice which carries the impression to the mind of other editors," he wrote to Reid, "that we are people of small consequence in the literary world, & indeed only triflers; that a novel by us is in no sense a literary event." His fear that the book would not be taken seriously rose almost to paranoia. Unaware that Hay had written the notice, he blamed Reid alone. Why, Twain threatened him, shouldn't he accept the blandishments of the *Herald* and write regularly for it if this is how the *Tribune* was going to treat him? Would the *Tribune* please do the notice again, and this time get it right? "Now just see if you can't do us a real outspoken good turn that will leave a strong wholesome impression on the public mind—& then command our services, if they can be of use to you." The anger, partly a function of his anxiety, was also the strategy of an author who believed he now had enough clout to intimidate those with the power to help make a market for his books. "Bilious?" he responded to Reid. "I was more than bilious—I was *scared*. When a man starts out in a new role, the public always says he is a fool & won't succeed. So I wanted to make every knife cut that could *help* us succeed, anyway."

But he never trusted Reid again, and what had been developing as a mutually supportive friendship quickly cooled down. Reid probably found Twain's letter distasteful, even insulting. Shortly before leaving for England, Twain encouraged Edward House, his friend from *Quaker City* days and a well-known journalist, to ask Reid to assign House *The Gilded Age* to review. While visiting Hartford in late April, House had read the novel in manuscript, with pleasure and great praise. From Twain's point of view, this was an opportunity for Reid to make amends. The publisher, who apparently disliked House, thought the proposal demeaning to the *Tribune*. He declined in no uncertain terms. "[Reid] is a contemptible cur," Twain wrote to Warner, "& I want nothing more to do with him. I don't want the Tribune to have the book at all." These were his last words as the *Batavia* pulled out of New York Harbor. Such incidents rarely if ever motivated Twain to self-examination; as was often the case, he transformed his unwarranted grievance into hostility.

4.

Just after mid-May 1873, accompanied by Livy's friend Clara Spaulding, a tall, thin, provincial Connecticut schoolteacher named Samuel Thompson, whom Twain had hired as his secretary, and a nurse, the Clemenses sailed from New York for Liverpool. He had with him the finished manuscript of *The Gilded Age* to deliver to Routledge. Bliss of course would publish it in the United States. Other than his two patented inventions and his quarterly royalty checks, Twain had no other source of income except a small dividend from five-thousand dollars' worth of American Publishing Company stock he had purchased. It was, he felt, an investment in himself, since his book sales accounted for most of the company's profits. Looking forward to having the means to buy additional stock, he told Bliss that he desired to be made a director of the company. He wanted to have as much control as possible over how much butter was put on his slice of the bread.

"Some people think I have no head for business, but it is a lie," he insisted, expressing his self-satisfaction about his astuteness in going to England to protect his copyright. As quick to praise as to blame himself, he took pleasure in his lack of debts, the prospect of substantial income from the new book and from lecturing, and the family's progress and happiness in Hartford since the beginning of the year. Though expenses were high, including regular checks to his mother and his readiness to help Orion, he was living within his income and expectations. That the house under construction might strain his resources seemed unlikely. Both Livy and the baby were in good health. Susy, nicknamed "Muggins," appeared to be as much blessed with good health as little Langdon had been cursed with bad. Both parents marveled at the contrast, the pleasure of having an amiable baby who fit naturally into life rather than one at odds with it. Livy was now comparatively healthy. The sea air and excitement put a touch of pink into her white cheeks. In Hartford, the social network at Nook Farm had embraced them both. Their friendships with the Twichells, the George Warners, and the Charles Dudley Warners had become intimately close. Smart, accomplished contemporaries, Lily and Susan Warner and Harmony Twichell provided daily companionship for Livy, particularly sustaining when her husband was away. Regular visits from her sister Susan and from her mother kept her two worlds happily connected.

Twain had also become a voice for Hartford charities and other civic projects, especially in the Hartford, Boston, and New York newspapers eager to print his words. To raise $1,500 for the poor, he gave his Sandwich Island lecture gratis. The Hartford Monday Evening Club, meeting twice a month from October to May, welcomed him as a guest and then, in mid-

February 1873, as a member. An elite group of twenty, including the reigning ministerial triumvirate, the intellectual society had been co-founded in 1869 by Horace Bushnell, Calvin Stowe, and J. Hammond Trumbull, the last an expert in New England Native American languages who provided *The Gilded Age* with the quotations, many in exotic languages, that prefaced each chapter; a whimsical joke in a serious, satirical book. At each meeting, rotating among the homes of the members, a short paper was read, followed by discussion, limited to ten minutes for each participant. Afterward, there was a light supper. The women of the house and other ladies graced the background as hostesses and friends, but not as participants. When, in March 1873, Twain gave his first paper, "The License of the Press," a "(bogus) *protest of the Publishers against the proposed foreign copyright,*" he combined comic relief and intellectual seriousness. His associates were delighted. He made laughter respectable. And he helped make Hartford a very desirable place to be, both for them and for him.

Though this trip to England was to be no more than a long working holiday, it confirmed his earlier impressions, reinforcing what was to be a lifelong approval of English life and culture. Restraint, modesty, politeness, courage, integrity, trustworthiness, loyalty, common sense—the stereotypes of the English character appealed to him, partly in contrast to American individualism, partly because of his own English heritage, but mainly because the English upper class, including the aristocracy, treated him well and made much of him. Eager to be loved and praised, he was soon to have to face definitively the question of whether he would allow himself to make fun in print of a nation that had opened its homes to him. When he had arrived in Liverpool the previous summer, he had been so unfamiliar with Britain that, getting a cab for an hour's sightseeing, he asked the driver to take him to Balmoral. Hours later, awakening from a daze, he needed sympathetic intercession from the authorities to get the cab driver not to insist that he pay the full fare. Local English justice treated the foolish stranger well. Now, in Liverpool, arriving on May 27, 1873, he could easily play the experienced traveler to Livy's innocence. Other than to set her feet on the Canadian side of the Niagara border, she had never been out of the United States, and she had seen little of her own country.

Settling into a small hotel in Hanover Square, they began a dizzying series of sightseeing excursions and social engagements. "My wife," he told a friend, "likes this awfully quiet [hotel] but I don't. I prefer a little more excitement." After four weeks, they moved to the huge Langham in Portland Square, in which he had stayed during his previous visit. Their "luxuriously ample suite" could contain visitors; there was a billiard room in which he could knock balls about. He took two days in mid-June to go to Ostend, Belgium, to do five letters about the visiting shah of Persia for the *New York Herald,* the change an expression of his anger at Reid: he had determined never to write for the *Tribune* again. Most mornings Thompson took dictation from him—mostly letters, perhaps notes for his book about the English, though by mid-July Twain felt enough frustration with his inadequacy in dictating—his "sentences came slow & painfully, & were clumsily phrased, & had no life in them"—that he decided to dismiss his secretary. Anyway, he was happily spending most of his time sightseeing and socializing.

Dinner invitations from Londoners came thick and fast. Twain accepted as many as possible, sometimes, where appropriate, with Livy, sometimes by himself. He dined with Thomas Hughes, author of *Tom Brown's School Days,* and Herbert Spencer, the sociologist and philosopher, and spent evenings at the Savage Club and the Cosmopolitan Club, where he met Robert Browning, whose works he admired more than any other contemporary poet's. He was introduced to Turgenev and Lewis Carroll. Friends from his previous visit embraced him again, particularly Moncure Conway. Henry Lee took pleasure in showing the family around the Brighton Aquarium. Livy and Clara Spaulding whirled about London, seeing the sights for the first time. With Joaquin Miller, the wild poet of the Sierras, now the American flavor of the season in London society, Twain did some late-night sightseeing and attended a celebrity-studded dinner in Miller's honor, hosted by Anthony Trollope. Next to Miller, Twain seemed quiet, almost shy. They got along well enough to plan a country excursion for later in the summer.

After visiting Stratford in late June, the Clemenses left London for Edinburgh. On their way north they stopped at York, "this queer old walled town," for a few days. Its ancient ruins embodied "the glory of English chivalry & romance." Edinburgh was a great delight, partly because Twain nearly succeeded in his intention "to be introduced to nobody . . . & go on resting." After six weeks of intense London social life, comparative anonymity seemed what the doctor ordered, especially for Livy, who soon needed the services of an actual doctor. The only one in Edinburgh whose

name Twain knew was John Brown, a writer in his early sixties best known
for his heart-wrenchingly sentimental dog story, "Rab and His Friends." A
quiet, charming, infinitely considerate man, Brown took to the Clemenses
immediately. He thought Livy beautiful. He wrote to a friend that she was
someone he had "better not see," because her beauty might "disquiet [his]
peace for life . . . such a startlingly pretty little creature, with eyes like a
Peregrine's, and better than she looks." Soon Brown's carriage began appearing regularly at their hotel door to take the family on drives, and his
unmarried sister, who ran his household, proved charmingly quaint. These
Scottish siblings seemed to Twain stellar embodiments of the best of the
national character.

In mid-August 1873 they visited Walter Scott's Melrose and Abbots-
ford. As a young boy in Hannibal, Twain had shared the widespread passion for Scott's romantic heroines and plots, and, though he still admired
his literary genius, he now thought Scott's romantic exaltation of chivalry
had been damaging in its influence on the manners and mores of the ruling class in the American South. Nonetheless, he eagerly purchased two
sets of the thirty-two-volume Waverley edition of Scott's novels, one for
himself, the other as a present for one of his Langdon relatives. Heavy-
hearted at saying good-bye to their friends, thinking that they would "probably never see them again," they left Edinburgh for Belfast. Everyone was
badly seasick except Twain. At the beginning of September they traveled
to Dublin, where they did the usual sightseeing, though he later regretted
that he had forgotten to visit Swift's grave. He did, though, reread *Gulliver's
Travels,* which he had first absorbed as an adolescent and had last read
in 1869.

By late September there were numbers of business and personal issues
to resolve. Bliss still had not provided Routledge with the plates for the illustrations for the English edition of *The Gilded Age*. In fact, Bliss had not
even settled on the date of American publication, except to assure the author and Routledge that he was making all possible haste. Livy, in the
meantime, was growing increasingly homesick. She missed her mother and
sister and her Hartford friends and wanted to settle on a definite date for
their return, which, however, could not take place before the British publication without Twain losing copyright protection. At least the question of
whether or not he would lecture in London had been settled. They needed
the money; they had been spending freely on "little odds & ends" for their

new house. These "odds & ends" were not all "little," though, and some were very expensive. In response to a suggestion that he visit Vienna, he pled family responsibilities and financial exigency. "I have been here 4 months; I have already spent ten thousand dollars—& the end is not yet! Is it to such a man that you blandly recommend Vienna?" Instead, he sent to America for more money and continued, "calmly & with courage," to purchase things for the new house and to fulfill his obligation to buy presents, including sealskin coats like his own for his mother and sister and Charley Langdon.

Soon he had reason to feel his purchases had been imprudent. In mid-September, a major New York bank with heavy investments in western railroad construction failed and a Wall Street panic sent the market plummeting. Stocks and bonds fell further, and foreign exchange was temporarily suspended. When, after a few disastrous weeks, the federal government reissued millions in Civil War "greenbacks" that had been retired, the immediate drama was over, though the panic became the prelude to a six-year-long financial depression that had grievous consequences. In London, Twain anxiously waited for each bulletin from New York. "The financial panic in America has absorbed about all my attention & anxiety," he wrote to John Brown. He had three thousand dollars on deposit in a New York bank that had suspended payments, though the bank assured its customers that they would be resumed. In the end Twain received his money in full, though he insisted, perhaps because of his general inability to make sense of numbers, more likely because of his inclination to turn situations in which people had made him uncomfortable into irrational grievances, that he had been cheated. After assessing their situation, the Clemenses went ahead with a brief visit to Paris, leaving Clara and little Susy in London. They worried, though, whether or not they should be pinching pennies, especially with regard to Livy's income from her Langdon investments. "You know if the firm is cramped," Livy wrote to her mother, "Mr Clemens can lecture and get money to pay our debts and get us home—Now Mother don't you and Charlie laugh at that, lecturing is what Mr. C. always speaks of doing when there seems any need of money."

When, in October 1873, he stepped onto the stage to give the first of seven lectures, "Our Fellow Savages of the Sandwich Islands," the crucial issues had been resolved. Appearing self-confident and with a quiet American swagger, so one British reviewer noted, the lecturer seemed "a comparatively young man, small in form and feature, dark-haired and dark complexioned. He has a good deal of the nasal tone of some portion of the Americans." His humor came supported by deadpan seriousness. He concluded with a flourish of beautifully descriptive rhetoric that left his large audiences in awed silence. After a final lecture in Liverpool on October 20, the Clemenses would sail for New York. But George Dolby, a well-known manager who had handled Dickens' lectures, had found a willing collaborator in his plan for Twain to offer another series of Sandwich Island lectures in London during the first three weeks of December, with the possibility of a lecture tour in the provinces. Dolby promised him full houses and plaudits. In addition, there seemed reason to think the British edition of *The Gilded Age* would be published in mid-December. Livy needed to go home. She desperately missed her familiar world, and she was now two months' pregnant.

One week after the *Batavia* docked in New York, Twain was back on the stormy Atlantic, this time on the comparatively huge and stable *City of Chester*. The first flush of lecturing in London through much of December sustained him. So too did Charles Warren Stoddard, his old San Francisco friend, the homosexual poet whom Twain thought the "purest male I have known, in mind and speech." Companionable, loyal, completely trustworthy, the well-traveled Stoddard, who had come to England in late October, happily accepted Twain's offer to pal around with him as a friend and secretary, with a small salary, which Stoddard needed. He hoped that Twain would use his influence to help him attain a consulship, the kind of government position that an impecunious poet could handsomely adorn. A good listener, he was a perfect foil for Twain's and especially Dolby's ribald jokes. Twain put him to work creating a large file for a book about the Tichborne perjury trial, some sessions of which Twain had attended the previous summer, fascinated, as always, by claimants. Stoddard's only flaw as a companion was his inability to keep his eyes open after midnight when his conversational employer was still wide awake and voluble. Some evenings Twain kept himself entertained and Stoddard awake by pounding out old favorites on the piano.

Why Twain chose to return to London rather than establish copyright by going to Canada, and why he returned to lecture for fees that he could have readily earned by lecturing in the United States, he never commented on. Since by this time he had, in his mind at least, given up the idea of writing a book about the English, that was not a motivation for returning. Perhaps he had not had enough of London and the English. An energetic, almost fearless traveler, he usually wanted more of what seemed a good thing, particularly applause, money, and adventure, wherever he needed to go to get it. The challenge was to harmonize those desires with his commitment to wife and home. He could be happy for periods of time without Livy, especially if he could keep the bond strong across the distance through letters. And he rarely felt the need to disguise from her both the pleasures he experienced when away and the desire he felt for her when they were apart. On the *Chester* "the time slides by in comfort & satisfaction," he wrote to her, "& I seem to enjoy every hour of it." From London he told her about his shopping trips and urged her to tell him *"all"* the Hartford gossip—"everything the neighbors say about each other," for "gossip of *any* kind, & about anybody is one of the most toothsomely Christian dishes I know of." On her birthday he provided the rhetorical flourishes that emphasized how much he missed her.

As the lecture series began, he felt a rush of adrenaline. On the day of each performance he worked off some of it in conversation, in billiard games, and in walks. The laudatory reviews and increasingly large audiences steadied his nerves. When he sent a note of invitation, as well as complimentary tickets, to Tennyson, he was pleased to get a friendly response. "An autograph note from him is a powerful hard thing to get," he boasted to Livy. Bored with the Sandwich Islands lecture, he decided to alternate it with a lecture from *Roughing It,* which required rehearsal and memorization. He had it prepared by the beginning of the second week of December. "Livy darling," he wrote to her, "I never enjoyed delivering a lecture, in all my life, more than I did tonight. . . . There were people there who gave way entirely & just went on laughing, & I had to stop & wait for them to get through. . . . Those people almost made me laugh myself, tonight." One night "thick blue smoke" from millions of coal fires, described as the heaviest London fog in twenty years, filled the concert hall, "so thick today at noon that the cabs *went in a walk, & men went before the omnibuses carrying lanterns.*" The first thing he said on stage was "Ladies and gentlemen, I *hear* you, & so I know that you are here—& I am here, too, notwithstanding I am not visible." London audiences and reviewers could not praise the *Roughing It* lecture enough. However, continuous heavy fogs diminished his audiences. He began to feel frustrated and discouraged, and by mid-December absence from Livy had begun to wear on him. "If I'm not homesick to see you, no other lover ever *was* homesick to see his sweetheart. And when I get there, remember, 'Expedition's the word,'" he wrote, using their private code for the urgency of his desire.

5.

After long absence, he was happy to be again in Hartford at the end of January 1874, though home was still Nook Barn. "I am *entirely* idle, & shall remain so for two weeks & possibly three," he wrote to Frank Fuller. "I *did* intend to lecture in New York & Boston, but my wife prefers that I should remain at home . . . & I honestly think I have not even a faint desire to do anything that does not meet with her enthusiastic approval." They went to Quarry Farm in the spring for Livy's confinement. On June 8, 1874, she gave birth to a girl of nearly eight pounds, whom they named Clara, after Clara Spaulding. To their relief, mother and baby had a relatively easy delivery. In the expectation that the child might be a boy, they intended, as they had for Susy, to name him after Henry Clemens.

When Twain visited Hartford at the end of June, he sent back to Elmira an impatient but glowing progress report on the house of their dreams. Turning off Farmington Avenue, he had his first glimpse of the new house and hardly recognized it, as "two months had made such charming changes in it." In fact, he was ecstatic. It seemed to him to be "a quiet, murmurous, enchanting *poem* done in the solid elements of nature. The house & the barn do not seem to have been set up on the grassy slopes & levels by laws & plans & specifications—it seems as if they *grew* up out of the ground & were part & parcel of Nature's handiwork. The harmony of size, shape, color,—everything—is harmonious. It is a *home*—& the word never had so much meaning before." Troops of workmen still constantly roved through the house. Though the servants had been installed in useable rooms, the family could not expect to occupy the house until at least September.

Even if she was disappointed with the news, Livy had her hands full with two children whose variations in health sent her into paroxysms of worry. When fresh cow's milk made Clara ill, she was breastfed by a local black woman. For a short while the infant's health faltered "so seriously as to scare everybody." When she got better, Susy became ill. Livy, exhausted, was beset by a series of illnesses that continued, on and off, for the rest of the year. Susan Crane, who had risen to sainthood in her brother-in-law's eyes, was the healthy, capable angel of the house. "It is such a comfort to me to know that if I *do* chance to wind up in the fiery pit hereafter, she will flutter down there every day, in defiance of law & the customs of the country & bring ice & fans & all sorts of contraband things under her wings. . . . [She will] be shunned by all proper angels as an eccentric & disreputable saint. I can believe a good deal of the bible but I never will believe that a heaven can be devised that will keep Susie Crane from spending the most of her time in Hell trying to comfort the poor devils down there."

That their original estimate for the cost of the house proved substantially low was for the moment a minor concern. By July 1874, they had expended about $40,000, excluding the land, the $10,600 cost of which they added to by purchasing small additional lots for a driveway, a greenhouse, and a protective barrier. With the cumulative cost of furnishing the house, the total expenditure between 1872 and 1876 rose to about $75,000, equal to about $1.5 million now, though neither the quality of the workmanship nor the furnishings could be reproduced for less than double that, given the high level of craftsmanship available at low cost in the nineteenth century and the cheapness of manual labor at a time when a wage of a dollar a day was considered reasonable. For example, Patrick McAleer, rehired after being fired for drunkenness in 1872, was paid fifty-five dollars a month for the skilled, responsible job of chauffeuring the family. Almost all their savings, and much of Twain's income, though apparently none of Livy's capital, went through the hands of Thomas Perkins, their lawyer and neighbor, for the ongoing costs of building the new house and to pay their regular bills.

Fortunately, Twain's income soared. Modest royalties still came from *Innocents Abroad* and *Roughing It. The Gilded Age* proved a financial success, though its critical reception was mixed and the large number of hostile reviews was galling to both of its authors. Some had a condescendingly nasty edge, particularly those highlighting the problems associated with dual authorship. Even the best of the critical reviews emphasized aesthetic weakness, the incoherence of a narrative in which the two plots seemed unreconciled. In his preface to the British edition, Twain had tried to forestall the possibility that the English would take his criticism of American political corruption as if it embodied his full view of the American scene, and indeed some British reviewers noted that Twain and Warner were as harsh on America as Dickens had been in 1843 in *Martin Chuzzlewit*. "In

America," Twain wrote, "nearly every man has his dream, his pet scheme, whereby he is to advance himself socially or pecuniarily. It is this all-pervading speculativeness which we have tried to illustrate in *The Gilded Age*. It is a characteristic which is both bad and good, for both the individual and the nation. . . . But I have a great strong faith in a noble future for my country. A vast majority of the people are straightforward and honest; and this late state of things is stirring them into action." Many American readers saw only the harsh criticism.

The hostile reviews pilloried the novel on two grounds, both morally censorious: Twain had used Warner to write half a novel with the intention of being himself rewarded as if he had written it all, and the satiric attack on American corruption so distorted reality as to be slanderously self-serving, biting the national hand that had made Twain the best-paid author in the country. The *Chicago Tribune* thought it a callous fraud, a puerile, vicious book by authors whose "names had become a sort of certificate of high character. It is a fraud to the reading public to append them to a trashy book. . . . Stupidity can be forgiven, but deliberate deceit—never." Though the worst of the negative reviews, it set only the outside parameter for many others. "It is a distortion of the life today in America," the *Boston Advertiser* stated, "to represent it as if knaves and simpletons were the only people of account." Twain had purposely not had a review copy sent to the *Tribune*. The *Herald*, like other papers and magazines favorable to Twain, gave the book a good notice, substantial and intelligent, with high praise for its satiric realism.

But, as Twain had feared, the absence of sustained humor disappointed many. Even some of the friendly reviewers had to work against that expectation. The *Atlantic Monthly* chose not to review it. At work on a novel, *A Foregone Conclusion,* to be published to considerable praise, including Twain's, and eager to have Twain as a contributor to the *Atlantic,* Howells was in an awkward situation in which silence was his best response. He highly valued cohesive structure and consistency of characterization. Twain had little sense of either and never would approach Howells' standards in these regards. The bad reviews depressed both Twain and Warner. "Warner felt the adverse criticism was for him," Twain recalled years later. But to their and Bliss's delight the book still sold very well, the royalties divided equally between the authors.

For Twain, in fact, the novel soon proved to be an even greater financial success, though in another form. The stage had had a longstanding appeal to him, from minstrel shows to Shakespeare in his Hannibal youth and from burlesque comedy to grand opera in his San Francisco days. In New York and London, he rarely missed a chance to see productions ranging from popular sentimental dramas to fashionably celebrated high art. His own platform appearances kept him sensitive to performance values, and over the years he had made tentative probes into theatrical creation. In England, Dickens had been powerless to prevent stage adaptations of his novels for which he received no payment and over which he exercised no artistic control. Adaptations of *Uncle Tom's Cabin* had produced profits for everyone but the author, who was often so totally excluded from the process as not even to know that her book was being staged until advertisements appeared. Theatrical piracy was a way of life. In both Britain and America, laws for protecting stage adaptations as intellectual property were rudimentary. In February 1873, a musical adaptation of *Roughing It* opened in New York. Augustin Daly, its producer and a prolific commercial playwright, claimed his play was based on a French source whose author and title he did not identify. His version had the same title as Twain's book and made use of several easily identified scenes. Twain was both flattered and annoyed.

A year later, soon after the December 1873 publication of *The Gilded Age,* Twain was furious to discover that a San Francisco journalist, Gilbert Densmore, whom he knew and otherwise felt friendly toward, had created a stage adaptation, which began performances in San Francisco in the spring. Twain and Warner had from the start anticipated the likelihood of a production. After completing the manuscript, they had registered a copyright for a "'Dramatic Composition' entitled *The Gilded Age: A Drama.*" When the popular dramatist Dion Boucicault expressed interest in doing it, Twain, on his way to England, warned Warner that he would "not consent to his having more than one-third." In London, he consulted with his English friend Tom Taylor, an experienced dramatist. Densmore, he soon discovered, had cleverly created a play based mostly on the character of Colonel Sellers, precisely what Twain himself had in mind. Sellers seemed to him theatrical gold, a Dickensian comedic figure, both gentlemanly and pathetic, a man of fundamental decency and honor caught in the grip of obsessive schemes for getting rich, the kind of memorable character that could be the basis for painfully riveting humor.

Twain threatened to sue. In a settlement, he paid Densmore four hundred dollars for his script and the cessation of performances. The copyright, Twain maintained, had always been his. Warner and Twain each relinquished dramatic rights in the characters the other had created. So Sellers now belonged to Twain alone. By July 1874, he had completed a five-act dramatization, drawing to some modest amount on Densmore's script. *"I entirely re-wrote his play three separate & distinct times,"* he explained to the *Hartford Times*. "I had expected to use little of his language & but little of his plot. I do not think that there are now twenty sentences of Mr. Densmore's in the play, but I used so much of his plot that I wrote & told him that I should pay him about as much more as I had already paid him, in case the play proved a success." The four hundred dollars had been for Densmore's plot, not his words. "I don't think much of it, as a drama, but I suppose it will do to hang Col. Sellers on," he wrote to Howells.

In early September 1874 he spent a week in New York, going each morning to the theater for three hours, helping "the actors at the rehearsals," so he thought. The West Coast comic actor John Raymond, who had appeared in Densmore's brief run, now performed in Twain's version. "We suppose (at least we *hope*) it will run twenty years, in this country." When the play premiered at the Park Theater on September 16, 1874, the author gave a brief curtain speech. President Grant and other notables soon attended. The play earned Twain, from its 115-night New York run and its tours, as much as he made from sales of *The Gilded Age*. "It pays me from five hundred to a thousand dollars a week," and Raymond the same, he reported. He wrote to his brother-in-law that his pay from performances in large cities was nine hundred dollars each night and, "in smaller towns" on its extended national tour, four hundred to five hundred dollars. As late as October 1876, he received a check for $1,616.16 for the play's first week in Philadelphia. Whatever the actual overall figure, he was profiting handsomely. The play was "a singularly emphatic success."

6.

Though New York was the commercial and theatrical capital of the country, Boston was still its literary center. When, in February 1874, Twain attended a dinner for Wilkie Collins at the St. James Hotel, the other guests included Whittier, Holmes, and Longfellow. Twain and Livy were Longfellow's guests for lunch at Craigie House. At the end of the year, a week before the one hundredth New York performance of *Colonel Sellers* in December 1874, Twain attended a dinner for twenty-eight *Atlantic Monthly* contributors hosted by its new publisher, H. O. Houghton. James Fields had sold the *Atlantic* to James Osgood, and, when Osgood's publishing firm retrenched during the panic of 1873 and the depression that followed, he in turn sold the magazine to Houghton. At the dinner, Twain responded to a toast to the president of the United States and to the female contributors to the *Atlantic* with a comic speech in which he commented that he was so staggered by the immensity of the subject that he needed to attack it in sections. He then proceeded to talk entirely about other things. It was an admirable dinner, Twain remarked, "quite as good as he would have had if he had stayed at home!"

Through much of 1874, he consolidated his position with the Boston cultural world, his attention directed more toward Boston than New York, primarily because of Howells, Aldrich, and the *Atlantic Monthly*. Howells indeed was the main human draw. After negotiating with Livy, who wanted to keep him at home as much as possible, Twain arranged with Redpath to lecture in Boston in March. Warner, meanwhile, invited the Howellses and James Osgood to be his guests at Nook Farm, intending to bring the Twains and the Howellses together for a few days. When it appeared that Redpath required Twain in Boston on the day of the visit, Warner and Twain were in a frenzy. "Warner's been in here swearing like a lunatic," Twain wrote to Howells, "& saying he had written you to come on the *4th*—& I said, 'You leatherhead, if I talk in Boston both afternoon & evening March 5, I'll have to go to Boston the *4th*'—& then he just kicked up his heels & went off cursing after a fashion I never heard of before." The visit was shifted to the sixth.

The day after Twain's lecture in March 1874, the Howellses and Osgood came down with Twain from Boston to spend the weekend as Warner's guests. Livy, who was pregnant again and recovering from a threatened miscarriage, liked Elinor Howells, with whom she shared a maternal temperament. Admiring the easy freedom of visiting between neighbors, Howells thought the Nook Farm community almost ideal, epitomized by their minister being addressed as "Joe." Twain urged Howells to move to Hartford. The house next door to Harriet Beecher Stowe was for sale. "I saw a good deal of Twain," Howells remarked, "and he's a thoroughly great fellow. His wife is a delicate little beauty, the very flower and perfume of *ladylikeness*, who simply adores him—but this leaves no word to describe his love for her."

When Howells next returned to Hartford he was to be the Clemenses' guest in the house they took possession of in September 1874. That summer, at Quarry Farm, with Livy preoccupied with the two children, Twain had returned to the book set in his Hannibal childhood. He made some minor progress, but much of his time was devoted to adapting *The Gilded Age* for the stage and writing two stories. One he named "Some Fables for Good Old Boys and Girls," a humorously satirical attack on false scientific reasoning and, indirectly, on the Judeo-Christian creation myth, the other "A True Story," a first-person account, in Twain's version of black dialect, of a story told by the cook at Quarry Farm, Mary Ann Cord. Working intently to create the illusion of a real voice, to translate actual speech into a literary analogue that would convey though its devices the illusion of authenticity, he created a brief first-person narrative, the power of which resides in the experience of the storyteller, a black slave woman in the South who has been separated forever from her husband and seven children. Working during the war as a cook for Union officers, she recognizes among the troops her favorite son. The reunion is tearfully joyous. Her endurance is her great strength. Her capability for joy never leaves her. "Oh, no, Misto C—, I hain't had no trouble," she concludes. "An' no *joy!*" Howells, though he thought well of "Fable," feared its Christian heterodoxy would alienate subscribers. "A True Story" he thought a small masterpiece, and soon convinced his *Atlantic* colleagues to pay Twain the highest per-page rate the magazine had ever paid in order to give fair compensation for such a brief piece.

However far Twain had gotten with the book about Hannibal, later to be called *The Adventures of Tom Sawyer*, it was a productive summer at Quarry Farm. In the spring, Susan Crane had constructed, a hundred yards above the house in a wooded area steps from the abandoned quarry that gave the property its name, an octagonal one-room wooden structure to serve as a writing studio for her brother-in-law. From the main house, renovated and designed, as were the grounds, in the fashion of mid-nineteenth-century country picturesque, Twain would walk each morning, after a light breakfast, up a winding path paved with rough stones, and stay until late afternoon, always skipping lunch, as was his year-round practice. A small table served as his writing desk. With a modest fireplace, a peaked roof, vine-covered outer walls, and a window in each of its eight sides, the study had a commanding view down the hill to Elmira and the river a few miles to the west, and to the tree-covered hills of southern New York State and northern Pennsylvania in the distance. It was to become his summer paradise, the place in which he would create much of his best and best-known writing.

When the family returned to Hartford in September, the Hartford-Elmira axis was firmly in place, though the Hartford house was still some months short of completion. With finishing work still being done on the first floor, they lived for a while entirely on the second. "We sleep in Ma's bedroom; eat in the nursery, & use my study for a parlor," he wrote to Orion. Twain soon moved his desk to the top floor, into the billiard room, since the second-floor room designated as his study proved to be too much in the center of activity even after the workmen had left. In August, leaving the children at the farm, they had gone to Fredonia to visit his mother and sister, and Livy became sick again. Consequently, much of the responsibility of the house fell to Twain. "I have been bullyragged all day by the builder, by his foreman, by the architect, by the tapestry devil who is to upholster the furniture, by the idiot who is putting down the carpets, by the scoundrel who is setting up the billiard-table (& has left the balls in New York), by the wildcat who is sodding the ground & finishing the drive-way (after the sun went down), by a book *agent,* whose body is in the back yard & the coroner notified. Just think of this thing going on the whole day long, & I a man who loathes details with all his heart!"

By November 1874 the house was sufficiently finished for him to take a holiday with Twichell, a walking tour from Hartford to Boston, an undertaking bizarre enough to elicit widespread newspaper accounts. After thirty-four heavily publicized miles, they gave up and took the train the rest of the way. "We arrive by rail at about 7 o'clock," he telegraphed to Howells. "The first of a series of grand annual pedestrian tours from Hartford to Boston to be performed by us, will take place *next year.*" Like everyone else, Howells thought the affair quite absurdly funny and knew that the project had been terminated, not postponed. But Howells did want Twain to continue writing for the *Atlantic Monthly.* "A True Story" was published in November, marking Twain's first appearance in the *Atlantic.* What about something also, Howells asked, for the January 1875 number: "some such story as the colored one?" "I have one or two things in my head," Twain responded, "but the trouble is I can't hope to get them out while the house is still full of carpenters." Howells asked again. "I find I can't," he replied. "We are in such a state of weary & endless confusion that my head won't 'go.'"

That same day he went for a long walk with Twichell. As they talked with their usual volubility, he began to tell Twichell "about old Mississippi days of steamboating glory & grandeur." Twichell said, "'What a virgin subject to hurl into a magazine!' I hadn't thought of that before," Twain wrote to Howells. He had, of course, though not as a series of magazine articles. The river book that had been in back of his mind since 1867 now found its occasion and its moment. He was soon at work on the first of a seven-part series, to be called "Old Times on the Mississippi." Though the still unfinished *Tom Sawyer* had already brought him back to Hannibal days, he would now plunge into both the real and fictional evocation of his formative years and places in ways that were to make a permanent mark on American literature and the American imagination.

CHAPTER ELEVEN

GOD'S FOOL

1874-1879

1.

Entering the fortieth year of his life, Twain spent the last months of 1874 and the first few of 1875 at his writing table in a corner of the top-floor billiard room, writing about his piloting days for the *Atlantic Monthly*. During the same period, though extending into the summer, he completed *Tom Sawyer*. Given to furious bursts of writing, he could sometimes produce as much as four thousand words at a stint. At other times household and business activities preempted writing for long periods. Over the years he grew confident that "ripeness was all," that when the unconscious and semiconscious forces at work had come into fullness they would, without intent on his part, resolve the problems that had previously baffled him. When a manuscript pronounced itself not ready to be finished, he put it aside. He never destroyed an unfinished manuscript, an expression of his sense of the potential usefulness to himself or to posterity of anything he wrote. He also had, for an impatient man, the surprising gift of volatile patience. He had learned by the end of 1875, despite moments of frustration, to trust in his gift's eventual effectiveness. When he died in 1910, he left a large number of unfinished manuscripts, many from late in his career, a testament to his lifelong practice but also to new obstacles that the Twain of 1875 never could have anticipated in his wildest dreams.

As he worked on "Old Times on the Mississippi" and *Tom Sawyer*, he had an initial audience of two: Livy, to whom each night he read the newest portion, and Howells, to whom he mailed the seven articles which the *Atlantic* published between January and August 1875, skipping the July issue. "You're doing the science of piloting splendidly," his editor assured him. "Don't you drop the series till you've got every bit of anecdote and remembrance into it." Howells thought Twain's combination of personal history and piloting fact brilliantly presented and likely to increase circulation. About the latter he proved to be wrong, mostly because large portions of each article appeared in newspapers around the country, directly reprinted from advance copies of the *Atlantic* the publisher provided in the hope of generating publicity.

Copyright laws in general protected neither author nor publisher. In September, Twain floated a proposal on the issue of international copyright, one of many efforts to better protect foreign and American authors. If Howells would get Longfellow, Whittier, Lowell, and Holmes to sign his petition to grant foreign authors American copyright, Twain would hire someone to attain hundreds of signatures of less well-known writers. He would then, himself, present it to the president for recommendation to Congress. Without protection for foreign authors, American writers had a fragile claim on other countries to respect their rights, and America was most at fault, since England at least provided a mechanism to protect American copyright interests.

Twain, though, also set his aim on a larger target, a radical extension of the forty-two-year copyright period in the United States. Championing international copyright was a first step without which the second could not be taken with any hope of success. "If we can ever get this thing through Congress," he wrote Howells, "we can try making copyright *perpetual* some day." It would benefit only the "one book in a hundred million" that "outlives the present copyright term—no sort of use except that the writer of that one book have his *rights*—which is something." He had reason to hope that he might be that writer. Why, he argued, should an author be different from any other owner of property? The law did not impose a statute of limitations on landowners, for example; private estates did not become public parks after a set number of years. Why should intellectual property be different? And even if an argument could be mounted on behalf of the public interest, why should writers be singled out to make such a sacrifice while every other entrepreneur whistled happily to the bank, knowing that the wealth he had earned or inherited could be passed on perpetually to his descendants?

What Twain had initially conceptualized as a likely nine-article series he soon decided would be no more than seven. "Old Times" he realized, threatened to preempt the Mississippi River book. "The piloting material has been uncovering itself by degrees," he wrote to Howells, "until it has exposed such a huge hoard to my view that a whole book will be required to contain it if I use it. So I have agreed to write the book for Bliss." He still owed his publisher a book to replace the South African volume for which he had accepted an advance. In February 1875, Bliss trumped him again on the issue of who owed who what. With encouragement from James Osgood, Twain gathered old sketches and essays, added new ones, such as "A True Story" and the unpublished "Some Fables for Good Old Boys and Girls," and wrote a preface. Osgood would publish it as a trade volume. When he informed Bliss, promoted from managing director to American Publishing Company president and whose board Twain now served on, Bliss argued against it. When Twain would not change his mind, Bliss shocked his author: "[He] went to his safe & brought back a contract *four years old* to give him all my old sketches, with a lot of new ones added!—royalty 7½ percent! I had totally forgotten the existence of such a contract—*totally.* Bliss said, 'It wouldn't be *like* you to refuse to first fulfill *this* contract.'" "The Old Fox" had his way again. *Sketches, New and Old* was published in July 1875 as a subscription book. Apparently Twain did not offer Bliss *Sketches* in fulfillment of both contracts. Or to pay back the advance in exchange for release from the diamond mine contract.

"You have the two greatest gifts of the writer, memory & imagination," John Hay wrote to him in December 1874, after reading the first two installments of "Old Times." Indeed, his memory was proving itself prodigiously active and inventive. His correspondence with Will Bowen had been the trigger that brought to life the dormant recollections that now surfaced with a particularity that made his Hannibal childhood and his river experiences primal. Memory, however, was not enough. *Tom Sawyer,* begun in 1872 and then put aside, had been his first attempt to take gold out of that mine. But it was only a tributary of the main stream, and though it was the second novel he had written it was his first solo attempt. Its brevity was a safeguard against novelistic inexperience, and its use of his Hannibal childhood guaranteed unity; but to create a definitive Mississippi book large enough for subscription publication he felt he needed to return to the river scenes and relive the river route, at least from Hannibal to New Orleans. In November 1874, he proposed to Redpath that the lecture agent accompany him in the early spring on "a lagging journey down the Mississippi, dining pilots & pumping stuff out of them for a book—& paying expenses & making money by talking," providing that he could finish *Tom Sawyer* by May. He had in mind, he told another correspondent, to "add fifty chapters more & bring the whole out in book form in November."

He also invited Howells, who seemed interested and whose expenses he offered to pay; then he substituted Osgood for an unwilling Redpath; then Osgood put himself on hold. When Livy's mother, whom he needed in Hartford when he would be away, became preoccupied with building a new house in Elmira, he postponed the trip. Howells vacillated. Twain urged that Howells and his wife travel with Livy and him; then, when the health of the wives eliminated that possibility, he proposed that he and Howells, with either Redpath or Osgood or neither, make the trip together. "Friend Bliss," he wrote at the beginning of March, "I've put off the Miss. River trip till June, & shall write a new book meantime," though he nowhere mentioned what that book might be. It seems unlikely to have been the unfinished *Tom Sawyer*, which hardly warranted being referred to as "new." Probably it was not the book he mentioned to Howells in July 1875 in which he would take "a boy of twelve & run him on through life (in the first person) but not Tom Sawyer—he would not be a good character for it." At the end of March he wrote to a friend, "Yesterday I began a novel," apparently the "new book" he had referred to in his letter to Bliss. "I suppose I am a fool, but I simply couldn't help it. The characters & incidents have been galloping through my head for three months, & there seems to be no way to get them out but to write them out. My conscience is easy, for few people would have fought against this thing as long as I have done. I certainly won't finish it, though, until I shall have completed one of my other books." The others, apparently, were *Tom Sawyer* and *Life on the Mississippi*. The writer who had made his fame with two autobiographical travel books had now begun thinking like a novelist.

In the end, Howells also declined to make the trip, and the Clemenses stayed on in Hartford for the early summer, where the weather remained unseasonably cool. Livy's health had been poor. Although almost never ill himself, Twain had some flu-like colds that were difficult to shake. There had been one scare with Susy, another with Clara. Each time illness struck, the specter of heartbreaking loss arose, partly owing to the trauma of Langdon's death but also because Victorian parents had good reason to expect a high incidence of infant mortality. Rather than go to Quarry Farm, they decided, perhaps on medical advice, that they would all benefit from sea air. In late July, *Tom Sawyer* now completed, they went to a rented farmhouse at Bateman's Point in Newport, Rhode Island, where Dan De Quille joined them for a week. Loyal and generous, Twain had offered to help De Quille complete his book on the Nevada silver mines, to be called *The Big Bonanza,* and to find a publisher. At Twain's invitation, De Quille came to Hartford, just as Goodman had come in 1873. De Quille was happy to have Twain's assistance, though he noted that Twain mainly skimmed through the manuscript before pronouncing it ready for publication.

Eager to have *Tom Sawyer* in the *Atlantic,* Howells urged Twain to extend the story to encompass the main character as a man as well as a boy. From Howells' point of view, it was not yet finished. "Don't waste it on a *boy,* and don't hurry the writing for the sake of making a book." Twain, though, had already made up his mind not to extend the story because "it would be fatal to do it in any shape but autobiographically" in the first person. To recast it from the first to the third person would require rewriting the novel. Besides, he did not think Tom Sawyer a suitable character for a first-person narrator. He insisted, "It is *not* a boy's book, at all. It will only be read by adults. It is only written for adults." Before delivering the manuscript to Bliss in November, he changed his mind and agreed with Howells: the success of *The Adventures of Tom Sawyer* would be measured by its appeal to children, especially young boys. It took Howells' analytical judgment to alter Twain's view of what he had accomplished. And Howells continued to play a decisive role as Twain's formal and informal editor. Amid a few suggestions for minor changes, he praised the novel effusively in a review for the *Atlantic,* calling it a book "which loses no charm by being realistic in the highest degree, and which gives incomparably the best picture of life in that region as yet known to fiction." Though Bliss's delay in publication from fall 1875 to late 1876 resulted in the review being put on hold, the "perfectly superb notice" of *Tom Sawyer* as "a book full of entertaining character, and of the greatest artistic sincerity" by an author who "has grown as an artist" exhilarated Twain.

Livy acted as his shield mostly on moral matters, Howells on stylistic. Livy sometimes encouraged him to rewrite considerably when she felt that the subject matter or the tone would make her husband vulnerable to being criticized by proper people. "You see, the thing that gravels her is that I am so persistently glorified as a mere buffoon, as if that entirely covered my case—which she denies with venom." When Howells returned the edited *Tom Sawyer*, Twain was delighted. What he had done "was splendid, & swept away all labor. Instead of *reading* the MS, I simply hunted out the pencil marks & made the emendations which they suggested," including shortening some of the episodes. On matters of propriety, Howells acted as a final screen to catch whatever Livy might have missed. Having "written & re-written the first half of [the fifth installment of 'Old Times'] three different times . . . at last Mrs. Clemens says it will do," Twain wrote to Howells. "I never saw a woman so hard to please about things she don't know anything about." But he recognized that it was in his interest to please her because she embodied the audience at large whose goodwill he needed to have. She helped him decrease the danger that he would be perceived as "a mere buffoon."

Propriety made its own demands, simply as the regulation of language and conduct in the world from which Twain earned his living. But so too did aesthetic and commercial considerations. And matching the kind and level of language to the character at issue was an aesthetic imperative. When both Livy and Howells let stand the phrase "and they comb me all to hell," he read the chapter to Livy's mother and aunt, "both sensitive & loyal subjects of the kingdom of heaven." To his relief, they did not protest. "I have noticed that a little judicious profanity helps out an otherwise ineffectual sketch or poem remarkably." "Profanity is more necessary to me than is immunity from colds," he wrote in response to Orion's pious counsel. Language considerations also were inseparable from his preoccupation with literary realism. Some punches of course had to be pulled, compromises made. But realism was the enemy of sentimentality, a distortion that Twain opposed in life and in literature. "I can see by your manner of speech," he wrote to his childhood friend Will Bowen in the summer of 1876, "that for more than twenty years you have stood dead still in the midst of the dreaminess, the melancholy, the romance, the heroics, of sweet but sappy sixteen. Man, do you know that this is simply mental & moral masturbation? It belongs eminently to the period devoted to *physical* masturbation, & should be left there and outgrown. Will, you must forgive me, but I have not the slightest sympathy with what the world calls Sentiment—not the slightest." If one could not be profane in public, at least one did not have to be sentimental, though Twain made exceptions, as the Victorians generally did, for certain idealizations, among them a lifelong belief in a pure class of females from Livy to Joan of Arc.

2.

Twain had two great teachers, experience and books, and the frequency and intensity with which he read widely in the popular literature of his era and in the classics of Western literature cannot be overemphasized. He desired to know—an autodidactic impulse he shared with many ambitious nineteenth-century Americans who had little to no formal education beyond grammar school. Twain was too early for the opportunity that land-grant universities would offer the next generation, and attending a private university was out of the question. An apprenticeship, whether in a counting house or law office or on a steamboat, served instead of an academic education except for the favored few who attended eastern universities. Other than for medicine and law, professional schools had only begun to exist. The ministry as a career was an exception, though its sectarian complications provided America at large with a much higher number of barely educated Baptist, Methodist, and Presbyterian preachers, like those of Twain's Missouri childhood, than graduates of Harvard, Princeton, and Yale divinity schools.

As a child, driven by curiosity, Twain immersed himself in the Bible, which he knew so well as to make Tom avoiding knowing it by heart one of the comic scenes in *Tom Sawyer*. He also read boys' books, adventure stories, romances, and how-to-do-it manuals, and then histories, biographies, travel books, works of religious advocacy, popular psychology and science, as well as newspapers and magazines that in the aggregate were anthologies of popular culture and thought. Also from early on he read novels by the score—Cervantes, Swift, Rabelais, Sterne, Fielding, Richardson,

Austen, Scott, Dickens, Thackeray, Trollope—and poets—everything by
Shakespeare, whose literary and biographical mysteries fascinated him,
and Milton, Pope, Byron, Shelley, Tennyson, and Browning. He ranged
backwards to the classics—Plato, Homer, and Virgil—and forward to his
American predecessors, from Franklin to Cooper, Emerson, Whittier, Lowell, and Stowe, and of course all the contemporary humorists who were his
rivals. Occasionally he detested a widely revered writer, such as Jane
Austen or Rabelais. His opinion of Scott changed from an early admiration
to a condemnation of his influence.

In the summer of 1877, telling Mary Fairbanks how a writer should be
totally immersed in his own work and thus consequently he had been reading little, he confessed that he could not "quite say" he had "read *nothing*.
No, I have read half of Les Miserables, two or three minor works of Victor
Hugo. . . . I have read Carlyle's wonderful History of the French Revolution, which is one of the greatest creations that ever flowed from a pen."
He had also read a favorable life of Marie Antoinette so bad that it "only
succeeds in making you loathe her . . . & swing your hat with unap-
peasable joy when they finally behead her," as well as a history of France
and part of a history of the Dutch Republic, and novels by Dumas and
Charles Reade. As soon as he could afford it, and especially when he at last
had bookshelves of his own, he began to buy books. From the time of his
residence in Buffalo, and even more in the new Hartford house, he created
a large private library. During his visits to England in 1873 and 1874, he
sent back boxes filled with books he had bought.

An eclectic reader, he made intellectual distinctions without being dis-
criminating. Everything was grist for his mill, substance for his curiosity,
and the source of literary ideas. He had a mind experienced in and delighted by logical argument. Science fascinated him, his vitalistic tenden-
cies often at war with his increasingly deterministic views. New inventions
he celebrated, evidence in support of his belief that technological progress
would narrow the gap between science and miracle. He welcomed the
typewriter and the telephone; he yearned for telepathy and flying machines, for instant transportation molecule by molecule from one part of
the globe to another. On the one hand, he took most such prospects seriously; on the other, he could always present the case humorously, aware
that the borderline between the unorthodox and the absurd was difficult to
draw. He was determined, though, never to be made a fool of, either by

those who claimed authority, regardless of efficacy, or those who made heterodox claims that needed to be tested by reason and evidence.

In London in 1873, he put phrenology to his personal test by visiting the leading phrenologist under a false name: "He examined my elevations & depressions & gave me a chart which I carried home . . . & studied with great interest & amusement—the same interest & amusement which I should have found in the chart of an imposter who had been passing himself off for me, & who did not resemble me in a single sharply defined detail. I waited 3 months & went to Mr. Fowler again, heralding my arrival with a card bearing both my name & my nom de guerre. Again I carried away an elaborate chart. It contained several sharply defined details of my character, but it bore no recognizable resemblance to the earlier chart." Of course he granted "that the prejudice should have been against Fowler, instead of against the art" but he added "I am human & that is not the way that prejudices act." Always a rational skeptic, he positioned himself on both sides of the rational divide.

Varieties of the human voice appealed to him—accents and modulations of speech, distinctiveness of dialect, his own long-cultivated Missouri drawl, the voices of American blacks—he delighted in the immense variations in speech American regions and ethnic groups provided. In *Tom Sawyer* he tried to capture the way boys spoke in his Missouri childhood, in "A True Story" and "Sociable Jimmy" the American black voice, to the extent that he could find convincing orthographic representations. Music without the human voice he found less compelling than voice as an instrument to express emotion musically. Orchestral music he enjoyed only moderately. Piano recitals he could sometimes tolerate, and soon Susy and Clara were to have piano and voice lessons. Livy had a sense of music as transcendence, as high art. She had a deep personal investment in high musical culture. Opera interested and amused her husband occasionally, though he had fun making fun of operas that bored him, a useful direction for a humorist with a wide audience, many of whom shared his artistic taste. He could, though, sit through entire performances of *The Messiah* and was sometimes genuinely moved by music for which he had no special affinity.

But the music that moved him most moved him immensely. From childhood on he had adored the simple songs of his midwestern world, the music of his religious community, especially its hymns, and would play on the piano and sing repeatedly such songs as "Swing Low, Sweet Chariot." Sometimes he had his own comic variations, such as "There was a horse named Jerusalem." He especially cherished the music of the black world of his childhood, his empathy with its dignity and power sustained throughout his life. It was particularly focused for him by his attendance in Hartford in 1872 at a concert of Fisk University's Jubilee Singers, whose performance riveted his attention. When the Jubilee Singers were in London in 1873, he volunteered a testimonial. "I heard them sing once," he wrote to George Routledge, "& I would walk seven miles to hear them sing again," an especially impressive claim, he explained, since he hated walking. Unlike the popular minstrel performers, white men in blackface, the Jubilee Singers reproduced for him the true melody of the plantations: "I was reared in the South, & my father owned slaves, & I do not know when anything has so moved me as did the plaintive melodies of the Jubilee Singers . . . for one must have been a slave himself in order to feel what that life was & so convey the pathos of it in the music."

3.

With America's centennial birthday approaching, Twain, like many Americans, began to have a heightened sense of the political scene. Reconstruction, though it continued to be a burden for the white South and a cause of division in the North, was overshadowed by two dramatic events that riveted Twain's interest in 1875–76: the Beecher-Tilton adultery trial and the hotly contested Hayes-Tilden election. In April 1875, when he attended Beecher's trial in Brooklyn, Twain had given up his belief in Beecher's innocence, though the trial ended in a hung jury and Beecher retained his pulpit and much of his clerical influence. Corruption at the highest clerical level, Twain felt, mirrored pervasive national corruption. "The present era of incredible rottenness is not democratic," he wrote to Orion, "it is not republican, it is *national*." He did not believe the nation was reflected in Charles Sumner, the abolitionist, pro-Reconstruction senator who had been physically beaten on the Senate floor by an infuriated southerner, but in Henry Ward Beecher, Whitelaw Reid, toward whom Twain now felt so antagonistic that he placed him in the company of notoriously corrupt celebrities, and Boss William Tweed, whose Tammany Club controlled New York City politics and made immense profits from graft.

Eager to elect Rutherford Hayes and keep the Republicans in power,

Twain believed that politics by itself was "not going to cure moral ulcers like these nor the decaying body they fester upon." When invited to appear in July 1876 at a "Congress of Authors" in Philadelphia to add his voice to the centennial celebration, politics was inevitably in the air. In response to the program's theme, he offered a brief eulogy of a key figure of the Revolution, the admirable Francis Lightfoot Lee, "a picture of the average, the usual Congressman" of that time. "It is vividly suggestive of what that people must have been that preferred such men. Since then we have progressed one hundred years. Let us gravely try to conceive how isolated, how companionless, how lonesome, such a public servant as this would be in Washington to-day." Widespread moral deterioration had made all congressmen, with rare exceptions, members of a class of native-born criminals, he joked seriously. Like Thomas Carlyle, the British essayist and social critic, Twain hoped for individual moral reformation. At the same time, he knew that human nature would always trump high ideals. Neither education nor religion would take nature out of human nature: man was a cursing, self-aggrandizing creature. If there was a God, there had to be a Satan. If there was prayer, there had to be profanity. If there was honesty, there had to be corruption. But the balance was important, in his own life and in the national life. And politics needed to be subordinated to morality. "St. Patrick had no politics," he wrote in March 1876 to the chairman of a Knights of St. Patrick's dinner to whom he had to send regrets. "His sympathies lay with the right—that was politics enough. When he came across a reptile, he forgot to inquire whether he was a democrat or a republican, but simply exalted his staff & 'let him have it.' Honored be his name."

And yet he feared that the election of a Democratic administration meant the abandonment of Reconstruction, nefarious trade and tariff policies, and monetary inflation. The 1873 depression, from which the country had been slowly recovering, would have its economic misery deepened. Writers whose books had been put on hold until after the election in the hope that a Republican victory would strengthen the market would find an even deeper bottom for book sales. "Get your book out quick," Twain wrote to Howells, who was writing a campaign biography for Hayes and whose wife was the candidate's cousin. Twain agreed with Elinor Howells: "If Tilden is elected I think the entire country will go pretty straight to Mrs.

Howells's bad place." To elect Tilden would be putting the fox in charge of the henhouse. It would reward the party that had supported slavery and opposed Lincoln. It would be somewhere between a crime and a sin.

In 1876, Twain's support of Hayes was more active than it was ever to be again for any candidate. The main specific issue was civil service reform. Hayes had promised to remove civil service from political patronage and to establish a merit system for government positions. To affirm his sincerity, he pledged that he would not run for a second term. Twain strongly supported reform. Still, he felt no embarrassment in planning to ask Hayes to award Charles Warren Stoddard a consulship. Proposals for reform did not include the State Department or generally any position higher than clerk. Northeastern Republicans of course supported Hayes. The Democrats, whose opposition to Reconstruction soon made the South a one-party region, also had widespread support among immigrant groups and the working class. The large Irish population voted overwhelmingly Democratic. When Hayes came to Hartford at the end of September 1876 for a campaign rally, Twain marched in a torchlight parade for his candidate. Tilden's supporters threw mud and rocks. At a mass meeting that night at Hartford's largest hall, Twain gave his first political speech. Like "nearly all the people who write books and magazines," he said, he had come forward because he saw "at last a chance to make this government a good government."

Twain had expected a sweeping victory for Hayes. On election night, as the returns came in, Twain cursed. Neither man had been elected. Four months later, the House of Representatives settled the election in Hayes' favor. His Republican supporters had made a deal with the contested Louisiana electors and the white southern senators, who were filibustering to prevent a final count and certification of the electoral votes. In exchange for the Republican Party abandoning Reconstruction and reestablishing white domination of southern political power, the senators guaranteed that the disputed electoral votes in Louisiana would go to Hayes and that the Senate would certify the result. Though Twain was exultant for the moment, years later he would acknowledge that the American people had actually elected not Hayes but Tilden. The centennial had been celebrated by "one of the Republican Party's most cold-blooded swindles of the American people, the stealing" of the election. And the instrument of defalcation had been the disenfranchisement and a second enslavement of the people whose emancipation the Republican Party had made possible.

4.

With the Hartford house fully furnished and fined-tuned, Twain's domestic life fell into comforting routines. Some mornings and full days he worked in the third-floor billiard room, preparing speeches, writing essays and fiction, composing a large number of business and personal letters. Chores, visitors, family, and impulsive projects occupied him frequently. A smoke cloud appeared wherever he was and remained wherever he had been. Livy had long ago lost her anti-smoking campaign. Consuming an average of eighteen cigars a day, addicted to the cheap sort that he had smoked as a young boy, he always reeked of tobacco, though apparently no one in his household or among his associates made that an issue. There was no prohibition on his smoking even in their bedroom, though it must have been a trial for Livy. He often extinguished his last cigar of the day just before turning over to go to sleep. Most evenings he spent time with his three ladies in family rituals that gave him great satisfaction. As soon as Susy was old enough, he and Livy read to her. Soon he was making up stories to tell the girls, at their request, often based on some item in the house, especially bric-a-brac, which would become the basis for a wildly inventive tale. With Livy alone, he read aloud from a manuscript when one was at hand, but often he simply shared whatever he was reading, from Plato to contemporary novels.

In London, in late 1873, he began implementing the recommendation of a shipboard doctor to drink "what is called a cock-tail," composed of "Scotch whiskey, a lemon, some crushed sugar, & . . . *Angostura bitters* . . . before breakfast, before dinner, & just before going to bed." "To it," he wrote Livy, "I attribute the fact that . . . my digestion has been wonderful—simply *perfect*." With the fussiness of a man who thinks he has discovered perfection in a formula, he instructed her to have the ingredients "put in the bath-room & left there" so that they would be there when he arrived: "Nothing but Angostura Bitters will do." This cocktail, and, later, straight Scotch whiskey, was to become his regular late-night soporific. When his sister urged him to join the prohibition ranks, he told her that he would rather go to hell. "I never would be able to make you comprehend how frantically I hate the very name of abstinence."

His domestic pleasures did not, though, eliminate anxieties. About twenty thousand dollars of his book and theater profits he invested in stocks, none of which seemed to flourish particularly. By temperament he wanted to make his money grow aggressively, but he had little feel for the value of investments; he depended on tips from friends, none of whom were professionals, and his own sudden impulses. Though Hartford and the house gave him many pleasures, the family had no sooner gotten settled than he proposed that they go abroad for a year or two or even three. He needed a subject for a book, and he was, for no discerniable reason, restless, as if the wanderlust of his premarital years was still a deep part of his personality. The Mississippi book, despite his having on hand the "Old Times" section, had come to a halt, and the voyage downriver had been indefinitely postponed. The unidentified novel had started with an energetic flourish that had abruptly dissipated, apparently forever, though by mid-1876 he had written about four hundred manuscript pages of a novel to be narrated by Huckleberry Finn. Unable to continue for reasons he could not fully identify, he put the manuscript aside, having gotten as far as chapter 16, in which the raft on which Huck and the escaped slave Jim, drifting downriver rather than to free territory, has been smashed by a steamboat, just as Reconstruction was about to be smashed by the Republican deal with the white South.

At last, in December 1876, Bliss brought out *Tom Sawyer* as a heavily illustrated subscription book. Routledge's London edition, from which American newspapers published excerpts, had already appeared months before. Howells' rave pre-publication review was the prelude to a widely favorable critical response, with some occasional uneasiness lest young readers be tempted to take Tom as a role model. Twain immediately had in mind a dramatization, about which he soon queried theater people. For Tom he suggested a female, the young daughter of Hartford neighbors, and though nothing came of that he soon became "a sort of father to [the] Young Girls' Club here," a group of a dozen young ladies between sixteen and twenty who met on Saturday mornings and to whom he gave talks and invited friends to do the same, an interest that discreetly related both to his model of Victorian female perfection and to Livy's education in Elmira.

When sales of *Tom Sawyer* at publication did not rise to the level of those of *Innocents* and *Roughing It* at publication, Twain criticized the increase in the American Publishing Company's overhead and, in his view, its scattering resources by publishing too many books. Were his books in effect sponsoring the publication of unsuccessful ones, the low sales of which resulted in reduced or nonexistent dividends? "I have a selfish interest at stake," he wrote directly to his fellow directors, with a copy to Bliss, in June 1876. "Tom Sawyer is a new line of writing for me, & I would like to have every possible advantage in favor of that venture. When it issues, I would like it to have a clear field, & the whole energies of the Company put upon it." He felt he was being deprived of money due him. And, by late 1876, with his royalties from *Colonel Sellers* declining, the financial shoe had begun to pinch again. As he told Howells, his ordinary and ongoing expenses were huge: "This recent bust-up in the coal trade hits us pretty hard. My wife's whole fortune is in coal, & so her income utterly ceases for the next five or six months to come."

The expensive Hartford house ran smoothly, with capable Livy in charge of domestic economy. Dinner was a family affair, not a widespread practice in upper-middle-class households. Twain insisted on having the children at the table, except when entertaining at dinner parties. Nursemaids and then a governess carried most of the physical burden of childcare, servants the general cleaning and cooking. "We have got the very best gang of servants in America," Twain told Howells, though his selective anti-Irish prejudice and Livy's determination to run an economical establishment required extra vigilance. Some servants drank the household beer too freely or got into sexual trouble, though clever servants usually had the upper hand. Patrick McAleer had settled into the stabletop apartment, his alcoholism either abandoned or controlled, his presence on the grounds and his work as chauffeur done with a satisfaction and spirit that made him invaluable.

By the end of 1875 the Clemenses had another servant who was to become even more of a family member. A black man, George Griffen, born a slave in Maryland, wandered up to the house one day, asked if he could wash windows, and charmed the Clemenses into making him their butler, an in-house servant who delighted Twain with his humor, intelligence, honesty, and good nature. His only fault was the difficulty he had learning to lie to unwanted visitors who came to the door. "But I have trained him," Twain wrote to Howells, "& now it fairly breaks Mrs. Clemens's heart to hear George stand at that front door & lie to the unwelcome visitor." Twain, though, found riotously funny George's awkward efforts to pretend that his employer was not at home.

Despite her husband's references to her as an invalid, Livy not only managed the household but doted on her children and gave them much of her time. "Susie [Susy] is so large a part of my life," she remarked in March 1875, "and I am so *desperately* fond of her." On the morning of their wedding anniversary in 1877, Livy announced to Susy, who was almost five, " 'This is my wedding day Susie, seven years ago today I was married!' 'Why, are you *married* mamma?' 'Yes I am married'—'Who to, to me?' 'No, to Papa'—'Oh to papa,' indicating by the tone of voice that it was all right if it was papa, that there would be no breaking up of the family." Three-year-old Clara seemed less precocious, somewhat in the shadow of her sister, more taken for granted, though Livy delighted in her good health and comparative placidity. Susy "has her mother's personal comeliness & her father's sweetness of disposition," Twain had humorously written when Susy was two years old. "When she gets in a fury & breaks furniture, that is a merit all her own—not inherited—at least only in a general way. I break a good deal of furniture, but it is only to see how it is made!"

Meanwhile, members of Twain's extended family continued both their financial dependency and their eccentricities. When Pamela's son, Sam Moffett, now in his early teens, desired a military appointment, Twain attempted to use his influence to help his nephew, though in the end he was unsuccessful. When Pamela's daughter, Annie Moffett, wanted to marry, Twain played the patriarchal uncle and lightly vetted the young man's qualifications. Orion's problems, though, were at a different level. After he had failed in attempts to establish himself as a journalist-editor in Hartford, New York, and Vermont, he and Mollie returned to the Midwest. Schemes burst from Orion's mind with dependable frequency. He had an idea for a novel, which turned out to be similar in plot to a recent Jules Verne success, and it took strong words to convince him that his justification that it was a "variant" was not sufficient. He still tinkered with hopeless inventions. When he and Mollie wanted to purchase a farm in Keokuk and raise chickens, Twain warned against it. Mollie began to get on his nerves also. He thought her standards of dress too high and her standards of economy too low, and it had become clear that she would never transform Orion into a reliable wage earner. As always, Sam found his brother's schemes and especially his changing views baffling, even painful. "I can't encourage Orion," he wrote in response to their mother's plea. "Nobody can do that, conscientiously, for the reason that before one's letter has time

to reach him he is off on some new wild-goose chase.—Would you encourage in literature a man who, the older he grows the worse he writes?
Would you encourage Orion in the glaring insanity of studying law? If he
were packed & crammed full of law, it would be worthless lumber to him,
for his is such a capricious & ill-regulated mind that he would apply the
principles of the law with no more judgment than a child of ten years." He
was no good for the ministry because he changed his religious views almost
every night. And when he did stick to something it was what he was least
qualified for. "If you ask me to pity Orion, I can do that," Twain offered,
and he continued to support him, just as he sent his mother and sister a
monthly pension. But he felt endless frustration, anger, and sadness at
what seemed to him Orion's wasted life.

Friends proved more companionable than his brother, particularly
Twichell and Howells and, to some extent, Aldrich. For business, Twain
went to New York. For companionship and fun, he went to Boston, where
he usually checked into the Parker Hotel but spent much of his time as a
guest of Howells' in Cambridge and, after 1880, at Belmont, just beyond
Cambridge, where Howells had built a house. Often he would go to Belmont in evening dress, after a lecture or dinner, and then stay overnight,
leaving his hotel room vacant. The two literary men would smoke and talk
into the small hours. In the morning, he'd borrow one of Howells' overcoats
to cover his formal clothes and return to the hotel. Aldrich's company often came at the price of Mrs. Aldrich's presence. Twain felt she disapproved of him, which indeed she did. His enthusiasms and humorous
eccentricities seemed to her coarse oddities, not appropriate in respectable
company. The Aldriches stayed with the George Warners when they visited
Hartford. The Howellses always stayed with the Clemenses. Between
1875 and 1878 Twain and Aldrich saw one another frequently, sometimes
in Hartford, mostly in Boston. The Nook Farm friends, both Charles Dudley Warner and George Warner, and the ever-present Joe Twichell, mixed
easily with the Boston friends. For his sake and for Livy's, Twain even went
to Twichell's services occasionally, after which he good-humoredly made
remarks such as "I notice how you pound the pulpit especially hard when
you have nothing to say." Twichell always responded with agreeable good
humor.

With Bret Harte, whom he had known longer than his Hartford and
Boston friends, he had a more complicated, precarious friendship. In late

spring 1875, Harte came to Hartford, searching for a house to rent, probably to be on hand to read the proofs of *Gabriel Conway,* the novel Bliss had contracted to publish and for which Harte soon signed a six-thousand-dollar contract for serial publication in *Scribner's Monthly.* His reputation as the golden boy of American literature had been eroded since his California successes by his unevenness. His failure to live up to the requirements of the ten-thousand-dollar retainer the *Atlantic* had paid him in 1871 had disenchanted the Boston literary establishment.

Off-putting with his prickliness, his heavy drinking, and his fashionable clothes, Harte was a handsome man beginning to show the wear and tear of middle age. Nevertheless, he still had great expectations for the subscription sales of *Gabriel Conway,* which Bliss brought out one month after *Tom Sawyer.* Twain may have been referring to *Gabriel Conroy* when he chastised Bliss for not arranging to give *Tom Sawyer* the American Publishing Company's undivided attention. At the same time, the stage had been calling both Twain and Harte, first separately, then together, not because either believed he had any great talent as a dramatist but because the theater offered estimable financial rewards. *Colonel Sellers'* success had put much-needed cash in Twain's pocket. Needing more, he wracked his brains for a successor.

Late in August 1876 Augustin Daly produced Harte's comedy *Two Men of Sandy Bar,* which failed badly under vicious critcism. Hurt and furious, Harte attacked the critics. "I think Harte has acted crazily about the criticism of his play," Twain remarked to Howells, "but he's been shamefully decried & abused." It was a response with which Twain could empathize. Having seen the play during the second week of its New York run, Twain had actually liked it. He worried that, like Harte and every writer subject to such attack, he himself might not do any better. In October Harte proposed that they coauthor a comedy and "divide the swag," as Twain put it to Howells. Twain wanted money; Harte *needed* money, desperately. Having just received a check for $1,616.16, his "clear profit on Raymond's first week in Philadelphia" with *Colonel Sellers,* Twain immediately agreed. Though they had little to no plot in mind, they had two characters. Twain would import Scotty Briggs from *Roughing It,* Harte a comic Chinese character named Hop Sing from *Sandy Bar,* a variant on "The Heathen Chinee" with whom he had had a great success. "This Chinaman," who could be taken as both the victim of injustice and, at the same time, a racial inferior for white audiences to laugh at, "is to be *the* character of the play," Twain told Howells. "Both of us will work on him & develop him. Bret is to draw the plot, & I am to do the same; we shall use the best of the two, or gouge from both & build a third." They had a title, *Ah Sin, A Drama*.

As soon as Harte left Connecticut, Twain went to work. "My plot is built—finished it yesterday—six days' work, 8 or 9 hours a day, & has nearly killed me." It was not to kill audiences, though. And it was to kill what already was not a very affectionate friendship. In mid-November, Harte again became Twain's houseguest. They worked together in the third-floor billiard room for two or three hours each day, Twain apparently more often at the billiard table than the writing desk. As they talked over the scenario, Harte filled in the script and the ersatz Chinese comic dialogue. Helped by Twain, he consumed a great deal of whiskey. Leaving him to continue with the play, Twain went to Boston just before Thanksgiving for two readings, his desire to keep in the spotlight and put some cash in his pocket once again overcoming his disinclination to lecture. With frazzled clothes, heavy debts, and no money, Harte kept drinking and writing, finishing the play by the time Twain returned. One night he stayed up till dawn, fueled by whiskey, to turn out a story for quick cash. To some extent, Twain actually admired his desperate endurance. Having lent Harte money, he wanted Harte solvent, partly for Harte's sake, mostly because he thought they could do each other a handsome turn with a successful play.

Harte returned to New York in mid-December, but the collaboration continued. By late February 1877 not only was the play done, the sanguine Twain happily reported to Howells, but the pair was "plotting out another one." When Harte, again broke, attempted to borrow a few hundred dollars from Twain for the purpose of going to San Francisco to "study Chinese character," Twain counterproposed that he put Harte on a salary at twenty-five dollars a week to carry him through their collaboration on this new play. Insulted, Harte rejected the offer, accusing Twain of exploiting his poverty and Twain and Bliss of cheating him on *Gabriel Conroy* royalties. Twain wrote on the back of Harte's angry letter that this was "ineffable idiocy."

Determined not to have any further dealings with him, Twain proceeded by himself to try to get *Ah Sin* produced. Charles Parsloe, the comic actor who had played Hop Sing in *Two Men of Sandy Bar*, agreed to take on the role once more. Daly, who staged the play, did a rewrite, particularly to make it more performable, since neither author had any mastery of stagecraft. Parsloe was, Twain boasted, "the best Chinaman that ever stepped on a stage," and Daly, Twain, and Parsloe edited and rewrote until little of Harte remained except his characters, most of whom he had taken from his 1874 short story "A Monte Flat Pastoral." Having convinced himself that his direction was essential, Twain went to Baltimore in late April to participate in daily rehearsals prior to its Washington opening in early May. Well received at the National Theater, the play then opened in New York to mixed reviews.

Harte tried desperately to be involved, especially to get information about rehearsals and progress. Parsloe, Daly, and Twain avoided him and his messages. Twain now hated Harte, he told Livy, as much as he hated John Raymond, whom he believed was cheating him out of some of his profits from the road tour of *Colonel Sellers* by padding expenses. When in mid-May Harte made another of many efforts to get information about *Ah Sin*, Twain told his lawyer, "[Tell Harte that] I have gone off on a sea voyage . . . that I left instructions with you to credit his indebtedness to me with any moneys received during my absence." Twain set to work in June on a comedy that he called "Cap'n Simon Wheeler, The Amateur Detective." "If the play's a success," he wrote to Howells, "it is worth $50,000 or more—if it fails it is worth nothing—& yet even the worst of failures can't rob me of the 6½ days of booming pleasure I have had in writing it." He also spent weeks, during a blistering July heat wave, supervising the rehearsals of *Ah Sin*. The actors, whom he thought stupid and slow, now at least had the benefit of a daily drilling from him. He told Livy, who urged him not to speak harshly in public about his former collaborator, "[Harte] will pay me $50 a day for my work here, or I will know the reason why—that is, if the play succeeds." As always, Livy attempted to provide perspective. "We are so desperately happy, our paths lie in such pleasant places, and he is so miserable, we can easily afford to be magnanimous toward him."

As opening night approached, Twain was ready with a self-congratulatory speech. "It is very short—& nothing in it," he assured Livy. "I've got a new swallow-tail, but I know I could not endure it in the sweltering theatre. I shall wear white linen. You see, if I wear a swallow-tail it is plain I expected to be called out, maybe *wanted* to be." As he watched from the rear, the audience seemed thick-headed, the play underappreciated. Still, he was hopeful. But "every time the audience roared" he knew that the low comedy element that audiences enjoyed, the critics would deplore. And he believed that without "the kitchen & the stable" elements, the play would not draw large enough audiences.

With mixed reviews, the play ran in New York only until early October. Though he put a bold face on the opening night reception, claiming that the play "was received with great enthusiasm by a large & brilliant audience," he knew that the financial rewards would be meager. After Parsloe took it on a brief tour, *Ah Sin* ended its life in Pittsburgh in early November 1877. The play was "a most abject & incurable failure," he admitted to Howells. Twain blamed Harte. The problem was in what of Harte's still remained, the footprint of its origin and even his name as coauthor. "It is full of incurable defects: to wit, Harte's deliberate thefts & plagiarisms, & my own unconscious ones. I don't believe Harte ever had an idea that he came by honestly. He is the most abandoned thief that defiles the earth." If there was to be any profit from the play, he did not want Harte to have a penny of it "till his entire indebtedness" to him was paid.

Twain's usual moral relativism when it came to human frailty had no tolerance for Harte. During the 1876 presidential election, Harte remained publicly neutral since he believed that friends of both candidates had promised him a position. Twain urged Howells, for the good of the country, to put in a bad word for Harte with the new administration once Hayes was in office. It had become a private vendetta, a personal hatred that belied his description of them as "cordial enemies." "Wherever he goes [Harte's] wake is tumultuous with swindled grocers, & with defrauded innocents who have loaned him money. . . . He is always steeped in whiskey & brandy; he gets up in the night to drink it cold. No man who has ever known him respects him."

The more generous Howells, who responded that he did not feel it right to destroy Harte's chances, reluctantly agreed to forward Twain's letter to the White House. Twain backed off. "Never mind about being bothered with the letter. I had to have an outlet to my feelings—I saw none but through you—but of course the thing would be disagreeable to you. I must try to get somebody to plead with the President who is in the political line of business & won't mind it." Newspaper rumors about why Harte did not get a position abounded, most of them painfully ad hominem. Harte blamed the secretary of state. When, the next year, President Hayes wrote his cousin-in-law about Harte's renewed request for a position, Howells recommended the appointment on personal grounds. He admitted that Harte's infirmities were many. "But," he wrote, "he is poor, and he writes with difficulty and very little." The appointment "would be a godsend to him." And, if he proved unworthy, he could easily be recalled. In April 1878 Harte was appointed to a minor consulship in Germany. Keen to keep their friendship intact, Howells never told Twain about his role in supporting Harte.

5.

There were other, more central frustrations. Though he was a devoted father and husband, domestic life sometimes seemed too much of a good thing. He also regularly became blocked and had to put aside manuscripts in progress. Though on the one hand Twain had too much to do, on the other he compulsively sought new projects, including additional books to start and new enterprises, like writing for the stage, into which he poured his energy until he became bored, or exhausted, or the enthusiasm had simply run its course. In March 1876 he urged Howells to organize a list of well-known American novelists to respond to a bare-bones, unsophisticated novella that Twain would write, "A Murder, A Mystery and A Marriage," with their own variations on the same plot. As with many such projects, profit mattered more to him than art.

Though he joked about being lazy, behind the drawl and shuffling walk was an obsessive fixation on action and an energy that kept him moving, both intellectually and physically. The trip to the Mississippi River valley, conceived in 1875, remained on indefinite hold. Between 1875 and 1878 he confined his travels to the Hartford/Boston/New York triangle, visiting Howells and Aldrich in Boston, putting his self-important nose to the grindstone of *Ah Sin* rehearsals in New York, and sometimes lecturing, despite his claim to Redpath that he was "at last one of those impossibilities which Nasby denies the existence of—a reformed lecturer." As always, he contradicted himself by proposing to Thomas Nast in summer 1877 what Nast had proposed ten years before—a series of joint lectures. This time it was Nast who declined. In May 1877, Twain got away for ten days with Twichell on a Bermuda holiday. "The real health-giving property of a sea-voyage," he noted, "is that a man eats like an animal & sleeps a dead dreamless stupor half the day & all the night."

Registering at their hotel under assumed names, they tramped around the island. The sunny weather and bright colors dazzled him, the start of a lifelong affection for the island, one of whose many attractions was that it could be reached easily from New York by boat. Eager to combine business with pleasure, he took notes for a long article, the aptly named "Some Rambling Notes of an Idle Excursion," an unorganized account of his Bermuda visit. When in June he read part of the manuscript to his family, he "got no applause," he wrote to Howells, who published it in the *Atlantic* in the four issues from October 1877 to January 1878. But, he explained, "they are a dull lot," though when he read them a recent piece written by Howells they responded "with shrieks of laughter & extravagant praise": "Oh, a name goes for everything with these people. If I had written it, they wouldn't have seen anything in it. Yet there are good things in it—I admit that."

After their 1875 summer in Newport, the Clemenses would not desert Elmira again for many years. In summer 1876 he found the octagonal studio at Quarry Farm so congenial that it established itself in his mind as the best place in the world in which to write. Increasingly, Hartford seemed the place to live all aspects of his life except sustained writing. Over the years, the Cranes were to enlarge the farmhouse to make it commodious for the two families. Susan and her mother, with servants, helped care for the children. Susy and Clara found farmhouse summer life earthy and healthy. With her sister and mother there, and her brother a regular visitor, Livy was surrounded by the people she cared most about. Looking after the children seemed easier at the farm than in Hartford, among other reasons because Susan Crane took charge of most of the household responsibilities.

When Twain found himself unable to continue with *Huckleberry Finn*, he conceived the notion of doing a book set in Elizabethan England, a development of his fascination with English history, its specific genesis probably his visits in 1873–74. Exactly what the plot would be was still undefined, except that he wanted to create a variation on the story of a young prince becoming a more humane king after finding himself having accidentally switched places with a commoner, a theme he had read about in a popular contemporary novel. Claimants he found, as always, a fascinating phenomenon. The plot turn appealed to him, its reconciliation of high- and low-class status in a common humanity expressive of his admiration of English social harmony. Keen on authenticity, he did linguistic research, with Shakespeare probably his main source. He soon took delight in writing in ersatz Elizabethan, which he convinced himself was exactly how those people spoke.

When he realized, as he read a sixteenth-century text, that Elizabethan society had a much greater freedom than his own in referring to bodily functions, his delight in bawdy language found its literary occasion. As he well recognized, it had to be a private one. Late in the summer of 1876 he wrote, in the form of a letter to Joe Twichell, "Date 1601. Conversation, as it was by the Social Fireside, in the time of the Tudors." A mixed group of Queen Elizabeth's courtiers casually discuss farting, masturbation, and sexual intercourse, as if having polite tea-time conversation. As he later said, he wanted to practice his "archaics." In fact, he wanted to get away from the standards of propriety represented by Livy and Howells. "I have always practiced doubtful things on Twichell from the beginning. . . . It made a fat letter. I bundled it up and mailed it." He described his fall afternoons with Twichell, on the return from their ten-mile Saturday walks: "We used to . . . lie down on the grass . . . and get out that letter and read it. . . . We used to laugh ourselves lame and sore." As did "1601," these readings provided the release of linguistic sexual clowning, a carnival of transgressive expression that made pervasive propriety tolerable.

At Quarry Farm, at the end of a happy afternoon in late August 1877, much of the Langdon family had made its way to the cooling breezes on top of the high hill, a handsome group in full skirts and dark suits despite the summer sun, an active, varied family harmonious in its hierarchies and at the apex of its happiness. Livy's mother soon joined her daughters, pulling up in a carriage with Charles Langdon's son, "little Jervis." Ida, Charley's wife, with two-year-old Julia, arrived behind them in a buggy with a "new, young, spry gray horse" that Ida happily drove. Later, as the sun began to set, Ida and Julia drove through the gate, returning to Elmira. John Lewis, the black tenant farmer, a stocky middle-aged man, was toiling up the hill from town, carting heavy manure in his two-horse wagon. Beginning to pick up speed, Ida and Julia began their descent. The family, which had gathered in front of the house for departures, waved back to Ida, who had turned her face toward the house. Suddenly Livy realized that Ida was driving too fast. She screamed, "Her horse is running away!" What had appeared to have been a good-bye wave had been a gesture of alarm, a cry for help. Twain and Theodore Crane "ran down the hill bareheaded & shouting." The carriage was descending at a speed that made, at the next sharp turn, a disastrous wreck inevitable. Twain's last glimpse showed the buggy "for one instant, far down the descent, springing high in the air out of a cloud of dust." His impulse was to shut his eyes "and so delay for a moment the ghastly spectacle of mutilation & death" he expected.

When he turned the curve, though, he saw *two* wagons, close together. Certain that one held mutilated bodies, perhaps corpses, he was astounded to see Ida and Julia alive and well. The other wagon was John Lewis', with its load of manure. Having seen the horse and buggy descending toward him at full gallop, he had turned his wagon across the road to force the buggy into a narrow V. In an instant he "seized the gray horse's bit as he plunged by & fetched him up standing." The family could hardly thank Lewis and reward him enough. Later, in "The Refuge of the Derelicts," a work he was never to publish, Twain retold this August 1877 incident as an exemplification of a time when his family's and his own good fortune was at its apogee, a golden age when miracles had been bestowed on him and those he loved. It served as a touchstone incident to measure just how far the fall was to be, to what an extent grace, or good luck, as he was more likely to think of it, was to be withdrawn.

At the time, Twain was also engaged in a serious dialogue about the clash between instinct and sublimation, the imp within versus the constraints of conscience. In a short story, "The Facts Concerning the Recent Carnival of Crime in Connecticut," read to the Monday Evening Club in January 1876 and then published in the *Atlantic* in June, he dramatized with humorous exaggeration the danger of getting away from one's conscience. "Crime" gave the narrator of "The Facts" pleasure. Conscience gave him pain. If only he could kill conscience or at least neutralize it, he could live a lifelong "carnival." When the visit of a puritanical aunt requires that he forgo smoking, he deeply resents the restraint her presence forces on him. Why should he have to renounce his pleasures because others call them vices? Suddenly there appears a "shriveled, shabby dwarf" who in every other way looks precisely like himself. It is his conscience. They do verbal battle. When, exhausted, Conscience falls asleep, the narrator, "with an exultant shout," pounces. "In an instant I had my life-long foe by the throat. After so many years of waiting and longing, he was mine at last. I tore him to shreds and fragments. I rent the fragments to bits. I cast the bleeding rubbish into the fire, and drew into my nostrils the grateful incense of my burnt-offering. At last and forever, my Conscience was dead!

I was a free man!" Aunt Mary flees. "Since that day my life is all bliss. . . . I killed thirty-eight persons during the first two weeks." He then "burned a dwelling that interrupted [his] view" and "committed scores of crimes." He was now having a sale to medical colleges of the bodies of assorted tramps and other nuisances he had stored in his cellar. They "can be had [at] a low rate, because I wish to clear out my stock and get ready for the spring trade."

Like most satirists, Twain preferred to be revered for his irreverence, to be praised for his merits though his merits revealed the demerits of others. But whereas "Facts" was a literary success, his attempt to be congenially subversive at a dinner hosted by the *Atlantic* in late December 1877 honoring its distinguished contributor, John Greenleaf Whittier, was a minor disaster. Boston's literary Brahmins—Whittier, Holmes, Emerson, and Longfellow—had Olympian status. With fifty younger *Atlantic* contributors, including Howells, Charles Eliot Norton, Charles Dudley Warner, and Mark Twain, they had gathered to celebrate Whittier. Speech after speech provided the usual sanctimonious if not unctuous praise. "Delicacy—a sad, false delicacy," Twain had written to Howells in September, "robs literature of the two best things among its belongings: Family circle-narratives & obscene stories." He had worked something of both of these into his speech, mainly the story, with dialogue, of an incident he claimed had been told to him fifteen years before in Nevada. Arriving at a log cabin in a lonely mining camp, he had introduced himself as Mark Twain. The "jaded, melancholy" miner responds that that is funny, as he is the fourth "literary man" to arrive in twenty-four hours. The three other "tramps" had identified themselves as Longfellow, Emerson, and Holmes. The miner says disparaging things about their manners, their appearances, and their personal habits. They had behaved badly, argued, drank, gambled, and cursed. These must have been imposters, Mark Twain tells the miner. " 'Ah—imposters, were they?—are *you?*' I did not pursue the subject," Twain concluded, "and since then I haven't traveled on my *nom de plume* enough to hurt. Such is the reminiscence I was moved to contribute, Mr. Chairman," Twain said, addressing Howells, who had introduced him as a humorist who never offended. His auditors ranged from stunned to indifferent.

Where was Conscience or his censors when he needed them? Clearly he had not run the speech by Livy. Howells tried to console him, but to no avail. "My sense of disgrace does not abate," Twain wrote to him a week later. "I see that it is going to add itself to my list of permanencies—a list of humiliations that extends back to when I was seven years old, & which keep on persecuting me regardless of my repentancies." The retentive memory that kept vivid the childhood experiences about which he wrote so effectively also kept fresh the humiliations that had burned themselves into his mind. "It seems as if I must have been insane when I wrote that speech & saw no harm in it, no disrespect toward those men whom I reverenced so much. And what shame I brought upon you, after what you said in introducing me! It burns me like fire to think of it." Howells continued to try to rationalize away the hurt. All those he talked to, he told Twain, regarded it as one of those fatalities "into which a man walks with his eyes wide open, no one knows why." Why not, he suggested, write to Longfellow, Holmes, and Emerson, whom he was certain made much less of it, if anything at all, than did Twain? "Gentlemen," he wrote to the Olympian trio, "I come before you, now, with the mien & posture of the guilty—not to excuse, gloss, or extenuate, but only to offer my repentance. If a man with a fine nature had done that thing which I did, it would have been a crime—because all his senses would have warned him against it beforehand; but I did it innocently & unwarned. I did it as innocently as I ever did anything." Longfellow responded with a sympathetic note. Emerson's daughter and Holmes assured Twain that no offense had been taken.

6.

From the deck of the SS *Holsatia,* as it sailed in mid-April 1878, the Clemens family, again accompanied by Clara Spaulding and with Rosina Hay, their German nursemaid, saw the New York skyline fade behind them. Beyond that, in the greater distance and fast receding, was the convivial Hartford life that they had taken up eight years before and the Hartford dream house they had occupied for the last four and a half. "The pictures are gone from the walls, the carpets from the floors, the curtains, the furniture, the books—everything has vanished away to the storage warehouse, & the place is empty, desolate, & filled with echoes." The servants had been discharged, except Patrick MacAleer, who was to stay in the apartment over the stable, guarding and grooming the horses, maintaining the grounds, and keeping the house secure. Finding a tenant would have been emotionally distasteful, the idea of strangers occupying the family inner sanctum unacceptable, but without one Twain would have to carry the irreducible expenses, such as taxes, without compensating income. Though the economic depression that continued to reduce Livy's dividends and his royalties had made them feel poor, such poverty was still at a level of affluence that did not compel them to take off the pinching shoe.

The decision to go abroad was not inexplicable. The cost of living in Europe was appreciably less than in America; the strong dollar would help, and usually there would be fewer fixed expenses. Germany itself had become fashionable among the American northeastern elite, the German language associated with high European culture, with Goethe, Schiller, Mozart, and Beethoven, and with the attractions of Wagner, the newest German musical star. Livy particularly desired that she and the children learn German. But the impetus for the trip had come from Twain. Livy had argued strongly against it when, in early 1876, a year and a half after occupying the new house, he first proposed that they go abroad that spring for an extended stay. It took almost another year of gradual persuasion for Livy to accept the inevitable. Even so, she successfully negotiated another delay. Though she would not hear of leaving even in spring 1877, she made it clear that she would accept departure at a later time. "Mr Clemens grows more and more determined to go to Germany next Summer," she wrote to her mother in February 1877. "I combat it and say the farm next Summer and Germany a year from next Summer if we have money enough—I don't know who shall come out ahead but I think I shall."

Twain's rationale was that he needed a subject for a new book. The projects he had under way, *Life on the Mississippi* and *Huckleberry Finn,* were stalled. In late November 1877, he had outlined the plot of *The Prince and the Pauper,* but apparently had neither imaginative nor financial impetus to move it forward. He played with the notion of doing it as a four-act play rather than a novel. "If I can make a living out of plays, I shall never write another book," he grumbled. Playwriting income, though, had come to a halt, his new effort unrealized, his desire to co-author a play with Howells on hold. No New York impressario had shown any enthusiasm for "Cap'n Simon Wheeler, the Amateur Detective." Anyway, Howells sensibly assured him, "You must not expect any profit out of [a play we do together] . . . I am the champion prosperity-extinguisher." Though Twain had worked on a burlesque account of a life of Methuselah and attempted to move forward with the story of Captain Stormfield's visit to heaven, neither seemed ready to be completed and neither had much commercial potential. And profits from *Tom Sawyer* had been disappointing, partly because the subscription sale price and consequently his royalties reflected the novel's brevity, but also because Bliss had found it impossible to stop American and Canadian publication of pirated copies.

Twain wanted a subject for a full-sized, copiously illustrated nonfiction subscription book. Since his greatest success had been with *Innocents Abroad* and *Roughing It,* a European itinerary as the structure for another travel book made sense. Germany was attractive, fashionable, and only semi-exploited literary territory—and picturesque Switzerland was nearby. However, so strong was Twain's distrust of his publisher that, a month before sailing, he signed a secret contract with Bliss's son Frank, who had set up his own firm, apparently while still retaining his position as American Publishing Company treasurer. The issue of the difference between a percentage royalty and half profits still rankled, and Twain was disappointed by how the senior Bliss had handled *Tom Sawyer.* That the relatively inexperienced, underfinanced son could successfully publish the new book was a delusion they both shared, at least for a while.

Before departure Twain visited his mother and sister in Fredonia and spent time terminating some valueless investments, including Nevada banking and mining stock purchased over the past half dozen years. "I never did meddle in the stocks without botching it," he told Denis McCarthy, but explained that he had no regrets: "I haven't lost $12,000 in the whole of them put together." Actually, that was a great deal of money. But he had an easy way of tossing off such losses as the price to be paid for his "foolishness" while at the same time taking his reluctant family abroad partly to tighten their belts. After four years of badgering, he succeeded in having his twenty-three thousand dollars returned to him from a friend who had persuaded Twain to invest in a new insurance company and had personally guaranteed the investment.

Always fascinated by technology, he attended a demonstration of a new invention, the telephone, installed at the *Hartford Courant.* The salesman urged Twain to buy stock, but, having recently been burned, he uncharacteristically resisted. The salesman reduced the price, offering him more stock for less money. He still resisted. "That young man couldn't sell *me* any stock but sold a few hatfulls of it to an old dry good clerk in Hartford for five thousand dollars. . . . We were gone fourteen months, and when we got back one of the first things we saw was that clerk driving around in a sumptuous barouche with liveried servants all over it." When a rumor spread that Twain had bought an interest in the *Courant,* he explained that his only connection was by telephone. In late 1877 the writer had a direct telephone line installed, one of the first in a private residence, between his home and the *Courant* office. It is "a great convenience to me when I want to send for something in a hurry; but the advantage is all on one side. I get all the benefit & they get all the bother."

The two-week voyage that brought the Clemenses to Hamburg had few pleasures other than the change from daily domestic routines. The seas were unsettled and varied. The girls were adored by the mostly German passengers. Almost everyone aboard, though, except Twain, had a queasy stomach. The rocking and wrenching ship forced them to their cabins, though seasickness abated and soon Livy had an "inexhaustible appetite." Twain enjoyed the company of Bayard Taylor, professor of German at Cornell and the newly appointed minister to Germany. Having departed with a large cash present from her mother, Livy felt rich. "I feel so much freer because I have that money," she wrote. She caught a heavy cold on the ship, and they rested at Plymouth before going on. Traveling slowly because of her persistent sore throat and tiredness, they went to Frankfurt-on-Main in early May, then to Heidelberg, their summer destination. "What a paradise this land is!" Twain wrote to Howells. "What clean clothes, what good faces, what tranquil contentment, what prosperity, what genuine freedom, what superb government! And I am so happy, for I am responsible for none of it. I am only here to enjoy." When rumors about war between Britain and Russia and the latest developments in the Beecher-Tilton scandal reached him, Twain feigned indifference—"For I am out of it all. . . . I don't read any newspapers or care for them. . . . I think I foretaste some of the advantage of being dead." They settled into comfortable rooms in the Schloss-Hotel high over the castle. Through its glass-enclosed balconies they had a spectacular view of the fast-flowing Neckar below and the Rhine valley beyond. At night the lights of Heidelberg stretched directly beneath.

As they settled in, Twain continued for a short while what seemed to him delightful loafing, though he continued to make extensive observations in a notebook he had begun in November 1877. It had been initiated for this European trip, its earliest entries about travel plans and anticipations.

His plan was that the notebook would be the first draft, that it would be to the finished book what his letters to the *Alta California* had been to *Innocents Abroad*. In Heidelberg, he contined to read extensively in German history, partly as background but also as possible material for insertion in the book. Romantic Germany appealed to him, particularly legends from its medieval and Renaissance past. The German language did not, except a comic pidgin German that amused him immensely. When, soon after arriving in Heidelberg, he provided Bayard Taylor with a physical description for a new passport to replace the one he had lost, he described himself as "5 Fuss 8½ inches hoch weight doch aber about 145 pfund; sometimes ein wenig unter, sometimes ein wenig oben . . . Ich habe das Deutche sprache gelernt und bin ein gluckliche Kind, you bet." Livy and Clara Spaulding were making progress with their language studies. They slaved over it "night & day," he wrote to Charley Warner, and looked "pale, jaded, & fagged out." "The thing that disturbs Livy is that the more she learns of the language the less she understands of it when spoken." Susy, by late July 1878, had made the best progress of them all. "She chatters away with almost as much ease as she does in English." But after a few weeks of lessons, her father decided that he would never be able to talk it.

A room in a small house on the other side of the Neckar, on a rise level with the hotel, seemed perfect for a writing studio, but after a short while he felt dissatisfied. The downhill walk was mostly at the start of the day, and he preferred to do his walking before writing. So he rented a room in a house high above his hotel, a 1,500-foot climb each morning, which took two hours from his ten A.M. departure and from which he had a stupendous view. "Then, about 5 or 5:15 I go loafing down the mountain again, find Livy & Clara in the Castle park, & listen to the band in the shadow of the ruin." The book itself gave him less pleasure. He could not readily connect his disparate notebook jottings, which remained fragments, unlikely material for a cohesive narrative. And he had little to write about since he had seen so little of Germany. He needed to collect travel experiences, and Livy and the children were not suited for some of the traveling he needed to do. Just as Livy had brought some of Elmira with her in the person of Clara Spaulding, Twain had arranged, at his expense, to import Joe Twichell to be companion and literary alter ego for six weeks of tramping. After wiring money into Twichell's account, he met him at Baden-Baden on August 1. When American newspapers gossiped about the arrangement, Twain remonstrated to Warner, "I bullyrag Joe into coming over here,—perfectly aware that nineteen-twentieths of the pecuniary profit & advantage are on my side—to say nothing of the social advantage,—& . . . one would imagine, from the newspapers that Joe is the party receiving a favor."

While the family went to Zurich, Mark and Joe, as they addressed each other, set off on an adventuresome journey, first to the Black Forest, then back to Baden-Baden and Heidelberg, then by flatboat up the Neckar, then at mid-August to Lucerne, where they rejoined the four ladies. Twain took extensive notes of the sort that provided prompts to memory and deep background. He enjoyed the traveling, but he had a sinking sense that the book itself was not emerging. He had assumed that *A Tramp Abroad,* like his previous travel books, would have a certain casualness of construction. But a successful casual construction needed a structural and experiential baseline to be casual about. In late August he decided, "It is no sort of use to try to write while one is traveling." There were too many interruptions and most of the time he was "too tired to write, anyway." He admitted to Frank Bliss that his initial concept, a diary or journal structure, seemed unworkable. He reported, "Since Twichell has been with me I have invented a new and better plan"; one feature of the new plan would be frequent use of Twichell as a foil under the name Harris, a familiar device with which he felt comfortable. "Therefore I shall tear up a great deal of my present MS. & start fresh." The new plan, which he had Twichell pledge not to reveal, was to write the book as a journey "announced as a walking tour, but actually making use of every other means of conveyance." It would be a sort of structural joke.

Often hiking separately, sometimes with the family, the two friends amused themselves with this and other ideas as they mostly railroaded across Switzerland. "When I was talking (in my native tongue) about some rather private matters in the hearing of some Germans one day," he wrote to Bayard Taylor, "Twichell said, 'Speak in German, Mark, some of these people may understand English.' " From Lucerne, they traveled to the Rigi-Kulm, then to Interlaken, then across the Gemmi Pass to Zermat and the Matterhorn, to Ouchy, Chillon, and Chamonix, where they admired Mont Blanc, and then to Geneva, where the family greeted them. After sadly saying good-bye to Twichell in early September, the Clemenses descended into Italy, assuring worried family at home that it was late enough in the summer for there to be no danger of infectious disease. From Turin they went to Lake Como, stopping in Bellagio, then to Milan, Venice, Florence, and Rome, traversing one of the most frequently traveled routes for literary Americans. In Italy the family did aggressive cultural sightseeing. Twain himself, partly content with memories of his 1867 visit, engaged more casually.

In Italy, he rethought his position in regard to the Old Masters. Although he still considered much of the reverence for them herdlike praise, he now granted that some were indeed "Masters," especially Titian, whose *Moses* he admired. Issues of high versus popular art were much on his mind. Whereas to Ruskin there was great beauty in Turner's impressionistic *Slave Ship*, why was it to him, Twain asked himself in his notebook, "what a red rag is to a bull?" It was, he concluded, because of his "noncultivation," the absence of an educated eye and taste. "How much we do lose by cultivation! It narrows us down. . . . And what will the cultivated people do in heaven?—for in the nature of things they will have to have 'popular' music there because of the crowd." And why was it that the contemporary visual artist was allowed a license in subject and treatment as great as that allowed the Renaissance artist while the writer's range had been "sharply curtailed"? "Fielding and Smollett could portray the beastliness of their day in the beastliest language; we have plenty of foul subjects to deal with in our day, but we are not allowed to approach them very near, even with nice and guarded forms of speech." Though he deplored the widespread practice of modern moralists covering male genitals on Renaissance statues, he asked why it was that Titian's *Venus*, "the foulest, the vilest, the obscenest picture the world possesses," could invite the gaze of any observer. "Well, let it go," the author of "1601" concluded, "it cannot be helped. Art retains her privileges, Literature has lost hers."

Increasingly irritated with Italy, Twain did his best to play the patient paterfamilias. Though disparate entries piled up in his notebook, actual work on his book was mostly on hold. Social engagements in Rome and Florence, especially with traveling Americans, had begun to be oppressive, as if the Hartford obligations from which they were on holiday had traveled with them. By mid-November 1878 they were on their way over the mountains to winter quarters in Munich, which they selected in order to continue their efforts to master German. A miserable first impression of the city was prelude to colds and cold weather: "I can't tell," he wrote to

Bayard Taylor, "at what moment Mrs. Clemens may take fright & flee to some kindlier climate." Almost by return mail they discovered, to their shock, that Taylor had died. Gradually, they all began to feel more affectionate toward, and more at home in, Munich. The women continued intensive language lessons. The city had enough culture and social life to keep all of them engaged.

In a rented studio, a short distance from their lodgings, Twain began attempting to turn his notes into a narrative. Though occasionally he wrote fluently and happily, it did not go well enough to give him sustained satisfaction. "My book is half finished," he wrote to Howells at the end of January 1879. And he exaggerated to Frank Bliss in February, "Yes, I'm still pegging along at the book & making pretty good & steady progress, though I continue to tear up manuscript." Though he had a talent for being amusingly calm on the surface of the written page, he was in fact (and between the lines) angry, bitterly hostile, and deeply unhappy for reasons he could not fully realize let alone explain. He had come to Europe for an extended creative holiday, for escape, rejuvenation, and an easy literary success. What he was attempting to escape he had of course brought with him— his moods, his self-criticism, his prejudices, his resentments. Some of his self-laceration appeared in a nasty letter about Bret Harte that he had written to Howells the previous June, from the comparative contentment of the Schloss Hotel, when the news came of Harte's consulship appointment. He could not stop stabbing, as if killing Harte was a repetition compulsion that enabled him to sustain his own life. After the Whittier dinner humiliation, he had declaimed to Howells, "I am a great & sublime fool. But then I am God's fool, & all His works must be contemplated with respect." But the book continued not to go well, its structure and tone a reflection of his repressed anger, his feeling of fragmentation, and a touch of panic inevitable in a man heavily dependent on his literary earnings.

Gradually, *A Tramp Abroad* began to emerge as a narrative with a congenial surface so bland as to be duplicitous, a melange of diverse material, much of it unconnected to any of the travel structure strategies he had devised in his mind. Drawing on his reading of German legends, he retold stories from books and made much of minor adventures. A digression helped him through the early part, "Jim Baker's Bluejay Yarn," a tall-tale comic version emblematic of his own situation as a writer, in which a blue jay keeps trying to fill a hole with acorns until at last he discovers that to do this he needs to fill the entire house, the roof of which the hole is in. Twain had many unfilled holes, he was very short of acorns, and the house was huge.

"I *hate* travel," he complained to Howells. "I *hate* hotels, & I *hate* the opera, & I *hate* the old Masters . . . no, I want to stand up before [every-thing] & *curse* it, & foam at the mouth,—or take a club & pound it to rags & pulp." The extent to which this rage was also self-absorption, expressed itself in much of *A Tramp Abroad*'s best writing, which focused on the au-thor's autobiographical past, highlighting a number of stories from his Han-nibal days, as if indeed he were going there in search of the real self that he could not readily discover in his European present. Incidents of partial or total self-deflation, even humiliation, inserted themselves into the text. He recalled the incident in Odessa in 1867, when he had mistakenly given a gold coin rather than a penny to a beggar in a church, then stole it back by stealthily replacing it with a Turkish penny. An even more devastating incident, combining humiliation and guilt, forced itself into the book. As a ten-year-old boy, asleep below deck on a steamboat, he had dreamed that it had exploded, as the *Pennsylvania* was to do, and that everyone was in danger of imminent death. Dressed only in his short nightshirt, without benefit of a fig leaf, he raced up to the deck, where a group of twenty or so women were knitting and talking. "Fire, fire!" he cried out, urging everyone to jump overboard. The ladies looked sweetly up at him and one said, "But you mustn't catch cold, child. Run and put on your breastpin, and then come and tell us all about it." He had expected to be a hero. Instead, he "crept humbly away . . . and never even cared to discover whether [he] had dreamed the fire or actually seen it."

After four months in Paris, from February to June 1879, and then a month in England, the entire family had had more than enough of Europe. It had been a cold winter and an inclement spring. In order to keep warm in London they had to have fires even in August. Paris and the French he disliked even more than he had in 1867. He amused himself with a fash-ionable balloon ascent and met President Gambetta. Paris seemed ab-surdly expensive in comparison to Germany and Italy, and both he and Livy worried that they were living above their means, though they always found justifications for expenditures. Street noises got on Twain's nerves regu-larly, Parisians seemed to have a gift for mercilessly overcharging visitors, and it seemed to both of them that what they missed most of all was American food. "Anywhere is better than Paris," Twain later advised a friend. "Paris the cold, Paris the drizzly, Paris the rainy, Paris the damnable."

In April 1879, four months before the family sailed for New York and for their Hartford home, he gave a dinner talk to the Stomach Club, a group of worldly American bon vivants living in Paris, his subject "Some Thoughts on the Science of Onanism." A brilliant, bawdy takeoff on the subject of masturbation, it was, like "1601," an expression of the subversive, anti-Victorian side of Twain that, perforce, found some of its best moments in private jokes. Stoically he accepted that he himself and everything he did was determined by forces beyond his control. Some were cultural. Some were genetic. All were implacable.

CHAPTER TWELVE

SUCH BEING MY NATURE

1879–1882

1.

Speeding by express train from New York to Chicago in November 1879, Mark Twain was exuberantly anticipating an event that would make national headlines: a three-day reunion of the soldiers of the Army of the Tennessee and the further apotheosis of General Ulysses S. Grant. Having served eight years as president, the taciturn Grant, who had recently returned from a two-year around-the-world trip during which he had been celebrated as America's greatest living hero, was rumored to be available for another term. Some Republican Party stalwarts thought him their best chance to retain the presidency. Others felt that his less than magnificent tenure in office warranted a new Republican standard bearer. Grant's limited administrative talents seemed less important than his heroic integrity. Famous for his imperturbability—his determination, emotional forbearance, and personal courage—Grant had been transformed by the advertising devices of post–Civil War America into an embodiment of the personal and national values that had won the war and unified the nation.

Bored and disgusted at endlessly revising *A Tramp Abroad,* Twain jumped at the chance to make the Chicago trip. He, too, he felt, had a contribution to make to the festivities, especially his own humorous twist on national unification. "We were the first men that went into the service in Missouri; we were the first that went out of it anywhere," he had told his Hartford audience at a dinner honoring "The Ancient and Honorable Artillery Company of Massachusetts." That he had been a reluctant warrior made him no less an apotheosis of reunification than Grant. He had become America's first coast-to-coast literary celebrity, himself an embodiment of the United States, a border-state man with one foot in California, the other in Connecticut. Lincoln and Grant's Civil War had made possible Twain's national career. No other literary figure, especially one who had been identified with the Confederacy, would have thought of going to Chicago, let alone anticipated being enthusiastically welcomed there.

Disembarking in New York in early September 1879, the family had gone directly to Elmira. "I was lucky to get through the custom-house at all," Twain wrote to Dan Slote, "because the ship was loaded mainly with my freight," including furniture and glassware. "Out of the poverty left on hand by an interminable European trip," he contributed twenty-five dollars to the Hartford Battle-flag Day Committee. He agreed to welcome a group of Georgian war veterans to the city. "Personal contact and communion of Northerners and Southerners over the friendly board will do more toward obliterating sectional lines & restoring mutual respect and esteem than any other thing that can be devised."

Expenses pressed, including assembling a staff of servants for the Hartford house. German-speaking Rosina Hay had returned with them to continue as nursemaid. The most significant addition was not to occur until the next summer when Katy Leary, a twenty-four-year-old skilled seamstress, the daughter of Irish immigrants who had settled in Elmira and whose older sister worked for the Langdons, came to Hartford as Livy's personal maid. Patrick McAleer, who now had seven children, remained in place. George Griffen had either stayed on salary or was rehired, though in employing a new black cook Twain had a seriocomic concern that she not be pretty, given the married George's propensities. The cook would have to be "strong enough & wise enough" to resist him. "I want him to live with his wife;" he added, "it curtails her immoralities, by diminishing her time for them."

Curbing his own expenses was more difficult, and he needed the income that publication of *A Tramp Abroad* would bring. But each time he believed he had finished he was annoyed to conclude that more revision was necessary. That the process now seemed endless suggested to him that the book was fundamentally flawed. Laboring at it for so long made him and it feel stale. Eager to have the final chapters, Bliss urged that the production process be started with dispatch. "I have been knocking out early chapters for more than a year, now—not because they had not merit," he told Twichell, "but merely because they hindered the flow of the narrative." In late October 1879 the family returned to Hartford. Livy was distressed by the challenge of getting "a house going that has stood empty for eighteen months." And many of their purchases had been broken in transit. At the end of the month, he wrote a letter declining to go to Chicago because of the unfinished book, but he did not send it, and in early November he accepted the invitation. The Chicago festivities, he hoped, would provide relief from tedious labor, refreshment for his sluggard spirit, something to set his mind and spirit stirring.

Arriving in Chicago a few days early, he was awakened the next morning at the Palmer House by Abraham Reeves Jackson, his medical companion from the *Quaker City* voyage, to begin the first of three exhilarating days, a celebrity among celebrities. Fred Grant, the president's son, invited Twain to two private receptions for Grant and Sherman, both of whom told him that *Innocents Abroad* had been their guidebook on their recent European travels. With George Warner he spent the afternoon surveying the city's rapid expansion since the devastating fire. After some theater visits, they caroused all night with twenty Chicago journalists whom he was delighted to cultivate and who were happy to share drinks and songs. "I was up at 6 AM & did not go to bed until 7 the next morning," he wrote to Howells. "[But] I have not at any time felt tired, & hardly even drowsy." The next afternoon he stood on the crowded second-story Palmer House balcony with a small group of select journalists and VIPs, reviewing the procession of marching veterans. "Gen. Grant came forward & was saluted by the cheers of the multitude." General Sherman was in full dress uniform. "When the head of the procession passed it was grand to see Sheridan in his military cloak & his plumed chapeau, sitting as erect & rigid as a statue on his immense black horse—by far the most martial figure I ever saw." That night Twain gave a speech at the welcoming reception, the main point of which was that he usually took hours to prepare an impromptu speech. Since this actually was impromptu, he kept it very short.

In the vast dining hall crowded with cheering men, Grant proposed a toast to the greatness of America. Fireworks flared. Martial music blared. At three-thirty A.M., Twain, the fifteenth and final speaker, stepped forward. Exhilarated but nervous, he looked at the celebrities around him and down at the faces of seven hundred veterans. Despite his request to be placed early in the program, he had been placed last, the notion being that, as a humorist, he would transform all lugubrious sentimentality into waves of laughter, the final note on which everyone would disperse. Four of the preceding speakers, Twain told Howells, "carried away all [his] wits" and made him "drunk with enthusiasm," especially Robert Ingersoll, who, evoking Lincoln, had toasted the volunteer soldiers who had saved the only people's government in the world. At a time when oratory was an art, when speakers memorized lengthy presentations, when public talk was stirring entertainment, Ingersoll's speech seemed better than any he had ever heard or could ever hope to hear again. Much of the magic, though, was in the occasion, not the texts. In cold print, they lost much of their effect. At a climatic moment "a bullet-shredded battle flag [was] reverently unfolded to the gaze of a thousand middle-aged soldiers most of whom hadn't seen it since they saw it advancing over victorious fields when they were in their prime." As Grant "stepped into view . . . somebody struck up 'When we were Marching though Georgia.' Well, you should have heard the thousand voices lift that chorus & seen the tears stream down." Twain loved every moment of it. He was now himself a member of the victorious team, an enlistee in the oratorical Union army.

Amid a flood of heroic verbiage, Twain touched the other side of male bravado with a clever reversal. Raising his glass, he toasted "The Babies. As They Comfort Us in Our Sorrows, Let Us not Forget Them in Our Festivities." The noisy audience came to a quick hush. What babies? What have babies got to do with this celebration of Union victory and with America's national hero? "We haven't all had the good fortune to be ladies," Twain began; "we haven't all been generals, or poets, or statesmen; but, when the toast works down to the babies, we stand on common ground, for we've all been babies." The child is father to the man, Twain reminded his audience. Babies were emblematic of the great leveling principle of democracies. All of them, including the "Commander in Chief," had started life in the same position. And babies, as all parents knew, were powerful creatures. "*One* baby can furnish more business than you and your whole Interior Department can attend to. He is enterprising, irrepressible, brim full of lawless activities. Do what you please, you can't make him stay on the reservation. Sufficient unto the day is one baby—as long as you are in your right mind don't ever pray for twins."

Having struck an almost universal chord of recognition, he assured them that all would be well for the future of the country. "The present crop" of babies, who were the nation's future leaders, would have the good fortune to wave a flag over a Republic "numbering 200,000,000 souls." It would be a great world power. "Let them be well trained, for we are going to leave a big contract on their hands." Among them are the great scientists, statesmen, and generals of the future. And in one of those cradles resides "the future illustrious Commander in Chief of the American Armies." He turned to Grant. So too did everyone in the room. Grant kept a straight face. So little is this future general preoccupied, Twain continued, with his future responsibilities that he is at this moment devoting his entire strategic genius to "trying to find out some way to get his own big toe in his mouth—an achievement which, meaning no disrespect, the illustrious guest of this evening turned *his* whole attention to some fifty-six years ago." All eyes went from Twain to Grant. And, Twain concluded, "if the child is but a prophecy of the man, there are mighty few who will doubt that he *succeeded*." Grant exploded into laughter. The wildly applauding audience rose to its feet. "I shook [Grant] up like dynamite, & he sat there fifteen minutes," Twain told Howells, "and laughed & cried like the mortalest of mortals." He laughed "till every . . . bone in his body ached," he wrote to Livy at five A.M. "I never was so proud in my life."

Returning to Hartford via New York, Twain savored his triumph. The compliments still sounded in his ears. "It was a memorable night. I never shall see its like again," he wrote to Orion, who had either quit or been fired by Bliss in 1872 and had returned to Keokuk, explaining that he had to return to Hartford immediately and could not visit. Skeptical, even cynical, about the frequent misuse of patriotic emotion for manipulative purposes, Twain had unreservedly identified with this celebration of national unity. Here he was, the son of slaveholding parents, who had fled Missouri to avoid service on either side, now a national celebrity so cleansed by his achievement as a writer and by the pleasure he gave as a humorist as to be chosen to speak at a banquet in honor of the general inextricably associated with Northern Republicanism and Southern defeat. The paradox reflected the reality that Twain no longer in any ideological way identified himself with the South. Missouri memories were strong and central to his imagination and his mannerisms. But the ideology that had been their context he had rejected. The novel narrated by Huckleberry Finn that he had put on hold was a reflection of the irony and the advantage of his southern origin. It took on the challenge of dramatizing the world of his childhood in a way that made literature out of both personal and national tensions. *Life on the Mississippi* was to be the nonfictional variant of the same challenges.

Grant did not become the Republican nominee in 1880. Though Grant and the war were a sentimental bonanza, political realities, particularly the stain of the Grant scandals and their association with the lingering depression of 1873, favored a new man. At a deadlocked convention, James Garfield was nominated on the thirty-sixth ballot. He also had served with distinction on the battlefield, had become the Speaker of the House, and had charmed his constituents with his amiability and honesty. This fresh face, with a keener, more forward-looking approach to the problems of industrialization, especially labor strife, seemed desirable. In support of the Republican candidate, Grant came to New England in mid-October 1880. Deeply respectful and personally fond of the general, whose taciturnity contrasted sharply with his own talkativeness, Twain joined a group of Hartford Republicans to escort him down from Boston. Headed by Twain, the welcoming committee had arranged a parade, a luncheon, and a formal reception at which Hartford's most famous resident delivered the main speech.

As in Chicago, Twain found just the right approach and turn of phrase to idealize the "First Citizen of the Republic," the soldier without peer, the peacemaker in international disputes, the man who, "being almost called—and yet not quite—to carry the standard of a great party for the third time . . . [had] sunk the hero in the patriot," and had put aside "all considerations of self" and devoted himself to the election of his party's candidate. And, Twain pointed out, he had refused in private life to engage in any commercial activity that might have a speculative end, to trade on his name for financial advantage. In any other country, he "would have been affronted in the same sordid way" as Wellington had been when the British government gave him a huge cash gift. But America did not do such things. "Your country stands ready, from this day forth, to testify her measureless love and pride and gratitude toward you, in every conceivable—

inexpensive way." Grant broke into a wry smile. That remark, Twain told Howells, "invoked the loudest shout, and the longest, & the most full-hearted that was heard in Hartford that day."

That same year Twain went to New York with Twichell to solicit Grant's influence in persuading the Chinese government not to abolish an educational program headquartered in Hartford that sent thirty boys each year to receive an American education. And on another visit to the ex-president in his New York residence, Twain took up the patronage cudgels for his friend Edward House, who had recently returned from an extended stay in Japan with a young Japanese "ward." Grant had anticipated the request and already attended to it. Twain urged Grant to write his memoirs. "I couldn't get General Grant to promise to write that book," he wrote to House. "But he sat down & spun out a lot of secret national history that would make a stunning chapter; says he does want to write that out before it gets too dim in his memory." Five years later, with Twain as his publisher, Grant would write every word of one of the most brilliant of American autobiographies.

2.

In late November 1879, soon after Twain returned from his Chicago triumph, Howells proposed that he speak in December at an *Atlantic Monthly* breakfast in honor of Holmes's seventieth birthday. Twain begged off on the grounds that he still had not provided Bliss with the final chapters and revisions of *A Tramp Abroad*. Actually, the day and a half that would be required for his attendance was not the main issue. His presence, he feared, would be another reminder of his speech at the Whittier dinner, a shame that still burned two years later. Charles Warner, though, strongly argued that Twain ought to go and "act just as if nothing had happened." Howells also pressed the case and the invitation. Twain soon agreed, though this time he made certain, perhaps with Livy's preapproval, that his text was flatteringly innocuous.

With Warner, Twain visited Howells' new Belmont house, where the friends enjoyed one another's company. At the breakfast on December 3, those who wished Twain well held their breath; others expected, probably even desired, another blundering performance from a man they considered a vulgar comic writer. His subject was plagiarism, his example his unintentional borrowing in the dedication to *Innocents Abroad* of an idea and turn of phrase that first appeared in a dedication by Holmes to a volume of poems. Twain had read and reread the book while sick in Hawaii in 1866. "Pride protects a man from deliberately stealing other people's ideas," he told his audience. The message between the lines was that, just as he had not consciously plagiarized, so had he not purposefully insulted the three Boston literary Brahmins in his 1877 talk. Shouldn't that put an end to any criticism, including self-criticism? He ended with glowing praise of Holmes's genius. Whatever his audience thought, his own sense of shame about his Whittier dinner performance diminished somewhat. It did not, though, entirely disappear. His tendency to cling to shame was relentless.

When in early January 1882 two friends, Charles Warner and Edward House, reported to him that Whitelaw Reid's *Tribune* had for months been regularly printing hostile references to him, Twain burst into fury. Having been angry at Reid for almost ten years because Reid had not selected House to review *The Gilded Age,* he was eager to believe the worst of him. When threatened, Twain divided the world into friends and enemies. For those he believed had attempted to or actually had damaged him, his imagination delighted in their extreme discomfiture, for which he had a ready vocabulary of damning references. The claim about the *Tribune* most likely originated with House, who felt that Reid had spoken abusively to him in 1873 during *The Gilded Age* contretemps. Now Twain was eager to believe that the *Tribune* had "been flinging sneers and brutalities" at him with "persistent frequency as to attract general remark."

Blinded by rage, Twain concocted a plan to write Reid's biography, a damning account of his shabby character and dishonorable life. Filling his notebook with promising slurs, he sketched its outline, working "day & night making notes & collecting and classifying material," including a trip to New York, "taking evidence while a stenographer set it down," as if he had nothing else to do or as if this were so important that it warranted setting aside everything else. When he confided the project to Howells, his friend was horrified. Twain responded to a nervous Livy's plea that he make certain before he continue that indeed the attacks had been "almost daily" and that their "number & character" would justify his plan. A search through the back issues of the *Tribune* produced only four references to Twain in the previous two months, two of them innocuous, the others far short of "malicious."

Shocked at how close he had come to making a public fool of himself, Twain immediately dropped what was under any circumstances an untenable project. His mountain had brought forth its "small mouse . . . and my three weeks' hard work have got to go into the ignominious pigeon-hole." To some extent he recognized it as a characteristic and humiliating stupidity. But there were others to share the blame. "What the devil can those friends of mine have been thinking about, to spread those 3 or 4 harmless things out into two months of daily sneers & affronts?" Warner had reported hearsay. House, though, had claimed to know that Twain was being vilified. Apparently Twain said nothing to him, and they continued to be friends.

Twain's torturous relationship with his publisher continued in the same vein. Although Bliss had allowed Twain to become a shareholder and director, the writer found it odd that the company never declared a dividend. At least he had been able to raise his royalty rate to eight and a half percent for *Tom Sawyer* and ten percent for *A Tramp Abroad,* though the increased royalty for the novel could not compensate for disappointing sales. Salesmen complained to Bliss that short books such as *Tom Sawyer* did not lend themselves to subscription sales. Perhaps because he initially had had such great success with subscription marketing, Twain was slow to see that shorter works needed a different method of distribution. His requirement that newspapers be prevented from publishing excerpts probably also worked against him. Subscription books got a boost from the added publicity and rarely lost sales if the selections were brief. Bliss knew this, but Twain could not get the concept into his head, and when a book did not sell as well as expected he blamed Bliss.

He had other complaints also, including Bliss's inadequate attempts to protect Twain's international copyright, as well as the necessity for him to correspond himself with his British publisher about the sale of plates, which he believed was his American publisher's responsibility. It was, though, the longstanding issue of his royalty versus half profits that gave him most concern. He could not shake the notion that he was being cheated. But, because he did not have access to the company's books, his attempts to document his belief proved futile. When he was at last granted an audit, he suspected that entries had been manipulated.

Frank Bliss's attempt to publish *A Tramp Abroad* had been both a father-and-son and an author-publisher folly, made possible partly because Elisha Bliss had in effect tried to take total control of the American Publishing Company. That put him at odds with his own partners and other directors, sending Frank off on his own. Perhaps Bliss had consented to his son's venture as part of his struggle with the other directors of the company. And perhaps, then, with Frank fading out of the picture, Twain believed that Bliss was still his best bet for successful subscription publication. When Frank could not carry off the project, his father used reassignment of the manuscript to himself to reassert control on his own terms. Apparently Twain thought he still owed Bliss a book, though how that could be in the face of his contract with Frank is unclear. Twain got assurances that the company would publish no other book in the nine months surrounding the publication of his. And he got Bliss to agree to half profits instead of a royalty. Twain, though, was once again in Bliss's hands.

Despite few reviews, *A Tramp Abroad* sold moderately well, better than *Tom Sawyer* but still noticeably less than his first two travel books. Its sales campaign (sixty-two thousand copies were sold within the first year) was led by Frank Bliss, who had returned to the American Publishing Company. The strong first-three-month sales did lift Twain's spirits, and Howells' and David Gray's laudatory reviews startled him into appreciation of a book that he had mostly disliked. Soon, though, when the sales flattened out, he consoled himself with inaccurate figures both as wish-fulfillment and as obfuscation.

In fall 1879, the fifty-nine-year-old Elisha Bliss became ill with heart disease. In September 1880 he died. Twain did not shed a tear for the "old fox." He soon got to see a balance sheet, and it was "enlightening." He had been right to be suspicious all along. His half profits on a cost basis for *Tramp Abroad*, when he and Perkins refigured it into a percentage, exceeded even the highest royalty that Bliss had conceded, let alone the seven and a half percent that he had sworn in 1872 was the equivalent of half profits. If Perkins had not dissuaded Twain from going to court, as Orion had urged, he calculated he would have earned about $60,000 more (to Pamela he raised that figure to $100,000), lost over the years because of Bliss's trickery. The half profits from the *Tramp* contract, he told Orion, gained him $20,000 more than he would have realized from a ten percent royalty.

Twain's analysis of the earnings and expenses reports was not necessarily accurate, his arithmetic often in the service of his emotions. But there is reason to believe that Bliss did, to some extent, swindle him. In fall 1880, having the latest half profits balance sheet in hand, Twain attended an American Publishing Company stockholders' meeting, at which he "stood up & delivered a lecture" to the directors, whom he assumed were co-conspirators with Bliss. The message was that the rascals had egregiously cheated him. And if Bliss were alive he would sue them for the money. Instead, he soon sold his stock and vowed never again to publish with the American Publishing Company. "My bitterness against [Bliss] has faded away and disappeared," he would write thirty years later. "I feel only compassion for him and if I could send him a fan I would."

3.

In regard to money, though, Twain had a worse enemy than Bliss. For over a twelve-year period, between late 1879 and the early 1890s, he devoted a great deal of his spare capital, and eventually much of his wife's, to various investments, primarily of three kinds: new inventions about which he became passionately enthusiastic, a publishing business that he founded and bankrolled, and the purchase of speculative stocks. "I must speculate in something, such being my nature," he told Howells in August 1883. Dividends were welcome but not his major object. With the soul of a venture capitalist, he preferred to gamble for the breakthrough, for the hope of a sudden surge rather than the slow accumulation of wealth. Occasionally he swore off business entirely, claiming that he had no head for it. What he meant was that he had no talent for or interest in details. He envisioned himself as a man of creative business ideas, an imaginative captain of industry whose subordinates would take care of everything else.

For much of the twelve-year period, he reserved enough of his and Livy's income to sustain their standard of living, though at the cost of heavy pressure to earn more and worry when things got unexpectedly tight. While the economy remained reasonably good, as it did through most of the 1880s, he acted as if it would always remain that way and that in any case one of his investments would produce a bonanza. When in 1893 the United States economy fell into a severe depression, he had little cash reserve: inventions he had invested in had not become marketable, and his stock investments, some of which were sound, declined with a sharply falling market.

In 1874, in Boston, Twain had bought one of the first typewriters, made by the fledgling Remington Company. It typed only capital letters. On his first attempt he wrote, "I AM TRYING T TO GET THE HANG OF THIS

NEW F FANGLED WRITING MACHINE, BUT AM NOT MAKING A SHINING SUCCESS OF IT." He soon could type as fast as he could write. And whomever he sent a typewritten letter to was so astounded at the novelty that he was invariably asked about it; that required another letter and the use of valuable time answering queries about the machine's wonders. Though he passed that first machine along to Howells, he soon had a new rented typewriter and was using it periodically. "I write so much plainer with the type-writer, than I can with the pen, that I expect every-body to applaud me for making the change," he wrote to a young friend. "As soon as you get used to the type-writer you will be offended when people write you in any other way." With his belief in the wonders of science, he felt lucky to be alive at a time when civilization was leaping forward into technological miracles. "Five hundred years ago—yes, one hundred years ago—I would have been in a fidget to die, in order to find out the mysteries of the world to come; but now I can't think of death with the right patience because I am so full of curiosity to see what other wonderful things are going to be done *here*. For we *do* live in an age compared to which all other ages are dull and eventless." The past deserved its due. Human nature had not changed. But inventive genius now had the encouragement of a culture eager for such miracles, especially in America, where the inventor, the engineer, and the builder, like Edison, became cultural idols. And whoever brought to market a better mousetrap had the chance to make a fortune.

His good friend from *Quaker City* days, Dan Slote, offered him the opportunity to invest in just such a better mousetrap. In 1878 he had lent Slote five thousand dollars to help rescue his stationery business, which was still putting out Twain's self-pasting scrapbook. The loan remained outstanding, though the firm had been reorganized and was in business again under a different name. Twain considered it a personal loan and expected it eventually to be repaid in full. That he took the firm's note as security may have encouraged Slote to think of it as similar to the firm's other debts. As usual, Twain was generous with friends and careless with details, and the writer's widely publicized prosperity made him a target for investment schemes and begging letters from friends and strangers. "I'm just about to start in on another ten thousand dollar venture—a patent," Twain wrote to Frank Fuller, with whom he soon was involved in financing an invention to power a whiskey still with a steam engine and then a "Vaporizer." "Want to come in?—in case it continues to look good? Slote is to run it."

He apparently soon "drew out of Dan Slote's speculation because my lawyer insisted that it was risky, although it promised mightily well & seemed to have a deal of money in it." In December 1879 Slote encouraged him to invest in a new engraving process called Kaolatype, in which a steel plate was coated with a layer of china clay (kaolin) through which an image was cut into metal. Molten metal was then poured into the matrix. The cold metal form provided a die or stereotype plate for printing engravings. It seemed to Slote and Twain that the invention would revolutionize the printing of engravings, especially of the sort with which Twain's own books were filled. Inspired by the idea, Twain had little difficulty persuading Slote to sell him the patent for five thousand dollars. He preferred total ownership.

For much of 1880 he increased his investment in it. His enthusiasm grew, especially in response to his own idea that the process could also be used to create brass stamps for imprinting ornamental titles and decorations onto book covers. So optimistic was he that by late winter 1881 he had put up "a building in New York for . . . brass-casting works (Twain-Sneider patent)," the "Office of the Kaolatype Engraving Company . . . S. L. Clemens President." Slote managed the office. The technician and inventor of the process, Charles Sneider, whom Twain had put on salary, was supposedly at work transforming Twain's brass stamp idea into a commercially viable process. The success of the enterprise depended on the validity of Sneider's claim to have developed an innovative chemical process that produced superior plates more accurately and at less cost than the current industry standard.

Eager to see the process at work, Twain made an appointment for a demonstration. The night before, the shop burned down. He made another appointment, this time at Sneider's own workshop. That also burned to the ground immediately before the scheduled demonstration. Twain was suspicious but still deeply committed. Sneider, and perhaps even Slote, he felt, was cheating him. Neither would produce receipts for ongoing expenses that Twain paid, and Sneider, although exclusively on Twain's payroll, apparently was also working on a gas-fixture invention. When it became clear that Kaolatype was useless for the purpose it had been originally conceived, Twain still was optimistic about the book stamp application. But Sneider had not yet shown positive results of any sort. Slote, he now worried, might be capable of fraud, especially since he had borrowed money for the stationery business "& then failed in a month or two," as if he had known that the failure was inevitable and the firm's note worthless. Still, in January 1881, as Twain encouraged Slote to make sub-licensing arrangements in Chicago and other places, he also ordered Slote, "[Don't] submit picayune trades to me . . . & don't ask me for advice in the d——d $2000 cases . . . I started in to be a Figure-Head President & that's what I *am*." As usual, he wanted someone else to sweat the details while he looked after the big picture. As he worried about his investment and how to put Sneider's claims to the test, a helping hand appeared.

Annie Moffett, the little girl whom he had amused in the Moffetts' St. Louis home in the late 1850s, had in 1875 married Charles L. Webster. Annie was twenty-three, Webster twenty-two. Brought up in Fredonia, New York, where Pamela and Jane Clemens now lived, Webster had been trained as a civil engineer, but he soon gave up engineering for business. In 1881, Fredonia business associates and possibly friends, the owners of the Independent Watch Company, represented themselves to Webster as being in need of additional capital. Would Webster attempt to interest his wife's famous uncle to buy five thousand dollars' worth of stock? What remuneration, if any, Webster was to have received is unclear. But the owners were "quite anxious that Mark Twain should become a stockholder," Pamela wrote to her brother. So they paid "Charley's expenses to go and see him" with a prospectus and the request to name a watch model for him. Twain succumbed, though he was in fact deeply worried about money, having sunk about fifty thousand dollars into the very uncertain prospects of Kaolatype. He had also decided that he himself would finance the publication of his new book, transforming half into full profits. His publisher would in effect work for him.

When, in mid-March 1881, a consultant gave Kaolatype a favorable report and Slote provided "handsome impressions" from Sneider, Twain felt immensely relieved. He could now afford, even at the high price of twelve thousand dollars, the purchase of a greenhouse and a one-hundred-foot piece of adjacent land. "If the utility of our invention was *doubtful*," he wrote to Slote, "I would allow my neighbor to go digging his blamed cellar, & build a house right in our faces . . . & in effect, block up the front of our house." At the same time he made arrangements for an extensive ten-thousand-dollar renovation to begin in June, while the family was in Elmira. The old kitchen would be torn down, a larger one designed and constructed, the entrance hall enlarged considerably, the ground floor entirely repainted, and the long driveway to the house reshaped and extended. All this on the basis of one consultant's informal report, and despite Twain's reservations about Sneider and Slote. Uneasy, he decided in early April that the nice young man from Fredonia, his niece's competent husband, might be the man to help with his business details, including investigating his New York employees. Webster was willing. Twain still believed "there was a fortune ready for the man who can find a way to cast fine nice brass book-stamps."

In April 1881, Webster's initial reports confirmed Twain's suspicions. At the end of the month he gave Webster "complete authority" over Kaolatype: "You will take entire control of the property & employees of the Company; you will hire whom you please, discharge whom you please; all moneys received & disbursed must pass through your hands, & you will be held responsible." Early in May, Webster had far more distressing news: there was no commercially viable Kaolatype printing or engraving process at all. Sneider's original patent was a fraud. Much of what he had stated he accomplished had not been done in the manner he claimed. The two fires had been set in order to avoid exposure. Slote, Webster thought, had most likely been a co-conspirator. By the middle of May, Twain instructed Webster to relieve Slote of all Kaolatype responsibilities and to establish whatever record he could in the event that Twain decided to sue. His five-thousand-dollar loan to Slote he now felt certain had been an earlier attempt to defraud him. In October he became convinced that Slote had also been defrauding him for years in regard to the sales of the self-pasting scrapbook. There seemed to be evidence that his old friend had been keeping two sets of books to conceal his theft.

Twain still believed his patent must be worth something. "The day that Kaolatype arrives at a point where it pays its own expenses, you are to have $900 of its stock," he told Webster. "Meantime, I wish to give you $100 of its stock, now, anyhow, & make you Vice President and Treasurer—also Manager." Webster would do his best for the company, but in the end Twain was to lose his entire investment. Ironically, the Independent Watch Company of Fredonia also proved to be a fraud. That five-thousand-dollar investment was lost, though apparently Twain did not hold Webster at fault. When Dan Slote died unexpectedly in February 1882 Twain refused to attend the funeral and privately cursed him to the grave.

But the urge to become rich was irrepressible, and he was not in the least discouraged, except momentarily, by these failures. The amount he invested between 1879 and 1883 was disproportionate to his and Livy's incomes and expenses, and some investments, like Kaolatype, produced substantial if not total losses. Between one investment and another, it seems likely that he lost about $100,000 in these five years, about 1.5 million twenty-first-century dollars, not including worthless stocks that would be debited years later. Though occasionally discouraged, sometimes depressed, and frequently angry about his monetary affairs, he was on the whole buoyantly optimistic. And he had the capacity for enthusiastic belief in what seemed to him sure things, no matter how many times certainties became worse than doubtful. The Vaporizer came to nothing. His $12,500 investment in a newly created engine factory in Hartford went down the drain, his losses limited by his inability, despite his desire, to buy even more stock in the company. He had invested "on the mere *prospect* of a profitable business. . . . No guaranty, I took all the stock I could get yet." He constantly had his finger to the wind, attempting to time market purchases. Almost always, he bought and sold unwisely, partly for the irresistible excitement, mostly for the dream of getting rich, somehow confident that his combination of brains and imagination would sooner or later strike the mother lode. His father's failed Tennessee land speculation may have influenced his compulsion, though he noticeably never invested in land, but there seems a direct line of connection between John Marshall's interest in tinkering and Twain's fascination with inventions.

Kaolatype was the first major failure. The second was to have a much longer, far more costly, life. Twain first heard of a new, fully automated compositor for setting and distributing type in late April 1881. A Hartford jeweler urged him to buy stock in a machine that had been invented in 1872 by James Paige, a thirty-nine-year-old Chicago-born inventor. In 1875, Paige had rented space—in partnership with the Farnham Type-Setting Company, which had agreed to provide the capital—at the Colt Arms Factory in Hartford. He set busily to work perfecting a demonstration prototype to attract investors. Hartford, though not a major industrial center, had two first-rate late-nineteenth-century high-tech factories and machine shops: the Colt Arms Factory and Pratt and Whitney, the engine designer and manufacturer. Skilled workmen were available. Costs could be better controlled than in a large city. And Hartford's insurance industry, among others, had created reserves in an age in which rich individuals were the primary sources of investment capital.

As an ex-printer, Twain had a special interest in the project and even some awareness of the issues. "I took $2,000 of the stock. I was always taking little chances like that—and almost always losing by it, too—a thing which I did not greatly mind, because I was always careful to risk only such amounts as I could easily afford to lose," he wrote inaccurately years later. When, soon after his initial investment, he visited Paige's workshop, he was dazzled. The machine seemed to him a technological marvel. "Here was a machine that was really setting type . . . with swiftness and accuracy, too. Moreover, it was distributing its case *at the same time*. . . . It began its work of its own accord when the type channels needed filling, and stopped of its own accord when they were full enough. The machine was almost a complete compositor." It worked at least as fast as four of the fastest human compositors could. The only thing it did not do was justify lines.

Encouraged by William Hamersley, Hartford City Attorney and president of Farnham, who proposed that he and Twain become the primary investors, he immediately put down another three thousand dollars. Much larger amounts of investment capital would be necessary to bring the machine to market successfully, but the potential profits, as Twain calculated, were dazzling. His figures exploded into the millions. Totaling his fantasy profits in advance was irresistable. Hamersley soon reported that he had raised another twenty-five-thousand dollars. When Hamersely asked Twain what he would charge "to raise a capital of $500,000 for the manufacture of the machine," Twain responded that he "would undertake it for $100,000." Hamersley said, " 'Raise $600,000, then, & take $100,000.' I agreed. I sent for my partner, Webster. He came up from New York & went back with the project." Webster and Twain set to work to raise capital from potential investors and buyers, especially newspapers like the *New York Herald*, which expressed interest in purchasing a large number should it prove successful. To Twain's surprise, customers hung back. Huge profits for Twain and others seemed possible, but only if the typesetter could be demonstrated to be reliable in pressroom and printing house conditions.

So convinced was Twain that success was imminent that, in late 1881, he decided "to pay the preliminary expenses . . . out of [his] own pocket." Starting in 1882, he regularly provided operating cash, for which he got stocks as security. In early 1883 the now sixty or so mostly small stockholders and investors, including Twain, demanded that Paige affirm that "the machine [is] now flawless." He did, orally. When the Farnham Company, which had invested about $90,000, withdrew, Hamersley and Twain renewed their efforts to raise at least $1 million for production. Meanwhile, Paige kept working to perfect his machine. Each success bred new problems that needed to be solved. In spring 1885 Hamersley proposed an elaborate buyout scheme in which Paige would sell the patent, "the whole thing *outright*," to Hamersley and Twain, who then would sell portions of the new company. That money would be used to finance the production of tens of thousands of machines, to be sold around the world, reaping immense profits for themselves. "I'd rather have $250,000 in non-assessable stock than $100,000 *cash*," Twain told Webster in April 1885. The imprudent investor sailed on, wafted by genuine belief in the machine, by irrepressible investment optimism, and by dreams of immense wealth.

4.

On a cold day in January 1881 screams came from the nursery as Twain raced up from the library on the first floor. He ran toward the fire, joined by the nurse, as flames enveloped the crib. The baby, her hair slightly singed, had been snatched from the crib and rushed from the room by the maid, whose terrified screams they both had heard. She had entered from Susy's room, where she had gone to make the bed. The first thing she had seen was "the rising gust of flame. . . . The bedclothes, the lace canopy, & even the *pillows* were blazing." The floor was covered with burning remnants. Flinging the bedding out the window, he and Rosa stamped out the fire, getting mild burns on their hands. Apparently a spark had flown out through the fireplace screen and lit the highly flammable materials.

"We are curiously pursued by disaster, latterly," he wrote to his mother-in-law. In fact, they had been lucky. The maid had been about to go downstairs to the laundry. "If she had passed out of Susie's other door instead of passing through the nursery, where would Jean & the house be, now! Or if she had been 4 seconds later, either!" There had been a similar incident the same week. Six-year-old Clara had also been snatched from her flaming bedding. Children were indeed, he granted, hostages to fortune, children and parents vulnerable to accident and "nature's changing course untrimmed." The latter was making its mark. As he observed to Livy at the start of his forty-fourth year, "Time is moving along at a more & more lively gait with us, every year—for, you see, we are growing *old*. . . . Still, what we lose of youth, we make up in love, so the account is squared, & to nobody's disadvantage." It was a benevolent, even sentimental, view of aging that later in life he found impossible to sustain.

The infant snatched from the bedclothes had been born in Elmira in late July 1880, the Clemenses' fourth child. She was given her grandmother's name, Jane Lampton Clemens, though always called Jean. Twain stayed up all night to be there when the baby emerged. She "is thoroughly satisfactory, as far as it goes," he wrote to Howells, "but we did hope it was going to be twins." For the first forty-eight hours the doctors thought the mother might not pull through. For six months she had spent long periods in bed, sick with this and that, frequently exhausted. Twain himself was having more bronchial and head colds than usual, but Livy suffered constant chills, fevers, and aches, vulnerable to every available microbe. Eager to protect her and the baby, Twain arranged for a private railroad car from New York City to Elmira. "This is the first time Livy ever made that trip without our arriving in a played-out condition. She shall always go by special car hereafter, until we bust."

That he had an invalid wife he rarely had occasion to forget, and Victorian marital responsibilities weighed heavily on Livy, who frequently felt inadequate. The fault, she had the wisdom to realize, was not entirely in herself. "Women must be everything," she complained to her husband a month or two into her pregnancy. "They must keep up with all the current literature," she wrote to her mother, "they must know all about art, they must help in one or two benevolent societies—they must be perfect mothers—they must be perfect housekeepers and graceful gracious hostesses, they must know how to give perfect dinners . . . they must dress themselves and their children becomingly and above all they [must] make their houses 'charming.'" On the one hand, she had seven servants. On the other, she was indeed frail, and the pressure to be the perfect wife, mother, and household supervisor took its toll. She was, fortunately, spared frequent pregnancies, perhaps because of poor health, perhaps because they took precautions. Whereas Livy had conceived almost immediately after marriage and then had had one child two years later and another two years after that, there had been six years between Clara's birth and Jean's. And though still well within the childbearing years, the couple was not to have more children. It seems likely there was method in their restraint.

On the one hand, Twain reveled in domestic pleasures, especially in the summers at Quarry Farm, usually his happiest time of the year, partly because his most productive as a writer. The other eight or nine months he felt burdened with business and domestic chores, including the huge pile of letters from strangers. Much as he complained, though, he chose this schedule because it suited him. It made summers at Elmira seem even better. It also kept Hartford from being a part of and identified with his imaginative life. On the other hand, he sometimes yearned for liberation from the confinement of domestic pleasures. Occasionally Hawaii rose up in his memory as a place where he could blissfully live a luxuriously carefree existence. "What I have always longed for, was the privilege of living away up on one of those mountains . . . overlooking the sea." He even made the first of a number of attempts to write a novel based on the life of a well-known Hawaiian character. At the same time, when he was not writing, he was surprised and bothered that he felt perfectly happy. For long periods of time at home in Hartford it did not distress him at all that he was not producing creative work; or, as he put it, he was only unhappy because he was not unhappy that he was not writing. "I don't want to be happy when I can't work; I am resolved that hereafter I won't be." Like many other resolves, this one was also subject to the mood of the moment.

Wonderful as the children were, one or more always seemed ill or at least worrisome. As good as Livy was at running the house, he often had to be a partner in domestic chores, especially in regard to children and servants. And he could rarely resist complicating matters by a burst of temper or a new business adventure or an expensive renovation. Quarry Farm was especially pleasureable in the summer of 1881. But when they returned to Hartford, work on the kitchen and downstairs had them camping out on the second floor while workmen made noise and dust in a "carpetless & dismantled house." Like most such supposedly limited projects, it seemed to go on forever. The house was not ready to be reclaimed until January 1882. "O *never* revamp a house! Leave it just as it was, & then you can economise in profanity." He unburdened himself even more emphatically to Howells: "A life of don't-care-a-damn in a boarding house is what I have asked for in many a secret prayer."

As for more heartfelt prayers, Twain's relationship with the Almighty was still contentious. Praying in any religious sense he had long forsaken. As a young man, he had not attempted the ministry because he had every qualification except belief. That he had an argument with God and Christianity kept him interested in, and sometimes preoccupied with, religious and philosophical issues, though he expressed his hostility with a genial lightness and amiability that might have allowed the uninformed to think he was a Christian. He felt he had a duty to Livy to attend church with her and their daughters when she required his presence, and his lack of religious belief did not prevent his attending services if he had some reason other than religious to do so. The family occasionally would go to South Church, where there was a fine choir that he enjoyed. More often they went to Twichell's church, where "congregational singing prevailed." The music had charms that the liturgy did not. One Sunday afternoon he had no money with him. The collection plate was making its rounds. Livy signaled that she also had no money. "There was no time for reflection, for the crisis was at hand. He met it heroically and in an original manner, for as the plate was thrust toward him, he looked calmly up to the young man who held it, and hoarsely whispered, 'Charge it, please!' "

Howells, also a nonbeliever, recollected after Twain's death, "I had asked him, if he went regularly to church, and he groaned out: 'Oh yes, I go. It most kills me, but I go,' and I did not need his telling me to understand that he went because his wife wished it. He did tell me, after they both ceased to go that it had finally come to her saying, 'Well, if you are to be lost, I want to be lost with you.' " He had courted her with passionate expressions of his desire to share her family's Christian belief and with promises to live a Christian life. By the early 1880s, they had both become nonbelievers, though the erosion of her faith in the 1880s suggests that her earlier commitment may have been based on needs she no longer had. In her parents' home, she made herself part of the ideological community they provided. In her own, she cast her lot with her husband. Later, he was to feel guilty that his influence had helped deprive her of a belief system that might have provided solace during unhappy times.

That there would be a future existence beyond the life of the body he strongly doubted, though both heaven and hell appealed to him as imaginative constructs. His interest, though, was in human attitudes and practices. He did his best to keep his mind off the future. The work and diversions of the day were sufficient thereunto. Orion exemplified the pernicious result of always thinking about tomorrow. "It isn't healthy," Twain told a friend. "One can't forecast his future. . . . *Every time one wastes a thought on the future he misses a trick in the present.* . . . Your work, today, dictates what your future shall be. . . . I have never taken thought about my future, & it has always come out about right." While not entirely true, this was true enough to characterize his general mind-set, as well as the absorbing present-ness about both Hartford life and Elmira summers. When, in 1880, Orion wrote his autobiography, Twain, who had encouraged him, sent it to Howells. It was, apparently, a powerfully stark confessional piece of writing. Howells, though, could not print it in the *Atlantic*. If it were to be printed someplace else, Howells advised, "I hope you won't let your love of the naked truth prevent you from striking out some of the most intimate pages. Don't let anyone else even see those passages about the autopsy. The light on your father's character is most pathetic." What feeling those passages evoked in Twain he never revealed.

5.

One of the advantages of Twain's huge cash flow was that he could readily afford to buy books, continuing the constant reading that had already made him immensely literate for a writer most of the world took for an intellectual lightweight. Usually his wide reading was reflected only indirectly in what he wrote, though books even as unpretentious as *Tom Sawyer* were as much grounded in literature as life. The main character, of course, was a partly autobiographical construction of a boy whose mind and feelings had been shaped by his fascination with stories. *A Tramp Abroad* took much of its force from the interplay between Twain's attempt to see Europe through fresh eyes and his deep engagement with Europe as a text known mainly through its folklore, legends, and romances, and to which he brought considerable reading sophistication.

When in summer 1875 he conceived of what became the most intellectual of his popular books, *The Prince and the Pauper*, some of the impetus came from an historical work he first read in 1874 and by which he continued to be influenced for decades, William Lecky's *History of European Morals from Augustus to Charlemagne*. Though he still read fiction, by the mid-1870s he had begun to concentrate on historical, philosophical, and psychological subjects. Lecky's preoccupation with moral theory, particularly with the conflict between those who believed people were born with moral feelings and those who believed human culture the source of morals, fascinated him. So too did Lecky's emphasis on education in determining human character. In both instances, Twain discovered in Lecky a well-developed, heavily documented, historically rich corroboration of his own beliefs: human beings are not born a certain way individually, though human nature is a pervasive constant; environment makes them what they are; education in the broadest sense determines character and performance. Lecky helped him develop his vision of the past, particularly the Middle Ages, as an embodiment of what nineteenth-century man still suffered from: irrational and exploitative superstition. Rationalism, Twain believed, was the bedrock of democracy; inherited superstition and a culture that bred frightened, medieval minds were responsible for most of the ills of the world

The Prince and the Pauper was Twain's first foray into historical fiction, and his decision to make it a book for children complicated the challenge: at the same time that he needed to appeal to a child's mind he also wanted to teach a civics lesson, the thesis of which was the transcendence of class division and the transformation of a feudal political structure by the power of education. The temporarily misplaced young king would learn about the shared humanity of commoners and nobles. The result would be a humane ruler, governing wisely and compassionately in the interests of all his people. The validity of royalism itself was not to be at issue. In fact, he assumed that its glamour would contribute to the attractiveness of the novel, the royal house of England and its genealogy a popular subject in the education of young Americans. The intellectual contradiction between royal glamour and democratic populism seemed not to disturb many Americans, and, though Twain was to play both sides of the fence, his strategy in writing *The Prince and the Pauper* would have the advantage of both. The young king's education would anticipate the triumph of a liberal monarchy in England and of democracy in America.

In summer 1883, as a spinoff of his and his family's enthusiasm for *The Prince and the Pauper*, he created an outdoor game to teach English royal genealogy. With energetic enthusiasm, he set out stakes at chronologically scaled distances to represent the monarchs and the dates of their reigns. Susy and Clara were thrilled. Little Jean's "interrupting assistance" helped keep him at it for eight hours one day. "I had to measure from the Conquest to the end of Henry VI. three times over—& beside I had to whittle out all those pegs . . . but was [still] full of my game after I went to bed— trying to fit it for *in*doors." Before falling asleep, he "contrived a way to play

[the] history game with cards and a cribbage board." It had dawned on him that, if transformed into a board game, this could be a moneymaker. "I might have known it wouldn't be an easy job," he wrote to Howells, "or somebody would have invented a decent historical game long ago." He set Orion and Charles Webster to work immediately "to see whether my game-idea is old or new," and his brother to create a prototype. "It is beautifully done, admirably done," he complimented Orion. He thought to capitalize the patent and sell shares in its value. By October 1883, he had "all the reigns skeletonized," and energy left over for long letters to Webster about the game's business and legal aspects. Webster dutifully did his work, but, in the end, the game turned out not to be marketable. At first Twain blamed Twichell, who passed on a letter Twain had written him to the *Hartford Courant* without Twain's permission. Twain's annoyance at his friend made him more about in the future in his confidences. When it came to an invention or an idea or an investment, he always feared being scooped.

Once work on the *The Prince and the Pauper* resumed in early 1880, he made quick progress. He was so eager to get back to the story that, contrary to usual practice, he worked at it energetically through the winter in Hartford. By the middle of March he had added 114 pages: "I thought that might almost complete it, but it doesn't bring it to the middle, I judge." Once again he was enjoying writing. "I don't see how a man who can write can ever reconcile himself to busying himself with anything else," he remarked in April. "There is a fascination about writing, even for my waste-basket, which is bread & meat & almost whiskey to me—& I know it is the same with all our craft. We shall find more joy in writing—be the pay what it may—than in serving the world in ways of *its* choosing for uncountable coupons." It was advice that he often lost sight of, though here the "coupons" were metaphorical. At Quarry Farm that summer he came close to completing the manuscript. And, as usual, he anticipated a successful stage adaptation from which he hoped to make as much as from the novel.

Still, he feared that those who defined him as a humorist would not give a non-humorous work of his the benefit of the doubt. Knowledge that it contained no humor, irreverence, or satire might curtail its sales. When Howells recommended two major changes, the insecure author eagerly accepted them. "[Howells] has read it; & he winds up his four pages (mainly of vigorous approval) with the remark: 'I think the book will be a great success unless some marauding ass who does not snuff his wanted pasture there, should prevail on all the other asses to turn up their noses in pure ignorance. It is such a book as I would expect from you, knowing what a bottom of substance there is to your fun; but the public at large ought to be *led* to expect it—and must be.' " Eager to hear as many helpful voices as possible, he read it to Lily Warner and asked Twichell to read it to his children. He queried Mary Fairbanks, another of his pre-publication advisors, about whether she would read it. He even gave serious thought to publishing it anonymously. "Well, I'll put my name to it," he decided in late December 1880, "& let it help me or hurt me as the fates shall direct." By mid-January 1881 he had finished, except for the historical notes.

Whether the book would appeal to children rather than adults, the same concern he had with *Tom Sawyer*, increased his anxiety. He desired to have both audiences. But he also feared he might miss his mark and have neither. The subtitle *A Tale for Young People of All Ages* emphasized his hope. In the end, he had the same luck he had with *Tom Sawyer*. He created a book that undersold his expectations at the time of publication but that, in the end, found the audience that made it, as a children's classic, both an estimable literary work and an ongoing merchandizing bonanza. Howells, who had resigned his *Atlantic* editorship to turn to full-time writing, did his best to proclaim its virtues in a pre-publication review in the *Tribune*, a conspiratorial end-run around Whitelaw Reid, who was away in Europe. "It isn't good journalism," Reid complained from abroad, "to let a warm personal friend & in some matters literary partner, write a critical review of him in a paper wh. has good reason to think little of his delicacy & highly of his greed." Neither Twain nor Howells shared Reid's scruples. "Howells's notice is superb," Twain wrote to his publisher. "And it will pitch the key for the rest of the American criticisms."

Overall the reviewers were friendly, even laudatory, with an occasional exception, mostly in Britain. The *Athenaeum* thought it "of Mr. Clements's many jokes . . . incomparably the flattest and worst." British sales in general, though, were good, and reviews "surprisingly complimentary," he wrote happily to Chatto, except those in the *Saturday Review* and the *Athenaeum*, "which were the reverse of complimentary, but it gave me no discomfort, because here we consider that neither of those papers would compliment the holy Scriptures, if an American had written them." A critical consensus treated *The Prince and the Pauper* as a book for boys or "for young people," one of the best in a long time or even ever. Twain might have wished for a judgment less limiting, but still it was an acknowledgment that he had at least hit one of his marks.

The problem that soon prevailed was not critical opinion but poor sales. James Osgood, now partnered with Benjamin Ticknor, had finally gotten his wish to become Twain's regular publisher. Liberated from Bliss and the American Publishing Company, Twain had proposed, probably by the summer of 1880, that he himself finance the publication of his new book. Osgood would handle the details, namely production and sales. For his labors Osgood would receive a royalty on each copy, reversing the prevailing relationship between author and publisher. A successful trade publisher with a distinguished list, Osgood had been eager to publish Twain since they had become acquaintances and then friends. Though he had not envisioned such an arrangement when he first pursued Twain, he now thought a relationship in which he risked no capital of his own worth trying, especially since it made him Twain's exclusive publisher. In 1877, without a long-term commitment from Twain, he had published *A True Story, and the Recent Carnival of Crime* as a trade volume. What he now probably found off-putting, though, was Twain's insistence that *The Prince and the Pauper* be published as a subscription book. Twain believed that he would know how to avoid what he considered Bliss's mistakes, and Bliss's successful strategies were there for them to emulate. Since he would finance the publication himself, he insisted that his interest be represented by Webster's presence in what would be Twain and Osgood's New York office. Osgood agreed both to subscription publication and Webster, partly because he so much wanted Twain. But Osgood's inexperience as a subscription publisher made him unaware of what he was getting into, publishing another *Tom Sawyer*–length book in a market in which buyers wanted quantity for their money.

When Osgood, fearing that it would siphon off the market, advised Twain against serial publication in *St. Nicholas,* the most prominent magazine for young readers, it was an error: readers of *St. Nicholas* were not subscription volume buyers. Livy and Lily Warner urged the *St. Nicholas* publication for its publicity value, but Twain, who should have known better, turned it down. At the same time, he continued trying to get a final accounting from the American Publishing Company. Eager to be paid for backlist sales, he railed against his former publisher's thievery and considered suing, partly because in his paranoia he suspected they were "working against" Osgood's subscription arrangements. Chatto and Windus published the first English edition in December 1881. Eleven days later Osgood published his, with the embossing on the ornamental cloth cover done in Twain's Kaolatype brass plate process, its only use ever. Advance subscription sales, though, were disappointing, and at the point when sales were irreversibly slowing Webster successfully urged Osgood to print an additional ten thousand copies. In the end, sales stopped at twenty-five thousand, and fifty thousand printed copies remained unsold. "I find myself a fine success, as a publisher," Twain lied to a correspondent. His new financial losses were added to those from his other business activities.

Even before *The Prince and the Pauper* came out, he and Osgood had committed themselves to the publication of his long-delayed account of Mississippi River life, though the contract was not to be signed until April 1882. He had, though, by then, lost confidence in Osgood's ability to handle subscription sales, though not before he had recommended him to Joel Chandler Harris, the Georgia-born editorial writer for the *Atlanta Constitution* and author of *Uncle Remus, His Songs and His Sayings,* which Twain had read to his daughters soon after it had appeared in 1880. Having begun a friendly correspondence, Twain, in June 1881, invited Harris to Hartford to discuss "some outlines of negro fables" he had, "one in particular being a 'ghost story,' " "The Golden Arm," a thriller he remembered from his childhood on John Quarles' farm that he had begun telling to select private audiences. "Old Uncle Dan'l, a slave of my uncle's . . . used to tell us children yarns every night," he wrote to Harris, "& the last yarn demanded . . . was this one. . . . We would huddle close about the old man, and begin to shudder with the first familiar words; & under the spell of his impressive delivery we always fell a prey to that climax at the end when the rigid black shape in the twilight sprang at us with a shout."

Twain now had more confidence in Webster than in Osgood. When he discovered that ten thousand copies of *The Prince and the Pauper* had been printed after sales had come almost to a halt, he believed Webster's untenable claim that the mistake had been entirely Osgood's. "I would like [Webster] to take pretty full charge of the matter of running the book," Twain told Osgood in October 1882, "if this will disadvantage you in no way." Similar in format and length to *Innocents Abroad* and *Roughing It,* the new book would be better suited to subscription publication. To write it, he needed, as he had always planned, to revisit the world of his past days on the Mississippi River. "Howells is still in the mind to go to New Orleans with me in November for the Mississippi trip," he wrote in July 1881 to a new literary friend, George Washington Cable. But he soon realized he would need a replacement. Howells was too busy with his own work and worries. Osgood agreed to be Twain's traveling companion. By late autumn 1881, they had decided to go west and then south in spring 1882. Twain was happy to pay all expenses. "Osgood," he wrote in December, "remind me to speak of a short-hand reporter to travel with us in the spring. I want a bright, companionable *gentleman*."

6.

Whenever Twain said something like "write this down," Roswell Phelps, the Hartford clerk he hired as stenographer, would take dictation on the run, mostly word for word, then transcribe it into longhand in a notebook each day. Twain also kept his own notebook in anticipation of the journey, though he mostly suspended using it during the trip. An earlier use of some of the same material had produced "Old Times on the Mississippi." Howells and the *Atlantic* readers had praised it without reservation, crediting him with capturing in an original voice experiences central to American self-definition, a brilliant combination of memoir and history almost perfect in its literary effectiveness. But how to write a full-length travel book that expanded the subject in an efficient way, how to fold or absorb "Old Times" into the new book, and how to give the new book its own artistic cohesiveness were challenges that apparently made him so anxious that he refused to plan for them. This was his usual practice anyway, but throughout the voyage and for the next year, as he struggled with writing, the lack of preparation kept him at an uneasy distance both from the new materials and from himself.

He had written pages of notes in the months before departure, and the notion that this would be a "standard work" had been central to the conception from its first appearance as an idea in 1862. From the start, *Life on the Mississippi*, unlike *Innocents Abroad* and *Roughing It*, had been conceived as containing a higher proportion of fully researched objective history than of personal narrative. *Life on the Mississippi* should be the first and only book readers need open to find out everything about the Mississippi River valley, from its geological inception to the late nineteenth century. From the start he assumed there would be a narrative, told in his own voice, much of it historical and cultural, a small portion of it autobiographical. It would also contain examples of his themes, embodied within inserted stories, one or two of which were already written, including the possibility of a section from the unfinished *Huckleberry Finn* to illustrate raft life on the river. It would also have an intellectual and theoretical point of view, arising from his lifetime of reading and observation.

The extent to which this journey he was now taking would become the book's narrative glue he had not fully worked out when he arrived in St. Louis in mid-April 1881, though he had already determined that the key structural device would contrast past and present Mississippi River valley culture. In St. Louis, the historical archaeology and the visual representations of change immediately struck him. It was what he had been expecting, but the sight of it solidified what he had anticipated would be one of his central themes. There were shockingly few steamboats at anchor. "In old days the boats lay simply with their *noses* against the wharf, wedged in, stern out in the river, side by side like sardines in a box. Now the boats lie end to end." The whistle of the triumphant railroad was everywhere. St. Louis had grown huge beyond recognition. One of his major reasons for the trip itself was to collect records in the form of interviews and newspaper files, anecdotal and vivid representations of what life there used to be like, and to contrast information about the past gathered from a variety of sources, including his personal experiences, with what he now would see with his own eyes. If it were to be only or even mainly a personal memoir, with his memory as its major source, he could very well have stayed at home.

Before leaving, he had committed himself to completing the manuscript by October 1881. Apparently he had forgotten his oath to Howells after finishing *A Tramp Abroad*: "Next time I make a contract before writing the book, may I suffer the righteous penalty & be burned, like the injudicious believer." To commit himself to complete a lengthy travel book in about four months was a characteristic combination of inattention and hubris. Probably he did not yet have a full enough grasp of the challenges, and the existence of "Old Times" may have contributed to his assent to the tight schedule. Nevertheless, as the spring came, he felt mostly eager, excited by the adventure ahead, pleasurably anticipating his plan to have

anonymity through an assumed name, the famous son of the river returning in temporary disguise to the scenes of his early life. That he was unlikely to be able to remain anonymous for long seems not to have occurred
to him or to have been calculated as part of the game. By the late 1870s
his face had become widely familiar through portraits and newspaper caricatures, his signature cigar, bushy hair and eyebrows, drooping mustache,
and beaked nose a cartoonist's delight. Many American newspapers, with
his approbation and often connivance, regularly highlighted his words and
activities in paragraphs devoted to celebrities, of which he was one of the
two or three best known in the country.

He also looked forward to connecting in New Orleans with two well-
known writers to form a triumvirate of literary celebrities. Joel Chandler
Harris had visited Hartford as Twichell's guest the year before. Twain had
come up from a summer resort on Long Island Sound to tell him in person
of his admiration, and he soon proposed that Harris unite with him on a
joint lecture tour. Shy and inexperienced, Harris declined. At the beginning of April 1882, Twain proposed that Harris meet him and Osgood in
New Orleans early in May. To Twain's delight, Harris agreed. He relished
meeting for the first time George Washington Cable, whose *Old Creole
Days* and *The Grandissimes* he admired immensely. He had in mind "a magnificent scheme," Howells later recalled, "for touring the country with
Aldrich and Mr. G. W. Cable and myself, in a private car, with a cook of
our own, and every facility for living on the fat of the land. . . . He would
be the impresario, and would guarantee us . . . at least seventy-five dollars
a day, and pay every expense of the enterprise, which he provisionally
called the Circus, himself." A man of intellectual and moral vision, Cable
was a veteran of the Civil War from a New Orleans cotton family in whose
trading business he had until recently been employed. The thirty-eight-
year-old Cable was now attempting to earn his living from writing. Twain
was soon to call him "the South's finest literary genius." Like Twain, he was
a southerner undertaking a racial journey, and his outspoken commitment
to black equality before the law was soon to make his life in the South untenable. Unlike Twain, he was motivated by a deeply felt Christianity, both
literal and visionary.

Soon Twain was steaming downriver on a boat named *Gold Dust*. Ahead
of him was the graveyard of innumerable river steamers. Beyond that was

Memphis, where Henry had died after the explosion of the *Pennsylvania*. On the river and along its shores was his young manhood as the southerner he once was, and ahead was New Orleans, where he had met his most strongly remembered young love. Out of some of this, and other things as well, he needed to make a "standard work" about Mississippi River valley culture. He had much to look forward to, and a great deal to sort out.

CHAPTER THIRTEEN

INFINITELY SHADED

1882–1885

1.

About a hundred miles above Vicksburg, Mark Twain awakened at four A.M. to stand alongside the morning watch. Ahead, what had been a hardly visible river path became a "glistening highway under the horizon," its muddy waters irradiating into an almost limitless distance as the *Gold Dust* steamed southward. It seemed, for a moment, as if the river had not changed and as if he himself were young again. For a few days, as the boat worked its way slowly downriver, he was having "a most serene & enjoyable time." Recognized by one of the pilots, he renounced his anonymity.

But change and distress regularly asserted themselves. An historically high flood earlier that spring had left human and topographical damage along the riverbanks. Between St. Louis, from which they had sailed on April 20, 1882, and Cairo he hardly recognized the river, so changed were its boundaries. Two years before, responding to a letter from a student of Laura Wright, his sweetheart of 1858 and now a teacher, who had asked him if he'd like to live his life over again, he replied that he would, but only under one condition, that he should "emerge from boyhood as a 'cub pilot' on a Mississippi boat & that I should by and by become a pilot, & remain one." In addition, he would require that it be summer always and that he have every condition of river and piloting perfection, so different from the reality that had been a significant part of his actual piloting days. And not only should he be famous for his piloting but he should require that he "be notorious" among English speakers: "And when strangers were introduced I should have them repeat 'Mr Clemens?' doubtfully, & with the rising inflection—& when they were informed that I was the celebrated 'Master Pilot of the Mississippi,' & immediately took me by the hand & wrung it with effusion. . . . I should feel a pleasurable emotion trickling down my spine & know I had not lived in vain."

His fantasy was of a time and a Sam Clemens that had never existed. In reality, his recurrent nightmare for years had been that he faced a sudden emergency and steered his boat to disaster. He and the river had changed, and romance had been beaten out of both of them. The river bottom between St. Louis and Cairo was lined with buried wrecks. When he imagined the ideal crew from among his former comrades, he could "call their names & see their faces, now: but two decades have done their work upon them, & half are dead, the rest scattered, & the boat's bones are rotting five fathom deep in Madrid Bend." The notion that he could ever be a pilot again was ludicrous for many reasons, including that he found that the river was brand new to him, as if it had been "built yesterday and built while [he] was absent." But in the pilot house he felt at home, as if he had never been out of it.

At the Kentucky-Tennessee border, he followed through on his earlier note to "ask about the old feuds" and had a long conversation, which he then dictated to Phelps, about the murderously quarrelsome Watson and Darnell families, to be used later in *Huckleberry Finn*. It was another association of the South with death. At Memphis, Henry's suffering rose before his eyes, his lifelong conviction that if he had acted differently his brother might still be alive. In the notes he made in preparation for the trip he had urged himself to "tell, now, in full, the events preceding & following the *Pennsylvania's* explosion," but to "*leave out*" the extraordinary anticipatory dream about seeing Henry's corpse laid out with white roses on his breast. He still could not bear to allow his mother to know about it. Eighteen miles above Vicksburg the hated William Brown came to mind. Long dead, and in Twain's mind deservedly so, he had been indirectly the cause of Henry's death.

At New Orleans, he stepped off the steamship into a city that he had not seen in more than twenty years. It had grown vastly, but otherwise it was remarkably the same, streets littered, gutters half full of water, sidewalks crowded with "casks & barrels & hogsheads," dust covering "great blocks of austerely plain commercial houses." Public hygiene seemed primitive, the above-ground cemeteries noxious repositories of infectious disease. With rare exceptions, architecture in New Orleans and throughout the South seemed to him imaginatively barren. A heightening of aesthetic sensibility about design and decoration had become a preoccupation in the North, the major magazines regularly carrying articles on the subject, and Twain had paid close attention to such matters in the creation of his Hartford house. Only the "lavish" use of electric lights impressed him, and the long sweep of the well-lit shoreline as he saw it from a boat struck him as the most beautiful sight he was to see in New Orleans. The South as a civilization seemed, in 1882, still close to its feudal origins. Later, when he wrote *Life on the Mississippi,* he would contrast past and present in parallel with the contrast between southern stasis and northern progress. Surprised that the war was the "chief topic of conversation," he may have noted a connection between southern economic desolation and some of its primitive public conditions, though the southern mind-set would have seemed to him at least equally responsible. Still, "it gives the inexperienced stranger a better idea of what a vast and comprehensive calamity invasion is than he can ever get reading books."

Meeting George Washington Cable soon after arrival, he was delighted with the short, thin, dark-bearded, immaculately groomed New Orleans writer and his family. Then Joel Chandler Harris arrived from Atlanta. Cable had his sharp edges, especially on matters of religious principle; Harris seemed to have none. During an afternoon and night at Cable's home, the host read to his friends, family, and neighbors from *The Grandissimes.* Twain admired Cable's mastery of Creole-French dialect. Neighborhood children, eager to see Uncle Remus, were disappointed that Harris was neither black nor old, as they had assumed. Since he was also too shy to read before an audience, they had to settle for Twain reading some of Harris' sketches along with his own. Treating his visitors as his personal guests, Cable delighted in taking them from site to site, from a sugar plantation to an industrialized ice house, the most technologically modern business Twain saw in New Orleans. The three literary luminaries even went to a cockfight, where, regardless of their views about Christianity, they compared the brutal, sporting entertainment with the Sunday morning service they had just attended. Sleeping well, napping in the early afternoon, drinking and eating moderately, starting out "in a fresh & vigorous condition every morning," he and Osgood endured a whirl of sightseeing and social invitations. But he had a book to write, and soon he was "reduced to lying," pretending "to have engagements which we have not, in order to escape others which we want to avoid."

Two days before leaving, they did take a tugboat excursion, steaming along swiftly for hours. Twain, at the helm, enjoyed the company of a number of riverboat pilots whom he had known years before. Seven ladies contributed gentility to the party. When he wrote home to Livy, he mentioned neither the ladies nor the most memorable element of the trip, an extraordinary parrot, a fixture on the boat that kept up a "constant stream of remarks, some irrelevant, some not," many profane and obscene. "Elaborate this," he wrote in his notebook. "Parrot makes extremely naughty remarks and the ladies gradually withdraw." When in *Life on the Mississippi* he did expand the incident, the parrot became a piercing representation of his own detestation of romantic falsity, as well as his awareness that his own cathartic tirades had their destructive potential. The parrot's and Twain's voice were, at times, eerily similar. And if he could not out-curse the parrot, he could at least equal him. As the excursionists sailed "up the breezy and sparkling river," singing popular old favorites, the "charming experience would have been satisfyingly sentimental and romantic," he was soon to write ironically, but for the parrot's "tireless comments upon the scenery and the guests," which "were always this-worldly, and often profane. He also had a superabundance of the discordant, ear-splitting, metallic laugh common to his breed,—a machine-made laugh, a Frankenstein laugh, with the soul left out of it. He applied it to every sentimental remark, and to every pathetic song. He cackled it out with hideous energy after 'Home again, home again, from a foreign shore' and said he wouldn't give a damn for a tug-load of such rot.' Romance and sentiment cannot long survive this sort of discouragement; so the singing and talking presently ceased; which so delighted the parrot that he cursed himself hoarse for joy."

An authentic voice and an admirable soul were, for Twain, conjoined in the black voices he regularly heard throughout the South. On the river below Baton Rouge he overheard "the big colored laundress on guard gossiping with a subordinate." They talked about money, distances, their lives on the steamboat. One of them remarked, "That's a mighty beautiful plantation." To which the other replied, "Lordy, Lordy, many a poor nigger has been killed there, jest for nuffin." The other wished she could have those old times back again for a moment to see what they had been like. "Oh, Lordy I don't want 'em back again for a minute. It was mighty rough times on the niggers." The other reminisced how she had once almost been sold downriver. "If I had been I wouldn't been here now."

For Twain, such voices were the antidote to everything false in the South. Sentimentality and romanticism had no place in the worldview of ex-slaves, whose experience had made them both tough and vulnerable, realistic and idealistic, antinomies that he himself embodied. Black voices spoke his language and his thoughts, and the issues they raised would reappear in his fiction. Whether or not God was responsible for human nature, the white world, he believed, was responsible for the condition of black people. Less than a year later, about to attempt once more to finish *Huckleberry Finn,* he was to make definitively clear, in a private letter, his view about the depredations that slavery had wrought. "I must remember, & you must also remember, that on every sin which a colored man commits, the just white man must make a considerable discount, because of the colored man's antecedents. The heirs of slavery cannot with any sort of justice, be required to be as clear & straight & bright as the heirs of ancient freedom. And besides, whenever a colored man commits an unright action, upon his head is the guilt of only about one tenth of it, & upon your heads & mine & the rest of the white race lies fairly & justly the other nine tenths of the guilt." It was a view even more unpopular in the late nineteenth century than at the start of the twenty-first. He felt himself, though, to be that "just man" whose special empathy with what blackness historically and culturally embodied unstopped his ears and his heart. It allowed him, in ways different from Harris and Cable, to create a novel about the shared essential humanness of blacks and whites. He was more than halfway there with *Huckleberry Finn,* which was as much an implicit element in his current travels as *Life on the Mississippi* was an explicit one.

As Twain was about to leave New Orleans, Horace Bixby steamed in, now the captain of the *City of Baton Rouge,* a handsome packet owned by the same company that owned the *Gold Dust.* Reminiscences about their piloting days overcame whatever residual tension remained from Twain's refusal in 1861 to follow his mentor into Union service. Now their situations were reversed. The young pilot had become a famous writer. The gruff, proud, river veteran was best known for having been Mark Twain's mentor, a subordination that had begun to irk him. Nine years older than Twain, Bixby seemed hardly to have aged. Captain Isaiah Sellers, central to one of Twain's two stories of the origin of his pseudonym, came up in conversation, the occasion for a litany about the decline of steamboating days. And if Twain hoped to hear his name sung out on the river, he was disappointed: "They do not call in the singing tone at the heaving of the lead as they used to, nor do they sing when leaving port."

With Twain and Osgood aboard, the swift *City of Baton Rouge* steamed upriver on May 6 and reached Natchez, to Twain's surprise, in less than twenty-four hours. When one evening a black man played the banjo and, with another black man, sang, Twain transcribed "Mary's Gone Wid de Coon," a sad song about a bereft father whose daughter has deserted him for an unsuitable lover. As they passed Vicksburg, dead friends like Sam Bowen, whose body had been washed away from his burial place when the river had eroded the shoreline, came to mind. So too did Henry.

On May 10, 1882, the *Baton Rouge* reached Memphis, on May 11 Cairo. "At 5 PM got to where Hat Island *was*. It is now gone, every vestige of it." After a one-day layover in St. Louis, Twain steamed northward on the *Gem City*. His first destination was Hannibal, which he had not seen since 1867, then Keokuk, a city he had once lived in, now Orion's home, and then St. Paul. As the packet approached Hannibal, his feelings became more acute, his attention to detail sharpened by his engagement with the landscape and people that had defined his life. Osgood had gone to Chicago, to rejoin him upriver. Phelps, who had injured himself falling down a flight of stairs, ended his part of the journey at St. Louis. Twain took over the notebook himself, and traveling alone gave him even greater opportunity to focus on himself.

Episodes and people from his childhood rose to his mind. Many of the people were dead and "now in heaven. Some, I trust, are in the other place," he wrote in his notebook. Tears burst from his eyes when he reached the familiar streets of his Hannibal home. "Alas! everything was changed," but he "recognized the mud. *It*, at least, was the same—the same old mud." He met with some childhood friends, particularly John Garth at whose home he was a guest, the first person to whom he had ever told a humorous story. For a while he felt like a boy again, at home in a place of innocence and beauty. But starker memories asserted themselves, incidents that embodied loss and anxiety, death and damnation, his own insecurities and hostilities—Lem Hackett's drowning, the drunkard Jimmy Finn, the jailhouse fire that killed the tramp to whom he had given matches, his efforts to make sense out of an often senseless reality, the cityscape from the high hill a panorama of houses in which he could have once found familiar people. "That world which I knew in its blossoming youth," he wrote to Livy, "is old & bowed & melancholy, now. . . . It will be dust & ashes when I come again." Now, at best, their descendants lived there. At worst, they had moved on, as had the Clemens family.

After three days of sentiment and sadness that were also "delightful days," he steamed to Keokuk, resuming what now seemed "this hideous trip," his "heart brimming full of thoughts" of home. He noted changes along the river, the new public works that tamed the Keokuk rapids, the growth in population and wealth in river towns such as Muscatine, Davenport, and Dubuque, which seemed another, better world than the retrograde South. The northwest was being rapidly settled, St. Paul and Minneapolis becoming cities, traffic hubs from which pioneers went farther westward and through which upper midwestern and northern products traveled eastward. River traffic, though, was modest. Passenger and freight trains blew triumphant whistles day and night. He had noticed at Hannibal that the boys fantasized about being railroad engineers the way he and his childhood friends had played steamboat games and aspired to be river pilots.

Approaching St. Paul, his heart was wrenched and his homesickness intensified by "a wretchedly poor & unkempt family on their way to the wilds of the Northwest." They bunked on the deck, in the cold, without blankets or pillows, though the exhausted woman and her children were allowed to sleep on the floor of the main cabin. Twain, adding five dollars from Osgood to ten of his own, asked a lady to give it anonymously to the family. Afterward, when he discovered that "they ate on deck, & of course had had nothing warm or nourishing," he told the chief clerk to put them at a table and charge it to him. "They were there this noon & evening at dinner & supper & ate like famished people. The woman stopped me afterward & asked if it was I that paid for their meals—& thanked me and broke down." When, that night, one of the girls awoke in fright, crying, Twain "comforted her & soothed her to sleep again." She reminded him of Clara. From St. Paul, where he and Osgood stayed three days, he traveled as quickly as possible to his Hartford home.

2.

Three men of consequence had died during Twain's Mississippi trip. Emerson, who had died in late April 1882, Twain and Osgood had visited a few weeks before leaving. Though the totemic New England writer had had no influence on his work and contributed nothing to his career, Twain paid his respects to Emerson as the highest representative of the Boston culture with which he had become affiliated through his association with the *Atlantic,* his friendship with Howells and Aldrich, and his marriage to Livy. Charles Darwin had died a week before Emerson. Twain recalled being introduced to him in 1879 at Grasmere, where, he felt, they were both embarrassed. Charles Eliot Norton, a friend of Twain's and Darwin's, had told Twain that Darwin "always read himself to sleep with [his] books." Twain took it as a compliment, as it was intended. The third death was of his Scottish friend, John Brown. That Twain, on his last visit to England, had foregone in his haste the opportunity to see Brown left him feeling regretful, almost guilty. Brown had seemed to him, in his role as physician, the embodiment of that profession at its highest and worthiest.

Roles were important to Twain, who played many, both within himself and in public, including the Hartford baron and the Boston literary celebrity. When it came to business, he was a New York entrepreneur and investment financier; in domestic life, a devoted husband and father. In another mood, he was a restless adventurer pining for Hawaiian simplicity and bachelor life in a boardinghouse. In accent, he was still a Missourian. In social and cultural values he belonged to the northeastern elite; in intellect, he was independent, satirical, and skeptical, particularly in regard to Christianity and what he considered inherited prejudices and stupidities. Using his own logical razor, he delighted in dissecting irrationalities. His own he had tolerance for, increasingly convinced that life combines contradictions into complicated unities, sometimes unstable but mostly cohesive amalgams that provide the reality of self and society. His own multiplicity was, in the end, singular. The spotlight of public self-analysis he found more attractive than private introspection. The literary and theatrical stages had long been absorbed into his self-definition. He made his living performing, but he could only make the living he did by being himself. That he combined many things made him especially entertaining and expressive, particularly on the national stage of America's attempt to define itself. "Here I am," Twain said. "I am you." But the "you" he presented often challenged sectional and national prejudices. In a speech to the New England Society of Philadelphia in 1881 he presented himself as the American amalgam. "I am a border ruffian from the state of Missouri. I am a Connecticut Yankee by adoption. I have the morals of Missouri and the culture of Connecticut, and that's the combination that makes the perfect man. . . . The first slave brought into New England out of Africa by your progenitors was an ancestor of mine—for I am of a mixed breed, an infinitely shaded and exquisite mongrel." Like himself, America was a mongrel singularity that could reach an even higher level of exquisiteness if it would understand and accept that many bloods and cultures flowed through its veins.

That he included black blood as central to the American coloration reflected his passage from slave-owning parentage to post–Civil War Republicanism. It also was inescapably central to his current preoccupation with southern black voices, and with completing two books anchored in the South. In addition to his notebooks, filled with interviews and personal observation, he read Cobbett, Coke, Freeman, Hamilton, Hulme, Marryat, Murray, Parkman, de Tocqueville, even Dickens' *American Notes*, a crash course in mostly substantial volumes. As usual, he read quickly and selectively. In June, when promises to send him books were not being quickly enough fulfilled, he asked Osgood to "set a cheap expert to work to collect local histories of Mississippi towns & a lot of other books relating to the river." From Cable, he got a New Orleans city directory. He was also prone to serendipity, to notice something relevant to his topic in a newspaper or a magazine like the *Atlantic,* the *Century,* or the *North American Review,* to which he subscribed and which in September carried an article titled "Architecture in America" and in October, "False Taste in Art."

As he began to write, the structural problem was formidable, the difficulty of keeping to his plan partly satisfied, partly undermined. To begin, he created two brief chapters on the physical and exploratory history of the river, then, with the clever title "Frescoes from the Past," he inserted a chapter, written for *The Adventures of Huckleberry Finn,* to illustrate the dominance of barges and keelboats before the days of the steamship. Following, with only modest changes, came "Old Times on the Mississippi," now chapters 4 to 17; then the newly written account of human nature, Brown, and the *Pennsylvania* catastrophe in chapters 18 to 20; then a brief bridge chapter; and, beginning with chapter 22, his return to the river after twenty-one years' absence. In intention, the rest of the book would deal with what he had seen in 1882, including his visit to New Orleans and how it compared to what had been before. There were to be two deviations from this plan, though it served indeed as the dominant pattern: autobiographical reminiscences prompted by his return to the scenes of his youth and interpolated stories, especially toward the end as he strained to finish the book, some only distantly relevant to a standard work and among its least engaging material. Black voices occasionally speak, though his formidable notebook entries containing black dialogue did not make it into the narrative, partly because they had less relevance to a standard work than to his novel-still-in-progress. He also worried about southern sensibilities: his readers were white, not black. Chapter 47, an explicit denunciation of slavery and the culture that depended on it, he dropped from the book before its publication in May 1883.

A book that he expected to write quickly proved laboriously slow. In June 1882 scarlet fever reached epidemic proportions in Hartford. When Jean came down with a suspicious rash as the family was about to leave for Elmira, panic set in. Dread quickly became fact. Other members of the household became ill. A surprisingly patient nurse, Twain ministered and kept vigil alongside Livy. Dr. Taft, the family doctor, did his best. By mid-July, everyone was well enough to leave for Elmira, where Twain settled into his studio, anxious to continue with the formidable task he had hardly begun. Orion provided an immediate distraction. When Charles Webster, who was managing what was left of the family's Tennessee land, put pressure on Annie Moffet to transfer the ownership of a piece of property from her name to his, Orion accused him of cupidity. Annie's mother, Pamela, expressed suspicion or, at best, disapproval. Orion flamed into accusations. Sam, called on to assess and resolve, at first thought there might be something to the accusation, then concluded there was not. He angrily reproached Orion. "I would like him to put his pen in the fire, since it was exactly as useful as a match in the hands of a child, & exactly as dangerous." He felt he had wasted a month, though it was closer to two weeks, on this family matter.

In November, Orion besieged his brother with a pressing plan for Twain to finance the installation of electric lights in Keokuk. Orion would manage that and their maintenance free of charge, and, from its stock profits, Twain would become rich. It would be a lot cheaper, Twain dryly commented, to increase his brother's "pension." Orion had not learned a thing in fifty years, Twain wrote to Howells, to whom he proposed that they collaborate on a comedy based on Orion's combination of hopefulness and stupidity. To Orion himself, in his gentler moments, he was more generous. "You are as good & kind as you can be, but you have no more this-worldly faculty than a babe." Soon he was to encourage Orion to sign a painfully ludicrous, even cruel pledge that he himself wrote, on the model of popular pledges to abstain from alcohol. "I solemnly swear that during the remainder of the present year & all of the year 1884, I will make no proposition of a business or literary nature to my brother, in writing, by telegraph, or other vehicle; neither will I ask his advice concerning any business or literary project of mine; neither will I submit any piece of writing to him for judgment or criticism. Neither will I lecture. . . . I will remind myself of the details of this oath at least once every week."

When by August everyone was finally well again, Twain returned to sustained work. However, Livy reported, "I have never seen him when he worked with so much difficulty . . . he so often comes down at night, with his head so sore and tired that he cannot bear to have the simplest questions asked him, or be compelled to talk at all." He felt tired, grim, headachy. "Every body here is well but myself," he was to write as late as mid-October, "& in my case some doctors think it is malaria, & some think it is laziness. I am taking medicine for both." He had written only fifty thousand words, and he needed to write thirty thousand more: "[It] will take me all the rest of this month to finish, & lucky if the 25 days will do it."

In mid-October he mailed some chapters to Osgood to use for the canvassers, optimistically reporting that he was almost finished, with a substantial portion at the typist's, the first time he switched from having a manuscript hand-copied. *Life on the Mississippi* was possibly the first literary manuscript to be typed. The typewritten page seemed friendlier than the handwritten, and more estimable for revision since more like the published page. But he still felt miserable: "my brain . . . stuffed & cloudy nearly all the time." By late October the final quarter of the book remained to be done, not to speak of revisions. "I shall finish my book this week I think," he wrote to Cable, "for I have already just finished writing all I don't know about New Orleans." It kept, though, dragging on. Its "unfinished & apparently unfinishable condition" plagued him even at the end of October, preventing him from doing anything else. He took to writing at night also, aware that he was using up his margin of energy and that he could not sustain double time for long.

"The spur & burden of the contract are intolerable to me," he wrote to Howells. To save time, he answered letters once a week, dictating dozens at a time. To House he complained, "What I write on one day I tear up the next. . . . In the work I have suffered two months of literary gout; all pain & no getting on." Revisions were necessary, both additions and omissions, including the difficult task of condensing material. It seemed to him that he had never before suffered so much while completing a book, though he had gone through the same agonies with *A Tramp Abroad,* his capability to complete a full-length subscription travel book set on a downward course since *Roughing It.* By Christmas 1882, when his secretary contracted scarlet fever, the book was still not finished. Dr. Taft thought Susy might be coming down with the dreaded disease, a possibility that made Livy's constant head and body aches worse. Twain himself was forced to bed by what was diagnosed as rheumatism. Livy "is fallen away to skin & bone," he told Osgood. In mid-January 1883 he was at last done, except for the inevitable review of the pages that Osgood had been setting in type as they arrived. Despite illness, both he and Livy read proofs.

Relieved to be done, he now worried about Livy's health. By early spring everyone else had recovered from the illnesses of the winter. But Livy's lingered, so much so that, in May, on his way to Canada to establish British copyright, he almost turned back at Boston. "We have a professional nurse," he had told Lawrence Hutton, a young New York essayist and critic with whom he had recently begun a friendship, "but I am the *main* nurse. . . . It is the slowest improvement I ever saw." Fortunately, the news from Hartford was good enough for him to go on, first to Montreal, where he and Osgood were guided, this time successfully, through the copyright process by a Canadian publisher, and then to Ottawa, where he was entertained by the English-Canadian elite, including the Marquis of Lorne, who became a friend. In late May he was lunched and dined and gave a talk "On Adam," out of whose neglect as the founder of the human species he made a comic ploy, at a Royal Literary and Scientific Society dinner. Lionized by the governor general and his wife, Queen Victoria's daughter

Princess Louise, he gave his hosts a private reading. When billiards, hikes, teas, and compliments kept him an extra day, he apologized to Livy, who he assumed would understand and even find amusing his need to use blacking on his shirt to disguise a hole in his borrowed formal coat. And when he returned home he noticed that she was mending. He expected that their imminent summer in Elmira would help her "come right up and be her old self within thirty days."

3.

From the first warm months of 1883 everything went well. The children were healthy, except for Jean's teething ills. Livy began to gain weight. "[She] is still a skeleton," he wrote to a friend, "but is freighting up at the rate of an ounce a day, & the prospect for ultimate recovery is quite bright." It had been an awful winter. But, with the onerous task of writing *Life on the Mississippi* behind him, Twain suddenly began to write in sustained high gear, with an exhilaration that he had not experienced since *Innocents Abroad*. Ripeness, he believed, was everything. When external pressure compelled him to finish a work in progress, he had great difficulty. When the choice about when to continue, if ever, was his, his personality and creative energies were most in harmony. A Romantic in this sense, he believed, with Keats, that if poetry does not come as naturally as leaves to a tree, it ought not to come at all. On the one hand, he sometimes had practical reasons for forcing the growth, and he could not afford to have too many unfinished manuscripts on his desk. On the other, if he respected the decision that the manuscript had made to become quiescent, he felt it more likely than not that it would come to life again. The novel that had been conceived as a sequel to *The Adventures of Tom Sawyer,* that had taken on a conceptual vision and life of its own in summer 1876 but that he had not been able to complete, now became a kind of extraordinary literary cakewalk, a sustained summer of high-wire flying that dazzled him into happiness.

From July to September 1876 he had written 146 of his manuscript pages, chapters 1 to 2½, and 5 to 8½ of *The Adventures of Huckleberry Finn.* Between November 1879 and March 1880, more than another 200, chapters 18½ to 21 and the prefatory "Notice." Within a week after touching ground in Elmira in mid-June 1883, he had regained momentum, though nothing in the narrative suggests what had prevented him from resuming previously. He was at the point in chapter 15 at which Huck replies to Buck Grangerford's asking if he knows what a feud is. The Darnell-Watson account that he had obtained on the river in spring 1882 would have been available to him previously, and he knew enough about such feuds all along. There seems to have been no narrative or thematic obstacle either in 1876 or in 1880. Perhaps the totality of the Mississippi River trip and the visit to Hannibal was sufficient to trigger his latent preoccupation with the characters and story. Black voices that had engaged themselves with his ear and his consciousness were more vocal than ever before, and probably he had been developing in his mind without conscious intention the black character Jim, whose downstream voyage carries with it issues that the black laundress and her helper discused in the dialogue he had recorded in his notebook. And, as much as he wrote with a sense of the past, the present had its impact on his formation of the story and the central relationship. The post-Reconstruction position of blacks in the South, where legal and economic exploitation were added to the race prejudice of the North, informed his development of Jim and Huck's situation. Cable, who visited Twain in Hartford in October 1882, very likely contributed to Twain's resumption of the novel by virtue of his own preoccupation with southern post-Reconstruction dehumanization and its continuation of aspects of slavery.

"Why, it's like old times," Twain wrote to Howells in July 1883. "I believe I shall complete, in two months, a book which I have been fooling over for 7 years. This summer it is no more trouble to me to write than it is to lie." His sudden enthusiasm for creating his game based on the history of English royalty filled the short interstices, a recreation, not a diversion, from which he returned to writing refreshed. "I wrote 4000 words to-day," he told Howells, "& I touch 3000 & upward pretty often, & I don't fall below 2600 on any working day. And when I get fagged out, I lie abed a couple of days & read & smoke, & then go it again for 6 or 7 days." He suspended his practice of reserving Saturdays and especially Sundays for his family. "I've wrought from breakfast till 5:15 P.M. six days in the week; & once or twice I smouched a Sunday when the boss wasn't looking. Nothing is half so good as literature hooked on Sunday on the sly." For all of July and much of August everything about life at the farm seemed magical. At night they all sat on the porch in the glow of the "wonderful moonlight."

There is, though, little to no romantic moonlight in *Huckleberry Finn*.

It is a world without innocence. And the only character who maintains the illusion that reality can be shaped to fit fantasy is the novel's supreme, often destructive, weaver of fantasies, Tom Sawyer, from whose callow imagination Twain protects the novel until its final third. "I had written 50,000 words on it before; & this summer it took 70,000 to complete it," he told Osgood. He would *"like* it," he asserted self-defensively, "whether anybody else does or not." He was perhaps concerned that Victorian high culture would find the main character unsuitable for proper literature, though at the same time he wrote to Howells that he liked it "only tolerably well"; he had remarked in 1876 that he might indeed "pigeon hole or burn the MS when it is done." It was not his practice, though, to burn manuscripts, nor did he "give 'em away," as he explained in a different context. "I *sell* 'em. It's my grub; it's the only way I've got to earn a dishonest living." As he expanded the fragment and completed it in August 1883, he was accustoming himself to the values of the narrative. And, by September, having committed himself to the moral seriousness of his themes, he had a high opinion of what he had written and an affectionate compassion for his main character. "I've just finished writing a book, & modesty compels me to say it's a rattling good, one, too," he wrote to his British publisher. He planned a late-fall Canadian visit to ensure British copyright, and he also had in mind again being the guest of the Marquis Lorne and Princess Louisa. Though Osgood was still to be the publisher of the new novel, he had made it clear the previous October that in fact Webster was to be in "full charge . . . of running the book."

Domestic order, meanwhile, suffered when Rosa, the German-speaking nursemaid, left to get married. She had, Twain surmised, not been away from the family for even a day in eleven years, partly the result of her isolation in America, but also an indication of her employers' nineteenth-century normative view of what was expected of servants. The two older girls, devastated, went into "deep mourning." "Poor Jean," though, "thinks she is coming back, & nobody undeceives her," Twain wrote to his mother. He rarely tired of recounting the amusing comments and activities of the three children, and especially of Susy, now a precocious teenager whose combination of innocence, wisdom, and articulateness seemed a special gift. A new nursemaid, also German-speaking, was hired before they left Elmira. So ambitious was Livy's cultural Germanophilia that the new servant, a recent immigrant, spoke no English at all. For days Livy worried whether her own German was good enough to allow her "to make herself understood." Anxiety, as it frequently did, gave her a debilitating backache. Returning to Hartford in mid-September 1883, they were relieved to be in the familiar care of Katy Leary.

Twain took his time with revision and, with Webster, planned the publication schedule. The virtues of the book would not overcome, Twain feared, a badly conceived and handled publication process. Livy, a rigorous proofreader and censor, apparently required only a few changes. Narrative cohesiveness, mostly determined by first-person narration in a compact story, made the rest of the revision process a happy one. Apparently none of *Huckleberry Finn's* pre-publication readers, including Howells, who suggested minor changes, was concerned about the latter third of the novel, dominated by Tom Sawyer's fantasy-story reenactment of a slavery-liberation drama for the recaptured Jim, who Tom knows has already been manumitted. Tom indulges, at length, his fascination with manipulating reality at the expense of Jim's dignity and freedom. Twain himself seems never to have questioned its appropriateness, even though Tom knows Jim has already been freed.

In December 1883, humiliated by Webster's ascendancy and Twain's scapegoating, Osgood offered to remove himself entirely from involvement, though he insisted that he did not deserve blame for the recent debacle: sales of *Life on the Mississippi* had been disappointingly poor. Twain maintained that books should not be printed until they had forty thousand subscription orders. He argued that publishing before they had reached that magic number had been the reason for the failure of *Life on the Mississippi,* a contention that Osgood found totally illogical. Accusatory, harsh exchanges followed. Twain tried to soothe Osgood's feelings. "I have never for a moment doubted that you did the very best you knew how—it is impossible to doubt that—but there were things about the publishing of *my* books which you did not understand. You understand them now, but it is I who have paid the costs of the apprenticeship." If that was true, then there was no reason for not allowing the now experienced Osgood to publish *Huckleberry Finn.* Various compromises were discussed, but then Twain decided that he would do better to control its publication himself. A scheme was proposed whereby he would become the sole financial backer and total owner of a new publishing firm, to be called C. L. Webster & Company, with Webster as editor in chief and chief executive officer at a salary of $2,500 a year. Twain felt confident that Webster, with his help, could do the job splendidly. After all, what did a publisher do? He selected books for publication, put them through the press, and sold them. Bliss had sold many books but mostly to his own profit. Osgood had meant well but bungled badly. The new company would combine Bliss's effectiveness with Osgood's honesty. And Twain would profit both as author and owner.

In early 1884 Webster began to organize the company. In April, they agreed to aim for December 1884 publication of *Huckleberry Finn*. "If we haven't 40,000 orders then, we simply postpone publication till we've *got* them." In the meantime, there was plenty of other business to handle, including acquiring other books for publication, though the cost of that and the additional cash that Twain began to put into the Paige typesetter, soon required more capital than he had readily available or available at all. Chatto brought out *Huckleberry Finn* in London in December. Excerpts appeared in the *Century Magazine* from December 1884 to February 1885, with a one-month overlap with Henry James's *The Bostonians*. Some of the same *Century* issues contained Howells' *Rise of Silas Lapham*. Finally, the American edition of *Huckleberry Finn,* under the Webster imprint, came out in February 1885. Though his name appeared only as author, it was widely known that Twain had become his own publisher. No one thought this an unwise arrangement. Many, though, were offended by the novel, which immediately began its enduringly controversial life.

4.

Overflowing with energy in Elmira in summer 1883, Twain had good-humoredly threatened Howells with an old mutual preoccupation: "If I were at home, we would write a play." Nine years before, while working on *Colonel Sellers,* Twain had helped Howells get a commission to create an English version of an Italian play. The expectation that a successful play would, night after night, transfer money from the pockets of patrons to those of authors had a gripping, fantasy-like immediacy that both Twain and Howells, like Henry James, could not resist. For the latter two, it was in part because their published fiction produced a comparative pittance. For Twain, it was because money-making schemes came naturally and his spending propensities were prodigious. *Colonel Sellers* had supported Twain's expensive life for about two years. Now Twain urged Howells to adapt *Tom Sawyer* for the stage. Howells responded, "I couldn't enter into the spirit of another man's work sufficiently to do the thing you propose." And he did strike out on his own, an unproduced farce called *The Parlor Car*. Three years later Howells had a minor success with *A Counterfeit Presentment*. "We shall yet write a play together," he responded to Twain's praise.

Twain proposed that they collaborate on a comedy about Col. Mulberry Sellers as an old man. "Your refined people & purity of speech would make the best possible back ground for this coarse old ass. And when you were done, I could take your MS & rewrite the Colonel's speech & make him properly vulgar & extravagant. For this service I would require only ¾ of the pecuniary result." By the next year the character had been refashioned into a sort of mad-scientist Colonel Sellers, inspired by Orion Clemens' personality and impractical inventions. Never loathe to repeat a commercial success, Twain felt certain that there was still more gold in the Colonel Sellers mine, provided they could hit on an attractive variant of the original formula. Twain also suggested that their play draw on the Lampton family's claim to be heirs to the Earl of Durham's estates. Mrs. Howells thought it a brilliant idea. Howells, who reread "every bit about Sellers" in *The Gilded Age,* concluded that there was another "great play in him yet."

Howells had recently, and reluctantly, been pulled into the orbit of Twain's enthusiasm for *The Library of Humor,* initially called *Mark Twain's Cyclopedia of Humor,* an unlikely project in everyone's but Twain's eyes. Osgood had agreed to publish, but protected himself with a contract in which Twain bore responsibility for seventy percent of whatever losses might occur. At its inception in 1881 Twain had in mind, in order to amortize the expense, a large but unspecified number of volumes. Charles Clark, managing editor of the *Hartford Courant,* signed on to sift through the books Osgood would obtain from a list provided by Twain, who would pay Clark's salary and expenses. Twain advised Howells, "Go through our said stack of selections, & knock out, approve—& add . . . if you want to." Howells had reservations. "I appreciate all you say," Twain replied, "& sympathize with your dread of manacles & fetters, & speculative uncertainties. Therefore we will . . . make it a distinct sum, $5,000, to be paid by me, whether the book succeeds or fails." There would be a three thousand dollars advance. When Twain and Osgood parted company in 1884, the *Library* became a C. L. Webster & Company project.

Twain's preliminary draft of the Colonel Sellers–Orion Clemens play combined two preoccupations, the dispossessed claimant and the scientist who expresses the nineteenth century's technological potential, though this scientist would be more or less mad, the victim of an overactive imagination and a deep streak of impracticality. Twain's interest in "mental telegraphy," his frequent experience that, when about to write to someone, that person usually was about to write to him, became an element in the farcical drama. On Twain's orders, Webster retrieved the preliminary draft of *Colonel Sellers as a Scientist* from the New York office safe and expressed it up to Hartford. Howells arrived at the Farmington Avenue mansion in early November 1883, and within a week they had a full-length version that both found engagingly hilarious. Everything thereafter was downhill. They had envisioned Raymond re-creating his earlier triumph, but Raymond would not undertake the role. When the play was finally staged, in 1888, it was an even greater failure than *Ah Sin*. Determined to get mileage out of his conception, Twain novelized it, but *The American Claimant* was neither a critical nor commercial success.

In 1884, with the publication of *Huckleberry Finn* still on hold till advance sales reached forty thousand Twain's mind was primarily on business. Between the end of summer 1883 and the publication of *Huckleberry Finn* in early 1885, he wrote mostly fragments. His attempt in January 1884 to write a novel set in Hawaii based on the life of Billy Ragsdale, the interpreter to the Hawaiian parliament whom he had met in 1866, came to nothing. Ragsdale, after discovering he had leprosy, gave up his career and marriage to commit himself to a leper colony. Though he was an unlikely subject for humor, Twain found him compelling. The underlying point of the book would be to "illustrate a but-little considered fact in human nature: that the religious folly you are born in you will *die* in, no matter what apparently reasonabler religious folly may seem to have taken its place." The project never got beyond a tentative outline.

At the same time, he created a dramatic version of *Tom Sawyer,* again a matter of business rather than art, as was his dramatic version of *The Prince and the Pauper.* Ideas for stories, some of them eerily prescient, regularly came to mind, including "a burlesque Frankenstein." Another was about marooned voyagers living "in interior of an iceberg" that had been luxuriously furnished with objects from their wrecked ship. There life goes on for a generation until "all found dead & frozen—been dead 30 years." Another idea for a narrative had the science fiction and Swiftean assumption that "we are all only the microscopic trichina concealed in the blood of some vast creatures veins, & that it is that vast creature whom God concerns himself about."

In May 1884, for nonliterary exercise, he took up the bicycle. He and Twichell amused themselves and others as they bruised their shins and nearly cracked their heads in an effort to master the popular high-front-wheelers. When he attempted to get literary mileage out of an essay, "Taming the Bicycle," he soon set it aside, either as not funny enough or too humiliating. Still not willing to admit defeat, he had a bicycle shipped to Quarry Farm, where he mounted it once, took a hard fall, and realized that the "hills are long & steep." That was the end of bicycling.

While proofreading *Huckleberry Finn* during the summer of 1884, he attempted to write a sequel, the first of a number of such attempts, which would take Huck and Tom to the Wild West. It would be, on the one hand, a literal fulfillment of Huck's decision to "light out for the Territory," on the other an extension of the novel's concern with racial issues into its most highly charged venue, the intersection between race and sex. He asked Webster to send him popular Wild West dime novels. At the start, he anticipated having great fun in sending the two boys westward, accompanied by Jim, including the opportunity to parody Wild West stories and their romanticized notion of Indians, which Twain had been disabused of in his Nevada-California years and had harshly dramatized in the character Injun Joe in *Tom Sawyer*. As usual, he had no detailed narrative plan. What he had intended to be a comic, satiric romp among easy parodic targets soon became unexpectedly complicated, and the stereotypes and the comedy soon become overwhelmed by events.

As they travel westward, the boys become attached to a pioneer family with two lovely daughters, one a beautiful seventeen-year-old. When Huck, Tom, and the Mills family assume that a group of Indians is peaceful, the family is massacred, except for the two girls, who are taken prisoner. So too is Jim. Frightened, remorseful, partly blaming themselves, Huck and Tom start off with the older girl's fiancé, Brace Johnson, a veteran frontiersman, to rescue the girls. The pursuit takes many days. Brace assumes that Peggy has been raped. When they discover her knife, Brace, partly believing, partly hoping, that she has killed herself, sends Tom and Huck ahead to find her body. But she is not at the deserted Indian camp. They tell Brace the lie, which he is eager to believe, that they have found her body and buried it. Now they hope to catch up to the Indians and rescue the younger girl. As in a nightmare, they find themselves able to follow their trail, but the Indians always remain just out of reach. Matters get even more gruesome, with dead men, rustlers, a dislocating storm, and a flash flood. As the boys pick up the trail once more, the manuscript ends. Peggy has been enslaved, a squaw to her Indian masters. Her younger sister's fate will be the same. Twain has nowhere to go with the story, except to places where neither he nor his Victorian readers could be comfortable. He put the manuscript aside, but, unlike *Huckleberry Finn,* it could not be resumed. Most of the summer, he reported to Twichell, had been "wasted in ineffectual efforts to work. I haven't a paragraph to show."

The summer of 1884 was also frustrating in that it also gave rise to one of the ugliest political campaigns in many decades, one that led Twain to make an uncharacteristic break with the past. There was widespread publicity given to the discovery that the Democratic candidate Grover Cleveland, a bachelor, had fathered an illegitimate child, even though Cleveland, the governor of New York, had acknowledged his paternity. From Elmira, Twain condemned the hypocrisy of the political circus. "To see grown men, apparently in their right mind, seriously arguing against a bachelor's fitness for President because he has had private intercourse with a consenting widow! Those grown men know what the bachelor's other alternative was—& tacitly they seem to prefer that to the widow. Isn't human nature the most consummate sham & lie that was ever invented?"

In political life, Cleveland's probity and support of reform were unimpeachable. Not so his Republican opponent, James G. Blaine. As Speaker of the House in the 1870s, in an atmosphere of widespread political corruption, Blaine had enriched himself by accepting money from the railroad interests in return for legislative support. Idealistic Republicans condemned him, and in 1884 withheld their support. For Twain, fidelity to principle superceded party loyalty, and once he had made his decision to support Cleveland he stuck to it with his usual stubbornness. It was, to some extent, a liberating moment, though easier for Twain than for many of his distressed contemporaries who had a more idealistically fervent attachment to the Republican Party. He had not devoted his commitment let alone his blood to the abolitionist and the Union cause. As outspoken a Republican as he had become, his Republican roots were comparatively shallow. They had, in fact, not been planted until his engagement to Livy, and his months in Washington in 1868–69 had increased his cynicism about politics in general. Among his Hartford friends very few became "Mugwumps," the name given to dissident Republicans. Even fewer went over to the party of "Rum, Romanism, and Rebellion."

But Twain vigorously championed Cleveland. Twice in October 1884 he addressed Mugwump rallies in Hartford, mainly to deny that he was a turncoat and to remind his Republican friends that it was indeed they who were going back on what they had said about Blaine before he became the nominee. Republican principle he upheld by voting against the Republican ticket. "Four days hence I shall have the pleasure of casting a vote against Mr. Blaine; shall vote the entire democratic ticket, from President down to town constable." Cleveland won a very narrow victory, the first Democratic president in more than thirty years. Soon after the election ten-year-old Clara wrote to her father, "Mamma made us take . . . off [the Cleveland medals that he had given them to wear] because she did not want every one to think that we were democrats." For Twain, it was a one-time apostasy, but a defining one.

5.

The day after the election he also began a new commitment, a four-*month* engagement with the American public, partnered on the platform by George Washington Cable. The traveling circus he had proposed in 1882 had never materialized. In 1883, such an extravaganza would, he believed, have helped sales of *Life on the Mississippi*. Now he had in mind publicity for *Huckleberry Finn*. He was, though, even more motivated by the prospect of excitement, adulation, and direct profit. None of his new ideas for books seemed compelling enough, and financial obligations pressed. "This trip's my last—forever & ever," he claimed. Such finality provided a celebratory and triumphant note to the venture, the last time to see Mark Twain in person. And though it would be only a two-ring circus, twinship had advantages. "[Cable] is a marvelous talker," he wrote to Howells when Cable came to Hartford for the first time. His Hartford performances in April 1883 had been, after a weak start, adequate. And, after elocution lessons to strengthen his voice, Cable's 1883–84 lecture tour had been successful. Reviews were good, audiences sizable.

Twain proposed to Cable's lecture agent, James Pond, a companionable, good-hearted Civil War major, formerly Redpath's partner in the

Boston Lyceum Bureau whom he had bought out in 1875, that Pond take ten percent of the profit for managing the tour. In turn, Twain would pay Cable, from Twain's ninety percent, $350 a week and expenses. To Twain's annoyance and Pond's discomfort, Cable counterproposed $450 a week. All in all Twain thought Cable worth that amount, but he had other reservations. Staying at Twain's Hartford house for a few days in January 1884, Cable came down with what turned out to be the mumps. Livy and the family attended to him during the next month, sending Mrs. Cable constant reassuring bulletins. Twain's sympathy gradually gave way to annoyance, even criticism. Cable seemed to him a whining, self-indulgent patient. "He's a bright good fellow,—but—Why, man, he made 280 times more fuss over his little pains," he wrote to House, "than you did over your big ones." When Cable was well enough to leave, Twain breathed a sigh of relief, though two of his children and Cable's nurse (presumably paid for by Twain) soon came down with the mumps. In May, Cable's New York friends floated the idea of a charitable fund to help support him. Twain was horrified that he might consent.

From as early as their New Orleans meeting in 1882, Twain thought Cable's religiosity sanctimonious and aggressive, his sin and salvation rhetoric abhorrent. At home with Presbyterians and Baptists, Cable bewailed Twain's lack of Christian commitment. Twain, though, suspected self-serving, even hypocritical narrowness behind all sectarian formalism. Cable criticized condescendingly what he thought Twain's financial extravagance, such as his predilection for taxis. Twain thought Cable cheap, even stingy. And now the penny pincher was pinching him. He had, though, promised Livy that he would do the lectures with Cable or not at all. He did appreciate Cable's virtues, including his good heart, his conversational talents, and his literary achievement, and no one else was a better fit.

Once the deal had been made, Twain was in high spirits. With Pond delegated to take charge of all details, Twain characteristically meddled when he felt like it and retreated behind his insistence on not being bothered when it suited him. He ruled out only Hartford and Elmira, on his longstanding rule that one should not make money off one's neighbors. For the sake of time and economy, and because of southern disapproval of Cable, Twain proscribed all locales south of Washington. Eastern and midwestern cities responded eagerly. Newspapers broke out into friendly clichés about the "twins of genius," but focused mainly on how much the writers would make, a subject more interesting to the public than any other aspect of the tour. The authors would share equal billing and time. But, Twain reminded Cable, "the audience must go away hungry, not surfeited." They needed to keep strictly to the two-hour length.

Between early November 1884 and a brief Christmas break they broke in the act until it was polished enough for Boston, then Philadelphia, New York, Washington, and Albany, where the president-elect greeted them, then westward to Syracuse, Utica, Rochester, and Buffalo, where the *Buffalo Express*, Twain's old newspaper, got the contrast right. Cable was a "precise, alert, brisk man of style," a "dapper sort, as polite as a dancing master." Twain was "the man from way back who has sat down by the stove at the corner grocery, gathered his cronies about him, and is telling a story as only he can tell it." Twain had filled notebook pages with different program alternatives, and as soon as the performances began he reconfigured. Audiences wanted at least as much Twain as Cable, usually more, and Cable had a tendency to stretch his time on stage, which Twain resented. More professionalism was called for, and more Twain, at least in the sense that he wanted to make sure the climaxes and conclusions were arranged for maximum audience pleasure. When attendance was thin at one of the Boston performances, Twain told Pond, "Louder advertising is absolutely necessary [including] men to patrol the streets with bill-boards on their backs—& if we then still have such houses as we had to-day & last night, it will mean that we can't draw & better quit." But Howells could not have been more glowing about the performance he attended. "I never enjoyed you more," he wrote to Twain. "You are a great artist, and you do this public thing so wonderfully well that I don't see how you could ever bear to give it up."

Audiences enjoyed and respected Cable. But their enthusiasm and their hearts went to Twain as the living representation of American character and storytelling. And that he was making a great deal of money representing their American-ness to them made him even more the embodiment of their own desires, of the national dream to be rich and famous. That he was, in his own eyes, "merely a starving beggar standing outside the door of plenty," as he told Howells, would have been bewildering to most Americans. He was widely believed to be a millionaire. "Mind, I am not in financial difficulties," he assured Howells, "& am not going to be." But for Twain, emotionally, there was no middle ground between being very rich and being poor.

"This trip's a great thing for my health," he wrote to Livy, "—haven't felt so robust in years." At Ithaca, he responded with an adrenaline high when after his performance Cornell students greeted him in a beer hall with enthusiastic applause. From northern New York they went to Buffalo and Toronto, then Ann Arbor and Grand Rapids, then Toledo, where Petroleum V. Nasby, in his civilian dress as David Locke, entertained them. In Washington, the lame-duck president visited them after the performance. So too did Frederick Douglass, a man Twain admired considerably more than Rutherford Hayes. "He came into the retiring room when the President was there," Cable wrote to his wife. "They met as acquaintances. Think of it! A runaway slave!" The tour itself had an African-American tonality: the *Huckleberry Finn* reading, about a runaway slave, had proved popular; Cable had Creole and black voices in his readings. Cable's controversial article, "The Freedman's Case in Equity" in the January 1885 issue of *Century Magazine,* advocating civil rights for blacks, and reparations, brought more public attention to the touring entertainers.

With the publication of *Huckleberry Finn* in mid-February 1885, prefaced by excerpts in the widely circulating *Century,* Twain's most controversial depiction of black-white relations began its public exposure. During the Christmas break, he had worried about the novel's advance sale. Though it had not reached the magic forty thousand, Twain and Webster decided that thirty would do. That it would sell much beyond that seemed unclear, though Twain was hopeful. In the next months he was to be mildly disappointed by sales that barely rose above fifty thousand. Outraged white voices complained not about the depiction of race but about moral vulgarity. Was the sympathetic depiction of two vulgar rapscallions proper reading for impressionable middle-class young people?

Everything considered, the principals did remarkably well together. Cable admired Twain's platform professionalism, his disciplined preparation, his consummate sense of timing. Mostly companionable, the two men sometimes banged shoulders, more annoyingly to Twain than to Cable. When Cable charged to Twain the expense of laundering clothes he wore during the break, Twain thought it a particularly infuriating example of Cable's cheapness. When Cable stepped on his colleague's time, Twain seethed. In mid-January 1885 he got Cable to agree to go on stage exactly at opening time and talk to the audience while it assembled, "telling them not to be concerned about *him & he* won't be troubled." It allowed them to end exactly after two hours. "The good effect is beyond estimation," he wrote to Livy. "Only half the house hears C.'s first piece—so there isn't too much of C any more—whereas heretofore there has been a thundering sight too much of him." Livy, though, regularly implored him not to allow himself "to get awry" with Cable: "He is good and your friend and it is an advantage to you to have him." Twain admitted that Cable, despite his "littlenesses, like Napoleon . . . is a brave soul and a *great man*," a reference to his courage as a southerner in speaking out for civil rights for blacks.

Cable's attempts to pressure Twain into at least the pretense of Sunday piety mostly failed. When they did not, Twain resented it even more. "You will never never know, never divine, guess, imagine, how loathsome a thing the Christian religion can be made until you come to know & study Cable daily & hourly. Mind you, I like him; he is pleasant company; I rage & swear at him sometimes, but we do not quarrel; we get along mightily happily together; but in him & his person I have learned to hate all religions. He has taught me to abhor & detest the Sabbath-day & hunt up new & troublesome ways to dishonor it." What Twain most resented, though, was that Cable cost him "$550 to $600 a week—that is, $450 a week & expenses," as he wrote in his notebook. "He is not worth the half of it."

Eager to have it over with, Twain counted the days, though he also had delightfully good times when he was in the mood, especially in Toronto in mid-February, where he went tobogganing with students from a young ladies' college. He sent a toboggan home to the children. Along the border of Lake Champlain, the landscape, he wrote to Livy, "is too divinely beautiful to describe." On the train westward to St. Louis, he had a reminder of the mind-set that *Huckleberry Finn* dramatized. He overheard a country boy, in easy hearing of a black woman, say to his older sister, "Mighty good clothes for a nigger, *hain't* they? I never see a nigger dressed so fine before." "She was thoroughly well and tastefully dressed," Twain wrote to Livy, "& had more brains & breeding than 7 generations of that boy's family will be able to show." In St. Louis his elderly uncle, James Lampton, visited him at his hotel. Twain had Cable listen through a partly opened door and transcribe Lampton's talk in order to demonstrate how closely it resembled Colonel Sellers'.

A few days later, keyed into childhood and family by seeing Lampton again, he arrived in Hannibal, his heart open to the impact of old friends grown even older than when he had last seen them. As in St. Louis and

Keokuk, where his mother embraced him for what they thought likely to be the last time, his performances were acclaimed. All three cities considered him their most famous native son. The childhood friend who had become deaf and dumb after falling into the freezing river while young Sam managed to make it to shore unscathed, shook his hand, putting a note into it. "This visit to Hannibal," he wrote to Livy, "you can never imagine the infinite great deeps of pathos that have rolled their tides over me. I shall never see another such day. I have carried my heart in my mouth for twenty-four hours." At a stop in Quincy, Illinois, he saw Wales McCormick, his raucous, good-humored, oversized, trouble-making companion at Anent's printing shop, and a decrepit old man who, when he had last seen him thirty-five years before, had been a conceited dandy. As Twain meditated on the river from the window of his railroad car, an idea arose for another sequel to *Huckleberry Finn*. "Make a kind of Huck Finn narrative on a boat—let him ship as cabin boy & another boy as cub pilot—& so put the great river & its bygone ways into history in form of a story."

His own history was part of his Keokuk visit. The *Daily Gate City*, a newspaper for which he had once written, trumpeted his coming, celebrated his arrival, and lauded his performance. A full house tramped to it through a fierce snowstorm. Twain and Cable, their train delayed, barely got there in time. His pensioners were in the audience, Orion still carrying in his pocket, seemingly indefinitely, a letter his brother had asked him to mail to Livy immediately. Afterward, Twain spent the midnight hours with his mother: "A beautiful evening . . . she is her old beautiful self; a nature of pure gold. . . . The unconsciously pathetic is her talent . . . & how naturally eloquent she is when it is to the fore! What books she could have written!" At eighty-six, Jane Clemens was frail, her memory fading. When he had worked his courage up, dreading the anticipated disappointment in her face, to tell her that he had faked his mesmeric trances as a boy in Hannibal, he was disappointed and then annoyed that she refused to believe him. She had a mind of her own, independent of evidence and supplication. He had told the truth then, she responded; he was not telling the truth now. " 'You are a man, now, & could dissemble the hurt; but you were only a child then & could not have done it.' And so the lie which I played upon her in my youth remained."

Cable and Pond left the next morning for Burlington, Iowa, where they were to perform that night. Twain stayed on to have another day with his

family. Soon he was in Chicago, Madison, Milwaukee, St. Paul and Minneapolis, then Chicago again, where he worked up a new program in order
not to repeat in cities they were visiting a second time. He took it to South
Bend, Lafayette, and Indianapolis, then to Columbus, Detroit, Toronto,
New York, Brooklyn, Philadelphia, Baltimore, and Washington. There he
wrote to Howells, "My four-months platform campaign is ended at last." So
too was the Twain-Cable relationship, which remained cordial but never
intimate again. An exemplar of pietistic virtues, Cable was, even in silence,
a reproof to Twain's ordinary and enjoyable vices. That kind of friend was
dearest when kept at a distance.

6.

At a late-night dinner in mid-November 1884 at the New York apartment of
Richard Watson Gilder, the *Century Magazine*'s editor, Gilder mentioned in
passing that General Grant had decided to write his memoirs for publication, with the understanding that the Century Publishing Company would
bring out the book. Late in 1881, Twain had first raised the subject of an autobiography. At that time, Grant had declined. He felt no urgency, and he
had little confidence in his abilities as a writer. By 1884, however, his circumstances had changed dramatically. The failure of his brokerage buei-
ness had left him in immediate need of cash, and now, with a diagnosis of
terminal throat cancer, he feared he would leave his family impoverished.
Taking up Twain's earlier suggestion, he had already written three Civil War
articles for the *Century*. Surprised and excited, Twain went the next day to
see the general and soon instructed Charles Webster to explore with Grant
his possible interest in an alternative offer, among other reasons because he
thought it likely that Webster & Company could make a great subscription
success of a book that the Century people seemed to be undervaluing.
Roswell Smith, the Century owner, and Gilder, themselves new to book
publishing, seemed also to Twain unaware of the value of Grant's memoir.
Inexperienced and ill informed, they had projected sales of about twenty-
five thousand copies, so Twain surmised, and consequently offered Grant a
standard ten percent royalty. In this case, Twain was right.

Eager to help the former president, whom he revered and thought
stingily treated by his country, Twain was convinced that as publisher he
could enrich Grant and make a reasonable profit for himself. Here was an
opportunity to do a good deed and at the same time further his own inter-

ests. Such a coup would make C. L. Webster & Company nationally prominent; it would attract other valuable authors.

While touring with Cable, Twain had neither opportunity nor energy to assert direct influence on Grant other than the initial discussion in which he pointed out that "the Century offer was simply absurd." As his deputy, Webster carried the campaign to Grant, his wife, and his two sons, including Fred Grant, the retired army colonel whom Twain had gotten to know in Chicago years before. Webster, at the same time, carried his own campaign to Twain, with a request for an ownership interest in the firm. He proposed that he receive one third of the net profits up to twenty thousand dollars and one tenth above, though he was to have no responsibility for the firm's liabilities. Perhaps Twain was simply not paying close attention. Or he was overwhelmed by a spasm of generosity. Or he thought that the Grant memoir profits would be so great that he would hardly suffer from sharing them. Perhaps he indeed bought Webster's argument that the memoir's success would be due to his "personal efforts and energy." "Additional care and responsibility will be placed upon my shoulders, and I must work, and think much harder," he wrote, though Twain on the basis of this had the right to wonder how hard Webster had been working heretofore: Had Twain indeed been paying Webster $2,500 a year plus expenses for a part-time job? In March 1885 Twain agreed to these terms. Like many of his business decisions, it might most readily be understood as the result of a missing screen of self-protectiveness that made him risk attractive rather than risk adverse. Or a belief in his luck, rising to the level of arrogance— his conviction that no decision of his own could bring him anything other than good fortune.

From the start the general asserted that, though he had no binding agreement with Century, he had a predilection to publish with them since the owners had suggested the idea and had treated him fairly. Webster pointed out that Twain had made the suggestion in 1881. Grant acknowledged that he had. In late November 1884, Webster made an offer, and Grant and his family mulled it over. The general still felt hesitant as a matter of honor. But, Twain argued, if the Century offer was inferior, how could honor and family be served? When Grant continued to be perplexed, Twain increased his bid, either a straight twenty percent royalty or seventy percent of the profits before expenses, which Twain estimated, on the basis of his projections, would be about $400,000, the largest sum any

American author had ever earned from a single book. When he described the offer to Livy, she worried that he would lose money on such an arrangement. Twain soon solidified Grant's confidence in him by proposing that C. L. Webster's competence to publish the book successfully be evaluated by independent experts and that the marketplace be tested by having other publishers bid. Smith and Gilder, initially only annoyed by Twain's intervention in a project to which they thought they had proprietary rights, were stunned by Twain's offer. It was soon clear that other publishers would match it. Smith and Gilder had lost whatever leverage they had, except Grant's sense of the courtesy due them. "I mean you shall have the book," he told Twain in late February, "but I wish to write to Mr. Roswell Smith, and tell him I have so decided. I think this is due him." Grant put his signature to the contract in March 1885, thereby insuring that his family would be well provided for.

For the rest of the year, Twain's mind focused on two concerns, *Huckleberry Finn*'s reception and bringing Grant's *Personal Memoirs* to successful publication. As Twain always worried would be the case for popular subscription books, *Huckleberry Finn* appeared in bookstores within a month of publication. The subscription boat often had a leaky hull, anonymous canvassers who found it profitable to provide copies for the retail trade. During the spring, sales approached fifty thousand, then paused. When the Concord Public Library in Massachusetts banned the book as unsuitable for children, Twain's commercial blood rose with pleasure. Such publicity would help sales. At the same time he resented what seemed to him the hypocritical stupidity of banning *Huckleberry Finn* when the library kept on its shelves books that were genuinely obscene, vulgar, and violent, like the Bible. The *St. Louis Post-Dispatch,* generally favorable to Twain, pointed out the counterproductiveness of the library's policy. "The directors of the Concord Public Library have joined in the general scheme to advertise MARK TWAIN'S new book 'Huckleberry Finn.' They have placed it on the Index Expurgatorius, and this will compel every citizen of Concord to read the book in order to see why the guardians of his morals prohibited it. Concord keeps up its recent reputation of being the home of speculative philosophy and of practical nonsense."

Reviews, though, were at best mixed. Twain's contemporaries did not, on the whole, think well of it. The regular pro-Twain critics lined up favorably, particularly Brander Matthews in the *Saturday Review,* Thomas Sargeant Perry in the *Century Magazine,* and Joel Chandler Harris in the *Atlanta Constitution.* Reviewers for the *Hartford Courant,* the *Detroit Free Press,* and the *San Francisco Chronicle* had words of high praise for the author's comic genius, his somber seriousness, the truth to fact of the realistic portrayals, and for the novel as a worthy successor to *Tom Sawyer.* So too did most British magazines, particularly elite journals like the *Athenaeum,* the *Westminster Review,* and the *British Quarterly Review,* which thought it "full of spirit and wit and drollery." American mainstream response was encapsulated by the *New Orleans Daily Picayune's* nasty satisfaction in remarking, "Mark Twain is having a great deal of trouble with his 'Huckleberry Finn.' He cannot swim in literature with it, and public libraries are rejecting it as trash that is not worth shelf room." The *Boston Herald* encapsulated the widespread distaste: "It is pitched in but one key, and that is the key of a vulgar and abhorrent life." The *San Francisco Alta California* saw it as "wearisome and monotonous," successful self-advertising rather than entertaining humor.

Review discussion paid no attention to the novel's depiction of black-white relations. Not until twenty years after its first publication did a reviewer refer to it, in passing, as an "antislavery tract." Shortly after Twain's death, Booker T. Washington, whose work Twain supported, contributed considerably to the twentieth-century transformation of *Huckleberry Finn* into a seminal American engagement with race. "It is possible the ordinary reader of this story has been so absorbed in the adventures of the two white boys," he wrote, "that he did not think much about the part that 'Jim' . . . played in all these adventures. [But] I do not believe any one can read this story closely . . . without becoming aware of the deep sympathy of the author in 'Jim.' In fact, before one gets through with the book, one cannot fail to observe that in some way or other the author . . . has somehow succeeded in making his readers feel a genuine respect for 'Jim.' . . . In this character Mark Twain has, perhaps unconsciously, exhibited his sympathy and interest in the masses of the Negro people." Twain was more disappointed by sales than by reviews, though he took satisfaction in neither.

The need to publish Grant's *Personal Memoirs* successfully kept his nerves keyed to a high pitch through 1885 and into 1886. From the start, his confidence was strong, the challenge great enough so that he felt the experience intensely. When Webster provided a thousand-dollar good faith binder to the Grants, Twain was shocked to discover that the penniless family needed it to put food on the table. In order to prevent creditors from attaching royalty payments, ownership of the manuscript was transferred to Grant's wife. The greatest worry, though, was that Grant would not live to finish his book. "He is failing steadily, & the disease is incurable," Twain wrote to his English publisher in March 1885.

With characteristic determination, Grant, who had "been hard at work dictating," finished the first of the two volumes by mid-May. He had also "closed up all the serious gaps that remained in the second volume," Twain noted, "but this morning's news suggests that he had possibly done his last work, for his disease has taken a new start." By early summer Webster had a number of presses at work producing volume one in an edition so large that other publishers could not find available printers for their books. To save Grant's failing strength, Twain regularly spent long hours at the general's New York apartment, sharing proofreading duties with Fred Grant and other members of the family, though he had to exert himself to limit Fred's desire to proofread creatively, as if he were co-author. Twain did not write a word of the memoir though newspaper rumors claimed that the nonliterary general required a ghostwriter or that Twain had to write much of it because the putative author was too ill to write anything at all. "Composition is entirely my own," Grant succinctly responded.

As the ex-president painstakingly raced with death, Twain was preoccupied with sales projections and the production process. From Quarry Farm, where the Clemenses joined the Cranes in mid-June, his mind was mainly on the feeble dying man, pen frequently in hand in Mount McGregor, New York, where he had gone to escape the summer heat. Twain's own pen also proceeded haltingly on "The Private History of a Campaign that Failed," a comic account of his two weeks in 1861 with the Marion Rangers, that *Century* sub-editor Robert Underwood Johnson had persuaded him to write. His connection to Grant played along the essay's satiric surface. The ascending officer and the fleeing volunteer had almost met on a Missouri battlefield. As Twain wrote about comic dishonor and civilian values, Grant wrote about tragic battles. To Twain, Grant embodied the commitment to "honor, duty, country" that the young Clemens had abjured and that the almost fifty-year-old writer had grown to admire in the West Point cadets whom he visited five times between 1876 and 1881.

In late June, he traveled to Mount McGregor. Rumors that Grant could not live much longer seemed true. Twain wrote, "The General is as placid, serene, & self-possessed as ever, and his eye has the same old humorous twinkle in it, & his frequent smile is still the smile of pleasantness & peace." Grant was "adding little perfecting details to his book." Back at Elmira, Twain seethed at published imputations that he had unscrupulously snared it away from the Century. "Every step has been taken in the broad daylight, & nothing concealed," he wrote in a self-defensive letter that he did not send. "Neither have I done anything unfair or in any way dishonorable." On July 23, 1885, Grant died. Five minutes afterward, bells tolled throughout the country.

From the windows in C. L. Webster & Company's Union Square office, Twain watched the funeral procession proceed up Broadway. Much of the dark-creped New York population lined the streets. At the same time, printing presses were churning out hundreds of thousand of copies of the two-volume *Personal Memoirs*. Seven large binderies were at work. By late October 1885, 320,000 sets had been subscribed. All Twain's available cash, including what he had earned lecturing and $100,000 he borrowed, went to pay production costs. "From now till the first of January every dollar is as valuable to me at it could be to a famishing tramp," he wrote to Howells. "I am kept so unceasingly busy by [publishing], that I cannot concentrate what I call my mind on a piece of literary work above the grade of narrative," he told Robert Underwood Johnson. "I am a business slave until the second volume issues." It did in March 1886. But he had found enough time in November to do another revision of his own war memoir. "It was immensely amusing, with such a bloody bit of heartache in it, too," Howells told him.

Soon Twain could exult that at last he was "totally free from debt." In the end, Grant's widow would earn about $400,000 and Twain about $100,000, most of which remained with the firm to fulfill his contractual obligation to provide all the working capital. His assets consisted of the value of the house in Hartford, stocks, most of which had depreciated in value, his share of the value of C. L. Webster & Company, his backlist, and his prospects as a freelance writer. Livy's investments remained intact, their value subject to ongoing economic cycles. And in the same month in which the *Century Magazine* published Twain's "Private History of a Campaign that Failed," C. L. Webster & Company published *Personal Memoirs of U. S. Grant*. Howells immediately read it "with a delight [he'd] failed to find in novels": "I think he is one of the most natural—that is, *best*—writers I ever read. The book merits its enormous success, simply as literature."

CHAPTER FOURTEEN

ONE OF THE

VANDERBILT GANG

1886-1891

1.

On an evening late in November 1885, with gas light glowing across rich mahogany surfaces and colorful Tiffany glass panels, a dozen guests bustled happily into the distinctive house on Farmington Avenue. They were all friends of the family, invited to celebrate a milestone, their hostess' fortieth birthday. Three days later, on the last day of the month, would be her husband's fiftieth. Tonight, though, was Livy's occasion. Joe and Harmony Twichell came in on the buzz of intimacy. The beautiful Lily Warner—along with Harmony, Livy's closest friend—accompanied by her husband, George, graced the dinner table. The other guests included a warm acquaintance, Joseph Jefferson, the popular actor who was continuing his forty-year-long starring role in *Rip Van Winkle*. Spirits were high. "[We] had a riotous time," the proud husband wrote to his brother.

At the moment, Livy's health was relatively good, at forty her elfin beauty still anchored in a slim figure. Her eyes retained their youthful luminescence. Gracefully negotiating her entry into middle age, she had much of the mother and little of the matron about her. Livy still studied German, arranged and supervised her children's lessons, and read closely in manuscript everything Mark Twain wrote. A realistic worshiper at his altar, emotionally committed and intelligently supportive, she was well established in her role as the wise censor to whom he deferred. He believed in her intelligent tactfulness, and he had a commitment to accede to her advice on such matters because he loved her at least as much as he loved getting his own way. Unlike most Victorian couples, they sometimes allowed other people to see them hold hands, which they did with furtive pleasure, as their thirteen-year-old daughter Susy noted in a biographical narrative about her father that she began to write at this time. To whatever degree passion's fire had given way to the domestic hearth, it apparently still burned, though, unlike the Twichells, who had nine children, the Clemenses had found a way to make five-year-old Jean their last. Livy's fragile health may have been the major factor.

"Livy & I love you both, & fervently wish you a long & happy life, & eventually a sufficient family," Twain teased the Twichells that Christmas. Their own smaller family seemed eminently sufficient. When, the next summer, thirty-seven-year-old Clara Spaulding married, her Hartford friends sent the newlyweds a handsome Persian rug, and Twain sent Clara advice based on "the accumulated riches" of his "seventeen-years' married experience." His golden rule for marital success was that neither spouse should be held accountable for intemperate exaggerations uttered in the heat of discussion. For "all conversations are but debates . . . & in them one is always apt to say more than he meant to say." Apparently he was referring mostly to himself. "And whenever he does that, just let him alone; don't call him to account—he will do that himself, every time." And "repentance," his own dominant mode in the aftermath of marital quarrels, "should never be put into words. Actions will show, & that is enough. . . . Words may start the fire again. After the little cooling-down interval, just drop into the old peaceful & cheery & loving channel again, the same as if nothing had happened. . . . There isn't time—so brief is life—for bickerings, apologies, heartburnings, callings to account. There is only time for loving—& but an instant, so to speak, for that." Clearly he was describing the tenor of his and Livy's marital accommodations, and the shadowy but constant awareness each had of the possibility of unexpected disasters. Both parents felt deeply fortunate in their marriage. And in their children. Yet little Langdon's death remained a reminder of the possibility that misfortune could strike again.

Like many non-Calvinistic Victorian fathers, he deferred to his wife's judgment as a mother who would understand daughters better than he and at the same time felt a special responsibility to provide them with a father's protective presence. With each daughter he developed a special relationship, though there were a number of common motifs, including his dominating pervasiveness. As a writer, and as a businessman, he worked mostly at home. As a household presence, he compelled his daughters' attention and admiration. His love for them, particularly as children, was unstinting. In return, he required total devotion, the unquestioned assumption that he was and perhaps always would be, other than their mother, the central figure in their lives. His status as a world-famous writer gradually became part of the children's awareness. Whether the family dined alone or with guests, he dominated the conversation, often striding around the room as he talked about people, politics, and life, with something to say about everything, sometimes amusingly, often angrily. His histrionic denunciations of fools and villains were both comically and awesomely compelling. The butler, George, was often so fascinated by Twain's dinner-time antics that he would stop serving in order to listen. Not everyone was as pleased. Hungry people waited and dinner got cold. His after-dinner storytelling, though, continued to fascinate the children—the tall tales he created when any one of them, usually now the youngest, demanded that he make one up about whatever came to mind.

The children and their father shared a love of animals, which included a household full of cats and usually a dog or two, and an endlessly fascinating donkey that he had shipped from the Midwest to Quarry Farm for their delectation. Each animal was given a name, usually comic, including cats named Sour Mash and Satan. Jean particularly bonded with her pets. Clara and Jean, who each got a horse as a gift, took to riding, and the horses made the annual round trip between Hartford and Elmira. Like most sisters, the girls sometimes quarreled. Clara became notorious for her temper—Susy also—and nursery room fights broke out regularly. Her mother, Susy wrote, believed that "if a child was big enough to be nauty, it was big enough to be whipped." "Here we all agreed with her," she added Livy was the disciplinarian who shared her society's genius for brainwashing children into acceptance of their combination of worth and worthlessness.

"Our very worst nautinesses," Susy wrote, "were punished by being taken to the bathroom and being whipped by the paper cutter. But after the whipping was over, mamma did not allow us to leave her until we were perfectly happy, and perfectly understood why we had been whipped. I never remember having felt the least bit bitterly toward mamma for punishing me, I always felt I deserved my punishment and was much happier for having received it." Apparently Clara was less subservient. Papa did none of the punishing, though he took such pride in his wife's disciplinary strategies that he published an article on the subject in the *Christian Union*. At first it caused the family amusement, then embarrassment. Soon "papa and mamma both wished I think they might never hear or be spoken to on the Subject of the Christian Union Article."

By 1885 the blossoming Susy, with a mixture of premature wisdom and youthful innocence, was beginning to make up her own stories, self-conscious enough about her father's qualities and success as a storyteller to describe them in her brief account of his life. Susy's relationship with her doting mother began to have sisterlike touches. A lover of poetry, she memorized, with seeming effortlessness, her favorite passages from Tennyson and Shakespeare. The parents happily collected Susy's misuses of language resulting in unintentional witticisms or insightful observations. Once, after brooding on her bad conduct, Susy said, "Well, mamma, you know I didn't see myself and so I couldn't know how it looked." Resenting Susy's precedence, Clara developed a special talent for willfulness and tantrums, though in a minor key. Physically adventuresome, she had tomboyish ways, with a penchant for loud, outdoor mischief. Quiet, introspective Jean was eclipsed by her older sisters.

The sound, though, that brought them all together was music, a strong interest for Susy and Clara, both of whom had good singing voices and took violin and piano lessons. All three children took part in family musical and dramatic events, especially a number of full-dress performances in 1885 and 1886 of an adaptation of *The Prince and the Pauper*, created by Livy, which they first put on, with an audience of about seventy people, as a surprise for their father. The house was transformed into a private theater. In the second performance, Twain played the role of Miles Hendon; Susy, the prince; Clara, the pauper; and Jean, Lady Jane Gray. Taught at home by governesses, sent out to local experts for music lessons, closely supervised and trained by their parents, the girls were subject to enrichment at every turn, even to the extent of being required to come to breakfast every day with a new fact that each had learned. By May 1886 the older pair was ready for formal schooling. Like their mother, they were belatedly to be entrusted to outside influences. At most, her parents vaguely imagined some literary or musical career for Susy's talents. Neither could contemplate the thought of any of the children leaving home, except briefly.

The paterfamilias celebrated his fiftieth on November 30, 1885. It was a muted celebration, mainly because Livy's fortieth took precedence, partly because the occasion struck him as one that lent itself to serious considerations. Fifty seemed old, not so much a signpost directing to what was to come but an announcement of what had already arrived. "I have never congratulated a person on being fifty years of age," he remarked. Only an enemy would do that. He struggled to respond graciously to well-wishers. "May you never be fifty," he wrote to Joel Chandler Harris, "till you've got to be, & then may we all be here to say the kind word that will mollify the affront of it." He thanked in print a group of friendly conspirators who had arranged the publication of a celebratory birthday poem by Oliver Wendell Holmes, who sent him the manuscript as a gift. "It was the pleasantest surprise I have ever had, and you have my best thanks. It reconciles me to being fifty years old." It also affirmed that the Boston literary establishment harbored no resentment for his 1877 Whittier birthday gaffe.

In letters and public appearances Twain was more good-humored and benevolently avuncular than at home, though on any occasion his temper might overcome his control, his recklessness cast aside its usual disguise of casual humor. He looked the friendly part, as well he could, a loving father, a happy friend, the national uncle with flowing auburn and gray hair, curling mustache, pipe or cigar in mouth, laughter at the ready. Like the rest of the household, Susy noticed his penchant for irreverence and, even worse, profanity. "Papa uses very strong language, but I have an idea not nearly so strong as when he first married mama." His full range would have dazzled Susy, who heard only "damns" and an occasional "God-damn," probably the strongest language she knew. "I prized my wife's respect and approval above all the rest of the human race's," Twain wrote years later in the margin of Susy's biographical manuscript. "I dreaded the day when she should discover that I was but a whited sepulchre partly freighted with suppressed language."

One day, in the bathroom, when the ordeal of shaving had been particularly vexing, he became enraged when he found some of his shirt buttons missing and others uncooperative. With the bathroom door accidentally left open, he exploded into a tirade. "In the midst of that great assault my eye fell upon that gaping door and I was paralyzed." Livy, in the bedroom, had heard every word. He determined that his best strategy would be to walk by without looking at her, as if nothing had happened. "You know how it is when you are convinced that somebody behind you is looking steadily at you. You have to turn your face—you can't help it." Livy's eyes flashed indignation. Contrite, he stood silently looking at her. "Then my wife's lips parted and from them issued—*my latest bathroom remark.*" He found the singer and the song so totally, hilariously incompatible that he struggled to keep a straight face. " 'There, now you know how it sounds' . . . 'Oh, Livy, if it sounds like that, God forgive me, I will never do it again!' " Both broke into convulsive laughter.

The temper that underlay the profanity had serious consequences within the impressionable family of young girls, who were not only awestruck by their father but also afraid of him. Livy had easy defenses against his intemperateness. Susy had a greater measure than her two sisters, though she too felt vulnerable. And they all knew that to ask him to desist doing something that gave them pain necessarily meant that he would do it again, as if by compulsion. He would then maintain that the response was unwarranted, or pass it off as a good-humored joke, or make a halfhearted apology. So harmless did he seem to himself, so lovingly devoted to his daughters, that the disconnection between his experience of himself and theirs of him was immense. In December 1886, "a thunderstroke fell," he confided to Howells. "[I] suffered sudden & awful disaster: I found that all their lives my children have been afraid of me! have stood all their days in uneasy dread of my sharp tongue & uncertain temper. The accusing instances stretch back to their babyhood, & are burnt into their memories: & I never suspected." Fortunately, he had the capacity to dramatize his pain, mainly by writing about it, which also allowed him to erase it, as if the more expressive his comments the quicker he could dismiss their substance and proceed without regard either to a lesson to be learned or a grief to be borne. His temperament was too self-protectively resilient to allow him to be anything but his egomaniacal self.

Deeply immersed in Hartford life, Twain had left his wandering behind, though sometimes a yearning to be free of routine emerged, partly a response to momentary frustration or, more likely, annoyance. Daydreams about Hawaii or Japan or Europe regularly surfaced. In winter 1884, he had hoped that they might soon have another European trip. "We want to go, but we can't well afford it," he wrote to a friend. "We have made but few investments in the last few years which have not turned out badly. Our losses during the last three years have been prodigious. Three or four more of such years would make it necessary for us to move out of our house & hunt for cheaper quarters." Livy found her usual combination of intelligent ways to make clear that she did not think it in their children's interest to disrupt their Hartford life and especially their Elmira summers. Nearby, Charley Langdon, who continued to manage Livy's money, was a friend as well as a brother. Livy's mother, always hospitable and generous, welcomed them to the Langdon mansion. At *her* midsummer birthday party, the children received most of the gifts.

That Twain spent much of his Hartford time in activities other than writing he took full responsibility for. Neither domestic obligations nor financial exigency required that he reserve book-length projects for Elmira. He mainly enjoyed household routines; the tone and activities of the home, regulated by Livy and George, expressed the master's personality more than anyone else's. Upstairs, in his study, he moved regularly between his two favorite surfaces, the billiard table and his writing desk, in a cloud of blue smoke, with as little or as much company as he wanted. Except when away on brief trips to Boston, New York, or Washington, each Friday night he assembled his local friends for billiards, stories, and cigars. As an off-color storyteller, he was first among them. When guests ran out of their expensive Havanas, he insisted they try his favorite, notoriously foul cheap cigars. The inevitable consequence was that, soon after they lit up, they said good night and departed. Later, George would find a trail of discarded cigars in the driveway. People always returned, however, for the pleasure of Twain's company. His friends came from various professions, especially Hartford's successful business community. "[Papa] is a very striking character," Susy lovingly wrote. "He glimmered at you," Howells recalled, "from the narrow slits of fine blue-greenish eyes, under branching brows, which with age grew more and more like a sort of plumage, and he was able to smile into your face with a subtle but amiable perception, and yet with a sort of remote absence; you were all there for him, but he was not all there for you."

2.

Between summer 1883, when he completed *Huckleberry Finn*, and 1889, Twain wrote only one book, which had its inception in his fascination with *Le Morte D'Arthur* and, like *The Prince and the Pauper*, had emerged from his reading and his visits to England. As a friendly critic was to remark, *A Connecticut Yankee in King Arthur's Court* is to *The Prince and the Pauper* as chess is to checkers. While reading Malory, Twain dreamed of "being a knight errant in armor in the middle ages." His mind immediately took a tellingly comic turn. Encased in armor, he couldn't blow his nose or "manage certain requirements of nature. . . . Iron gets red hot in the sun—leaks in the rain . . . freezes me solid in winter. Suffer from lice & fleas. . . . Can't dress or undress. Always getting struck by lightning. Fall down, can't get up." Trapped in a time warp, he had "the notion & habits of thought of the present day mixed with the necessities of that." Soon he envisioned a battle between medieval knights and a modern army equipped with machine guns.

In June 1885, anticipating Grant's imminent death, he prepared a eulogy for the *Hartford Courant*, quoting at length from the eulogy for Sir Launcelot in *Le Morte D'Arthur*. Its "noble and simple eloquence," he remarked, had not been equaled until the Gettysburg Address. Late in the year, some of the defining ideas of the story and situation of his main character became specific, particularly the emotional distress of a modern Connecticut man who finds himself twice and doubly dislocated, first by his transference to medieval England, then by his return to late-nineteenth century England. He grieves for his Arthurian sweetheart. "He mourns his lost land." Whatever the satiric intent, the dominant tone was to be nostalgia and tragic loss. The title he had in mind was "The Lost Land." He would bring it out, he thought, as "a holiday book."

Despite his intention to get it done soon, self-inflicted obstacles intervened, particularly business considerations, one of which was that Webster & Company, committed to bringing out one subscription book a year, had no place in its schedule until 1889. Two books from which he hoped to earn handsome profits were ahead of his own in the pipeline. Since it was his pipe, he could have rearranged the schedule, though at considerable embarrassment, if not cost. With Grant's memoir fully published in March 1886, he sent Webster to Rome to negotiate for the rights to Pope Leo XIII's authorized biography, to be supervised by the pope but written by Father Bernard O'Reilly, though about the exact degree of papal involvement and the specific nature of the narrative the contractual language remained vague. It was an opportunity he had started pursuing the previous fall, his eyes a-dazzle with dollar signs. He assumed that its purchase would be a requirement for Catholics. That the pope and his collaborator might not create an interesting narrative was not a consideration or seemed irrelevant. With little excess income and pervasive illiteracy, working-class Irish and German Catholics were not a likely book-buying public. Asking his own Catholic servants if they might buy it apparently never occurred to him. With Webster & Company's cash reserves swollen from its share of the Grant proceeds, a gold-bound presentation copy to the pope seemed to Twain well worth its three-thousand-dollar cost in publicity value.

When in May 1886 news reached him that the contract had been signed, he and Twichell agreed that he would make "a vast amount of money." "You did well to go to Rome, & you did wisely to spend money freely," Twain told Webster. In October 1886, Twain's Catholic servants went into ecstasies when a rosary blessed by His Holiness arrived. Livy begged Webster to acquire three more so that each servant could feel equally blessed. Twain himself took this with a straight face, though he grumbled when the pope made Webster a Knight of the Order of Pius, "He ought to have made me an Archangel." Delighted at the canvassing pamphlet, so attractive it would "sell a Choctaw Bible," he felt certain that the book was "going to *go*, sure." In the end, its sales were disappointing and contributed only a little to Webster & Company's balance sheet.

The other book that had precedence was General Sheridan's *Personal Memoirs*, for which Twain began negotiating in late 1885. As a publisher with an affinity for the topic, Twain felt especially attracted to factual accounts by distinguished warriors, partly because of his success with Grant but also partly by temperament. His admiration for Sheridan rose to Carlylean hero worship. Unlike politicians, warriors were relatively untainted. Webster, he assured Sheridan, had conducted a brilliant publishing campaign for Grant as well as for *Huckleberry Finn*, an exaggeration of his views in the service of acquiring Sheridan's book. This new memoir was to be Webster & Company's major 1888 publication, the sales of which he

hoped would repeat the success of Grant's. For a writer often satirically antisentimental, the list he acquired in 1886–87 was dominated by God and
country, including a biography of "Grant in Peace"; *The Genesis of the Civil
War;* a book by the widow of General Custer; and two books by Henry
Ward Beecher, his autobiography and *Life of Christ.* Not all were to see
publication, but the sales of those that did were as disappointing as those
of the pope's biography.

Eager to see Twain devote more time to writing, Howells encouraged
him, in January 1886, to get on with his idea about "the Hartford man waking up in King Arthur's time": "There is a great chance in it. I wish I had a
magazine, to prod you with, and keep you up to all those good literary in-
tentions." By February, spurred on by this encouragement and his own enthusiasm, he had written the first few chapters, which he read to Livy and
his daughters. In November, when he read from his manuscript to the Military Service Institution at Governor's Island, New York, the name of the
main character was Sir Robert Smith of Camelot, to be renamed Hank
Morgan, a Yankee from Connecticut, a Twain-like humorist, a shrewd engineer, and a military mind of the first rank, much like Grant.

"Only two or three chapters of the book have been written, thus far," he
responded to Mary Mason Fairbanks, who had expressed concern that it
would satirize the Arthurian legend. "I shall leave unsmirched & unbelit-
tled the great & beautiful *characters* drawn by the master hand of old Malory," he assured her. "I am only after the *life* of that day, that is all: to
picture it; to try to get into it; to see how it feels & seems." His claim that
"the story isn't a satire peculiarly, it is more especially a *contrast,*" could not
be sustained by a reading of the chapters he had already written or by his
general plan for the book. From the start, his notebook entries were as bit-
ingly satiric, psychologically painful, and culturally angry as the complicated, subversive book he was to write; and the target was to be as much
nineteenth-century inhumanity as medieval superstition. Typically,
though, he assuaged Mrs. Fairbanks' anxiety with an affirmation of her romantic medievalism so gracefully expressed that he managed an illusion of
credibility. The Arthurian "Dreamland" would not lose its "pathos and tears
through [his] handling," he assured her.

Apparently he added little to the manuscript between February 1886
and his reading in New York in November. As he confessed, "If I peg away

for some weeks, I am safe; if I stop now for a day, I am unsafe, & may never get started right again." And though he was soon to immerse himself in seminal books such as George Standring's *People's History of the English Aristocracy,* Macauley's *History of England,* Carlyle's *French Revolution* (already read and twice reread now), and William Lecky's two books, *Spirit of Rationalism* and *A History of England in the Eighteenth Century,* in the margins of which he made extensive notes, he did most of this reading in 1887. He wrote little in summer 1886. Concerned that his increasingly frail mother was living on borrowed time, he and Livy decided they would give the girls the opportunity to see Jane Clemens before it was too late. Livy's mother and brother they saw regularly; their paternal grandmother the girls had few to no memories of. It was now or perhaps never, even though it meant journeying in summer heat. From Elmira, in late June, "to avoid the awful railway journey" they took the lake route, embarking from Buffalo. If lake travel should prove unpleasant, they would take the railroad from Cleveland. All in all, though, it turned out to be comfortable enough. From Duluth, they took the train to St. Paul and then Keokuk. "We expect to do our eating with you," he wrote to Orion, "but we wish to sleep in the boarding house on the other side of the street, & Livy will not hear of any other arrangement. There will be 6 of us—five & a servant."

They had "four or five days & nights of hell-sweltering weather in Keokuk." He later joked to his mother, "I burnt a hole in my shirt . . . with some ice cream that fell on it," and the bishop of Keokuk "did not allow crying at funerals, because it scalded the furniture." "By and by, when my health fails, I am going to put all my affairs in order, & bid good-bye to my friends here, & kill all the people I don't like, & go out to Keokuk & prepare for death." His death jokes usually had an emotional point, and family friction increased the heat. Soon after returning to Hartford, he apologized to his sister: "I love you, & I am sorry for every time I have ever hurt you; but God almighty knows I should keep on hurting you just the same, if I were around; for I am built so, being made merely in the image of God, but not otherwise resembling him enough to be mistaken for him by anybody but a very near-sighted person." The trip as a whole, though, was "the pleasantest & completest pleasure trip a family ever took." As close as he was to Hannibal, he did not take his family to see the place of his early life and the crucible of his literary imagination, perhaps because he had been there less than two years before, perhaps because their curiosity about that part of his life was satisfied by his books and conversation. It was a visit they were never to make.

Between summer 1886 and summer 1887 his mind was intently on his non-literary business affairs; to the minor extent that his life as a writer had any priority, it was in regard to *Colonel Sellers as a Scientist*. Only Howells' cold feet prevented it from being produced in spring 1886. Twain himself had reservations. He feared that if it was badly received the damage might spill over to Webster & Company. "I won't allow that play to be played this year or next, upon *any* terms," he assured Charley Webster, since it "isn't worth a damn & is going to fail." But he nevertheless soon proceeded with negotiations and signed a contract for production. At first hesitantly, then with more certainty, Howells raised his fear that not only would they make no money from a stage production but that they would suffer embarrassment. "It *is* a lunatic whom we've pictured and while a lunatic in *one* act might amuse, I'm afraid that in three he would simply bore. . . . Neither of us needs the money it might make, very badly," he wrote to Twain in early May, "though we would like it, and it won't make us any reputation, even if it succeeds." When a determined Howells telegrammed a definitive request for withdrawal, Twain undid his agreement with the actor Alfred Burbank and the producer Daniel Frohman, who behaved graciously in an arrangement that penalized the two writers only seven hundred dollars between them.

Actually, Twain *did* need the money and was contemplating a steady flow of theatrical cash that would help with the capital Webster & Company required and especially with the money he had committed himself to provide for the Paige typesetter. In February 1886 he had taken a fateful step, a partnership with Paige that required that he pay the inventor's development costs, three thousand dollars a month, while the typesetting machine was being perfected, as well as Paige's annual salary. In exchange, Twain was to own a large part of the profit from its sale and rental, some portion of which he could sell to raise capital, a large amount of which would be needed to manufacture the typesetter. Its superiority to its two competitors required, so it seemed to Twain, that thousands of newspapers purchase or rent large numbers. Once more, he was sitting on a gold mine. He would have a huge share of the profits and not necessarily have to share them with anyone. All that remained was to bring the gold to the surface.

Filling his notebook with typesetter plans and calculations, he had little time for *A Connecticut Yankee* until early 1887, and then only indirectly. When Matthew Arnold, whom he had entertained in Hartford during the poet's 1883 visit, published an article on Grant's memoir that criticized American boasting and vulgarity, Twain was furious. Arnold's criticism of America's attraction to "funnymen" he thought directed specifically at him. The context implicated Grant particularly, whom Twain believed the most perfect gentleman imaginable, his *Personal Memoirs* beautiful and guileless. Arnold's focus on Grant's supposedly defective grammar seemed both inaccurate and wrongheaded. As Grant's publisher, Twain could feel himself equally charged in any criticism of Grant's command of English.

When, in late April 1887, Twain addressed a reunion of Connecticut's Army and Navy Club, he fired back at Arnold with his own heavy artillery, demolishing Arnold's grammar and defending and extolling Grant. Arnold's death the next year prevented him from publishing his response, but, overall, the incident contributed to Twain's gradual rethinking of his earlier praise of English social and political harmony. His own Mugwumpism had made him a more independent political thinker, his temperament increasingly volatile and occasionally radical by the standards of his community. He had lost his tolerance for status and political power based on heredity rather than merit, both in the distribution of power in America and what seemed to him medieval English conservatism. Even his earlier disapproval of labor unions began to fade. Probably kick-started into work and new directions by reading Standring's *People's History,* he returned in summer 1887 to *A Connecticut Yankee.* The case against English corruption, stultification, and injustice, embodied in its ruling class, from its inception to its present empire, seemed incontrovertible. In June, in his antiroyalist frame of mind, he observed from afar the feudal pageantry of Queen Victoria's Jubilee and the brainwashed cheering of working-class crowds that lined the streets of the procession.

Escape from such concerns waited in Elmira, where Quarry Farm provided its habitual magic. The children amused themselves in their playhouse. Livy happily recuperated from a difficult winter. Twain began to have one of his best writing stints since the summer of 1883. The manuscript quickly grew from three to twenty chapters. By mid-July, the book was "nearly half done," he told a correspondent. It still had no title, but the novel's satiric attack on nineteenth-century irrationality, superstition, and oppression was firmly in place, a representation in the feudal past and the technological present of the harrowing prevalence of unnecessary human pain. In the end, *A Connecticut Yankee* argues, everything goes wrong. Inertia, evil, and stupidity are powerful and triumphant forces. In the larger pattern, little had or would change. But within the individual human life, change did occur, as he recognized that he had changed from when he had first read Carlyle's *The French Revolution* in 1871. "How stunning are the changes which age makes in a man while he sleeps," he remarked to Howells. In 1871 he had been a moderate liberal, suspicious of revolutionary radicalism. "Every time I have read [*The French Revolution*] since, I have read it differently—being influenced & changed, little by little, by life & environment . . . & now I lay the book down once more, & recognize that I am a Sansculotte!—And not a pale, characterless Sansculotte, but a Marat. Carlyle teaches no such gospel: so the change is in *me*—in my vision." Some change was loss, some gain. But "*nothing* remains the same."

By the last week in July, he was writing "without rest or stop," he told his Hartford business agent, Franklin G. Whitmore. "As the book is worth thirty or forty thousand when finished, I can't afford to stop to read agreements, write letters, or anything else. . . . When this spurt of mine breaks—which I hope won't be soon—I'll come down to earthly business again." August started well, with "splendid progress," though it was soon clear that he would not finish with "Smith of Camelot" for another year. "I had a sort of half-way notion that I might possibly finish the Yankee at King Arthur's Court this summer," he wrote his English publisher, "but I began too late, & so I don't suppose I shall finish it till next summer." That he might accelerate by dictating occurred to him as an idea worth pursuing. Aware that Thomas Edison had produced a marketable recording machine, he wrote to the inventor in May 1888. "I had had the hope that if I could see you I might possibly get my hands on a couple of phonographs *immediately*, instead of having to wait my turn. Then all summer long I could use one of them in Elmira, N.Y., and express the wax cylinders to my helper in Hartford to be put into the phonograph here & the contents transferred to paper by type-writer." After a few canceled appointments, they met at Edison's New York studio. The demonstration seemed promising, but Twain proceeded with *A Connecticut Yankee* in his usual longhand. Twain's esteem for Edison and his business sense soon had him pursuing a possible Edison autobiography for C. L. Webster & Company's list, but that too did not work out.

Since the earliest practical date to start canvassing for subscription sales was January 1889, and since he once again intended not to publish until advance sales reached forty thousand, Twain put the manuscript aside when he returned to Hartford in late September 1887. He resumed in summer 1888, writing chapters 21 to 24. He intended to finish in October, his timing an effort of pleasurable propinquity since he also expected the Paige typesetter to be finished that month. In fact, the novel was not to be completed until March 1889, the typesetter never. *A Connecticut Yankee* would sell poorly, only thirty-two thousand copies during the first year of publication. Critical response was mixed to bad, with the exception of a few glowing reviews, mostly in friendly places, particularly in *Harper's Monthly,* by Howells, who had become editor. Some hostile critics and even those that might otherwise be friendly thought it "a ponderous political pamphlet," and its radicalism offended some. Though he had refined what Livy had highlighted in the manuscript as vulgarities, it still seemed coarse to many Victorian readers, and British reviewers were especially offended by the attacks on monarchy and church, despite Twain's self-censoring. Most of his royalties stayed with Webster & Company to fulfill his obligation to provide capital and sustain a cash reserve.

3.

Webster & Company managed to hold its own reasonably well between 1885 and 1887. As a firm owned by Twain and run by Webster, it had the disadvantage of depending entirely on Twain for capitalization and on Webster for efficiency. From the start, Twain was stretched thin, and even thinner when he began to fulfill the obligations of his February 1886 agreement with Paige: he had no source of income other than his writing, and he had not thought through the possibility that he would be required to contribute some or even all of his royalties to Webster & Company if the firm should need capital. With good reason, Webster worried that Twain's commitment to Paige would divert money from the publishing company. In a pinch, Twain could sell some of his stock, though his holdings were not worth enough to staunch an ongoing drain. For the time being, Livy's money was apparently off-limits.

In 1886 *Huckleberry Finn* produced a small profit, and Twain's 1885 contract gave him seventy percent of the profit from his new books, sixty from his old. Unfortunately, though, everything else Webster & Company published either made or lost small amounts, with the exception of Grant's *Personal Memoirs*. And its great success actually proved a liability: it encouraged Twain and Webster always to think that another such success was imminent, and it allowed Webster justification for his desire to be the captain of a more imposing ship. Since Twain's capitalization obligation made him responsible for everything from paper clips to salaries to production and advertising costs, he had strong incentive to keep costs down. Webster's contract, negotiated in anticipation of *Personal Memoirs* success, provided an annual salary of three thousand dollars regardless of profits, one third of the profit up to twenty thousand dollars, and ten percent thereafter, only a small portion of which could be withdrawn. He had little incentive to keep costs down. As long as the firm remained viable, he collected his salary. Without additional bestsellers, Twain might collect nothing, even if his own books sold well, and, if expenses exceeded income, he was obligated to make up the difference.

From the start, Webster had a whipsaw reality inflicted on him. Sometimes his uncle by marriage demanded detailed accountings. At others, the God *in absentia* allowed His nerve-wracked deputy to run His universe. The success of Grant's *Memoirs* kept Webster credible through much of 1886, but Twain felt he was not getting precise or timely enough answers to his questions, particularly about cash and costs. Webster trusted the details to the bookkeeper, Frank Scott, on whose monthly accounts he signed off. Apparently Webster had neither ability nor inclination to check Scott's accounting. His own command of the figures was loose; there was never consideration of an outside audit. Concentrating on acquisitions and production, Webster apparently was unaware that Scott was not fulfilling his instruction that monthly statements be sent to Twain. Those that Twain received, he had difficulty understanding. Oversight and control were minimal when, as early as spring 1886, Scott began pocketing money from the firm's accounts, including some *Huckleberry Finn* royalties, though most of the twenty-five thousand dollars he embezzled over the next year came from profits from Grant's *Memoirs*. In late summer 1886, suspicion aroused, the firm's lawyer advised a watchful approach. He also advised that Scott not be questioned, fearing that if he were alerted he would do even more to cover his criminality or actually flee. When in March 1887 Scott's crimes were exposed, a furious Twain blamed Webster.

Webster now promised a full accounting, which would "also show the firm's indebtedness to [Twain], as *author*." When on April 1 they signed yet another new contract, it retained the clause that stipulated that Twain should "not be called upon to perform any service or to take any supervision of the business." Webster was to remain totally in charge. Twain agreed to raise his salary to $3,800 a year, the additional $800 to compensate for what Webster had lost to Scott's embezzlement. Apparently Webster had a statement reconstructed from the destroyed ledgers, demonstrating to Twain's satisfaction that under his management the business was splendidly profitable.

But in fact it was not going well. Webster had enlarged the staff considerably. The handsome offices at Union Square were more costly than the old. "I woke up 6 weeks ago," Twain wrote to Orion in September, "to find that there was no more system in the office than there is in a nursery without a nurse. But I have spent a good deal of time there since, & reduced everything to exact order & system . . . even Webster can run it now—& in most particulars he is a mere jackass." Nervous and nerve racked, Webster had no more control of the business details than before, and he resented that Fred J. Hall, his assistant, who had started as a stenographer and was now in charge when Webster traveled, seemed to have more of Twain's confidence than he did. Then his health became an issue. He had a cough that would not desist, and the long hours he worked exhausted him. At work and at home, he snapped irritably. Often he was lethargic and depressed, and his family worried that he was on the brink of collapse.

Through the rest of 1887, Webster and Twain struggled to find a bestseller. Twain constantly put a huge dollar value to almost every potential or actual acquisition. He had an irrepressible rosy-colored calculator in his mind, which calculated only big numbers. "My valuation of Beecher's book goes up as much as double what it was," he told Webster. When Beecher's death did not allow his projections to be put to the test, Twain nevertheless bewailed the "clear loss" to the firm of $100,000. Not to worry, he assured Orion. "We've got a safe full of MS books that are as good as government bonds." A full pipeline, however, was a competitive disadvantage for new acquisitions, given that two books a year were all that Webster could bring out, only one of which could get star subscription treatment. That made it imperative that that book sell well. In most cases, Webster & Company was unfortunate in the books it published and unfortunate in those it missed. When calm, Twain acknowledged his penchant for poor choices. "Don't make the mistake of overvaluing my opinion," he wrote to an author in January 1887. Twain and Webster chose books because they thought they would sell. Usually they were wrong.

With a new statement in hand, it occurred to Twain that if his contract could be interpreted to mean that he was responsible for a total of seventy-five thousand dollars to the firm rather than for funds that would sustain an ongoing seventy-five-thousand-dollar capitalization, thirteen thousand of the thirty thousand dollars on hand, added to the sixty-two thousand he had already put in, would fulfill his obligation. And then he would be entitled to two thirds of the remaining seventeen thousand. He needed the money for personal expenses and for his Paige typesetter costs. How much exactly he was supplying Paige is difficult to determine, but it was not less than three thousand dollars a month. "Curse all business," he complained. "I can't understand even the ABC of it." He continued to act as if he believed he did. More and more responsibility for Webster & Company devolved onto Hall, an adequate businessman in his late forties who took gingerly to his new importance. By September 1887 it had become obvious that Webster's faltering health, described as neuralgia typified by "exacerbation," sensitivity to sound, and "acute pain of the nerve," had made him dysfunctional. "We did not know you had been seriously ailing until Mr. Hall's first letter," Twain wrote gently, in his capacity as uncle by marriage, "& did not realize the full extent & severity of it. . . . It is plain that you have had an exceedingly hard summer."

Convinced that his arduous work on Grant's *Personal Memoirs* had ruined his health, Webster expressed his willingness to resign, though he still desired to continue the partnership. "My duty to wife & family tells me I must not relinquish any part of my share." In early 1888, to Twain's great relief, Webster removed himself from active participation. The man who had been Twain's minor scapegoat he now elevated into the main reason for Webster & Company's difficulties. "How long he has been a lunatic I do not know," he wrote in his notebook, "but several facts suggest that it began . . . while the 1st vol of the Grant Memoirs was in preparation." By the end of 1888, Webster's temporary retirement had become permanent. His small partnership share in the firm he sold to Fred Hall for less than he thought it worth.

Twain's own nerves on edge, he now gave free rein to his merciless condemnation of Webster. "I have never hated any creature with a hundred thousandth fraction of the hatred which I bear [for] that human louse, Webster," he wrote to Orion in July 1889. In late April 1891, at forty years old, Webster died. "[He] left this dying injunction," Twain scathingly remarked in his notebook, "that upon his monument be this inscription after his name: 'Publisher of Gen. Grant's Memoirs & Knighted by the Pope.'" But to his niece Annie, Twain succeeded in being empathetic and loving. "There are no words," he wrote to her, "that can bring solace at such a time; the most that one can do is to offer one's strong sympathy, & this we do out of our hearts. Charley was a great sufferer, & to him death is peace, & a grateful release from intolerable pain. When death takes this merciful form it is a benefaction, & the grave a refuge." He meant with genuine kindness the stoic call to the blessings of a final resting place. Later, he was to extend it to others whom he loved, and to himself.

4.

Twain's affair with the Paige typesetter fell into four stages: his initial involvement between 1881 and 1883, his sudden passion in 1884–85, his total commitment between 1886 and 1890, and his disillusionment starting in 1891. It finally ended in 1894, though Twain continued to believe in the machine's superior virtues. He fell in love with what he felt to be the realization of perfection, a machine that would with unfailing reliability equal the speed of at least six highly skilled typesetters. He had a deep iconic and emotional connection to the printing press. As a writer, he communicated through type, the magic of raised hot iron letters transforming idiosyncratic handwriting into universal representation. This machine married his fascination with technology to his irrepressible desire to become rich.

When in 1881 Twain first invested in the typesetter, its completion seemed imminent, if not within months then within a year or two. But each instance of correction and improvement required, as Paige saw it, disassembling then reassembling the entire machine, which took three months, sometimes considerably longer. Until spring 1885, Twain's investments were only occasional sums of money, making him one of many, along with and then after the Farnham Company, who thought it sensible to bet modest sums on an invention that had great promise. In 1885 Paige offered to "sell the whole thing *outright*" to Hamersley for $350,000 and a $500 royalty on each machine sold in the United States. Hamersley proposed that Twain, using his connections and fame, sell their ownership to a well-financed company that would give each of them $250,000 cash above their purchase cost. Twain had at last found, he thought, his long-sought gold mine. But no company or investors were forthcoming with the capital required to buy the patents.

Beginning in February 1886 Twain's mission was to provide money to keep Paige at work as he perfected the typesetter and to raise capital for manufacture. He accepted Paige's assurance that it would take no more than six to eighteen months to overcome minor imperfections, particularly the machine's tendency to break type, which caused it to stop running until the pieces had been removed. Twain estimated that three thousand dollars a month would keep Paige going, including seven thousand dollars a year salary in monthly installments to continue until he realized a sum equal to that as "a net yearly profit." This was an estimable sum, though one that, with strain, Twain felt he could manage, providing that expenses did not increase or extend beyond the projected period. He had reason to believe that Pratt and Whitney, in the facilities of which Paige worked, would allow a considerable and increasing debit to be settled at a more convenient time. "Every expense connected with making the model machine cannot reach $30,000," Paige had asserted at a meeting in Twain's billiard room a few weeks before Twain signed on, "can't possibly go *over* it." Twain never doubted that their machine would show itself superior to three typesetters now or soon to be on the market, the most formidable of which, as it turned out, was Ottmar Mergenthaler's "Linotype" machine. Twain scoffed at the competition. Apparently faster and more versatile, Paige's machine seemed a high-tech paragon of inventive genius, while Mergenthaler's seemed a boring workhorse that got the job done without style or distinction. By 1886, however, the Linotype was already at work at the *New York Tribune*. Paige still had tinkering to do.

In exchange for his investment, Twain was to have a five-hundred-dollar royalty on every machine sold. Though the typesetter seemed to Twain ready for demonstration in spring 1886, Paige decided that effective line justification needed to be added. "Business sanity would have said," Twain wrote in 1890, "put it on the market as it was, secure the field, and add improvements later. Paige's business insanity said, add the improvements first and risk losing the field. And that is what he set out to do. To add a justifying mechanism to that machine would take a few months and cost $9,000 by his estimate, or $12,000 by Pratt and Whitney's." Twain reluctantly agreed, assuming that it would be done quickly as an improvement to the present machine. "There could be no sense in building a new machine," he later remarked, "yet in total violation of the agreement, Paige went immediately to work to build a new machine, although aware . . . that the cost could not fall below $150,000 and that the time consumed would be years instead of months." An implacable personality, immensely skilled in his own work, Paige, "a most extraordinary compound of business thrift and commercial insanity," was as obsessed as Twain, who gradually realized that he had put (and was incapable of withdrawing) his financial well-being into the hands of a man over whom he had little to no control.

Twain's commitment, though, remained unshakable, even as estimates of the amount necessary to manufacture increased between 1886 and 1891: conditions changed, arithmetic varied, "improvements" raised costs, figures were mostly speculations, and Twain's calculations were obsessively self-serving. Also, there were various outstanding obligations, structured as royalties to be paid investors. And, as Twain needed money for himself and capital for manufacture, he brought in other investors (after additional negotiation with Paige, including consideration of foreign rights) to whom he sold fractions of his own royalty. It soon became clear that the second part of his mission would be even more difficult than the first. The estimate of capital required rose from less than $1 million to more than $3 million, though at times Twain projected even larger figures, which it seemed to him investors could easily be persuaded to provide. To his surprise, he met resistance. It gradually dawned on him that until the successful demonstration of a finished machine there was little to no chance that any investors would provide the necessary capital for manufacture unless they too were true believers. His own rosy projections would do him no good without a convincingly superior machine that would reliably outperform the competition.

His mind was soon on training operators for the trials, his mental calculator constantly projecting numbers in regard to comparative speed of the Paige typesetter and its rivals. A year later, though, his nerves and financial resources were wearing thin. When his Nevada friend Calvin Higbie asked for a loan, Twain had to say no. His obligations, he explained, were stretched to the limit. "If I had half of the money which the newspapers credit me with, you should have that $20,000 per this mail." He could not even accommodate Livy's desire to spend the summer of 1887 in Europe to give the girls a taste of European culture. Anyway, he couldn't go to England without his machine, he explained to an English friend. "One doesn't go abroad & leave his soul and entrails behind."

When, in Elmira in summer 1887, he tried to insulate himself from typesetter business to work on *A Connecticut Yankee*, his success was erratic, particularly because he expected that an imminent report would bring news that the machine was completed and demonstrations could be scheduled for the fall. Revised expenses considerably exceeded previous estimates. Early in July, cash was needed for a new motor. With almost none on hand, he considered selling some bonds at a loss. Pratt and Whitney anxiously pressed for payment. Twain found his main solace in his imaginative sales projections: "There is a market in the world for 5,000 machines now, without regarding the 5,000 that will be salable a very few years later on." By Christmas 1887 he felt caught in a repetitive nightmare: no matter how close the typesetter appeared or was thought to be to completion, it remained tantalizingly unrealized. Paige always insisted on another minor improvement, another test to run. In August, Twain instructed Whitmore to sell some of his stock, again at a loss.

But on the last day of 1888 he sent a note to Livy, probably from the machine shop to the Farmington Avenue house: "Happy New year! The machine is finished & this is the first work done on it." A few days later, exultant, he wrote to Orion. "At 12:20 this afternoon a line of movable type was spaced and justified by machinery, for the first time in the history of the world! And I was there to see. It was done *automatically*—instantly—perfectly." The machine was "the most amazing and extraordinary invention ever born of the brain of man." It was now "completed and perfect. Livy is down stairs celebrating."

For the first half of 1889 he exulted in his conviction that his gamble had paid off. Here was a machine that fulfilled his fascination with technological beauty, an invention additionally wondrous because it was in the service of culture. Even the argument that it would create profits by putting laborers out of work failed to daunt him, despite his newborn sympathy for organized labor. Every labor-saving invention, he argued to Howells, whose labor sympathies and sense of justice were making him sympathetic to socialism, "takes a livelihood away from 50,000 men—& within ten years *creates* a livelihood for *half a million.*" The flood of profits that would make him a millionaire seemed about to break through the dam of delay that had held it back for so long. But, no matter the level of Twain's confidence, he still had not provided the only evidence that would turn a speculation into an attractive investment: a convincing demonstration that the machine would be durable and cost-efficient enough to outperform its competitors. Short-term demonstrations under controlled circumstances would not do. When a representative of the *New York Herald* watched a demonstration in March 1889 and observed that the machine had transposed type, Twain took it as a warning that "doubtless the only wise thing" was "a public exhibition & with a *perfected* machine; not a 2-hour glimpse of it, between trains, but a 6-months day-&-night exhibition, 24 hours in the day, & with trustworthy representatives of the big newspapers to watch it *all* of that time, & *then* report it." But for the desperately cash-short Twain, such a lengthy trial period would extend his days of ongoing expense and no income.

In April 1889, unable to resist Paige, Twain consented to one additional minor improvement. Bereft of cash, he got a reluctant Charley Langdon to invest five thousand dollars. Susan Crane also came through. That spring he approached Clara Spaulding's husband and soon got Clara to invest five thousand dollars though other friends were too prudent to cooperate. Potential investors' names ran through Twain's prospecting mind, usually with detailed figures in his notebook about what amount he would sell them and how much each would make. An exasperated Charley Langdon, about to leave for an extended European trip, reviewed Twain and the machine's history of broken promises and required his brother-in-law to provide a statement from Paige asserting that the machine would be *"finished."* Twain instructed Whitmore to fill in "such-and-such a date" and "insert it in the telegram," then "name a sum [the investor] can't possibly find fault with, for time is short & the corner I am in is distressedly tight." It was too late for Twain to adhere to the adage he had written into his notebook in late 1888: "There are two times in a man's life when he should not speculate: when he can afford it, & when he can't."

Fortunately, at the end of the summer, Langdon and Company repaid fifteen thousand dollars that it had borrowed from Livy. The first use of his wife's money to pay his business debts, it allowed him to stave off Pratt and Whitney. Livy's investments were still being managed by her brother, though in 1886 she either initiated the thought or had responded to her husband's suggestion that he handle her stocks. "I thought she was going to put her affairs into my hands," Twain wrote to Whitmore, "but thanks to goodness she has left them with her brother." He was busy enough mishandling his own. Capital for manufacture now became a concern again. Raising large amounts continued to be impossible.

But success seemed at hand. "I can have no stoppage upon *any* pretext," he insisted in August 1889. He demanded no more experiments, just ordinary testing and fine-tuning, in preparation for exhibiting the machine to potential investors, to see if speed could be increased and reliability made more certain. Trial runs kept the machine at work through much of the year. His frustrations and anxieties as the typesetter's major financial backer he kept separate from his ecstatic delight in its abilities. "I want to show you my type-setting machine," he wrote with proprietary zeal to Howells. His total investment, estimated at between $150,000 and $200,000, was about to be, he believed, repaid, "every cent of it," from his share of the profit "on the very first (unasked) order," which he expected imminently from a major New York newspaper.

Eager to strike a definitive blow for capitalization, he persuaded Joe Goodman to leave his California retirement ranch to take charge of raising money from rich investors. Goodman and Twain had access to various western mining millionaires, like John Mackay and Senator John P. Jones, the Nevada "Silver King," friends from *Territorial Enterprise* and *Roughing It* days. But he was able to sell only a few royalties at a thousand dollars each. Twain assured Sue Crane that her three shares would soon each be worth ten thousand dollars. They would no longer, he instructed Goodman, sell small numbers of shares but only large amounts to a small number of capitalists. Goodman began over a year of cross-country travels for strategy sessions and for meetings, practicing his sales pitch on both coasts. So confident was Twain that in December 1889 he signed a new contract with Paige, this one even more potentially self-damaging and disadvantageous than any he had signed before. It obligated him to raise a huge sum at the risk of severe penalties. "Papers are now being drawn," he exultantly told

Goodman, "which will greatly simplify the raising of capital; I shall be in supreme command; it will not be necessary for the capitalist to arrive at terms with anybody but me."

Certain that the machine was ready, he went to Washington to press Senator Jones to invest substantially. A demonstration would be scheduled for midwinter. When Jones responded encouragingly, Twain concluded that he had a commitment from him to invest $100,000 or $200,000 and gave him a six-month no-cost option to form a stock company. "Jones standing at our back," Twain wrote to Goodman, "with his purse in his hand, is an object-lesson & easily understandable by proposed customers." So great would his profits be, Twain calculated ($20 million soon, $150 million over the life of the patent), that he might buy up all of New York City, he joked with Katy Leary. But when Jones was ready to come to Hartford in mid-January 1890, he was put on hold, as was everyone, by Paige's decision once again to withdraw the machine from exhibition, this time to install an "air-blast." A disappointed, bewildered Twain chafed. It seemed an incomprehensible decision. "Paige & I always meet on effusively affectionate terms, & yet he knows perfectly well that if I had him in a steel trap I would shut out all human succor & watch that trap till he died."

Paige promised that the improved machine, with the air blast, would be ready for demonstration by April. News from reliable sources that an improved version of the already partly successful Mergenthaler Linotype had passed muster gave Twain additional unsteady moments. Livy saw signs of exhaustion and desperation in her husband's face. "Youth . . . I want to see you happy much more than I want anything else. . . . Oh darling it goes to my very heart to see you worried." There were other ways to make a living and more economical ways for them to live, she reminded him. When, at last, in June 1890, Jones and Mackay came to Hartford to observe a demonstration, they were cautious and willing to invest only five thousand dollars each. Humiliated, broken-hearted, and angry, Twain was in no position to have even the bitter satisfaction of turning them away. Even that pittance was better than nothing, and he still relied on Jones to form a stock company to raise capital for manufacture. "Now here is a queer fact," he mordantly wrote to Goodman soon after his disappointment with Jones and Mackay. "I am one of the wealthiest grandees in America—one of the Vanderbilt gang, in fact—& yet if you asked me to lend you a couple of dollars I would have to ask you to take my note instead." Still, the machine would redeem him. When he needed cheering, he would go to Pratt and Whitney and "sit by the machine" for hours. With Paige, he went down again, in the hot August weather, to Washington to try to answer Jones's objections.

Still determined to win, in that same month he signed an option to purchase all Paige's rights for $250,000, payable in six months. Jones still promised to raise the capital that fall. "I am resolved to stick tight to the thing till I haven't any money left; & then I will hand it back to Paige & keep my royalties. . . . My mind is at rest," Twain wrote to his brother, "& I feel entirely fearless as regards the future." But nothing went right. He and Goodman could not raise the $250,000. His purchase option lapsed. Old and new bills kept coming due. Paige continued tinkering and incurring costs. And Pratt and Whitney also seemed to Twain at fault for not providing as many workmen and not giving the priority to the typesetter that he believed their contract required. When Jones suggested that instead of a few large investors, they might do better to try a larger number of people of modest means, Twain embraced this change of tactics.

But Jones, who had exuded optimism, had by mid-February 1891, the date of the expiration of his option, raised nothing. By late February, Twain was reduced to pleading with him, "Take $75,000 worth of the royalties for $50,000 & pay it in installments of $1,000 a month; or take $50,000 worth for $25,000 & pay cash down. You will get your money back ten times over—& I shall be saved." He had spent forty thousand dollars on the machine, he told Jones, that he would not have spent if the senator had not committed himself. But he had little to no recourse. Jones had been advised by people he trusted that the Mergenthaler Linotype had reached a standard of reliability that made it preferable to the Paige compositor. Twain's perfect machine had one disastrous flaw: it broke down too often. Its delicate precision could not take heavy pounding.

A devastated Twain now sent back Paige's bills unpaid. He could not have paid them even if he had wanted to. "Mr Clemens . . . desires me to say," Whitmore was instructed to tell Paige, "that he is not making any further advances for the type machine." To Orion he proclaimed his disenchantment, not with the machine but with Paige. It was all Paige's fault. "I've forsook the machine (this is possible), & never wish to see it or hear it mentioned again. It is superb, it is perfect, it can do 10 men's work. It is worth billions; & when the pig-headed lunatic, its inventor, dies, it will instantly be capitalized & make the Clemens children rich [from the royalty he had retained]." Twain had at last turned into his father. The typesetter had become his version of the Clemens family's Tennessee land.

Broke, he needed to earn money to pay ordinary expenses. Webster & Company's balance sheet left him responsible for bills and bank loans, so there could be no help from that quarter. Fortunately, he had no typesetter debts, only a huge financial emptiness that might have contained the almost $200,000 he had wasted. For the next eighteen months he scurried to turn out literary work, rushed and inferior, to earn money to pay for the family's bread, and also its cake, in the form of their expensive Hartford life, which no longer seemed sustainable. In October 1890 Livy requested from Langdon and Company ten thousand dollars due her. Only five thousand was available. Her own capital could not be made liquid in short order without possible damage to the company. Probably the dividends from her investments had for some time been helping pay Hartford expenses. But the capital remained tied up by family as well as financial cords. "I wish there was some way to change our manner of living," she wrote to her mother, "but that seems next to impossible unless we sell our house. I wish there was no one in this world troubled for money, while there are so many so frightfully troubled I think we can only be thankful that it is as well with us as it is, even if there is only five thousand dollars with J/L. and Company." The Elmira family, though, would not disappoint her. "I want to thank you too Mother sweet for letting Mr Clemens have the ten thousand dollars. It seems so much easier and better to borrow in the family than out of it. At any rate it is easier for us whether it is for you or not. Mr Clemens was as pleased by Charley's suggesting it as he was by the entire arrangement."

By early 1891 they were making plans to live a cheaper life in an extended European residence. They would do their best not to think of it as a voluntary exile but as a cultural opportunity for their daughters. It was, though, they both recognized, the bitter result of Twain's financial irresponsibility. This interruption of their Hartford life, which they assumed would be temporary, was not something any of them wanted. He felt that he had failed his family and that all the fault was his.

5.

So engaged was he for these years with his typesetter and Webster & Company that he found time for only one sustained literary work, *A Con-*

necticut Yankee, and for the less time-consuming *Colonel Sellers as a Scientist.* In 1887, he published "English as She Is Taught" in the *Century*: a brief essay glossing amusing answers gathered from questions posed by a Brooklyn schoolteacher to her students. A more incisive essay, "Letter from the Recording Angel," he did not publish for the same reason he did not publish dozens of later essays and stories—neither his nor Livy's sense of his professional well-being would permit it. A satiric attack on Christian hypocrisy, it is an anticipation of his more sustained later attempts to write the biography of Satan he had proposed as a youngster in Hannibal. "A Petition to the Queen of England," humorously requesting that he should not be taxed on his English income, he did publish in the December 1887 *Harper's Monthly.* To the Hartford Monday Evening Club he delivered a paean to the American workingman whose empowerment he believed would be the final deathblow to oppressors, "the king, the capitalist, and a handful of other overseers." In the talk "On Foreign Critics" he condemned the "sham liberty" of England and the encrusted European antidemocracies. The claim that America's commitment to democracy, personal liberty, and technological progress somehow did not add up to a "civilization" equal to that of Europe infuriated him. On the contrary, he argued that America had far surpassed European oligarchies in what really mattered and what civilization in fact was about.

His own obligation to social justice he took quite seriously. Visiting Yale University in late 1885, Twain met one of the first African-Americans admitted to the law school, later a distinguished civil rights advocate, and he arranged to pay the young man's expenses. He also agreed, with the law school dean, to support another black student. Twain forcefully emphasized that he believed reparations were called for both in personal and communal acts. But when in February 1889 he thanked those at a Yale Alumni Association banquet for an honorary master's degree, he kept the tone and subject matter light. Both he and Livy felt proud that he was the first humorous writer to be so honored. But the old thorn still pricked. It was an article of faith in the Clemens family that Mark Twain was not taken seriously enough, his claim to attention undermined by the public's view of humor as a low genre. "He is known to the public as a humorist," Susy wrote, "but he has much more in him that is earnest than that is humorous." With the publication of *A Connecticut Yankee* few of those paying attention could doubt that. But not everyone was paying attention, and the balance of danger soon would be tipping in the other direction as fewer and fewer close readers found his new work funny at all.

Not that there was much new work. As early as 1885, his family observed the decline of his literary commitment as he plunged into business activities. "Mamma and I have both been very much troubled of late," Susy noted, "because Papa, since he has been publishing Gen. Grant's book, has seemed to forget his own books and works entirely." His assertion that "he didn't expect to write but one more book" disturbed them, unsettling their sense of what made him the important man he was.

When in 1890 he returned to literary work in order to rebuild his "wasted fortunes," the best idea he could come up with was a novelization of *Colonel Sellers as a Scientist*. That he recast the play to put most emphasis on the claimant theme reflects the complexity of his own relationship to claims, partly of lineage but also of self-identity and ownership; the satiric mockery of Sellers' invention, which he believes will earn at least $5 million, is likely to have been done with some self-awareness. Twain was probably one of the few readers to think funny his reworking of *Colonel Sellers* into *The American Claimant*. Most reviewers did not. Twain found it sidesplitting, especially as he wrote it. He had, in February 1891, "completed the first four chapters in 4 days—9,000 words—(1/15) of the book," he exuberantly told Orion. The *London Morning Leader* baldly expressed the general judgment: "A book by Mark Twain without any of Mark Twain's humor cannot be other than dull and disappointing." Serialized in the *New York Sun* in early 1892, it earned very little for its author or his publishing house, which brought it out in May as a book for the retail trade. In a radical and desperate redefinition, a reluctant Twain, at Fred Hall's urging, decided that Webster & Company would move into trade publishing. Twain had at last accepted that the high noon of subscription publishing had passed.

His attempts to profit from dramatizing his narratives, though, continued. The success of his adaptation of *The Gilded Age* was the model he hoped to replicate. He recognized that *Huckleberry Finn* was not readily adaptable, and that he was not the best person to attempt it. And he had already tried and failed with *Tom Sawyer*. But, from the start, *The Prince and the Pauper* had structural compactness and dramatic episodes that lent themselves to the stage. A few years after its publication Twain attempted a dramatization. When no producer expressed interest, he consulted

Howells, who in May 1884 prescribed a revision Twain was not willing to undertake, partly because he disliked such tasks. "I'd rather take a dose of medicine," he told Howells. Encouraged by Susy, Livy turned her own hand to it. She had in mind a script for home performance, a surprise to celebrate her husband's completion in March 1885 of his reading tour with Cable. She used her husband's abandoned script as the basis for her own. In April 1885, the family and friends acted a version that Twain had expanded for the occasion, and Twain himself performed the role of Miles Herndon when the Warners' son Frank fell ill. Both performances were a celebratory dress-up time for the Nook Farm community: "one of the prettiest private theatrical performances I have ever seen," Twain wrote to James Pond.

Sometime in 1886 Ed House encouraged him to revise the dramatization for stage production. "*That* would be nice," he granted in December, "but I can't dramatize it. The reason I say this is because I *did* dramatize it, & made a bad botch of it. But *you* could do it. And if you will, for ½ or ⅔ of the proceeds, I wish you would. Shan't I send you the book?" When House, who had collaborated on a few successful commercial plays, expressed interest, Twain instructed Webster to send it to him. "I've done up my absurd P & P dramatization, & will express [the manuscript] to you to-day or to-morrow." In mid-spring 1887, House reported that "A few days ago the complete scheme of the play developed with an effectiveness that I had not expected to arrive at so soon. The mere writing of the scenes and acts ought not now to occupy a great deal of time."

Frequently in pain from crippling gout and in need of money, House imagined that dramatizing *The Prince and the Pauper* would make him financially secure. A supportive friend, Twain had attempted to persuade Bliss to publish a book that House had written about Japan. House's Japanese companion, whether mistress or caretaker or both, elicited no Hartfordian moral questions. Like House, she was a welcome visitor, and House himself became a favorite of the children, especially Clara. House assumed that his oral and written communications with Twain constituted an agreement, as good as a contract, which in his mind stipulated that he had an exclusive right to dramatize the novel. House settled in Farmington Avenue for the full summer of 1887, where he intended to work hard on the dramatization. It was a welcome refuge from his New York life. Before Twain left in June for Elmira, House read him either a detailed sketch of act 1 or the act itself—accounts differ—and stated his thoughts about the rest of the play. Apparently Twain responded approvingly.

By the end of summer 1887, when he left Hartford, House may not have added much if anything to what he had read to Twain in late May or June. Without any specific schedule commitment, he may have felt that it would get done at his leisure. Between summer 1887 and mid-1889, House said nothing about his dramatization-in-progress. Preoccupied with Webster, Paige, and *A Connecticut Yankee*, and with a memory that rarely served him well on such matters, by late 1888 Twain had only the vaguest sense of what he had agreed to. To his recollection, he had given House a shot at dramatizing *The Prince and the Pauper* but nothing had come of it. The specific language of their exchanges had gone out of his mind. That it could be construed as a legally binding contract never occurred to him.

When in early December 1888 Abby Sage Richardson, a young New York writer, editor, and actress, asked if Twain would collaborate with her on a dramatization, he urged her to do it herself. Soon he wrote up a contract, stipulating, among other things, that a well-known child actress, Elsie Leslie, would need to be enlisted, that Richardson would have until March 1889 to get the script done, and that the producer Daniel Frohmann needed to be brought on board shortly. He reluctantly consented that one performer should play both roles, a strategy that Richardson also urged. When in February 1890 House learned that Twain had made an arrangement with Richardson, he was furious. It seemed a stab in the back. Twain was bemused, and a little distressed. "House seems to have a claim," he wrote in his notebook. "I will go & see what it [is]. I can't imagine, myself, [that it can amount to anything.]" "I remember that you started once to map out the framework for me to fill in," he wrote to House. "However, I never thought of such a thing as your being willing to undertake the dramatization yourself—I mean the whole thing."

But he recognized that he might have made a contract he had no right to make. "I must live up to it," he wrote to House, "unless there is an earlier contract in existence. If you have one, send me a copy of it, so that I can take measures to undo my illegal action, & I will at once proceed in the matter." Since House had not said anything about it for some time, Twain had assumed that he had "gradually abandoned" the idea: "I still remember somewhat of the sketch you made for a part of the first act. But I do not remember that it was anything more than that, or that you were then thinking of writing the act yourself." He was being truthful, not just strategic, when he told House, "I would naturally have preferred you, who I knew could write plays. . . . My memory may be all astray; I cannot help that; such as it is, I have to depend upon it, whether to my hurt or help. I supposed I had a full right to make that late contract, & I made it. If you have a previous one, I beg you to send me a copy, & I will come as near setting things exactly right as possible." Apparently not a word of his written exchanges with House had stayed in his memory.

He now, in effect, had two contracts in place, both of which implied but did not stipulate exclusivity. He also was in the process of losing a friend, and he could not make things "right" except perhaps at the cost of paying damages to one party or the other, which he does not seem to have considered, among other reasons because he could not fully accept the validity of House's claim. Twain wanted and expected House to withdraw. When House refused, Twain felt betrayed. How could House stand in the way of his making some desperately needed money? After all, it was *his* book. He had no compromise to offer. Neither did House. As words turned bitter, only complete withdrawal would have been acceptable to Twain and complete vindication to House. Twain was in the "no good deed goes unpunished" frame of mind. It all proved a painful mess, which Twain responded to with characteristic anger and vituperation.

Richardson's dramatization had a glamorous Broadway premiere on January 20, 1890. Twain made a witty curtain speech. Leslie was highly praised. The play received generally good notices. Livy, though, like her husband, thought the adaptation demeaned the book. And it had a disappointingly short run. Soon after the opening, the courts granted House an injunction against Twain's profits. Even worse, the court mandated that his profits go to House. "I *must* have some rights somewhere, & I wish to know what they are," Twain complained. By mid-February, bruised and sick of both playwrights, what he most wanted was "to stop the present piece, & also . . . prevent House from reinstating the present piece or playing his own," which indeed did have a short production in October 1890. There were now two productions, he bewailed, "one in the hands of a pirate, the other in the hands of a person who is the same thing without the name." That House's play was halted by an injunction from the Frohmann faction did Twain no good. An account in the *New York Times* left an impression unfavorable to Twain: "MARK TWAIN HAULED UP/A SUIT OVER

'THE PRINCE AND THE PAUPER.' E. H. HOUSE SAYS HE WAS AUTHORIZED BY TWAIN TO PREPARE THE PLAY AND THAT HIS IDEAS WERE STOLEN."

Ironically, Twain's unearned reputation for sharp business acumen worked against him. Sympathy went to House, whom it was assumed Twain was trying to cheat. "Like the majority of writers, Mr. House has not had occasion to cultivate commercial habits. Mark Twain, whom he makes the principal defendant in the preliminary proceedings, as will be done also in the suit to follow, is well known to be a conspicuous exception to this rule of business carelessness among literary men." Of course it was Twain's carelessness that had created the problem. Legal proceedings took more than a year. The suit was eventually dropped, the friendship irrevocably ended, and House took his place, with Bliss and all those whom he believed had tried to cheat him, in Twain's damnology. "Any mention of the stage," he told Howells in April 1890, "brings House to my mind & turns my stomach. What a gigantic liar that man is!—& what an inconceivable hound." His name thereafter was usually followed by the epithet "May he burn in hell!"

During the summer of 1890, the family deserted Elmira for a summer colony of artists and intellectuals, the Onteora Club, near Tannersville, New York. Mary Mapes Dodge, the author of *Hans Brinker and the Silver Skates* and the editor of *St. Nicholas Magazine,* anchored Onteora. Two of Twain's young New York friends were residents in 1890, the critic Laurence Hutton and the Columbia University professor of English and public intellectual Brander Matthews. Livy and the girls found congenial company. Susy's and Clara's artistic aspirations were encouraged: Susy studied French and Clara took piano lessons. The convenient rail connections to New York and Washington probably were attractions to Twain, and with no sustained literary work at hand, preoccupied with business, he had less need of Quarry Farm. The decision to try an alternative was also influenced by Theodore Crane's death the previous summer. After a stroke had disabled him in September 1886, Crane had survived three additional years, under intense care, some of this time at the Hartford house. Her husband gone, Susan Crane, with Charley and his family in Europe, stayed at the Langdon townhouse to help care for Mrs. Langdon. Livy would have to do the housekeeping at Quarry Farm. "Nine months of the year is quite enough of that for me," she confided to a new friend, the Louisiana writer

Grace King. When they decided that Livy's proposal that they spend the summer in Europe was impractical, Onteora became a reasonable second best.

In the hot Washington summer Twain lobbied Jones and others for money for the typesetter. At Onteora he tried to relax, though the heat distressed him. "Please send me a summer suit as soon as possible for the weather is terrifically hot here," he wrote to his New York tailor of the first of the white suits that were to become his sartorial signature. In New York, he sweated some of the business perils of C. L. Webster & Company, eager to make it a paying investment, or at least collect the interest to which he was entitled on his seventy-five-thousand-dollar capital. Fred Hall's best was insufficient to allow Twain to draw money from his investment. On the contrary, the ongoing deficit required everything of Twain's to be ploughed back into the firm. One of its few sales successes, the eleven-volume *Library of American Literature,* surprisingly proved a cash-flow burden rather than a cash cow. Somehow Webster & Company had committed itself to pay its subscription salesmen full commission on all eleven volumes at the time of the initial sale, though the purchaser paid for one volume at a time, delivered periodically over a two-year period. So the cash-short publisher was out money until receipts caught up to outlay. Bank loans were required to stay afloat, and now there was interest to be paid. Twain's own royalties had to be diverted. When he met Edward Bellamy in January 1890, soon after reading *Looking Backward,* his own social consciousness had been sufficiently liberalized by sympathy with the poor and sharpened by his dysfunctional experiences as a capitalist to make the author of *A Connecticut Yankee* an admirer of another, though different kind, of reformer. But capitalism, he granted, had not failed him. He had failed it. Somewhere between a Mugwump and a radical, he remained, unlike Bellamy, an ardent capitalist.

His stature, even his celebrity, provided emotional buoyancy even during times of distress. He had a magical capacity to brighten into amusing, slyly instructive conversation, no matter what burdens he carried. Usually, though, he had more conversational magic for friends and strangers than for his immediate family. And he had genuine interest in meeting writers he admired, one of whom, Robert Louis Stevenson, he met in New York in April 1888. In response to a letter from Stevenson, they arranged to meet in Washington Square Park, where they sat on a bench, talking for hours.

In summer 1891 the youthful Rudyard Kipling extended his world travels to visit his idol at Elmira. He simply showed up one day, unexpected, relatively unknown to Twain. Soon Twain was an avid Kipling fan. Walt Whitman, whom he seems never to have met, he exalted, in a letter contributed in 1889 to a festschrift volume, as an heroic figure, the poet of the American democratic ethos and of American technological progress. Strongly identifying with his version of Whitman, he read and admired *Leaves of Grass*. Poets he gave special license to. They should not, he wrote, be expected to be moral, though he did not explain what he meant by "moral."

He was not being accurate when he begged off contributing a list of favorite poets to the *Century* with the claim, "All the poetry which I have read in twenty years could be put between the lids of one octavo. I do not read anything but history & biography." Browning was the poet he most adored after Shakespeare. He assumed with pleasure the role of leader-teacher of Browning to a group of Hartford ladies, including Livy. "I used to explain Mr. Browning—but the class won't stand that. They say that my reading imparts clear comprehension. . . . Moral: don't explain your author; read him right & he explains himself." When asked the what-authors-would-you-take-to-a-desert-island question, he responded that his list would contain "Shakespeare; and Browning; and Carlyle (*French Revolution* only); Sir Thomas Malory (King Arthur); Parkman's *Histories*. . . . *Arabian Nights*; Johnson (Boswell's), because I like to see that complacent old gasometer listen to himself talk; Jowett's Plato," and he added "*Pepy's Diary*." Shakespeare stood supreme, though by the late 1880s he had enlisted in the ranks of those who argued that Bacon was indeed the author of the plays. "Mama revolts," Susy noted, "at the mere idea, but papa favors Bacon, and so do I."

With a mind of her own, Susy's mind was unmistakably much like her father's. So too was her sensibility. She desired to please and model herself after him. At Thanksgiving 1889, the usual games of charades were preceded by "a brief little fanciful play. [It] was written by my eldest girl, & was played in the drawing-room by herself & two sisters & a couple of school-girl friends." In October 1890, after she (and Clara also) had passed the Bryn Mawr entrance examination, she tested her personality against the new experience of living away from home. Bryn Mawr was both a revelation and a burden. "It is by long odds the best female college in the world," her father boasted. As they waved good-bye to her, "Our train was drifting away," he wrote to his sister Pamela, "& she was drifting college-ward afoot, her figure blurred & dim in the rain & fog, & she was crying."

At first Susy flourished, to some extent. Within a short while, she and one of her classmates, an attractive, bright girl from New Jersey, Louise Brownell, were in love, a deeply emotional attachment without any necessary physical expression other than hugs, and not unusual among young Victorian women who were well protected from the casual company of men. The educational challenges Susy met well, but, shy, seemingly aloof, and always identified as the famous writer's daughter, she was deeply homesick. Eager to encourage her independence and aware that Susy's attachment to father and home threatened her long-term development, Livy tried to keep father and daughter at a reasonable distance, though she felt deeply enough her daughter's unhappiness to commit herself not to force her to stay at Bryn Mawr more than one year if her spirits did not improve. Her father missed her terribly, though, and took every chance, with Livy and alone, to visit her at school.

When invited to give a reading, he eagerly accepted and came to Bryn Mawr in March 1891 for his performance, another chance to see his daughter and be the center of attraction in Susy's world. Probably wishing that he wouldn't appear at all but without the courage to tell him so, she begged him at least not to include in his program "The Golden Arm," which she thought too sensationalistic for a highbrow audience. He promised he would not. As always, such a promise made him incapable doing anything but the reverse. Susy could not (but of course fearfully could) believe her ears. Following his every cue, the audience burst into startled shock when, after his pregnant pause to a silent house, he shouted the climatic words, "You did!" Weeping with anger and humiliation, Susy fled. During much of 1890–91 she was increasingly fragile, and a little unstable. Literally sick with longing for home, she gave up college, returned to Hartford, and prepared to leave with her family for Europe. Part of her did not want to go. She did not want to leave Louise Brownell.

6.

As much as Twain loved his mother, distance and her mental deterioration had kept them apart in the 1880s. Their relationship since he had left Hannibal as a teenager had been based on the unspoken assertion that his love for her flourished best at a distance. He apparently had no desire to spend other than occasional moments with her, and he had bought for three hundred dollars a month both Orion's financial stability and a home for his mother. He did it out of generosity and loyalty, but also self-interest. That his mother might live with him was out of the question. Orion and Mollie had taken on the burden and relieved him of everything but paying for it. Short visits, as in summer 1886, were best. That year his mother's mind had still been active, but her memory was disappearing. "She knew my face; knew I was married; knew I had a family, and that I was living with them. But she couldn't, for the life of her, tell my name or who I was. So I told her I was her boy. 'But you don't live with me,' she said. 'No,' said I, 'I'm living in Hartford.' 'What are you doing there?' 'Going to school.' 'Large school?' 'Very large.' 'All boys?' 'All boys.' 'And how do you stand?' said my mother. 'I'm the best boy in that school,' I answered. 'Well,' said my mother, with a return of her old fire, 'I'd like to know what the other boys are like.'" As a child in Hannibal, he had been the best boy in that town, but those "nearest and dearest" to him, especially his mother, "couldn't seem to see it," he complained. His mother, as she faded, still gave precedence to the pleasure she took in her own wit than to his feelings. It was a trait he shared, the consequences of which in his own life, and for his own children, he insufficiently appreciated.

Jane Clemens' failing health kept him additionally aware of his own aches, particularly rheumatism in his right hand, arm, and shoulder that sometimes made holding a pen painful. Other than that, he seemed as energetic as always, and still adventuresome enough to make a second attempt to master the bicycle. Mortality, though, was a more formidable problem than scraped knees. Signs of aging provoked unavoidable confrontations with the prospect of the end game. At every birthday he complained. He was in no mood, nor was the rest of the family, for his fifty-fifth in November 1890. At Bryn Mawr, where he had gone to bring Susy home for Thanksgiving, he felt sadly commemorative as Livy's forty-fifth approached. "Livy Darling, in two hours it will be your birthday & so I am already celebrating it with gratitude that you are still among us & of us & that you belong to me. Time is drifting remorselessly on, & soon you will know what I knew so many years ago—how it feels to be 45. I would like to experience it again." They had both been badly frightened by a "savage attack" of diphtheria that came on with terrifying force and had seemed for a few weeks in March and April 1888 as if it were going to kill her. In spring 1889 she contracted "pink eye." The infection was difficult to get rid of, and, when the worst was over, she was for a while almost blind, with devastating headaches; her condition was miserable for almost half a year. By late summer, she still could barely read. "We are all growing old," he wrote to his sister, whose visit had been postponed because of Livy's illness, "we live wide apart, & we may never have a chance to meet again."

Warnings from Keokuk that his mother was fading fast required, in August 1890, another interruption of the Onteora holiday. For nearly a decade Jane Clemens had suffered "mental tortures—hallucinations which . . . often took the form of malignant persecutions & insult as any other. . . . She had as a rule a worn & haunted look." It was "an infinite pity," he wrote to Orion, "that poor old Ma must drag her tired life out in so much needless suffering." After one last, heart-rending look at his mother's ravaged face, he abruptly took the train back from Iowa. He had received a telegram from Whitmore about Paige typesetter business that he misinterpreted to mean that he was needed in Hartford, and then blamed Whitmore, though his anxiety about finances produced the mistake. He had nothing but unreserved "admiration & gratitude," he wrote to Orion, "for the lovely & patient way" he had cared for their mother "all these trying years": "It is beautiful—& beyond me." On October 27, 1890, Jane Clemens, at the age of eighty-seven, died. Her famous son accompanied her coffin to its Hannibal grave, alongside Henry's and John Marshall's. "It appeased my sorrow to see that that look was wholly gone from her face when she lay in her coffin, & that in its place was serenity & peace."

In poor health, Livy still found energy to devote to her own eighty-seven-year-old mother. Though she had all her faculties, Mrs. Langdon seemed close to the end. When, on his way back from Hannibal, Twain spent a Sunday with his mother-in-law in Elmira, Livy wished she could have been there. She felt constrained, though, not to spend the money for the trip. In late November the Clemenses were called to Elmira for what seemed certain to be a deathbed watch. The vigil was shattered by a telegram from Hartford. Jean was seriously ill, with a high fever. There was no immediately satisfactory diagnosis. While Livy stayed with her mother, her husband took the first train back to Hartford. Jean seemed to have had a seizure. "I ought to be there to [be] a support to Mrs. Clemens in this unspeakable trouble, & so ought Susy & Clara; but Jean pleads to be not wholly forsaken; so, when the death-telegram falls, I think I shall stay with Jean & send Susy & Clara to their mother. I have fed so full of sorrows, these last weeks that I seem to have become hardened to them—benumbed." On the night of November 26–27 Mrs. Langdon appeared to be dying. But, after a time "she got quiet & slept." Sue and Livy sat by her bed through the night. "I wish she would be released in her sleep," she wrote to her husband. Mrs. Langdon died the next night.

It was a mournful Christmas, the end of a harsh year. Susy returned to Bryn Mawr; Clara to her music, practicing five hours a day on the piano and violin; Jean to her quiet, withdrawn childhood, recovered from what none of them would know until some years later was an episode in an illness that would be lifelong. "I feel so much older since mother was taken away," Livy confided to Grace King. "I am very lonely for her." Twain's morale was equally low, his personal distress inseparable from his financial woes. At moments, he still expected that the typesetter fiasco would be resolved satisfactorily. Some reorganization and new financing might redeem his investment, though there was little for him to do but hope and cajole. Webster & Company's affairs especially preoccupied him because he believed cash would be forthcoming. Added to the Langdon ten thousand dollars, it would make possible a year or more in Europe.

Twain himself would rather have gone to some place of exotic escape, like Hawaii. His family had heard him "sigh for the islands every year for twenty years," but Hawaii was not a reasonable alternative to Hartford. Paris, Geneva, Germany, and Italy were, and in Germany the ailing parents could take curative baths and find balm for bodily aches and wounded hearts. The girls would have valuable artistic and cultural opportunities. Livy's health "has determined us to go to Europe," he told Howells, as if that were the whole story. The family wanted to go, he insisted. Necessity, he pretended, was not at issue. If it was to be only a year or so that they would be away from Hartford, that would be bearable, Livy surmised, though they would miss their lovely house and intimate friends. For Twain, distance from the scenes of his financial disasters would not have been unwelcome. Most of all, with the dollar formidably strong against every currency except the pound sterling, Europe promised a reduction in living expenses. Why, he reflected, could he not buy time to repair his fortunes, though he gave no thought to the likelihood that there would be counterbalancing new expenses, that without a determination to reduce their standard of living, significant savings were unlikely. Either he did not consider renting or did not choose to rent the Hartford house, though some items were sold, like the piano, and the staff reduced to the caretaker. The thought of putting the house into the hands of strangers would have given them a sacrilegious shudder. George and Patrick were no longer to be in his service, and he did his best to find them new jobs. Kate Leary, along with Susan Crane, was to sail with them.

By mid-May they were "in the rush & turmoil of preparation for a long absence in Europe," though for how long was unclear. On June 6, 1891, they sailed from New York on the French liner *La Gascogne,* bound for Havre. The three girls tearfully left behind beloved pets and servants and friends. "We all regarded this break in a hitherto harmonious existence as something resembling a tragedy," Clara was later to write. When everything was said and done, they were going into financial exile.

CHAPTER FIFTEEN

EXILE & DESOLATE

1891–1895

1.

A chastened Mark Twain, eager to get his professional life back on track, leaned his face into the wind of exile and opportunity. "I have been an author for 20 years & an ass for 55," he confessed, with a touch of self-dramatizing pride. Numbers of turning points in his life had begun with sea voyages: the young San Franciscan sailing westward to Hawaii in 1866; the crossing of the Isthmus in 1867, which brought him to his new East Coast life; the roving correspondent for the *San Francisco Alta California* steaming eastward to the Holy Land, an assignment that resulted in *Innocents Abroad* and his introduction to Livy; the Atlantic crossings to Europe in the 1870s in search of subject matter. Those were voyages of optimism and ambition, directed toward a burgeoning future. This, now, was to be different, an attempt to undo the past, to repair the damage he had done, without the advantages of youth or optimism. He knew as he sailed in June 1891, on the most beautiful days "the Atlantic ever saw," that the change was not in his stars but in himself. On the one hand, he thought in terms of his lifelong good luck having changed. On the other, he blamed himself for his family's straitened circumstances. His rheumatism persisted. So did his anxiety about money.

He would have to find subjects to write about and churn out prose, whatever its literary value. The thought of writing a travel book repelled him, though circumstance made that a logical genre to pursue. As a compromise, he committed himself to write six disparate travel articles for a thousand dollars each for the McClure newspaper and magazine syndicate. That would provide some cash and, he assumed, little burden. Later, perhaps, with additional material, they might form a book of travel sketches, allowing him to publish a book without, so to speak, having to write one. The Langdon ten thousand dollars would not last more than a year or two, especially for the support of an entourage of eight, though Susan Crane would pay her own way. His unpublished story "The Second Advent," written in 1881, came to mind, perhaps because he thought he might revise it for publication, more likely because it expressed a favorite observation of his—that Jesus, having come once, would not return. And there would be no second coming for him, either. He soon jotted into his notebook one of his favorite Jesus jokes in the black dialect that for him epitomized intuitive and worldly wisdom combined: "Come yo' seff Lawd, doan sen' yo' son, dis ain' no time f'chillun."

But why, he asked himself, couldn't Huck and Tom come again, favorites with the book-buying public, embodiments of his personal revivification, agents of his literary rebirth. As he tried to imagine their reappearance, he discovered, to his horror, that they expressed the mind and condition of Mark Twain in 1891. The Huck and Tom he now imagined had also grown old, and they too had made egregious mistakes. "Huck comes back," Twain wrote in his notebook shortly before sailing, "60 years old, from nobody knows where—& crazy. Thinks he is a boy again, & scans every face for Tom & Becky etc. Tom comes, at last, 60 from wandering the world & tends Huck, & together they talk the old times; both are desolate, life has been a failure, all that was lovable, all that was beautiful is under the mould. They die together."

2.

After a week in Paris, in pursuit of health, culture, and economy, the family went to Geneva, where the girls remained with Susan Crane. The two invalids went for five weeks to Aix-les-Bains to take the baths and catch their breath, the first of a series of fashionable health spas they submitted to during the summer and fall of 1891. Twain's rheumatic right arm and hand ached badly, a condition particularly debilitating for a man who needed to make his living holding a pen. Fortunately, he did not take his affliction as punishment for misuse of his talents. But he had other reasons for critical self-reflection, including continuing to take at face value Fred Hall's mildly upbeat predictions about Webster & Company. In fact, Hall had insufficient cash to cover expenses, the success of *The Library of American Literature* remained a draining liability, and the twenty-five-thousand-dollar debt to the Mt. Morris Bank needed to be regularly renewed, though Hall's evasions and his own optimism convinced him that the debt was being reduced. Also, he had not given up entirely on the Paige compositor. When an opportunity soon came to sell his royalty interest, he insisted on stipulations that anyone but he would have realized would kill the deal. He was not yet ready to let go. Paige, he believed, was the problem, not the machine. As he took the waters at Aix, part of his mind regularly drifted westward, his ears straining to catch the voices from which he still expected to hear good news.

Twain hoped to make his spa visits do double-duty. "I could write reams & volumes I'm so hungry to get hold of a pen, & the place & the air are so inspiring . . . [but] my arm won't let me." The six McClure syndicate letters, to be published in the *New York Sun,* had to be manufactured. He made halting progress. After soaking his rheumatic arm every day, by the fifth week he could write for an "hour or so at a time." Two weeks later it was as bad as it had been before. The casinos and the scenery had their attractions. But the waters stank, whether drunk or dipped in, and the doctors were self-serving entrepreneurs. Like other spas, Aix provided serene semi-seclusion; physical pampering, if one did not drown or poison oneself; and light entertainment, if one did not overfrequent the baccarat table. But this widely advertised "paradise" for rheumatics where "all diseases [were] welcomed, and satisfaction given or the money returned at the door," did not give him back the use of his right hand.

And Livy's health remained fragile, the main concerns intermittent breathlessness, lack of energy, and chest pain. Sometimes headaches forced her into seclusion and darkness. The diagnosis of heart disease had started to emerge and had become tentatively accepted by early 1891. The cleverest of spa doctors generally knew that the sulfuric waters widely touted for gout, rheumatism, and liver conditions also provided a quiet setting that benefited hypertension. The most optimistic or venal proclaimed that their general modality could cure anything. Spa treatments, of course, could do nothing for Livy's heart directly: they did, though, encourage rest. At Aix, she was liberated from the responsibility of running a household and, indeed, during this first year of their travels Susan Crane carried most of the household burden; Katy Leary did the semiheavy lifting; local servants did the rest. "They fed us well, they slept us well, & I wish I could have stayed there a few years & got a solid rest," Twain concluded.

Soon they all went to Bayreuth, for culture, and then to Marienbad for the waters and a strict regimen of walks, sulfuric water, and mud baths, along with a sparse diet. Bayreuth immersed Livy, Susy, and Clara in the Wagner cult. Piano teachers encouraged Clara to think of a career as a concert performer, though the encouragement was tentative. Neither parent imagined a career for any of their children other than one that some special talent mandated. Otherwise (and desirably) it was assumed they would follow their mother's precedent. As enthusiastic about music as her sister, Susy had a fine but "small" voice that she hoped to develop. She too would have lessons. Jean apparently had no talent worth mentioning. As the youngest, only her general education was at issue, but that included concerts and operas, and Livy had booked seats for nineteen Wagner performances.

For Twain, it was an occasion to create for the McClure syndicate a humorous complaint, "At the Shrine of St. Wagner." He felt "like a heretic in heaven," he wrote, "the one sane person in the community of the mad . . . the one blind man where all others see." As with his other encounters with European high art since *Innocents Abroad,* he was indeed a sophisticated heretic, determined to be true to his own taste. That required a level of evaluation and cultural positioning that made him a thoughtful philistine, partly a pose and usually an effective attempt to embody American straight talk and existential frankness. It was, paradoxically, as sophisticated a performance in its own genre and mode as Wagner's in his, though it made his high-culture wife and daughters uncomfortable.

Much of summer 1891 he spent in France, Germany, and Switzerland, including a visit to Heidelberg, where they stayed in the same hotel rooms they had occupied in happier days fourteen years before. "I was a skittish young thing of 42 [then]," he remarked, when disappointed that two women whom he had known as comparative children did not recognize him. His mind continued its gloomy cast. "Hell or Heidelberg," he wrote in his notebook. "Whichever you come to first." When he was in a foul mood, widespread and deeply habitual European deference to power infuriated him. "The first gospel of all monarchies should be rebellion," he wrote. Russian despotism particularly disgusted him. Before leaving America, he had stated his support for an anti-czarist freedom movement. "The idiotic Crusades were gotten up to 'rescue' a valueless tomb from the Saracens; it seems to me that a crusade to make a bonfire of the Russian throne & fry the Czar in it wd be some sense." Cutting aphorisms about human nature and practices increasingly came to mind, including about Columbus Day that "it was wonderful to find America, but it would have been more wonderful to miss it," an appropriate comment for a man who had taken himself and his family into exile.

In counterpoint to his increasingly bleak view of human nature, in late 1891 the ideal embodied in Livy began to have a renewed focus in a historical figure in whom he had long been interested. They traveled close to Joan of Arc's birthplace. His revival of interest in Joan might also have been, in part, a reaction to France's newborn enthusiasm about its national heroine. Fascinated by Joan's life and character, he began to buy and read everything about her he could. She seemed an embodiment of beauty and courage, an antidote to the moral ugliness of his modern world. That she was a virgin adolescent spoke to his Victorian admiration for feminine purity. That she was a courageous warrior against a corrupt church and state spoke to his partly concealed rebellious anger. The idea of writing a French companion piece to *The Prince and the Pauper* came to mind, an historical novel focused on the life of this heroine.

Switzerland, where they arrived in early September 1891 and of which he had happy recollections, had among its attractions its republican independence. With Twichell he had hiked the Swiss Alps, collecting material for *A Tramp Abroad*. Now he needed to gather material once again. Three of the six essays committed to McClure had been written but not sent. His rheumatism, though, continued to make writing difficult. But even if he had the stamina, he did not have the will to go on a walking tour. Also, he had no obvious companion. Instead, he hired Joseph Verey, his guide from 1878, to arrange the details of a solitary trip down the Rhone, including buying a flatboat, engaging a boatman, and organizing a floating tour from Lake Bourget to Lyons and Valence, then to Avignon and Arles. There he would take the train to Montpellier. In mid-September he left the family in Lausanne. In his notebook he listed Henry James's ten-year-old account of the same route, *A Little Tour in France*. Drifting downriver reminded him of rafting, and his attempt to revivify Huck and Tom under the title "New Adventures of Huckleberry Finn," soon to be developed into *Tom Sawyer Abroad,* was probably in his mind. He also had in mind a long article or short book based on his Rhone trip, perhaps to be incorporated into accounts of other such tours. After a few days of rain, the weather improved, as did his spirits. Still, his impressions and notes did not cohere sufficiently to point him in the direction of an effective essay. The spirit, energy, and point of view, humorous or otherwise, necessary to bring disparate materials together flagged.

Livy wrote home that they were going to keep house in Berlin, in a "pleasant sunny" inexpensive flat that she and her sister had made a quick trip from Lausanne to procure. It was on the first floor of a building in a seedy area. She had no idea of the character of the neighborhood, which turned out to be more or less satisfactory for the fall and early winter. By the new year they were to move into handsome apartments in the first-class Hotel Royal on Unter den Linden. Berlin had been chosen partly because of its music resources and also its fame as the most advanced center of medical science. Livy could have the best doctors. In late November, Twain's over-optimistic interpretation of a statement from Fred Hall, detailing C. L. Webster's accounts, lifted his spirits. Safe and happy haven seemed imminent. "I shall be glad when the ship comes in!" he wrote to Hall, a dangerous metaphor for a man constitutionally unable to see business reality. Still "badly crippled by rheumatism," even if he could not write, he could observe and socialize.

Suddenly they had the stimulation of a great capital, the autumn bustle, quaint customs, and German culture of which delighted them all, except Susy. Her Berlin was a dark reflection of her mood, the seriousness of which her parents continued to underestimate, important elements of which they remained ignorant of. Livy resumed German lessons from a female professor whom she called "one of the most intellectual women" she had ever met; Jean took lessons from a governess; and Clara, now the student of a well-known piano teacher, had her own circle of friends, some of them German, and a social life in which invitations were frequent. The least happy, Susy, desperately missed Louise Brownell, with whom she exchanged letters of desire and despair. "Ah, Louise if I could only see you!

I am so afraid—*Don't forget me!*" Her confidence, even hope, that she could one day, like her father, be a successful writer disappeared almost entirely. Voice lessons had some promise. But she had little faith that her "small voice" could ever be big enough to enable a career.

With his works widely translated into German, his well-publicized face recognizable to the German elite, the celebrated author was a lion to be seized. Welcomed by the American ambassador, William Walter Phelps, and his assistant, Theodore Bingham, Twain soon was at home at the embassy and in American and German drawing rooms. Both men, who provided introductions, quickly became friends of his. When a note came from Poultney Bigelow, a well-connected American journalist working in Europe, offering another introduction, Jean remarked, "At this rate, papa, there presently won't be anybody left for you to get acquainted with but the deity." Even the recently enthroned Kaiser Wilhelm II wanted to meet the famous humorist. German officers and aristocrats Twain had met apparently spoke interestingly of him to the king. Twain noticed that this kaiser, who twenty-two years later helped lead Europe into World War I, kept domestic peace with a heavy hand. In a speech to the Brandenberg parliament, the kaiser "complained sharply" about those dissatisfied with the government and urged them to leave Germany. "The speech has made a great stir," Twain wrote in his notebook. When a mob of the hungry unemployed gathered in front of the palace, "bread was distributed to them, but they threw it away." When "crowds of the proletariat" drifted onto an aristocratic riding ground, the emperor, with his family, "rode out as usual . . . to show that they [were] not afraid."

In late February 1892, Twain sat at the kaiser's right hand at a black-tie dinner hosted by a German general who, of all things, had married one of Twain's St. Louis cousins. Etiquette required that guests speak only when spoken to. To Twain's delight, the emperor spoke highly of some of his books, which he had read. When Twain presented his own view on a matter the kaiser had raised, the table fell silent. "I had committed an indiscretion." Thereafter the kaiser did not address him at all. For years afterward he wondered if he had been purposely rebuked. In 1906 an American diplomat recently returned from an audience sent him the regards of the kaiser, who had wondered why he hadn't done "any more talking at that dinner." In the actual presence of royalty, Twain was far from a radical. When, later in the year, the British ambassador to Germany introduced him to the Prince of Wales, who sought out the introduction, Twain enjoyed walking with him arm in arm. "I would like to be Emperor a while," he wrote in his notebook. He felt himself, at some moments, an emperor of sorts, and at home in the company of generals and kings.

Though the Berlin winter of 1891–92 had satisfactions, the cold weather and hectic social schedule were tiring. Doctors advised more medical spas and a warmer climate. Chilled after a speech in an overheated hall to a crowd of Americans, Twain felt his lungs become congested; his condition was serious for a day and a night. Livy wrote to Alice Day, "I was really frightened, then he lay and slept almost in a comatose state . . . so unnatural that it was frightful." He spent two weeks in bed, amusing himself with self-aware partial misinterpretations of the political news in the German newspapers. The reading kept him in "a state of excited ignorance," which he enjoyed.

Leaving the children with Susan and Katy Leary, the couple went for a week to a small village in the Harz Mountains. Twain was soon back in bed again, and doctors urged a warmer climate for both of them. Leaving the family in Berlin, they went to Mentone for March. "I leave Monday," he wrote in late February, "for the Riviera to get back my strength. . . . I am going to have a long holiday from writing, now." He had barely managed to complete the six articles for McClure. Impulsively, he translated a German children's story only to learn that it had already been copyrighted for American publication. He played in his mind with two new stories conceived as short novels, a comedic account of the absurd adventures of Siamese twins and a new adventure of Tom Sawyer and Huck Finn. His earlier nightmare of Tom and Huck as old mad failures gave way to a brighter revivification of his young characters, though the details of what was to become *Tom Sawyer Abroad* were still unclear to him. Exigency pressed, though. Livy vowed they would cut their expenses for the next year. But when she received fourteen thousand dollars from her Langdon investments, encouraged by Hall's optimistic reports, they reinvested it in the publishing firm.

Unfortunately, Mentone seemed even colder than Berlin. They spent March sitting around a stove, trying to keep warm, though Twain enjoyed the seclusion: "just us two & the ocean, which is booming at our door." They made plans for their European future, which seemed to extend indefinitely ahead, though a return to Hartford, which Livy and Susy deeply missed, was taken as a certainty. But when? Livy felt "pangs of homesick-ness" and longed to see "the dear old Hartford home and friends." But they had no plans to return "at present." Italy was much on their minds, for themselves and for Susan Crane, who had never been there. They arranged for the family to meet them in Rome in early April. They would stay in Italy till August, then go for the autumn to Nauheim, a German health spa that specialized in heart disease. But all were eager to return to Berlin, the girls especially. Jean missed the school she had been enrolled in and liked; the others missed their admired music teachers. Livy preferred Paris, for the girls to learn French. "Mr Clemens says if we had one more girl to be ed-ucated we would have to go to Africa to find the teacher she wants."

The family soon had a happy month in a hotel in Rome, near Trinita dei Monti, with a side trip to Naples. Twain saw again the Italy he had seen in 1867. They arrived in Florence in late April 1892 and had what were re-puted to be the best accommodations, but the hotel's ancient dirt and "gi-gantic fleas that threaten your life" depressed him. Florence did not. Florentine resources would provide a piano teacher for Clara and a voice teacher for Susy. The climate, they believed, would prove salubrious for Livy, though they significantly overrated the Florentine winter, which they assumed was dry and warm. In the first half of May Florence was gorgeous, and they were warmly welcomed by the English and American expatriate community. Williard Fiske, a forty-seven-year-old Dante expert from a dis-tinguished New England family, took them on a house-hunting day trip to Fiesole. Ultimately, Janet Duff Ross, the writer-daughter of well-known Victorian travel writer Lady Duff Gordon, found them the Villa Viviani, which they immediately liked. Halfway up the Settingnano hill, an elegant but unpretentious sixteenth-century building, large but manageable with a few servants, the neglected villa seemed perfect for them.

When they left Florence in mid-May, first for Venice, where they spent ten days comfortably at the luxurious Hotel Danieli, then Milan and Lake Como, where they stopped at Cadenabbia, "looking across to Bellagio & the snow-clad peaks," then northward through Switzerland to Germany and Bad Nauheim via Berlin, Fiske, their new American friend, had agreed to look after the formal details and to obtain furnishings. Mrs. Ross man-aged hiring servants and having the house scoured in preparation for their return in September. To Livy's disappointment, Clara successfully made her case to spend her winter in Berlin for music instruction. Susy would get a voice teacher in Florence. What Jean would do was unclear, though tutors were the likely resort. Livy would keep warm, at least to the extent that a Florentine winter would allow.

3.

Christmas 1892 they spent in the Villa Viviani, where they had arrived in September after a summer and fall of hopes raised and hopes dashed. "[We had] great times here last night," Twain wrote on Christmas day to Clara in Berlin. "Jean had a tree & it was a very nice one indeed . . . & the candles were startlingly bright." Actually, Livy was ill and Susy depressed. His own spirits were high, though only for the moment, not the result of holiday cheer (he had begun to resent Christmases, without either the energy or desire to celebrate them lavishly, as they had in Hartford) but mainly because he had just completed "Those Extraordinary Twins," which he had started in August at Bad Nauheim. He had made "better speed" than he had made "for a great many years" on that and on the manuscript of what would become *Tom Sawyer Abroad,* a draft of which was under way. His right hand functioned almost normally now, the rheumatic pain much less frequent.

He brooded, though, about money, and about Livy's health, and also about Susy's depression and her sense of uselessness in Florence. Clara's social improprieties in Berlin also concerned him. When Clara allowed herself to be the only woman in a room with a large number of men, her parents were disappointed and angry. And Livy missed her desperately. "Don't get used to being away from us my darling and have such a good time in Berlin that you feel content to stay away from us . . . I cannot bear to have you so far away from me and such a big piece of your life I am not sharing in." Livy burst into tears every time she read one of Clara's happy accounts of her cosmopolitan life. Susy, who envied Clara's escape, found an occasional companion in one of Janet Ross's nieces, Lina Duff Gordon. But, generally, as autumn turned winter gray, she felt trapped in an alien world. She spent much of her time alone, reading, with occasional forays into Florentine life, where she felt out of place, and regular voice lessons, which seemed unfruitful. "Reading all day can get tiresome. As for writing I never think of that nowadays," she wrote to Louise. "I should love to, but I can't now anyway, and I don't ever expect to be able to."

When they had arrived at Nauheim in June 1892, Twain felt heartened, almost exhilarated, by two doctors pronouncing Livy's condition "curable, & *easily* curable," he wrote to Clara. Soon the family was "in the clouds." "The bath physicians say positively that Livy has no heart disease & will soon be sound & well again. That was worth going to Europe to find out," he told Orion, experiencing an Orion-like elevation of mood that had him happily singing his favorite "humping jumping Jesus" lyric. Early in the summer, Susan Crane and Susy traveled in Switzerland for six weeks, Susan to continue on to America. Livy, who relapsed in the face of her sister's departure, did her therapeutic duty at Nauheim, and her husband enforced the doctor's peremptory order that she have absolute rest, which ruled out a quick trip to Brussels to see her brother. "Lord protect her from any more partings until she [has] weathered this disease & grown able to bear them!"

When, in September, they left for Florence, she developed such painful and ceaseless headaches that the family took two weeks to make the journey. Laudanum and analgesics helped, but she was little better by Christmas. Her sleep was regularly broken by a thirst from "excessive dryness of the mouth & lips" and a bad taste. Susy's Christmas was equally distressed, though from different sources. "I do think it is hard to be young. One is so horribly *alive* and has so much *temperament* one can't bear things well." She found it especially difficult to bear her father's constant scrutiny, his teasing and disapproval. Christmas festivities were muted by the general mood of the household, though Florentine winter weather was at its best, the sky sunny, roses blooming in the garden.

A visit in October 1892 from their friend the American writer Grace King enlivened them all, especially Susy, who thought Grace "her old fascinating self," the most brilliant "woman talker" she had ever heard. Livy, though, spent much of her time resting on a sofa, depleted by "one of her lasting dysenteric attacks." "It's heart-breaking to see her, so weak & wasting away." Twain wrote to Clara. He had his literary work to enliven him, though he also enjoyed King's visit. And he delighted in the striking views from the windows and terrace looking westward down to the rooftops of Florence, "the ever-changing aspects of Florence." In contrast, if only she were strong enough, and "had a little more money," Livy wrote to Clara, she would pick up Susy and fly to Berlin for Christmas.

Fred Hall had begun in spring 1892 to send five hundred dollars each month, supposedly the interest on Livy's loans and Twain's capital. In fact, behind the confusing bookkeeping, the money came from operating capital for ongoing expenses. For the firm to survive, expenses would either have to be cut or profits increased or more money borrowed. Cost-cutting was difficult. Even if the book trade were not in semi-depression, the firm had no reasonable hope of increasing sales. And who would lend C. L. Webster & Company money other than Twain? Twain, though, thought his publishing company was now on the right track. And news in May about a revival of plans to manufacture the Paige compositor had excited him. Chicago investors were negotiating a contract with Paige to finance a factory there. Still a believer, Twain once again did flamboyant mental calculations. He decided to sell a portion of his royalties for cash or, better, to sell an option on his royalties.

With Livy's blessing, he impulsively left from Nauheim for America in mid-June 1892 for a brief visit to protect and pursue his interests. When he arrived in New York, the news was dismal. The deal had apparently fallen through. The Chicago investors were also finding out how difficult a negotiator and partner Paige was. Then the news got a little better. So, with Fred Hall, he immediately took a train to Chicago. The brief Chicago visit revealed that nothing favorable was imminent. "Nothing *but* a Co can manufacture," he wrote in his notebook, "& P. is determined there never shall be one, except on his own terms—& they will never be granted." In Hartford for a short visit, he wisely resisted calling on Paige. In New York, he again pursued selling an option on his royalties to the same on-again off-again investor who had earlier been interested. That also fell through. By mid-July, he was back at Nauheim, the only pleasurable part of his trip the two swift, comfortable sea voyages. "I came away thoroughly disgusted with my flying visit," he wrote to a friend. His finances did not look in the least better by the end of the year, though it helped that checks arrived regularly from Hall and that he could anticipate royalties from novels-in-progress and some magazine fees for short pieces.

One, "The £1,000,000 Bank-Note," was a fitting rags-to-riches story, which he had had in mind since 1879, about an impoverished young American who makes use of a million-pound note given him as part of a bet between two wealthy London brothers, but which no one will cash. The young man, oddly named Henry Adams, has done nothing to deserve what he discovers is in effect a million-pound line of credit. When a society dazzled by the size of the bank note showers him with opportunities to make money, Adams need do little else than make good use of what others thrust on him. Soon he is living luxuriously among the London elite. At the home of the American ambassador, he and a friend of the ambassador's daughter fall instantly in love. Her name is Portia Langham, as much a representation of Olivia Langdon as Adams is a projection of Twain's fantasy of himself financially redeemed. "It's a noble & elegant tale," Twain wrote to the editor of *Century Magazine,* which published it in January 1893, an odd description by a man who had driven his family into comparative semipoverty by his financial speculations but for whom no savior had yet appeared. In the story, Adams marries Portia Langham; one of the wealthy brothers turns out to be her stepfather. It was a comforting fantasy that gave its title to a volume of disparate pieces published by Webster & Company in February 1893.

In the nonfictional world, the Clemens marriage, which had been so financially secure, now faced previously unimaginable insecurities. And, with the poor business climate in America deteriorating even more, it began to seem that a European exile might be theirs for a long time. Father and Clara seemed "quite weaned" from homesickness and American life, a worried Susy noticed. "Clara wants to live and die abroad and is urging mamma to let her prepare for the concert stage." And they all agreed that Livy's health had not "sufficiently improved to make it possible for her to go back." Jean seemed perfectly content. Susy wanted to go home. Lonely, desperately missing Louise, she felt out of place and with little to do. Only the mother and eldest daughter grieved for Hartford and their lost life.

Twain, now into a good work rhythm, began to value some of the advantages of their European world. Since he believed he had no choice anyway, he made the adjustment. When depressed, he had the revivifying capacity to invoke the pleasures of the moment, including his unflagging hope that his ship would come in. Fortunately, after New Year's Day 1893 and through the spring, the inhabitants of Villa Viviani had some better days. Susy's spirits rose, temporarily, in the first flush of Florentine cultural and social life. "I have seen Sara Bernhardt twice this week in *Adrienne Lecouvreur* and *La Tosca* . . . and met the great Salvini at dinner. . . . Florence is sweet after all." At one of the occasional balls to which she was invited, Susy was smitten by a suave, charismatic Italian whose hot and cold advances baffled her until she discovered he was married. By late winter,

Livy had a few good days, though much of the time, following doctor's or-der, she remained supine. One afternoon a week she allowed herself the luxury of being at home to visitors.

Soon the family was on a drop-in basis with the Rosses at Villa Castag-nola, renamed Villa Ross. Boccaccio had supposedly written *The De-cameron* there. Often Twain would take a shortcut downhill through the fields and across the Florence-Settignano road. Always invited when the Rosses had interesting guests, Susy and her father happily went to dine when Sir Henry Layard, the British archaeologist of Ninevah fame, visited in mid-March 1893. "Mrs. Clemens, one of the most charming and gentle of people, was already in very bad health," Mrs. Ross later remembered, "and her husband's devotion, and almost womanly tenderness to her, was very touching. One evening we persuaded him to sing some of the real ne-gro songs; it was a revelation. Without much voice and with little or no knowledge of music . . . he moved us all in a wonderful way." Still, there were many moments when Twain was alone, sometimes by choice at his writing table, or by default. "It is lonesome," he wrote to Clara one night early in February, "& I turn to you for company. Susy has gone downtown to a ball . . . & Jean & Mamma are gone to bed. There's nothing to think about, nothing to talk about, nothing to write about—so there is nothing for you & me to do but look at each other across Germany & the interven-ing lands & be silently sociable."

What sustained him was his writing. The novel he had been at work on since spring and summer 1892, "Those Extraordinary Twins," had been go-ing through various changes. Frenzied writing sessions in November and December 1892 transformed the story. A second narrative, barely con-nected to the first and comprising a book equal in length, was simply added on. What had been a comic novel focusing on the predicament of Siamese twins now also contained a blistering attack on the theory and practice of racial superiority in the pre–Civil War South. Renamed *Pudd'nhead Wilson*, it returned Twain, with a vengeance, to the world of his childhood. Unlike *Huckleberry Finn*, it highlights irony rather than humor, a novel about a boy in the process of developing a humane conscience, a novel of ideas about the naturalness of human depravity. The Mississippi River, still flowing downstream, is unredeemed by any touch of innocence or love. "Down-river" is different only in quantity, not kind, from upriver life, and though the novel ends with the restoration of justice for the characters and the community, the tone and taste of even that are metallic to the tongue.

Though the setting evokes much of the steamboat Americana of a small Mississippi River town, it both is and is not Hannibal. Dawson's Landing, also on "the Missouri side" of the river, is "half a day's journey, per steamboat, below," not *above,* St. Louis. Like the actual Hannibal, though not like the partly whitewashed town of *Tom Sawyer* and *Huckleberry Finn,* it is "a slave-holding town, with a rich slave-worked grain and pork country back of it," in which the brutalities of slavery are a prominent part of everyday life. Aphorisms that he had been writing for years, and some new ones, he placed as prefaces to the chapters. Many were sardonic, such as "All say 'How hard it is that we have to die'—a strange complaint to come from the mouths of people who have had to live"; others were witty, even funny, though usually with a touch of revelatory frankness, such as "When angry, count four; when very angry, swear." In late winter 1893, he sent the manuscript, to which he had added an irrelevant foreword, to New York to be typed. He hoped that a typewritten version would give him a better opportunity to revise it successfully.

As soon as it was off his hands, he turned to other books in progress. In 1892 he had decided to write a life of Joan of Arc, though he may not have started the writing until early 1893. "The priests of Church got fat things out of the enemies of France by stealing her & burning her, perhaps they can turn a neat political penny with France, now, by insulting soiling her sacred memory with the tardy gift of a brass halo," he wrote in his notebook in December 1892. He had in mind creating a golden halo for Joan. *Tom Sawyer Abroad* needed only polishing. Accidentally afloat in a technologically miraculous balloon, Tom, Huck, and Jim sail eastward from St. Louis to Africa, where they have various adventures, some of which are recounted with interest and verve. Huck is the narrator, though he engages with few of the issues of his earlier embodiment, with the exception of one fine passage about Jim as a human being. The mad inventor has a touch of James Paige. Tom is the irrepressible storyteller intent on making reality cohere to his imagination, Huck the skeptic who notes that Tom "got all that notion out of Walter Scott's book, which he was always reading." When the balloon reaches Africa, "Jim's eyes bugged out, and he began to stare down with no end of interest, because that was where his originals come from." To an Americanized black man, Africa is as exotic and foreign as it is to his white companions.

In the end, the balloon's occupants and the narrative have nowhere to go but home. Unlike *Huckleberry Finn, Tom Sawyer Abroad* is genuinely a boy's book. Twain's childhood reading of *Arabian Nights* contributed some of its exotic touches. Jules Verne's *Five Weeks in a Balloon,* the 1869 publication of which had prevented Twain's completion of a sketch about a balloon flight around the world, was a model. He also may have remembered Orion's science-fiction manuscript imitating a popular Verne novel. Still, without himself making much of a literary case for it, *Tom Sawyer Abroad* engaged Twain in the writing. He had high hopes for its financial success.

Soon after Susy's twenty-first birthday in March 1893, Twain sailed from Genoa for New York into "the usual brilliant sunshine, the usual soft summer weather." His business affairs had gone from bad to worse. On his most recent birthday he had remarked, "57 yrs. old. I wish it were either 17 or 97." Though he could not know it, this was to be the first of three round-trip crossings in the next twelve months, the down payment on eight in a three-and-a-half-year period. "People wonder why I go so much," he was to say to an American audience in 1895. "Well," he joked, "I go partly for my health, partly to familiarize myself with the road." On Susy's birthday he described his life in a letter to Susan Crane, using a metaphor that he now frequently deployed to express his sense of what had happened to him. "I dreamed I was born, & grew up, & was a pilot on the Mississippi, & a miner & journalist in Nevada, & a pilgrim in the Quaker City, & had a wife & children & went to live in a Villa out of Florence—& this dream goes on & on and on, & sometimes seems so real that I almost believe it is real. I wonder if it is? But there is no way to tell; for if one applied tests, *they* would be part of the dream, too, & so would simply aid the deceit. I wish I knew whether it is a dream or real."

In his waking life, he had many moments in which he indeed wished that life was a dream from which he would awaken to be financially secure, redeemed from exile, and at home again. His actual dreams, many of them recurrent nightmares, fascinated and frightened him, including his obsessive vision of himself as a steamboat pilot steering his boat to disaster. In early March he had "the dream again—no noticeable difference in the details." A complementary narrative, written soon before his departure for

America, "Extracts from Adam's Diary," expressed his worry about Livy's health. It is the monologue of a reluctant Adam who at first does not want to share his world with Eve and who, grudgingly, forfeits his independence, an innocent who has no name for the new creature made from his rib, and who is resentfully bewildered about events over which he has no control. Years later, Adam concludes, "I see that I was mistaken about Eve in the beginning; it is better to live outside the Garden with her than inside it without her. At first I thought she talked too much; but now I should be sorry to have that voice pass out of my life. Blessed be the chestnut that brought us near together and taught me to know the goodness of her heart and the sweetness of her spirit!"

With Twain's ship a few days short of landfall, the ocean turned rough, a suitable prelude to his six-week visit. Since the Chicago financiers had become active again, probably in response to signals from Paige that this time he would be cooperative, Twain once again wanted to encourage the formation of the venture. He also wanted to option or sell a portion of his royalties for much-needed cash. Perhaps the Chicago investors might like to purchase an option as an expression of their confidence in the compositor? And if not, then perhaps a New York investor? In the mid-1880s Webster had complained that Twain was drawing money from the publishing company to support the typesetter. Now, ironically, Twain hoped to get money from his typesetter royalties to provide support to Webster & Company, which was gasping for cash. "My dear darling child," Livy responded to one of his self-blaming, semi-despairing letters from New York, "you *must not* blame yourself as you do. I love you to death, and I would rather have you for mine than all the other husbands in the world and you take as good care of me as any one could do." Apparently recalling Hall's comment of March 1892 that it might be necessary "to continue the $15,000 bank loan another 6 or 8 months or a year," Twain was unhappily surprised that the debt was now forty-five thousand dollars. Additional bank credit was unavailable. Soon he was huddling with his partner about their business problems, and about *Pudd'nhead Wilson*. He agreed that it needed substantial revision.

New York literary circles welcomed him, though business concerns preoccupied most of his time. He dined with Howells, whom he had not seen in two years; Mary Mapes Dodge, soon to publish *Tom Sawyer Abroad* in *St. Nicholas Magazine*; and Rudyard Kipling, now living in Vermont with his American wife. He had dinner with Andrew Carnegie, whom he urged Hall to approach as a possible investor or even purchaser of Webster & Company. A few days later, he lunched at the Carnegie residence, where his charm made him welcome but his pitch got nowhere. Carnegie knew better. "Put all your eggs in one basket," he advised Twain, *"and watch that basket."* Charles Warren Stoddard joined him for a lunch hosted by Kipling. Another night he dined with Clarence Rice, a distinguished ear, nose, and throat specialist, physician to rich and famous New Yorkers, especially in the entertainment world. Having come to America for typesetter business, he pursued it first in New York, at the offices of the Connecticut Company, one of Paige's entities. The Company claimed that fifty machines were "well along in building" and that one would be finished July 1. But in fact, since the present factory's capacity was only one machine a day, a new factory to turn out five a day *would* be built "when location decided on."

The Chicago trip, accompanied by Hall, turned out to be worse than fruitless. Sick on arrival in mid-April 1893, he took to his hotel bed, wracked by the flu. By the time Twain was on his feet again, there was no reason to stay in Chicago. Actually, there had been no reason to come other than his impulsiveness and his desire to see for himself whatever there was to see, which turned out to be nothing. The Chicago investors had no interest in optioning his royalties. They were indeed serious about financing the Paige compositor, but on reasonable terms. And it was not even certain that there existed *one* demonstration machine that could be trusted to a sustained test. Paige himself, in Chicago to negotiate terms, visited Twain twice at his hotel room. When Twain asked him if how he had treated him troubled his conscience, Paige played the misunderstood victim. "He said it broke his heart when I left him & the machine to fight along the best way they could." He "shed even more tears than usual." An extraordinary talker himself, Twain could not help appreciating Paige's verbal brilliance and the contradictions of his character. "He could persuade a fish to come out & take a walk with him. When he is present I always believe him—I cannot help it. . . . He is the most daring & majestic liar," and "absolutely frank in his confessions of misconduct."

Disappointed that he was not well enough to visit the Chicago world's fair, he stayed eleven days in bed with what the doctor thought was pneumonia. When he returned to New York, he was still so sick that he was unable to see a "grand naval parade" in the harbor. After a short time at a hotel, he accepted Dr. Rice's invitation to convalesce at his home on Irving Place. The Rices came and delivered him to a comfortable bed. He had less than hopeful news for Livy, who now worried more about his illness than anything else, though he was well enough by the beginning of May 1893 to visit Elmira. "All the family here are bewitchingly lovely & lovable," he wrote Livy, whose heart ached with homesickness at these words. As he "mounted the hill" at Quarry Farm "& approached the arbor on the summit," he wrote to Susy, he saw that the children's playhouse had a new roof and that his octagonal study was "just as it always was." "[It is] as lovely & cozy & full of charming color & comfort as heaven. I wish you were all here, to stay a year. The city lies steeped in Sunday peace & serenity & sunshine down yonder, & the distant hills & the mottled skies are just as they used to be—they have nothing to say of the familiar voices that have fallen silent & the lives that have vanished & become a dream. . . . We have had dinner & long talk about all of us coming here, Mamma & I to have reposeful times in the autumn & winter seclusion & you girls to have gay times down town . . . & in skirmishes in NY & Hartford—God grant that these things may be."

His words probably gave more pain than solace. "My trip was merely wasted time," he wrote from Villa Viviani to William Phelps at the end of May 1893. "I was sick abed with grip almost the whole time, got no chance to do what I went to do, & had to hurry out of the country to keep from getting nailed to my bed permanently. I'm afraid to go again." Yet Livy reported to a Hartford friend, "Mr C. is much more desirous of getting back than he was before this last trip. . . . [But] I think we must stay away a little longer." In fact, they all accepted that it would be much longer. Money was tighter than ever. "We are at heavy expense, now, in breaking up housekeeping. . . . We are skimming along like paupers, & a day can embarrass us," he wrote to Fred Hall. He was particularly worried about the Mt. Morris Bank debt. Any Paige compositor income, he had realized, was "a long long ways off": "I am terribly tried of business. I am by nature & disposition unfitted for it & I want to get out of it."

Despite his effort and investment, including Livy's much-shrunken resources, he calculated that Webster & Company's liabilities exceeded assets by $100,000, not including the $170,000 "the firm owed Livy and him. He had a proposition to make. "Will Harper, or Appleton, or Putnam give me $200,000 for those debts and my two-thirds interest in the

firm? . . . I don't want much money. I only want first-class notes—
$200,000 worth of them at 6 percent, payable *monthly*. . . . Such a deal
would make it easy for a big firm to put in a big cash capital & jump the
[*Library of American Literature*] up to an enormous prosperity. Then your
one-third would be worth a fortune." It was an unrealizable fantasy.
Neither Hall nor Twain were in a position to help the other, or to solve
their mutual problem. And other issues aside, as Hall pointed out to Twain
in June, why would any firm pay anything at all for Webster & Company?
As if matters weren't dismal enough, the business climate soon turned
abysmally worse. The stock market crash later that month made it difficult
for even more debt-worthy businesses to raise money through the normal
channels. For Webster & Company, it was impossible.

As they had planned, the Clemenses said good-bye to their Florence
friends with a large reception at the start of June 1893. When it "went off
well," they felt they could "leave Florence with a clear social-conscience."
They left the Villa Viviani, first to go to Munich to consult a heart specialist, who recommended the health spa at Krankenheil. A quick visit in
search of rooms revealed it to be "the most unattractive spot in Europe."
The doctor, though, insisted. Twain was soon able to report the incredible
news: "It is just decided at last, by the highest expert authority in Europe,
that Mrs. Clemens has nothing the matter with her that cannot be cured.
This is a relief, after two years of the other opinion. The uplift is not to be
described. Mrs. C. is now making good & steady progress. . . . Two American & three European doctors [had told us that] she had incurable heart
disease." Who was to be believed? Clara joined them from Berlin. Livy had
determined that Paris was to be the family's winter destination. At breakfast
in late July 1893, thirteen-year-old Jean burst into tears. It was her birthday
and she was "deadly homesick." Susy, who had been sent on to France, was
ordered by her teacher to the baths at Franzenbad, to strengthen herself for
voice lessons. In a decision made just ten days before departure from
Krankenheil, Twain suddenly determined that he was once again needed in
New York. Webster & Company was about to go under.

So too was Twain, or at least it seemed to him that he was so close to
the financial abyss that to remain at such a distance from the scene of his
fate was simply impossible. His nerves could not bear it. "I feel panicky,"
he wrote to Hall early in July 1893. "I have never felt so desperate in my
life—& good reason, for I haven't got a penny to my name, & Mrs.

Clemens hasn't enough laid up with Langdon to keep us two months." He had reason to worry that soon he would not be able to pay his ordinary bills, let alone live in a city as expensive as Livy soon realized Paris to be. Whatever their feelings about the Hartford house, the falling real estate market would not allow them to realize much of its previous value. Selling at any reasonable price would be difficult.

During July and August, Twain got the best relief he could at his writing desk, where he plunged into revising *Pudd'nhead Wilson*. Livy and Fred Hall had given him the same advice: make one unified book by eliminating most of the original narrative. The full-length treatment of the twins he put entirely aside. He now centered the story on "the murder & the trial." Even Livy, "the most difficult of critics," approved of the new version. "Formerly she would not consent that it be published either before or after my death." What had begun as a discarded short story now succeeded as a novel. "This time it suits me. One story is gutted-out, the other one properly finished up & concentrated, & the bulk reduced to 58,000 words." What would *Cosmopolitan,* the magazine with the deepest pockets, though one that Livy thought too common for her husband to publish in, pay for serial rights? He urged Hall to do his best for him. "I do not sleep, these nights, for visions of the poor-house."

In the next weeks, as liquidity plummeted, the financial markets panicked—the start of a worldwide depression. Businesses collapsed into bankruptcy, particularly debt-bloated railroads, and more than six hundred banks failed. Massive accounting fraud and fraudulent stock schemes, previously a concealed crack, now opened into a visible chasm. Much of the gilt peeled off the Gilded Age. For the remainder of his life Twain was to live in an economic climate considerably different from that of his post–Civil War prosperity. And the labor-management conflicts of the 1880s had already produced widespread working-class bitterness. After the June 1893 stock market collapse, longstanding unemployment and low wages were followed by massive layoffs, then further wage depression. Labor agitation became more radical. The voice of the newly formed Populist Party demanded that corporations be reined in, railroads be nationalized, a graduated income tax be instituted, senators be elected by popular vote, and trade unions be protected from union-bashing. Washington, though, overwhelmingly favored business, and many businesses were reeling. Webster & Company was a mere paper cut in a body politic undergoing major bleeding. To its owners, though, the consequences of its likely failure seemed no less cataclysmic than the collapse of Goliaths like the Erie and the Northern Pacific railroads. With close to $200,000 in liabilities and $50,000 in assets, Twain's share had not the slightest hope of a buyer. "I am not made for business," he repeated to Hall; "the worry of it makes me old, & robs life of its zest. I wish you were able to buy me out yourself." Hall knew better. And he soon made Twain squirm with the claim that, by selling out to anyone, he would damage any chance Hall had of keeping the firm afloat and saving his own interest.

On shipboard, Twain tried to distract himself by playing horseshoes with Clara, but he inevitably worried about what would confront him on arrival. Hall welcomed him to New York by confirming that there was no cash on hand and banks were not lending money; on the contrary, they were declining to refinance loans that came due. Webster's debt to Mt. Morris Bank was a frightening liability. Still, Twain preferred "to be on this side in the midst of the trouble, instead of on the other, impotent & walking the floor." Fortunately, their notes were not imminently up for renewal. But unless he could quickly raise eight thousand dollars to satisfy other pressing creditors, Webster & Company would be dead. While her father remained in the city, Clara was dispatched to Elmira to reacquaint herself with her Langdon cousins and benefit from the cooler country weather. Having recently spent more time with her than ever before, her father had developed an increased fondness and respect for his daughter's character. Later in the month she sang at a concert, the first public exhibition of her musical talents.

Twain, mournfully and anxiously, took the train to Hartford, where he spent a full day toward the middle of September consulting with two of his billiard-playing businessmen friends about borrowing money. At the end of the day he recognized that Hartford would not be forthcoming. "Money can not be had, at any rate of interest whatever, or upon any sort of security, or by anybody." Asking his Hartford friends had been a great humiliation; it was an even greater humiliation to have been turned down. He did have, though, one professional ace in the hole, a card that he had thought he would never have to play again. "Well, when the worst comes to the worst I can go to India & Australia & lecture. I can clear off these debts easily in that way." But he abhorred the notion. "If I must, I must—but nothing short of absolute necessity will drive me." Still, he assured Livy, "I don't feel uncheerful, & you mustn't, my darling." It was a brave show, and partly sincere.

Companionship offered some solace, particularly that of Dr. Clarence Rice, suitable and eager for Twain's company. With his family on summer holiday, the two went "bachelorizing," the well-known doctor and the famous writer handsome figures at New York theaters and restaurants. Twain was regularly recognized, even on the street. One night they spent hours watching billiards experts at play, other nights they played themselves. Twain was fascinated by the spectacle of a boxing match. Despite his bad cough and head cold, they were "having good sociable bachelor times together," he wrote to Clara. The violent coughing, though, produced a rupture for which Charley Langdon recommended a truss. Twain seems to have taken his brother-in-law's advice even though Dr. Rice disagreed, and he wore one for the rest of his life. By the end of the year, when the cough persisted with "little or no relief from medicines," Twain went to see a Madison Avenue doctor for a "mind cure." "He sat with his face to the wall & I walked the floor for ½ an hour." That midnight he remarked, "Don't know if he is the reason, but I haven't coughed since." The effect of the pre-Freudian therapy did not hold. Each morning Twain was up at seven A.M., frantically pursuing every conceivable scheme to raise money. From Hartford, when financial "ruin seemed inevitable," he asked Susan Crane to send him money, if she could. He could not afford, he told her, to have any shame now. In Elmira, Susan and Ida Langdon Twain's sisters-in-law, immediately traded securities for negotiable bonds sufficient to raise five thousand dollars.

To his relief, in mid-September, before Susan Crane had actually sent the money, he no longer needed it. Clarence Rice introduced or reintroduced Twain to oil executive Henry Huttleston Rogers, whom they ran into accidentally in a hotel lobby. Twain remarked to Clara that he had first gotten "acquainted with him on a yacht two years ago." His memory may have been faulty, however, for in 1892, a little over a year before, Twain referred in his notebook to meeting the "President of the Standard Oil Company & a hell of a fellow all around." This was on the SS *Lahu* in heavy seas, and a description more likely to fit Rogers than anyone else. Twain could have believed he had met the president of Standard Oil rather than a vice president, which Rogers was. Alternating graceful charm and steely aggressiveness, Rogers was a notorious tycoon in an age of well-publicized robber barons. One of the triumverate that ran Standard Oil, he had risen from Pennsylvania old-field wildcatter to one of America's wealthiest men. Unlike Rockefeller, he regularly kept his eye on the stock market and owned large blocks of shares in related industries. A gifted entrepreneur, he had the business morals of his environment, meaning that nothing had or could stop him. Four years younger than Twain, at the age of fifty-four he was an embodiment of Gilded Age success, respected and envied by much of the world.

A charming companion, Rogers knew how to negotiate, compromise, and seduce, both in boardrooms and dining rooms. His personal generosity made him a valuable friend and supporter. His charities were widespread, especially in his hometown of Fairfield, Massachusetts. His low-key bonhomie was infectious, his sense of humor dryly bawdy, his love of hearty male companionship as great as Twain's—for dining, jokes, billiards, cards, off-color stories, humorous teasing, and yachting excursions. A man who also valued culture, he read when he could, and one of his literary idols was Mark Twain. Made aware of Twain's problem by Dr. Rice, Rogers instantly offered to help. He invited Twain to meet him that afternoon at his office at the Standard Oil building. Twain left with a check for four thousand dollars to pay the pressing creditors, probably understood between them as an interim investment in Webster & Company or a loan to keep it solvent while Rogers looked into the possibility of further investments or some disposition of the firm that would return the cash advance.

Twain's prayer, so to speak, had been answered by the kind of angel he had believed in and could believe in, one who came in a form like himself, though the richer self he had always hoped to be. At an unspoken level, Twain and Rogers knew this loan was a personal statement of support for a man Rogers admired and wanted to know better. "We were strangers when we met, and friends when we parted half an hour afterward," Twain later wrote. That night, "entirely worn out mentally & bodily," Twain had enough energy left before falling asleep to write Clara, "The best new acquaintance I've ever seen has helped us over Monday's bridge." It was a return of the good luck that he had come to think had deserted him.

4.

What had been anticipated as a home visit of no more than a few months began to appear, by October 1893, likely to extend to at least the end of the year, perhaps longer. Much as he missed Livy, Twain now had hope that, with Rogers's help, he might not only keep Webster & Company alive but see his long-awaited Paige royalties. "There's no telling when we are going to leave America," he told Clara. "I see no early prospect." His publishing firm was stable for the time being. Rogers' money had stayed creditors, and the Mt. Morris loan was not up for renewal. Rogers also had arranged to have the incubus of *The Library of American Literature* lifted off Webster & Company's chest. His wealthy Chicago son-in-law, William Benjamin, a collector of books and manuscripts, a part-time publisher and a partner in a rare book firm, bought it for fifty thousand dollars, to be paid in installments. The money gave Webster & Company a little breathing room, and by late October Twain was free to concentrate on what could be made of or, if it came to that, salvaged from the Paige compositor.

Enjoying relative freedom from scrutiny, Clara wanted to stay in America, but Livy refused to allow it. "No, it would not be cheaper for me to leave you in America, there would be too much expense of longing for you to make it profitable." Clara reluctantly sailed at the end of October, returning via Berlin, a roundabout route she insisted on that angered her parents, concerned that she was not paying attention to proper escorts and propriety. Depressed, Susy admired her sister's outgoing attitude and courage. "I would rather be locked up in a box *alone* for the rest of my life than gather up courage to go out into the world and enjoy myself. And so you see as I admire you and love you and am infinitely interested in you without being afraid of you—you're just everything in the world to me! Oh I *have* such a shuddering horror of being found fault with and criticised and yet I manage to do more things that merit criticism in a week than others do in a year." Neither parent realized how much she felt they found fault with her. Livy of course chafed at her husband's extended absence, partly because of the difficulty an entirely feminine household encountered in Parisian life. Mainly, though, she just missed him. His rationale for remaining had to be at least partially interpreted as self-indulgence, if only because he occasionally expressed what a good time he was having. By late in the year, newspapers were referring to him as "the Belle of New York."

Lonely at Rice's house when the doctor was away, Twain had, by the end of September 1893, ensconced himself in a "deliciously quiet," handsomely carpeted, elegantly furnished huge room at the top of The Players Club, "with an open fireplace, two mirrors, six electric lights, seven gas burners, and 24 pictures on the wall." It had the innovative advantage of an electric light above his pillow. The cost was three dollars a day and less than a dollar for three meals, though he almost always lunched and dined on the town. In November he was guest of honor at a Lotos Club dinner celebrating the inauguration of its new home on Fifth Avenue, near 45th Street. A few days later he was the celebrity among celebrities at a "beautiful & impressive" memorial service at Madison Square Garden for Edwin Booth, the actor most instrumental in the founding of The Players. "All of the distinction of New York was massed in that place," he wrote Livy. "I seemed to be personally acquainted with half of the people there." The theatrical toast of the New York fall season, the actor and impresario Henry Irving had given him a free perpetual pass to all his theaters, which he now made use of, and Irving and his touring manager, Bram Stoker, his *Dracula* four years off, joined a number of Twain's friends as small investors in the Paige compositor. With Howells, Twain went to see Irving perform and attended a dinner party for Irving and Ellen Terry. A longer Hartford visit with Clara in October seemed, he felt, to have given him back his youth again. He particularly enjoyed seeing the Twichells. Charley Warner came to New York frequently now, and Twain once again appreciated what good company he was. Livy might have had mixed feelings as she read his words. If her generosity of spirit prevented her from being resentful, she must indeed have felt ordinary human envy. If only the whole family had come to New York, he exclaimed to Livy, as if that had been something he had raised in August. But he had not.

In November, from his perch at The Players, he looked out onto Gramercy Park's unseasonable May-like greenery. "What magnificent weather it is," he told Livy, who complained of bitter Parisian cold, "& we have had weeks of it. Cool bracing air that makes you feel fine and vigorous, & such flooding sunshine! It's the boss climate of the world." The city had once seemed unfriendly, even boorish. Now its eagerness to celebrate him made him feel at home, his well-being only marginally undermined by the absence of his family. Except for his cough, he felt healthy, despite an occasional newspaper story claiming he was seriously ill. "Don't you be troubled a bit about my health. I am in splendid condition," he assured Livy. "I take good care of myself. I wear gum shoes in wet weather, & a chamois skin vest next my hide when I put on my swallow-tail." He felt almost inexhaustibly energetic. "I play billiards till 3 in the morning," he boasted to Susy, "& have got more health & vigor than I know what to do with." In late November, at a dinner in his honor, a high-level American diplomat told him that "he had seen three little parcels of books which had made a strong impression on his memory; one was in the private parlor of the President of the Chilean Republic, one was on Bismarck's private writing-desk, & the third was in the boudoir" of the Empress Eugenie. Each contained copies of *Tom Sawyer* and *Huckleberry Finn*.

His general well-being, though, was qualified by his desire to return to his writing desk. "I must get to work or my spirits will go down," he told Livy. "Many a time I think of Joan of Arc." He regretted that he had not brought the manuscript with him. "I am going to resume work on my great big *anonymous* romance in which I have aforetime written 93,000 words," he insisted, "& that is no less than a *third* of the book." He began tinkering again with "Captain Stormfield's Visit to Heaven," which he delighted in recounting at dinner tables to transfixed attention. He told Orion, whose monthly stipend he had been forced to halve, that he had just "mapped out a long novel . . . & will bury myself in it to-morrow & be heard of no more & answer no letters till the back of it is broken, some weeks hence. I shall prodigiously enjoy writing it." When Livy complained of sleeplessness, he responded that he was sleeping well, "though the people in my story," tentatively called "Tom Sawyer's Mystery," "go galloping through it most of the time, raising the devil."

His major literary effort was seeing *Pudd'nhead Wilson* through serial publication. When he discovered that the esteemed *Century* copyeditor had made unauthorized changes, he was apoplectic. "I said I didn't care if he was an Archangel imported from Heaven, he couldn't puke his ignorant impudence over my punctuation." He had for a long time held a brief against meddlesome proofreaders. He now inserted into *Pudd'nhead Wilson's Calendar,* "God made idiots. This was for practice. Then he made proof-readers." And the *Century* was reluctant, as usual, to pay what Twain felt appropriate. "I do not venture to suggest prices any more," an annoyed Twain told Gilder, "because on the three occasions when I made the attempt the editors were shocked. They gave me to understand that I was degrading my art to a trade." The *Century,* under pressure, paid him $6,500. When *Pudd'nhead Wilson* began publication in December 1893, to continue until June, compliments came thick and fast from New York friends like Laurence Hutton and Brander Matthews. By mid-January 1894, the

praise swelled into a gratifying chorus. Spring publication in England produced mostly laudatory reviews of this "vigorous indictment of the old
social order of the South." Fred Hall thought *Pudd'nhead* "clearly & powerfully drawn." "[He] would live & his take his place as one of the great creations of American fiction. Isn't that pleasant," Twain exclaimed, "—&
unexpected! For I never have thought of Pudd'nhead as a *character*, but
only as a piece of machinery." He expected Webster & Company to publish the American edition in the fall.

His friendship with Rogers also enhanced his enjoyment of the city. He
was welcome, both socially and at Rogers' eleventh-floor Standard Oil office on lower Broadway, where Rogers' much-valued executive secretary,
Katherine Harrison, made him comfortable whether Rogers was there or
not. Reclining on a sofa between the back of Rogers' desk and the windows
commanding the harbor, he amused himself by reading, watching Rogers
at work, and looking out at the magnificent view, which included the recently erected Statue of Liberty. Upstairs, in the executive dining room, he
dined with men of power, the arrangement, he boasted, providing him with
privileges in the best club in town, infinitely better than the Lotos Club or
The Players.

And Rogers' involvement with the Paige compositor suddenly made
Twain a much more formidable factor. Early in November 1893, Rogers
went to Chicago to examine the machine and to have it evaluated by his
expert, authorized to do so on Twain's behalf. At the machine shop, where
a typesetter was being prepared for trial, Rogers soon had a good grasp of
the machine's problems. He also had a clear sense of the difficulty of inte-
grating the Chicago interests and the Connecticut interests, to both of
which Paige had sold rights in the typesetter and both of which he prevented from moving ahead by postponing final agreements for manufacture. To make Twain's royalties profitable, Paige, the Chicago investors,
and the Connecticut Company would have to be contractually reconciled
into a new company; the Chicago investors and Paige would have to reac-
knowledge Twain's royalty rights by entering into a revised agreement with
him; and the typesetter would need to be sold in large numbers. Rogers began secret discussions to hammer out exact terms with the Chicago
groups, who came to New York in early December and who wanted Twain
to accept stock in exchange for his royalty rights. "Mr. Rogers represented
the capitalists," he told Livy, "who are expecting to take hold, & I repre-

sented my royalties." Secrecy was imperative. "If Paige finds out he will get so extravagant in his demands that it will be impossible to deal with him."

By mid-December 1893 all but a few minor details had been resolved. The terms provided Twain with the right "to demand & receive any time during 3 years, $240,000 cash, or $500,000 stock," or keep his royalties, which he would do. The Chicago investors acceded to such favorable terms at least partly because Rogers had agreed to become an investor, for which Twain received a commission of 750 shares, an outright gift from Rogers since the only reason he invested was to help Twain. "We furnish $120,000 cash," Twain remarked, with some self-indulgence in regard to the pronoun. Rogers and Twain were to share equally in the profits from the revised agreement, in effect now partners. It looked very promising, he wrote to Livy, who wanted to come as soon as possible to New York. Paris, without her husband, was worse than useless. It was cold, depressing, and unfriendly. "If you should come home and [Paige] should *not* sign!" he responded. "And don't you see? *When* he signs you are independent from that moment & may do whatever you please. . . . But surely you are receiving letters by this time which show you that . . . we [are] pointed straight toward success, as far as in us lay to make success. . . . I am only in Hell when I think for a moment of Paige's not signing—but that is a thing I seldom think of."

Four days before Christmas 1893, the partners sped toward Chicago, discussing general strategy in considerable comfort. The Pennsylvania Railroad president had provided his private car, handsomely stocked with food, whiskey, and cigars for his eminent guests. Twain hoped that this Chicago visit would allow him to cable to his family in Paris news that would make them "all jump with jubilation." Still, his low opinion of Paige's character kept him wary. Before negotiations began, Rogers instructed Twain on specific strategy, the execution of which was to be left in Rogers' hands. At a sumptuous apartment on Michigan Avenue they met the Chicago company principals to prepare for the crucial negotiation with Paige's lawyer, which was to take place that night. As the Chicago people had feared, Paige rejected Rogers' terms. "I may as well be frank with you, gentlemen," Paige's lawyer said. "Mr. Paige will never concede *one* of these things. Here is a proposed Company of $5,000,000. Mr. Paige has consented to be reduced to a fifth interest. That seems to me to be concession enough."

Twain alerted Rogers to Paige's usual pattern. "Whenever I have found a capitalist, he has immediately gone to work underhand to persuade that capitalist to withdraw until he (Paige) could get me and others out of the way, then he would give said capitalist better terms & the two would have the whole of the swag." Twain and Rogers accurately surmised that Paige wanted to split the Chicago from the Connecticut investors and make new arrangements with the Chicago people alone. The next day, ready to depart, they waited to learn whether or not Paige had accepted. After a leisurely breakfast, they prepared to make their train. "The absence of a message meant what was to be expected," Twain wrote to Livy. "Paige was holding out & wouldn't sign." Rogers arranged one last meeting. "At the end of an hour Paige had retired from position after position until he had conceded every detail but one; & there he took his stand. It was the matter of stipend. He was offered $5,000 a year till his dividends should aggregate $100,000 in three successive years. He said he could not *live* on it. That his *immediate* debts, for which he was being daily hounded, aggregated more than $5,000 . . . he could not accept those terms, & it would be useless to discuss the matter further." His lawyer tried to persuade him otherwise. Paige insisted he would sue the Connecticut Company and have their contract annulled. "That ended the Chicago campaign. There was nothing overlooked or left undone that *could* have been done, except the raising of Paige's stipend to his fancy figure of $3,000 a month—& we were all opposed to that."

Rogers and Twain, though, were convinced that Paige would have to come around. Otherwise he would get nothing, since it was obvious, to Twain's satisfaction, that his hated partner and adversary was next to impoverished. "I am full of pity & compassion for him," he told Livy, "& it is sincere. If he were drowning I would throw him an anvil." Soon after Christmas, Twain received "the great news"—Paige was ready to sign. The lawyers began organizing the restructuring. Twain stayed in New York. "So long as the contract is not signed in Chicago," he explained to Livy, "I should die at sea if I started. Upon that contract depends our very bread & meat"—as if he had no earning power as a writer. While he waited, "it rain[ed] invitations," though he went only to private dinners. The invitation he never declined was to Rogers' home, where Mrs. Rogers, an invalid, always remembered to have a glass of milk by Twain's place at dinner. With Rogers, he visited Fairhaven, the site of Rogers' country house and his benefactions to his boyhood hometown. Twain happily said a few words at the dedication of a new town hall and post office Rogers had funded. With Dr. Rice he took long midnight walks, usually after luxuriously dining out, the doctor's wit and laughter keeping him amused. He played billiards regularly with Rice and Rogers, who had a billiards table at home.

Impatient, fatigued, and wracked with a cough for which Rogers gave him homeopathic powders, he nervously anticipated a favorable resolution. Then, he told Livy, he would bid " 'Farewell—a long farewell—to *business*! I will *never* touch it again!' I will live in literature, I will wallow in it . . . I will swim in ink. Joan of Arc—but all this is premature; the anchor is not down yet." In mid-January 1894, so excited by a telegram just received on what seemed to him "a great date in [his] history," unable to sleep after playing billiards for hours with seemingly inexhaustible frenetic energy, he telegraphed Livy, "Look out for good news." *"Nearing Success,"* he telegraphed her on January 19. By early February the anchor was down, everything signed. Fifty thousand shares were divided among investors. Paige retained the largest amount, 10,000; Rogers the second largest, 7,000, Twain 1,500 plus his additional 750 and what remained of the royalties that he had not exchanged for stock. A share was ostensibly worth ten thousand dollars, though selling at a fifty percent discount because of risk. In his room, undressing, he suddenly realized, with tears almost starting from his eyes, "I & mine, who were paupers an hour ago, are rich now & our troubles are over!" Euphoria dominated. "Wedding-news," he cabled Livy on their twenty-fourth anniversary, *"Our ship is safe in port.* I sail the moment Rogers can spare me." "We rejoice with you and congratulate you on your well-earned success," she responded.

That all this had not put one penny in his pocket seemed irrelevant to his euphoria. Two conditions for success had been met: a unified company had been put in place to manufacture a compositor for a trial run, and his share of potential profits, if the trial should succeed and machines be sold, had been secured. But success in a trial run and in competition for sales remained a shadowy unknown. What he owned was a sizable amount of high-risk stock in a company that still needed to prove itself. Somehow he assumed that a good market existed for the shares he now held. "I mean to ask Mr. Rogers," he wrote Livy, "to let me sell some stock to the other big Standard Oilers—the Rockefellers & Archibald." And he commissioned the Elmira area Standard Oil representative to sell a block. Rogers must have been amiably appalled.

There were also other business concerns that kept Twain from leaving: his hope that arrangements would be made to liberate him from Webster & Company; a suit against Frohman for restitution of his royalties paid to House; discussions with Frank Mayo about dramatizing and performing in *A Connecticut Yankee* and *Pudd'nhead Wilson*; and an interest that had been expressed in financing a magazine using his name and over which he would have oversight. In early February 1894 he still believed he had important reasons to stay in New York. Eventually, Rogers convinced him that there was no need to remain. Three days before sailing on March 7, he wrote to his benefactor, "You have saved me & my family from ruin & humiliation. You have been to me the best friend that ever a man had, & yet you have never by any word made me feel the weight of this deep obligation." Leaving his power of attorney with Rogers, he sailed for Southampton, satisfied with what had been accomplished. He hoped never again to be separated from Livy.

5.

Less than four weeks after arriving in Paris in March 1894 he again sailed to New York, alone. During the months in which his and Rogers' attention had focused on rationalizing the Paige complications, Webster & Company, though barely breathing, had been maintained on life-support. In mid-February, Twain had turned to Rogers for advice, though in back of his mind he probably hoped Rogers would come to the rescue here as he had done with Paige. After discussions with Hall and examination of the books, Rogers recommended stringent economies, including a contraction of office space. Some of the space could bring in income, little of which was coming from book sales. Rogers hoped for the best but did not think the company could be kept alive much longer without additional capital, the infusion of which he thought would be ill advised. "He is fast coming to the opinion that I had better assume the debts & close up the concern, & turn over my books to the Century Company on the best terms I can get. They want my books badly, but don't value any of the others," Twain wrote to his wife.

He cursed a long litany of scapegoats, especially Webster, "let him rot in peace," his own stupidity in taking so little of the Grant *Personal Memoirs* profits, and also Hall, who he was now convinced had given him false figures to encourage his investing more of Livy's money in a ship Hall knew was sinking. Always a creative revisionist, he now accused Hall of tricking him into signing the second of the two Mt. Morris Bank notes. By Twain's accounting, Webster & Company owed him $110,000 and Livy $60,000. It had business debts of about $83,000 and assets of $60,000. "I am going to get out," he told his sister Pamela, "at *whatever* loss." In March his hopes were raised by Rogers' view that survival rather than honorable death was possible. But the new officers of the Mt. Morris Bank, which previously had been friendly, declined to cooperate. In mid-April, the bank refused to renew two five-thousand-dollar notes that came due. When Twain arrived in New York, bankruptcy seemed the most likely scenario.

Disappointed, Livy would not allow him to leave Paris without explaining why she had to be left behind again. Why could her health not be served as well at Quarry Farm as in wintry Paris? That would allow them all to return to America. Once again, the answer was that the trip itself would be deleterious. The doctors believed "she would lose all she has gained." And indeed her health did seem better than when he had left. Susy's, though, was worse. Twain urged that she try the Parisian version of mind cure. Elinor Howells had convinced him that "hypnotism & mind-cure are the same." William James, whom he had met in Nauheim and saw recently in New York or Boston, also equated hypnotism with mind-cure. Twain soon found it infuriating that there was "no mind-curist" to be found in Paris. "Now the minute I get my matters here in safe shape & rake in some money for your use, I mean to rush over & get Susy & fetch her to Hartford & board her with Lilly Warner, & let her have mind cure from the same person who cured Lilly Foote." Alice Day, sending pamphlets to a skeptical Livy, recommended Christian Science. The way they speak of Mrs. Eddy, the founder of the movement, "gives me a sense of bad taste," Livy responded. On his Hartford visit in mid-January, he took seriously Harmony Twichell's offer to have Susy live with them. Perhaps returning to Hartford might do more for her health than anything else. That was not, though, a separation Livy could contemplate.

In the end, Livy consented to his returning alone. The long exile had indeed made her at times nervous, even hesitant, about going home, and, like her husband, she had come to believe that only European spas and doctors could restore her health. With warm spring weather having come early, Paris seemed almost pleasant. And she had so much benefited from an "electrical treatment" for weight gain that they thought it might be best to endure another Paris winter in order to continue it. As for the economic rationale that had driven them abroad in the first place, it remained in effect, but exile made no more financial sense than it ever had. Twain's willingness, even eagerness, to conclude that Europe was still an effective way to economize suggests that at times he preferred staying abroad. The peripatetic European life suited him, and staying in hotels postponed making a decision about selling the Hartford house. Only if the Paige compositor became a commercial success would their Hartford life be possible again.

In New York he settled into his old rooms at The Players, which had been readied for its honored member and valued resident. But to his disappointment he discovered that his representative in Elmira had not sold any of his Paige stock, a failure he attributed to incompetence rather than to the value of his offering. He had hoped to use that money to save Webster & Company. After discussions with creditors and after considering various possibilities, including a gradual liquidation that would repay creditors in full, Rogers' advice was now unequivocal: bankruptcy was the only practical course. Everything of value was already in Livy's name, except Twain's Webster & Company copyrights. The sixty thousand dollars that Webster & Company owed Livy had been secured by preferred notes, which put her at the head of the line. Rogers soon arranged for that indebtedness to be forgiven in exchange for Twain's copyrights. The intellectual property now, so to speak, belonged to Livy, leaving nothing to be attached.

Rogers and Twain had hoped that an agreement could be negotiated allowing Webster & Company's gradual repayment of its $80,000 indebtedness, $29,500 to the bank, and the rest to assorted creditors while the firm remained in business. That seemed to them and Livy more honorable than immediate liquidation. To Twain's shock, the bank refused—it wanted its money or liquidation. The other creditors, hoping to get a larger sum against each dollar owed, were willing to wait. "I have lost 84 pounds in the last 24 hours," Twain wrote to a Hartford friend. "Not meat, but moral fat." Rogers had persuaded the creditors to settle for fifty cents on each dollar, though he supported Twain's intention to repay in full. Though it was a business bankruptcy, it still was, by the standards of their community, tinged with shame, and Twain and his wife strained to keep their heads high. Worried that her husband and Rogers were not being fair to the creditors, Livy urged them to implement arrangements that met the highest moral standards. "Nobody finds the slightest fault with my paying you with all my property," Twain reassured her. "There is nothing shady or improper about it. We make no concealment of it."

When Alice Day expressed thankfulness that at least Livy retained her "separate fortune," Livy confessed, "Unfortunately a good deal of my money has gone too. I will not write more about it except to say the two most important things, that there was nothing dishonourable about the failure, and that the debts will all be paid." Langdon company business losses, the devaluation of real estate, and the fall of the stock market had reduced her inheritance considerably. Their single most valuable investment remained the Hartford house. "I for myself would have rather mortgaged our house and raised money in that way but I suppose it was not best, my brother objects strongly to my doing that, he says sell your home when you must but never mortgage it, because then there would be not only the expense of keeping the place up but also the interest on the mortgage." She now reconciled herself to the loss of her husband's entire Webster & Company investment. When asked to meet Twain at Rogers' office, Fred Hall still hoped that Rogers had arranged for a rescue or at least a reprieve. To Hall's shock, he was informed that the firm was to go into receivership immediately: "Mr. Clemens and I walked to a law office on Wall Street where the necessary papers were drawn up and signed." Twain felt immediate relief, almost happiness. When he sailed back to France in early May, all that remained of Webster & Company's affairs was the mopping up.

Rejoining his family in Paris in May 1894, he wanted to focus as much as possible on *Joan of Arc*. He hoped it would be ready for serial publication in the fall. Partly, he wanted to be at the head of the still increasing international fascination with France's revivified national heroine, though, to Twain's disgust, she was in the process of becoming a beatified St. Joan and a tool of reactionary French Catholicism. During the voyage across he worked at the first of what he thought would be three articles analyzing and ridiculing eighteenth- and nineteenth-century classics of British and American fiction, the first of which, James Fenimore Cooper's *Deerslayer*, he thought "the most idiotic book [he] ever saw." By the time the boat docked, he had most of the Cooper assault finished. Springtime Paris had attractions, though the Twains were primed to leave at the first sign of heat. They soon repaired to the resort town of Entretat, recommended by Susy's doctors. After a brief visit, they rented from August to October a "little chalet . . . situated quite back from the coast" (since the doctor did not want Livy too near the water), with "a beautiful view." It had been offered to them, including servants, on reasonable terms. While Susy, at intervals, continued to be depressed, Livy's heart condition remained their major concern, now complicated by what seemed to be gout or an arthritic condition that stiffened and pained her fingers.

The most immediate heart pain, though, came from Clara, whose urge for independence pursued various avenues of expression, including a mountain-hiking excursion with friends, the prelude, Livy knew, to an attempt to establish herself in Berlin rather than Paris for the winter. But, though he admired the idea of energetic Alpine heartiness, Twain shared his wife's concern for propriety. There must be proper escorts and companions, always. "No, I cannot feel as you do," Livy responded to Alice Day's unwelcome compliment, "that we are wise to let Clara out from under our wings . . . *I do not at all at all like it*. I am never satisfied except when we are all together. I have told Clara that this is the last time I shall ever consent to it. . . . I *hate* it all this having a young girl away from her family and it is the last time, I think, except for visits."

In New York, Rogers attended to Webster and Paige business. Before his friend's departure, he had taken Twain aside privately: "If you get short, draw on me." Henry's wife, Abbie Rogers, confided to him her view that her husband would be lonely without Twain's company, which touched him even more when the news came at the end of May that she had died following surgery to remove a tumor. When Twain soon had a chance to comfort his friend in person, he was drawn to tears by Rogers' description of what it was like to awaken each morning "expecting to see her" and then the shock each day of the new reality. "Let us be spared this, my darling," he wrote to Livy. "May we die together." His condolences also went to Rogers' fifteen-year-old son, Harry, a teenager with a sense of humor whom Twain liked. He encouraged the young heir to call him "Uncle Sammy." In June, Howells was in Paris for a week during which the friends of twenty-five years spent part of almost every day together, though this too was tinged with sadness. Within hours of arrival, Howells learned that his father had been stricken with paralysis. "Clemens was very kind and brotherly through it all," he later wrote.

In 1885, Howells had published what Twain thought a beautiful story. *Indian Summer* gave him, he told Howells, "gracious glimpses of his lost youth," filling him "with a measureless regret" and building up in him "a cloudy sense of his having been a prince, once, in some enchanted far-off land, & of being in exile now, & desolate—& lord, no chance to ever go back there again. That is the thing that hurts." It hurt even more now, and would get worse, Twain knew. Howells' daughter, Winifred, had died in 1889 after years of illness. Of all their parents, only Howells' stricken father remained. There was reason to think Livy would not have a long life. Susy's ill health frightened her parents, though they could not have even remotely guessed at the turmoil into which her recent London meeting with Louise Brownell, traveling in Europe, had thrown her. When it became clear that Louise would leave Europe without their meeting again, her anguish became expressive. "I cannot, *cannot* bear it! . . . Oh I have *lost* you and can do nothing. I am so miserably helpless, I love you so. . . . This being apart *breaks* my heart. But you will not go. It is a *nightmare*. It isn't true. My darling, beloved." Understandably, Susy shared none of her inner life with her mother. And the maturation into adulthood that Clara insisted was her right, and that Susy also desired, had the potential to reduce the Clemens household to two lonely elderly people whose children had been everything to them. "It's Jean's birth-day—14 years old, think of that," he wrote Livy from New York. "No children left—I am submerged with women." And women who wanted lives of their own.

What kept the couple most on edge for the rest of 1894 was their awareness that financial redemption still depended on the success of the Paige compositor. Except for occasional moments of panic, Twain refused to think about what he might have to resort to if the machine failed. From New York a desperate Fred Hall pressured him to be involved in the liquidation of Webster & Company, and particularly in the issue of whether the Mt. Morris Bank had conspired to force the assignment to creditors. "I have no authority & can do nothing," Twain wisely responded. "If the assignment was a put up job I knew nothing of it, & never in the least suspected it." Happily free of Webster & Company, even if at such a high price, he had no desire to reopen wounds, to scratch at finalities that then would take even longer to heal. Paige was another matter.

There was as yet no Paige crisis, but Twain's restlessness and his desire to see Henry Rogers drove him once more to cross the Atlantic. In New York, in mid-July 1894, the main order of business was keeping company with the bereaved Rogers, as well as refining arrangements with Webster

& Company's creditors. Twain also negotiated an agreement with Henry Mills Alden, the editor of *Harper's Monthly Magazine*, and Harry Harper, its owner, to publish the still unfinished *Joan of Arc*. As the Webster wrap-up continued, Livy detected signs of slippage. She urged that not only Twain and Rogers treat all the creditors honestly but that they should also "help them in every possible way. It is money honestly owed and I cannot quite understand the tone which both you Mr. Rogers seem to take." Harper agreed to pay five thousand dollars for magazine rights to the first part of the novel if, as Twain desired, it was published anonymously (he feared that his reputation for humor would influence *Joan's* reception), but an additional twenty-five percent or thirty percent "if the secret got out." Rogers shed some tears in private conversations with Twain, and talked at length about his wife's last moments and what she had meant to him. In intervals of escape from New York heat, Twain joined a group of Rogers' family and friends staying at a plush resort hotel on the south shore of Long Island, where he socialized happily and rested. When popular demand pressured him to perform for the hotel guests a version of "Captain Stormfield" that he had done one evening for his friends, he consented. It was a great hit. From the large veranda, he could see "all day the ships slip by . . . & at night one has the stars & the moon & the distant winking of the light-houses."

Twain's concentration, though, was mostly on the machine being prepared for trial at the *Chicago Herald*. He assumed success. His shares, he still believed, would make him rich. He found it difficult, though, to confess to Livy that another of his reasons for coming to New York, his desire to find someone to buy his Paige stock at a reasonable price, had not and could not be realized. As usual, on the one hand he managed good times in New York, especially at the Manhattan Beach resort. On the other, he felt "tortured by a conscience": "[It] howls & tugs & pulls & upbraids & reproaches—an infernal conscience which is twins—the one twin pulling one of my arms and saying 'Come—sail!'—the other one tugging at the other arm & saying 'Stay where you are & settle your business matters!' "

At Etretat, where he rejoined the family in mid-August 1894, he returned to work on *Personal Recollections of Joan of Arc, By The Sieur Louis de Conte*, which soon seemed to be writing itself. He hoped to finish before leaving for Paris at the start of October. Livy, who was doing well, had decided they would "venture on house-keeping . . . for economy's sake."

The improvement in her health they credited to her electrical treatment in Paris, which she planned to resume. She urged her husband "to drop the lecture platform" from his mind and "go straight ahead with Joan until the book is finished." According to her accounting, they now had enough household money for the next eight months. What she would not consent to was another separation. Early in September, with manuscript piling up, Twain needed a rest. "I drove the quill too hard, & I broke down—in my head," he wrote to Rogers. When he resumed, his pace dragged, though he felt that the slower pace and his family critics resulted in higher quality: "The madam & Susy are prompt & frank about squelching inferiorities. . . . They make me proud of it myself." By the end of the month he had almost finished book 2, aware that the final book would be difficult and would need "a good while, much study & thinking, & very great pains-taking in the writing." Suddenly, in Rouen on their way to Paris, Susy, whose spirits had perked up at Etretat and who actually began writing a story, became sick. Her lungs were congested, and she ran a high fever. They stayed two weeks in Rouen until she had recovered enough to travel. He arrived in Paris, as did Livy and Susy, exhausted from illness, nursing, and sleep-lessness.

After a month at a hotel, they moved into a rented house, at first glance "more comfortable & homelike than the hotel." Just before moving in, though, Twain became ill with what was diagnosed as gout in an ankle. It was painful and prevented him from walking, and soon he had it in the other ankle. Able neither to walk nor write, he stayed mainly indoors for more than a month, which made him restless and miserable. The house turned out to contain mainly small rooms, oddly placed, and, as usual, the anticipated savings hardly materialized. At least, he remarked, their rental had been furnished by its American owner who liked bright colors, not by the usual drab Frenchman who preferred tomblike interiors. French taste was a mystery to him, and he particularly resented condescending French criticism of America. Other than Napoleon, he considered French history a rogues' gallery of incompetents, and French culture relatively cultureless, mostly cream-puff, a hostility he gave vent to by drafting "some articles" in response to a book attacking America by the novelist Paul Bourget. "France hasn't any [civilization] to speak of," he explained in a letter, "except what she got at second-hand."

By late November he had made no progress on *Joan*. "I am pretty impatient to get to work again," he wrote to Rogers. It certainly would not be finished, as he had hoped, that fall. As he approached writing about his heroine's trial, he was aware of the trial that autumn of another French patriot in whose innocence he believed: Alfred Dreyfus, who was convicted of treason in December 1894. "I have now lost two solid months & am away behind-hand on my engagements. It will take me all the winter to catch up." He did manage, though, to correct proofs for the *Harper's Monthly Magazine* serial publication of Book 1 of *Joan*.

Trials of the Paige compositor had begun in late summer 1894, and his eyes were constantly on the mail in hope of news. He urged Henry Rogers to send him a newspaper that had some portion set by the typesetter. When one arrived, it was "healing for sore eyes. . . . It affects me like Columbus sighting land." He predicted that the "Mergenthaler people will come & want to hitch teams with us." The Chicago, the Connecticut, and the Rogers/Twain interests seemed to be working together harmoniously. Everyone awaited the test results. By late October, he felt a restrained euphoria. "Things couldn't well be going better at Chicago than they are," he wrote to Rogers. "By & by our machines will be perfect; then they won't stop at all." There were problems, though, particularly the frequency of jamming and error, that gave him sufficient pause to regret that they hadn't used the older of the two existing machines. He almost screamed across the Atlantic, "When the machine is in proper working order, it *cannot make a mistake.*"

Either the machine in Chicago was *not* in proper working order or it could not hear Twain's shout. The *Herald* people complained that correcting errors took too long. It's not the machine, Twain insisted, it's the operator. Fire the bad operators and get better! Henry Rogers' engineer produced an "account of the machine's misconduct," which Twain had in his hand in mid-November, detailing one breakdown after another. Rogers went immediately to Chicago. "Great guns, what is the matter with it!" Twain was bewildered and frightened, blaming himself for what he now considered a mistake in strategy. He could have saved Rogers from disappointment by having insisted that "none but a thoroughly perfect machine" be exhibited. His impatience had pressured the mechanics to rush into performance a machine that still needed work. If only they had allowed two more months for tinkering. Then it would have passed with flying colors. This was, though, he believed, a temporary setback, not a final defeat.

But on Thanksgiving Day 1894, Twain's house of cards began to collapse. A letter from Rogers was put into his trembling hands. He thought to himself, as he opened it, "Clemens, stand by for a cyclone! for if Mr. Rogers finds it wise & best to remove his supports from under that machine, your fine ten-year-old dream will blow away like a mist & you will land in the poor-house sure." Just back from Chicago, Rogers expressed strong doubt that the machine would ever prove successful. It was too complicated, too fragile, for daily pounding in a printing shop. It was all too human. Extremely good at what it could do and sometimes did do, it could not do it with machinelike regularity.

Realizing that the *Herald*'s decision almost certainly would not be favorable, Twain collapsed into panic. His next defense was a default strategy. "I am catching around for straws to swim ashore on, in case of disaster." If he should decide to withdraw, whatever money remained from "the wreckage," he suggested to Rogers, perhaps should be invested in Mergenthaler stock bought before his withdrawal became public knowledge. Since Paige would have to sell his patents to Mergenthaler cheaply, he and Rogers would at least profit from the increased value of Mergenthaler stock. He assumed without warrant that there would be some money saved from the wreckage. Embittered by Paige's culpability in the machine never being brought to market, he urged Rogers to help make certain that Paige suffered equally in the collapse.

Depressed, he attempted to get relief by burying himself in work; otherwise, there would be "a sudden inquest & a verdict 'died of the blues.' " Three days before Christmas he learned that Rogers, his experts and his business sense having brought him to the conclusion that the machine would never be commercially viable, had thrown in the towel. "I *seemed* to be entirely expecting your letter," Twain responded. Still, as resigned as he believed he had been, the news hit him "like a thunderclap." In a manic fog, he went to book passage to New York. "I must be there & see it die." Livy tried to reason with him as ideas for resuscitation whirled through his mind. Gradually, by bedtime, he seemed more rational. Then, unable to sleep, he became manic again. He smoked and thought until dawn. Then he wrote to Rogers with a half-dozen ideas. He was still in denial. *"Don't* say I'm wild. For really I'm sane again this morning." But he was not, quite.

By New Year's Day 1895 he was resigned to the wisdom of dissolving the company. "I couldn't shake off the confidence of a life time in my luck," he explained to Rogers. The only luck that had come his way in the Paige affair had been Rogers' help. If he had had him from the start, he told his friend, they both "should have had the good luck to step promptly ashore." Shaken to the depths of his being, he feared that his luck, having deserted him, might never return. In the few days after New Year's a sober accounting of his situation produced stark conclusions. His two great business gambles had failed, irredeemably. "I ought to have knocked CL Webster & Company in the head 3 years ago when it owed only $16,000," he wrote to Rogers. "That would have been a good time to shove the machine out of my dreams, too."

Slowly, in the next weeks, he started again to breathe, though it was not ever again to be the air of optimism that previously had fed his energy and enthusiasm. Despite the financial and psychological wounds, he still had his natural resiliency and Livy's unvarying support. As long as they honorably provided for the Webster creditors, she believed, they themselves would be spiritually sound, if not actually improved by this trial. Her health, better than it had been for years, and Susy's comparative equilibrium during the last months, were blessings. Clara flourished. Jean's fainting spells and odd lapses were puzzling but not distressing. Except for recurrent coughs and painful attacks of gout and neuralgia, Twain himself was in excellent health.

Disappointment sent him back to his writing desk, for solace, for pleasure, for profit. In January 1895, he spent brief periods polishing *Tom Sawyer Detective,* then worked hard at Book 3 of *Joan,* which he soon told Mary Fairbanks was finished. And there were other assets: the uniform edition that the Century Press proposed and that Rogers wanted Harper & Brothers to publish; and his own copyrights, which Rogers and Livy felt certain would prove a profitable long-term resource if managed properly. There was also the knowledge that renting the Hartford house would relieve the two-hundred-dollar monthly maintainenance costs, as well as the possibility of the dreaded round-the-world lecture tour, which now seemed a necessity.

Still, he could not resist a moment of self-deception. The lecture tour would not be "for money," he told Rogers, but to get Livy and him away from "the phantoms & out of the heavy nervous strain for a few months." If either Susy or Clara would agree to accompany them, Livy would consent. It was, though, only for the money. They could think of no other way to pay the debts of C. L. Webster & Company. Perhaps, he speculated, he could contractually hire himself out "to Mrs. Clemens as a platform-reader & thus escape trouble from [his] creditors." If he had to do again what he so much hated, and what he had resolved never again to do, Livy, at least, would accompany him. Two of the daughters would stay part of the time with Elmira relatives, part with Hartford friends. It would mean that the entire family would go home again in the summer, at last, to Quarry Farm. And even if the round-the-world trip should take a full year, at the end they might be solvent again. Their European exile would be over.

CHAPTER SIXTEEN

DISAPPOINTMENT TO THE END

1895–1896

1.

Steaming southwestward from Vancouver in late August 1895, the Clemenses were beginning a new chapter in their lives with yet another voyage. Twain had last journeyed across the Pacific in 1866, to what had proved for him to be the blessed islands of Hawaii, launching his post-California career. Without the success of his Hawaii letters to the *Alta California,* there most likely would have been no *Innocents Abroad.* Now necessity demanded that they voyage so far westward that it would eventually become eastward. As their ship, the *Warrimoo,* left North America behind, Twain began anticipating new scenes and pleasures. He had always wanted to go to the Orient. Turning toward his long-imagined reencounter with Hawaii, he felt himself at home again, in the sense that he was usually more at ease on shipboard than on land. Clara, more like her father than either of her sisters, accompanied them, craving change and adventure. Susy's general health seemed too fragile for such a voyage, and she craved the opportunity to be once more in an American home. Jean was simply too young, and there were questions about her health as well. The eldest and youngest daughters were to stay half the year in Elmira, the other half with Hartford friends. Livy consoled herself that they would reunite in London the following spring, and at least she would have with her the daughter on whom she felt the need to keep the closest watch.

The departure from Vancouver seemed almost an escape. "You are in such a state of mind that you seem to worry about everything," Henry Rogers wrote to Twain in mid-July 1895. He ruefully acknowledged that Rogers' administration of his affairs amounted to a full-time job: "Look here, don't you think you'd better let somebody else run the Standard Oil a week or two till you've finished up these matters of mine? Why *I* can keep you busy, you don't need any outside industries." If Rogers had attached himself to a much-loved humorist to mitigate the unpopularity of monopolistic wealth, such ulterior motivation escaped Twain. Rogers also paid far more in labor and energy than any public relations advantage could amount to. Twain's only payback had been his insistence that Webster & Company decline, sight unseen, a book attacking Standard Oil, hardly a consequential matter. From the start, friendship dominated the exchange and, naturally, all the material gifts came from Rogers. Creditors pursued Twain through much of the spring and summer. When, in July, the only creditor to seek a judgment brought suit, Twain, Frederick Hall, and Rogers testified in a New York courtroom. Livy feared newspaper publicity. Her husband worried that an attempt would be made to attach box-office receipts from his inaugural lecture, scheduled for Cleveland in mid-July. Twain and Rogers were in the mood to fight, but Livy "was ill, over the situation." Twain "at once administered the only medicine that could stop her from getting worse." He would compromise or pay in full.

Working closely with Twain, Rogers handled his negotiations with Harper & Brothers, advising the author about their projected uniform edition. Since Harper and Frank Bliss were at odds, the series could contain only titles Twain had published with Osborne and Webster. Bliss, who owned rights to everything of value before *Life on the Mississippi,* would not relinquish them. Absurdly, the American Publishing Company now also owned rights to *Pudd'nhead Wilson,* which Twain had signed away, against Rogers' advice, without anticipating that it would give Bliss additional leverage in his struggle to publish a collected edition. In April 1895, Twain complained to Rogers, "Bliss is an ass. It would be a mistake to publish with him on any terms," though why Twain thought Bliss more of an ass in April 1895 than when he had contracted with him to publish *Pudd'nhead Wilson* the previous spring is unclear. "I've signed a lot of contracts in my time," Twain confessed, "and at signing-time I probably knew what the contracts meant—but 6 months later everything had grown dim and I could be *certain* of only two things, to-wit. 1. I didn't *sign* any contract; 2. The contract means the opposite of what it *says*." *Personal Recollections of Joan of Arc* he committed to *Harper's Magazine* for serial publication.

At the end of February 1895, Twain had sailed alone from Paris for a three-week stay in New York to settle additional publication arrangements. He was still as depressed as he had been for much of the winter. Waiting for Bliss to clarify his position, for Century to make an offer, and for Harper details to be resolved irritated him. Soon Twain and Harry Harper agreed that, at the conclusion of serial publication of *Joan*, Harper would publish the novel in book form. The arrangement was for *Harper's Monthly Magazine* to pay about twelve thousand dollars for serial publication of *Joan of Arc* and *Tom Sawyer Detective* and whatever additional royalties the books would earn. The contract was signed in late May, in Elmira, to which, after four years of European wandering, the family had at last returned. "I have great hope that by a year from this coming Fall we shall be able to settle down in our own home and live there."

But their estimate that it cost them about two thousand dollars a month to live, despite economies, sobered their arithmetic and their plans. Twain was legally obligated to pay the Webster creditors a substantial sum by the end of the year, and little to nothing could be expected from Livy's inheritance, though the possibility that they would soon be able to liquidate a Buffalo property she had inherited, worth about fifteen thousand dollars, briefly raised their spirits. He mostly turned down requests from editors for short stories and essays. As absolute sums the fees were attractive, but he felt it cost more time to write a short piece than he could afford. He found that it took less work to write "a big book or a wagon load of criticism" than a short story, especially since, as Twain wrote, "one can't charge for the work, but only for the result." Backlist royalties produced a few thousand a year. For new work he could no longer count on selling fifty thousand copies as he had in the high days of subscription publication. Trade books sold fewer copies generally and, in the midst of a severe depression, the public was hardly buying books. Even a uniform edition would have to overcome sales resistance. He could feel the lecture tour noose tightening. "If I go on that trip," he wrote to Rogers in early February, "I may possibly get a book of travel out of it; & books of travel are good sellers in the subscription trade." He still failed to appreciate that the subscription market was dying. Estimated travel expenses were at least ten thousand dollars, but he had reason to believe that, with good planning and management, he stood to profit considerably. Regardless, as he confessed to Rogers, "I've *got* to mount the platform next fall or starve."

No sooner had he returned to Paris in April 1895 than the family went into its usual decamping frenzy. Their nerves were strained, their spirits tired, and they alternated between excited determination and anxious misery. "After a long period of homesickness," Clara later recalled, "my sisters and I had become attached to life abroad." They were "now aghast at the prospect of leaving" their Paris life, though Clara spoke more for herself than her sisters. On some nights neither Twain nor Livy could sleep except with the help of whiskey. It was wonderful to be famous, miserable to be poor.

From Paris in the middle of April he cabled his acceptance of terms offered by a Melbourne impresario, the former music critic and newspaperman Robert Sparrow Smythe, who had managed Henry Stanley's Australian tour. During a visit to Hartford in 1882, Smythe had urged Twain to visit. Other Australian voices had called out to him. Now he had a compelling reason to respond. As they prepared their Paris departure, they intended taking the Pacific voyage without any daughters, partly because of expense. But when Livy, still economizing, declined to take a maid, Clara, with her usual peremptoriness, decided that she would go. Her parents said no. Since "the experts" seemed to think that she was "a musical genius," they did not want her studies to be interrupted. Clara, though, apparently anticipated that life in Elmira or with Hartford friends would be too boring. Her parents soon acceded. "Livy & Clara go with me around the world, but Susie refuses because she hates the sea," he wrote to Orion. Jean, scheduled to enroll at Elmira College, could not "spare the time from school." When they sailed for New York in mid-May, they were all, except Twain, in high spirits. He hoped to make better progress completing *Joan of Arc* at Quarry Farm than he had in Paris. For much of the winter he had been "tired to death all the time," he confessed to Rogers. "My head is tired & clogged, too, & the mill refuses to go. It comes of depression of spirits, I think, caused by the impending horror of the platform."

They were happy to be once again on the bucolic hillside. "Livy looks young & fresh & spry," he wrote to Orion. But he had "a world of work to do & mighty little time to do it in." Bliss surprised him with a handsome offer for the prospective travel book, which he decided to accept if Harper did not object, though as usual he overestimated how many copies would sell. His mis-estimates led him to decide not to contract for a series of magazine articles for which *Harper's Magazine* was eager. Occasional eruptions of the death rattle of Charles L. Webster & Company put him into a sweat during an already hot summer. He resuscitated his 1885 lecture tour programs, listing and rearranging the usual suspects, such as the jumping frog, the blue jay, the golden arm, and excerpts from *Huckleberry Finn,* but that hardly scratched the surface of the challenge. So as never to repeat himself in the same city, he had to plan three different platform programs, and two selections from *Joan* seemed suitable, giving him the additional advantage of publicizing the book. He decided he would "break the incognito in Sydney in September for the sake of having something to contrast with the broad-farcical jumping Frog & such."

His preparation schedule was made even more onerous by illness. Soon after arriving in Elmira, the gout returned in his right leg. Worse, he developed a "pretty malignant boil on the other," he told Harry Harper at the end of May, explaining why he had been able to do little more than reduce Book 3 of *Joan of Arc* "to a couple of magazine installments." A subcutaneous infection from an unknown source produced a large pocket of pus covered by inflamed skin. The boil was technically a carbuncle, "as big as a turkey's egg." It needed to be lanced, drained, and bandaged. In an age before antibiotics, such infections at best took a long time to heal. The Langdon family doctor lanced it, and it drained slowly. Confined to bed, Twain was in physical pain and mental anguish. Concentration proved impossible, boredom insufferable. His general constitution, though, was robust. His one glass of hot whiskey as a soporific each night gave him mostly sound sleep. As much as he hated being sick, he hated being old. With his sixtieth birthday approaching, there was nothing youthful about his appearance, other than the occasional twinkle. A compelling American icon, he had ripened into a combination of sage and eccentric. But the age part he did not like. "I have detested old age from my infancy, and anything that removes from me for a few moments the consciousness that I am old is gratifying to me."

In mid-June, he wrote, "I'm perishing with idleness." A hoped-for visit to Hartford in 1895 became impossible. They had also wanted to see

Pamela, but "Papa's illness," Clara wrote, also ruled that out. "There is more Clemens now than carbuncle," he told Rogers. "It puts the balance of importance where it properly belongs." Progress, though, was excruciatingly slow. "The boil abolishes literary lusts," he wrote to the *Century* sub-editor. Three weeks later it "sloughed out a big hunk of decayed protoplasm like a Baltimore oyster . . . & left a corresponding raw cavity" in his leg. He was encouraged: "it will heal fast, now." He expected to be well enough by the end of June to prepare his readings. But he could not even put on clothes, let alone do any mental work, until the end of the first week in July, when he had to travel in sweltering heat to a New York court "to undergo the shame born of the mistake [he] made in establishing a publishing house." It was an unhappy return to mobility. "I can't make any more financial mistakes; I've nothing left to make them with," he confessed. He still could put little to no weight on his left leg. How, he wondered, would he be able to stand for an hour and a half before lecture audiences, the first of which was scheduled for mid-July 1895 in Cleveland? "I've got to *stand;* I can't *sit* & talk to a house."

The first of two trial readings disappointed him, though his performance at the Elmira reformatory seemed "a roaring success." The American part of the tour had been arranged by his friend and tour manager James Pond to sweep as far north as possible to avoid extreme heat. San Francisco had been scratched, to Twain's bitter disappointment. August performances there would be hopeless, Pond believed, because San Franciscans would be on vacation. Instead, the tour would head to Michigan and across the Great Lakes to Minnesota, North Dakota, Manitoba, Montana, Wyoming, Washington, and Vancouver, their port of Pacific departure. Thirty percent off the top would go to local hosts and arrangements. Of the remainder, one fourth was to be Pond's, three quarters Twain's. At a minimum tickets were to be a dollar; audiences were anticipated to be not fewer than 500 and as many as 1,500. Pond hoped, and Twain assumed, that there would be a lecture series in England in the spring and an East Coast tour the following fall. He calculated that he would need a year and a half to repay the Webster debt.

2.

What he had not counted on was the heat, the cultural unevenness of their northwestern route, and the demonstrations of affection that his presence and predicament evoked from many Americans. Sometimes his travels had the flavor of a triumphal procession. At others there were spaces and empty seats, the latter infrequent but galling. Sometimes there were too many people, as at his inaugural lecture in Cleveland on July 15, 1895, which he judged a "dead failure." There were "250 chattering news boys on the platform" behind him in the broiling hot Music Hall, 4,200 people in front. Though he began well, with a newly created comic introduction delivered with a straight face, explaining that he had undertaken this tour to propagate his infallible scheme for the moral regeneration of mankind, he had to fight heat and noise. The trick of his scheme, he explained, was to commit as many transgressions as possible but to learn from them. "Suppose that every time you commit a transgression . . . you lay up in your heart the memory of the shame you felt when your sin found you out, and so make it a perpetual reminder and perpetual protection against your ever committing that particular sin again." Thus, the more transgressions, the closer to perfection. Since it's impossible to invent or create any new sins, how hard, he proposed, could it be to get through all 354? In the end, moral perfection; and he himself was an example of the scheme's success.

Since examples of misconduct would comprise the first part of his program, he began with the story of "the stolen watermelon," an opening and a segue he was to use many times in the next year. Then the "Jumping Frog" and the "Character of the Bluejay." "A True Story," renamed "Aunty Cord's Story," and "The Golden Arm," both with African-American tonal and thematic inflections, became fixtures. So did the autobiographical account of finding himself alone with a corpse in his father's office. "I got *started* magnificently," he wrote to Rogers, "but inside of half an hour the scuffling boys had the audience's maddened attention and I saw it was a gone case; so I skipped a third of my program and quit."

That he would "speak on morals" became the usual newspaper announcement heralding his arrival. Within a month, he crafted more than thirty selections into the three programs, some longtime chestnuts, others new, all examples of human character and conduct. They were representations of "Mark Twain at Home," his general title to signal that the spotlight was on the personality of the performer. Each item was capable of being slotted into almost any position in any program. At Livy's suggestion, he soon included a few sentimental selections to give audiences a reprieve from laughter, on the notion that contrast increased the effect of both modes. *Joan of Arc* was not yet available to represent sentiment. Harry Harper had argued against his revealing his authorship so soon; so had Livy. By the time he reached Minneapolis at the end of July, he felt he had gotten program "No 1" perfected. Audiences seemed to agree. "I am at work *all* the time on my lectures," he wrote to Rogers, "on board the trains & everywhere." Though he used the word "lecture," his performances consisted of memorized selections from his published works, reworked for oral presentation and linked by scripted introductions and transitions, the items arranged into a scheme whose came from their dramatization of his personality and ideas. When he discovered that program number 2 was thirty-five minutes too long and offered to stop at the end of the scheduled hour and a half, his audience insisted he continue.

A sparsely filled house was rare as the Twain caravan moved westward, first by steamer across Lake Huron to the summer resort of Mackinac, Michigan, with a side performance at Petoskey, then through the locks into Lake Superior, to Duluth and Minneapolis, to Crookston, North Dakota, north into Winnipeg, back across the border and westward to Great Falls, Butte-Anaconda, Helena, and Missoula, and on to the northwest via Spokane. Railroad travel in stifling hot weather exhausted them all. Schedules often forced long waits at railroad stations in early morning or late-night darkness. His talent for cursing helped, and Livy usually found a way to soothe her husband's grumbling.

As they traveled, James Pond, Twain's manager, had one of the newly popular Kodak cameras and took striking photos of pioneer farmers in the Plains states, scraping an existence from arid land, including one of Twain dressed in jacket and tie attempting to persuade a raggedy Norwegian immigrant child to sell him one of her kittens. Her parents slouch warily by their ramshackle cabin, their long-suffering poker faces unreadable. Especially in the mining communities there was massive unemployment, deserted towns, exploited landscapes, and abysmal poverty, partly the result of depression, partly of unregulated capitalism. When they reached Helena, his carbuncle needed dressing "only once a day," he wrote to Frank Fuller: "Within a week it will be entirely well." He felt better enough to tolerate a few excursions with boosters eager to show local glories to the great man. In the wealthier cities he relaxed at late-night dinners hosted by prominent men's clubs, partly an opportunity for self-advertisement.

And there was much to see that stirred Twain into a renewed appreciation of American and Canadian beauty, especially the wheat fields of the upper Midwest, "a horizon-girdled waveless ocean of green," he wrote in his notebook, a repository of observations for the travel book to come. "Seas & seas of wheat. . . . The roads are as black as tar the soil is so rich." At Mackinac, the air was "superb & invigorating." At Winnipeg, on a "sunny Sunday morning," he heard "the happy laughter of the only bird that *does* laugh by nature—the martin," his "favorite as a boy." He had not heard it since childhood. At first sight of the high mountain vistas, with their "splendidly bracing & life-giving air," he felt himself back a generation into his early manhood. "You *must* hire a private car some day and take a swing through this splendid country," he wrote to Rogers.

Frequent examples of puritanical anti-working-class Sunday restrictions made him less happy. At Butte-Anaconda the foul copper-mining stench nauseated him, part of the paradox of the American West, such healthy beauty, such deadly depredation. At Fort Missoula, the guest of honor for a dress ceremony performed by the "colored regiment or army corps—25th U. S. infantry," he marveled at former slaves transformed into some of the best soldiers in the United States Army. "They all have the look & bearing of gentleman." The thirty-piece band played and the regiment sang beautifully. All the officers, though, were white. A few days later, he remarked in his notebook, "Let Jim tell Huck what he knows about Canada, the *real* home of the free." Much had changed since the days of the Underground Railroad. He appreciated what had changed, but many important things had not, and now, as usual, he had his eye on the condition of blacks in America. Northern blacks were controlled by law and prejudice. Lynching had become a forceful tool of race dominance in the South.

White America, though, treated Twain well; he was a celebrity who discovered that he had a huge reserve of goodwill and affection in the hearts of ordinary people. His universal readership since *Innocents Abroad*, his attention to publicity, which made him a friendly household commodity, and his reputation as a platform performer insured large audiences; and he was traveling a lecture route to places that rarely if ever had a chance to be entertained at this level. Spectacles like the circus or the horse races seemed comparatively ordinary. The chance to see and hear Mark Twain was a once-in-a-lifetime event. Aware of expectations, he did not want to disappoint. A subpar performance made him irritably self-critical. As his command of his materials improved, so did his consistency, though inevitably there was the occasional bad night when either he or his audience fell short.

Still, as he left the Midwest for the high plains and then the mountains for the coast, his spirits rose. After eighty-two consecutive days of dressing the carbuncle, it finally seemed healed. After twenty-eight days on the road, his status as more than a popular performer had sunk in. Indeed, earlier in the summer, when news that he would lecture to pay his debts began to circulate, he had begun to realize that many Americans, in a nation suffering from economic depression, identified with his plight and honored his determination. At first in trickles, then in torrents, letters of condolence came from strangers, some with gifts of money—"one-dollar bills . . . from here and there and yonder—from strangers—and I had to send them back"— and others offering large contributions, as if he were a national monument in need of repair. At railroad stations, in small towns, in auditoriums after his performances, people reached out their hands to touch him.

By the end of the American part of his tour his finances seemed less onerous, more promising. Averaging a profit of more than five hundred dollars a performance, it seemed to him that he might pay his Webster & Company debts more quickly than he had anticipated, perhaps in less than a year. He might not need to lecture in England or America at all. "My eyes have been opened by this lecture trip across the continent," he told his nephew, Sam Moffett. "I find I have twenty-five friends in America where I thought I had only one. Look at that house in Cleveland, in the dead middle of July, with the mercury trying to crawl out of the top of the thermometer." Those "unknown friends" did not come mainly to hear him talk. "No; they came to shake hands & let me know that they were on deck & all was well. I shall be out of debt a long way sooner than I was supposing a month ago." That he had such friends was "a compliment worth being in debt for." In fact, he humorously reasoned, it was immodest of him to talk about paying his debts: "By my own confession I am blandly getting ready to unload them onto the whole English-speaking world." Still, all that mattered was that his indebtedness would be over much before he had expected. He felt momentarily wonderful. Lecturing was no trouble at all. He assured his nephew, in a playful riff of euphoric exaggeration, "Lecturing is gymnastics, chest-expander, medicine, mind-healer, blues-destroyer, all in one. I am twice as well as I was when I started out; I have gained nine pounds in twenty-eight days, & I expect to weigh six hundred before January. I haven't had a blue day in all the twenty-eight. My wife & daughter are accumulating health & strength & flesh nearly as fast as I am. When we reach home a year hence I think we can exhibit as freaks."

While Pond and his wife trained eastward with a pouch full of photos to show the Quarry Farm contingent, the Clemenses boarded their small Canadian-Australian mail steamer, the RMS *Warrimoo*. They were disappointed at its accommodations in comparison to the Atlantic liners they were used to, disgusted at the prevalence of roaches and rats, and concerned about the ship's seaworthiness. On its approach to Vancouver, it had gone aground on a reef. Repairs required delay, and there was time to arrange an additional lecture in Victoria, British Columbia. At Portland he had enjoyed a "splendid house, full to the roof" despite stifling heat. In Olympia, Oregon, the theater had been only half full. In Tacoma, there was "a big house & a great time." His audience at Vancouver on August 16 adored the performance, despite his hoarseness, the start of a bad cold. At his late-arranged Victoria lecture, the governor general and his wife led the enthusiastic applause. When "a kitten walked across the stage behind" him, "the audience laughed in the wrong place" which he did not understand until after the performance.

He accommodated reporters serially, for local consumption, with a widely distributed interview to his newspaperman nephew in Seattle, an interview for the *Seattle Times*, and another for the United Press. His Australian tour manager made sure the free publicity was widely reprinted there. On August 17, Clara reported to her cousin, "[Sailing] seems quite indefinite. . . . The longer we stay on dry land, the happier I am." In a spare moment Twain wrote to Kipling, rumored to be going to India, that he would soon return the compliment of the visit Kipling had made to Elmira. "I shall arrive next January & you must be ready. I shall come riding my Ayah with his tusks adorned . . . & you must be on hand with a few bottles of ghee, for I shall be thirsty." Finally, the captain was satisfied with the ship's repairs. "It is midnight, & we sail at 8 tomorrow morning," Twain wrote to Rogers on August 22. "Big house & a good time last night. No more talking to do for a week; then—possibly—a talk in Honolulu." His cold was better. He was, though, "threatened a little" with another carbuncle: "But it is not a strong threat. I have been to the drug store & laid in materials for a war upon it, so as to be on the safe side." They all kept their fingers crossed that the *Warrimoo* also would be on the safe side.

3.

As they sailed into lovely late-summer weather, Twain looked forward to restorative quiet and comparative isolation. The crew's inattentiveness and the ship's inconveniences irked them all. Still, despite occasional curses at the ship and the shipping company for allowing them to sail on a vessel in which safety was not certain, he began to feel that he would like this voyage to continue indefinitely, perhaps partly because of "a most disagreeable" recurrent dream of appearing before a "lecture-audience in [his] shirt-tail." The family of three spent hours reading on deck and playing their favorite shipboard games, shuffleboard and cards. "The weather has been divine," he wrote to Rogers. "For the past three days the sea with the sun on it has counterfeited the intense & luminous blue of the Mediterranean."

On August 30, 1895, they approached Honolulu. "In a couple of hours after dark we shall be [there]—too late to lecture, & I am not sorry," he wrote in his notebook. "We sail at 11 in the morning. . . . I got mighty tired platforming before we left America, & shall be glad to remain quiet till we reach Australia." The money for five hundred tickets already sold would have to be returned. When the captain ordered his crew to change into white uniforms for the tropics, Twain bought a white suit from the ship's store. Docked in the outer harbor, they learned that cholera had that day killed five people in Honolulu. "This first little boat that brought the ill news," Livy wrote, "asked if Mark Twain was aboard." No one from the *Warrimoo* would be permitted ashore, not even the passengers whose destination was Honolulu.

In the daylight, the view from the ship was as beautiful and alluring as he had remembered it. Looking down in the "luminous blue water," he saw "2 sharks playing around laying for a Christian." That night, from shipboard, the sunset was spectacularly beautiful, "the vast plain of the sea . . . rich in color—great stretches of dark blue, others of purple, others of luminous bronze." Toward the shore white surf broke across and into variegated green tones. "The rounded velvety backs of certain of [the mountains] made you want to stroke them as you would a cat's back." His cabin became stifling hot. Since no food could be taken aboard, meals became even more unattractive. At midnight on September 1, the *Warrimoo* raised anchor, sailing southwestward toward the Fijis. Twain had not been able to set foot on the blessed island that had remained in his imagination since 1866. It was a deep disappointment, and he was never to have the opportunity again.

Two weeks later, fifty miles from Sydney, he watched schools of phosphorescent porpoises streak across the ship's bow. In the black night the surface of the sea "was not distinguishable." An eight-foot porpoise "would look like a glorified serpent 30 to 50 ft long, every curve of the tapering long body perfect," the color of a "glow-worm & wonderfully intense." Usually averse to any exercise except walking, he had become, after a few days of aches, the ship's shuffleboard champion, and boasted about it to Rogers. "Mr. Clemens seems entirely well again of his cold," Livy wrote to her sister. "He is pretty cheerful—in fact he appears entirely cheerful—but underneath he has a steady, unceasing feeling that he is never going to be able to pay his debts. I do not feel so, I am sure if his life and health are spared to him that it will not be long until he is out of debt. Won't that be one joyful day."

Crossing the equator, he felt languid, washed out. His descriptive eye, though, remained bright. A flock of flying fish was "a flight of silver fruit knives." A total eclipse of the moon, "a saucer of strawberry ice." The equator fascinated him: the storms, the doldrums, its effects on the passengers. Soon the Southern Cross appeared, then the Magellan Clouds. At the Fiji Islands the natives reminded him of the Hawaiians in 1866, "splendid half nude natives with their brown mops of hair. Fine race—both sexes." Keenly attracted to what was prohibited, he admired a civilization in which natural things were not forbidden. If fishing had been forbidden in the Garden of Eden, he seriously joked in his performances, Adam would have gone fishing. That would have been "so *natural*. It wasn't that Adam ate the apple for the *apple's sake,* but *because* it was prohibited. It would have been better for us . . . if the serpent had been prohibited—then Adam would have eaten the *serpent*."

In his six-week Australian visit he played to full houses in the provinces of Victoria and New South Wales, from Sydney to Melbourne to Adelaide and smaller cities, a triumphal procession by a writer many Australians considered the greatest living English-language author and the world's superlative humorist. His merest gesture, even his presence, set people laughing. Flattered that such a writer had come all that way, Australians were primed to celebrate his visit. Always a curious traveler, he made himself as knowledgeable as possible with a cram course, started on shipboard, on Australian history and society. His small stack of books avidly grew larger as he traveled. An experienced manager, Robert Smythe had inundated newspapers and billboards with publicity. Reporters and editors cooperated. With his cascade of white curly hair, Twain was recognized almost everyplace. With the usual eagerness of colonials, Australians were keen to see and ogle the most famous colonial of them all.

Clara and Livy, who accepted invitations for excursions and parties, made Australian friends as well. To her discomfort, Livy found herself also a celebrity, or at least a celebrity appendage. She was shocked when her photo and Clara's appeared in a Melbourne shop window. Her husband took it up with the proprietor. "My wife is so troubled by the exhibition of her & our daughter's photographs . . . that for her sake I write to ask you to remove it. She is not used to publicity & cannot get reconciled to it." Australians, Twain thought, had much in common with Americans. Unlike the reserved British, they had a breezy, brash informality, an eagerness to meet strangers and publicize visitors. When, during his walks on Sydney streets, strangers requested loans, he immediately declared with convivial informality that he was so glad to be in Australia, to which he had come to earn money to pay off debts that had left him impoverished.

The strategy usually worked. So too did his stage performances. "Really I am almost in love with the platform again," he wrote to Henry Rogers. Sydney, Melbourne, and Adelaide papers praised him effusively, with an occasional exception. "I think Papa never talked to a more enthusiastic audience," Livy wrote about a characteristic reception. "They were entirely uproarious, taking a point almost before he had reached it. The house was packed. . . . A young fellow who sat next me . . . began to pound his sides as if troubled with stitches in them. . . . And so it goes, it is constant unceasing adulation of papa and most appreciative words about him. They . . . seem to know most of [his work] by heart." At one town his talk on the difficulties of the German language offended a contingent of German-born Australians. In Sydney, pursued by reporters and invited to receptions by the local elite, including a former and the present prime minister, he put his foot into his mouth with gauche comments about free

trade and federation, two controversial issues. He soon learned to say little to nothing about Australian political matters.

Wife and daughter dutifully attended his performances. Curious Australians watched to see if they laughed at jokes they had heard repeatedly.
In hotel suites, when Twain pontificated to newspaper people, humorous
riffs memorized through repetition, Livy and Clara tuned out what they
had heard so often. In private and public company his combination of humor and benign incisiveness fulfilled the public's image of Mark Twain.
His deadpan delivery, his idiosyncratic version of a Missouri drawl, the
slowness of his speech, the exoticism of his colloquial "at home" performances, delighted audiences, including those he spoke to at dinners in his
honor. In a speech to Melbourne's Yorick Club he reminisced at length
about his Mississippi River days, a rare public evocation of the sentimen-
tally revisionist and selective expression of his memories. "[At that time]
fogs and dark nights had a charm for me. And that is one of the very advantages of youth. You don't own any stock in anything. You have a good
time, and all the grief and trouble is with the other fellows. Youth is a lovely
thing, and certainly never was there a diviner time to me in this world. All
the rest of my life is one thing—but my life as a pilot on the Mississippi
when I was young—Oh! that was the darling existence. There has been
nothing comparable to it in my life since." He was, the next month, to turn
sixty, Livy fifty. These were not birthdays either of them felt like celebrating. The change of decades preoccupied him. "[He] is so impressed with
the fact that he is sixty years old," Livy wrote to Susan Crane. "Naturally,
I combat that thought all that I can, trying to make him rejoice, that he is
not *seventy*."

Australia impressed him with its conquest of a new world, the great distances overcome, the cities created and countryside cultivated: skyscrap-
ers in Melbourne; vineyards on the hills; sheep ranches the size of small
countries; beyond its southeast corner, a vast, mostly unexplored continent. Much reminded him of the American West at an earlier time, the dialectic between the gold rush mentality and the urge to put down roots.
Slow railroads and railroad discoordination from province to province irritated him. Twain filled his notebook with observations, his way of process-
ing experience. The position of women in Australian society fueled his
preoccupation with the differences between savagery and civilization,
which had been a strong interest since *Pudd'nhead Wilson*. "One of the

signs of savagery," he observed, is a civilization "where equality between man & woman is furthest apart," adding that "no civiliz[ation] can be perfect until exact equality between man & woman is included." Yet the so-called most advanced civilizations continued to treat women as inferior.

Still, he admitted, he was not going to make a public issue about this, or about his views on nature and God. "There is nothing kindly, nothing beneficent, nothing friendly in Nature toward *any* creature, except by capricious fits & starts. . . . Nature's attitude toward all life is profoundly vicious, treacherous, & malignant." But most human beings were too irrational and blinded by fear to see the truth, evidence of which was an ever-present part of their own physical lives. Before he landed in Sydney, nature had resumed torturing him in the form of a new carbuncle halfway between left knee and ankle. It plagued him for weeks until an Australian surgeon lanced and drained it. "Badly crippled," he needed to cancel social engagements and recuperate in bed. His gradual recovery did not make him feel any the less certain that nature had worse in store for him, and everyone else. "It is the strangest thing," he wrote in his notebook, "that the world is not full of books that scoff at the pitiful world, & the useless universe & the vile & contemptible human race—books that laugh at the whole paltry scheme & deride it. Curious, for millions of men die every year with these feelings in their hearts. Why don't *I* write such a book? Because I have a family. There is no other reason." He was being absolutely honest, in private. Direct public expression of such views the public did not desire and would not tolerate from a humorist.

After six exhausting weeks in Australia, they sailed to Tasmania, arriving too late for Twain to lecture, then to the southernmost port of New Zealand's South Island. Forced by quarantine to remain in Sydney Harbor, Smythe had relinquished his charge to his capable son, who became Twain's lecture agent for the rest of the tour. On the three-day voyage to New Zealand, Twain found irresistible the request that he entertain his fellow passengers, among them the Irish nationalist Michael Davitt, whose speaking tour had already intersected with his. Ceylon and India were next on his schedule, then South Africa, where British settlers, eager to overthrow the Boer regime in Transvaal, had been ratcheting up British-Boer tensions. In Australia and New Zealand, British sovereignty seemed more nominal than real. "Can't see that the British govt has any more authority here," he wrote, "than she has over the constellations."

As he had come to see in the American West and Hawaii, "All savages & semi-civilized countries are going to be grabbed." European powers would either destroy or subjugate native populations as the circumstances warranted. "Whatever civilization seizes a savage country stamps ruthlessly the savages out when the populations are small." Land, natural resources, and markets were the rewards. In every case, Twain wished "England might be the grabber, not France. India is better off for being grabbed by England. She has had 800 years of the foreign yoke anyway, & the English is the most beneficent she has had." England rationalized government, maintained national defense, created schools, educated a civil service, and built an infrastructure. The English language united its speakers in a worldwide English-speaking union. It provided government, values, and culture, the best of what the world had to offer. He preferred independent republics on the American model, but in the meantime Britain was the least predatory colonial power, and it gave back value for what it took.

But he also clearly heard the plangent voices of native peoples dispossessed of their lands and even their lives. His visceral antipathy to what had seemed to him the savagery of the Indian tribes in Nevada and California had not allowed him to transcend the cultural biases of his frontier world. For the native Hawaiians, dominated politically and then destroyed by European diseases, he had had an erratic sympathy. Now his longstanding compassion for enslaved blacks and his detestation of postReconstruction iniquities provided the base for a gradually extending concern about the exploitation of all native peoples. His admiration for (and envy of) South Pacific and Asian sensual vividness also helped him to think beyond Victorian Anglo-American stereotypes. Difference he now thought a good thing. And since stupidity and barbarity were so rampant in his own culture, he thought it hardly sensible to condemn those vices in others, especially as the condemnation usually was based on ignorance and racial stereotyping. He had, gradually, transformed himself into someone who thought less in Eurocentric racial terms than did most of his contemporaries, and his racial categorizations, often value neutral, emphasized that all human beings were equally human. Even his antipathy to American Indians would not have prevented his realizing that the genocide that characterized white treatment of Australian Aborigines and New Zealand Maori tribes had its North American counterpart. On a sunny day, as he sailed between Tasmania and the adjacent islands, formerly prison camps, he heard in his mind the voices of "the poor exiled Tasmanian savages [who] used to gaze at their beloved land & cry; & die of heart-break." In New Zealand, he sought out and admired the Maori, their crafts, their culture, their efforts to survive as a people. So too did Livy, who began a small collection of Maori artifacts.

New Zealand's landscape thrilled him, though the four-day sail from Tasmania to South Island seemed the worst they had experienced: bad weather, distasteful food, foul sanitation, an overcrowded, stinking ship—a "floating pig-sty," Twain remarked, "with her 1500 Christians crowded into 'accommodations' more proper for 25 cattle." From the tip of South Island they ferried northward along the east coast, accompanied by Smythe and a German-speaking maid who had been attending them since their arrival in Australia. Dunedin and Christchurch provided full houses. They sailed to Wellington and then up the west coast to Auckland and around North Island, making a full circle back to Wellington. "We leave for Auckland next Saturday on nothing but a row-boat I am sure," Clara remarked. Any site that offered an audience had been addressed or was now scheduled. Distances were great, rural areas huge and sparsely populated. To make the trip financially sound, he had to travel frequently and far, though people came as much as a hundred miles to hear him and, in one case, two hundred. Audiences, with rare exceptions, treated him as the long-awaited charismatic celebrity, the genial, wisdom-purveying humorist personified. Whatever he said, they found it funny or riveting or both.

Six weeks in Australia and then six in New Zealand seemed barely enough to attend to duties and to sightsee, the tension between duty and desire a constant feature of Twain's life on land. On shipboard, he usually was in blissful heaven with little to do and long stretches of free time. On land, great distances and slow transportation limited his opportunities. He particularly regretted not visiting the bustling gold fields of Australia. A severe chest cold and discomfort from his carbuncle further limited his sightseeing. Now and then he broke down entirely and needed bed rest, which he spent smoking and reading, especially books about the countries he was visiting. Much of his touring was restricted to scenery along the routes between two cities in which he had engagements. At those times, though, he was all eyes and pen, filling pages with observations he expected to incorporate into his book—anecdotes, intellectual comments, cultural questions, exquisitely framed descriptions of landscapes and people.

"We have had a most delightful 6-weeks lecture-campaign in NZ," he wrote Henry Rogers on December 12, 1895. "This is merely a note to say we sail in an hour for Australia; & thence, after a few days, for India—say about the first week in January." They would sail from Sydney; a week in Australia would provide the opportunity to make up performances missed when he had been bedridden in Melbourne. During the day he played billiards. Christmas the Clemenses spent in Melbourne, New Year's Day 1896 in Adelaide, saying good-bye to Australian friends who filled the family's cabin on the *Oceana* with flowers. The only way to determine the date and time of departure was to check at the dock every day.

To Rogers he continued to send the profits, a total of about $7,500 before leaving Australia. Sometimes he felt upbeat about the accumulating proceeds, at others disheartened at how long he estimated it would take to satisfy his creditors. On the one hand, father, mother, and daughter had begun to get used to the wandering life. On the other, Livy deeply valued the actuality and the ideal of home. Twain often enjoyed himself considerably, though the wear and tear ground him down. Inconsistently and naturally, he both loved being on the platform and resented having to sing for his supper.

It had been his decision, though, to undertake this particular tour. It would have been more efficient first to try England and America, the most concentrated English-speaking markets, and then, if he still needed money, the more distant outposts. To an extent, he chose to lecture around the world for its publicity value. The announcement had a uniquely dramatic flair. But his lifelong restlessness contributed to the itinerary, and, most of all, an around-the-world tour would take him to exotic lands, to places to which he had never been and had always wanted to go.

4.

As they sailed 2,500 miles northwestward from Australia to the Indian subcontinent, they were, in a sense, on their way home. From India to America was less than the distance they would have to travel if they turned around and sailed east. They did not, though, feel that any return at all was imminent. Hartford still seemed out of the question. "Oh dear me!" Livy exclaimed. "I wonder if we shall ever get our debts all paid, and live once more in our own house. To-day it seems to me as if we never should." London, where he had determined he would write the travel book, offered opportunities to lecture profitably if he needed the money. Susy eagerly expected to meet them there in the spring. But it soon appeared more likely that they would need until midsummer to finish the tour, especially if the South African visit remained on the schedule. From New Zealand, Livy had broken the disappointing news to Susy. "Everything takes longer than we expected. We have been hindered here and there and it is now evident that we shall not get through with Africa before July if we do then." It was not because they had dawdled or indulged themselves, she explained. "We have done steadily our work all the time, we have not loitered one day for sight-seeing. In fact we are really seeing nothing of the wonders of this land that we ought to see. We have passed by so much for lack of time that I sometimes wonder if papa will not lack material for his book. . . . We are here for a definite purpose, and that purpose is not pleasure seeking." Yet, she admitted, "in spite of that we get much pleasure by the way."

For Twain, the supreme pleasure of the trip was India, though health problems continued to curtail his activities. The thirty lectures he planned had to be reduced to twenty, at a forfeit of about two thousand dollars in profits. Though the pernicious carbuncle tendency desisted, chest colds dominated, exacerbated by his performances, his voice occasionally reduced to a croak. Doctors insisted on bed rest. Indian food and water wreaked havoc with their stomachs and bowels. Smythe had to go to bed for a week. "We get up many mornings at six, and as a rule are not in bed before twelve, and I very rarely lie down in the day-time. Don't you think I must be pretty strong and well?" Livy wrote to Jean. To their shock, parts of India were hotter in the winter than America and Australia in the summer, which gave them what seemed nine consecutive months of dust, noise, and sleeplessness.

Despite the heat, the week-long voyage from Australia to Ceylon was mostly restful, particularly for Twain's tired voice. On the Indian Ocean all seemed "everlasting peace & tranquillity . . . infinitely comfortable & satisfying," the *Oceana* the cleanest, most spacious ship he had ever been on. Delighted by its superb library, he read a stack of novels. His bad cough subsided, then returned, then seemed "miraculously cured by a few garglings with diluted listerine." When they stepped off the boat in Ceylon, everything changed. The colors were "dazzling yellows and greens in shades one never finds in America anywhere," Clara noticed. For the first time they were in a "sumptuously tropical" world, the vividness of which dazzled Twain's eyes. He felt surrounded by "wild beauty & life." Lustrous black skin, turbans and sarongs of every color, brighter and deeper than any he had ever seen, crowded streets and outdoor markets set against a land-scape of greens, browns, and multicolored flowers with a variety he had never imagined, sent him into a sensory whirl. "The most amazing variety of nakedness & color—& all harmonious & fascinating."

After a day in Ceylon, they sailed northwestward on the *Rosetta* into the Arabian Sea and up the coast to Bombay, their first Indian destination. Ar-riving late on January 18, 1896, he went immediately to bed with his "in-fernal cough": "It does not improve. I wish it was in hell." Livy and Clara began sightseeing. Confined to the small world of his room, Twain found it immense, filled with sounds different from those he had ever heard be-fore—the quaint accents of the English-speaking Indians, the raucous ho-tel noises beginning at five in the morning, the mellifluously grand aristocratic titles like "the Begum of Bhopal" to which he added his own comic inventions, the "Slambang of Gutcheree . . . the Hoopla of Hellas-plit" and "his highness the Juggernaut of Jacksonville."

When the German hotel manager, without any explanation, cuffed a Hindu servant, Twain was jarred: "It carried me instantly back to my boy-hood and flashed upon me the forgotten fact that this was the *usual* way of explaining one's desire to a slave." The servant meekly accepted the as-sault. As a boy, Twain recalled, he had thought such treatment natural, though he had also felt "sorry for the victim and ashamed for the punisher." The incident brought to mind his father's regularly cuffing their slave boy for any little infraction, and occasionally lashing him. Writing this in his notebook, to be expanded later into a powerful passage for his travel book, awakened additional memories of master-slave interactions that he had ob-served in Hannibal, including the accidental murder of a slave by his mas-ter "for merely doing something awkwardly, as if that were a crime." Suddenly, in the confines of his hotel room, he felt himself transported back to the world of his Missouri childhood. He was now in two places at once, their distances connected by the power of memory and by the con-junction of similar social structures, separated by continents and genera-tions. Throughout his Indian travels he was aware that both those vectors met in him.

As in Australia, but even more so in India, he did not think his hosts

ready for self-governance. Just as, in Twain's view, American post–Civil
War blacks needed compensatory support, the impoverished masses of the
Indian subcontinent needed to be brought to a higher level of education
and well-being, a challenge on a far greater scale than even in the American situation, before self-rule could be viable. He observed in *Following
the Equator,* "India does not consist of cities. . . . India is one vast farm,
one almost interminable stretch of fields with mud fences between. Think
of the above facts; and consider what an incredible aggregate of poverty
they place before you." Native peoples should rule themselves, he believed. But nineteenth-century India was the result of thousands of years
of non-Western conquest and enslavement, of an Oriental society in which
an elite class of Indian potentates controlled huge wealth, with life-and-
death power over hundreds of millions of impoverished people. British rule
seemed comparatively benign and enlightened. He still sustained his
satiric hostility to English aristocratic misrule, but that was within the context of a materially advanced and democratic culture. In Britain and America, one could distinguish between the baby and the bath water. In India,
so much seemed bath water, and it, like the River Ganges, was badly
polluted.

As always, he was invited to lunch and dine with the privileged and
powerful, both British and Indian, at various government houses and impressive palaces. Elite clubs extended honorary memberships. At the Bombay Yacht Club, Livy and Clara attended a ball. Indian proprietors asked
for testimonials to what fine establishments they ran. Railroad authorities
arranged private cars and sometimes special trains. His most memorable
moments had to do with indigenous life. At the Towers of Silence in Bombay they had a glimpse though an iron gate, opened to admit a funeral procession of a "row of vultures" that had "fringed the top of the tower wall . . .
flying down" into the sacred place to play their important role in a Parsi funeral. A young Parsi prince who had heard him in London years before invited them to an elaborate, well-attended ceremony, where they were
entertained "by gaudy professional boys—wonderfully graceful creatures."
Once, close to midnight, they were driven through rat-infested, plague-
ridden Bombay streets, on which hundreds of natives slept wrapped in
blankets, to a betrothal ceremony in a brilliantly lit house just one
street away from the urban misery. "Gaudy & gorgeous decorations—a

bewildering dazzle. No women present—but the comely & shapely little bride came & shook hands. . . . She is 12 years old. . . . *He* (about her age) didn't turn up—gone to bed."

After three well-attended lectures, they left Bombay by train at the end of January 1896. Six of their ten days there he had spent in bed. The local and national press reported his lectures as events that did honor to India. After stops at Poona and Baroda, where the Maharaja gave him the unhappy pleasure of his first elephant ride, they traveled 1,200 miles eastward to Calcutta, with lecture stops at Allahabad and Benares. The usually impatient man observed that he would "always like to wait an hour for [a] train in India." They usually waited even longer. To his astonishment, he never grew tired of the spectacle of colorful native life at the stations. At Allahbad "everybody came [to his lecture] in his own private carriage apparently, with 2 or 3 turbaned footmen." In the street, "small naked beggars" stood and repeated "apparently the same words" every half-hour. "[Religion]," he later wrote, "is the *business* of Benares, just as gold-production is the business of Johannesburg." Temples, holy men, beggars, pilgrims—it was "a religious Vesuvius." His wife and daughter must also have noticed the widespread worship of Shiva as a phallus, religion as sexual energy and reproduction.

The dirt, disease, and superstition warranted mockery, some of which he provided in satiric passages in *Following the Equator*. But sincere religious belief he respected, especially in comparison to widespread Christian hypocrisy. "In these countries the *whole* people are religious;—profoundly, sincerely, heartily religious in Xian ones it is 1 in the 10." At the confluence of three holy rivers, they observed the spectacle of the Ganges. The power of religious faith to overcome material reality bewildered and amazed them. For Hindus, the Ganges provided both cemetery and river of purification. Hindu theology he had little interest in and mostly dismissed, but he was fascinated by the psychology of religion and its manifestations.

Like most Western travelers in India, they had Indian servants because it was expected, and also to help negotiate situations they knew little about. To their surprise, sleeping cars and hotels did not provide bedding. In fact, guests at private homes were expected to bring their own and also their own servants. They found themselves being served even at palaces by the two servants they had hired. One seemed to Twain uninteresting, the

other he named "Satan," expressive of Twain's lifelong collegiality with his
favorite companion among symbolic creatures. "I only liked Manuel, but I
loved Satan." Satan made them all dizzy with his frenetic activity. As his
valet, Satan dressed Twain "from head to heel in spite of my determination
to do it myself, according to my lifelong custom." At first he was embarrassed to appear even partly dressed in front of the man, whose petite good
looks had enough of the feminine to send Twain's normal gender boundaries out of equilibrium. But as soon as he made a mental adjustment he
found his valet's constant presence unthreatening, the totality of his personality attractive, even his loudness, which the rest of the family could
not stand, and his bossiness with Indians. Twain delighted to see him in
action, especially at railroad stations. It "humiliated" the others, though.
When Satan's predilection for alcohol emerged, Clara and Livy insisted
that he be fired. Twain resisted but after a few awkward episodes gave in.

On arriving in Calcutta, Twain went to bed with the severe cold he had
caught on the seventeen-hour trip from Benares. Still, he fulfilled three
lecture commitments in one week. "I am shut up in the hotel starving it
out," he wrote to Susy, "& so, instead of river parties & dinners & things,
all three of us must decline & stay at home." He soon recovered enough to
be dined and feted by the lieutenant governor and to accept the honor of
inspecting the Calcutta Garrison. Since the supposedly "cold weather" in
Calcutta felt roasting hot, they went to Darjeeling, seven thousand feet
above the Bengal plain, a raised platform on the eastern spur of the Hi-
malayas, from where they could see the highest peaks in the world. It was
a wild, lovely, and comfortable holiday.

Leaving Calcutta in a private railroad car provided gratis, they watched,
as if looking through a screen, the bustling Indian panorama. On the far
side of the Ganges they transferred to a private sleeping car, which took
them overnight to the terminal for the ascent to Darjeeling on a miniature
narrow-track train, with canvas roofs and sides open to the air. The forty-
mile ascent on a switchback road took almost nine hours. The views of
the Bengal plain were spectacular, and after seven hours, at six thousand
feet, they ascended into clouds, then descended into Darjeeling. Neat
European-style bungalows and mountain flowers dotted the hillside. Wind
chimes tinkled in the breeze. The air was crisp, invigorating. To their delight, Darjeeling looked like an Alpine village. It was almost as if they were
back in Europe. The next day, since everything was immersed in clouds,

they consoled themselves at the crowded, colorful regional market. The next morning they awakened to a clear vista. From his second-floor bedroom window, wrapped in blankets, smoking his pipe, he gazed at Kichingunga, "& 2 other great peaks . . . only about a thousand lower than its neighbor Everest, the highest mountain in the world." Clara ran off to attempt a higher, better vantage point. Twain remained slouched in the window, smoking his pipe, gazing into the distance. Two hours later the clouds closed in again.

He took delight in the descent from Darjeeling, the open train taking curves at what seemed double the speed of the ascent. "We have lectured, & seen the Himalayan mountain that is 29,000 feet high," he wrote to Charles Henry Webb, "& have met a man who conversed with a man who knows the man who saw a tiger come out of the jungle yesterday & eat the friend of his who had just put on his breech-clout & was starting out to pay calls, for we have to pass right by that spot & he will probably want some more." It was as if he were once again in his Hannibal childhood, having adventures he could then only read about. The excitement brought out the Tom Sawyer in him. "We started in rugs & furs," he wrote to Henry Rogers, "at a dizzy toboggan gait . . . & stripped as we came down, as the weather gradually changed from eternal snow to perpetual hellfire."

His remaining weeks in India, though, had in them more chore than play, and on the next leg they all began to show fatigue. They left Calcutta again, traveled northwest to Lucknow, and then to Cawnpoore and Agra, where they stayed in a spacious bungalow provided by the English governor, on to Jeypore, where the heat was intense, and Delhi, then northward to Lahore and Rawalpindi, at the Afghanistan border. His lectures were cumulative economic punctuation marks in an immense landscape of long train journeys. In the end, Livy calculated that, since so many performances had had to be canceled, after their expenses they had made only about a thousand dollars: "But it has been a most charming trip. We have enjoyed every minute of it," she exaggerated to her sister, "and it is better material for Mr. Clemens' book than Australia or Africa."

Twain kept himself amused as best he could, and continued to take notes. At Jeypore they were almost all sick. Since smallpox was a threat, Clara and Livy were vaccinated. The English doctor urged that Twain cancel his engagements and "rest a week or ten days." Smythe joined them, and he too immediately became sick. Twain, though, was well enough to be dazzled by a festival procession of Hindu idols. English courage and folly continued to entertain him, including the high incidence of venereal disease among the soldiers because English "cant" would not allow vetting the health of prostitutes. Still, wherever he went in India and around the world, he felt he was part of a worldwide Anglo-Saxon fraternity, and he had not the slightest inclination to "go native," no matter how deep his sympathy for the Indian people or excitement by Indian beauty. He was an observer, a writer, an American, an Anglo-Saxon.

At Agra, they visited the Taj Mahal, a required tourist stop, which he admired but to which in *Following the Equator* he attempted a fresh approach by discussing how prepackaged images determine what we see when we actually are, at last, in the presence of the thing itself. When he arrived, close to midnight and with two carriages of visitors, the "splendid full moon" began to go into eclipse. After an hour, it was total, "an attention," he noted, "not offered to a stranger since the Taj was built." He may have wondered if perhaps his luck was returning. At Jeypore, a doctor warned him to leave India soon. The unhealthy monsoon season was about to begin. When "the *real* summer" comes, he wrote to Rogers, "Satan himself has to knock off and go home and cool off." In Calcutta, two hundred people were dying of cholera every day. They took the warning, which fit their schedule anyway. "I think this must be a most terrible land in the summer," Livy wrote to Jean. At Lahore, on March 19, 1896, he noted that it was Susy's birthday. She was twenty-four years old. Her father, Clara noted, appeared fatigued and depressed.

5.

Two weeks later, as they sailed into the calm waters of the Indian Ocean, Twain began to shake some of the weariness from his bones. He did it mainly by sitting still, smoking, and reading, absorbing himself during the three-week voyage to Mauritius, the French island colony off the South African coast, in a stack of travel, history, and science books, particularly a lengthy study of a particular ant population. Its conclusion that every ant recognized every other member of its colony through vision gave Twain's resentment of human limitation an additional focus, since people could remember a comparatively small number of faces. A Swiftean mood returned, in which he saw human beings as "the most odious race of pernicious vermin that Nature ever suffered to crawl on the face of the earth," especially all those who had done him injury, like Charles L. Webster and Elisha Bliss. If it were not for Webster, this tour, he had convinced himself, would have been unnecessary.

Still, under sunny skies, his anxiety about paying off his debts gnawed at him less than usual. Reading, and the writing he did regularly in his notebook, transported him to a happier, compartmentalized place. Gently rocked by the ship's motion, gazing at the tranquil horizon, he felt peaceful. He wished the voyage would never end. Livy, though, brooded unhappily. Cockroaches infested their steamy cabin. They were "as large as mice and more familiar," Clara remarked. Mother and daughter slept on deck most nights. Twain's health, actually better than it had been for some time, worried Livy. But her mental anguish focused on the lengthy list of creditors, what vast stretches of time it would take to pay them, and the difficulty of sustaining her faith in their eventual return to Hartford. She would have given a great deal to be there now, and to see Susy, who had moved there from Elmira. "I feel," she confided to her sister, "that our going home and inhabiting our own house is far in the distance. Very, very far. You know I have a pretty good courage, but sometimes it comes over me like an overwhelming wave, that it is to be bitterness and disappointment to the end."

If they had not decided to pay the creditors in full, they would have had a smaller rock to roll uphill. They might already have been at the top, or close to it. Livy's puritan sense of honor had driven her argument that creditors must be paid dollar for dollar. Henry Rogers had argued that Twain's capital as an author resided in his reputation, and doing what almost no one else did would increase its value. They were paying a high price for what now seemed to him a dubious honor. Later he was to have additional reason to question their judgment, and additional bitterness. "Do you remember, Livy, the hellish struggle it was to settle on making that lecture trip around the world? . . . But once the idea struck us we couldn't shake it. Oh, no! for it was packed with sense of honor—honor—honor—no rest, comfort, joy—but plenty of honor, plenty of ethical glory."

Slogging on with the work at hand, they sailed from Mauritius, where they had two weeks of rest enforced by quarantine and the absence of an English-speaking audience. In early May 1896, they disembarked at Durban, on the east coast of South Africa. "We feel now that the back of our journey is broken," Livy wrote, "and that we are started toward home, at least toward England." Twain urged his wife and daughter to stay in comfortable Durban rather than be subjected to his tiring travel schedule. The South African winter would soon begin and, though "the days [were] warm, coolness [began] with sunset." As he traveled, a seven-week South African version of his triumphal Indian tour, he missed Livy terribly. Though she wished she could help lighten his burdens, particularly his self-criticism, she accepted that he had little capacity for conversations about misery. Cursing came more easily than intimacy, at least partly, he explained in his notebook, because he "came of an undemonstrative race." Apparently he had his father, more than his mother, in mind. "We seem each to be compelled," Livy observed, "to carry much alone our own burdens."

With Smythe, he carried his one-man performance, oiled by practice into perfection, south to Port Elizabeth, then to Johannesburg and Pretoria in the Transvaal, the seat of the Boer government, then to Queenstown and Bloemfontein in the Orange Free State. Railroad officials provided their famous guest with private cars, often with a toilet, a rarity. Overflow audiences packed the performances. Here, as elsewhere, he was an international celebrity, the equal of any. Audiences were either exclusively British or Boer, and always white. From the moment he stepped ashore, the South African political pot, which had been boiling over, fascinated him. British and Dutch-speaking settlers, uneasily scattered among one another in varying proportions throughout separate states, controlled South Africa. In Cape Colony, the British dominated; in the Transvaal, the Boers. Between was a huge cultural divide. Each accused the other of discrimination against their white minorities. Both treated the indigenous black population with paternalistic disdain, though the Bible-thumping Boers added brutality to contempt. At Johannesburg the manager of a huge gold mine told Twain, "We don't *call* our blacks slaves, but that is what they *are,* & that is what we mean they shall remain."

In December 1895, a British colonial administrator, Leander Jameson, with a company of armed volunteers including a few Americans, encouraged by the autocratic Cape Colony prime minister Cecil Rhodes, had invaded Transvaal with the expectation that dissatisfied British settlers would join in overthrowing the Boer government. Jameson hoped to unite all of South Africa under Queen Victoria's rule. Instead, his band found itself outnumbered and was badly bloodied. The furious Boers imprisoned the survivors. Rhodes denied responsibility. In London, her Majesty's government was quietly sympathetic to its imperial warriors but unwilling to defend, let alone be complicit in, naked aggression. British South Africa and the British Empire, though, were widely perceived to be responsible for the raid.

Having learned about it in February 1896 while in India, Twain was eager to interview the participants. As an American, he was welcome in Boer South Africa, among other reasons because recent British-American disagreement over the Monroe Doctrine and Venezuela had raised tensions to a level that threatened war. It could not be assumed that he would be pro-British. In Australia and India, reporters frequently asked their distinguished guest his view on the Venezuela affair. Twain succeeded in not putting his foot in his mouth. Comity between the two Anglo-Saxon nations, he regularly responded, was essential, war unthinkable. Twain felt deeply relieved when, late in 1895, the Venezuelan conflict moved toward a peaceful resolution. In South Africa, his sympathy was with the British, though not with Jameson. In fact, he had more interest in and sympathy for South African blacks than for the British or the Boers. After all, he angrily remarked in his notebook, it had been their country first. Europeans thought they had a right to steal other people's property if the rightful owners were not Europeans. Colonialism was nothing but and no better than theft, though he continued to believe that the British version was better than anyone else's, certainly than the Boers', who seemed to him retrograde political reactionaries.

At Pretoria and Johannesburg, where he gave ten performances, officialdom welcomed him with the keys to the city. His first-night audience in Pretoria consisted mostly of "direct descendants of the old Boers." It took a while for him to warm up this tough audience. Once he had, they were responsive. Johannesburg audiences seemed filled with people claiming they knew him from Nevada and California mining days, to whom he responded, "Of course, of course," but privately remarked that he didn't know any of them. One good lie, though, deserved another. When a man showed him the copy of *Innocents Abroad* he had given John Riley in 1870, he was reminded that he had once made a South African investment, sponsoring Riley's search for diamonds in exchange for detailed notes on the basis of which he had hoped to write a best-selling book. "Must pretend that Riley told me we owned de Toite Pen & Kimberley mines." It would make a good joke and a good story.

A raw frontier town, Johannesburg had been transformed by a huge gold strike into an African version of what Virginia City had been in the early 1860s. Miners were everywhere. Most of his socializing, though, was with British residents. After almost every performance he joined his American friend Poultney Bigelow, who was writing newspaper dispatches, for brandy, cigars, and late-night conversation. He usually held court for interviewers in the late mornings while in his hotel bed; it was convenient—and good newspaper copy. He diplomatically avoided any but bland comments about South African politics and was evasively circumspect about Cecil Rhodes, whom he despised. At its best, British colonialism was generous in its treatment of native populations; at its worst, it was Rhodes. At a dinner in his honor at a private home, twenty distinguished British guests were joined afterward by twenty leading Boers in an effort to bring the communities together. Twain humorously addressed them about "the curse of *party* loyalty" and the destructiveness of extreme nationalism.

Accompanied by some English residents, Twain, with the permission of the authorities, who probably thought it a good thing for him to describe to the world their humane treatment, visited the English and American prisoners; their condition and eventual disposition was of intense concern in South Africa and London. Negotiations were in progress, rumors flying. With an armed guard at his elbow, he was taken on a tour of the facilities, introduced to the detainees, and then, sitting on a box, allowed to address a large group in the courtyard. "Explained to the prisoners," he later wrote in his notebook from a transcription Smythe had made, "why they were better off in the jail than they wd be anywhere else; that they would eventually have gotten into jail anyhow, for one thing or another, no doubt . . . that it would be better all around if they remained quietly where they were & made the best of it; that after a few months they wd prefer the jail & its luxurious indolence to the sordid struggle for bread outside; & that I wd go & see Pres. Kruger & do everything I could, short of bribery, to get the government to double their jail-terms."

There is no indication that the prisoners found this funny. When a Boer newspaper printed Twain's response—that the prisoners were now living in luxury—to a reporter's question about prison conditions, his irony backfired. The government cut their rations. A few days later, he visited President Kruger to request leniency. "Everybody says he has a kind heart. His wife present, a motherly old lady, simply & cheaply dressed, with a hospitable handshake. . . . He said he felt friendly toward America & it was his disposition to be lenient with the American captives." By the end of May 1896 all but four prisoners were liberated. "Kruger, it is said," Twain wrote in his notebook, "threatened to resign unless this was done." In mid-June the remaining four were fined twenty-five thousand pounds each and set free. When Rhodes, whose culpability was widely assumed, declined to promise that he would never again "meddle in Transvaal politics," he was banished. He was instead to find his type of paradise just to the north, in what became Rhodesia, now Zimbabwe.

From Pretoria, Twain made his way back, lecturing along the way, to Durban, from where, with Livy and Clara, he sailed south to English-dominated Port Elizabeth and then Cape Town on the west coast. There were annoyances, like being awakened each morning at an early hour by a waiter bringing coffee he hadn't ordered and didn't want, and then, as soon as he had fallen back asleep, returning to collect the cup since it was needed to serve others. Essentially the same lecture scenario repeated itself from city to city. Large crowds. Enthusiastic hosts. Sometimes he bore it happily, the self-satisfaction of a successful performer. Other times he still chafed at the necessity of having to perform.

There were also pleasures, including a brown-green landscape that made him think of Texas. Clara and Livy, still under the influence of India's lushness, found South Africa dull. With his talent for focus and transformation, Twain did not. America was on his mind. "I could frame glimpses, with my hands, of rocks & grassy slopes & distant groups of trees that were exactly American—New England, New York, Iowa." The colorful singularity of "*one* blossom in this blossomless Africa—a cactus with a foot-long tongue of flame standing up out of it as red as the coat-of-arms at the head of the page"—sent him into descriptive ecstasies. It was a landscape of a sort that always had appealed to him, like Minnesota wheat fields or Keokuk sunsets. He found even more fascinating the variety of skin tones of South African blacks. Shades of darkness had an attractive luster that he took pleasure in. To his mind, God had left out something important when he had created bleached white skins. Black voices and speech patterns appealed to his ear, too, as if he were hearing voices in the Missouri night. "These darkies [are] just like ours. . . . The women have the sweet soft muscial voice of ours, too. I followed them a couple of miles to listen to the music of their speech & the happy ripple of their laugh."

American images and memories superimposed themselves on the South African reality.

What he most wanted to hear, though, as they began counting down the days until departure, were actual American voices, especially Susy's and Jean's, which they expected to hear soon. They were all reconciled to spending the next year in London, and perhaps returning to America the year after. Departure from South Africa would at least bring their homeless voyaging to a stop. London had that and other attractions, including familiarity and appropriateness. It offered them all a life. Meanwhile, Twain went to Grahamstown, Cradock, then Kimberley, where he visited the De Beers Company mines. The honored guest was allowed to hold a fistful of raw diamonds. Just a few of them, he undoubtedly thought, would have solved his financial problems.

At Cape Town, he learned that his friend, the actor Frank Mayo, four years younger than he, had "died of heart disease in a railway train near Denver," on tour with his stage adaptation of *Pudd'nhead Wilson*. It would have been enough to frighten even a man who believed in heaven. Exhausted, Twain was "tired of the platform . . . tired of the slavery of it, tired of having to rest-up for it; diet myself for it . . . deny myself in a thousand ways in its interest. Why, there *isn't* any slavery that is so exacting and so infernal." At last, in mid-July 1896, they sailed from Cape Town for Southampton, England. "I hope I have trodden [the platform] for the last time," he wrote to Henry Rogers, as the SS *Norman* steamed northward.

6.

Livy had, in June, instructed Susan Crane to prepare Jean and Susy for departure about "the fifth of August" but not to fix an exact date. *"I don't want them really to start until we send a cable saying 'come.'* Because if they start before getting a cable from us they might find us in the bottom of the sea when they reach England, or on our way to America." In fact, Twain, Livy, and Clara reached Southampton safely at the end of July 1896, after a stop in Madeira, where they were delayed a few days. They had traveled fifty-three thousand miles without accident or misfortune. Livy now sprained her ankle. Her pain, Twain wrote to Howells, was matched by her despondency "when she found she couldn't run around the country house-hunting." The long-anticipated cable had been immediately dispatched, and their American left-behinds, accompanied by Katy Leary, were expected to arrive by the middle of August.

Within the week, Clara and her father found a comfortable house in Surrey, an hour from London, sufficiently close to return the same day. They had decided they would prefer to spend their first three English months in the country, not far from London but sufficiently distant to provide "the luxury & rest of writing a book or two after this long fatigue & turmoil of platform work & gadding around by sea & land." Also, the prospect of having their daughters to themselves before settling in London for the winter appealed to them. As soon as her ankle was healed, Livy began searching for a London residence. Clara would resume her piano lessons as early as September. Jean would go to school, near home, or perhaps in London. Susy's disposition was unclear. What would her health permit? Would it allow her to resume training for a singing career? It had been a difficult, complicated year for her, but not an entirely unhappy one. In fact, despite some lonely moments, she had maintained remarkable good cheer. It was not easy to be Mark Twain's talented daughter, but it was also less a burden to her than it had been previously, at least partly because her health had improved. The separation may have contributed to that.

Back in August 1895, as soon as her parents and sister started westward, Susy, at Elmira, brooded. "I am often deeply cast down with the thought of how I have failed to be what I should have been to you all. . . . But perhaps I shall have a chance to try again. In any case, you know I love you all and could not have wanted more to be a 'nice child.' The only difficulty is that our duty doesn't end with wanting." For much of the year she focused her energy on an effort to transform herself. "I have become determined to get hold of a philosophy that will if possible straighten me out morally, mentally, and physically and make me less of a burden to myself and others. I am tired tired of all my sins . . . this hitch, this discord, this restlessness making every undertaking impossible, and spoiling and frittering away my life."

She wanted a calmer center of self. She wanted to be able to be a harmonious member of the only community to which she felt a desire to belong. She wanted to be well enough "to leave Elmira and all its bores" to rejoin her family: "[You] brilliant, experienced, adorable people, to whom I belong, and to rejoin you in Europe!!!" Remaining behind had been a voluntary exile, an attempt to work to some happier resolution the elements of her personality and nervous system that had frustrated her ambitions, made her ill, and reduced her to feeling a burden to those she loved. "If I ever can be with you again, I shall stick like a burr indeed! There will be no extricating and separating me from you again! We are such a congenial family. It seems to me no one ever understands us as we understand each other. We do belong together."

Within four months of separation, she indeed had made progress, primarily through the help, she believed, of what was referred to as "Mental Healing," which sometimes meant Christian Science but also any one of the many faith healing ministries that treated emotional and physical distress. Hypnotism, the "talk-cure," electrical shock, the passing of hands, contact with higher powers, the many varieties of spiritualism popular since the mid-century, all had their partisans. In Paris, convinced of the extraordinary powers of the mind, including telepathy, Twain had urged his daughter to try hypnotism. Livy was enthusiastic. In Hartford, Katy Leary was incredulous about "one Spiritualist—a kind of healer—a woman." "Susy, she used to go to her, and she made passes over Susy's throat—to make it strong so she could sing good." One time Katy overheard the woman tell Susy that she had been at a concert the previous night with her husband, who enjoyed it so much. *"Now her husband had been dead twenty-five years,* and I know it! When I heard that I just called out, 'Rats!' and Susy said: 'Oh, Katy! Katy!'"* Susy had insisted to Katy that the woman might have been "the worst kind of a Spiritualist . . . but [was] a good healer." Like his daughter, Twain believed in the power of suggestion to heal and transform. So did Livy, whose early years of illness probably came to mind. More important, they did not particularly care from what source help came: they wanted Susy to get better.

Between September 1895 and the new year, Susy tried a number of such engagements. When she felt distress, she and her medium would talk, hold hands, concentrate silently together; when they were apart, they would set a time to be in communication mentally. In these "absent treatments" she would concentrate on her healer's mind. Verbal mantras and visual images helped. Almost always, she felt better, and the improvement gradually sustained itself. Throat and voice problems that had plagued her disappeared. She could sing again, though she did not resume lessons. Her difficulty with writing diminished, and she began to compose little things. Feeling more socially at ease, she started to make visits, including one to

Louise Brownell in New Jersey and to a new friend, Lily Burbank, at a home "full of historionic characters," where she had a wonderful time. In late winter she had an exciting three weeks in New York. "I have learned how to meet people with . . . comfort thro' the help of mental science," she told Clara. It was a happy, heady feeling.

Visiting with the Howellses and Dr. Rice and his family, she enthusiastically recommended the city to her parents, both of whom had already begun to think of a modest New York apartment as their best alternative to the Hartford house they could not afford to live in. New York's cultural liveliness seemed to Susy almost European, on a level with Paris and Berlin. By early spring, she had moved from Elmira to Hartford to stay with Alice Day and her husband as their guest in the Clemenses' much-loved Hartford house, which the Days had rented. Just as she had been bored with the young people in Elmira, so she found her Hartford contemporaries pallid, but she took pleasure in the company of family friends: the Twichells, the Warners, and the Days. When the Days ended their rental, she became the house guest of Charles and Susan Warner. Katy Leary, who had a small apartment nearby, helped look after her. In Hartford, as the warm summer weather came on, she spent much of each day in the shut-down Farmington Avenue house, where she would accompany herself on the piano as she sang.

When the cable instructing the children to depart for England arrived early in August 1896, Katy went to Elmira to collect Jean. Susan Crane and Charley Langdon accompanied them to New York to purchase tickets and see them off. Katy, to help Susy pack, went to Hartford, where she found her ill. It did not seem serious. But soon she had a high fever, her discomfort exacerbated by torrid weather. They were scheduled to sail the next day. When Susy begged that they wait till nightfall to go to New York, Katy agreed. Later that afternoon, she realized how feverish Susy was. Because she wanted her favorite faith healer to treat her, Susy insisted that Katy not call a doctor. "No! Nobody will treat you but the doctor," Katy responded. "I'll get him now, myself." He diagnosed early-stage spinal meningitis.

As soon as they got the news, her aunt and uncle left their New York hotel for Hartford. Susan Crane cabled the family in England on August 4, telling them only that there was a delay. Departure was postponed until the twelfth. On the seventh she felt forced to telegram that Susy was ill, slightly. In Surrey, the Twains worried that only something serious would have warranted postponement. "We have been expecting disastrous news," Twain wrote to Rogers, "and it has come this morning; in the form of— silence. . . . It means that Susy is still ill." They responded to the silence by urging that Susy be moved to someplace cooler than Hartford, perhaps Elmira. Livy began to panic. There was a ship leaving from Southampton the next day. Livy and Clara packed, in case a telegram should come with bad news.

The next day a cable arrived, but it had no news, only the instruction that they should wait for a telegram that would come the next morning. Twain went to the Guildford post office. He waited all day. Nothing came. Just before closing time, he cabled Hartford that they were going to Southampton to take the boat the next day; they should send the telegram there. At Southampton, there was a message. "The recovery would be long but certain." They still did not know what the illness was. To Twain, there was an instant flood of relief. Susy would live. Livy did not allow herself any optimism. And whatever the outcome, she wanted to be with her daughter as soon as possible. To remain in England was out of the question. Clara and Livy steamed out of Southampton on Saturday, August 15. Twain, his heart wrung with pity for his wife, waved from the dock until they disappeared from view. They had agreed that he would remain behind to keep the home fire burning, so to speak, and to search for a larger Guildford house to have ready when Livy brought all his children back.

As Twain lay in bed, he thought, "The calamity that comes is never the one we had prepared ourselves for." His intuition told him that when next he saw his wife her "dear head [would] be grayer," which would be so whether Susy recovered or not. But after so much moderately happy traveling to have the last leg of the voyage such a worrisome one! It was, he believed, all his fault. And, he lamented, he did not even have the capacity to express his feelings to her, except by letter. "I am not demonstrative; I am always hiding my feelings. . . . I could not tell you how deeply I loved you nor how grieved I was for you, nor how I pitied you in this awful trouble that my mistakes have brought upon you. You forgive me, I know, but I shall never forgive myself while the life is in me." Never for a moment did he doubt that his financial sins were the cause of this calamity. If he had not wasted their money on business schemes for which he had no real competence, they would not have had to leave their Hartford home. He would not have had to lecture to pay his debts; the family would not have been separated; Susy's life would not now be threatened; Livy would not now be suffering in parental hell. "Be good & get well, Susy dear," he prayed from afar, "[and] don't break your mother's heart."

His own was broken in the early hours of Tuesday, August 19, 1896. He received the saddest cable of his life. "Susy could not stand brain congestion and meningitis and was peacefully released to-day." She had died on the evening of the eighteenth Hartford time. Livy and Clara were still steaming westward, two days away from New York. The next morning, Clara was told the captain wished to speak to her. He put a dispatch into her hands, with the headline, "MARK TWAIN'S ELDEST DAUGHTER DIES OF SPINAL MENINGITIS." She returned to their stateroom. "Nothing was said. A deadly pallor spread over [Livy's face] and then came a bursting cry, 'I don't believe it!' And we never did."

Livy and Sam leaving New York City rented
house, about late 1901

Twain, with a gift bouquet
at the Hannibal railroad station during
his last visit, June 1902

Twain, with John T. Lewis, during his last visit to Quarry Farm,
Summer 1903

Villa di Quarto - Castello (Firenze)

Postcard, Villa di Quarto, about 1904

Clara and Sam on *Prinz Oscar* from Italy to New York,
with Livy's body, July 1904

Twain, the cynosure of attention, with Clara,
New York, about 1905

The Paige typesetter

Isabel Lyon, Jean, and Twain, New Hampshire, May 1906.
Clara tore the photo to eliminate Lyon from the historical record.

Twichell and Twain, 1905

Twain in a characteristic place,
New York, Winter 1906

"Grandfather" Twain with two of his Angelfish,
Stormfield, 1908

Twain in the billiards and Angelfish room at Stormfield,
1908 or 1909

Twain, with a favorite kitten, Stormfield, 1908

A melancholy Twain about 1908

Twain and Henry Rogers in Bermuda,
March 1908

Twain in his Oxford University gown, Jervis Langdon, Jean,
Ossip, Clara in her bridal dress, and Joe Twichell,
Stormfield, October 6, 1909

Twain disembarking in New York, April 4, 1910, two
weeks before his death

CHAPTER SEVENTEEN

SUNDAYS IN HELL

1896–1900

1.

On Christmas morning 1896, Twain awakened in a rented house in Chelsea, London. The day felt funereal. "The Square & adjacent streets are not merely quiet, they are *dead*. There is not a sound." Once or twice he heard "the rumble of wheels come out of the sepulchral distance." For Twain, Jesus had been born but had never risen and would never come again. So too Susy was irretrievably dead, no matter how much he dreamed of her, no matter how intensely she existed in his sleep visions.

The difference between dream life and real life, always a preoccupation, had become even less distinct. If Susy's death were a dream, then he, Livy, Clara, and Jean might soon awaken. "I cannot believe it," he wrote to Susan Crane, "cannot realize it! It is a dream, & will pass, & Susie will come again." But he knew that she would not. On Christmas afternoon, he noticed people "going around with doleful accordions & pious wailings." It suited his mood. When the family breakfasted, no one mentioned that it was a holiday. The previous month, they had refused to acknowledge Thanksgiving or their birthdays. The text of the fall and winter season was *In Memoriam,* which Livy read repeatedly from a collection of Tennyson that had belonged to Susy. Gradually, it joined with other healing touches to take away her sharpest pain, though great pain remained, and lingered and lingered as she brooded about what had happened. "I have always had much courage even when things seemed hard," she wrote to Grace King, "but now I have none. I long to be with Susy." Livy "has nothing in the world to turn to," Twain wrote to Twichell. Even six months after Susy's death, each day, all day long, Livy sat alone, wondering "how it all happened, and why." Twain reread sections of *In Memoriam*. "It is a noble poem," he granted. But it provided no relief, its concluding affirmation of a "God of love" a proposition that his experience and personality gave him no reason to believe. His own "martyrdom" seemed beyond bearing. "I bear it as I bear all heavy hardships that befall me—with a heart bursting with rebellion."

Life had given the humorist a blow so hard that what had always been his ambivalent relationship with humor had now gone from curdling to sour. "I cannot always be cheerful, and I cannot always be chaffing," he was to tell the Society of Pilgrims in London in 1907. "I must sometimes lay the cap and bell aside, and recognize that I am of the human race like the rest, and must have my cares and griefs." That was his temperate public mask. But grief, anger, loss, debt, and exile gave much in his life a bitter, often elegiac edge. "Thunderous outbursts of bitterness shading into rugged grief became characteristic," Clara later recalled. "He walked the floor with quick steps and there was no drawl in his speech now."

As always, he felt personally at fault for some large portion of what had happened, but malevolent forces beyond his control, he believed, had also done much damage, including the endless history of genetic inheritance that had formed his character and everyone's. His longstanding inclination to believe that human destiny was determined by forces over which individuals had no control became a settled conviction. "Luck has turned her back on me for good, I reckon," he wrote to Henry Rogers a month after Susy's death. "My luck is down," he told Franklin Whitmore when he realized he had forgotten to instruct him to renew insurance on the Hartford house. "If the insurance failed for a day the house would burn down."

His view that there were dark elements within human nature and in the natural world had been there from the start, from as early as his depiction of pietistic hypocrisy in *Innocents Abroad*, of avarice in *Roughing It*, of the dehumanizing world of slavery in *Huckleberry Finn*, of the realities of slave-society ideology in *Pudd'nhead Wilson*, of the interactive folly of feudal past and nineteenth-century present in *A Connecticut Yankee*. By 1896, what he had believed all along, though in a lesser degree, and often disguised—partly to create Mark Twain as a humorist but also to sustain the entirety of his role as best-selling author, husband, father, and citizen—became the explicit text of his writings and his daily life. He had established a pattern, since his debacle with Paige and Webster & Company's bankruptcy, of alternating between self-blame, fury at his betrayers, and angry denial that a just God existed. All in all, the humorist had concluded that the universe was a nasty cosmic joke. And Sunday seemed the worst day of the week, Christmas the worst of the year, except for the anniversary of Susy's death.

When in September 1896 his family arrived in England, he wanted to know every detail about his daughter's last days. From Katy Leary he learned directly, from Livy through what she had been told. In August, in the hot Hartford house, his feverish daughter had insisted on dressing herself each day. She had hallucinated about a famous long-dead opera singer with whom she conversed about the great career she, too, would have. As she lay on her couch, listening to the noises from the street, she would say, "Up go the trolley cars for Mark Twain's daughter. Down go the trolley cars for Mark Twain's daughter." When she found a gown of her mother's hanging in a closet, she kissed it and cried. To her it seemed Livy herself, or Livy's corpse. As the bacterial infection spread, brain tissue swelled. Suddenly she lost her sight. "I am blind, Uncle Charley, and you are blind," she exclaimed. Leaning down toward her, Susan Crane heard her quietly say her last word, "Mamma." She lay in a coma for two days. Each morning, as he had since she became ill, the gardener brought a basket of roses. Jean and Katy were with her at the end. "[At least] she died in her own house," Twain wrote from London, as if this were consolation to Livy, "not in another's . . . died where she had spent all her life till my crimes made her a pauper & an exile. How good it is that she got home again." Hartford was thereafter always to be, for him, "the City of Heartbreak."

When the news of Susy's death arrived at Guildford, he began playing "billiards, and billiards, & billiards" until "ready to drop to keep from going mad with grief." As Livy's ship approached New York, friends and family waited, including Howells and Twichell, who said to Katy, "I don't know how I'm going to tell Mrs. Clemens! I don't know how I can ever talk to her about Susy!" Clarence Rice went out to the ship to be a doctor to her misery. They all worried that her heart might fail. The coffin had been set up in the same room in the Langdon home in Elmira in which Twichell and Thomas K. Beecher had married Olivia Langdon and Samuel L. Clemens twenty-six years before. There Livy may have gotten some of her husband's letters, probably mailed to Hartford and brought to Elmira. She may have expected a telegram telling her that he was on his way. Instead, he had written that he had been telling himself repeatedly, "I shall never see her again, I shall never see her again. *You* will see the sacred face once more—I am so thankful for that. But though my heart *break* I will still say she was fortunate; & I would not call her back if I could." Susy was buried on August 23, 1896, near the grandfather she had never seen.

If her father had sailed on the eighteenth or nineteenth and if the burial had been delayed three or four days, he might have arrived for the funeral, at worst a few days late. He preferred, though, to wait in England for the remnant of his family to return to him. He stayed because he anticipated there would be no solace for him in America. And he had a plan for partial recovery, even if unspoken, which may have contributed to his decision. It was simple and reliable: work, work, work. He had a book to write, one that would earn money he desperately required. And it needed to be an entertaining book that did not reflect his misery. "I myself can keep cheerful," he told Rogers, "much more so than the others—for I have my work." He wrote to Twichell, "I work all the days, & trouble vanishes away when I use that magic." What Livy and Clara most wanted was for him to be productive again. "Never did he write more continuously," Clara later recalled. In work, he could be his best self or at least the self that sustained his life.

"We are a broken-hearted family . . . and such I think we must always remain," Livy confided to Mary Fairbanks. At least her husband, though, went to his study "directly after breakfast and works until seven o'clock in the evening." "I work seven days in every week, & seldom go out of the house," he told Rogers. In bitter moments, he criticized the friends he had trusted to look after Susy. They had let him down, primarily because they had allowed the sensitive girl to come under the influence of mental science. Both he and Livy were now convinced that "spiritualism" had weakened her and made her vulnerable to disease. Earlier, both had encouraged her involvement with Christian Science. Now, with his propensity to find scapegoats, he blamed what he had previously recommended. "Susy you know," he wrote to Alice Day, "was simply killed by mental science & spiritualism, without the least exaggeration. A murder it was, a demented cold-blooded unforgivable murder." And those who were on the scene and had not stepped in to stop this homicide were at grievous fault. "If she had had only one wise & courageous friend among the crowd of friends in Hartford," he wrote Rogers, "we should not have lost her." It was as if spinal meningitis had played no role at all. Soon Mary Baker Eddy's variant of mental science and particularly the grand priestess of Christian Science herself were to become targets of scorn.

When not depressed or furious, he was, as always, satirically observant, resilient in his confrontations with disappointment. In his compulsion to create ineluctable chains of irrational connections, he even found Charles L. Webster to blame for Susy's death. If Webster had not lied to him, trapping him into huge indebtedness, then he would not have had to lecture around the world; if he had not lectured, Susy would not have been separated from the family, which had left her alone and vulnerable to mental science and caused her death. Ergo, Webster had killed Susy. And if he had not spoken on Webster's behalf to his sister Pamela when Webster was courting Annie Moffett, "the lousy scoundrel and thief" would never have become part of their lives. Often the villain was the damned human race in general, and on Sunday walks with Jean and Clara he blasted human selfishness with a vehemence that for the first time impressed Clara with the depths of her father's "sinister doctrine" that seemed to rule out the possibility of any moral progress for the individual or the race. Such a view seemed to her pernicious, and in her idealism, as they strolled through London streets, she argued with him. "Often the battle continued," she later recalled, "after we reached home, weary in body if not in mind."

By mid-December 1896, he had written about a fourth of *Following the Equator* and completed an essay, "Man's Place in the Animal World," apparently started before Susy's death and resumed in October, though not to be published in his lifetime. It had particular propinquity now, a deflationary description of human nature that moved him fully into the darkest end of a continuum that had seemed to many readers dark enough in *A Connecticut Yankee*. He was, he told his future readers, renouncing his "allegiance to the Darwinian theory of the Ascent of Man from the Lower Animals": "It now seems plain to me that that theory ought to be vacated in favor of a new and truer one . . . to be named the *Des*cent of Man from the Higher Animals."

Daily life made its demands, including a visit to the Carlyle House, now turned into a museum, mostly with American donations, he noted, though Carlyle had excoriated America; the search for the house in Chelsea that they rented; his efforts to hire servants, particularly a cook, a series of whom went in and out the revolving door, including one they fired because her boyfriend took all his meals in their kitchen; and the toting of books back and forth to the London Library and the Chelsea Public Library. As always, his intellect and curiosity drove him to spend a great deal of time reading. He needed to consult books relevant to *Following the Equator*, stacks of which he brought home.

Speculations and demonstrations—historical, cultural, psychological, anthropological, theological, and scientific—fascinated him. Why are we the way we are? Who or what is responsible? Among other books, he read closely William James's *Principles of Psychology*. The power of habit interested him, and his own seemed useful examples, especially since he had in mind continuing the autobiographical accounts he had begun in 1885. "Nothing can kill one habit but another," he concluded. "To successfully kill the habit of drinking you must gain the habit of driving away the *desire* to drink, the moment it intrudes." The new habit would kill the old one. He had no desire to stop smoking. Unlike Livy, as the new year approached he began gradually to grieve less, or at least to grieve less grievously. Early in January 1897, he began a series of recollections of Susy in his journal, which became an expression of, and a partial liberation from, grief.

Dreams and their nature preoccupied him, dreams as prophecy, warning, and self-revelation, the nature of dream time and the relationship between sleep and consciousness. "While you sleep," he noted, "you are dead; & whether you stay dead an hour or a billion years the time to you is the same." It puzzled him that when he closed his eyes he could conjure up "miniature faces with precise detail" though he had no talent for drawing. They were always "dark-colored" faces, and totally unfamiliar. "How can I invent them? And what is it that makes perfect images in my dreams?" He hypothesized that he had two selves, a day self and a dream self. "Waking, I move slowly; but in my dreams my unhampered spiritualized body flies to the ends of the earth in a millionth of a second. Seems to—& I believe, *does*." His dream self had that previous night found itself "in the presence of a negro wench." Vividly sensual and erotic, she sold him a mushy hot apple pie, another of which she was eating herself. She made him a "disgusting proposition" but he was not surprised by it. When he made "a chaffing remark" that embarrassed her, she pretended that he had misunderstood her. "I made a sarcastic remark about this pretence, & asked for a spoon to eat my pie with. She had but the one, and she took it out of her mouth in a quite matter-of-course way & offered it to me. My stomach rose, &—there everything vanished." But he felt strongly that "it was not a dream—it all *happened*." Its vividness was indelible. "I had never seen that girl before . . . but dead or alive she is a reality; she exists, & she was *there*."

More than ever before, he was redefining the terms of realism for life and for fiction. Dream life lent itself to another kind of fiction. Myth and fable could convey ideas and situations before which realism faltered. An idea for a novel taking place in heaven and hell came to mind, his personal version of the Demeter and Persephone myth. In it a woman like Livy, who is in heaven, has been searching for her daughter "for a long time." She is watching hell "but not expecting her daughter to be there. Musing, she hears a shriek & her daughter sweeps by—there is an instant of recognition by both—the mother springs in, perceiving there is no happiness in heaven for her any longer."

2.

During winter and spring of 1896–97, as he stared his financial situation in its uneven face, his guess as to when his debts would be repaid oscillated between another year and as many as four. To cut expenses he would have resigned from the Lotos Club, but his colleagues had presented him with an honorary life membership in summer 1895. Now he considered resigning from The Players. He decided, though, that its inexpensive accommodations had more value to him than what he would save. "It is my house & home when I am in New York." His business affairs, fortunately, were in more competent hands than his own. Henry Rogers, for all practical purposes his literary agent and money manager, was very much at work on his behalf. While Twain, in London, kept his pen grinding, Rogers worked at the complicated negotiation between Harper, Bliss, and Twain, and the stressful negotiation for a final settlement with the Webster & Company creditors. He also acted as repository for the lecture profits and whatever else Twain earned beyond living expenses, some of which he invested in equities. Rogers' shrewdness and insider information began to produce the same, though proportionally smaller, profits for Twain that he made for himself. Though Twain still believed he needed another series of lectures in England and America to put him over the top, he told James Pond that the lecture platform was now out of the question. He had no heart for public appearances, which would, he felt, put his well-publicized loss and grief on display. And reason to believe that he could complete righting his financial affairs without additional lecturing gradually emerged.

A tempting alternative was a subscription relief fund initiated by the *New York Herald*. His friends there and its publisher, James Gordon Bennett, took seriously newspaper reports that Twain was living in poverty in London. Another rumor, more amusing than hurtful, also contributed to the belief that he needed help. When a cousin, James Ross Clemens, a medical doctor residing in London, became seriously ill, reports circulated in American newspapers that Twain was dying or actually dead. No, Twain cabled to a New York reporter, "The report of my illness grew out of his illness, the report of my death was an exaggeration." When a *Herald* interviewer pierced his defenses, he responded to the pointed question about his health that of course he was dying but not "any faster than anybody else."

In June 1897, he cabled Bennett to put a stop to the *Herald*'s public subscription, announcements about which had already been published and some money collected. Livy objected strenuously. He did not. "This way out," he told Bennett, "would not have occurred to me, & a year or two ago my self-love would have rebelled; but I have grown so tired of being in debt that often I think I could part with my skin & my teeth to get out." He tried to convince Livy, but it seemed to her shameful, as long as he could work and they could scrimp, to "shift" their burden to other people. "My wife won't allow me to accept any money so long as I am not disabled," he explained. To occasional offers of help from individuals he invariably responded, "I shall work out of debt by my own exertions." Not only, though, did he think the subscription acceptable but he was curious to see just how much his friends and the public valued him. He was unhappy to discover that, after a number of months, the collection amounted only to a little more than two thousand dollars.

Another scheme he thought more likely to gain Livy's approval. "Intimations" reached him that New York friends would like him to give a benefit lecture at the Waldorf Hotel. This was different enough from a lecture tour as not to qualify as lecturing at all. A dozen millionaires would sign an invitation that would be widely publicized. One seat would be sold to the highest bidder at auction, the others privately at prices up to a hundred dollars. After New York, Chicago and San Francisco would do the same. He had millionaire friends in both places. "Now if that scheme could be worked—well, it appeals to my vanity, I *would* like to sail up like that, & go into history as the only lecturer that had ever made so immense a scoop in any country." His old friend and New York entrepreneur Frank Fuller would be the perfect person to manage it, partly because Twain's lecture subject would be "an explanation of how [he] came to lecture to $35 in money & 3,000 deadheads in Cooper Union [in May 1867] when nobody in New York had ever heard of me but you." His words would be accompanied by "lantern portraits" of distinguished people, including Grant, Greeley, Emerson, Whittier, and Howells, who had sent regrets, and portraits of the few who had not, such as "Boss Tweed . . . & a few Sing-Sing people," with accompanying comment by Twain about each. An alternative was a satirical lecture on the Jameson raid. "Would either of them 'go' & pull me suddenly out of debt?" If so, Livy's income would enable them to "go home & live in a modest way" in their Hartford house. Fuller responded enthusiastically. One or a few such benefit lectures would produce a huge profit for a minimum effort. When, in late June, Twain approached Livy with what seemed this desirable proposal, she again objected. It seemed like cheating. If he were going to lecture again, he would have to do it the old-fashioned way. When Livy proved unalterable on the issue, he told Pond that he would "go home & lecture all fall & winter."

Six months before, at the end of December 1896, Rogers had worked out two contracts in addition to the agreement of May 1895, further refining the uniform edition project, one item of which provided a ten-thousand-dollar nonreturnable advance from Frank Bliss for *Following the Equator.* Others satisfied Charles Warner's rights in *The Gilded Age,* negotiated a working relationship between Frank Bliss and Henry Harper about their separate editions, and assured Harper that it could publish a complete uniform edition. Tossing in his sleep, Twain worried about the contracts and whether the parties, particularly Bliss, would sign. In March 1897 good news lifted his spirits. "It is like a new start in life," he responded to Rogers. "You are the best friend a man ever had, & the surest."

Bliss came to London in June 1897 to consult about plans for sub-scription sales of *Following the Equator,* which Twain worked on through the winter and spring. Livy edited out marginal and questionable material. He praised her "twenty-five years of valued service as [his] literary advisor and editor" in a dedication he intended to have included in the British edi-tion of *Joan of Arc.* He finished a rough draft of *Following the Equator* in mid-March. That was "gutted" by one third and revised. It seemed three quarters done and, to Twain, quite good. "Four-fifths of it had been writ-ten, & is now undergoing Livy's second revision, & my third," he wrote to Orion at the end of March. His decision to conclude with the departure from India, a more colorful point at which to end than South Africa, he re-versed under pressure from Livy and Bliss, in whose judgments South Africa needed to be included. He would not be entirely finished until August.

Rogers and Twain had reason to hope that in the hands of Harper and Brothers Twain's backlist would begin to make handsome profits whatever the sales of his new books. Frank Bliss seemed the weak link. Livy, who de-scribed Bliss as "sleepy and timorous," reminded her husband that she and Rogers had urged him to deal exclusively with Harper. Twain hoped Bliss would default on the ten thousand dollars, which would void the contract. Bliss did pay it, though, and sales of *Following the Equator* did turn out to be mildly disappointing. Even that might not have persuaded Twain that subscription publishing was dying. Evidence was beside the point. Bliss, not the subscription trade, was to blame. Moreover, *Joan of Arc,* a Harper trade book, was not selling well. The uniform edition, though, would prove a long-term bonanza, and Twain's stories and essays, for which there was demand, obtained the highest fees paid. "This is a strange time for my mar-ket value to go up," a pleased but puzzled Twain remarked. In early sum-mer 1897, though, as the family prepared to leave London, he was still nervous, mainly because of the outstanding Webster & Company debts. And Livy had said absolutely no to his lecturing in America.

They were, in fact, about to travel in the other direction. At the end of June 1897, after almost a year in England, observing Queen Victoria's ju-bilee procession from a reserved seat in the Strand, he indulged in a retro-spective consideration of the British Empire from the first great London procession celebrating the victory at Agincourt in 1415, the vivid details of which he imagined through the narrative of a "spirit correspondent," to this second great procession celebrating Victoria's sixtieth year of rule. A New York newspaper syndicate treated their temporary reporter as the world-wide celebrity that he was. Arrangements were made to get him, unseen, to the seat that had been reserved in another reporter's name in a grandstand occupied by distinguished guests from throughout the empire. His reportorial bodyguard noticed that Twain attracted more attention in his part of the grandstand than did the parade itself. With his tongue only partly in cheek, Twain enumerated the advancements in civilization that had occurred on Victoria's watch. It was a case of serendipity, not cause and effect: at least Victoria had done nothing to hinder progress. Under her aegis the British Empire had become the supreme world power. The world still seemed to him considerably better off with this empire than without it.

As he watched the gilded brilliance, then focused once again on his work, the misery he felt at Susy's death declined to a background hum. Only at occasional moments of sentiment or nightmare did it rise to a roar of pain. James Ross Clemens, "Dr. Jim," a newly discovered cousin, became an occasional companion. That he was a medical doctor was helpful. Twain consulted with him about a four-year-old groin rupture and whether to have surgery. With Bram Stoker he attended the theater. In summer 1897 he jotted into his notebook theatrical dialogue for a satirized character somewhat like Colonel Sellers but based on Frank Fuller. " 'Are you an American?' 'No. I am not an American. I am *the* American.' " Poultney Bigelow, who came round for walks and late-night conversations, had also suffered the death of a child. Twain felt compelled to make a list of people he knew who recently had been struck by misfortune. "Since bad luck struck us it is risky for people to have anything to do with us." In the spring he began to leave the house regularly, for business, for short excursions, for limited sociability.

Fortunately, the family had to confront the potentially healing regimen of daily tasks, which for all of them included the small challenges of London life, and for Clara the attempt to channel her musical talent into plans for the future. Twain helped both girls obtain bicycles, the modern kind with two wheels of equal size. A rented piano, on which Clara practiced daily, was set up in an upstairs room. When their neighbor, a *Times* journalist whose bedroom was on the other side of the wall, complained, Twain was politely firm, then disdainful. Six months of exchanges with this unhappy neighbor became both an irritant and an amusement. And Clara played on.

At a concert in November 1896, she got or had confirmed the idea that her musical destiny depended on becoming the pupil of the Viennese piano teacher Theodor Leschetizky. His name had become enough of a household mantra by June 1897 for Twain to write a comic sketch in which a first-person narrator describes himself as a "pupil of Letchitizky." Like Livy, he believed in Clara's talent. He considered that, if he were to lecture again, Clara might also perform, a father-daughter evening of entertainment. But as the family ratcheted its energies into high gear for departure, there were three concerns about the ladies of the household. One was Livy's eyes, though a recent surgical procedure had produced good results. Another was Jean's ongoing illness, the diagnosis of epilepsy having been made in New York the year before, which they had now almost fully accepted. There had been an attack, and probably Susan Crane or Charley Langdon, or both, had brought her down from Elmira to a specialist. Almost immediately, there had been a second; a third a year later, followed quickly by two more. They chose not to tell Jean the nature of her illness. His third concern was Clara's desire for a concert career.

On the one hand, he took pride in the praise she received. On the other, he preferred no career at all for his daughter, especially not a career that would subject her to publicity, judgment, and emotional risk. Livy also preferred something more modest, preferably a conventional marriage. But Clara was determined, and her parents sufficiently ambivalent not to oppose her overtly. They would uncomplainingly pay for piano lessons, and Clara pounded away at her practices long enough and with sufficient talent to make her ambitions credible. When she insisted on Vienna, for Livy the conclusion was simple and unalterable: if Clara needed to go, then they all needed to go. She required, her parents believed, supervision to keep her from indiscretions like those she had committed in Berlin and which she took pleasure in flaunting. Also, world-famous Viennese doctors might be able to cure Jean's illness. Beyond that, Livy had sworn that she would never again allow a daughter to be separated from her.

From London, they went to France, then Switzerland for the summer. Autumn would be time enough for a Vienna stay. A small Alpine village not far from Lucerne called Weggis proved beautifully cool and curative. Twain suddenly found himself filled with literary ideas and energy, the start of a two-year period that produced some of his most startling writing. Susy's death and his decade-long financial recklessness, the two banes of his life, now became part of a creative goad. He had much in his feelings, much on his mind, to write about, though the challenge of finding an effective literary form gave him difficulty from the start. The primary event of his recent life, Susy's death, demanded its literary due, a poem to memorialize the one-year anniversary on August 18, 1897. The parents spent the day apart. Livy went off to brood and suffer, spending "the day solitary in an inn in an unknown town up the lake." He worked on his memorial poem. No spoken reference to Susy passed their lips. "There was no August day in which I was in my right mind—& there never will be an August day, perhaps, in which I shall be sane. It is our terrible month. It is a whole month of awful anniversaries," he wrote in September 1897. Since he had little to no talent as a poet, Twain's "In Memoriam" does not transcend the limitations of its Victorian clichés. Its claim that "the light" that represents Susy "surely . . . will come again" has a sentimental falsity when expressed by a man who did not believe in life after death. Still, writing it no doubt was therapeutic, and the publication of "In Memoriam" that November in *Harper's Monthly* had its place in the widespread Victorian anxiety about the relationship between the living and the dead.

Twain's own experience also expressed itself that summer in a striking prose piece, "Which Was the Dream?" never entirely completed and not to be published in his lifetime. He had begun it, a representation of his preoccupation with dreams, failure, and loss, in London in May 1897, and came close to completing it in August. Even had it been finished, Livy probably would not have permitted publication. It also had genre and structural problems he could not readily overcome. In the story, an American general who has gained glory in the Mexican War, now a United States senator and widely viewed as a president-to-be, is married to his innocently beautiful but wise childhood sweetheart with whom he has had two daughters. He narrates his story after a selection from his wife's diary sets the scene. The day is the birthday of eight-year-old Bessie, a playwright and prodigy, "the foundation of [whose] nature is *intensity*." All the Washington elite is to attend, reminiscent of the parties and theatricals at the Twain Hartford house. The family's luxurious life in Washington has been made possible by his wife's inherited money.

The general, though, has placed his business affairs entirely in the hands of a cousin, whom his wife has warned him against. On the night of the birthday celebration, their house burns down. He discovers that his business agent has not renewed their fire insurance. He also discovers that his cousin has forged his name on documents, defrauding the general and others who have invested in a nonexistent gold mine. Having lost large sums because they had trusted him, the investors will not believe his explanations, especially since his creditors have documents to which his cousin has signed his name in a perfect replica of his actual signature. When accused of forgery, he collapses and falls into a coma. Eighteen months later, when he awakens, he finds that he has been ministered to by his loving but impoverished family, that his old West Point colleagues have believed in his innocence, and that the country at large has either likewise believed in him or at least forgiven him. All he has been guilty of is a gentleman's trust in others. And naiveté. His honor as a gentleman survives.

Unfinished but coherent, the story embodies Twain's fantasy of self-exculpation. The arrogance, negligence, and stupidity of Twain's actual business conduct are absent from the story. At the end, the general is redeemed by the love of his family and public recognition that he meant no harm and has behaved honorably, though not wisely. Despite its obviousness, the story is eerily effective as autobiography, partly because the reader cannot be sure to what extent its author is aware that it is a self-serving fantasy. As an autobiographical document, it is at a minimum a psychological snapshot of one way that Twain, at certain times, managed his misery. Livy may have been unshakably depressed, but Twain's emotional register, as usual, alternated between despair and creative engagement. His energy for writing and observation sustained itself. And as much as the August anniversary oppressed him, it did not prevent his carrying on. "We are gathering cheerfulness & healing of the spirit," he wrote, "& that is the best profit of all. Susy would have loved this place." He hoped that the cold would "hang back long enough" to allow them to stay in Switzerland until October. "It promises very well. This is paradise." In the Alpine sunlight even his finances seemed less gloomy. The expenses were astoundingly low. "I am a cheerful man these days," he wrote to James Pond. "It is the madam's economical genius that is accomplishing this. She knows where every penny goes, & that it doesn't go unnecessarily."

He was also, by late August, after the usual struggle with unsatisfactory copyediting, finished correcting *Following the Equator* proofs. "I know more about punctuation in two minutes than any damned bastard of a proof-reader can learn in two centuries," he complained. That he had been able to write a travel book in which grief played no role was testimony to his professionalism and his use of his pen as catharsis. Still, it had pushed him hard. "It was the only book I have ever confined myself to from title-page to Finis without the relief of shifting to other work meantime; & I would rather go hang myself than do the like again." Its completion liberated him for more attractive work. "I have mapped out four books this morning, & will begin an emancipated life this afternoon, & shift back and forth among them & make them furnish me recreation & entertainment for three or four years to come, if I last so long." The beneficiary of a compulsive inability not to write, he used the phrase "mapped out" loosely. One scheme projected at book length an expository discussion of human nature and the human condition. Two probably had to do with briefly expressed notebook ideas for stories that made use of microbes and microscopes, a long-considered trope to dramatize man's minuscule place in the vastness of the macroscopic universe. Perhaps he had in mind combining a dream-voyage narrative and the microscopic world.

In London, while writing *Following the Equator,* he had deviated from the factual narrative into a fiction, "The Enchanted Sea-Wilderness." A disastrous voyage, it is captained by a man who had heretofore considered himself "born lucky." The ship is sucked into the "Devil's Race Track," a mysterious current that carries it to a graveyard for ships named "The Everlasting Sunday." Though he omitted this fragment from *Following the Equator,* the story had a powerful hold on him. In his notebook he sketched out a parallel narrative, a voyage to Australia in which characters, based on people such as the Gillis brothers and Joe Twichell, represent different belief systems. An atheist, "humorous, kindly, large-hearted," is based on Robert Ingersoll, a Presbyterian on Twichell. The two are "fond of each other. "If all Xns were like you," the atheist says, "heaven would not be such a hell of a place as it is." "Let us make him happy here if we can," the Presbyterian says. "We know whither he is going." He was storing up narratives that dramatized both sides of his emotional struggle: dream visions and voyages of total loss, and fantasies of rescue and revival. Loss predominated.

Two other story ideas also came to mind. The first, referred to as a "New Huck Finn," he probably originated in spring 1897. It appears not to be one of the four he sketched out in late August. Hannibal returned to his mind with great force and with entirely different coordinates than in the days of *Tom Sawyer* and *Huckleberry Finn*. His surprise and delight at the sudden appearance of his old favorites, the Jubilee Singers, at Weggis in mid-August 1897, raising money for Fisk University, may have stimulated Hannibal recollections. After an evening performance, they came "up to the house" the next morning and gave the Clemenses a private performance. "They are as fine a people as I am acquainted with in any country." George Griffen was also on his mind: the news of the death of the family's black butler had recently reached him. Twain thought he might write a sketch of this extraordinary man. "He was with us 18 years," he wrote in his notebook when assembling recollections of Susy. "He was always betting: Susy always trying to reform him. When he won a bet he always told us about it at breakfast—so that she could hear it." The retrospective mood cast his mind back to his childhood: memories of skating on the Mississippi, Jim Wolf and the cats, and Nicodemus Dodge; contributions to his autobiographical jottings but also part of his effort to plot out a "New Huck Finn."

Other real people and events suggested other fictional possibilities. "Hellfire Hotchkiss," an extended story intended as a novella, contained his father, mother, and Orion, barely transformed. Hellfire herself is an extraordinarily talented, brave young woman so attracted to and successful at masculine activities that she raises issues of gender identity that fascinated Twain, a representation of his inner struggle about female roles. The cross-gender and cross-dressing elements seemed the other side of the coin of his conventional desires for his daughters and wife. He had taken at least one opportunity to dress as a woman for public fun and for a photographer, and he had made cross-dressing important to the plot of *Pudd'nhead Wilson*. "Hellfire Hotchkiss" remained unfinished, like "Huck Finn and Tom Sawyer Among the Indians," because Twain's imagination took him into dangerous complexities that his Victorian prudence could not pursue to a conclusion.

And the "New Huck Finn" also remained a fragment, though a sustained one that came within sight of completion. Its plot proceeds from the plot of *Tom Sawyer, Detective*, with Clemens family members and history providing ideas for the story. Twain considered introducing, in a subplot, "Orion as T's uncle." The Tennessee land could be worked in. When Tom is the cause of Orion fighting a duel, it gives Orion "an immense chance to make solemn preparation for death." His will gives "10,000 acres of Tenn land & a pocket knife to this one, 10 & another trifle, & 10 to every church he has ever belonged to & finally $4 each. Disposes of about half of Tennessee, without stopping to count acres." Colonel Sellers, "an immense admirer of Orion's talents . . . is his second." Huck is the narrator. At Bram Stoker's suggestion, Twain reintroduced the duke and the dauphin.

The narrative, though, is less revealing than the notebook jottings. There race considerations dominate, brutish black-white hostility and also anti-Semitism, to which his fury at the French treatment of Dreyfus had given focus. He considered working into the story a version of "the Lev'n boys—the first Jew family ever seen" in Hannibal. Before, the town knew Jews only as mythic unrealities. Suddenly, there was an actual Jewish family there. Latent anti-Semitism is stirred up by a "German youth. . . . The shudder visited every boy in the town—under breath the boys discussed them & were afraid of them. 'Shall we crucify them?'" Tom, though, "stands by" the Levin boys, "& fights for them." The description ends abruptly.

Nothing about the Hannibal Jews appears in "Tom Sawyer's Conspiracy." A slave trader, a fake slave, and a murder do; but the most powerful notebook ideas on race are absent, including a "negro smuggled from Va in feather bed when lynchers were after him." He is in fact guilty of horrible crimes. In a plot variation under consideration "whites seized the slave nurse & hanged her for poisoning the baby while another party was scouring the woods & discovered the baby's uncle in suspicious circumstances, hiding something & charged him (Tom or Huck discovered him) & he confessed; & he arrived in custody just after the innocent slave girl had been lynched—or Tom & Huck shall save her." In these notes, slavery and racial hate brutalize both blacks and whites. The victim returns in kind what he has received from the victimizer.

Another plot possibility occurred to Twain, parallel but less sensational: "Tom is disguised as a negro & sold in Ark for $10, then he & Huck help hunt for him after his disguise is removed." In the end, only this last contributes to "Tom Sawyer's Conspiracy," with an important change: Jim is again, as in *Huckleberry Finn,* the unwilling tool of Tom's cruelties. The townspeople are tricked into believing he is a runaway slave who has murdered a white man. The king and duke, with forged documents, enter the courtroom, claiming the alleged runaway is theirs. Tom denounces them as the real murderers. As he is about to provide proof, the story stops. Twain went no further, perhaps because he did not like what he had done, perhaps because he saw no readership for the tale, even if he could conclude it successfully.

Twain also returned to his Hannibal childhood in an exercise that put back into the world of Tom Sawyer the realities previously excised in the interest of sentiment and sales: the older Twain's realistic view of what Hannibal and its people had actually been like. Not intended for publication, "Villagers of 1840–3" may have been conceived as a preliminary casting of characters and life stories for the "New Huck Finn," which was never to be written. It took the form of a Hannibal census consisting of thumbnail biographies and character sketches: many designated by their actual names, like John Robards, others thinly disguised, such as John Marshall Clemens as "Judge Carpenter," with his *"Wife,* Joanna. Sons: Oscar, Burton, Hartley, Simon. Daughter, Priscilla," a list that contains Jane Clemens, Orion, Henry, Sam, and Pamela. "Villagers of 1840–3" has a concise frankness that makes it a distinctive work of art, the part-factual, part-fictional census as literary form, a variation on the short story that puts human lives into cosmic perspective and also captures the individual human pattern. For example, *"Bill League.* Married the gravestone-cutter's daughter. 'Courier.' Became its proprietor. Made it a daily & prosperous. Children. Died." Or *"Blankenship.* The parents paupers & drunkards; the girls charged with prostitution—not proven. Tom a kindly young heathen. . . . These children were never sent to school or church. Played out & disappeared." The dominant refrain is "This lot all dead now." And even in the less conclusive instances, the deadpan tone, the concise summaries, the selective facts and images, the listing of popular songs of the day, have an unflinching funereal force, the rich particularities of individual lives reduced at best to quiet fading and stoic ends, at worst to loss and ruin.

None of these painfully realistic Hannibal fictions were to be published in Twain's lifetime. He was to maintain his popular image, the humorously satiric and genially avuncular embodiment of America's nostalgia for small-town life, the Norman Rockwell of American prose. Later, Howells was to call him, memorably, "The Lincoln of our Literature," which he is, suggesting that he also embodies the darker, tragic strains of American experience, though it also implies that, like Lincoln, he provided in his prose a redemptive vision, an optimism earned through painful experience. But, in fact, he is also the anti-Lincoln of our literature, who looked unflinchingly, for himself though not for his public, mostly in unpublished works, at the nasty underside of American and of human life in general: its brevity, selfishness, and meaninglessness, its hypocritical religiosity, and its devotion to mammon. All human life, Twain concluded, begins with false hope and inevitably imposes loss and pain. No redemption of any kind inheres in its random nature.

3.

After midnight, from the top floor of his workroom at the Hotel Metropole in late September 1897, Twain looked down at the expanse of Vienna's Morzinplatz. The stone pavement of the great square, vacant except for sleeping cab horses, counterfeited "the stillness and solemnity of death." "I've seen nothing of Vienna except what is visible from the hotel window," he complained to Henry Rogers. His old nemesis, gout, kept him confined. Still, he could see a great deal. Lights stretched and curved along the Danube Canal, "a broad Milky Way of innumerable lamps." In the distance, Vienna's newest wonder, the Ferris wheel in the Prater, blinked in the tired darkness.

In what seemed absolute stillness, his imagination moved from restful meditation to dramatic vision. There, leisurely strolling across the square, he saw a living exemplification of the other main story idea he had envisioned and begun to sketch out in Switzerland. Amid flashes of literary lightning, he saw in his mind's eye, strolling in his direction, Satan himself, the much-feared childhood terror from whom he had hidden under his Hannibal bedroom blankets as lightning flashed. Now there was a rush of wind, a flash of light. Suddenly, raised up from the street below, at his side in his workroom, was Satan himself, in the form and dress of an elegant Viennese gentleman. "It was being whispered around that Satan was in Vienna incognito," he was soon to write, "and the thought came into my mind that it would be a great happiness to me if I could have the privilege of interviewing him. 'When you think of the Devil he appears,' you know."

That month, in Vienna, he had written the first nineteen pages of the story of a young stranger with supernatural powers, the nephew of his infamous namesake, visiting St. Petersburg, the Hannibal of Twain's boyhood. A plot, the intent of which is to reveal greed, superstition, and stupidity, begins. Twain had perhaps been concentrating on the manuscript late into that September night. He had, though, been thinking of Satan since childhood, first as the Christian God's agent sent to punish evildoers, boys like himself threatened with hellfire forever; then as a grand mythic figure, the forceful rebel, like Milton's Lucifer, embodying the creative energy with which Twain the young writer had identified.

Satan, though, had additional uses that particularly appealed to him: the devil could be made to talk sense, Twain's countervoice to Christian dogma and God's nonsense. Christianity had enslaved the Western world with self-serving clerical institutions specializing in punishment and slaughter, pillars of wealth and power instead of love and charity. And Christian theology had brainwashed people into believing that in a universe in which God was ultimately responsible for everything, human beings, his creations, were to be held to account for their actions and thoughts. Religions and philosophies that claimed that people were independent moral agents and that a just God, rewarding good and punishing evil, guided individual and cosmic destiny were perpetrating a cruel hoax. And people steeped in superstition, clericalism, and irrationality, dependent for survival on lords of the church and state, were in no position to see the truth. If there were a God, he was either a madman, a fool, or a villain, and certainly he was a sadist who destroyed innocents like Susy for his self-serving reasons. Satan could be Twain's surrogate, his voice of dissent.

Vienna, Twain soon realized, was the right city in which to create "the St. Petersburg fragment." It seemed the devil's territory, though not the Presbyterian devil of the American frontier. Vienna's devil came in the form of an upper-class gentleman who loved life's sophisticated pleasures, an habitué of the best coffee houses, who smoked only the finest tobacco. Vienna is Satan's urban utopia: a mixture on the one hand of hedonistic culture and beauty, on the other of authoritarian corruption and anti-Semitic degradation. It is, Satan affirms, "my favorite city. I was its patron saint in the early times before the reorganization of things, & I still have much influence here, & am greatly respected."

In November, in a revised and expanded "St. Petersburg Fragment," Huck and Tom become Austrian boys in a semi-medieval eighteenth-century Catholic world who are befriended by "Philip Traum," the pseudonym of the protagonist of "The Chronicle of Young Satan." As the boys' teacher, Traum provides object lessons in the cruelty, cowardice, and stupidity of the human race, its cosmic insignificance, the hollowness of its claims to progress, the hypocrisy and viciousness of "Christian Civilization." Human beings live, according to Young Satan, "a life of continuous and uninterrupted self-deception." When he recommends the liberating, revivifying power of laughter, which has the power to blow humbug and evil "to rags and atoms at a blast," his young pupils are "too much hurt" by Satan's depiction of human contemptibility to laugh. The humorist, who had discerned so much worth laughing at, now finds that human misery makes laughter too painful to bear. Twain's reworkings between 1898 and 1908 of Young Satan's visits to earth, "Schoolhouse Hill" and "No. 44, The Mysterious Stranger," have, like most of what Twain had written since *A Connecticut Yankee,* little about them that is funny.

The family's accommodations in Vienna had not been easy to arrange. Twain, apparently, had not thought reservations necessary. To their shock, scurrying along the Ringstrasse and within the central city, they found nothing suitable. It was not until trying eight more hotels that they happily moved into the Metropole, an imposingly large, well-worn establishment famous for a chef who attracted an aristocratic clientele. Once management realized who Twain was, it made him an offer he couldn't resist: a seven-room top-floor suite with a balcony for $460 a month, with all meals for five people included. When it became clear that its attractions exceeded those any private house could offer, they decided to stay. And Vienna in general was eager to welcome the distinguished visitor. His appearance had been heralded in the newspapers as much as three weeks prior to his arrival. Pursued by interviewers, he slyly remarked that he had come to find material to write about, which he apparently expected Viennese readers to take as an attention-catching joke. Some felt eager to be written about. Others found the prospect disconcerting: Vienna already had enough homegrown satirists, and a foreign one might say unfavorable things. Its ruling classes were not eager to be teased by an American writer. From the start, Twain's ironic jokes, despite the goodwill and self-congratulations with which he and Vienna greeted each other, created a linguistic disconnection that resuled in some misunderstandings.

Leaving unpacking to others, Clara and her father bounced through unfamiliar streets to Karl Ludwig Strasse 42, where they had an appointment with Theodor Leschetizky, at sixty-seven (five years older than Twain) the most famous piano teacher in Austria, if not Europe. A Galician by birth, he had debuted as a soloist at the age of nine with an orchestra conducted by Mozart's son. At ten, he studied in Vienna with a protégé of Beethoven's among whose other students was Franz Liszt. At age thirty-two he became head of piano instruction at the St. Petersburg Conservatory, then returned to Vienna. The most talented pianists of the next generation, among them Paderewski and Arthur Schnabel, became his students. In the 1890s, Viennese musical culture still retained the patina of the Mozart and Beethoven legacy, and Leschetizky was one of its commanding figures.

Filled with trepidation, Clara wanted to learn if she was good enough to be his student. Twain wanted to determine whether the family should unpack. Although they could not know it, they had no reason for uncertainty: Leschetizky recognized the mutual self-interest of celebrities. Having Mark Twain's daughter in his studio would be an asset. A clever businessman-musician, he had in place a piano-teaching factory in which his best students taught those just beneath them, and those taught others, and so on, in an arrangement allowing a large number of aspiring pianists to have the status of being his pupils. From this, he made a handsome living. Twain also most likely did not know about "Leschy's" reputation as a sexual roue who had found some of his students irresistible enough to have married four of them. Clara, who knew of his reputation, would not have found it a disincentive. So nervous was she in the cab that she purposely got her father started on a monologue about the "damned human race" in order to distract attention from herself.

When ushered into the great man's presence, she was startled at the disparity between her mental image of this musical giant and his inconspicuous stature. Leschetizky spoke halting English. Twain usually botched spoken German. Clara's conversational German, though, was excellent. After awkward preliminaries, she went to the piano, her heart beating wildly. Leschetizky soon rendered his judgment to her father in rapid German of which Twain did not understand a word but kept insisting, in German, that he did, in the hope that that would get Leschetizky to stop. Twain asked, and kept repeating, "Are we to remain in Vienna?" Finally, with Clara's help, he learned that the master had said yes. For the time being, he explained, since Clara would need preparatory work to make up deficiencies, one of his assistants would give her lessons. Immensely relieved, father and daughter concluded that Clara had passed the audition.

From the start, the city provided friendly people and activities. Livy began emerging from her seclusion, gradually acceding to regular entertaining at the Twain suite and to returning social calls. Cards and invitations came from Viennese eager to meet the American genius. To a greater extent than had been the case in their other residences abroad, Twain found that the American embassy embraced him as a national treasure, the only American artist so well known and liked as to be treated with honors similar to those a former president might receive. The American minister, Charlemagne Tower, was a Twain enthusiast. Augmenting his State Department pittance from his own wealth, he entertained handsomely in a city used to lavish diplomatic affairs. Twain happily starred at the ambassador's party on July 4, 1898, and for two Thanksgivings was the guest of honor at Tower's open house, attended by most of the two hundred American medical students studying at the prestigious University of Vienna. The young specialists-to-be made Twain their avuncular icon and buzzed around a flirtatious Clara. Viennese medicine dominated advanced knowledge in a wide range of specialties, including neurology, one of whose innovators, the relatively unknown Sigmund Freud, was a great admirer of Twain and was himself at work on his own book on dreams and dreaming. They probably met in February 1898, after one of two public readings Twain gave for charity.

Through Leschetizky, and partly in Clara's service, Twain attended more concerts and operas in Vienna than the total number he had ever attended before, and also because he was needed as an escort. Musical performance was inextricably woven into Viennese social life, and Leschetizky regularly invited the family to sit in his box at the Hofopera. Handsomely slim in his tuxedo, his curly white hair a colorful flag of identification, Twain was widely noticed. The newspapers regularly remarked that he had attended such and such performance or had been a guest at such and such occasion. He did not in the least mind. Sometimes, when he minded the musical performance, he left after the first intermission. Lightly melodious Italian opera entertained Twain more than stentorian seriousness, and he had more affinity with Johann Strauss, the elderly "Waltz King," than with classical symphonic compositions. When, in November 1897, he met Strauss at a concert, Twain accepted the composer's invitation to sit in his box. At least once the family had Leschetizky, with other Viennese friends, as their guest for dinner at the Metropole.

In December 1897, Twain attended a dinner party at which he made friends with Countess Misa Wydenbruck-Esterhazy, a thirty-eight-year-old widow at the pinnacle of the Viennese social and artistic world. Her aristocratic pedigree had prevented her pursuing a concert career as a singer. To compensate, she had become the premier patron of Viennese musical society, along with her friend Princess Pauline Metternich, both supporters of Gustav Mahler—the artistically and ethnically controversial conductor of the Vienna Court Opera—and other luminaries. Twain soon began attending the Esterhazy-Metternich salon, an elite stage for charity performances and reputation-making, where he met Mahler, August Strindberg, Erich Korngold, and Bruno Walter.

The countess took special interest in seventeen-year-old Jean Clemens, arranging that her own daughter be her constant companion, relieving her parents' worry that, if alone, she might in an epileptic convulsion swallow her tongue and choke to death. Moody, unpredictable, and sometimes disturbingly hyperactive, Jean remained ignorant of the seriousness of her illness. Her parents continued to explain bouts of nausea and spasms as "fainting spells." Attacks, though, came with increasing frequency, and Vienna's medical resources, they hoped, might be able to help her. With a letter from their New York doctor, they took her to Herr Dr. Heinrich Obersteiner. He confirmed the diagnosis, but neither he nor anyone could do more than minister to its side effects. With bitter anger, Twain began reconciling himself to the likelihood that his youngest daughter would be the lifelong victim of a chronic, perhaps fatal, illness. What, he wanted to know, had she or he done to deserve this?

As usual, no matter how embittering his personal poison, Twain's resilience and energy sustained him. Livy's health seemed as strong as it had ever been. Robust and willful, Clara flourished, and met a talented young conductor and pianist, Ossip Gabrilowitsch, one of Leschetizky's pupils and a close friend of Mahler's, whom, after interruptions and vicissitudes, she would marry more than ten years later. She happily practiced four or more hours a day; every few weeks Leschetizky listened and gave her advice. At selected times, though, the family dinner table was funereal enough to keep even Clara's spirits down. "All anniversaries, of whatever sort," Twain wrote in his notebook, "perished with [Susy]. As we pass them now, they are only gravestones." All the survivors bore a burden of guilt. Clara suffered the further deprivation of her own birthday being obliterated from the family calendar. Her twenty-fourth, in June 1898, went by completely unnoted, a circumstance that may have added another layer of resentment. But, like her father, she had the temperament and stamina to carry on, and she felt the obligation to make up to her mother for Susy's absence.

Viennese literati were also eager to celebrate Twain's presence. Eduard Potzl, premier humorist and satirist for one of Vienna's best newspapers, immediately became a close friend; sympathetic currents of temperament and ideology connected the two. With excellent English and a sly sense of humor, Potzl made easier Twain's entrée to Viennese cultural and political life. He served Twain and himself well early in October 1897 with a Sunday newspaper sketch, an imagined encounter in which "Herr Mark Twain" attempts to converse with two Viennese workmen who speak a heavily inflected street dialect. The result is comic misunderstanding, a sketch of a sort Twain himself might have written, which announced his arrival in Vienna to a large audience of newspaper readers.

In late October, when Twain addressed the Concordia Society, Vienna's prestigious press club, only the second foreigner ever to be granted that distinction, most of Vienna's press corps was there. The most prominent directors and performers in Viennese theater and music, including Mahler, many of the city's best-known editors and publishers, among them Theodor Herzl, and a large contingent of its most distinguished writers attended, though apparently the formidable Karl Kraus did not. Some diplomats were there, including the American ambassador. Twain's subject, a ten-minute variation in German on a topic on which he had previously written—the German language—amused his audience enough to produce thunderous applause. Much of it was for the man, not the talk. Apparently acoustics were bad. His German struck some as more puzzling than funny. And if they took his humorous indictment "The Difficulties of the German Language" good-humoredly, the next day's newspapers did not: they grumbled that the talk was tactless, his German pedestrian.

Almost nothing in Austrian public life, Twain quickly realized, was not political. Vienna was the battleground for Austro-Hungarian ethnic tensions. Different views of the empire and of human value were struggling for dominance, sometimes to the point of blows. Deep-rooted, outspoken anti-Semitism was the common coin of daily speech. Right-wing nationalists, who despised enlightenment Europe, expressed open contempt for inferior races, particularly Jews from Central Europe, large numbers of whom had recently settled in a Vienna ghetto and whose presence antagonized the Viennese working class. That facilitated longstanding middle- and upper-class anti-Semitism turning against assimilated Jews, many of whom were successful in the professions and the arts. By the early 1890s, liberal Vienna was quickly disappearing, and by 1897 it was gone: one was either a philo-Semite or an anti-Semite. If there were many Jews in an organization, as in the Concordia Society, it was pilloried as philo-Jewish. In opposition, anti-Semitic journalists had their own society and their own newspapers, a polarity established throughout Viennese professional life. Racial politics and nastiness were the order of the day, smelling out Jews a preoccupation.

To the anti-Semitic Viennese it seemed unmistakably apparent that Twain was a Jew. He had a hooked nose; he was a liberal; he was known to believe that Dreyfus was innocent; he also hung around with Jews (though Potzl was not Jewish, the playwright Sigmund Schlesinger, with whom Twain agreed to collaborate, was; so too was Theodore Herzl, whose play *The New Ghetto* Twain attempted to translate into English); and, finally, Twain had good things to say about Jews. References to "der Jude Mark Twain" began to appear regularly in the anti-Semitic press. At best, he was a "charming Jewish humorist." Other slurs were considerably less sly.

Twain's respect for Jews had its peculiar though admirable slant. Like much nineteenth-century European philo-Semitism, his was framed in generalizations about an entire race. In Twain's case, the generalizations were positive, perhaps partly an overcompensation for widespread negative characterizations. Much of Twain's pro-Jewish feeling, though, had its origin in personal experience. Vienna reinforced his longstanding belief that Jews were smarter than other people. "The difference between the brain of the average Christian & that of the average Jew—certainly in Europe—is about the difference between a tadpole's & an Archbishop's," he wrote in October 1897. "It's a marvelous race—by long odds the most marvelous the world has produced, I suppose?" He never seems to have met a Jew he didn't like. The people of the Bible fascinated him from childhood on, as did their distinctive role in the Christian imagination, from Bible class in Hannibal, to the Levin boys, to the boatload of Protestant patriarchs sailing to the Holy Land in the *Quaker City*. A few American Jews, like Adoph Sutro in Nevada and California, became much-respected acquaintances. In 1890 he had responded to a questionnaire sent by the editor of the *New York American Hebrew* to prominent American Christians, asking whether they had personally observed anti-Semitism and what they could suggest "be done to dispel the existing prejudice." Twain wrote a long reply, praising Jewish charity and family loyalty, explaining anti-Semitism as an irrational manifestation of inherited prejudice. That "rudimental Christian antipathy to the Jew [would] disappear" seemed unlikely. Jews had his sympathy as unjust victims of local persecution and of generic slander as Christ-murderers whom Christians demonized both because he abhorred injustice and because he found Christian psychology perverse.

Since his residence in Paris in 1895, Twain had become obsessed with the Dreyfus case, a focus for his longstanding detestation of the French national character, especially its authoritarian Catholic and Royalist reactionaries. At a time when Twain was immersed in his life of "the Maid of Orleans," Joan of Arc's persecutors seemed alive and flourishing. "Wild editorials" in anti-Semitic Paris newspapers about "Dreyfus's sham trial and unjust condemnation" shocked him. French caricatures of Dreyfus regularly depicted him with Negroid features. Between 1894 and 1896, Dreyfus and French contemptibility were the subject of notebook tirades, and undoubtedly of Twain's conversations also. Probably in 1896, while writing *Following the Equator,* he wrote two brief versions of a story, later for convenience called "Newhouse's Jew Story" and "Randall's Jew Story," which he claimed to have heard in 1860 while a cub pilot on the *Alonzo Child.* It may have been intended for inclusion in his travel book, a parallel to the passage about his father's mistreatment of a slave. A Jew, traveling on the Mississippi, rescues a young slave girl from the hands of a nasty professional card-player who has won her from an elderly, foolish, but kindhearted planter. When the brutal cardsharp refuses to take money for the return of the girl, the Jew, whose courage puts to shame the other passengers, kills him in a duel. "A very superior man," Mr. Randall says. "And the finest thing of all was his risking his life out of pure humanity." Twain brought race prejudice and anti-Semitism into compassionate conjunction.

When in late 1897 Dreyfus supporters publicized new and potentially exonerating evidence, Twain excitedly proposed to his British publisher that he write an introduction or a number of prefatory chapters to an anthology of newspaper writings about the case. The only costs would be for a researcher and translators. Chatto declined because he did not think there would be sufficient reader interest, and Twain put the project aside. But when the French army officer Ferdinand Walstin Esterhazy, for whose treasonous crimes Dreyfus had been punished, was brought to trial, Twain complained that Chatto had caused them both to miss a golden opportunity. In Vienna, he expressed his pro-Dreyfus view publicly and helped convince Austrian anti-Semites that their distinguished American guest was a Jew. His reverence for Emile Zola, one of Dreyfus' strongest defenders, knew no bounds. "A grand figure," he wrote in letter to the *New York Herald*, "standing there all alone fighting his splendid fight to save the remains of the honor of France. . . . Ecclesiastical & military courts made up of cowards, hypocrites & time-servers can be bred at the rate of a million a year & have material left over; but it takes five centuries to breed a Joan of Arc & a Zola."

Between his arrival in Austria in autumn 1897 and departure in spring 1899, Twain for the first time saw anti-Semitism as a civic phenomenon, a part of accepted political activity and discourse, one of many threads woven into the nationalistic issues tearing at the Austro-Hungarian Empire. "The Jewish question" became inseparable from the larger conflicts. He seized the opportunity in November 1897 to attend a series of contentious, scandalous sessions of the Austrian Parliament that made headlines in Europe and America. Austria's two leading politicians, Dr. Karl Lueger, mayor of Vienna and head of the Christian Social Party, and Georg von Schonerer, leader of the German Nationals, were openly anti-Semitic. Jews were handy scapegoats. Should Jews be allowed to hold office? To be judges? Generals? University professors? Were they not potentially dangerous subverters of Austrian purity? Lueger blamed Jews for the economic miseries of Austria's small businessmen; Schonerer viewed them as enemies of German cultural supremacy in the empire. In the larger battle, the Christian Social Party defended its Catholic-based small-business constituency against the German National support of big business and of German cultural dominance over Czech, Bohemian, and Hungarian constituencies. Language was a particular sore point. Should Czech be given legal parity with German in Czech-speaking parts of the empire? Tempers flared. Revolution and dissolution threatened.

A widely noticed presence, Twain was welcomed to the visitors' gallery, to which he obtained a ticket through a Viennese novelist and translator of Bret Harte. After a pro-Czech deputy spoke eloquently in a marathon twenty-four-hour speech, the Reichsrat became even more raucous than usual. Bitter taunts and slurs, including anti-Semitic invectives, were flung around the chamber. "There was hammerings with fists," Twain noted, "chokings, threatenings with chairs, a wound made with a penknife." In an attempt to stifle the opposition, the conservatives forced through a motion permitting force to maintain order. The Socialist deputies protested noisily, and then seized the rostrum. Twain couldn't have been more thrilled to be a witness to history. "[Sixty] policemen marched in and cleared the Presidium of 10 Social Democrats by violence." When the police also cleared the visitors' gallery, Twain was hustled out into the corridors. Fortunately, an English friend from the press gallery steered him to a seat there. He lost, he wrote to Twichell, "none of the show." Within days he was at work on a dramatic essay, "Stirring Times in Austria," which *Harper's Monthly* published in March 1898.

4.

Late in an evening in mid-December 1897, a cablegram from Keokuk arrived at the Twain hotel suite. Seventy-three-year-old brother Orion had died that morning. They had not seen each other in more than ten years, a separation that had become easier as Orion's eccentricities intensified with age. While the younger brother's love had never been extinguished, his patience had long ago run out. Since their mother's death and Twain's departure for Europe in 1891, even their once frequent correspondence had diminished. Within hours of receiving the cablegram, he wrote a letter of condolence to his sister-in-law. "I & all of us offer to you what little we have—our love & our compassion." He instructed Franklin Whitmore, in Hartford, to "send to Mrs. Orion Clemens $50 *extra* when you receive this, because of her heavy immediate expenses. Continue to send her the usual $50 per month."

As he would always do in any expression of condolence after Susy's death, he cast his words to the widow in the rhetoric of blessing, which the mourner of the moment may not have been happy to hear, and with reference to his own loss. Mollie may have felt an extra stab of pain at his evocation of her only child's "escape from this life thirty-three years ago." Orion, so unlike himself, he implied, "was good—all good, & sound; there was nothing bad in him, nothing base, nor any unkindness. It was unjust that such a man, against whom no offence could be charged, should have been sentenced to live 72 years. . . . The bitterness of death—that is for the survivors, & bitter beyond all words, it is. We hunger for Susy, we suffer and pine for her. . . . She & Orion are at peace, & no loyal friend should wish to disturb them in their high fortune." Later they were to learn that Orion's death had been quick and peaceful. "It does seem a beautiful way to go when ones time comes," Livy wrote. For Twain, his brother's death remained distant, almost abstract.

As the winter of 1897–98 turned to spring, the family's routines continued: receptions, concerts, theater performances, salon visiting, introductions to new people, including royalty. They were busily preoccupied with Austrian politics, bouts of essay writing, stabs at translating and writing plays, Clara's piano practice, Jean's illness and lessons, including her study of Polish, Livy's rheumatism and her resilience as she carried on as wife and mother—all of which fashioned a mirror image of normalcy different only in that it was happening in Vienna rather than Hartford. At the same time, they were sometimes desperately homesick. "We are hoping that Clara can complete her piano-education by next Spring," he wrote in June 1898, "& end our exile. Then we shall go home, & shall be deeply content to burn the trunks & stay there. I like Europe—I like it very much indeed—but I am two or three thousand years old sometimes, & I don't like so much paddling around."

They were also, with the outbreak of the Spanish-American War in April 1898, defensively pro-American. Austria's special relationship with Spain made the American invasion of Cuba and the dispatch of a fleet to the Philippines deeply unpopular. "[It is] almost like being in the enemy's country to be here," Livy remarked, "and now we shall soon find ourselves hated." Twain approved of the military action. Autocratic Spanish brutality disgusted him; the Cubans deserved American help. "I think we ought to have taken hold of the Cuban matter & driven Spain out fifty years ago." It seemed to him, so far, a war in which America had the moral high ground, a war not of invasion but of liberation.

They had only one reason to remain in Vienna or to remain abroad at all—Clara's studies. At long last financial redemption had come, and money was no longer an issue. One month after arriving, struggling to finish various narratives, still smarting over the hell of having had to write *Following the Equator* without the least desire to do so, he had instructed Rogers to pay the Webster & Company creditors pro rata thirty thousand dollars in three equal installments, not including the small amount the Grant estate claimed, another small individual debt, and thirty-four thousand dollars owed Mount Morris Bank. He did not have enough to pay the bank, and he resented the Grant claim. The delusion that his debts kept him from writing, or from finishing projects, sustained him. "I am writing hard—writing for the creditors," he wrote to Rogers in mid-December 1897 as he worked on "Stirring Times." "For the first time in my life," he reported in late December, "I am getting more pleasure out of paying money out than pulling it in."

The profits from the 1895–96 lecture tour, the royalties from *Following the Equator,* his meager but profitable newspaper work, the advances from Bliss and Harper, Rogers' investment of a thousand here and there, payment Twain had earned from articles, and some dividends from the Langdon estate added up to a considerable amount. Every investment Rogers made prospered. When Rogers cabled that an investment for Twain had produced a $16,000 profit, his ecstatic friend cabled back, "Splendid bird, set her again." His executive secretary, Miss Harrison, kept track of the details and reported to Rogers, who reported to Twain. In early January 1898, after the Webster debts had been paid except the three exclusions, $33,862.72 was still owed, $23,334.62 on hand. "I have abundant peace of mind again," Twain wrote, "no sense of burden." In February 1898 the bank offered a settlement compromise and Twain accepted. When, in March, the *London Times,* quoting John MacAlister, reported that the most famous literary debtor since Sir Walter Scott had now worked himself free, Twain thanked his London friend. "You could not have done me a greater favor. . . . When I look back on those three black years. But I am looking the other way now." That ordeal was over. "I want to be able to come & die at home. . . . Funerals are too expensive here for my means." By the end of 1898 he could tell Howells, with relief and satisfaction, that Livy, a more reliable arithmetician than he, had done an end-of-year accounting: "We own a house & furniture in Hartford . . . my English & American copyrights pay an income which represents $200,000; & . . . we have $107,000 cash in the bank."

But no sooner was he free of debt than he became transfixed by a new scheme he once again believed would make him rich. In March 1898, Livy mentioned that her afternoon guest had spoken about a young Austrian who had invented a marvelous carpet-weaving machine. Twain immediately wanted the patent rights. "I would like to have the opportunity to raise the capital & introduce it in America." Was it too late? No, the response came. Jan Szczepoanik and his business manager met with Twain the next day. Within twenty-four hours he had made up his mind. He soon persuaded the two Austrians to give him a two-month option at a price of $1.5 million, which he would pay in installments. If he sold American rights, his commission would be twelve percent. Twain was ecstatic. The next day, a representative of an American carpet company, eager to purchase what Twain had already optioned, came to the Metropole with financing in hand. Twain, though, did not allow the subject even to come up. "I was afraid," he wrote in his notebook, "he would offer me half million dollars [cash] for it. I should have been obliged to take it. But I was born with the speculative instinct & did not want that temptation put in my way."

For the next month he filled his notebook with Paige-like calculations. A remedial learner, he still could not get it into his head, despite the Paige debacle and Rogers' guidance, that inventions were riskier investments than established companies with balance sheets showing assets and earnings. He immediately attempted to lure Rogers into the scheme. "I've landed a big fish to-day. He is a costly one, but he is worth the money . . . because America has got to buy him whether she wants to or not." At great length he detailed the huge profits awaiting them. Rogers recognized the familiar Twainean rhetoric. While waiting for a reply, Twain got to know Szczepoanik, who had "a laboratory 3 or 4 stories high, in the centre of Vienna" and "inventions enough in his head to fill it to the roof. . . . He is going to be the European Edison, I suppose." Fortunately, Twain had no money of his or Livy's to invest. Rogers replied with a dash of cold water, some unpromising preliminary data, and a negative expert opinion. "When I hear from you next," Twain responded, "I shall know its American value. . . . I know you are doubtful about patents." But if he did not think this one practical, what about another, a machine that made "blankets & other cloth out of peat?" When Charley Langdon, visiting in Vienna, showed no interest in the carpet machine, Twain had sense enough not to mention peat. By mid-May he confessed the difficulty of making the strong case he believed both inventions warranted. Gradually, as Rogers' silence made clear that no investment money would be forthcoming, Twain was forced to let his option run out.

As summer 1898 approached, the family was steered by the Countess Esterhazy, their aristocratic friend who had taken a special interest in Jean, to the two-story Villa Paulhof, just off the main street but still privately sit-uated between steep hills, in the village of Kaltenleutgeben, fifteen miles from Vienna. They would be neighbors. The town had the additional ad-vantage of well-known hot baths presided over by a medical establishment that could provide therapy for Livy, Clara, and Jean. Moody and frenetic, with seizures once a week, Jean took bromide daily, prescribed for her absent-mindedness. It was the Clemens family sedative and sleeping med-icine of choice. They stayed at Villa Paulhof from late May to mid-October 1898, except for a ten-day excursion to the Saltzkammergut in August, al-most every minute of which Twain hated. The vacation was propelled by Clara's desire to be with friends and the family's inclination to have a look at the famous mountain landscape. Livy, they felt, also needed a break from housekeeping. But facilities were primitive; insects buzzed; Twain found the weather unexpectedly hot. At Kaltenleutgeben he had been hav-ing one of his most productive summers, and both before and after the ten-day break he wrote with more enthusiasm and success than he had since his summers at Quarry Farm in the mid-1880s. This was, though, a differ-ent or at least a much changed Mark Twain.

That winter, in December 1898, he found himself compulsively read-ing a study of the psychological theories of J. F. Herbart, an early-nineteenth-century German philosopher and psychologist who believed that the individual consisted of multiple selves, and that these different selves establish reality for the individual by their constant competition with one another for self-preservation. Continuous identity is a fiction, and the mind has no independent generative power of its own. Partly in response, Twain created, from April to June, a draft of a substantial manuscript, *What Is Man?* It expressed his deterministic views in a lengthy dialogue. Something called *he* was aware of something called *his mind,* which acted with a frightening and humiliating independence. Livy and Clara hated it. Publishing it seemed out of the question. "So, all these months I have been thinking the thoughts of illustrious philosophers, & didn't know it. I merely knew that they were not my thoughts; that they all came from the outside; that neither I nor those philosophers nor any other person has ever had a thought [that] was his own." Thus, Twain concluded, "Man's proudest pos-session—his mind—is a mere machine . . . so wholly independent of him that it will not even take a suggestion from him, let alone a command. . . . [So] our pride in it must limit itself to ownership—ownership of a

machine—a machine of which we are not a part, & over whose performances we have nothing that even resembles control or authority. It is very
offensive."

Years before he had made a similar argument to his mother about her
pride in her Lampton inheritance. Herbart's theory corroborated his own
view, developed over the last decade and reinforced by Susy's death: multiple selves make cohesive human identity and individual responsibility impossible; a Darwinian struggle for survival between our multiple selves
determines who we are and our fate; human beings have no reason to glo-
rify the human mind as if it were a conscious, self-directed, and moral
force; man and nature are inseparable elements of a common kingdom;
there is no moral and providential force in nature or the universe; whatever
fancy words are used to describe human thought and action, everything is
ultimately motivated by the struggle for survival and pleasure; and man's
dominant characteristic is selfishness, both at large and on the genetic
level. Consequently, it would follow that Mark Twain was not to blame for
the Webster & Company bankruptcy, the Paige debacle, the family exile,
or Susy's death. These were, like Jean's epilepsy, things to curse and blame
on a nonexistent God, forces beyond any individual's control or responsibility, referred to as "God" out of habit and convenience. Most of what he
would write thereafter would reflect, in one variation or another, this deterministic view.

At Kaltenleutgeben he worked again on *What Is Man?* and began a long
never-to-be-completed fiction, "The Great Dark," the story of a nightmar-
ish sea voyage through an endless ocean that is in fact a drop of water. In
a quick burst he wrote "Concerning the Jews," an essay locating the origin
of anti-Semitism in Gentile jealousy and hatred of Jewish business success. "My Platonic Sweetheart," a short story combining his notion of multiple selves and of dream existences with sentimental autobiography, he
had ready to send off by early September. When editors proved resistant,
he withdrew it from consideration. "I hold myself your servant & friend,"
he told the editor of *Harper's Monthly,* "for rejecting the 'Platonic Sweetheart.' I thought it was good; I think differently, now." By late summer and
early fall 1898 he was in high gear, one result a short story about human
greed as both individual and communal, "The Man Who Corrupted
Hadleyburg."

By November, he was ready for another try at his biography of Satan, a manuscript he called "Schoolhouse Hill." Like "Chronicles of Young Satan," he left this unfinished. In its six chapters, it again brought young Satan to St. Petersburg, where he becomes Huck and Tom's much-admired friend. The Hotchkisses appear, again thinly disguised versions of his family, especially Orion, a man who "changed his principles with the moon, his politics with the weather, & his religion with his shirt." Becky Thatcher, by name, is a character. All St. Petersburg/Hannibal is in awe of young Satan, "the miraculous boy" of prodigious talent and essential goodness who becomes known as "Forty-four," a representation of one of Twain's own multiple selves, the boy he partly saw himself as having been and the creative writer he had become. His extensive notes sketch out a satirical series of scenes. Early in Satan's visit, "he takes Huck & Tom to stay over Sunday in hell—gatekeeper doesn't recognize him in disguise & asks for tickets. . . . They see papa Satan on his throne." When they try to help suffering creatures, "the police interfere. They wipe the tears of the unbaptised babies roasting on the red hot floors—one is Tom's little niece that he is grieved to lose—still, as she deserves this punishment he is able to bear it." In November and December 1898 he set the stage for the main part of the narrative. Then he abruptly stopped. Apparently, he could see ahead only a series of lesson-teaching magical performances. That was enough, or too much of the same thing. As with the other Satan fragments, he put it aside.

5.

In fall 1898, after a long summer in Kaltenleutgeben, the family resumed Vienna life at the recently built Hotel Krantz, a centrally located neoclassical structure with all modern comforts. It was, in Twain's view, the equivalent of New York's luxurious Waldorf. At the Villa Paulhoff, Twain had learned that an anarchist had stabbed the empress Elizabeth at Geneva in the name of the working people and in hatred of upper-class privilege. Now, in mid-September, from the windows of their large eight-room suite overlooking Neuer Markt, he watched the coffin contaning her body join her royal predecessors in the small, white-walled Capuchin church on the far side of the square.

Twain was distressed and of two minds. He deplored the assassination. But who was really guilty of the crime? "This man?" he wrote in his notebook. "No—militarism, which burdens & impoverishes & maddens. Royalty is itself the E's murderer before the fact." More such murders, he believed, would come in the next decades. Still, he recognized that he him-self desired and enjoyed, as the most famous writer in the world, the re-wards of privilege. He believed "nobilities" to be foolish, but wrote, "If I were a citizen where they prevailed I would do my best to get a title for the consideration it furnishes—that is what we want. In Republics we strive for it with the surest means we have—money." From his privileged viewing position at the Hotel Krantz, Twain observed the spectacle and took notes for an article: the sand-covered city streets in hushed silence, the muffled sound of horses' hoofs, the tolling of the bells, the costumes of the nobil-ity, the soldiers from every part of the empire in ritual parade splendid "in red, gold and white," and the solemn entrance of the corpse, answering only to the unadorned name Elizabeth, "a poor sinner," into the mau-soleum of her ancestors.

No sooner had the Clemens family settled into the Krantz than Clara announced she was giving up the piano. Instead, she would prepare for a concert career as a singer. Her parents were astounded, though not dis-pleased. It would have taken greater talent than Clara's to overcome the smallness of her hands and the limited reach of her fingers, a liability greater than she had previously allowed herself to believe. The opportunity for taking stock at Kaltenleutgeben may have brought her to a long-developing realization. When a lady whom Livy believed "a competent judge heard her sing and said 'Why do you go on with the piano when you have a voice; the piano is so much less recompensing than singing and the work so very much heavier,' " Clara's parents found a rationalization for a decision Clara had already made. In back of their minds was their disin-clination for their daughter to have any career at all. "When Clara is away from me for a day the sense of loneliness is so great," Livy confessed, "that it makes me hope that it will be many a long day before any one succeeds in persuading her to leave home." Obviously, she hoped that voice lessons would be less a threat to the integrity of the family than the piano. Twain did not at all disagree with his wife. And there were excellent voice teach-ers in London and New York.

Still, they remained in Vienna until May 1899, partly because they had already made arrangements to be there but also because Viennese life had become familiar, the friendships rewarding, the activities interesting. Clara began voice lessons with a well-known retired diva. Though Jean's illness distressed them, for public consumption she was mostly fine. "We are all usually well," Livy remarked, "and I have not known Mr Clemens for years to write with so much pleasure and energy as he has done during this last Summer." She had a sense, though, of that too coming to an end. "Sometimes I have felt almost frightened lest it be his swan song but it continues and he seems well so I take great comfort in it." In December 1898, Twain insisted to Frank Bliss that widespread newspaper reports were false. "I am not 'making the effort of my life,' & I am not finishing *any* book. And I am not expecting to, very soon.'

Only three works in progress compelled his long-term interest: his autobiography, "The Chronicle of Young Satan," and "Schoolhouse Hill." "A good deal of the Autobiography is written," he wildly exaggerated to an editor, "but I never work on [it] except when a reminiscence of some kind crops up in a strong way & in a manner forces me; so it is years too early yet to think of publishing—except now & then at long intervals a single chapter, maybe." He had an independent piece, "My Debut As a Literary Person," which he would consider publishing. "The Man That Corrupted Hadleyburg" and "Concerning the Jews" had been placed in *Harper's Monthly*. A series of about fifty cynical, semi-obscene quatrains in the manner of the *Rubiyat of Omar Khayam* he thought to print privately and sell as a high-priced collector's item, but he soon reconsidered.

Returning home was already much on their minds when news of Mary Fairbanks' death reached them in late 1898. Since Jean had gotten no useful medical help in Vienna, perhaps doctors someplace else could do better. "If it weren't for my sister we should probably remain one more winter in Vienna," Clara wrote, "but there must sometime come an end to our wanderings." Twain had in mind a long summer excursion to Scandinavia and St. Petersburg, a brief stay in London, then departure for New York in October. The excursion would be a holiday from work, which "does not go well, to-day," he told Twichell in January 1899. When his autobiographical efforts also seemed fruitless, he "abandoned" that. He did write at a quick pace four magazine articles on Christian Science: "[They] contain nothing offensive against the lay Christian Scientist, & they confess that he is probably going to do much good; but they make remorseless fun of his pudd'n-headed little Goddlemighty, Mrs. Eddy, & her jackass 'Key' to the Scriptures." Do you want them suppressed, though? he asked Frank Bliss. He was concerned they might damage prospects for the uniform edition.

In March, they all went to Budapest, their second visit since arriving in

Austria. Twain lectured for charity, at a banquet celebrating the jubilee of the emancipation of the Hungarian press. No matter how many times he swore off lecturing, no "final farewell," even to the voluntary platform, proved the last. As for returning to Hartford, they still feared the expense, as well as the likelihood that Susy's death would live for them too painfully in that house on Farmington Avenue. Also, they had grown used to being in a more cosmopolitan world than Hartford could provide. Clara needed the best voice teacher available in America, and that would be in New York. Livy would do everything she could to have their home where Clara was. For Twain, Howells, Henry Rogers, and Laurence Hutton were in New York. The Lotos Club and especially The Players were second homes to him. But could they afford to live in Manhattan? Twain sent out inquiries.

Though Viennese good-byes had a touch of sadness, he was eager to leave. "The salt water will smell heavenly to me after this long privation." On May 25, Twain had a private audience with Emperor Franz Joseph I, who seemed less remarkable than any of the other royalty he had met in Europe. Twain had little to say about the small, austere man whose empire would soon vanish. Viennese friends and newspapers were informed that their departure for London was required by business demands. In fact, London had become Twain's summer destination primarily because Clara wanted to study voice there. At the last moment, rather than risk rough seas, they took the train to Prague, Numburg, Cologne, Brussels, Calais, and then the ferry to Dover.

On the last day of May 1899 they arrived in London, where familiar faces greeted them, including these of Poultney Bigelow, Andrew Chatto, and literary editor John MacAlister. Twain's newly married nephew James Clemens still lived in London. His Savage Club colleagues welcomed him back. Unexpectedly, the family went to Broadstairs for ten days because Clara had been "ordered . . . by the doctors" to recuperate by the sea from an unspecified illness. She had often been unwell during the spring, and anything that affected her voice required instant attention; rest and a change of scenery were most frequently prescribed. Within a week of arrival, Twain gave a speech at the Savage, the first of a series of invitations he accepted that month. The great American humorist was back in town, and the newspapers made certain everyone knew. "We are still in exile," he wrote to a friend, "but are eagerly expecting to see our lost land again before next winter's snow flies."

Late in the month they revised their summer plans. Instead of staying in London, they would leave immediately for as much as three months in Sanna, Sweden, a place they had learned of only recently. At the suggestion of Bigelow, Livy had taken Jean to the London office of Jonas Henrik Kellgren, a sixty-two-year-old Swedish-born therapist, the founder of a medical theory and therapeutic practice called the "Kellgren Treatment," which was much like osteopathy. Twain oscillated between skepticism and enthusiasm. The "Swedish Movement Therapy," as it was alternatively known, consisted of intense muscle and bone manipulation, intended to stimulate nerve endings, the dullness of which Kellgren believed caused most illnesses. Drugs of any sort were forbidden, and diet and a disciplined daily regimen were essential. To her parents' delight, Jean showed immediate, but minor, behavioral improvement. Livy's heart leaped at the possibility of a cure. Since nothing else had helped, Twain thought the Kellgren treatment, which claimed success with epilepsy, worth trying. The time specified for therapy, though, was to be no less than six months, and probably longer. Kellgren's summer institute in Sanno offered the most disciplined immersion in his therapeutic practices.

In their enthusiasm and barely restrained optimism, the Twains decided that they would go to Sanna for the summer and then stay in London, at least until January 1900, perhaps even through the winter, to give Jean the benefit of continuing her treatment at the Swedish movement's London Institute. On July 5, 1899, they sailed for Sweden. "We are here till October taking the Swedish movement-cure," he wrote to Laurence Hutton. "I am taking it myself, though there's nothing the matter with me." In the end, he was indeed the family member who benefited most from the treatment. Kellgren, he confided to Henry Rogers, relieved what no physician had ever been able to, his "semi-annual itching piles." Otherwise, except for gout, his health was remarkably good. And his resilient constitution was always stronger than his illnesses. Clara, who stayed in London and would join the family later at Sanna, was in excellent health, her illnesses more temperamental than organic, the result of stress about career and tension with parents. Livy's heart disease produced no events. She did have frequent exhausting bouts of diarrhea; her winters were possessed by flu and infections; and she too had developed gout.

After a week at Sanna, Jean's improvement was "astonishing." Her father wrote in his notebook. "We hardly venture to talk about it lest it presently turn out to be only a transient flurry." Two days later she "fell in a spasm striking her head. . . . A bad convulsion; she lay as if dead. . . . They are working at her now. She is better." As the months at Sanna went by, and then another full year in London with thrice-weekly sessions at the institute, Jean had periods of noticeable improvement. They were always followed by relapses, sometimes moderate, often severe. Kellgren calibrated a long-term, if unsteady, improvement, but a cure was certain, he believed. So too did her parents. Whether Jean would have done as well without Kellgren at all no one can say, and even Twain, who became the family's premier convert to Swedish movement therapy, and then to osteopathy, regretted that Kellgren never kept case histories and consequently had no records to cite.

In Sweden, Twain at first thought he was in "Hell (Sanna Branch)"— early rising, bad coffee, earthen privies, relentless flies, primitive living quarters, exhausting treatments, and a rigid day-long schedule. Soon he realized that the exercise made him feel good, especially since others did the work for him. With no distractions, the routine became pleasant. And the landscape appealed to him, particularly the changes of light. He had lots of free time in which to write, and he worked on aphorisms and some manuscripts he had brought. Soon he felt disciplined and light spirited. Within two weeks, he was blowing the Kellgren trumpet for himself and his family and to anyone who would listen. Despite his interest in microbes, he retained his belief in the curative value of spas and tonics. "I take it myself," he wrote to Richard Gilder, "mainly for the refreshment of it. Damn all the other cures, including the baths & Christian Science & the doctors of the several schools—*this* is the satisfactory one! Every day, in 15 minutes it takes all the old age out of you & sends you forth feeling like a bottle of champagne that's just been uncorked." Twain had convinced himself that "this system, like surgery, [was] a science," whereas all other forms of healing were "as variable, indefinite & unscientific as religion."

After their return from Sanna in October, the full year that they remained in London was not a particularly productive, let alone happy, time for Twain. In three- to six-month increments they extended their stay, with the intention of going again to Sanna for a second summer. Jean apparently benefited, and the family certainly believed she did, from her sessions at the institute. There was satisfaction when she went for a longer period than usual without an attack. Attacks, though, did occur, and Kellgren and his associates engaged with them as if they were wrestling with the devil. The exercise itself apparently did Jean good. That she was the center of caring attention probably helped her self-esteem, the heavy emotional burden borne by a young woman gradually realizing that a chronic illness would deprive her of career, marriage, and children. That she did not get worse at least seemed promising. But when, in November, Twain realized that the Kellgren system was "being practiced all over America . . . under the new name of 'Osteopathy,'" he was angry that they had remained in London under the impression that it was the only place for such treatment, and by December 1899 Livy was discouraged. Maybe osteopathy could do better. But they had already committed themselves to a furnished flat at Wellington Court, Knightsbridge, a busy area close to Hyde Park, for seven and a half months. Half the rent was paid in advance. "If only I had found this out in September, instead of yesterday," he wrote to Rogers, "we all should have been located in New York the 1st of October."

Since the flat was too small to have a private writing area, Twain went most days to the offices of Chatto and Windus, where his publisher provided space. Some of his work was his usual personal and business correspondence, some an effort to reignite stories he had started, including the never-to-be-completed "Which Was the Dream?" which he also had worked on at Sanna. A threatened bankruptcy and then reorganization at Harper and Brothers concerned him, though the emergence of Colonel George Harvey, the owner and editor of the *North American Review,* as president of the reorganized firm and then editor of *Harper's Weekly,* had Rogers' approval. He urged Twain to hold steady with Harper, though Twain fretted about the arrangement that had the American Publishing Company bringing out the uniform edition and Harper everything else. With his usual bad judgment on such matters Twain thought Bliss more likely than Harper to produce profits for him. The absence of a clause giving him cancellation rights in his November 1898 revised contract with Harper annoyed him. That Christmas, in London, he thought he had reason to complain that Harper was urging "all books upon Christmas buyers but [his]." At least, though, they were "straightening up & going on with business." In the end, Harper under Colonel Harvey was to do at least as much for Twain as Twain for them.

The previous spring, in Vienna, he had started another version of his Satan opus. Between May and October 1899, in London and at Sanna, he revised "The Chronicle of Young Satan," extending his exposure of Christian and clerical brutality and the conflict between Christian practices and the moral sense in a series of new episodes. In spring and summer 1900 he tried again, dramatizing the irony of Father Peter going mad at the same time that he is exonerated of the crime of which he has been falsely accused. Triumphant, all-powerful, brilliantly intelligent, Satan highlights the folly and cruelty of the human species. With Theodor under his wing, he flies around the globe to provide examples of how worthy human beings are of dismissive laughter. The narrative remained unfinished. Since Twain had again written himself into a semi-structureless, open-ended expectation of more adventures, there seemed no viable way to bring it to a close. Once more, he had not "started it right."

In spring 1900 he got off to an excellent start, he believed, on a new business venture, his debt-free status and Henry Rogers' investments on his behalf reminding him, so he seriously joked, that he was a capitalist. Some of Livy's coal stock, its value severely depressed for thirteen years, had recently gone up considerably and was now worth $100,000. She owned $75,000 worth of other stock that her brother held for her, probably a remnant of her original inheritance. In view of his comparative affluence and despite Livy's attempts at economy, it seemed to Twain "that it was about time to look around & buy something," he wrote to Rogers in March.

As usual, his investment choice was fueled by imagination, not financial sense or prudence. The product that attracted him was Plasmon, a food additive in the form of a powder made of albumen, extracted from "the waste milk" of dairies, a pound of which, so the experts claimed, contained "the nutriment of 16 pounds of the best beef." He had heard about it two years earlier in Vienna, where it had first been developed. A Berlin company had been formed, and scientific evidence and analysis, statistical and sales projections, and a company prospectus had been produced in support of a sales pitch to encourage investment. "The scientific testimonials are strong enough to float Gibraltar," he told his friend and fellow investor, John MacAlister, to whom he urged that they propose to "deliver in Calcutta or Bombay, carriage free, 2,500,000 of Plasmon per month to the end of the famine for £50,000. . . . We shall clear £20,000 a month on the business."

Twain hoped to persuade Plasmon's Viennese proprietors to sell him an exclusive option for British and American rights, but the British rights had already been purchased by a small syndicate. Elected a director of the British company in which his five-thousand-pound (twenty-five-thousand-dollar) investment bought him a one-sixth ownership, he began attending monthly board meetings. His mental and notebook calculator went furiously to work with fantasy arithmetic. He needed, he recognized, to be joined by deeper pockets than his own. "I think it would be well," he urged Rogers, for Standard Oil to "buy control of the company." Rogers did his usual careful investigation and declined to participate, despite Twain's blandishments. So too did Andrew Carnegie, whom he approached in late May 1900 via a letter to Carnegie's young daughter, with whom he had not had any contact since she was a little girl. Carnegie did not invest in Plasmon. Twain schemed, also unsuccessfully, to get the British tea magnate, Thomas Lipton, interested. In the end, over the next eight years, Twain invested fifty thousand dollars, all of which he lost.

He did genuinely believe in the supplement. "I take it in cold milk—all lumpy—not half dissolved," he wrote to Chatto, to whom he sent a pound as a gift that was also an advertisement. "It has completely cured my ancient curse of indigestion." When William James, who suffered from debilitating heart disease, wrote to him in April 1900 about whether to try the Kellgren cure in Sanna rather than a German spa again, Twain recommended both Kellgren and Plasmon. James had graciously included in his letter praise of Twain the writer, some of whose essays he would have been in sympathy with. "You are bound to get one advantage, happen what may," Twain responded. "[Kellgren] will put your nerves & your circulation in better shape than they are now, & thus improve your general health. . . . It is my conviction that Kellgren can modify any ailment, & can cure any that is curable. In typhoid, scarlet fever, influenza, & all such things, he is a master-hand." Life at Sanna Twain praised as vigorous and restful, despite the flies and the accommodations. If he were to return, which he intended to do that summer, he would live on Plasmon.

In a few years this odd but compatible couple, Twain and William James, were to be allies in a principled and more public venture, the Anti-Imperialist League. Twain at first strongly approved of the American invasion of Cuba in 1898, and also applauded Admiral Dewey's destruction of the Spanish fleet in Manila Bay. Authoritarian, anti-democratic Spain needed to be forced to lift its heel from the neck of those it oppressed. In

New York, Theodore Roosevelt, a war hero with immense national appeal, was performing nobly in his anti–Tammany Hall crusade. But, as Howells wrote Twain, he was also the man "who did more than almost any other to bring on the war, and now [wanted] to have a big army and navy, and go in for imperialism." America, which had committed itself to self-governance for Cuba, was in the process of reneging on its promise. Commercial and investment interests believed they would profit more from Cuba if it was an American semi-protectorate. American forces were at work pacifying the Philippine Islands. The pro-democratic and pro-independence Filipinos who had expected American support were, instead, hunted and attacked. When the peace treaty of 1898 gave America the same rights that the Spanish had had, the Filipinos fought back. By 1901, they were brutally defeated. The "war for humanity," Howells wrote to Twain, had been turned "into a war for coaling-stations." Twain was appalled, and furious. It seemed a betrayal of American values and of the moral superiority of this democratic republic to the European powers.

Britain he still respected, even loved, despite its flaws—corrupt aristocracy and imperial history. When England suffered more than a little humiliation, Twain felt pained. The Cecil Rhodes–provoked humiliations in South Africa were followed in 1899 by war between the British and the Boers. Twain believed the Boers in the right, though his loyalty was with the British. In London, English losses produced mourning crepe and black sadness. The war went badly, but then, in 1900, a string of British victories destroyed Boer dominance. "London wild with joy & noise all day & until two hours after midnight," Twain wrote in his notebook on May 19. President Kruger fled to Europe to plead his cause. The Boer states were formally annexed. To Twain's horror, America now was beginning to resemble Britain in its aspect that he most deplored.

As summer 1900 approached, they decided that another stint at Sanna was unnecessary because American osteopathy would be the treatment of preference for Jean. In May they found a large comfortable house at Dollis Hill, a suburb three miles from London, where Jean would go thrice weekly to the Kellgren Institute. In early July, in a pouring rain, they took possession of what seemed to him "the dirtiest dwelling-house in Europe—perhaps in the universe," which servants soon scrubbed clean. It was "a rather lucky strike" for them, "a farm, with hay & forest trees & sheep, & plenty of space & seclusion," he wrote to Richard Watson Gilder, editor of the *Century*. The house was leased till mid-September. Clara continued singing lessons. Her father resumed work on "The Chronicle of Young Satan." Long summer days on the park-like lawn, sheep grazing nearby, provided restful quiet. Still, they were both anxious to be under way. When he came down with one of his severe attacks of gout, he could hardly dress himself, let alone walk. He spent much time in his pajamas, in bed or on the lawn. On August 18 they observed "Our Day of Mourning, for our lost daughter, who died this day four years ago." But what came frequently to mind was going home. "I am getting heart-breakingly anxious," he had written on New Year's Day 1900, "to get home & never budge again. I am due to die this year, according to a trustworthy prophecy of thirty-five years' standing & I must not get caught out, on the wrong side of the water." Nervous and eager, they sailed on an American ship, in mid-October 1900, for New York. They had been in exile for eight years.

CHAPTER EIGHTEEN

SWEETHEART OF MY YOUTH

1900–1904

1.

Come home to America, Howells had urged. So too did Twain's heart. He had been an exile too long, essentially since 1893. He was now out from under the pressure of debt, and he had in the works a contract with Harper and Brothers that would regularize his income from royalties. Rogers' stock market forays kept his money growing. His independent speculative enthusiasm, Plasmon, was under reasonable control. Clara Clemens, who showed determination to go off as she pleased anyway, could study voice in America, and American osteopathy, Twain now believed, could do as much for Jean's epilepsy as Kellgren. At Twain's request, his nephew Samuel Moffett, now a New Yorker, had scouted out capable osteopathic doctors in Manhattan. And he himself could write anywhere. Anyway, he told Howells in May 1899, "I have intended to stop writing for print as soon as I could afford it. At last I can afford it, & have put the pot-boiler pen away." Writing for himself was another matter.

Though the Clemens family exaggerated its financial limitations, determined to protect itself from extravagance by thinking poor, it could indeed afford to live anyplace; Hartford, though, was out of the question. Susy's death, they had at last realized, made it impossible for them. It was, in fact, only a matter of when, not if, they would dispose of the house, since he considered the taxes and maintenance costs outrageously high. Real estate agents, word of mouth, and the help of Frank Doubleday, an up-and-coming publisher who became a friend, helped him locate a satisfactory house at a reasonable rent at 14 West Tenth Street. He quickly began, in October 1900, to establish a New York presence. The Clarence Rice–Henry Rogers circle re-embraced him, delighted to have their famous friend back in their midst. Laurence Hutton at Princeton, where Twain went in mid-November, a widely noticed guest at a football game, and Brander Matthews at Columbia provided literary and intellectual company. Social evenings with Richard Gilder, the *Century* editor, and his family became regular sustenance.

The most familiar embrace came from Howells, the active resumption of an intimacy that had remained strong over the years. Once again the friendship became the rich texture of both men's lives. Even on days when not together, each had the other in mind. Howells, who had lost his daughter in 1889, had more than the usual sympathy with Twain's bereavement. In late 1897, from Vienna, Twain had sent him a photo of Susy. The dead girl's angelic eyes affected him "as the eyes of Winnie sometimes did," Howells responded. "The night after the picture came I dreamed of seeing you in Vienna, and after some joking at our first meeting I put my arms round you, and we cried into each other's necks, like two sad old children. . . . I am sorry not to see you as I used, but I shall always love you." Twain expressed his love for Howells less directly, in the familiar tone of his letters and by his confessional openness. "We are all hoping to end our long exile," he wrote to him, "& see you then and have a time!" Ever generous, Howells had an infinite store of praise, in private and public, for his friend. "You have pervaded your century almost more than any other man of letters, if not quite more; and it is astonishing how you keep spreading." Twain's own self-appreciation made him less available to praise Howells, though he did, when the occasion required or when not distracted by self-concern. Howells continued to contribute importantly to drawing elite attention to the high seriousness of Twain's achievement.

At a popular level and as a media event, Twain remained the center of attention. At dockside, to satisfy reporters, he gave a group interview, newspapers eager to trumpet the return of the exile and get from his lips some witticism to print. New York papers heralded the celebrity's return,

emphasizing his honorable triumph over debt, another stage in the transformation of a literary giant into an American icon. His awareness of his
public image expressed itself, among other ways, in his now employing a
press clipping service. Only the president of the United States was more
likely to be recognized. An habitual stroller, he liked nothing better, as soon
as they had settled in on Tenth Street, than to walk around town and to
travel on public transportation. When a taxi driver overcharged Katy Leary,
Twain harangued the newspaper-reading public with accusations of highway robbery, exaggerating the amount of overcharge in his self-righteous
insistence that justice be meted out to malefactors. He was rarely too tired
to write indignant letters to editors. One afternoon, while chatting with
Twain at the corner of 42nd Street and Fifth Avenue, Finley Peter Dunne,
the author of the "Mr. Dooley" newspaper columns, noticed how much attention they were attracting. He urged Twain to go with him to the privacy
of his club. "What's the matter with staying here?" Twain responded.
Dunne said, "But aren't you embarrassed standing here in these crowds
talking to a celebrity?" Twain "answered like a man coming out of a trance.
His eyes were wide open and staring. He stammered, 'wh-wh-why, do you
think these people are looking at you? Why, you conceited fellow, they're
looking at me!' "

New York elite society could not get enough of him. Eight years away
had exponentially increased his attractiveness as a public-relations and a
self-celebrating commodity. In his first six months in New York, eager to
cooperate but also to protect his time, he struggled to limit the number of
invitations he accepted, especially for public appearances. The right balance, though, was difficult to find. Some invitations were irresistible, starting with a dinner in his honor at the Lotos Club on November 10, a
reception at the New York Press Club, a speech to the Society for American Authors, a dinner hosted by the Nineteenth Century Club, and the St.
Nicholas Society Banquet on December 6. He graced eleven more such
occasions in the next four months, at all of which he gave memorized
speeches on serious subjects, such as the reconciliation of North and
South at a Lincoln's birthday celebration and an attack on municipal corruption at a City Club dinner, the latter the first of many contributions to
the reform effort that would in 1902 defeat Tammany Hall.

When the appearance of Winston Churchill, a warrior for the British
Empire, now in New York hawking his recent account of his Boer War ex-

periences, evoked outrage among antiwar New Yorkers, Twain presided over a huge assembly gathered at the Waldorf-Astoria to hear Churchill speak. In a brief introduction, Twain extolled English-American kinship, a marriage between the best of Britain and of America, embodied in the marriage of Churchill's parents. Britain had many pro-liberty credits, he granted. America, though, had remained purer than Britain, until recently at least. "I think that England sinned in getting into a war in South Africa which she could have avoided without loss of credit or dignity—just as I think we have sinned in crowding ourselves into a war in the Philippines on the same terms. . . . We have always been kin: kin in blood, kin in religion, kin in representative government, kin in ideals, kin in just and lofty purposes; and now we are kin in sin, the harmony is complete, the blend is perfect, like Mr. Churchill himself, whom I now have the honor to present to you."

Graceful as his phrases were, they barely disguised his outrage, some directed at Britain and most at his own country, about which his expectations had been higher. Apparently, "according to an anonymous listener" whose report differs from the censored newspaper accounts, Twain began his introduction with a venom that even the sophisticated Churchill must have found discomforting: "Fellow thieves and robbers! I take it that this audience consists of English people and Americans, so I commence my remarks, fellow thieves and robbers—the Americans in the Philippines and the English in South Africa. But never mind, we're *kith* and *kin* in *war* and *sin*." From the moment he returned to New York, he felt an inner urgency to speak the truth about American aggression in the Philippines. His careful reading of the treaty that ended the Spanish-American War had forced him to conclude that the United States favored military subjugation of Cuba and the Philippines to enforce commercial dominance. The promise of self-governance was a ploy.

Livy did not oppose his outspokenness, at least partly because she strongly shared his views. Howells, his closest New York friend other than Rogers, opposed the expropriation of the Philippines as strongly and outspokenly as he did. From Hartford, the cautious Twichell warned Twain about the danger to his popularity and purse. "I'm not expecting anything but kicks for scoffing, & am expecting a diminution of my bread & butter by it," he responded. But, everything else being equal, he would speak his piece, and not because he thought himself a better patriot or more moral than others. "I am only distressed & troubled because I am befouled by these things. That is all." He argued that, like everyone else's, his motives were selfish. He needed to relieve himself of his distress. The only way to do that was to oppose publicly what he felt was damaging his country.

McKinley's reelection in November 1900, with Theodore Roosevelt as his vice president, gave added bite to Twain's disapproval of American policy. McKinley had campaigned on America's obligation "to confer the blessings of liberty and civilization upon all rescued people." To Twain, this rhetoric represented an abandonment of America's longstanding refusal to join the European powers in colonial conquests. Suddenly America was being transformed from the republic of his childhood into a predatory international power. Roosevelt he scoffed at. As a young man, Twain had been a shill for American dominance in Hawaii and had approved Burlingame's vision of American influence in China. Now he felt angry terror at this betrayal of the principles established by the Founding Fathers. It voided American uniqueness, that which differentiated it from the rapacious European powers. It undermined constitutional government at home, he later wrote in his autobiographical dictations. "For fifty years our country has been a constitutional monarchy, with the Republican Party sitting on the throne." A large standing military and constant action abroad would further undermine constitutional liberties at home. Hypocritical self-justification would sap the country's moral fiber and self-respect.

The "blessings of civilization" argument assumed that non-Christian foreigners needed redemption. Twain largely kept to himself the extent of his alienation from most aspects of Christian theology, but he had always openly detested clerical hypocrisy. When American missionaries in China insisted that, like their European colleagues, they deserved compensation for losses during the Boxer Rebellion, Twain could not contain his contempt. What was this "civilization" they were bringing to China? Since some of the most "terrible offences against humanity" were being "committed in the name of Politics" against a brutalized population in the slums of New York, "civilization" needed repair at home, not abroad. And if the missionaries' idea of civilization was what was on exhibit in China, perhaps the vice-ridden slums of Christian New York were to be preferred. When, on Christmas Day 1900, the *New York Sun* reported that the American Board of Foreign Missions urged that the Chinese be compelled to pay "fines amounting to THIRTEEN TIMES the amount of the indemnity . . .

to pay for the propagation of the Gospel," Twain, in a white fury, wrote "To the Person Sitting in Darkness," ironically addressing non-Christian natives to convince them that the forces of "civilization" were doing great things for them. Its publication in February 1901 in the *North American Review* filled his mailbox with reviling letters from strangers.

To Twain's disgust, hawkish patriotism had made the war popular. He received "one or two letters from . . . dear friends hotly reproaching him," Livy wrote to Annie Fields. "Other friends are silent, so we feel their disapproval." He began a satirical political fantasy, "The Secret History of Eddypus, the World-Empire," in which American democracy, enervated by material prosperity and by political monarchism of the sort represented by Roosevelt, collapses. A new world order ensues. Christianity is replaced by Christian Science. Mrs. Eddy becomes worldwide monarch and pope. A character called "Mark Twain . . . sometime Bishop of New Jersey," a "revered priest of the earlier faith" who had been hanged in A.D. 1912, has left to future generations a written account of the change from the old to the new order on which this "secret history" is based. After two months of fiddling, he put the manuscript aside. In October 1901, at the Yale Bicentennial, he apparently overheard Roosevelt, who the month before had succeeded McKinley, remark, "When I hear what Mark Twain and others have said in criticism of the missionaries, I feel like skinning them alive!"

Twain's brief "Salutation Speech from the Nineteenth Century to the Twentieth," published in the *Herald* at the end of December 1900, reached an even wider audience and would have angered Roosevelt even more. The New England Anti-Imperialist League printed it on small cards and distributed it nationally: "I bring you the matron called CHRISTENDOM— returning bedraggled, besmirched and dishonored from pirate raids in Kiaochow, Manchuria, South Africa and the Philippines; with her soul full of meanness, her pocket full of boodle and her mouth full of pious hypocrisies. Give her soap and a towel, but hide the looking-glass."

2.

"So many dinners . . . so few books," Howells remarked to Thomas Bailey Aldrich about Twain in November 1901. For much of 1900–1 he dined and spoke at a pace that would exhaust even the most dedicated self-publicist. What Howells only partly appreciated, though, was that this activity expressed a reengagement, even if to excess, that partly redressed his eight years of absence. It was flattering to be sought after. And he rightly judged that it served a legitimate need, much of it emotional, to be once more, even if briefly, at the center of American life. The ongoing consequences of the Spanish-American War were the focus of some public appearances, but there were other issues to which he also devoted himself, particularly his outrage at corrupt New York City politics. With Howells and others determined to promote social justice and civic decency, he became a leader of the anti-Tammany reform movement, helping elect Seth Low mayor in November 1902. At a meeting of the Male Teacher's Association, Twain proclaimed that he would indeed teach patriotism in the schools. But he would "throw out the old maxim, 'My country, right or wrong,' and instead . . . say, 'My country when she is right.'" In early 1901 he addressed the annual meeting of the Hebrew Technical School for Girls at Temple Emanu-El. "I've been in favor of women's rights," including the ballot, he told them. "I see in this school the realization of a project I have always dreamed of. Why, do you know, when I looked at my gray-haired old mother, with her fine head and noble thoughts, I really almost suspected, toward the last, that she was quite as capable of voting as I was." In February, he helped raise money for the University Settlement Society whose lower East Side "House" provided free educational services for impoverished slum-dwellers, most of them immigrant Jews.

As he had done before, he protected himself from adding to the many letters he wrote almost every day by printing engraved cards declining lecture invitations. His royalties, his article fees, and his dividends from investments were sufficient to sustain him; in fact, they produced a surplus from which he increased his Plasmon investment to fifty thousand dollars and bought, with Henry Rogers' guidance, more stock in solid companies. "My axiom is—to succeed in business, avoid my example," he told a banquet audience. Colonel George Harvey, whom he saw regularly and counted a friend, continued trying to tie Twain more tightly to the Harper empire, particularly to find a contractual way to make the press and its monthly and weekly magazines his exclusive publication venues. Though Twain chafed at the realization, his days as a best-selling author of new books were over, and Harvey had the market sense to know that Twain's major assets were his backlist and his short pieces for the magazine trade. His celebrated name was an attraction on covers and contents pages, and Harvey was willing to pay to have it. When James Pond proposed a ten-lecture tour for ten thousand dollars, Twain declined, happy to tell Pond and anyone else who asked that he had given up that detestable activity forever. Charity readings were another matter. Two or three a year seemed reasonable, partly for the flattering attention and to keep his hand in, mostly in the service of causes he believed in and to accommodate friends. But, he insisted, they were to be at private homes only, without notice or availability to the press.

By late spring 1901, Livy had had enough of the West Tenth Street house, ostensibly because it seemed impossible to keep sufficiently warm through the winter. In actuality, she felt deprived of a residence she could properly call her own home. Still, the family had good reasons to stay in or close to Manhattan. Clara took regular singing lessons. Under the aegis of a professional manager, more attracted by her lineage than by her readiness, she gave two performances that winter, one in Washington, the other in Hartford. As always, she was plagued by colds and voice problems, nervous insecurity inseparable from both. Her parents chaperoned her and did what they could to minister to her needs, though neither had any notion that they might have helped her most by leaving her alone. In Washington, they had the doctor twice before the performance. In Hartford, Clara struggled with a bronchitis infection. Finally, claiming that she needed more lessons and that her agent was "unreliable," she gave up for that season. Her parents wished she would give it up forever. "We do not oppose her," Livy remarked, "for of course that is not best—but we are very sorry indeed that she wants this public life."

Jean's medical regimen kept her under Dr. George Helmer's care, osteopathic treatment still attractive to her parents who were greatly relieved that, whatever the cause, her attacks came less frequently. Dr. Helmer, now also Twain's physician, treated him successfully, so he thought, for bronchitis and other winter ills. His gout, though, resisted osteopathic skills. In February 1901, in Albany, he amused the New York General Assembly's Committee on Public Health with one of his patented arguments, mixing humor, reminiscence, and common sense on behalf of the movement to license osteopaths. In opposition, the representative of the medical association urged the legislature to dismiss Twain as a mere humorist "whose condemnation of American policy in the Philippines would have gotten him mobbed if anybody had taken him seriously." He calmly responded with a one-hour presentation extolling osteopathy and the logic of giving people the freedom to be treated in a regulated way by trained osteopaths. "I like osteopathy," he declared. "It is quicker and you don't have to take any medicine." The *New York Times* chastised him as "a public enemy," "a defender of quacks."

With the prospect of a New York City summer looming, he and Livy visited Saranac Lake in the Adirondack Mountains, where they did "some heavy traveling & brisk running around," searching for a summer house. The date of departure awaited Dr. Helmer's permission. Clara, who was pleased that Ossip Gabrilowitsch, Leschetizky's successful protégé who had paid off and on again attentions to her since their Vienna days, was in New York, would stay behind, at least part of the season. During the next two years Ossip proposed twice to Clara, and twice, after Clara had accepted and to Livy's disappointment, the engagement fell apart. The city had its attractions for Twain also, but at a pace that left little time for work or for his sister Pamela, who now lived uptown, or his nearby niece, or his nephew, now a well-settled journalist who commuted from New Rochelle. "I have done very little," he wrote a friend. "There is too much speechmaking here." He and Livy, though, did find time to try visiting Susy through a spiritualist, a reluctant effort on his part. "I judge that nothing is going to come of this matter. At least it looks so unpromising—& also so silly & so cheaply visionary." They soon gave up. Susy, he felt, had presence enough for him through ordinary means.

Late in June 1901 they had a good enough report from Dr. Helmer to take the train to the mountains. "The Lair," near Ampersand, a rustic, comfortable log cabin, small but manageable, its prow extending over the water, its views across and down the lake, turned out to be a summer paradise. The days were mild, the nights cool, the surrounding forest a "primeval wilderness." He loved the isolation. Without newspapers or telephone, he was beyond the reach of the stock market and soliciting letters. Jean's outdoor activities kept her brown and limber, though a few unusually hot days threatened to make her ill; they all feared something might set off an epileptic attack. She also had a vocation of sorts. With her parents' encouragement, she had learned to type, for the purpose of copying her father's manuscripts and taking dictation, particularly to help with the stacks of letters that took up so much of his time.

Twain puttered with small things and unfinished manuscripts, and he may have attempted to dictate some autobiographical reminiscences.

What he wrote, he added to his "stacks of Literary Remains," much of it placed in what he described as his "large box of Posthumous stuff," including what he referred to as his "hundred year book," his autobiography, not to be published until a century after his death. Sam Moffett tried to revivify a Clemens family obsession, John Marshall's Tennessee land. The remnant, he thought, might have value in the reserved mineral rights. "How strange it would be" if at last it should be valuable, Livy wrote. For more than "sixty years the family have expected riches from it." She gave him modest encouragement, including money to pay for preliminary investigation. Her husband thought it nonsense. "It has always brought disappointment to the family."

Early in the summer, the real estate agents they had set in motion and their own inquiries turned up a large house in Riverdale, the "old Appleton homestead," a stone residence on a large piece of riverfront property with more than twenty rooms, including a huge living-dining area. Enticing views sloped down lawns to the Hudson and its river traffic. They had not intended to leave Manhattan. Suddenly, though, the idea of semi-country privacy at the reasonable rent of three thousand dollars a year, with an option for a second at the same rate, appealed to them. Grand Central Station was twenty-five minutes away, close enough for Jean's medical treatments, Clara's lessons, and Twain's Manhattan activities. Livy, at last, had given in to the inevitable and consented to putting the Hartford house on the market, mostly because she expected to use the proceeds from the sale to purchase a house in the New York area. Twain, who valued the property at $110,000—what they had paid initially, plus what they had added—agreed to list it at $60,000. Unfortunately, the market was not interested even at that discounted price. Livy vetoed advertising, which seemed to her distasteful. Buyers would have to seek them out. Though she began looking for a house to buy, she was determined to buy nothing new until the old was sold.

In August, Twain had the pleasure of a two-week vacation within his vacation, a trip on Henry Rogers' newly purchased reconditioned steam yacht, the *Kanawha,* a handsome 227-foot vessel reputed, at its twenty-two-knot cruising speed, to be the fastest of its class sailing the East Coast. Twain came aboard in New York on August 3 with Rogers, Clarence Rice, and Rogers' son-in-law, and the group sailed northward. At Bar Harbor, Maine, Tom Reed, the ex–Speaker of the House known as "Czar Reed," a

Republican Party stalwart with a strong independent streak who had opposed the Spanish-American War, joined them. Neither Twain nor Livy mentioned that Twain had been at sea on August 18, 1901, the fifth anniversary of Susy's death.

In late-summer weather, usually on the porch over the lake, he once again did a stint of hack-writing of the sort he had claimed he would never again do, partly because Colonel Harvey pressed him to provide something for *Harper's Monthly*, mostly because he had an idea he considered amusing, a parody of the Sherlock Holmes craze. *A Double-Barrelled Detective Story*, a 205,000-word novella that he wrote in two weeks, is a minimally amusing burlesque, the interest of which derives from three elements: the depiction of a brutalized wife, a revengeful son's search for his father in the American West, Australia, India, and Ceylon, and the appearance of a Holmes burlesque namesake. He had for a long time "planned to make fun of that pompous sentimental 'extraordinary man' with his cheap and ineffectual ingenuities," he wrote Twichell, who had introduced him to Conan Doyle's novels—"but the plan wouldn't sprout; I have planned again, several times. . . . But this time I've pulled it off." It was an attempt at nonserious amusement, an entertainment for *Harper's* readers, for which Harvey would pay handsomely. It was also a step in a process that Harvey hoped would commit Twain to supply a set amount of material annually, an exclusive arrangement in which Harper would pay him a yearly retainer, the details of which were yet to be worked out.

If *A Double-Barrelled Detective Story* was a light amusement, "The United States of Lyncherdom," also written late that summer, was a furious response to the increase in the number of public murders of black men without benefit of judicial proceedings or constitutional protections. It was warmup for a full-length book to be called "History of Lynching in America" or, alternatively, "Rise and Progress of Lynching." "The thing I am full of, now," he wrote Frank Bliss in late August 1901, "is a large subscription book," the bulk of which would contain newspaper accounts from around the country gathered by researchers he would employ. "Yesterday I wrote an acid article on the subject . . . for the *North American Review*. . . . In it I . . . implore the missionaries to come back from China & convert their own Christian countrymen." If desirable, he could reserve the essay for an introduction to the book. A few days later he had changed his mind about the entire project, realizing the value of the "Southern trade" to both him and his publishers. "Upon reflection . . . it won't do for me to write that book." "The United States of Lyncherdom" remained unpublished until 1923.

In late September 1901 they took up residence in Riverdale. As always, Quarry Farm remained a second home, though attenuated by time and change. Livy's brother and sister were the relatives to whom they were emotionally closest, though age, illness, and loss had made Livy and Sam more inward and isolated. In New York, Twain puttered with radical ideas in manuscripts that remained unpublished fragments and commented angrily on almost daily bulletins about brutalities from the American South to South Africa to the Philippines. In late September, he attended the celebration at Yale at which he was awarded an honorary degree, but he largely kept to his intention to do less after-dinner speaking, though that still allowed for a number of appearances, the most memorable an address on Scots humor to the St. Andrew's Society. That irresistible invitation came with urgings from his friendly acquaintance Andrew Carnegie. Livy ran the house and family; Jean went regularly to her New York osteopath; Clara bustled from singing lessons to concerts to social events. "Jean is getting along fairly well; her mother's heart & gout bad; Clara in pretty good shape; I healthy as granite," he reported to the Aldriches.

The Riverdale house proved almost a perfect residence, its major deficiency that it was not permanently theirs. "We are ourselves dwellers in remoteness & tranquilities now, with the river & the Palisades in front & the woods behind, & seldom have to go to the City." When inquiries about whether it might be for sale met discouragement, Livy began searching for something near the Hudson with enough land for Jean to have horses and outdoor life, ultimately finding a house in Tarrytown priced at forty-five thousand dollars. To be suitable it needed an addition, which meant it would not be habitable until the next winter. The Hartford house remained unsold. Livy's heart, though, was set on Tarrytown. They closed the deal in May 1902.

During the search Twain had a six-week reprieve, a West Indies excursion that turned out to be a carnival of sensual delight. In mid-March, his suitcases filled with summer clothes, he took the train, with Henry Rogers, John Archbold, another Standard Oil executive, Tom Reed, Clarence Rice, and George Harvey, to Palm Beach, Florida. The *Kanawha* awaited them at Miami. It was Susy's birthday, Twain remarked in his notebook. At Nassau, where they took on coal, "the sea was beyond imagination." Each day brought the gratification of white, velvety sand, intense blue skies, pellucid water, and changing varieties of color and form. At Hog Island they had a "fruit debauch," a feast unavailable in the north, out of season. With Archbold he "swam far out into the enchanted solitudes & rode the rich seas for half an hour."

As they sailed for Havana, a route Twain, "as chief of the itinerary committee," had determined, they all stayed on deck to escape the heat below. Twain urged Rice, who was constantly seasick, to try Plasmon, but the doctor declined. During a storm, Twain heard Reed "grunting and blaspheming, and butting the bulkhead, carrying on. Then he appeared up there in his pajamas, and he was going it. Well, he said: 'I couldn't stay in my berth at all; it's wet.' 'Why,' I said, 'you old thing, you ought to be ashamed of yourself—scared to that extent.' " In Havana Harbor the ruins of the *Maine* looked like "a Brobdignagian tarantula in his death-squirm." On Good Friday, Kingston, Jamaica, seemed quiet and dull. When a storm threatened, the *Kanawha* took shelter in a bay. That afternoon they were pulled by fast mules through "the most prodigal & marvelous exhibition of tropical vegetation imaginable. . . . It was a grand day, & makes all other days of the trip poor & commonplace by comparison." As they sailed in a sweeping circle around Jamaica, set course for Nassau, then steamed toward New York, they played cards in the "poker chapel," dined elegantly, played practical jokes, and drank and dozed considerably, a sophisticated, profane group of accomplished men who enjoyed one another's company. Each, whether he felt himself so or not, was treated as first among equals.

In June 1902 he took a different kind of voyage, into recollections of childhood and the realization of changes that returning to Hannibal inevitably evoked. When the University of Missouri offered a Doctor of Letters degree, he gave up the thought that they might spend the summer in Venice, an idea motivated by their desire to keep an eye on Clara, who had sailed for Europe in late April, supposedly chaperoned but essentially at liberty. They had reason to think she sought time there with Ossip Gabrilowitsch. Twain deeply objected, but silently, it seems. Venice, with its heat and tourists, would have been an absurd summer place, and they could do little anyway to control Clara. Flattered by Missouri's offer and thinking that this might be his last chance to visit Hannibal, he accepted the honorary degree.

Livy wanted "very much to go," but her husband thought the trip would be too tiring for her, and he would probably be less able to focus on himself and his past if he did not go alone. Before leaving, he instructed Franklin Whitmore to sell the Hartford property immediately, even for as little as forty thousand dollars. He wanted it disposed of before he returned, certainly before the family left Riverdale for a summer cottage at York Harbor in southeastern Maine, which he had rented for six hundred dollars for five months. It was forty minutes by trolley from Howells' summer home in Kittery. With Howells he was emotionally closer than ever. That fall and winter they had spent many hours together in New York. After each visit, Howells walked Twain back to Grand Central Station. "He has no time table," Howells told Aldrich, "but all the gatemen and train starters are proud to know him, and lay hold of him, and put him aboard *something* that leaves for Riverdale. He always has to go to the W.C., me dancing in the corridor, and holding his train for him. But they would not let it go without him, if it was the Chicago limited! What a fame and force he is!" To Twain's disappointment, the "rich Chicagoan" whom Whitmore felt certain would appear to buy the house once he had been allowed to advertise "Mark Twain's House For Sale" had not materialized. What did especially surprise Twain, though, was one Hartford offer: "A Hartford man has said to me, 'If the house were out of the way, the land would promptly sell for $35,000; it is a prime site for several purposes.' Is that true? What could we get for the house & stable as old materials?" If the house were not sold to some appreciative person, he would rather tear it down than have it some day "degraded to base uses."

As Twain prepared for his Missouri trip in late May 1902, his notebook entries expressed his reawakened autobiographical impulse, that hundred-year book, selections from which he had promised Harvey he would consider publishing in a Harper magazine. A letter from Jim Gillis, "dear old Unreconstructible" from California mining days, also revivified the past. "How should I imagine that you & Jim & Steve could still be above ground," he responded, "when I haven't had a line from any of you for ages? . . . Come as far as Columbia, Missouri, you three, & strike hands with me there the 4th of June; otherwise we shall not meet again on this side of the grave—& certainly not on the other." At the same time, he got a letter from Joe Goodman, the firmness of whose handwriting put him in mind of the shakiness of his own. "I shall be 67 at the end of the year, & sometimes I feel old, but not often. But I am persistently old in this: my this-world interests are decaying, & my other-world interests have already disappeared. Wine & beer do not invite me anymore, & it has taken me 5 months to drink one bottle of Scotch whiskey, my pet of all brews. But I smoke all day, & I get up twice a-night to do the like. When I get smoked out—well, it will be a sign!" He departed for St. Louis and reached Hannibal in a valedictory mood. He was still here, and in good health, but others were fading faster, and he fast enough.

Hannibal embraced him, and dead companions proved to have as much presence as the living. He visited his father's, mother's, and Henry's graves at the Mount Olivet cemetery, to where their remains had been transferred. "Almost every tombstone recorded a forgotten name that had been familiar and pleasant to my ear when I was a boy there fifty years before," he later wrote. An aged John Robards was his primary host, along with Helen Garth and Laura Hawkins (now Mrs. Frazer). He posed for photos in front of what had been the family house on Hill Street. With surviving companions, he toured Hannibal, visited Bear's Creek, and climbed Holliday's Hill, looking "out again over that magnificent panorama of the Mississippi River, sweeping along league after league, a level green paradise on one side, and retreating capes and promontories as far as you could see on the other, fading away in the soft, rich lights of the remote distance. I recognized then that I was seeing now," he told the Hannibal High School graduation audience on May 30, "the most enchanting river view the planet could furnish."

It was "an intensely emotional week," he told his audience at the University of Missouri. "I experienced emotions that I never had expected, and did not know were in me. I was profoundly moved and saddened to think that this was the last time, perhaps, that I would ever behold those kind old faces and dear old scenes of childhood." It was a sentimental farewell, the other side of the coin of what he conveniently left out: the darker realities that coexisted in his memory, which he had recounted in "Villagers of 1840–3." He had returned to Missouri as the homecoming king, a narcissist's fantasy realized, the celebrity who gave to the town he left as a boy its greatest claim to fame. He had kick-started the image and the industry of Hannibal, the home of Tom Sawyer, Huckleberry Finn, and Mark Twain.

3.

In June 1902, with Livy and Jean, Twain sailed on Rogers' *Kanawha* to Kittery, Maine, where they settled into a modest cottage in York Harbor called

"The Pines." Clara was in Paris, scheduled to join them later in the summer. On the sail up, Jean seemed on the brink of an epileptic attack. If they had not had the privacy of the yacht, "it would have been equivalent to being in hell," he wrote to Rogers. "The scare & the anxiety would have been unendurable." Livy stayed up with her most of two nights, "& so the convulsion was staved off." At York Harbor, the attack came. "I have seen it only three times before, in all these fiendish five years. It comes near to killing Mrs. Clemens every time." It probably took a combination of accidental and intentional absence for him to have seen it only three times before.

The Hartford house still remained a source of anxiety. Even at a cut-rate price, it had not been sold. Livy particularly felt the strain, enough to agree, at her husband's urging, to postpone indefinitely the Tarrytown addition. They were glad "to be out from that uncomfortable pressure," though they still planned to move there in the autumn and squeeze themselves into what they recognized was insufficient space. When in early July a midwestern businessman made what at first glance seemed a viable offer to buy the Hartford house, they had a heart-flurry of hope. Railroad bonds, supposedly worth fifty thousand dollars and paying a five percent dividend, "to be issued a year or eighteen months hence," were offered as security, in effect a disadvantageous trade rather than a cash payment. The buyer wanted to take possession in October. Realizing that this was "too deep" for him, Twain turned to Rogers. "You might as well put your deed up against so much brown paper," Rogers advised. "Don't let me influence you too much, but do be careful. It is much easier to keep out of trouble than it is to get out. You and I know that of old." Twain took Rogers advice, though he soon urged Whitmore to "get rid of the house" under whatever terms: "Sell it for a song. So that I can tell Mrs. Clemens that that burden upon her spirits is gone."

A decline in Livy's health worried him. Her gout had gotten worse. Muscles were stiff and joints sore and the effects of various medicines had become inseparable from the illnesses they were supposed to alleviate. When she had osteopathic treatments, which she stinted on to save money, she felt debilitating aches for weeks. Something catastrophic was on its way, Twain believed, the result of "five years of constant anxiety" about Jean. Severe heart flutters returned. Hypertension was severe, breathing impeded, a sign of either heart congestion or asthma or both. Soon her need to sit upright in order to breathe became "a nightly experience."

Eager to do for herself, Livy had to have daytime attendants to force her to stay inactive. Doctor and husband lied to her: they were not in the least worried, they asserted; her condition was not life-threatening. Such assurances did little to allay her fear. The resemblance of this deception to the plot of a story he was writing gave him moments of bitter reflection. The story, "Was It Heaven? Or Hell?," which he had begun late in the spring and continued working on through July and early August, dramatized some of the death-anxiety trauma at the heart of Twain family life. It was eerily appropriate now, and soon became even more so. Twin maiden aunts attend to their sick niece and her daughter, each of whom has become fatally ill but does not know the other is dying of the same disease in another part of the house. Having laid her head upon her mother's breast and, under pressure from her stern aunts, asked forgiveness for her sins, the daughter has caught the disease. The Presbyterian sisters, who believe lying is an unforgivable sin, are persuaded by the attending doctor not to tell the daughter or the mother of the other's condition. For the mother, knowledge of her daughter's death would be the heaviest blow possible. The aunts, whose narrow Christianity the story attacks, collaborate on a fictional scenario for humanitarian reasons. But their religious training is at war with their hearts. When mother and daughter die without knowing the other's fate, an angel comes to pronounce judgment on the sisters. The story concludes: "Was it Heaven? Or Hell?"

At seven in the morning on August 12, 1902, Livy became "violently ill." "Telephoned, & Dr. Lambert was here in ½ hour," Twain wrote in his notebook. "She could not breathe—was likely to stifle. Also she had severe palpitation. She believed she was dying. I also believed it." The doctor took "heroic measures." By noon, the crisis abated. Whether it was congestive heart failure or hypertension and a panic attack or some combination of these or other things is not clear. Various doctors then and later disagreed. Howells told Aldrich that it was "organic heart disease and nervous prostration." Immediately a telegram went to Elmira. "She is low-spirited & wants you," Twain told Susan Crane, "& frankly says the rest of us are not valuable comforters. The truth is, she won't *let* us be. We try our best to keep hidden the doctor-secrets, but she [is] sharp, & penetrating, & hunts us through all our shifts and dodges, & worms everything out of us, & then the results make her low-spirited."

Two doctors were enlisted for almost around-the-clock attendance, a

New York physician and an osteopath "with an allopathic diploma." One began staying overnight at the cottage. Coming directly from dockside in New York, Clara arrived that same night. The doctors, intending to keep Livy as unexcited as possible, allowed Clara but not her father into the sickroom. "It proved . . . good medicine," Twain wrote to Rogers. By habit and by personality, his presence would, the doctors believed, cause Livy emotional distress. He began to sleep at a neighbor's cottage. Katy took long turns beside Livy's bed, as comforting as a familiar piece of old furniture and slavishly useful. Jean hovered in the background. Father and daughters did what they could to transform the cottage into a private hospital, including ordering a special bed from Boston. For the time being, Livy could not be moved. "Of all the impossible places for the meeting of emergencies promptly & successfully, this is the impossiblest," he told Rogers ten days later. When their telegram from Boston arrived two hours after Susan Crane and Charles Langdon themselves had arrived, Twain lashed out at Western Union. It gave him pleasure to do so. At least, he felt, he was doing *something*. Over the next week occasional indications of improvement proved unreliable. "The illness drags along," he moaned. "There is never any *great* improvement; never anything to rouse us & make us jubilant." Worst of all, for the first time in a lifetime of poor health, Livy felt "doubtful." She, who wanted very much to live, had apparently seen death.

During August and September, Twain occasionally had afternoon guests. He and Howells drank tea and smoked cigars on the veranda, voices hushed in order not to disturb the patient. When on a rainy day Howells visited "on his way to a reception," he seemed as "sweet & lovely as ever." To give himself relief from worry about Livy, Twain worked on "Tom Sawyer's Conspiracy" and revised "Was It Heaven? Or Hell?" After reading the latter, Clara was shaken by what seemed a prophetic anticipation of their conspiracy to keep the truth from her mother. What lies would they have to tell next to disguise their conviction that she was likely to die? Twain complained to Frederick Duneka, his Harper editor, "I have been—in literary matters—helpless all these weeks. I have no editor—no censor." For the first time, though, Clara filled that role. And he could not shake from his mind the prediction made twice by a professional clairvoyant in the last seven years—that in his sixty-eighth year he would become unexpectedly "very rich." The subject, which had become a family tease, obsessed him. It had deep roots in his life: the connections between the Langdon family wealth, the fortunes he had failed to make, the trials his failures had inflicted on his family, and Livy's longstanding poor health. How ironic it would be, he thought, if he became a wealthy widower.

In late August 1902, after a few good days, Livy proposed that they go to Elmira. Susan Crane encouraged the plan. Twain looked into railroad arrangements. The doctors, though, recommended against any journey until she could sit up in a chair for much more than the ten minutes a day that now taxed her limit. To cheer his wife, Twain assured her that he had no objection to the Tarrytown house addition. When Livy clung to the idea of Elmira, he resisted. Getting back to Riverdale would be difficult enough. Then, in late September, she had a relapse. Convinced that worry rather than something organic had been the cause of this "heart-attack," as he now referred to it, he attempted to show her that money was not a problem. For example, they had an offer of fifty thousand dollars for the Tarrytown house, five thousand more than they had paid. Neither brought up the Hartford house.

With Howells he went to Boston, where he made arrangements for an "invalid car from York Harbor to Riverdale without [special] charge," the entire cost $339. Clara fired the nurse and hired another, a likely savior, Twain believed, the start of a pattern of high expectation and quick disillusionment. Clara took charge of their departure from "The Pines." Colder weather and rainstorms made them eager to leave, and they all thought spirits would be raised by returning home. Jean, her father noticed, had not had an attack for almost ten weeks. It seemed a miracle, but, he told Duneka, explaining why it took so long to get manuscripts typed, "[She] isn't strong & sometimes can't stay at the machine more than an hour a day, & some days we don't allow her to work at all." In mid-October Livy was carried into her Riverdale bedroom, hardly the worse for travel. It was a great relief to them all to be again in a familiar house, and to resume their New York life.

Though in the next nine months Livy returned from the abyss, she never became other than an invalid again. In late October 1902, Twain convinced himself temporarily that there was no heart disease at all. Livy suffered from "a vigorous case of nervous prostration," he told Poultney Bigelow. Absolute rest was the major prescription. No excitement of any sort. Life in the winter and spring of 1902–3 became an exercise in white lies, physical separation, and deadly silence, a prescription that placed an additional pall on their lives. Twain soon confessed that he was "a little troubled about Clara, whose anxieties [were] telling on her." With Katy and a hired nurse, she attended Livy around the clock. He and Jean were mostly forbidden the patient's presence: it was generally agreed that he was incapable of not saying the wrong thing, and the sight of Jean, a reminder of the ever-present possibility of an epileptic attack, had the potential to raise Livy's blood pressure to dangerous levels.

When, at Christmas, Jean came down with pneumonia, two doctors came to the house, one of whom occasionally stayed overnight, especially as Jean worked through a month-long life-threatening crisis. With her father and Katy, Clara created a fictional life for Jean in order to explain the absence of the Jean-associated sounds Livy usually heard and the changes in Clara's schedule. "[Livy's] heart is bad," he confessed to Susan Crane, "[and] Clara is sure it will not be able to bear the shock." When Clara slipped, Livy pounced. Clara cleverly told more lies to weave herself into credibility, reaping the reward of her well-earned, longstanding reputation as a truth teller. Twain marveled at his daughter's brilliance and wrote up a long account, with dialogue, of the strange scenario. "The whole thing would be funny," he remarked to Susan, "if it were not heart-breakingly pathetic & tragic." Despite all his practice, he himself, he recognized, was "but a poor clumsy liar, whereas a fine alert & capable emergency-liar is the only sort that is worth anything in a sick-chamber."

To some extent, he was cut out of even the medical loop. "The house is a hospital, & the expenses phenomenal," he told Frank Bliss. Clara handled the doctors. Sometimes his information came from overheard telephone conversations. Occasionally he hovered outside Livy's door, listening. "For the first time in months I heard her break into one of her girlish old-time laughs. With a word I could freeze the blood in her veins." The word would have been about Jean's condition. And he knew enough to know that he could not trust himself not to say what he should not say. Months passed without his getting permission to see her, and visits were short, often no more than five minutes. Convinced that their separation was in the interest of her health, he accepted it stoically, among other reasons because he believed himself to blame for her illness. "It grieves me so to remember that I am the cause of your being where you are. I wish—I wish—but it is too late. I drove you to sorrow & heart-break."

Still, he missed her desperately, and with Clara busy taking singing lessons and attending to her mother and the doctors, and Jean staying upstairs doing "wood-carving, or outside prowling in the fresh air," he was lonely. Usually he wrote notes to Livy twice a day, hundreds of them through the winter and spring, some carefully restrained accounts of his day, others touching evocations of his love for her. He had not had occasion to express such focused tenderness since his letters to her as a young man. These notes now had an elegiac, autumnal tone. "I love you darling old-young sweetheart of my youth & my age, & I kiss you good-night." Occasionally they blew the trumpet of shared hope into the darkness of a reality they both preferred to deny. "The summer is here. Cheer up. My best beloved. We shall be happy again."

4.

Antagonism to Mary Baker Eddy provided some focus for the writing he did in winter and spring 1903. Twain had nothing against Christian Science itself. But "making fun of that shameless old swindler, Mother Eddy, is the only thing about it I take any interest in. At bottom I suppose I take a private delight in seeing the human race making an ass of itself again— which it has always done whenever it had a chance." The manuscript was growing into a book, which he expected to publish soon. The Harper team, led by the sociable, well-connected George Harvey and his tactful subeditor Frederick Duneka, placed few limits on how far they would go to keep Twain happy. The limit was approached only when he had something he desired to publish that might alienate book buyers or magazine readers, like a book attacking Mary Baker Eddy. The claim that he did not mean it to be an attack on Christian Science itself was hardly meaningful in the circumstances. Harvey assured him that Harper would publish it, though at a later, unspecified time.

Eager for a better arrangement for his backlist, Twain struggled to bring the competing parties together. He wanted the American Publishing Company to enter into cooperative leasing agreements with other publishers or to co-publish or, if not, to sell its interest outright to Twain. Harper & Brothers wanted either a better arrangement with Bliss's company or to eliminate it entirely. Twain went to Hartford in June 1903 to try "to reconcile the Harper quarrel upon perfectly just & fair terms." Harvey arrived at a practical solution. In order to obtain the American Publishing Company's

Sweetheart of My Youth   ⇒ *601*

only asset of value, he would buy the company. Bliss capitulated. Harper at last had exclusive rights to Twain, past, present, and future. Only the details needed to be worked out, and Twain wanted to be certain that the new contract, unlike previous ones, would have a time limit. Harvey acceded to all Twain's requests, including a sunset clause, and guaranteed Twain a minimum $25,000 a year for five years. Twain needed only to provide two essays or stories, one for summer, the other for Christmas publication. Since a substantial portion of earnings from new books and from his backlist in various editions, once the $25,000 had been accounted for, would go to him, he had sound reason to anticipate an annual income of about $100,000. Among many sweeteners, Harvey agreed to advertise Twain prominently in each issue of *Harper's Weekly* and *Harper's Monthly Magazine*. In early October 1903, he signed. He was now a member of a team with a shared financial interest. The uniform editions would be the gold mine for which all his life he had been searching.

A celebration that both anticipated the contract and lubricated the wheels of the negotiation had occurred the previous November, a sixty-seventh-birthday banquet at the Metropolitan Club hosted by Colonel Harvey. Sixty prominent people assembled, many of them writers, including Howells, Gilder, Booth Tarkington, Hamlin Garland, Richard le Galliene, and Henry Van Dyke; others, such as Henry Rogers, Tom Reed, August Belmont, Adolph Ochs, and John Hay, now secretary of state, were men of influence and wealth. Some were old friends, including Twichell; others more recent New York friends. It was a party for Twain and, through Twain, for Harper, which had regained stability under its new regime. As master of ceremonies, Harvey orchestrated a genteel Twain roasting. Twain contributed to the humor by pretending that he was so perturbed that he was going to stand and reply immediately. When his time came to deliver his memorized speech, he moved himself and his audience with his praise of Howells, Hay, Twichell, and Rogers. He toasted longstanding friendships and time's passage, and evoked in a delicate, beautifully rendered passage his best friend of all, who could not be there and whom he had met "in the same year that I first knew John Hay . . . and Mr. Twichell—thirty-six years ago—and she has been the best friend I have ever had." The day before had been Livy's birthday. At the Riverdale house it had been celebrated in hospital-like silence.

Livy was constantly in mind, whatever events he turned out for, including Woodrow Wilson's inaugural as president of Princeton, at which Twain bantered with ex-president Cleveland and President Roosevelt. In his own way, though, he gave absolute prominence to Livy's recovery, which came haltingly and slowly. Since his absence of religious belief still distressed her, she was deeply gratified when he pretended to have changed his view about personal immortality. People, she argued, needed to believe in a reunion with departed loved ones. More than anything, though, she wanted him to show his "better side," which she believed still existed, even if now hidden. "Your present attitude will do more harm than good. You go too far, much too far in all you say. . . . People forget the cause for it and remember only the hateful manner in which it was said. *Do* darling change your mental attitude, *try to change it.* . . . You can if you will— if you wish to. Think of the side I know; the sweet dear, tender side—that I love so. Why not show this more to the world? Does it help the world to always rail at it? . . . Why always dwell on the evil until those who live beside you are crushed to the earth and you seem almost like a monomaniac. Oh I love you so and wish you would listen and take heed."

He did his flawed best, eager to please her, and often failed. But at least he would not publish things she disapproved of. Self-censorship by omission seemed sensible. When his deterministic bleakness caught the eye of a clever reader, he confessed, "What I have tried to do & what I still try to do, is to allow only a little to leak out. . . . This has been a strain upon me for thirty years. I have put this restraint upon myself & kept it there all these years to keep from breaking my wife's heart, whose contentment I value above the salvation of the human race." He would never publish *What Is Man?* except in a small private edition. But he also recognized that Livy's advice had resonance in his own self-interestedness. "99 parts of me are afraid, & my wife, who is the bulk of the remaining fraction, forbids it."

For the first time he had a full-time secretary, a capable assistant eager to take on any task he required, from writing letters to taking dictation to handling household clerical chores, even to chaperoning Clara and Jean. Isabel Van Kleeck Lyon, a petite, dark-haired, thirty-five-year-old daughter of a Columbia University professor, born in Farmington, Connecticut, and once a governess for the Whitmores in Hartford, had literary interests and idolized Twain. Smart and intellectually lively, Lyons had little to no interest in money or material things. Initially, in June 1902, her name had been raised by the Whitmores as a possible secretary for Livy. Crowded quarters at York Harbor, in conjunction with Livy's collapse in August, prevented that interview, and Livy soon had more need of doctors than of secretarial help. Her husband, though, could make good use of Miss Lyon's services. In November 1902 she unflinchingly accepted the meager salary of fifty dollars a month and room and board to work for a man she revered. Twain started by dictating letters to her.

Sick himself with recurrent bronchitis, he was forced to bed for most of April and part of May 1903. When he was well and Livy could travel, they went to Quarry Farm. To fulfill his *Harper's Monthly* commitment for a Christmas story, he soon wrote "A Dog's Tale," a sentimental and, at the same time, bitterly cynical anti-vivisectionist story ostensibly about how selfishly and cruelly human beings treat even their well-deserving pets. It was, among other things, a gift to the animal-loving Jean. But it was also, in its slightly disguised autobiographical elements, another lament for Susy. A cruelly insensitive master blinds and kills the puppy-child of the mother dog who narrates the tale. She cannot understand why. She is given to believe that if she waits by her puppy-child's grave the puppy will, like a flower, sprout from the earth and be reborn. At about the same time as he wrote "A Dog's Tale," he noted that in 1847 he had "witnessed the post mortem of [his] uncle through the keyhole." It was his father's body he had seen dissected. Such displacements brought the death and dissolution of loved ones as close to home as he could bear.

He took heart, though, from signs that Livy was recovering, at least enough to be upright more often and then, as the weather warmed, to sit out on a porch. To her relief, the Tarrytown house was leased by an eager tenant with an option to buy "at $7,000 more" than they had paid for it a year before: "Purchase terms, cash down." It was the only real estate on which Twain ever made a profit. Livy was considerably cheered by the sale, at long last, of the Hartford house. Between January and May 1903, Twain and Whitmore kept knocking down the price. He had determined he would have it torn down if it were not sold soon. "For the Lord Jesus H. Christ's sake *sell or rent that God damned house*," he wrote to Whitmore in early April. "I would rather go to hell than own it 50 days longer." He managed to avoid the fiery pit by about twenty days. The knock-down price, about $25,000, finally attracted a buyer. Livy sent Whitmore a list of furniture to be sold and items stored. They had lived happily in the Hartford residence for almost twenty years; they had suffered as its self-exiled owners for another ten.

Still weak, Livy was confined mostly to a wheelchair. By spring 1903 there was talk about where to spend the next year. Where would be best for Livy? Doctors recommended removal to a warm climate, perhaps Florence, perhaps Pasadena, California. Remembering the good year they had spent at the Villa Viviani, Livy preferred Florence. In May, Twain started inquiries about a villa, putting Florentine friends to work immediately, but from the start the search went badly. Apparently no one bothered to point out that the average Florentine winter was rainy and cool, that villas tended to be poorly heated and cavernously damp, and that the most attractive were already taken on long-term leases. In addition, medical care was not likely to be of the best, and dealing with servants in a language they hardly knew would be troublesome; Clara and Jean might find themselves spending much of their time with a depressed father and a dying mother; and getting there and back from New York certainly would be exhausting. The doctor who recommended Italy may never have been there, or may have been thinking of Sicily. And Twain was rarely disposed to think realistically about options across a full range of considerations. A winter in nearby Georgia, or Florida, or the Bahamas, or even in distant Pasadena, would have been a sensible alternative. As was so often the case, he made the least prudent decision.

5.

As they sailed for Genoa from New York on October 24, 1903, he strained to keep his comic bearings and balance. Despite an initial storm, passage on the *Princess Irene* went well. Livy endured "the voyage marvelously . . . as did "Clara & Jean . . . & far better than the trained nurse," who, along with Katy Leary, accompanied them. Isabel Lyon, with her mother, was to join them in Florence in November, to continue her work as his secretary. Still wheelchair- and bed-bound, Livy took fresh air on the deck, much as she had sat long hours on the porch through the summer at Quarry Farm. She could not sleep though, Twain complained, mostly because of noisy fellow passengers.

At their destination what counted most soon went terribly wrong. The residence that they had rented sight unseen, Villa Reale di Quarto, in the hills three miles west of central Florence, looking southwest toward the Chianti Hills and Valombrosa, was a house for a small army, not a small family. A cavernous four-story seventeenth-century building of no architectural distinction and with more than forty rooms, it had no central focus. A series of small walk-through chambers off floor-length bisecting hallways did not lend themselves to livable let alone intimate subsections for the six of them. "God himself couldn't start through it on a given excursion & not get lost," he told Howells. The furniture was spare and shoddy, the stone and plaster cold and unadorned, the heating system remedial. The new inhabitants huddled unhappily in a series of rooms on the ground and first floor. While the rose and ilex garden was lovely and the surrounding cypress woods dense, from below their living quarters and under Livy's room they began to noticed a less attractive smell. "It transpires," he discovered, "that the house-sewage goes directly into cesspools *under the house*—almost under Mrs. C.'s room!" Outraged, he insisted that the cesspool be drained immediately.

Accident seemed to have arranged almost everything to distress them. The large, lovely, handsomely designed garden seemed perfect for Livy's convalescence. But for much of November and December 1903 there was little sunshine. "We have heavy fogs every morning, & rain all day," he told John MacAlister, his English Plasmon partner. Language proved a vexing problem with servants, though friends and acquaintances helped. A local Italian priest proved to be a genial, kind, and tactful neighbor whom they all soon adored. Still, much of daily life was an uphill battle. Doctors proved unsatisfactory, the situation no worse than Twain's usual experience but compounded by the language difficulties. Livy's illness and the bad weather depressed him, and it took forever to get from the relatively isolated and huge estate to anywhere else in Florence.

Worst of all was their difficult landlady, Countess Massiglia, the American-born widow of an Italian count, who apparently considered Twain privileged to be required to pay in advance the two-thousand-dollar yearly rent. While her tenants occupied the main house, she lived in an apartment over a stable fifty yards away. The servants and groundskeepers answered to her, and she considered the entire domain still under her control. Twain was soon in a slow burn and then a rage. When the distant outer gates needed to be left open to allow the doctor to make his daily call, the countess had them closed. When they needed to be kept closed at night for safety, she had them left open. By New Year's Eve 1904, he had finally succeeded in having a working telephone installed, but it immediately ceased working and was out of service for a month. A better name for Villa Reale di Quarto, he remarked in his notebook, would have been "Calamity House."

In early January 1904, the news of Mollie Clemens' death arrived and seemed to warrant only an entry in his notebook and a passing sigh. As he did for the death of their friend Henry Stanley in May, he kept the news from Livy. To fulfill part of his Harper obligation he worked on two essays, revisiting Joan of Arc with the idealistic enthusiasm of his earlier years and attempting to amuse with "Italian with Grammar." Dictating autobiographical reminiscences to Isabel Lyon, who, with her mother, occupied a cottage next to the main house, gave him focus and allowed him to pass time writing in a genre he found congenial. He could stop and start almost effortlessly. Soon he fetched out the "Chronicle of Young Satan" manuscript and experimented with dictating additional narrative, probably the inception of "No. 44, The Mysterious Stranger," his last attempt to write the Satan story. A devoted secretary, Isabel picked up where she had left off the previous spring.

In early February, the countess's favorite donkey, who had the run of the estate and who liked to bite whatever was available, an activity that included the recent removal of a local peasant's thumb, charged Isabel, apparently with intent to harm. It took her three weeks to recover from her nervous collapse. "[The countess's] presence poisons the whole region," he wrote to Rogers. In retaliation, he supported a number of legal suits, including the thumbless peasant's. With Clara and sometimes Isabel, he went villa hunting. As soon as they found the right one, they would buy it. And as soon as Livy was well enough, they would move. She would live once again in a house of her own.

But the pervasive problem was Livy's condition. Her "trained nurse" left for America on December 7, 1903. With unwarranted optimism, Livy had decided that they no longer needed to carry the expense, but within the month she had a severe relapse, with night sweats and a high temperature, and she became increasingly depressed and despairing. Desperate, at the start of the new year Twain pleaded successfully with his old friend Dr. William Baldwin, now in practice in Rome, to come to Florence with his "mind & conscience all prepared to commit a lofty & righteous deception—if need be—to save Mrs. Clemens' life. Tell her that you want to make a more thorough examination by the light of the last few days' regime, & then tell her there is nothing the matter with her heart that need alarm her. I was born with an incurable disease, so was everybody—the same one that every machine has—& the knowledge of the fact frightens nobody, damages nobody; but the moment a *name* is given the disease, the whole thing is changed: fright ensues, & horrible depression, & the life that has learned its sentence is not worth the living." Baldwin brought with him a new invention, "one of those machines for measuring the might of the blood." The visit cheered them all. Clara, alarmed that her mother "should have these fearful attacks so frequently," soon urged him to make a second visit.

On their wedding anniversary in February 1904, Twain did his best to keep out of his voice the bitterness he felt about her suffering. "It's a long time ago, my darling, but the 33 years have been richly profitable to us, through love, a love which has grown, not diminished, & is worth more each year than it was the year before . . . dearest old Sweetheart of my youth." If either of them deserved such misery, he felt that he did. And he hated the Villa Reale di Quarto. "When we first arrived here she was twenty times better than she is now," he told Duneka. At her better moments, she had the energy to bewail her situation, to tell her family that she did not want to die. Still, as much as they feared for her life, neither Clara nor Jean actually expected her to die, and they all tried to carry on, against great odds, with a semblance of normalcy. Jean took long walks and kept silent about her mother's and her own affliction. There was little for her to do, and as usual she had her best moments with the animals on the estate. More than any other member of the family, she had a hidden life, the open secret of which was that it was not much of a life at all. For Clara, the strain was immense. Trapped where she did not want to be, her career and her romance on hold, she was pushed to the breaking point. In early February, she erupted. "I was seized," she wrote to Dorothy Gilder, "by something and began to scream and curse and knocked down the furniture. . . . In my father's presence I said I hated him, hated my mother, hoped they would all die and if they didn't succeed soon I would kill them." The cathartic release was followed by remorse and shame. She feared that her mother had overheard her.

At long last, in April, the weather became lovely. Clara exerted herself to attend to her mother and to check on and encourage the doctors, one of whom, Dr. G. W. Kirch, an Austrian doctor popular with the American community in Florence, Twain put in charge. At Twain's insistence, he came to the house daily, helped in dealing with practical issues, and played long hours of billiards with his patient's nervously bored husband. In her bedroom, cut off from much of the world, Livy required that her family provide accounts of what they had been doing each day. Anyone out at night stopped by before going to bed. Carrying on as best she could with Florentine life, Clara gave two concerts in early April, each "a triumph," Twain wrote in his notebook. "[She] astonished the house—including me—with the richness & volume of her voice. . . . Livy woke up & sent for her to tell her all about it near midnight!" The next night Livy had an "awful attack." She struggled desperately for breath. A week later she had another. A trained nurse was now on duty all day. Katy slept in the room at night. Clara was allowed one hour with her mother, Jean banned. So too was her husband.

Through it all he kept to his work schedule with some regularity. It was, as always, his strongest defense against anxiety and collapse. His bleakest mood was embodied in a short story he wrote, ironically, for the Christmas 1903 number of *Harper's Monthly*, about the corrosive result of living with speculative fantasies of great wealth. In "The $30,000 Bequest" a once sober, conservative couple turn their imaginations and consequently their lives over to their certainty that they are about to inherit thirty-thousand dollars, though under the condition that they do not inquire about when the money will come. Their mental stock market speculations become more real to them than anything else. In their fantasy, they grow rich over the years through the wife's skill as a speculator in, among other things, coal. But she waits too long to sell. The next day, the market crashes. "I am to blame," she cries, "do not forgive me. I cannot bear it. We are paupers! Paupers, and I am so miserable." But, her husband consoles her, they still have the actual and untouched thirty thousand dollars in the unclaimed bequest. By accident, they discover that their benefactor has played a cynical joke on them. He had died a pauper. "Money had brought him misery, and he took his revenge upon us, who had done him no harm." They of course had done great harm, to themselves. As Livy lay dying, Twain found a way to blame himself for a central misfortune of their lives and at the same time exculpate himself. Even if the irony of the story's couple blaming someone else reclaims the author's culpability, the most revealing turn is making the wife, not the husband, the compulsive stock market speculator.

Livy approved of the autobiographical dictations that he read to her on occasional evenings. Whereas before he had written or dictated such recollections without a theory to justify his practice, at the beginning of 1904 he had a revelation. "You will never know how much enjoyment you have lost until you get to dictating your autobiography," he told Howells; "then you realize that you might have been doing it all your life if you had only had the luck to think of it." This newly conceived multi-volume autobiography would be, he believed, an antidote to the twenty-eight-year copyright limitation: the new material would be published as "notes" to "existing books," adding fifty percent new matter to each, which would allow a new copyright. What he had "struck" was the idea that the genre permitted, even encouraged, structure by association, spontaneous description and argument, faithful to its author's mental movements.

For a writer who had usually fallen short as the creator of unified narratives, this theory put the highest value on what he did best. Slips and inconsistencies were part of the natural organism. And, since mind was the highest matter and did not conduct its most self-revealing activity in well-shaped structures, the supreme autobiography should take its shape from the flow of its creator's mind. Narrative beginnings, middles, and ends would be subordinated to associative processes. One thing would always lead to another. And no matter how evasive, self-justifying, and even deceitful the author, he cannot help but reveal his deepest self to the reader. Suddenly he felt liberated, to write as little or as much, in whatever sequence his mind suggested, about whatever he wanted to write about. His facility for dictating transformed impromptu speech into literary art.

In early May, Katy reported, "Mrs. Clemens is really and truly better!" It was for him a moment of heartwarming happiness. But, wisely, he allowed himself only the moment. "We take not to-morrow's word any more," he wrote Twichell. "Too many times they have breathed the word of promise to our ear and broken it to our hope." To his numbed surprise, she continued to get better. He felt the sheer pleasure of seeing Livy looking "bright & young & pretty," as if the "pallid shrunken shadow" that she had become had been replaced by the young woman who had been the light of his life. To help keep up her spirits, he kept hunting for villas. Soon he found one for summer rental on which he put down a deposit mainly in order to be able to report that they would be moving imminently. "It doesn't look as if we could ever move her there, but Clara & I pretend with all our might."

Limited to visits of no more than five minutes, he did not have much time with his wife in which to pretend. "It was too pitiful . . . to see the haunting fear in her eyes . . . & hear her say, as pleading for denial & heartening, 'You don't think I am going to die, do you? oh, I don't want to die.' " Some days he made additional brief visits, for seconds, to put his arms around her and kiss her brow. She slept sitting up, leaning her head against a board, afraid that otherwise "the choking horror" would strangle her. He now took breakfast in bed and, as usual, never had lunch. Clara and Jean kept as busy as possible, usually in distant rooms in the villa or away entirely. Miss Lyon took dictation when Twain called for her; he himself rarely left the grounds: "It does get deadly lonesome on the days when the pen refuses to go & I can't work." The doctors, though, seemed able to do nothing for Livy except administer subcutaneous injections of brandy or morphine when she seemed to be fading. The standard treatment with digitalis and bromide did no good. The morphine may have been the key element in Livy's confidence in Dr. Kirch. Twain wished he could fire them all.

For a few days she again seemed better, so much so that after one of his evening visits Twain went to the piano and began to pound out the Negro spirituals that he loved. Perhaps he played "A Horse Named Jerusalem," the favorite of his Missouri days and associated with his Holy Land adventures. Or "In the Sweet By and Bye," the song that he always associated with the day, in New York in 1867, on which he had first met "Livy Langdon, a sweet young slender girl & beautiful." An organ grinder had been playing it in the street as he approached the St. Nichols Hotel. "In our engagement-year some of us often sang it, evenings, along with other songs."

Clara sat with Livy on the afternoon of June 6 while Katy was out. Livy felt wretchedly sick, unable to breath. The day nurse gave her oxygen. Twain visited briefly, and Livy talked eagerly about spending the summer at the newly rented villa. At eight P.M. the nurse sent him and Clara away. Katy came in at about nine P.M. "I've been awful sick all afternoon," Livy told her. Clara was in the parlor, her father in the dining room. "You'll be all right now," Katy said. She leaned over, taking her patient in her arms. Livy took "a little short breath," Katy remembered. "Then she fell right over on my shoulder." Twain came back to the bedroom, either on his own or because Katy had fetched him. Clara also. The nurse and Katy "were holding the oxygen pipe to her mouth," trying to revive her. He bent toward her and looked at her relaxed face. "I think I spoke—I was surprised & troubled that she did not notice me." Clara and Jean broke into tears. "They put their arms around their father's neck and they cried, the three of them, as though their hearts would break." Then the two girls took their father by the hand and led him out of the room. He came back at eleven-thirty P.M. Within two hours Livy's haggard face had been transformed. "How sweet she [looked] in death, how young, how beautiful, how like her dear girlish self of thirty years ago," he wrote to Twichell. He went down again at two-thirty A.M., and then "at 4, 5, 7, 8—& so remained the whole of the day" until the embalmers came at five. "Then I saw her no more. In all that night & all that day she never noticed my caressing hand—it seemed strange."

Dr. Kirch examined the corpse and started the paperwork. "The immediate cause of death," the certificate recorded, was "paralysis of the heart." For the long voyage home, "the body was embalmed by the attending physician . . . & [their] vice consul came out to the villa & put the requisite seals upon the casket." Katy, who had dressed Susy for her burial, began to do the same for Livy. "I kept my promise, and put on her the dress she wanted, the beautiful lavender silk dress, and the stockings and little slippers that matched."

Having prepared so long for this moment, Twain met it characteristically. He sent a telegram to the Langdons in Elmira. Livy's brother noted that he received the news on the thirty-seventh anniversary of the sailing of the *Quaker City*, the voyage that had brought Mark Twain and the Langdon family together. "An hour ago the best heart that ever beat for me & mine went silent out of this house," he wrote to Richard Gilder, inquiring if he could rent one of Gilder's Berkshire cottages for the summer. It would be a place for them to go after the ceremony in Elmira. At three A.M. he was still writing letters "out of a heart that is filled with bitterness & rebellion," he wrote to his brother-in-law. "It was heart failure & instantaneous," he told Rogers. He was now, he felt, a wandering derelict, without the guiding hand and star that had kept him safe. "I was beginning to hope, & half-believe, she would get well. It is a thunder-stroke." As Livy's body was laid out, Clara wailed and crouched under the coffin. She wanted to stay there. For the next weeks, as they prepared for departure, Clara slept in Livy's bed. "I am tired & old," Twain wrote to Howells. "I wish I were with Livy."

CHAPTER NINETEEN

THE DAMNED HUMAN RACE

LUNCHEON CLUB

1904—1910

1.

Under a late-summer sun, Mark Twain chatted with Henry James at the New Jersey seashore home of George Harvey. The two literary titans, who had dominated post–Civil War American literature, had each recently crossed the Atlantic, James to return from his home in England for his first visit in twenty years to the city of his birth. Twain had come home that June 1904 with his wife's body and two shattered daughters, one two thirds of the way to a nervous breakdown. He faced, in a year and a half, his seventieth birthday, and James would face his eight years later, a milestone they and their society considered not the start but close to the end of old age. Neither would add anything of major significance to what he had already accomplished, and neither thought much of the other's work. James was alienated by Twain's commercial success; Twain by James's stylistic obscurity. The more James stayed away, the less he missed America; the more Twain was absent, the more he wanted to return. There was, though, not the slightest personal animosity between them. "The weather, the air, the light etc. are delicious, and poor dear old Mark Twain," James wrote, "beguiles the session on the deep piazza." Twain would have called it a "porch."

There was, though, a sentimental bond between them. Henry's brother William suffered from a disease of the heart similar to what Livy had died from; the patients had crossed paths, shared doctors. The novelist's visit to America was, among other things, an expression of concern about his brother. With William and their deceased sister, Henry was, as William put it, "a native of the James family, and [had] no other country." Livy and the Langdons had been Twain's existential homeland. "I am a man without a country," he wrote. "Wherever Livy was, that was my country. And now she is gone." He returned with a firm sense of his need to be replanted in his proper soil, and he agreed with Howells that "if any man who *can* live in America comes to Europe he deserves all he gets." He had needed to get through Livy's dying. Now he needed to get through the depression and heartache of mourning. "I thank you out of a heart that is hurt beyond healing," he responded to Laura Hawkins. Details and arrangements had to be managed, and his two unstable daughters looked after. "How thankful I am, that her persecutions are ended," he wrote the night of her death. Her suffering had made him value his own life less. It also reinforced his hostility to Judeo-Christian theologies. "I wish I could find a pulpit that could rationally excuse and justify Nature's atrocities—such as persecuting & harassing & torturing unoffending people," he wrote to Rogers. "I cannot keep my temper when I think of these wanton & unforgivable malignities; & as I think of them several times a day I lose my temper often."

From Florence, in June 1904, Twain and his two daughters had gone to Rome. Before leaving, he had a hostile confrontation with Dr. Kirch, whose bill he thought outrageous. He was being charged at twice the usual rate, including for the billiard-playing and other social time as if they were professional hours. In Rome, Dr. Baldwin wrote his colleague an angry letter, a copy of which he gave to Twain. Kirch would continue in the next year to try to get Twain to pay in full. Lawyers, lawsuits, and mediators were brought to bear. When, late in June, traveling slowly, the family arrived in Naples, he was anguished to discover, at three P.M. on the day of the scheduled four P.M. departure, that the death certificate and the certificate from the American consul necessary for Livy's body to enter the United States had not been delivered to the *Prince Oska*. The body, which had been placed aboard the ship, would have to be brought ashore. Dr. Kirch, he assumed, had not forwarded the papers. It seemed to be blackmail: if Twain would not pay up, his wife's body would remain in Italy.

The hesitant captain and reluctant authorities worked around the regulations. "I made a personal declaration & swore to it before the Vice Consul & satisfied the captain. If I had been an unknown person, we should have been in awful circumstances." He argued that the captain would do better taking the legal risk than the newspaper publicity resulting from such a barbarous act. Newspapers around the world had noted Mark Twain's wife's death. Telegrams had come from friends and strangers. Theodore Roosevelt and his cabinet had sent their condolences. In fact, the president had instructed customs in New York to let through everything associated with Twain without examination or question, which Twain did not yet know. All this was frenetic foreground to his inner distress. As always, he had the energy to explode at slights, to magnify justifiable discomforts, such as every passenger having to be vaccinated when smallpox was discovered among steerage passengers. He commented in his notebook that "people who travel in an immigrant ship belong in the insane asylum." Standing on deck in the sunny breeze, as the *Prince Oscar* sailed westward, he thought of the corpse in the darkness below: "31 years ago we made our first voyage together—& this is our last one in common." He felt despairingly lonely. And he imagined how lonely Livy must be. Clara and Jean kept to their rooms. Suddenly, in self-deprecatory panic, he realized that he could not remember Livy's face—"I was never in my life able to reproduce a face. It is a curious infirmity—& now at last I realize it is a calamity."

He was to see her actual face once more, in the living room of the Langdon home in Elmira, in the same room in which, thirty-four years before, they had been married. As he had done then, the Reverend Joseph Twichell presided, now "in a breaking voice. . . . The same voice that had made her a wife . . . committed her departed spirit to God." That afternoon she was buried next to her parents and Susy. He had his eyes on the gravesite directly next to hers. Not yet ready, if ever he would be, to think of himself as a widower, a few days later he joined Clara, Jean, and Katy Leary in Lee, Massachusetts, at the summer cottage they had rented from the Gilders. The two horses that had been Livy's last gifts to her children and which had been sent ahead with the butler had arrived. Clara, who had been breaking down, and whom he had tried to persuade not to attend the funeral, got worse. "Sick, heart-broken, unrestful," she entered a sanitarium in New York. Illness kept her mostly confined and entirely away from her father for much of the next year. At the end of July, Jean fell from her horse. The horse was killed, Jean badly but not permanently hurt. That September, Twain's sister, Pamela Moffet, died at the age of seventy-seven. Soon, at his direction, his adaptation of a favorite poem of his, associated also in his mind with Susy, was carved on Livy's marble memorial: "WARM SUMMER SUN SHINE KINDLY HERE,/ WARM SOUTHERN WIND BLOW SOFTLY HERE./ GREEN SOD ABOVE LIE LIGHT, LIE LIGHT—/GOOD NIGHT, DEAR HEART, GOOD NIGHT, GOOD NIGHT."

2.

Twain, who in October 1904 executed his "last will," had almost six years more to live. "The world is black today, & I think it will never lighten again," he wrote on the day of Livy's death. It did lighten, but he never stopped mourning her absence. He was never to be less than lonely in his private moments. As much as he tried to find companionship in his daughters, he compounded his lifelong habit of controlling possessiveness with a yearning for their company stronger than any reality could fulfill. Clara would not give up her life to him the way Livy had. Jean, who would have, could not, at least for the time being. Her illness prevented that, and her father often found her presence trying, especially as his patience and strength diminished. He did not define fatherhood as self-sacrifice, though he was willing to make some sacrifices but not others. Still, he had to live. And to live he needed to reimmerse himself in work, including articles and stories required by his contract with Harper. That meant providing what the reading public expected, if only in occasional short pieces.

Spending the summer of 1904 in New York on business, including house-hunting, with Henry Rogers' help he negotiated a three-year three-thousand-dollar-a-year lease for 21 Fifth Avenue, a stone mansion on the southeast corner of 9th Street, a house large enough for him to cover the floors with forty-four Oriental rugs. He liked the location, not far from where they had lived after returning from Europe in 1901. Close by was the Grosvenor Hotel, where he stayed while 21 Fifth Avenue was being renovated. Hotel life had always suited him. But he had two daughters to look after. "With Mrs. Clemens gone my life has lost color & zest, & I do not value it," he wrote to John MacAlister, but, he conceded, "I must live for my daughters."

A house was a necessity, though it would turn out that neither Clara nor Jean lived there consistently during his tenancy. With rooms for guests, for Isabel Lyon, and for the servants, and with an immense combination living room and library, it was a baronial residence. The renovations, including a new heating system, kept Jean and Katy Leary in the Berkshires and Twain many nights with Rogers on the *Kanawha*. He spent a few days at Rogers' son-in-law's Great Neck estate, then went to the Grosvenor until late November. Clara, in isolation at a private sanitarium uptown, kept in touch by phone and letter. He bade her "a long farewell" in November. "I feel like sending you one more fluttering goodbye before the bars are bolted," she responded. "You are a cunning little man and very touching with all your thoughtfulness." Though there may have been some slyness in calling him "cunning," there was also much love. "I hope that soon I shall hear you are beautifully situated with companionable friends about you."

He was, though, to have a difficult winter. When friends conspired successfully to have him readmitted to The Players as an honorary member (he had been expelled when he had not paid dues), he accepted. But, though the club was only a short distance from his new residence, he stayed away. When Rogers dropped by, as he did often, Twain treated him to bitter outbursts, though, as he told Twichell in an attempt at humor, he did not think Rogers should serve both as safety valve for his cosmic bile and as financial advisor. Twichell should handle the former, Rogers the latter: it would be a more equitable distribution of the workload. Anyway, a clergyman was a more appropriate audience for a diatribe against existence, a profane-laden expression of how life was worse than a profanity—a blankness, a nothingness, at best a dream that left him dislocated about what was real and what was not. Had his life with Livy been real? Was this life without her real?

In this bleak mood, he accepted only a few invitations, including one to a small dinner party given by the second Mrs. Rogers, celebrating his own sixty-ninth birthday. Gradually, the Rogers family, particularly the daughters, were becoming Twain's family also; it was the only household that he went to as if he were a welcome relative. Mai Rogers became his particular favorite, one of the first expressions of his need to find young, daughter-like women to fill the vacuum left by Livy's death and his own daughters' extended absences. Sometimes, to keep him company, he had Clara's "splendid cat," Bambino. When in mid-December 1904 he developed a severe cold and painful gout, he spent six weeks in his room. He was still in bed, his favorite place, he told Mrs. Andrew Carnegie early in January, declining an invitation: "[I] expect to stay there till the whiskey runs out, for I read, smoke, write, & am very comfortable & seldom sober." He was also depressed.

At the end of the month, he "hobbled downstairs" for the first time in five and a half weeks. With the folding doors open and the retrieved furniture, the sitting-dining room looked like the lost Hartford home. "It broke my heart," he wrote to Susan Crane. "I sat & looked out at the storm & listened for hours while Miss Lyon played on the orchestrelle," a player-piano-like organ, purchased for $2,600. He chose the "pieces—dirges, funeral marches, &—saddest of all—wedding marches. The wedding is never otherwise than a tragic event, & all present should be clothed in black, & upon the wedding-bell should be written 'A day is coming when one of these hearts shall break.'"

He still attended to business and politics, less productive but hardly less acidic than before. Roosevelt's 1904 campaign elicited "A Brief Biography of Government" in the form of a satiric private letter to George Harvey. Roosevelt's expansion of the powers of the presidency Twain thought threateningly monarchical. "What he wants, he takes. It will be best again to elect him Government of the United State on the eighth of November next. Otherwise he will take it anyway." Appreciative of Roosevelt's thoughtfulness at the time of Livy's death and always affable with him, he had mostly harsh things to say privately. "For twenty years I have loved Roosevelt the man & hated Roosevelt the statesman & politician." He thought in public office Roosevelt was "insane and irresponsible," but he granted in the same breath, "We are all insane, each in his own way." In June, when a Panama Canal procurement ripoff surfaced, he exploded at great length to Twichell, reviewing what he considered the ignoble, dishonest career of a loudmouthed, publicity-seeking, deceitful politician.

Between November 1904 and February 1905, Twain wrote two Browning-influenced prose monologues, "The Czar's Soliloquy" and "King

Leopold's Soliloquy." The former, also influenced by Carlyle, is the psycho-pathic boast of a cynical czar who despises the stupidity of a world that al-lows him to rule; the latter an amoral defense by the King of Belgium of his brutal rule of the misnamed Congo Free State. "I have never read *Sartor Re-sartus*," Twain responded to his *North American Review* editor, "& so I did not know [Carlyle] had been handling the subject." He had, in fact, added to his library and signed his copy of *Sartor* in 1888. George Harvey thought the small circulation *North American Review* rather than *Harper's Monthly Magazine* the best Harper venue for "The Czar's Soliloquy." When Harvey declined to publish "King Leopold's Soliloquy" at all, Twain blamed Freder-ick Duneka's Catholicism for its being "buried." It was eventually published under the auspices of the Boston-based Congo Reform Association.

Increasingly, Twain had his claws sharpened for his publisher, whom he suspected of undermining his projects behind his back. When things did not go exactly his way, he had, in what Isabel Lyon called " 'Uncle Mark's' savage moods," nasty words for Duneka. In saner moments, Twain rather liked the subeditor, who proved a pleasurable billiards companion and whose wife he found charming. At other moments, explosively intemper-ate, he built up a case against Harper—they were "tricky & dishonest." When he believed Harper was not fulfilling the contract clause requiring that Twain's work be prominently advertised in each issue of *Harper's Mag-azine,* he tore into Harvey as if he were an enemy. Tactful, conciliatory, clever enough to know that his author's mood would change, Harvey grad-ually brought Twain to a more reasonable approach. In his own domain as imperial as Roosevelt, Twain imperiously reminded Harper of its obligation to publish his Christian Science book and revealed that he had a new book in mind for which he desired anonymous publication. From that Harper could anticipate nothing but red ink.

From his own financial misrule he had almost entirely abdicated, and he had the good sense to refuse to invest, though pressed to do so, beyond the dollars he had already put into American Plasmon. His faith in the product itself was undiminished. So too was his confidence in the man-agement of British Plasmon from which he had been receiving £350 quar-terly dividends on his £5,000 investment. That, along with the competence of his London friend and codirector John MacAlister, had earned his com-plete support. But with no return at all on his American investment, he had, beginning in early 1903, developed reservations not only about the competence but the honesty of the directors. "I am warned from sources which I respect," he wrote to the chief officer, "that the company is crooked, & has private schemes which will not bear the light." When requests for detailed information were disregarded, he threatened, then instituted, litigation. Gradually, but not till 1904, did he learn that he had been denied bonus shares he was entitled to under the terms of his purchase. His informant was the twenty-nine-year-old treasurer of the company, Ralph W. Ashcroft, the English-born son of a Congregational minister whom Twain described as "truthful, honorable, careful . . . a bright & good business man & very efficient manager." His praise was not entirely misplaced, though to some extent it reflected Ashcroft's eager commitment to Twain's interest and his willingness to act on its behalf.

When in September 1904 a Plasmon stockholder, willing to pay assessments to which Twain and others objected, attempted to attach the company's assets, Ashcroft removed documents, patents, and checkbooks from the Plasmon office and brought them to 21 Fifth Avenue. With a literary bent and a juvenile lack of discretion, Ashcroft attacked the enemy faction with a Byronic parody and with insulting letters. When a court upheld the Twain faction, Ashcroft celebrated, proposing that they send an "embossed cut of crowing rooster" to the losers. Twain wisely reined him in. In effect, his $32,500 American Plasmon investment was already down the drain. But he appreciated Ashcroft's loyalty and his talents. Like Twain, he was obsessively fascinated with financial speculations. And soon Ashcroft was, gradually but noticeably, becoming Twain's business agent, more a functionary than an advisor but still with influence, much as had been the case at first with Webster. Ashcroft began to make investment suggestions, some of which Twain took, such as putting six thousand dollars into the Spiral Pin Company, in which Ashcroft's uncle was a major investor. When the hairpins turned out to be useless, Twain of course lost his money. Fortunately, in regard to large matters, Rogers was always there for balance and anchor.

Isabel Lyon was another source of much-needed stability. By 1904, she had become an indispensable functionary, the manager of his household and daily affairs. Some responsibility he put in Katy Leary's hands, and in late February 1905 he sent her to Dublin, New Hampshire, to look at summer houses. "The bearer of this . . . knows by old & seasoned experience just what we want," he wrote to a Dublin resident, the well-known landscape painter Albert Thayer. At 21 Fifth Avenue, Katy was servant in chief.

She was, though, more personal than household servant, her time mostly devoted to Clara and Jean, just as she had attended to Livy. Twain would not have left Jean in the Berkshires without Katy. She knew Clara's moods and needs, perhaps better than anyone, and got on well with Isabel. "We are a very peaceful household," Lyon wrote to Harriet Whitmore. "Katie is good & valuable beyond words." Isabel found life at 21 Fifth Avenue the fulfillment of her wildest fantasy. When Twain wanted to dictate, she was on hand. When he needed company, she was there, eager to snatch every pearl as it dropped. When he wanted entertainment, she played the orchestrelle. Aware that she had extraordinary exposure to the great man, she began a diary centering around him; his moods, his dress, his habits, his entertaining comments. She began to fulfill one of what had been Livy's functions, listening to his manuscripts-in-progress as he read them. She herself could not have been happier doing anything other than being of service to him.

By late spring 1905 his depression had lightened. He still wore mourning clothes, and mourning continued. But he felt a quickening, an anticipation of summer in the country and of returning to unfinished manuscripts, particularly "No 44, The Mysterious Stranger." He was honest in his claim that, intellectually, he had no love for life: he accepted existence because he needed to live for his daughters; without him, they would have no means of support. And writing still engaged him. "I have led a turmoilsome life this winter, & am tired to the bone," he told Aldrich. Clara had to have an appendectomy in early May; the next week, though, Twain joined Jean in Dublin. He rehired Patrick McAleer, now in poor health, a favorite of Jean's who shared her passion for horses. Katy Leary attended to New York duties, particularly the tearing up of the house again for "new heating arrangements." Two other servants came up. So too did Isabel, her pen at the ready to take dictation, her hands to play the orchestrelle for long hours. "Good place to work?" he soon responded to Clara, now in a rest home in Norfolk, Connecticut. "I should say so! My! to think that I've written 30,000 words here! That used to take a kind of a forever." He was at work on a variation of his science-fiction horror tale "3,000 years among the microbes." "I read a chapter aloud every night." Soon he was at page 240. "It beats the record," he boasted. "The best record before was in Florence. . . . This is the same output (31,500 words) but the time is considerably shorter." His major preoccupation for the next months was "No 44." He took pleasure in his daily word count, the numbers equal to a strong heartbeat, an affirmation of being alive.

When in July hot weather overwhelmed his resolve to visit Clara at Norfolk, he let Jean go alone, a reunion their father's absence made more enjoyable for the sisters. Jean did well through the summer, "prospering," he told a friend. Clara had her ups and downs, including, her father remarked, "one of those intervals that come in nervous prostration when a whole year's progress vanishes in a week & the patient work must be done all over again." Until Jean's visit, Clara had been forbidden any family callers. But, a month later, hobbling from a gout attack, Twain traveled to Norfolk, with a stopover in Boston and Hartford, for a one-week visit that apparently went well enough. Depressed and lonely, Clara seemed glad to have her father's company. Her doctor's permission for her to resume voice lessons in the fall cheered her. Father and daughter continued an earlier conversation about Clara becoming his official biographer. That he could have thought such a venture realistic seems bizarre. He may have been using it to bring them closer together, hoping it might raise Clara's self-esteem. In mid-June he announced to her, "I'm appointing you & Jean to arrange & publish my 'Letters' some day—I don't want it done by any outsider. Miss Lyon can do the work, & do it well . . . & take a tenth of the royalty resulting."

When he discovered that the Twichells had a $1,500 debt they could not foresee repaying, he sent them a check, explaining that an investment had unexpectedly produced that gain. Consequently, it was "tainted money"; he would be relieved to be relieved of it. They gratefully accepted. It was, in fact, Rogers' charity: at Twain's request, Rogers gave Twain the money, agreeing that Twain take the credit. His beneficiaries' effusive thank-you letter he forwarded to Clara. "I want her to see what a generous father she's got," he told Rogers, "& what grateful praises people whom he's saved from dire distress can pour out on him. I didn't tell her it was you, but by & by I want to tell her, when I have your consent; then I shall want her to remember the letters. I want a record there, as she is to prepare my Life & Letters when I am dead."

Duneka urged that a story Twain had written, "Extracts from Adam's Diary" needed a companion, "Eve's Diary," which he wrote in mid-July. Beside it, "Adam's Diary" seemed "coarse & poor," just as he himself had always felt coarse in comparison to Livy. A plangent depiction of Eve's goodness, its self-portrait is an elegy to his dead wife. Adam's voice appears only in the final sentence at Eve's grave: "Wherever she was, there *was* Eden." Livy's absence, especially since he was also without Clara, made him lonely no matter what company he had. Clara's report from Norfolk that she now felt calmed and restored reminded him of how anxious he had made Livy by his words and deeds. "Dear heart, I am gladder of the spiritual peace which has come to you than I can tell you. I was a criminal toward your mother in that matter," he wrote to Clara, "& can never forgive myself, but for her sake—& yours & mine—I shall try my very best never to treat you so." But, after attending a wedding in early September, he reported to Clara that the bride's "poor old father," losing his beautiful daughter, "was a pathetic figure to see, after that star had sunk below his horizon. A wedding is an awful disaster to a family." Clara could not have missed the point.

For weeks in October 1905 he was "drunk . . . with the autumn foliage." Monadnock was "a rippled & ruffled landscape of hellfire toned down for Sunday consumption." Flames were still there "but the fierce anger all gone—softened down to mottled yellows . . . smitten through with a jet of sunlight, the whole avalanche daintily luminous." It had been, he told a friend, "the pleasantest summer" they had ever had, "on either side of the Atlantic." He had already arranged to rent for the next summer, after visiting to test its views, a large cottage higher up the mountain slope. The first touches of winter chill in late October sent him to Boston for two weeks of socializing, then to New York. Jean and the entourage went home in early November. Clara was already there, ready to resume lessons, but Jean worried them all. Late in the summer she had a series of attacks, accompanied by violent physical and verbal outbursts. Desperate, she began to see her only hope in "surgical examination & possible operation." "She is heavily afflicted," her father cursed, "by that unearned, undeserved & hellish disease." So too was he, as he felt the burden of her presence. He wished, primarily, for her cure; secondarily, for her absence. Or at least to have someone else responsible for her. He appointed Clara. "Assume full & sole authority in the house," he commanded. "Require that all complaints be brought to you—none to anyone else. Allow no one but yourself to scold or correct a servant. All of this is for Jean's sake, & to keep her out of trouble." He was, he felt, not up to the task. His seventieth birthday was approaching.

When the time arrived, he did not have any difficulty celebrating, in early December 1905, at a star-studded banquet hosted by George Harvey and paid for by Harper. Despite Twain's narcissistic, semi-paranoid grumbles, Harper continued to treat its regal lion with a generosity reflecting his stature and his value. A forty-piece orchestra from the Metropolitan Opera played for more than two hundred guests at Delmonico's. Most of the literary establishment of the East Coast attended. Each guest received a gift of "a foot-high plaster bust of Mark Twain." As toastmaster, Howells' witty revision of "Oh King, live forever" into "O King, live as long as you like!" affirmed in comic terms that Mark Twain was now the literary "King" of the world, a royal title that he came to like. It also was absolutely clear to him, though, that he could not live as long as he liked.

Responding to Howells, he humorously reviewed, in a carefully crafted presentation, his birthdays and his habits. In his artful quasi-Missouri drawl, he created, as he always did, the illusion of casual spontaneity and mellow amiability. He concluded, appropriately, with imagery drawn from the sea voyages embodying the restlessness of much of his life and which he now used to epitomize the port of old age at which he had arrived, allegedly happy and content. "I am seventy . . . and would nestle in the chimney corner, and smoke my pipe, and read my book . . . wishing you well in all affection, and that when you in your turn shall arrive at pier No. 70 you may step aboard your waiting ship with a reconciled spirit, and lay your course toward the sinking sun with a contented heart." His delicately humorous speech ended with a sentimental cliché, a rhetorical lift over which he had an easy mastery and could draw on for any appropriate occasion. The audience was deeply moved. It rose to its feet and applauded. Like all his powerful sentiments, Twain believed it and in it for the moment. But he was not at all contented or reconciled.

3.

One indication of his disenchantment with all things human and sentimental, except his reverence for Livy, was his proposal to Howells, Harvey, and "Mr. Dooley," that they form the "Damned Human Race Luncheon Club." Though it seems to have met at most a few times, with Twain as "President pro temp," the name expressed his pervasive private attitude. Fortunately, his attitude had "attitude": a rarely repressible energy despite occasional expressions of battle-weariness and many references to three score years and ten. And no matter how despairingly and disparagingly he spoke about the "damned human race," he continued to try to make some aspects of it better. In the winter and spring of 1906, he spoke at various benefit performances, one of them a relief meeting for victims of the San Francisco earthquake. "We must not let our minds dwell upon the dead," he told the audience. "After life's fitful fever they rest well." He urged that sympathies be for the living. He had pledged never again to speak to an audience that "paid to get in," so he told them, "You didn't pay to get in here; you're going to pay to get out." Most of his appearances reflected ongoing sympathy for particular causes or peoples, including a fund-raiser for the Tuskegee Institute; a benefit for the New York Association for Promoting the Interests of the Blind, an expression of the same sympathy he epitomized as the host, at 21 Fifth Avenue, of a dinner party for Helen Keller; and a benefit performance, one of whose stars was Sarah Bernhardt, for Jewish victims of Russian pogroms.

Russia continued to be much on his mind, his hatred of czarist brutality and his hope for a democratic revolution. But in April 1906, shortly after enthusiastically introducing at a fund-raising banquet the anti-czarist pro–working class Russian writer Maxim Gorki, he withdrew his support when the *New York World* revealed that the woman Gorki had introduced as his wife was his mistress. Probably the Russian embassy had leaked the story. Used to European sophistication on such matters, Gorki had unwittingly destroyed his usefulness as a fund-raiser and rallying force in America for the anti-czarist cause. The *World,* fighting a circulation war, pounced on a paper-selling scandal. Every major newspaper, including the *New York Times,* gave it headlines. Soon Victorian prudence trumped ideological sympathy. Ever the self-protective pragmatist in such matters, Twain blamed Gorki for failing to know about or take seriously American mores. "It is less risky for a stranger to dance upon our Constitution in the public square than to affront one of our solidified customs. The one is merely eminently respectable, the other is sacred." Twain regretfully but decisively distanced himself, though with not as much of an unseemly rush as did many others.

Public engagement with public issues took some of his time. With George Harvey as his guest, he went to the White House for dinner in late November 1905, mostly for the purpose of speaking about King Leopold. Did the United States government not have a moral obligation to rally the international community against Leopold's criminality and genocide? Gradually an answer came from Roosevelt, whom Twain detested anyway, and a morally sympathetic State Department: American national interests were not at stake; there was no domestic constituency for brutalized black Congolese. Twain's outrage was followed by annoyance. He needed to revise "King Leopold's Soliloquy," which had been composed, partly, to persuade the government to intervene. When he awakened one morning to find himself, to his distress, "tacitly committed to journeys, & speeches, & so on" on behalf of the Congo Reform Association, "perfectly appalling activities," he disengaged himself from his speaking engagements. "To do these things would infallibly lay further burdens upon me. . . . I should find myself tangled up in the Congo matter [and] my instincts & interests are merely literary . . . & I scatter from one interest to another, lingering nowhere. I am not a bee, I am a lightning-bug." Partly out of rationalizing self-interest but mainly because of frustration and despair, he had come to the conclusion since his "last visit to the State Department . . . that the American branch of the Congo Reform Association ought to go out of business, for the reason that the agitation of the butcheries can only wring people's hearts unavailingly—unavailingly, because the American people unbacked by the American government cannot achieve reform in Congo." It was an accurate assessment.

Two new friends from a younger generation came into his life that winter and spring. Charlotte Teller was a young married writer with whom Twain had a brief but intense flare of friendship that served her well and that may, for Twain, have had a touch of unacknowledged eroticism. An aspiring playwright with strong socialist views who lived a literary but still conventional life, Teller belonged to a progressive writers' community, the "A Club," housed a few streets from Twain's Fifth Avenue house. In late March 1906, she volunteered to approach Twain, hoping that he would accept an invitation to meet a number of Russian revolutionaries who were staying at the club, among them Nikolai Tchaikovsky, the composer's younger brother. Twain, they hoped, would be helpful in furthering their cause, particularly if he would consent to the use of his name and be present at a dinner and at a fund-raising rally. Isabel answered the door. Charlotte, whom she thought "young and delightfulish," was asked to return that afternoon with Tchaikovsky. She introduced him to Twain, "both of them white haired and most distinguished in appearance." When she told

Twain, as she took the opportunity to do, that she had written a play about Joan of Arc, he found the topic irresistibly personal, connected both to the start of his career and his idealization of Livy. He invited her to return the next morning to read the play to him. "I did, and when I finished he was much moved. . . . From that day I saw him almost every day for nearly three months."

Lonely and eager for companionship, Twain took delight in Teller's intelligent, self-assertive company. Coyly engaging and attractively expressive, young enough to be his daughter but happily not, she kept him regular company at home; they exchanged lightly flirtatious letters. Twain, who volunteered to read her manuscript, gave advice and assistance, including introducing her work to producers. The Gorki fiasco did not affect their relationship, at its most intense during spring 1906. When he left for the summer, he continued by correspondence, long letters to his protégé praising her "beautiful play. . . . It is full of life & energy & character." Relieved and delighted to be able to confirm her talent, he invited the head of Appletons, a prominent publisher, to 21 Fifth Avenue. He came at once "& we talked an hour. He likes her book & is going to publish it; & I asked him to sell the serial rights . . . and he said he would do it with pleasure." Charlotte was "one of the happiest persons in America last night."

When his friend from Nevada days, Calvin Higbie, requested help placing a manuscript, Twain happily consented, but after reading it he sent Higbie a frank report of his opinion, justified by his claim that they were both honest men in their own way. He could do nothing to help. Generosity and loyalty were not enough. In Charlotte's case, though her talent proved not to be sustaining or stellar, she had provided a manuscript he could back. And he was personally susceptible. "You are launched, now, & well and prosperously," he told her in October 1906. She had a theatrical agent and a possible producer. By the end of the year, the intensity of his interest had diminished considerably. There were no more tête-à-têtes, no more long letters. Starting in 1907, he found other ways to fill the need that Charlotte had helped satisfy. And, when newspapers reported a likely marriage between Charlotte and Twain, he had Isabel Lyon orchestrate denials. When the same newspapers reported the same of Twain and Isabel, they suspected it had been revengefully instigated by Charlotte.

On a morning in January 1906, reclining in his large bed with Venetian hand-carved posts, wrapped in his deep crimson silk robe, he began the first of a series of autobiographical dictations that were to serve a double purpose: to comprise the major part of the book to be published one hundred years after his death and to provide information for the creation of an authoritative biography. "I am saying these vain things," he dictated, "in this frank way because I am a dead person speaking from the grave. Even I would be too modest to say them in life. I think we never become really & genuinely our entire & honest selves until we are dead—& not then until we have been dead years & years. People ought to start dead, & then they would be honest so much earlier." In the pale winter light that came through north-facing windows, he spoke with self-satisfying and self-aggrandizing frankness to an audience of two, one the man he had recently determined would be his biographer, forty-five-year-old Albert Bigelow Paine, the other Paine's stenographer, Josephine Hobby, now on Twain's payroll. In the next two years, Paine was to establish a primacy that made him, eventually, the one indispensable member of the entourage.

A handsome midwesterner, Paine was twenty years old when, in 1880, he settled in St. Louis to become a proficient photographer and dealer in photographic supplies. In 1895 he came to New York to pursue literature, his first love. Profits from his photographic business may have financed the initial stages of his New York career. Co-author of a volume of poems, he began to earn his living writing fiction for children and adults, a talented journeyman capable of straightforward prose and eager for success. Victorian to the bone, he valued discretion, propriety, and achievement. In 1899 he became an editor, under Mary Mapes Dodge, of *St. Nicholas Magazine,* the premier literary magazine for children. His 1901 novel *The Great White Way* fixed in popular consciousness an epithet for Broadway's theatrical district. By 1901, when he met Twain, to whom he had sent one of his two recent novels, he was a member of The Players, where he rubbed shoulders with men of achievement and distinction. Twain responded to Paine's self-introduction with the claim that he had actually read his presentation copy. With a biography of Thomas Nast, Paine had, by 1904, established himself as a respected member of the New York literary establishment. When Twain's friendship with Nast prompted a request from Paine to see Twain's side of the correspondence, Twain cooperated.

At The Players' dinner honoring Twain in January 1906, Paine's dinner companion leaned toward him and said, "You should write his life." He took this as "a pleasant courtesy," he later claimed, and gave it no weight. Probably, though, given that he was the biographer of Nash, it was not the furthest thing from his mind. As the company drifted apart, he asked Twain to be allowed to come to visit, "an impulse" of the moment, he later recollected. Twain responded, "Yes, come soon." Within days, he was sitting by Twain's bedside at 21 Fifth Avenue. When conversation eventually got round to his autobiography-in-progress, Twain said that "he had hoped his daughters would one day collect his letters; but that a biography—a detailed story of personality and performance, of success and failure—was of course another matter, and that for such a work no arrangement had been made." He then turned his "piercing-agate-blue eyes directly upon me," Paine later wrote, and said, "When would you liked to begin?" Had Clara, who had already been asked, turned it down? Had her father decided that she was not the right person to do it? Had he consulted with her at all? Was there an understanding that she would edit the letters but not write the biography? Within moments, Paine was anointed. Within days, he was at work.

Between January and June 1906, Twain had sessions four or five days a week with Paine and Hobby. Paine's initial proposition that Miss Hobby be Paine's employee Twain had rejected. The documents, he insisted, would belong to him, for publication in his one-hundred-year book, as he should choose. Hobby took dictation; Paine took notes; Isabel Lyon moved between foreground and background, ready for correspondence and other duties. Paine and Hobby concentrated on the past. New business went through Isabel's hands. Each day, Hobby typed his dictation to provide hard copy for Twain to edit. Paine's own notes included some that had gone into the stenographic record, but they also contained material that had not, elicited by questions he was free to raise at any point in the session. As Twain got used to the process, it was rare that he could not resume with as much fluency as he had had before any interruption. In April, Howells, who had already heard much about Twain's theory of biography, got in the mail a small sample of the large manuscript that had accumulated in four months. He found it compelling, though its frankness shocked him, especially Twain's account of Orion's unwittingly getting into bed with a lady. "You really *mustn't* let" that happen. Howells, though, wanted to see "every word of the 578 pages before this, which is one of the humanest and richest pages in the history of man. If you have gone this gait all through you have already gone further than any autobiographer ever went before. You are nakeder than Adam and Eve put together."

The nakedness, though, was not a Rousseau-like account of his sexual life. His subject was everything under the sun but that: his family, his childhood, the development of his views about God, man, religion, and politics, and his opinions about his contemporaries. Much, but far from all, was bile raised to the level of vituperation, diatribes against those against whom he held grievances. In June, he was, he told Howells, "in the middle of a history of Bret Harte," which he was about to break off, as his principle of composition allowed, for "a newer hotter interest tomorrow." His only structural obligation was to follow whatever at the moment interested him most strongly. At the end of the month, he was "dictating some fearful things" about the depiction of God in the Bible, the absurdity of Christian theological arguments, and the impossibility of man making moral choices and, therefore, being responsible for his actions. These comments, he told Howells, are "for no eye to see but yours until I have been dead a century—if then. But I got them out of my system, where they had been festering for years—& that was the main thing." The conventional Miss Hobby was uneasily fascinated; Paine and Lyon were admiringly riveted. Twain found the dictation energizing, and it still left him with time on his hands. "I'm not overworking," he assured Clara, "oh, my land no! I dictate 2 hours in the morning, about 4 days per week; & read & revise an hour or two, afternoons, with Miss Lyon for audience. I do nothing, after that, but cripple time—I can't really kill it."

But his second summer in Dublin, New Hampshire, in 1906, proved disappointing. Upton House was uncomfortably large and impersonal, the constant wind always blowing harder than lower down the slope. One resident called it "The Lodge of Sorrow." The nearest neighbors were too far to encourage visiting, and, torn between the pleasure and pain of solitude, he issued few invitations to New York or Boston friends. "The rest of the household walk & drive, daily, & thereby they survive. But I am not surviving. I am in a trance. When I have dictated a couple of hours in the afternoon I don't know what to do with myself until ten o'clock next day. . . . The Garden of Eden I now know was an unendurable solitude. I know that the advent of the serpent was a welcome change—anything for society." Though he complained, he did nothing to alter the situation, except trips to Fairhaven and New York, where, pursuing legal action against Harper about the advertising clause in his contract, he hated the noise and heat.

As company, Katy Leary, the servants, and the rest of the entourage were background. Jean spent her days at a cabin up the hill, carving wooden animal figures. "[She] mourns," he wrote to Clara, "because she is the only member of the family who has no calling, & she is accomplishing nothing in the world. It touches me; it is pathetic." The much-esteemed Patrick McAleer, whom both he and Jean adored, had died of stomach cancer in February. In respect and affection, Twain had been a pallbearer at the funeral in Hartford, which he had little desire to visit, though he arranged for a lunch at the Hartford Club for Twichell and other old friends. When he read a reworked story, "Wapping Alice," to Harmony Twichell and her Saturday morning discussion group, Harmony felt smoldering resentment that he dared present a story about sexual escapades and transvestitism to respectable female company. Less factotums than companions, Paine and Lyon provided what friends do without being acknowledged as such. Isabel was now nicknamed "The Lioness," the maiden aunt member of the household, an inferior with influence and a touch of maternal authority. Two new kittens, Sackcloth and Ashes, brought smiles to his face. But what he sorely lacked was someone like Howells. For Twain, it was a lonely time, and, despite Jean's pleas, he would never return to New Hampshire.

Reversing his preference for posthumous publication, he began to consider imminent publication of excerpts from his dictations. A number of publishers expressed interest; he desired to keep his name prominently in print; and the prospect of handsome pay appealed to him. George Harvey, who had at first seemed uninterested, responded enthusiastically to the invitation to come to Dublin to read the manuscript and, if he liked, make excerpts, in consultation with Howells, for publication. Twain's 1906 contractual obligation was fulfilled by "A Horse's Tale," a sentimental novella featuring the young Buffalo Bill, and a gracious, laudatory article about Howells, even the more precious because any such essay is a rarity in Twain's career. Harvey had probably learned that Twain might publish excerpts outside the Harper empire if Harper should decline, which Twain would have been free to do, and that he had invited McClure, who wanted to syndicate excerpts for newspaper publication, to examine the manuscript. Harvey, who was revamping the *North American Review* into a fortnightly with "*a purely literary* section," thought that selections from Twain's autobiographical writings might be a way to get the changed magazine off to a good start.

At the end of July 1906, he arrived at Dublin. He liked what he read, and chose five ten-thousand-word selections, mostly from narrative material evocative of Twain's childhood and youth. In total, he segregated about a hundred thousand words from what was now a quarter million. And "very nice culling he did, too," Twain remarked. He was to continue dictating, off and on, until 1909, the dictations the major literary effort of his last years. Though he returned to "No 44, The Mysterious Stranger" in 1908, his energy for sustained work other than bursts of autobiography decreased considerably. By spring 1908 he confessed that he wished he had "energy enough to resume work on one or two" of his half-finished books—"but this is a dream, and won't ever come true."

He did, though, in 1906–7, have energy for billiards, his favorite and only exercise other than occasional walking, and for frequent public speeches at civic and fraternal occasions in New York. When in 1906 Rogers revealed that Twain would receive a billiard table as a Christmas gift, the writer was overjoyed enough to ask, shamelessly, to have it delivered months early. He would then, he told Rogers, have more time in which to enjoy it. Rogers of course complied. In preparation for its arrival in late October, Twain had his bedroom turned into a billiard room, his study into his bedroom. His persistent journey of thousands of miles around his billiard table began almost immediately. The room became where he spent more time than any place other than his bedroom, and where he often entertained friends.

Though he had hardly played before, Paine, who in fall 1906 was sleeping more nights in a room set aside for him at 21 Fifth Avenue than in his Connecticut home, found himself cajoled into picking up a stick. Given the circumstances, both players were surprised at the younger man's proficiency. He soon was Twain's daily and often nightly billiards companion, a status that helped transform him from semi-hired biographer to affectionate friend. Twain sometimes took their games casually, amusing himself by having one of the kittens snuggle into a table pocket and sometimes redirect a ball. Mostly, though, he was fiercely competitive and a disgruntled loser. Paine now devoted himself full-time, it would appear, to Twain and the biography, billiards included. How he managed this financially is unclear. Twain does not seem to have paid him a salary, though he probably paid occasional work-related expenses. Since Harper would publish the biography, perhaps Harvey provided an advance. Paine did continue working for *St. Nicholas* until 1909 but gave the magazine less of his time, if any, than he gave Twain.

With his energy diminished, Twain proclaimed that, after more than sixty years of labor, he was on a well-earned permanent holiday. Whereas through much of his life he had joked about being lazy, he now embraced leisure. His earnings from his Harper contract and other royalties from copyrights produced about seventy thousand dollars a year between 1906 and 1909, excluding what he earned for the autobiography selections in the *North American Review*. That money he set aside for a new project. Gradually, he had become disenchanted with 21 Fifth Avenue. It and New York seemed dark, gloomy, and damp, a place where his bronchitis flourished.

In spring 1906 Paine persuaded him to buy a seventy-five-acre tract of land in Redding, Connecticut, near Paine's home, an hour and a half by train from Grand Central Station. It was conceived of, at first, as a real estate investment. Soon he decided to build a house there for himself, with Howells' son, John, as architect. Since it was to be built with the money from his autobiographical articles, he proposed calling it "Autobiography House." Two conditions were established: the cost should not exceed twenty-five thousand dollars, and he would not see the house until completed. John Howells and Clara gladly took charge, though Clara's contribution turned out to be mostly long-distance demands, including an expensive change to accommodate her insistence on having her own bedroom suite. Isabel did most of the daily hands-on managerial supervision. Twain had been involved in most stages of the creation and renovation of the Hartford house, and that had ended badly. This one he would move into, like a king, as Lyon regularly referred to him, after his minions had prepared it.

4.

Resplendent in a scarlet robe, in June 1907 Twain happily received from the rector of Oxford University an honorary doctoral degree. For an Anglophile who had never himself gone to college, an honorary degree from Oxford outranked degrees from Yale and Missouri. He could hardly stop referring to it, and boasting. Early on he had been dismissed as only a humorist, at best a somewhat better one than now forgotten figures like Petroleum V. Nasby, Josh Billings, and Artemus Ward, but this humorist had long since transcended humor's lowly berth. Partly it was a sign of the increasing respect in which American literature was held in England, as well as Twain's long, ambivalent, but always mutually respectful relationship with the English reading public. "The King . . . has always wanted a scarlet robe," the ever-worshipful Isabel Lyon wrote in her diary.

Colorful costumes had always appealed to him. In December 1906 he made a sensation in Washington when he appeared before a congressional hearing on copyright, threw off his dark cloak, and revealed himself entirely in white, even to his shoes. Ordering a half-dozen white suits for the winter, he began wearing white all year round, partly because he thought white hygienic, but also the better to stand out from any crowd. "I go out frequently & exhibit my clothes," he told Clara in February 1907. "Howells has dubbed me the Whited Sepulchre." When he went to Maryland to appear at the naval academy, he "talked in a snow-white full dress, swallow-tail & all, & dined in the same. It's a delightful impudence. I think I will call it my don'tcareadam suit. But I think I will always ask permission, first, saying 'Dear madam, may I come in my don'tcareadams?'" The scarlet Oxford gown he wore to any occasion at which it would not be totally inappropriate, and at some inappropriate ones also, such as when he introduced Clara at a concert. He would shamelessly upstage anyone.

The Oxford invitation had compelling attractions, among them a last good-bye to his English friends who besieged him with invitations, from which he selected the Royal Garden Party at Windsor and the lord mayor's dinner at Mansion House, among others. He gave numbers of speeches and many interviews, and lunched with James Barrie, Max Beerbohm, and George Bernard Shaw. With Ashcroft managing his schedule, he restricted himself mostly to daytime events. The British press made Twain its lead front-page story throughout, and the English-speaking world amused itself with a cartoon representing Twain in his bathrobe walking from Brown's Hotel to a nearby bathhouse while Ashcroft, formally dressed, followed, a parody gentleman-valet. Clara, worried that her father's eccentricities might embarrass them all, reminded him, as Livy had regularly done, to behave himself in public. Usually, though, publicity meant more to Twain than propriety. Clara had decided not to accompany him, partly to ensure that Isabel Lyon would not go. If Clara went, he had insisted, Isabel must also come. Apparently he preferred to have neither. Jean desperately wanted to go, but the previous fall she had been forced into a sanitarium. In early 1906, during an epileptic attack, she had tried to kill Katy Leary. Twain worried that he might become the object of one of her violent episodes. When her doctor, who believed it damaging for Jean to live with her father and that she needed a controlled environment, recommended that she be semi-institutionalized, Twain agreed.

Oxford's traditional historical pageant, with three thousand Oxfordians dressed in historical costumes from the Middle Ages through the eighteenth century, sent him reeling with delight. "Once I turned a corner & came suddenly upon an ecclesiastic of A D 710 & up went his two fingers in prelatic blessing, as he called me by name & made me welcome to his long-vanished day; & I met Charles I in the same way—oh, Charles to the life! And he also was cordial. And James I, & Henry VIII, & Friar Bacon, & no end of others—I came upon them everywhere, & always it was a charming & a thrilling surprise." For a writer for whom English history had been a lifelong passion, it was a heady experience.

The radiance, though, did have an elegiac shadow; the pageant was also an image of transience. He felt himself fading into history. Despite regular self-exaltation and claims of pleasure, happiness was increasingly compromised by difficulties and deaths that preoccupied him. He sent a list of his Hannibal childhood companions to Laura Hawkins Frazer, asking her to strike through all those no longer alive. Clara's concert career he detested, and he worried about her health. So run down did he himself feel that in early January 1907 he went, with Twichell and Lyon, to Bermuda for a week. While he was away, Thomas Bailey Aldrich, "that lovely spirit," died at the age of seventy. On his return, Howells came to commiserate with him. Then, within moments of Twain's return from England in early July, Henry Rogers had a stroke. It affected his speech and his left arm and leg, and the newspapers reported that he was dead or about to die. Though he was soon functional again, he was never to be fully himself.

In summer 1906, Twain urged Howells to build next to him in Redding. "I'll sell you the site for $25," he wrote, promising that Howells' son would tell him that "it is a choice place." Howells responded, "I would come and build next to you, but you ask too much for your land. $25 for a ten acre lot? No, sir." When, a year later, Harvey returned the *North American Re-*

view to a monthly, the new format could contain fewer excerpts from the autobiography, and Twain immediately had financial palpitations. Expenses for Jean and Clara were high. His domestic payroll was sizable. He decided to abandon the Redding project. Clara consoled him: "I am really exceedingly glad you have decided again against the Redding house. . . . The result of building would have been great expense, some dissatisfaction, loneliness and a new burden." When John Howells pointed out that it would cost as much to halt as to finish, he reversed his decision. Harvey agreed to guarantee two thousand dollars a month regardless of other considerations. And his savings of fifty-one thousand dollars in the Knickerbocker Trust Company, most of it earnings from the *North American Review,* was more than adequate for the house.

When in October 1907 a bank run forced the Knickerbocker not to honor withdrawal requests, Twain contained his anxiety as best he could. "He walked up and down singing 'Swing low, Sweet chariot.' The kind of a song," Isabel noted, "that means his heart is very heavy." In a public letter, he urged other depositors to accept the terms of a proposed bank reorganization. In the end, despite nasty letters from Twain alleging criminal culpability, the Knickerbocker repaid depositors in full. All in all, his financial anxieties proved unwarranted, though a general downturn allowed Harper to guarantee his annual retainer only through 1908. Regardless of emotional alarms, his cash flow remained stable and sufficient.

Two visits to Bermuda, his favorite retreat from winter weather and balm for his bronchitis, kept him mildly cheerful, the first in late January 1908 with Ashcroft, the second for six weeks in late winter to early spring with Lyon and Rogers. Rogers boarded the boat noticeably feeble, the only sign of the stroke he had suffered. In Bermuda, Twain played golf with Woodrow Wilson. The future president was a golfer, Twain not. Without consistent literary work, and with Clara often away on concert and Jean in exile, he found himself emotionally at loose ends. One daughter now had little time for him, the other he had sent away.

When Jean, who had two passionate desires, never to criticize her father and to live at home again, bitterly complained that she hated her newest protected living situation, her father lamely replied, "Evidently there is something that has been kept from me." Jean's surrogate targets were Clara and Isabel. "But that is right," her father continued, "& as it should be, unless it is something that I could remedy. Clara, Miss Lyon, &

Mr. Paine keep all sorts of distresses from me, & I am very thankful for it—distresses which they are aware I could not remedy. . . . They know I desire this; for I am taking my holiday, now after 60 years of work & struggle & worry & vexation. . . . But wherever there is anything that depends upon *me* & *my* help, I want to know all about it." Jean could not have felt this other than as the slam of a door in her face.

Paine, Lyon, and sometimes Ashcroft provided company. In New York, Howells provided companionship. Rogers less, now. Twain spent evenings at some of the many hospitable hearths at which he was welcome, but loneliness still weighted his spirits. Images of Livy and Susy were regularly in his mind's eye. From early on he had been, at first erotically and then emotionally, fixated on the beauty of adolescent females. With his own daughters he had had an empathetic engagement that allowed him to be one of them, to cross-dress into a playmate, creating games that transported him into realms of carnival-like pleasure, as if he were himself a child again. With his daughters' adolescence long gone and without grandchildren, he began to collect young girls he met and corresponded with into a private club of which he was to be the only male member. "I am 73 & grandchildless," he explained, "& so one might expect the whole left hand compartment of my heart to be empty & cavernous & desolate; but it isn't because I fill it up with schoolgirls." With a strong sense of himself as a grandfatherly ancient, he saw no taint in it. Besides, his playful eccentricities were known worldwide. And when it came to performance, there was no one more morally Victorian. His young friends' mothers trusted in his geriatric harmlessness. Fortunately, his new hobby made no one uncomfortable except Clara, who learned to live with it.

The first of a series of grandfatherly obsessions began when, just after his seventieth birthday, he introduced himself to fifteen-year-old Gertrude Natkin. There was, sometimes, a coyness, an elaborateness, even a relentlessness about his passions that had a touch of the monomaniacal and a hint of the pathological. But he was not a danger to the girls, and he was lonely for what they could provide. Always chivalrous, he treated them with clinging courtesy and courtly compliments. Sometimes he was hard put to keep their attention, though he played cards, took walks, told stories, escorted them to the theater, and even accepted invitations to speak at their occasions. He preferred that they not exceed sixteen years of age. He began to keep elaborate lists, which included their ages, organizing them into two overlapping clubs, one of pen pals in various countries who had introduced themselves to him in letters, the other named from his Bermuda associations, for whom he had membership "angelfish" pins made. The girls of his "Aquarium" he saw in New York, on a few occasions at their homes, and then, after he occupied the new house in the summer of 1908, at Redding.

On his trip to England in June 1907, he met Carlotta Welles, who reminded him of Susy. In London, he became attached to a sixteen-year-old Atlanta schoolgirl, Frances Nunnally, whom he nicknamed Francesca and took with him to many events. On the return voyage, eleven-year-old Dorothy Quick, from New Jersey, found him fascinating. To New York dockside photographers the cute combination was irresistible, white hair, scarlet robe, and feminine innocence. Dorothy, whose visits were a great success, became one of his most cherished companions for much of 1907. In Bermuda, twelve-year-old Helen Allen, the American consul's daughter, became a favorite. Three more Dorothys were added to the club: Butes, Harvey, and Sturgis. Three New York girls were enlisted, Irene Gerken, Margaret Blackmer, and Marjorie Breckinridge. In the end, there were to be thirteen angelfish.

In June 1908, the youngest was twelve, the oldest seventeen. Their framed photographs lined the walls of his billiard room at the Redding house. Creating comically formal club rules and regulations amused him. "It's a frisk-about lot, my angel-fishes," he complained. "I can't keep enough of them in the Tank to make a show." Letters helped. Paine's thirteen-year-old daughter Louise lived so close by that she could swim regularly in the tank. But, as he wrote to Dorothy Quick in January 1908, "I wish a person could rent you or buy you."

When in good temper, he was as amiable as ever, especially with friends like Rogers. In bad, he had uncontrollably irascible moments, with little regard for the feelings of others, especially those most vulnerable, such as his daughters and Isabel. He attempted to keep his profanity private, and mostly succeeded. Isabel worshipped her king, no matter what, and forgave him anything. She wanted only to serve, though sometimes she had tremors that verged on breakdown. She succeeded, though, in exercising her competence daily. With other guests, she consumed her share of Twain's scotch whiskey. So did he. Mostly it resulted in a happy drunken haze for them all, and Twain's tottering seemed to her inseparable from his charm. His habit of prowling the house in a bathrobe and old slippers, which disgusted Clara, she thought endearing. And Twain lavishly praised her work on the Redding house, almost a full-time job by itself. "She will make an admirable job of it if she survives," he told Jean.

Clara kept away from her father's temper, though she made demands of her own, especially monetary, a self-protective assertiveness. They had an ongoing bantering conversation, often by letter, about her wish to be as famous as he, a topic on which he had the upper hand. When she boasted that her concert audiences were "better than Mark ever done," he demolished that claim in no uncertain terms. "But you are coming along, dear, you are coming along." Jean he crushed entirely, with a semblance of kindness intended to soften his assurance that father and Dr. Peterson knew best. Her feelings were of no concern, not because he did not love her but because he had, at times, no idea of his brutality, at others because he selfservingly believed that people could not change at all. Nothing Jean could say made a difference, and Clara was less than helpful. The best Jean could make of her situation was that her father was being influenced against her. Increasingly, in her mind, Isabel Lyon—whom she at first tried to court as an ally—was the villain.

But not to her father or to Ralph Ashcroft, with whom Isabel flirted and who seemed increasingly fond of her. And not to Paine, who took long walks with Lyon at Redding, their subjects literary and philosophical and also of course their most intensely shared interest, the man to whom they were both dedicated. When a tense issue of access to letters arose between Paine and his subject, Lyon helped the biographer smooth things over. In a speech at a Lotos Club dinner in his honor in mid-January 1908, Twain introduced Paine as his biographer: "[He] has been right at my elbow for two years and a half, making notes, and under these circumstances if he doesn't know me, who does know me?" When Katy Leary reported to Twain that she had seen Paine going through "private papers and letters" to which he had not been granted access, Twain felt his privacy invaded, his trust abused. This was presumption, and possibly with ill intent. He instructed that the manuscript box be locked. "When Paine discovered this move against him, he came to me in distress," Isabel wrote, "begging me to use my influence with Mr. Clemens, who could always be swayed by the last person caring to build up a prejudice or to break one down."

Paine also had gotten, without Twain's knowledge, letters from Howells and Samuel Moffett, both of whom assumed Twain had approved the request. "I don't like to have those privacies exposed in such a way to even my biographer," Twain wrote immediately to Howells. "A man should be dead before his private foolishnesses are risked in print." Apparently he had forgotten that it had been agreed that the biography would not appear until after his death. He had, though, promised the letters to his daughters as part of their inheritance, "for bread-and-butter's sake." Publishing large extracts let alone full letters in the biography might undercut their value.

His injunction to Howells was too late. Paine had already read the letters and made copies. He had seen Twain on such intimate terms with Paine, Howells explained, that he "should not have hesitated to offer him all" of them. Anyway, Paine was absolutely trustworthy, and, Howells assured him, there was nothing embarrassing in the letters. Isabel argued that Twain should do nothing to jeopardize Paine's biographical enterprise. By late January 1908, the issue had been resolved satisfactorily.

So too had a related cause of concern, his daughters' financial future. Ashcroft had come up with a brilliant idea. Why not incorporate all Twain's business activities into the Mark Twain Company? Fees for the commercial use of his name could be put on a methodical basis. Most important, if the new company were to own his copyrights, could not the copyright life of his books be extended considerably? Twain embraced the idea. Ashcroft was given power of attorney. By early 1908 the Mark Twain Company was well under way, Twain president, Ashcroft secretary and treasurer, Isabel, Clara, and Jean directors.

His factotums rowed Twain's domestic and financial boats competently. The passenger, though, began to falter. In Bermuda in late March 1908 he found enough sunshine to "beat the bronchitis." "Mr. Rogers was pretty poorly when we came down here," he wrote Clara, "& Miss Lyon was not much better off, but both are in much improved condition now. There was nothing the matter with me. Yet I seem to have improved a little myself." In fact, it was impossible to tell how much his persistent cough came from bronchitis and how much from smoking, what doctors had for years described as a "tobacco cough" and which he had been advised was hard on his heart. Gout and associated pains he hardly complained about. Occasional dizziness and a fainting spell or two did not seem serious. Billiards provided exercise and relaxation.

At Redding, a new billiard table graced one of the most handsome rooms in a house he adored and in which he felt at home as soon as, on June 28, 1908, he walked through the door. He spent the first night playing billiards with Paine. "I realize that I haven't had a real home, until now, since we left the Hartford one 17 years ago," he wrote to Mrs. Rogers. "It is a long, long time to be homeless." Perched high on a hill with a commanding view of the countryside, the compact but large structure, an Italian villa with a loggia rather than a Connecticut country house, was both distinctively foreign and comfortably domestic, a tribute to John Howells' skills and to Isabel's. "Miss Lyon has achieved wonders, I think." Twain's bedroom, study, billiard room, and all the entertaining and functional facilities were on the first floor, Clara's suite, Jean's room (in name only), three guest bedrooms, and the servant bedrooms on the second. He never wanted to go back to 21 Fifth Avenue.

Before settling in he had a duty to perform: to attend the dedication of a memorial to Thomas Bailey Aldrich in Portsmouth, New Hampshire. The discomfort of getting there in the July heat and the program's tediousness irritated him. His love for Aldrich, though, overcame every obstacle except Mrs. Aldrich, who had never liked Twain and whom he had detested from the start. Beside Twain on the platform, Howells whispered that Aldrich would have treated the stiffness of his wife's formal program as if it were "an old time minstrel show." The two old friends had a sense of their time together growing short, their lives declining. Abandoning his memorized eulogy, Twain spoke spontaneously, which he almost never did, about his recollections of his friend, particularly an incident in which Aldrich had pretended to console him for their finding many of Twain's books in a bookstore and none of Aldrich's. "You see your popularity has all gone," Aldrich had said. "I'm popular now. He's sold out all my books." Back at Redding, Twain excoriated Mrs. Aldrich in a long dictation session.

When he received news that his forty-eight-year-old nephew, Samuel Moffett, had drowned in the surf at a New Jersey beach, he left his bucolic contentment to attend the funeral in New York. "I was gone two days," he wrote Jean, "& the shock of the tragedy, & the blistering heat, & the heavy black clothes & the pathetic sight of the broken-hearted family, was a heavy drain upon me & struck me down; but I am getting over it now, & indeed am about as well as I was before I went." But the strain may have been more serious than he would admit. "The doctor had half an idea that there is something the matter with my brain," he wrote to Mrs. Rogers. He had been knocked out "by something akin to a sunstroke." It may, indeed, have been a ministroke. His most serious complaint was of "over-fatigue," a recurring condition. In small spurts, he boasted, he was "as brisk & active a young thing as there is in any country." Twain continued to feel vaguely ill. Indigestion, which he usually controlled by short bursts of fasting and for which he tried other treatments, such as an "electric vibrating machine" and osteopathy, resolved itself into "protracted heartburn."

A burglary at Redding in mid-September 1908 produced a commotion and a countryside pursuit. Miss Lyon came on the burglars in the act. She screamed. They fled, followed by wild shots from the butler's gun. Silver pieces of sentimental value were stolen. Twain took it in good spirits, posting a notice to future burglars: "There is nothing but plated ware in this house now. . . . Please close the door whenever you go away!" But the servants were spooked, particularly by the isolation of the house, the name of which Twain changed, at Clara's insistence, from "Innocents at Home," which had embarrassed her, to "Stormfield." All the servants quit. "Not a woman in this house has had a whole solid hour's sleep since," Twain wrote Howells. "They drop into feverish cat-naps, & at the very slightest & almost inaudible noises they spring to a sitting posture, panting & gasping & quaking. It is pitiful." Clara fled to New York, where she rented an apartment of her own, the better to carry on her life without her father looking over her shoulder. Miss Lyon stayed in bed with nervous tremors.

He had additional reasons for discomfort. In mid-November, not giving it a second thought and later claiming he had forgotten ever doing so, he signed documents giving Ashcroft and Lyon power of attorney over his business affairs. He had every reason to trust them. They had been apparently scrupulously honest and loyal, and he had no desire even to oversee let alone manage details, including signing checks. Clara was useless in such matters, partly because she was often in New York or on concert tours. Her father paid all Clara's expenses. Lyon made out the checks and occasionally urged, at his insistence, frugality on both daughters, each of whom increasingly resented Lyon's position. Both felt humiliated at their need to bring every bill to Isabel, their economic lives apparently under her control. Clara worried that Lyon and Ashcroft's influence would prove detrimental to her. Her worst nightmare was that her father would marry Lyon. An attractive woman with a penchant for flirting, Isabel had suitors, including Ashcroft. Next in horror was the possibility that Lyon would poison her father against her, jeopardizing support for her career and even her inheritance. A real but lesser anxiety was that Lyon's residence in her father's house might cause tongues to wag.

Another complication arose at the end of 1908. Clara, apparently, was having an affair with her accompanist, a well-known minor pianist named Charles Wark, with whom she traveled in Europe on tour. In September 1908 the *New York World* gossiped that the engagement of Twain's daughter "to Mr. Charles E. Wark of this city, has been rumored." Such language usually signaled that the principals were lovers. Isabel knew about Wark; Twain didn't, and Clara suspected Isabel of leaking the story to the press. Wark stayed at Stormfield a number of times, in a guest room and as Clara's professional associate. Clara feared her father's response if he should have his suspicions raised, especially since in 1903, when she was deeply involved with Gabrilowitsch, he had written an impassioned essay, published in *Harper's Weekly,* blasting the destruction of a father's happiness by a daughter's seducer. Seduction of an innocent was a crime. "There is no age at which the good name of a member of a family ceases to be part of the property of that family." He probably most likely had Clara and Ossip in mind. Now, in late 1908, Gabrilowitsch was spending long periods in New York, and, at the same time rumors surfaced about Clara and Wark, he was about to reassert himself as Clara's suitor.

Soon Isabel and Clara negotiated a cease-fire, which required Clara to cease attempting to damage Isabel in her role as secretary and Isabel to eliminate, by marrying Ashcroft, any possibility of a romantic association between herself and Twain. Isabel agreed to say nothing about Wark. No doubt she and Ashcroft were companionably attracted to each other, though later Isabel claimed, plausibly, that she had married him to protect her position with Twain. Her idea was that, married, they could be an even better team, loyally dedicated to the interests of the great man. And Clara would have fewer reasons to fear her. For a short time the truce held.

In March 1909, Howells came to the new house for his first visit. Though Twain complained of ongoing indigestion, the two friends had a grand time together, Twain's spirits high enough for him to stand early each morning near Howells' bedroom door, calling out his name. When Howells looked out, Twain "was in his long nightgown swaying up and down the corridor; and wagging his great white head like a boy." Literary discussions took some of their time. Twain had recently complimented Howells on a

Harper's Weekly article on Edgar Allan Poe. "To me," though, he told him, "his prose is unreadable—like Jane Austen's. No, there is a difference. I could read his prose on salary, but not Jane's. Jane's is entirely impossible. It seems a great pity they allowed her to die a natural death."

Soon he had his own literary news. He had decided that his autobiographical dictations had been faltering because the presence of a stenographer inhibited him, like having a lecture audience. You were not talking to yourself. And if the person taking dictation was "a religious person, your jaw is locked again." He had a better idea. He would write letters, never to be sent, to his closest friends. "I will fire the profanities at Rogers, the indecencies at Howells, the theologies at Twichell. Oh, to think—I am a free man at last!" Very few such letters got written, and he was far from free.

That same month, domestic hell broke lose. At the start of March, Isabel went to Hartford to her mother's and to be among friends, in order to "try to beat a threatened breakdown," Twain wrote to Jean. With Isabel away, Clara made shocking accusations: Lyon and Ashcroft were thieves! They had been stealing money for their own personal use from Twain's accounts. What was her evidence? She had none. How would she then prove her case? A thorough investigation by a lawyer she had hired, and an independent accountant would, she asserted, support her accusations. To his credit, Twain defended his retainers at length and with conviction. But, to satisfy Clara's strong-willed certainty, and, given the seriousness of the charges, he consented to a preliminary investigation.

Ashcroft readily agreed, but Clara demanded that in addition all records relating to financial transactions during Ashcroft's tenure be examined by professional accountants. Twain balked, fearing that that would be felt as an insult so severe that Ashcroft would not be willing to remain in his employ. At a minimum, it would make impossible a trustful relationship. "While we are hunting eagerly for *dis*service, are we forgetting to hunt for service? It is a thought which does not make me feel very comfortable." Isabel Lyon "came to your mother as secretary, at $50 a month. She has never asked for more. Yet she has been housekeeper 4 or 5 years. . . . She could not have been replaced at any price, for she was qualified to meet our friends socially & be acceptable to them. . . . And she has been a house builder. . . . Would you have undertaken that job? I think not. Could we have found anybody, so competent as she, to take it? Or half so willing, or half so devoted? . . . Anybody can get his mind poisoned, & I have not

wholly escaped, as regard Miss Lyon. But it is healthy again. I have no suspicions of her. . . . She has not been dishonest, even to a penny's worth. All
her impulses are good and fine. . . . And what shall I say of Ashcroft? he
has served me in no end of ways, & with astonishing competency—bril-
liancy, I may say." He had gotten Twain out of the ongoing Plasmon complications with the least possible loss. His business genius had conceived
of the Mark Twain Company. Now, to satisfy Clara, everything was to be
put on a business basis. "Nothing is as it was," he lamented. "Everything is
changed. Sentiment has been wholly eliminated. . . . All duties are strictly
defined. . . . Stormfield was a home; it is a tavern, now, & I am the land-
lord."

In the preliminary investigation, the accounts tallied. One minor detail
was restructured. He had given Lyon a cottage on the Redding property
and a five-hundred-dollar Christmas gift toward redecorating. He had lent
her a thousand dollars to cover the remaining cost, which Lyon had taken
from the household funds. But there had been no formal document
recording the loan. Ashcroft gave Twain four notes for two hundred and
fifty dollars each. "Jesus, what a week!" Twain concluded the excruciatingly
long letter to Clara, which he thought ended the matter.

In mid-March 1909 Twain bemusedly attended the Lyon-Ashcroft wedding in New York. He took Isabel's rationale at face value. "It won't make
any difference in my life with the King," she wrote to a friend. "I'll stay
right here." Ashcroft "will come when he can to be with us both. . . . You
know that this thing wouldn't be happening if I could live without this dear
and wonderful man." As a marriage of convenience, its aim was the king's
well-being. Twain had no reason to be concerned, other than ordinary prudence. His daughters' equal shares in his estate were secured in his will.
Lyon and Ashcroft's power of attorney gave them power only over business
matters, though their decisions could indeed affect the value of his estate,
but it concerned him so little that even the fact of it seemed to have gone
out of his mind.

Twain's defense of his retainers, though, fell on deaf ears. Clara had determined that Ashcroft and Lyon should go, the charge a means to a predetermined end. She also had an ally. Jean now saw her chance to get back
at Lyon, whom she blamed for her banishment. Once Clara began her
campaign, Jean brought up her comparatively light artillery of complaints
and accusations. With the support of her doctor, who came regularly to

Stormfield and whom Twain respected, and her friend Mary Lawton, she nagged her father ceaselessly. The "poor old man is being driven almost crazy," Mrs. Paine wrote to her husband, "and he said until three weeks ago he was happy and well off, but since then it has been h—— and that if things did not get better he would cut his G—— D—— throat."

The battle was over control and possession. Ashcroft and Lyon needed to fight back. But criticizing Clara would eventually force Twain to defend his daughter. In the end, she was not replaceable; they were. And Clara knew she could manipulate her father, particularly his paranoia about being cheated, his ability to turn on a dime against those he believed had betrayed him. She fired volley after volley against the enemy: Isabel had used the household money to buy clothes for herself; she had never intended to pay back the money she had spent renovating her cottage; an examination of the records would reveal disbursements unaccounted for. Lyon and Ashcroft presented documents to show that Twain had approved every expenditure. And they proposed that Lyon act henceforward only as Twain's social secretary, not as housekeeper, to eliminate any concern about her handling money and keeping records.

Clara increasingly gained the upper hand. "You will give Miss Lyon her notice right away I hope," Clara urged in early April. Her father's only path to peace required capitulation, and he wanted peace most of all. He soon sent Isabel a cold note of discharge. By the middle of the month the Ashcrofts were gone, never to return to Stormfield. At Clara's urging, he agreed to try the experiment of having Jean return home to live with him, and, with Clara's help, to run the household. "Dear child," he wrote to his youngest daughter, "you will be as welcome as if it were your mother herself calling you home from exile!" Jean moved into Stormfield, never again to live anyplace else, while Clara mercilessly pursued the Ashcrofts. She and her now converted father wanted not only justice but vengeance. She enlisted Rogers to undertake a thorough investigation of Twain's business records, which the Ashcrofts turned over in full. She pressured and frightened Isabel to return the cottage Twain had given her as a gift. Twain revoked the Ashcrofts' power of attorney, which they relinquished without resistance. Apparently, it had never once been used. In the end, the investigation revealed no criminality.

Cast out of paradise for sins they had not committed, the Ashcrofts fought back, in the interest of their reputations, in the courts and the press. Convinced that Clara had been right all along, Twain counterattacked with a book-length dictation blasting his former employees. The screed was petty, sanctimonious, and self-demeaning, and as a factual account egregiously unreliable. His treatment of Jean he blamed entirely on Isabel. "It's the first time I've treated the subject with a pen," he told a friend in August 1909. "I have enjoyed it, for I am full of malice, saturated with malignity. I feel nearer to the Lord than I ever was before. I feel as he feels of a Saturday night when the weekly report is in & He has had a satisfactory clean-up of the human race." The newspapers presented the Ashcrofts' side of the case favorably. Returning to her mother in Hartford, Isabel found her Hartford friends, some also Twain's, warmly sympathetic. They knew Twain well enough not to be surprised. The comprehensive examination of household accounts during the Lyon-Ashcroft stewardship produced only small cash expenses that were unaccounted for. Ashcroft responded that of course that would be the case when there were many small daily disbursements. Clara continued to maintain that they were thieves.

The coin of Twain's loyalty had flipped to its other side—profane contempt. The Ashcrofts, he argued, had obtained his signature on the power of attorney fraudulently, by hypnotizing him or by forgery. They were indeed thieves. And he wanted them punished, preferably behind bars. "She and Mr. Ashcroft so worked Father," Jean explained to Twichell, "that he was as clay in their hands and the climax of their actions was the signing of a general power of attorney to them, individually and together, which gave them the power to do anything they chose with every sort of property Father now has, and might at any time possess." Any reminder of the Ashcrofts brought curses to his lips and pen. Isabel Lyon "was a liar, a forger, a thief, a hypocrite, a drunkard, a sneak, a humbug, a traitor, a conspirator, a filthy-minded and salacious slut pining for seduction & always getting disappointed," he wrote to Clara in March 1910. "At this very day," he confided in one of the last notebook entries of his life, "Ashcroft is manufacturing forgeries to rob Clara with when I am dead." He literally cursed them till the day he died.

5.

When Twain stepped off the train at Grand Central Station on May 19, 1909, Clara met him with the grim news that, during the night, the man he was coming to visit, Henry Rogers, had died of a stroke. She had hastened to be the first to tell him and to brace him. Newspaper reporters were there. "This is terrible, terrible, and I cannot talk about it," he told them. Paine rushed down from Connecticut to join him at the Grosvenor, from which he soon went to be a pallbearer, carrying the body of a beloved friend who had served him well. Feeling weak, unwilling to converse with family mourners, he did not attend the burial at Fairhaven. Clara and Paine sat with him in the hotel room. "He had a helpless look," Paine noticed, "and he said his friends were dying away from him and leaving him adrift." Under such circumstances, Jean's recall from banishment turned out to be a blessing. With unexpected competence and energy, she took charge of Stormfield, and as housekeeper she was superlative. "How glad I am that Jean is at home again!" he instructed Paine to tell her, though he sought redemption by sometimes telling her himself. "Clara has virtually forsaken her NY quarters, & she lives with me nearly all the time, now. So I've a family again, you see." He self-protectively but now with a tentative touch maintained that her exile had been "necessary for her recovery, but I hope it will never have to be repeated."

In early June 1909, as a favor to one of his angelfish, he addressed the graduating class of St. Timothy's, a girl's school at Catonsville, Maryland, near Baltimore. The heat, the humidity, the fatigue, the dozens of cigars, left him breathless. "I have a curious pain in my breast," he told Paine, who had accompanied him. He hoped it was his usual indigestion, and, when he rested briefly, the pain disappeared. As they walked on, though, he put his hand to his chest. "That pain has come back." His face turned gray. "It's a curious, sickening, deadly kind of pain. I never had anything just like it." It was what some of his recent apparent indigestion may have been— angina. At Stormfield, Dr. Quintard, Clara's internist but now the family doctor, put him to bed, telling him he was to move as little as possible and desist from smoking.

"It is heart-disease," he told Frances Nunnally. The doctor had no doubt that Twain was suffering from "tobacco" heart. The irony struck him. "I am well aware that I ought to laugh at *myself*—& would if I were a really honest person. However the victory over me is not much of a victory after all, for it has taken 63 years to build this disease. I was immune *that* long, anyway." He was ordered not to "go out of sight" of the house, he told Rogers' son-in-law, "nor walk more than half a mile on a stretch; nor run up stairs; nor do any other customary or agreeable thing; & moreover, I must cut my smoking way down! It isn't going to happen. I shan't diminish it by a single puff." Actually, he tried to desist. "But it was too lonesome, and I have resumed—in a modified way: 4 smokes a day instead of 40. This will have a good effect. On the bank balance." "You would better come [to visit me] very soon," he told George Harvey, "because I am preparing for another world, & yesterday afternoon & last night the prospects were good. I am practising for all emergencies—both directions, up & down: with wings in the morning, parachute in the afternoon."

Nature, though, did not find it easy to dispatch him. By September he had made enough of a recovery to pretend that, except for easily tiring, he was perfectly capable of some activities he enjoyed, such as entertaining angelfish and encouraging a well-attended charity concert at Stormfield for the Mark Twain Library in Redding, initiated by his gift of hundreds of books and for which he had been collecting a dollar donation from every visitor to the house. More than five hundred people attended. At the piano, Ossip Gabrilowitsch accompanied Clara. Wark had been dismissed; Ossip and Clara were reunited and became engaged again. Twain introduced them.

Though confined to the house and surroundings, he pretended that he recognized nothing but the advantages that being convalescent provided. He had the perfect excuse to decline invitations of any sort. "It is an ideal life for a lazy person, & I was born lazy. When I found that Dr. Quintard was curing me," he joked, "I discharged him." He felt fine twenty-three out of twenty-four hours. During that one hour, though, the pain was excruciating. Drugs relieved but didn't limit the number of attacks. He stopped using medicines and tried an osteopath. No help. He tried gallons of hot water, which gave some relief. When Clara argued that his pain was due to indigestion, he ate less. "Therefore the pains & I are getting to be strangers." But only temporarily. In October and November 1909 he felt well enough to write. It was his last sustained effort, and, though "Letters from the Earth" remained a fragment, it had some of the literary brio of earlier works in its attack on the stupidity of human nature and Christian theology. He took satisfaction in a service Ossip rendered him, something he had not himself been able to accomplish and for which he was "most thoroughly grateful: he has squelched Clara's 'career.' She has done with the concert-stage—permanently, I pray. I hate the word. I never want to hear it again."

On a bright October day, "decked out" in a white suit and resplendent in his Oxford scarlet gown, Twain gave away the bride. Twichell came from Hartford to perform the ritual. Langdon relatives arrived from Elmira. Family friends assembled; letters, telegrams, and telephone messages kept Jean and Paine exhaustingly busy. A radiant Twain supervised. Oddly, unexpectedly, he now had a son in the form of a son-in-law, though when he tried the unfamiliar word it came hesitantly. When the newlyweds left for New York, to sail for Germany and an indefinite European residence, he thought it likely he would never see Clara again. His assumption was put on hold when Ossip, in New York, had an appendicitis attack that required surgery. After a month of recuperation, the couple sailed, a departure that Twain preferred not to witness. He did not know, as she herself would not for at least a month, that Clara was pregnant.

At the advent of cold weather, Twain sailed for Bermuda, on the urging of Dr. Quintard, accompanied by his valet and by Paine, now also his business manager. He rarely tired of comparing favorably, with self-congratulatory triumphalism, Paine to Ashcroft. Distress at the state of his finances flared up while he was in Bermuda, triggered by the long-expected failure of American Plasmon. Paine assured him, though, that he need not worry about his Harper income. Unnerved by her father's anxieties, Jean looked for ways to cut Stormfield expenses, though cutting staff was incompatible with entertaining on the scale her father desired.

In Bermuda, where he arrived on November 18, he became the houseguest of the American consul, though he kept his comfortable hotel rooms throughout. The consul's wife and angelfish daughter delighted in having "Uncle Mark" at their home, though fifteen-year-old Helen Allen was not always as pliable as he would have liked, and she had an interest in boys that distressed him. With Paine and the Allens, he took three-hour-long carriage rides. The mornings he spent in bed. "Everything—weather included—is in perfection here now." Most social invitations he declined, though he went to Government House, whose request had "the quality of a command." Angina pain came less frequently. The news of the death of Richard Gilder, who had seemed so happy at Clara's wedding, was kept from him. "The doctors are certain that my father too has this horrible heart disease," Jean wrote to a friend. Twain found unawareness increasingly congenial. He stopped his lifelong newspaper reading because of lack of interest: "I do not seem to be in the world or of it at all. Its affairs are not mine. Never in my life before perhaps, have I had such a strong sense of being severed from the world, & the bridges all swept away." Even more tellingly, he had lost interest in billiards.

Returning home a few days before Christmas 1909, he made no attempt to be anything less than his crusty anti-Christian self about the holiday. Early in the year he had shocked Jean's Euro-centered assumption that the Virgin Mary was white. "What is there about it that's shocking?" "Can't you see, papa? The idea of saying the Mother of the Saviour was *colored*. It's sacrilegious." "Sac—oh, nonsense! Jean, in her day the population of the globe was not more than a thousand millions. Not *one-tenth* of them were *white*. What does this fact suggest to you?" "I—I don't know. What does it suggest, papa?" "It most powerfully suggests that *white was not a favorite complexion with God*. Has it since become a favorite complexion with Him? . . . There is nothing important, nothing essential, about a complexion. I mean, to me. But with the Deity it is different. He doesn't think much of white people."

Jean had welcomed her father with overflowing attentiveness, the house prepared for Christmas, the tree half trimmed, gifts partly wrapped. He had responded happily, with Clara gone, to the only daughter he had left. They had "two splendid days together." When a telephone inquiry about his health came two days before Christmas, he cabled the Associated Press: "I hear the newspapers say I am dying. The charge is not true. I would not do such a thing at my time of life. I am behaving as good as I can. Merry Christmas to everybody! Mark Twain."

The next morning, the day of Christmas Eve, at seven-thirty A.M., his bedroom door opened. Katy came to his bedside and said, "Miss Jean is dead!" She and another servant had been nearby while Jean took her morning bath. They heard nothing unusual. When she realized that Jean had been at her bath an unusually long time, she went to the door. Jean did not respond. She entered. Perhaps Jean had had an epileptic attack and blacked out. She may have drowned. Perhaps she had had a heart attack. What exactly killed her is unclear. There was, now, an actual death to report. Paine sent out a press release. Dr. Quintard filled out the death certificate. Katy dressed Jean in the gown she had worn for Clara's wedding.

As her father could all too clearly visualize, Jean's cure was to be effected by the Elmira cemetery, where she would be buried beside her sister and mother. He would be happy to join them soon. But not to accompany Jean, displayed in her coffin in the living room at Stormfield on Christmas Day. "How sweet, & peaceful Jean was . . . with that classic face!" he wrote to Joe and Harmony. "I saw Livy buried. I will never consent to see another dear friend put under the ground." Snow began to fall. He had Paine play Jean's favorite Schubert "Impromptu" on the orchestrelle. From his window he "watched the hearse and the carriages wind along the road and gradually grow vague and spectral in the falling snow, and presently disappear." A few days later he was "already rejoicing" that she had been "set free." "It is always so with me. My grief for the loss of a friend is soon replaced by gratitude that the friend is released from the ungentle captivity of this life. For sixteen years Jean suffered unspeakably." She was now set free "from the swindle of this life."

Waiting with subdued impatience for his own freedom, at a deep level of organic resistance and resilience he was committed to having nature determine the timing. He would play out the string as if there were no connection between his will and his ending. Life in the body had its protocols. On New Year's Day 1910 the pain in his chest came back. And, as he wrote to Clara, he was "so glad" that Jean was "out of it and safe—safe!" Remorse for the obtuseness that had kept him ignorant of her qualities for so long alternated with relief. In Germany, Clara remorsefully pondered why it had happened. "If only I had never quarreled with her about anything." On his way to Bermuda for "an indefinite stay," Twain visited overnight in New York with his niece, Charles Langdon's daughter, Julia, and her husband. It gave him comfort to know that they and his Langdon nephew, Jervis, were actively involved in the Mark Twain Company. Howells joined them for a few hours of conversation, which they realized might be their last. As Paine walked him home, Howells said, "I turn to his books for cheer when I am down-hearted. There was never anybody like him; there never will be."

In Bermuda, as a guest of the Allens, attended by his own butler, he had no desire to return to Stormfield. At Twain's suggestion, Paine had moved into the house with his family as indefinite guests to keep it companionable for when he might return. Katy was still housekeeper. "The main thing is," Clara stressed, that Paine, with legal safeguards in place, "should *never* be allowed the kind of power that the Ashcrofts got!" In Bermuda, dubbed "the Islands of the Blest," where "my raft has landed me," Twain was "as happy as any other shipwrecked sailor ever was. I shan't go 'home' till . . . oh, by & bye. I don't know when—There's no hurry. Hurry? Why, there's no hurry about *anything*, suddenly the hurry has all gone out of my life." Solicitous letters from Clara and news from Paine smoothly flowed into his quiet life and occasional excursions. "You are nearer and dearer to me now than ever," he wrote to Clara, who needed reassurance. "Of my fair fleet all my ships have gone down but you; but while I have you I am still rich." Expenses, he told Paine, should be reduced by selling some land and discharging some servants: "I shall probably see Stormfield but seldom, hereafter, & then only flittingly." Clara would probably never return, he thought. In fact, she had decided to come home in May. "He seems so alone," she wrote to a friend. "I don't know why you should love me," he wrote to her. "I have not deserved it."

Angina pain limited his Bermuda activities, which he did not mind, though he minded the pain. In mid-February 1910, he had enough of a burst of interest in his investments to order Paine to sell a badly performing stock. A week later he came down with his old nemesis, bronchitis. Late in the month, it was so severe that it was difficult for him to talk. With Helen Allen as secretary, he dictated his letters; his estate and Clara's inheritance were on his mind. "Sometime or other I am going to die," he wrote Paine and his lawyers. Watch out for Ashcroft "because it will then begin to rain swindles & forgeries." As if reaching for a source of energy, he had some active sessions of bilious name-calling that soon gave out. His cough lingered. He had a telegram sent to the editor of the *New York Journal*: "Not sick enough to excite an undertaker." He had enough focus to read *A Connecticut Yankee,* which he had not read in thirty years. "Prodigiously pleased with it," he found it "a most gratifying surprise."

In late March he wrote to Paine that he might return sooner than his scheduled April 23 sailing "if the pain in my breast does not mend its way . . . I don't want to die here, for this is an unkind place for a person in that condition. I should have to lie in the undertaker's cellar until the ship would remove me & it is dark down there & unpleasant." Ironically, his bronchitis had nearly disappeared. The chest pain, though, became almost constant and hardly bearable. His father, whom he almost never mentioned, came to mind. "My father died this day 63 years ago," he wrote to Clara. "I remember all about it quite clearly. I miss Jean so!"

Without telling him, Paine booked passage and sailed for Bermuda with opiates and hypodermic needles supplied by Dr. Quintard. Clara had been cabled to return from Europe immediately. At the Allens', Twain was cosseted and nursed. His resilience faltered, though occasional flickers of humor did not. When Paine arrived, Twain felt sufficiently well to take a drive. Return passage had been arranged for April 12, 1910. In bed much of the time, he dozed. Paine read to him. Then a series of angina attacks began on the eighth. With some slight improvement on the eleventh, he was barely able to board the ship, though once under way he seemed better. On the second day of the two-day voyage, he suddenly had great difficulty breathing. Paine thought he would not make it to New York. "I am sorry for you," he told Paine, "but I can't help it—I can't hurry this dying business." He requested a lethal injection. Paine urged him to hold on for Clara's sake. With calm resolve, he ordered Paine to make certain that, when the moment came, he would not "be stimulated back to life."

At dockside, the press corps waited. As he was carried past friends and the friendly crowd to the train station, the cold air chilled him. He felt his chest clutched by another but comparatively mild attack. Quintard and another doctor accompanied him to Redding. On the train, he glanced at the newspapers and breathed freely. Stepping out of the carriage at Stormfield, he greeted the household, and went to bed. Two days later Clara and Ossip arrived. She may or may not have revealed by sight or word her four-month pregnancy. Probably Katy knew immediately. Twain seems not to have known.

"Father has been so ill since we arrived here," Clara wrote on April 18, "that he has not been able to talk at all. . . . He has slept some today and had less distress from short breath but is nevertheless most *distressingly* ill. I pray that by tomorrow he will be suffering less." Opiates kept him drowsy and pain-free. His mind began to wander. He could hardly talk, and when he did words seemed not to come or to make little to no sense. On April 21 he wrote in a barely legible handwriting to Clara, "Dear You did not tell me, but I have found out that you . . ." He asked for his eyeglasses and a pitcher of water. As the sun was setting, he quietly died.

On the twenty-third, Shakespeare's birthday, huge crowds passed before the coffin in the Brick Church in Manhattan. Joe Twichell said a brokenhearted prayer. The nation bordered itself in black for a moment of mourning, as if a well-liked president had died in office. Later, at a memorial, Howells put into words Twain's "congeries of contradictions . . . but contradictions confessed, explicit, positive. . . . I wish we might show him frankly as he always showed himself. We may confess that he had faults, while we deny that he tried to make them pass for merits. He disowned his errors by owning them; in the very defects of his qualities he triumphed, and he could make us glad with him at his escape from them." His body was brought to Elmira, where he shared familiar earth with Livy, Susy, Jean, and little Langdon.

Two days after his funeral, Harmony Twichell escaped; so too, later that year, did Elinor Howells, William James, and even Mary Baker Eddy. Twichell died in 1918, Howells in 1920, at the age of eighty-three, his final celebration of his friend a short, beautiful book, *My Mark Twain,* in which he recalled the great writers he had known. "They were like one another and like other literary men; but Clemens was sole, incomparable, the Lincoln of our literature." Clara gave birth to a daughter at Stormfield in August 1910. Katy Leary, in Clara's service at first, lived till 1934. Clara, who became a widow in 1936, remarried another pianist, a compulsive gambler who commandeered most of her money, and died in 1962 at the age of eighty-eight. In her last years many of her father's letters and manuscripts were sold to pay expenses. Twain's granddaughter, his only descendant, committed suicide in 1964. There are no heirs. There has been no one like him since.

NOTES

TITLE ABBREVIATIONS

CR   *Mark Twain: The Contemporary Reviews*. Edited by Louis J. Budd.
          Cambridge: Cambridge University Press, 1999.

DW   Dixon Wecter, *Sam Clemens of Hannibal*. Boston: Houghton Mifflin,
          1952.

Frear   Walter Francis Frear, *Mark Twain and Hawaii*. Chicago: The Lake-
          side Press, 1947.

HHR   *Correspondence with Henry Huttleston Rogers, 1893–1909*. Edited
          by Lewis Leary. Berkeley: University of California Press, 1969.

Leary   *A Lifetime with Mark Twain: The Memories of Katy Leary*. Written by
          Mary Lawton. New York: Haskell, 1972.

L1–L6   *Mark Twain's Letters* [1853–1875]. Edited by Dahlia Armon, Edgar
          Marquess Branch, Richard Bucci, Victor Fischer, Michael B. Frank,
          Kenneth M. Sanderson, Lin Salamo, and Harriet Elinor Smith.
          Berkeley: University of California Press, 1988–2002.

LLMT   *The Love Letters of Mark Twain*. Edited by Dixon Wecter. New York:
          Harper and Brothers, 1949.

MFMT   Clara Clemens, *My Father, Mark Twain*. New York: Harper and
          Brothers, 1931.

MMT   William Dean Howells, *My Mark Twain*. New York: Harper and
          Brothers, 1910.

MTA   *Mark Twain's Autobiography*. Edited by Albert Bigelow Paine. 2 vols.
          New York: Harper and Brothers, 1924.

MTAD   Mark Twain, Additional Dictation. Mark Twain Papers, Bancroft Library.

MTAQ   *Mark Twain's Aquarium*. Edited by John Cooley. Athens: University of Georgia Press, 1991.

MTB   *Mark Twain: A Biography*. By Albert Bigelow Paine. 3 vols. New York: Harper and Brothers, 1912.

MTBus   *Mark Twain, Business Man*. Edited by Samuel Charles Webster. Boston: Little, Brown, 1946.

MTE   *Mark Twain in Eruption*. Edited by Bernard DeVoto. New York: Harper and Brothers, 1940.

MTHL   *Mark Twain—Howells Letters*. Edited by Henry Nash Smith and William M. Gibson. 2 vols. Cambridge: Harvard University Press, 1960.

MTHHR   *Mark Twain's Correspondence With Henry Huddleston Rogers 1893–1909*. Edited by Lewis Leary. Berkeley: University of California Press, 1969.

MTL   *Mark Twain's Letters*. Edited by Albert Bigelow Paine. 2 vols. New York: Harper and Brothers, 1917.

MTLP   *Mark Twain's Letters to His Publishers, 1867–1894*. Edited by Hamlin Hill. Berkeley: University of California Press, 1967.

MTMF   *Mark Twain to Mrs. Fairbanks*. Edited by Dixon Wecter. San Marino, Calif.: Huntington Library, 1949.

MTOA   *Mark Twain's Own Autobiography*. Edited by Michael J. Kiskis. Madison: University of Wisconsin Press, 1990.

MTP   Mark Twain Papers. Robert H. Hirst, general editor. Bancroft Library, University of California, Berkeley.

NBK   Typographic transcriptions of Mark Twain's unpublished notebooks, 1891–1910. Mark Twain Papers. Bancroft Library, University of California, Berkeley.

N&J   *Mark Twain's Notebooks & Journals* [1855–1891]. Edited by Frederick Anderson, Robert Park Browning, Michael B. Frank, Lin Salamo, Kenneth M. Sanderson, Bernard L. Stein. 3 vols. Berkeley: University of California Press, 1975–1979.

OFG   Carl Dolmetsch. *"Our Famous Guest": Mark Twain in Vienna*. Athens: University of Georgia Press, 1992.

PA   Susy Clemens. *Papa, An Intimate Biography of Mark Twain*. Edited by Charles Neider. New York: Doubleday, 1985.

SCH   Gary Scharnhorst. *Bret Harte: Opening the American Literary West*. Norman: University of Oklahoma Press, 2000.

SK   Laura E. Skandera-Trombley. *Mark Twain in the Company of Women*. Philadelphia: University of Pennsylvania Press, 1994.

SP   *Mark Twain Speaking*. Edited by Paul Fatout. Iowa City: University of Iowa Press, 1976.

TIA   *Traveling with the Innocents Abroad: Mark Twain's Original Reports from Europe and the Holy Land*. Edited by Daniel Morley McKeithan. Norman: University of Oklahoma Press, 1958.

Travels   *Mark Twain's Travels With Mr. Brown.* Edited by Franklin Walker and G. Ezra Dane. New York: Alfred A. Knopf, 1940.

MARK TWAIN'S WORKS

Mark Twain's writings exist in many editions—first editions, reprints within his lifetime, collected editions within his lifetime, collected editions since his death, modern reprints (including many paperback editions, most of which are reprints of existing texts), and modern scholarly textual editions. In the case of the latter my quotations are from the Mark Twain Papers and Works of Mark Twain, University of California Press, Robert H. Hirst, general editor: *The Adventures of Huckleberry Finn* (2001) in the Mark Twain Library [*HF*]; *The Adventures of Tom Sawyer, Tom Sawyer Abroad, Tom Sawyer, Detective* (1980) [*TS*]; *A Connecticut Yankee in King Arthur's Court* (1979) [*CY*]; *Early Tales & Sketches*, vol. 1, 1851–1864 (1979) [*ET&S1*] *Early Tales & Sketches*, vol. 2, 1864–1865 (1979) [*ET&S2*]; *Fables of Man* (1972) [*FM*]; *Hannibal, Huck & Tom* (1979) [*HHT*]; *Huck Finn and Tom Sawyer among the Indians, and other Unfinished Stories* (1989) [*HFTS*]; *What Is Man?* (1973) [*WIM*]; *Which Was the Dream? And Other Symbolic Writings of the Later Years* (1966) [*WWTD*]; *The Prince and the Pauper* (1979) [*P&P*]; *Mysterious Stranger Manuscripts* (1969) [*MSM*]; *Roughing It* (1993) [*RI*]; *Satires and Burlesques* (1967) [*S&B*]. While these are the preferred editions, undoubtedly readers will be drawing on whatever editions are available to them, though in a number of instances the material is unique to some of the above editions. Those quotations from Twain's works with a source indicated in the exposition are not cited in the endnotes. The abbreviations I use for other Twain works I cite are as follows: *IA, Innocents Abroad; ISD, Is Shakespeare Dead?; FQ, Following the Equator; GA, The Gilded Age; LM, Life on the Mississippi; JoA, Joan of Arc;* OT "Old Times on the Mississippi"; *PW, Pudd'nhead Wilson: TA, A Tramp Abroad.*

UNPUBLISHED LETTERS

The main repositories of unpublished letters and manuscripts are the Bancroft Library, University of California, Berkeley; the Beinecke Rare Book and Manuscript Library, Yale University; the Berg Collection, New York Public Library; Mark Twain House, Hartford; and Vassar College Library. Additional letters are archived in dozens of other libraries and in private collections around the world. The files of the Mark Twain Papers at the Bancroft Library, the premier source for Mark Twain studies, contain copies of every locatable letter and manuscript and secondary files on most aspect of Twain's life and world. Unpublished source materials are quoted from the Mark Twain Papers (MTP) unless indicated otherwise.

660 *Notes*

NAME ABBREVIATIONS

ABP: Albert Bigelow Paine
AC: Andrew Chatto
AD: Augustin Daly
AT: Annie E. Trumbull
ANC: Andrew Carnegie
AO: Mrs. Augusta Ogden
APC: Mrs. A. P. Cosgrove
BA: Bayard Taylor
BM: Brander Matthews
BT: Benjamin Ticknor
C&W: Chatto & Windus
CC: Clara Clemens
CDW: Charles Dudley Warner
CEN: Charles Eliot Norton
CEP: Charles E. Perkins
CH: Calvin Higbie
CHW: Charles Henry Webb
CL: Charles Langdon
CN: Gertrude Natkin
CS: Clara Spaudling
CT: Charlotte Teller
CTH: Carl Thallitzer
CW: Charles L. Webster
CWS: Charles Warren Stoddard
DAY: Alice Day
DB: David Watt Bowser
DDQ: Dan De Quille [William Wright]
DG: David Gray, Sr.
DS: Daniel Slote
EB: Elisha Bliss
ECS: Edmund Clarence Stedman
EH: Edward H. House
EP: Edward P. Parker
ERR: Emilie Randel Rogers
EW: Elizabeth Wallace
FAD: Frederick A. Duneka
FC: Mrs. Frank Cheney
FEB: Francis [Frank] E. Bliss
FF: Frank Finlay
FFU: Frank Fuller
FGW: Franklin G. Whitmore
FJH: Fred J. Hall
FS: Frances Skrine

GF: George Fitzgibbon
GFG: Gerald Fitzgerald
GH: George Harvey
GK: Grace King
GW: George Warner
GWC: George Washington Cable
HA: Helen Allen
HB: Hjalmar H. Boyesen
HC: Henry Clemens
HH: Henry Harper
HHR: Henry Huddleston Rogers
HL: Henry Lee
HMA: Henry M. Alden
HR: Henry Robinson
HW: Harriet Whitmore
IVL: Isabel V. Lyon
JB: John Brown
JBP: James B. Pond
JC: Jean Clemens
JCH: Joel Chandler Harris
JGB: James Gordon Bennett
JH: John M. Hay
JHT: Joseph H. Twichell
JL: Julia O. Langdon
JLC: Jane Lampton Clemens
JMC: John Marshall Clemens
JR: James Redpath
JRC: James Ross Clemens
JRO: James R. Osgood
JRY: James Russell Young
JTG: Joseph T. Goodman
JWP: James W. Paige
KIH: Katherine I. Harrison
KJG: Karl and Josephine Gerhardt
LB: Louisa Brownell
LH: Laurence Hutton
MAC: John Y. MacAlister
MB: Margaret Blackmur
MC: Mary E. [Mollie] Clemens
MDC: Moncure D. Conway
MLB: Margaret L. Bowes
MMF: Mary Mason Fairbanks
MP: Muriel Pears
MR: Mary Rogers

NB: Nancy Brush
OC: Orion Clemens
OLC: Olivia Langdon Clemens
OLL: Olivia Lewis Langdon (Mrs. Jervis L.)
PB: Poultney Bigelow
PCM: Pamela Clemens Moffett
RIH: R. I. Holcombe
RUJ: Robert Underwood Johnson
RWA: Ralph W. Ashcroft
RWG: Richard Watson Gilder
SB: Sylvester Baxter
SC: Susy Clemens
SLC: Susan Langdon Crane (Mrs. Theodore Crane)

SM: Samuel E. Moffett
SW: Susan Warner
TBA: Thomas Bailey Aldrich
TC: Theodore Crane
TSB: Thomas S. Barbour
USG: Ulysses S. Grant
WB: William Bowen
WC: Mrs. William R. Coe
WDH: William Dean Howells
WFG: William F. Gill
WWB: William Wilberforce Baldwin
WM: Wayne MacVeagh
WR: Whitelaw Reid
WW: William Winter

INTRODUCTION

p. 2. "When I was born": SP 393.
p. 4. "Whenever": MT/KLG, May 1, 1883.

CHAPTER 1

The facts of Clemens' family background and his early years are established in a variety of disparate sources, among the most prominent of which are *Mark Twain's Letters*, vol. 1, 1853–1866 (1988) and vol. 5 (1997) (the References section of each volume provides full bibliographical information for the notes, which are the most reliable sources of factual information about Twain's life); Dixon Wecter, *Sam Clemens of Hannibal* (1952); Samuel Charles Webster, *Mark Twain, Business Man* (1946); Minnie M. Brashear, *Mark Twain, Son of Missouri* (1934); *Mark Twain's Autobiography* (1924); Albert Bigelow Paine, *Mark Twain: A Biography* (1912); and *Mark Twain's Own Autobiography* (1906–1907), edited by Michael J. Kiskis (1990). Three other sources warrant mentioning: Twain's published and unpublished letters over his lifetime, often but not always unreliable about dates; a large number of specialized articles, which I cite only when I quote but which are listed in *Mark Twain's Letters*; and a series of investigations by Edgar Marquess Branch of Clemens' career as a steamboat pilot, which form the basis of Appendix B of *Mark Twain's Letters*, vol. 1, and which provide additional facts in two later publications, *Men Call Me Lucky: Mark Twain and the "'Pennsylvania'"* (1995) and "Bixby vs. Carroll, New Light on Sam Clemens's Early River Career," *Mark Twain Journal* 30: 2 (Fall 1992), 2–22.

p. 6. "My mother knew": MTA1, 90–91.
p. 9. "less than": MTA1, 3.
p. 11. "A lady came in": DW, 44.

p. 13. "bilious fever": *DW*, 51.

p. 14. "the substance": *MTB*, 9–10.

p. 15. "hopeless expression": *DW*, 77.

p. 15. "Stern, unsmiling": *DW*, 67; *HFTS*, 104.

p. 16. "My own knowledge": MT/RIH, September 4, 1883.

p. 16. "every old": *MTA*1, 106–8.

p. 16. "my mother used": *SP*, 386.

p. 16. "they left me": *SP*, 387.

p. 17. "I asked my mother": *MTA*1, 106–8.

p. 17. "to make them": *MTA*1, 275–82.

p. 18. "if he had ever": *ISD*, 2.

p. 18. "meditating": *ISD*, 2.

p. 18. "Being loaded": *LM*, 54.

p. 19. "just at bedtime": *MTA*2, 174–76.

p. 19. "plunged in": *LM*, 54; *MTA*, 179–86.

p. 20. "For a time": *MTA*2, 174–76.

p. 20. "They were all": *MTA*1, 219–21.

p. 20. "In my schoolboy days": *MTA*1, 99–102.

p. 21. "he had the sheriff": RIH/MT, August 29, 1883; *DW*, 72–73.

p. 21. "Kind-hearted": *MTA*1, 123–25.

p. 21. "The 'nigger trader' ": *MTA*1, 123–25.

p. 21. "a dozen": *MTA*1, 123–25.

p. 22. "There were grades": *MTA*1, 199–223.

p. 22. "mild domestic slavery": *MTA*1, 124–125.

p. 22. "lump of iron-ore": *FQ*, 38.

p. 23. "for impudence": *FQ*, 38.

p. 23. "harmless slave boy": *FQ*, 38.

p. 23. "singing, whistling": *MTA*1, 99–102.

p. 23. "It was on": *MTA*1, 99–102.

p. 23. "In the little": *MTA*1, 99–102.

p. 24. "whose head was": *MTA*1, 99–102.

p. 24. "staged him in books": *MTA*1, 99–102.

p. 24. "I can see": *MTA*1, 109–15.

p. 24. "the turn to the left": *MTA*1, 109–15.

p. 24. "how very dark": *MTA*1, 109–15.

p. 25. "the wild blackberries": *MTA*1, 109–15.

p. 25. "through the black": *MTA*1, 109–15.

p. 26. "ignorant, unwashed": *MTA*2, 174–76.

p. 26. "the annual procession": *LM*, 3.

p. 26. "also had a small": *MTA*2, 99–102.

p. 27. "had gathered the glory": *MTA*2, 99–102.

p. 27. "We were all": *MTA*1, 179–86.

p. 28. "I was glad": *MTE*, 107–10.

p. 28. "In all my life": *MTE*, 107–10.

p. 28. "ceased to be": *MTE*, 107–10.

p. 29. "An old farmer": *SP*, 362.

p. 29. "eighteen or twenty": *MTA*1, 179–86.

p. 29. "It took me awhile": *MTA*2, 212–19.

p. 29. "There was not": *SP*, 433.

p. 29. "Mary Miller": *MTA*2, 212–19.

p. 30. "Inspired by something": *MTE*, 234.

p. 31. "the age at which": *MTE*, 118–30.

p. 31. "a long, dusky": *IA*, 18.

p. 32. "That man had been": *IA*, 18.

p. 32. "Do you believe": *DW*, 115–19.

p. 32. "In a burst": *DW*, 115–19.

p. 33. "Even the *Democratic*": *DW*, 115–19.

p. 33. "My father died": MT/CC, March 24 and 25, 1910.

p. 33. "exceedingly straightened": *ISD*, 6.

p. 33. "died a natural death": *LM*, 554–59.

p. 34. "You will doubtless": *MTL*1, 3.

CHAPTER 2

p. 35. "forest of masts": *L*1, 10.

p. 36. "the printers have": *L*1, 14.

p. 37. "1 large Bible": Appraisal, May 21, 1847, of the personal property left by JMC at his death. Marion County, Missouri, Probate Court File No. 358, Palmyra, Missouri.

p. 37. "Like Aunt Becky": *ISD*, 13.

p. 37. "the oratory was": *SP*, 432.

p. 38. "desired earnestly": *SP*, 432.

p. 39. "There was an old horse": *MT-Bus*, 39.

p. 39. "it burst upon": *MTE*, 111–15.

p. 39. "out of mischief": "The Turning Point of My Life" (1910).

p. 40. "always failed": *MTA*1, 275–82.

p. 40. "had attained to": *MTA*1, 275–82.

p. 40. "promoted from": *MTA*1, 275–82.

p. 40. "One day when": *MTA*2, 93–95.

p. 41. "I had one comfort": *MTA*2, 283–85.

p. 41. "carry off nearly half": *MTB*, 15.

p. 41. "I think": *MTB*, 15–16.

p. 41. "reduced the subscription": *MTA*2, 285–86.

p. 41. "The office rent": *MTA*2, 285–86.

p. 42. "If he were there": *SP*, 200.

p. 42. "a barbecue": *SP*, 201.

p. 42. "and if he got through": *MTP*.

p. 42. "full of blessed egotism": *SP*, 202.

p. 43. "Being of a *snaillish*": *ET&S*1, 62.

p. 43. "a formidable looking": *ET&S*1, 65.

p. 44. "in print was": *MTB*, 90.

p. 44. "wrote East": *MTE*, 235–36.

p. 45. "An Apprentice to": *L*1, 2.

p. 45. "taken a liking": *L*1, 16.

p. 46. "The man's whole soul": *L*1, 16.

p. 46. "I reckon I had": *L*1, 4.

p. 46. "trundle-bed trash": *L*1, 10.

p. 47. "I shall ask favors": *L*1, 17.

p. 47. "I always thought": *L*1, 29.

p. 47. "plenty of work": *L*1, 3.

p. 47. "I was only 15": MT/APC, April 11, 1885.

p. 48. "Many and many": MT/APC, April 11, 1885.

p. 48. "switched off": *L*1, 23–24.

p. 48. "loaf the rest": *L*1, 19.

p. 48. "A chairman": *L*1, 31.

p. 48. "which was right": *L*1, 22.

p. 49. "When a stranger": *L*1, 30.

p. 49. "would have whittled": *L*1, 23.

p. 49. "so many foreigners": *L*1, 28.

p. 50. "would come to St. Louis": *L*1, 33.

p. 50. "I asked a lady": *L*1, 34.

p. 50. "out of place": *L*1, 40.

p. 50. "a fine looking": *L*1, 41.

p. 51 "what vast progress": *L*1, 42.

p. 51. "sitting upright": *MTA*1, 281–82.

p. 51. "went to bed": *MTA*1, 281–82.

p. 51. "[He] extracted": *LM*, 47.

p. 52. "a large, cheap place": MT/Frank E. Burrough, December 15, 1900.

p. 52. "the mob were in": *LM*, 51.

p. 52. "You have described": MT/J. H. Burrough, January 1, 1876.

p. 52. "brain full of dreams": *ET&S*1, 8.

p. 53. "an eloquent": *L*1, 48.

p. 53. "She will doubtless": *L*1, 51.

p. 53. "the shrieks of the poor horses": *L*1, 51.

p. 54. "old and faithful": Deed Record "O" of Monroe County, Missouri, 240; Mark Twain Shrine, Florida, Missouri.

p. 54. "Pilot of one": *L*1, 59.

p. 54. "five dollars a week": *MTB*, 104.

p. 56. "I believe it was": MT/Isabel S. Bohon, July 29, 1907.

p. 56. "Ah, Annie": *L1*, 64.

p. 56. "It is the burning": *N&J1*, 21–23.

p. 57. "Good-bye": *ET&S1*, 125.

p. 57. "a tropical empire": Henry Nash Smith, *Virgin Land: The American West As Symbol and Myth*. Cambridge: Harvard University Press, 1950, p. 154.

p. 57. "fifty or a hundred": *L1*, 66.

p. 57. "I believe that": *L1*, 66.

p. 58. "One day in the midwinter": *MTA2*, 288–89.

p. 59. "conversation [is] murdered": *ET&S1*, 386.

p. 59. "lay aside": MT/?, December 29, 1905.

p. 60. "the boys and girls": *LM*, 5.

p. 60. "I wished I could": *LM*, 5.

p. 60. "I sat speechless": *LM*, 5.

p. 61. "Here, take her": *LM*, 6.

CHAPTER 3

p. 62. "about to scrape": *LM*, 6.

p. 63. "I either came": *LM*, 6.

p. 63. "My boy": *LM*, 6.

p. 63. "learned to be": *LM*, 6.

p. 63. "went on the river: MT/PCM & JLC, October 25, 1861.

p. 63. "had decided": *MTBus*, 33.

p. 64. "She was": *LM*, 6.

p. 64. "fires were fiercely": *LM*, 6.

p. 64. "Your true pilot": *LM*, 6.

p. 64. "touched bottom": *LM*, 6.

p. 65. "When I get": *LM*, 8.

p. 65. "Well, taking you": *LM*, 8.

p. 65. "is an instinct": *LM*, 9.

p. 65. "The face of the water": *LM*, 9.

p. 65. "groups of Italians": *L1*, 72.

p. 66. "There's depth": *L1*, 73.

p. 66. "No Protestant child": *Letter from the Earth* (1909).

p. 67. "she was a very": MT/DB, March 20, 1880.

p. 67. "somehow always happened": *L1*, 112.

p. 67. "parted from L": *N&J3*, 153.

p. 68. "I seldom venture": *L1*, 77.

p. 68. "I cannot correspond": *L1*, 77.

p. 68. "I am in a bad way": *L1*, 94.

p. 69. "Here's a romance": MT/SLC, July 27, 1906.

p. 69. "fatherly": *LM*, 19.

p. 69. "dread in [his] heart": *LM*, 19.

p. 69. "malicious, snarling": *LM*, 19.

p. 69. "Instead of going": *LM*, 19.

p. 70. "He came up": *LM*, 19.

p. 70. "The pleasure of it": *LM*, 19.

p. 70. *"struck him"*: *LM*, 19.

p. 70. "You have been": *LM*, 19.

p. 71. "Had another pilot": *L1*, 81.

p. 71. "These good-bys": *MTA1*, 307–12.

p. 71. "before he went": *MTBus*, 37.

p. 72. "In case of disaster": *MTA1*, 307–12.

p. 72. "cleared away": Edgar Marquess Branch, *Men Call Me Lucky: Mark Twain and the* Pennsylvania. Ohio: Miami University, 1985, p. 11.

p. 73. "From one end": Branch, 24.

p. 73. "senseless": Branch, 31, 36.

p. 73. "We all felt": *MTBus*, 36.

p. 73. "floating bodies": Branch, 32.

p. 74. "Pray for me": *L1*, 82.

p. 74. "They had no way": *MTA1*, 307–12.

p. 74. "We were not sorry": *L1*, 84.

p. 74. "unpainted white coffin": *MTA1*, 307–12.

p. 74. "almost crazed": *MTBus*, 36–37.

p. 76. "What's the grandest thing": *L1*, 96–97.

p. 76. "The first electric": *MTE*, 9–10.

p. 77. "shouldered": MT/Jeff Thompson, March 28, 1874.

p. 77. "rather lucky than": *L*1, 97.

p. 77. "At that time": *SP*, 294.

p. 78. "I got personally": *LM*, 18.

p. 78. "in blissful ignorance": *L*1, 88.

p. 78. "in fine, fancy": *L*1, 88.

p. 79. "I think that I may say": *L*1, 87.

p. 79. "the New Orleans market": *L*1, 103.

p. 79. "We stored": *L*1, 103–4.

p. 80. "a gay party": *L*1, 118.

p. 80. "Ma was delighted": *L*1, 117.

p. 80. "*gasping* and straining": *L*1, 117.

p. 81. "whole future welfare": *L*1, 110.

p. 83. "It will be a great": *L*1, 114.

p. 84. "Uncle Sam": *MTBus*, 61–62.

p. 84. "He was obsessed": *MTBus*, 60.

p. 84. "He had come": *MTBus*, 60.

p. 85. "[We] mounted and rode": Absalom C. Grimes, "Campaigning with Mark Twain" in *Confederate Mail Runner*. 1912; reprint, New Haven, Conn.: Yale University Press, 1926.

p. 86. "desire to kill": "The Private History of a Campaign That Failed," 1885.

p. 86. "I thought he needed": *MTBus*, 39.

p. 87. "took along": *RI*, 2.

CHAPTER 4

p. 90. "an Indian child's . . . arrived at": *RI*, "Supplement A," 669–72.

p. 91. "through two outlets": *RI*, 12.

p. 92. "situated in a flat": *L*1, 133.

p. 92. "It never rains": *L*1, 139.

p. 92. "an honest man": *RI*, "Explanatory Notes," 574.

p. 93. "I have been": *L*1, 132.

p. 95. "infernally lazy": *L*1, 147.

p. 96. "If nothing goes wrong": *L*1, 156.

p. 96. "convinced Orion": *L*1, 159.

p. 96. "old St. Louis chums": *L*1, 166.

p. 97. "in such a way": *L*1, 167.

p. 97. "ground, anywhere": *L*1, 189.

p. 97. "As far as I can see": *L*1, 192.

p. 98. "Keep this entirely": *L*1, 193.

p. 98. "I shall never look": *L*1, 195.

p. 98. "Two years' ": *L*1, 205.

p. 98. "I have got": *L*1, 205.

p. 98. "I have struck": *L*1, 207.

p. 99. "a large, strong man": *L*1, 225.

p. 99. "within ten days": *RI*, 40–41.

p. 99. "as long, now": *L*1, 221.

p. 99. "I never have *once*": *L*1, 236.

p. 100. "I have written:" *L*1, 231.

p. 100. "The company": *L*1, 252.

p. 101. "had heard": *RI*, 22.

p. 101. "We intended": *RI*, 22.

p. 101. "the Lake burst . . . homeless wanderers": *RI*, 22–23.

p. 106. "I feel very much": *ET&S*1, 194.

p. 107. "As I remember it": MT/Miss Cohen, July 18, 1899.

p. 107. " 'Mark Twain' ": MT/John A. McPherson, May 29, 1877.

p. 107. "No; the *nom de plume*": MT/John B. Downing, August 18, 1881.

p. 108. "there was a howl": William Wright, "Salad Days of Mark Twain." *San Francisco Examiner*, March 19, 1893, 13–14.

p. 108. "being burned alive": Effie Mona Mack, *Mark Twain in Nevada*. New York: Charles Scribner's Sons, 1947, p. 267.

p. 108. "only doing": *L*1, 244.

p. 109. "It is misery": *L*1, 251.

p. 109. "Can't you let me": *L*1, 245.

p. 109. "I used to try": MT/OLC, December 19 and 20, 1868.

p. 109. "I don't mind": *L*1, 145.

p. 109. "Once, when I was": *SP*, 520–21.

p. 110. "If I had any": *L*1, 260.

p. 110. "I pick up a foot": *L*1, 252.

p. 111. "Mark Twain": *L*1, 252: *Daily Territorial Enterprise*, Sunday, May 3, 1863.

p. 111. "giving the Unreliable": *L*1, 247.

p. 112. "to see the sea-horses": *L*1, 255–56.

p. 112. "I do hate": *L*1, 255–56.

p. 113. "they all say": *ET&S*1, 312.

p. 113. "Mark said we might": *L*1, 310.

p. 113. "As soon as he opened": *L*4, 62–63.

p. 114. "that Irresistible": *L*1, 270.

p. 115. "his inimitable way": *SP*, 45.

p. 115. "the editorial slaves": *L*1, 269.

p. 115. "She is friendly": *L*1, 274.

p. 116. "causing her": *L*1, 278.

p. 116. "with a brass band": *L*1, 282.

p. 117. "I had rather die": *L*1, 282.

p. 117. "the Flour Sack": *L*1, 289.

p. 117. "Sammy Clemens": "A Misconception," *Virginia City Evening Bulletin*, April 2, 1864.

p. 117. "Whatever blame": *L*1, 288.

p. 118. "conveyed in every word": *L*1, 291.

p. 118. "Mr. Stephen Gillis": *L*1, 290.

p. 118. "undignified and abominably": *L*1, 293.

p. 118. "another challenge": *L*1, 296.

p. 119. "*If you can spare it*": *L*1, 299.

p. 119. "Having made my arrangements": *L*1, 301.

CHAPTER 5

p. 121. "no bother": *L*1, 308.

p. 122. "Heaven": *ET&S*2, 10.

p. 122. "& begin on": *L*1, 315.

p. 122. "I have got": *L*1, 304.

p. 122. "Working his right": *L*1, 305.

p. 122. "a reportorial assignment": *L*1, 305.

p. 123. "The entire audience": *SP*, 1–2.

p. 124. "By nine in the morning": *MTE*, 254–62.

p. 124. "with considerable warmth": *MTE*, 254–62.

p. 124. "I don't work": *L*1, 310.

p. 124. "I am taking": *L*1, 312.

p. 124. "at 10 in the morning": *L*1, 312.

p. 125. "His head": *SCH*, 29.

p. 126. "high-toned": *L*1, 315.

p. 126. "privately aside": *MTE*, 254–62.

p. 126. "on the world": *MTE*, 254–62.

p. 127. "avoiding": *RI*, 59.

p. 127. "It was somewhat": *SP*, 378.

p. 127. "I was once": MT/WB, March 20, 1882.

p. 128. "[The inspiration] which enabled me": *ET&S*2, 128.

p. 129. "What has become": *L*1, 313.

p. 130. "first class Literature": *N&J*1, 70.

p. 130. "always soberly": *MTE*, 360–62.

p. 130. "one of the most": *MTE*, 360–62.

p. 130. "One of my feet": *N&J*1, 74.

p. 131. "Coleman with": *N&J*1, 80.

p. 131. "If I can write": *L*1, 321.

p. 131. "over the mountains": *N&J*1, 81.

p. 131. "[Though] it makes my heart": MT/James Gillis, January 26, 1870.

p. 132. "There were no vacancies": *RI*, 62.

p. 132. "had a very comfortable time": *ET&S1*, 142.

p. 132. "I don't approve": *ET&S1*, 190.

p. 133. "Bear these rules": *ET&S1*, 195.

p. 133. "with a strapping": *ET&S1*, 238.

p. 134. "They did all": *ET&S1*, 248.

p. 134. "I have gone": *L1*, 324.

p. 135. "merry gentlemen": *L1*, 325.

p. 135. "a talent for": *L1*, 323.

p. 135. "Go forth": *L1*, 323.

p. 135. "a 'call' to": *L1*, 322.

p. 136. "brotherly partiality": *L1*, 323.

p. 136. "set all New York": *ET&S1*, 271.

p. 136. "After writing many": *L1*, 327.

p. 137. "I don't know": *L1*, 327.

p. 137. "Mark Twain is": *San Francisco Examiner*, February 10, 1866.

p. 137. "Verily, all is": *L1*, 327.

p. 137. "I will only": *L1*, 328.

p. 138. "a book": *L1*, 329.

p. 138. "will have to be written": *L1*, 329.

p. 138. "the subject will be": *Virginia City Union*, January 23, 1866.

p. 138. "being chained": *L1*, 326.

p. 138. "valuable now": *L1*, 326.

p. 138. "That worthless brother": *N&J1*, 112.

p. 139. "because there would": *L1*, 329–30.

p. 139. "letters of introduction": *L1*, 333.

p. 139. "If I come back": *L1*, 333.

p. 140. "like a couple": *N&J1*, 92.

p. 140. "something like mumps": *N&J1*, 189.

p. 141. "twenty-two passengers": *Frear*, 263.

p. 141. "Take that water": *Frear*, 264.

p. 141. "shamed the pale heavens": *N&J1*, 193.

p. 142. "how firm a hold": *N&J1*, 190.

p. 142. "This King has never: *N&J1*, 151.

p. 142. "I am now": *Frear*, p. 282.

p. 142. "It is a matter of": *Frear*, 271.

p. 143. "alone about": *Frear*, 276.

p. 143. "hurry and bustle": *Frear*, 277.

p. 143. "Tom cats": *Frear*, 276–77.

p. 143. "If I were not": *Frear*, 279.

p. 144. "All small villages": *N&J1*, 133.

p. 144. "Beloved by all": *N&J1*, 199.

p. 144. "Kanakas will": *N&J1*, 228.

p. 144. "The king": *Frear*, 289.

p. 145. "More missionaries": *N&J1*, 233.

p. 145. "no care-worn": *N&J1*, 200.

p. 146. "a hollow human": *Frear*, "A Strange Dream," 253–55.

p. 146. "I never spent": *Frear*, 322.

p. 146. "two pretty": *L1*, 337.

p. 146. "Sam liked to ride": *Frear*, 57.

p. 147. "I wish you": *L1*, 339.

p. 147. "opening the old sore": *L1*, 341.

p. 147. "It is Orion's duty": *L1*, 341.

p. 148. "half a dozen": *Frear*, 319–21.

p. 148. "loved and cherished": *N&J1*, 150.

p. 148. "baffling winds": *N&J1*, 227.

p. 148. "small blame": *Frear*, 378.

p. 149. "My name is": *Frear*, 75–76.

p. 149. "They didn't charge": *L1*, 343.

p. 150. "never tried": *L1*, 344.

p. 150. "California is proud": *L1*, 347.

p. 150. "that could beam": *MTA2*, 124.

p. 151. "won't suit those planters": *MT/WR*, January 3, 1873.

p. 151. "who had been": *Frear*, 334.

p. 151. "[Burlingame] hunted me up": *L1*, 347.

p. 152. "Avoid inferiors": *L1*, 346.

p. 152. "I speak feelingly": *Frear*, 361.

p. 152. "kept half a dozen": *N&J*1, 129.

p. 152. "more immoral": *N&J*1, 120.

p. 153. "the midst of": *Frear*, 409.

p. 153. "with a great": *N&J*1, 133.

p. 153. "a devilish saddle-boil": *N&J*1, 132.

p. 153. "Horrible": *N&J*1, 174.

p. 154. "We are abreast": *N&J*1, 134.

p. 154. "the first *twilight*": *N&J*1, 135.

p. 154. "fully as level": *N&J*1, 137.

p. 154. "Pacing the deck": MT/OLC, December 19 and 20, 1868.

p. 154. "We see *nothing*": *N&J*1, 137.

p. 154. "Eloquence Simplicity": *N&J*1, 143.

p. 154. "But of the 15": MT/OLC, December 19 and 20, 1868.

p. 155. "No alien land": *SP*, 246.

p. 155. "Marry be d——d": *L*1, 359.

p. 155. "Every rag:" *N&J*1, 162.

p. 156. *"side by side"*: *N&J*1, 163.

p. 156. "Home again": *N&J*1, 163.

CHAPTER 6

p. 157. " 'Mark Twain' ": *San Francisco American Flag*, August 14, 1866.

p. 158. "presented a bill": *L*1, 355.

p. 158. "I have got a spirit": *L*2, 58.

p. 159. "naturally lazy": *L*1, 357.

p. 159. "the best reporter": *L*1, 361.

p. 159. "You bet your life": *L*1, 358.

p. 159. "There seems to be": *Californian*, August 25, 1866.

p. 160. "exquisite appreciation": *N&J*1, 176.

p. 160. "I am utterly": *L*1, 367.

p. 160. "I write their": *ET&S*2, 150.

p. 162. "DOORS OPEN": *MTA*1, 242–43.

p. 163. "Mark Twain in Trouble": *Californian*, September 29, 1866.

p. 163. "The house was gloomy": *RI*, 78.

p. 164. "They have the consolation": *Oakland News*, October 10, 1866.

p. 164. "the Western Character": *San Francisco in 1866 by Bret Harte, Being Letters to the Springfield Republican*. Edited by George R. Stewart and Edwin S. Fussell. 1951, p. 83.

p. 165. "He said he had": *SP*, 606.

p. 165. "a natural pride": *L*1, 364.

p. 165. "the most valuable": *Virginia City Territorial Enterprise*, October 31, 1866.

p. 166. "Everybody says": *L*1, 369.

p. 167. "Use the pruning knife": *San Jose Evening Patriot*, November 22, 1866.

p. 167. "the old city": *SP*, 17.

p. 167. "leaving more friends": *L*1, 373.

p. 167. "A man's boots": *N&J*1, 245.

p. 167. "If anybody can": *N&J*1, 246.

p. 168. "A great burley": *MTE*, 244.

p. 168. "He believed that": *MTE*, 245.

p. 168. "got off some": *Travels*, 19.

p. 169. "But above all": *N&J*1, 251.

p. 169. "rather travel": *N&J*1, 253.

p. 170. "Such liquid, languishing eyes": *Travels*, 41.

p. 170. "hot corn, carved cups": *N&J*1, 259–61.

p. 170. "The dizzy heights": *N&J*1, 268.

p. 171. "& was shoved": *N&J*1, 273.

p. 171. "Verily, the ship": *N&J*1, 277.

p. 171. "to promise not": *Travels*, 67.

p. 171. "This Key West *looks*": *N&J*1, 280.

p. 172. "they put me in": *N&J*1, 286.

p. 172. "Time presses me": *L*2, 10.

p. 173. "a few days after": *San Francisco Evening Bulletin*, February 1867.

p. 173. "the most liberal": *Travels*, 110.

p. 174. "The scenery": *Travels*, 85.
p. 174. "She did her work": *Travels*, 106.
p. 174. "Webster's Unabridged": *Travels*, 99.
p. 175. "earlier than any": *Travels*, 92–94.
p. 176. "Send me $1,200": *L2*, 17.
p. 176. "We doubt if any": *New York Times*, January 29, 1867.
p. 178. "a clergyman of some": *Travels*, 114.
p. 178. "You don't look": *L2*, 16.
p. 178. "No veto": *L2*, 18.
p. 179. "Will you allow me": *New York Evening Post*, March 9, 1867.
p. 179. "Mark Twain, of literary": *New York Dispatch*, January 6, 1867.
p. 180. "began to swell": *MTE*, 143–45.
p. 180. "Son of a Bitch": *L2*, 30.
p. 180. "Come & engineer": *L2*, 8.
p. 181. "the Californians in town": *L2*, 10.
p. 181. "snap up a joke": *Travels*, 136.
p. 181. "busy visiting": *Travels*, 131.
p. 182. "I could write": *Travels*, 134–35.
p. 182. "on those old-fashioned": *Travels*, 143–47.
p. 182. "Mark Twain that is now": *Keokuk Gate City*, April 5, 1867.
p. 182. "You shall never know": *L2*, 354.
p. 183. "damnable errors": *L2*, 39.
p. 183. "Beneath the surface": *CR*, 29, 25.
p. 183. "I hate both": MT/Mr. Buell, December 29, 1905.
p. 183. "This fidgetty": *Travels*, 261.
p. 183. "what notabilities": *L2*, 23.
p. 184. "Frank, I want to": *L2*, 34.
p. 184. "With all this": *L2*, 38.
p. 184. "from everybody except": MT/FFU, May 27, 1897.

p. 185. "I was looking for": *MTBus*, 92–93.
p. 185. "1. Horace Greeley": Program: Cooper Institute/The Sandwich Islands, May 6, 1867.
p. 186. "the government has": *New York Evening Post*, May 17, 1867.
p. 186. "one magazine article": *L2*, 45.
p. 187. "a solemn, unsmiling": *Travels*, 276.
p. 187. "I am wild": *L2*, 49–50.
p. 187. "An accusing conscience": *L2*, 57–58.
p. 188. "preached from": *N&J2*, 332.
p. 188. "all such moneys": *L2*, 53, 57.
p. 188. "I say good bye": *L2*, 58.

p. 189. "I am going": *L2*, 54.
p. 190. "I am *fixed*": *L2*, 50.
p. 190. "I hope they will": *L2*, 63.
p. 191. "and all eyes": *L2*, 66.
p. 191. "ruling spirit": *N&J1*, 336.
p. 192. "Is Captain Duncan": *N&J1*, 340–41.
p. 193. "Madame, these attentions": *N&J1*, 348.
p. 193. "a deep, splendid": *N&J1*, 349.
p. 193. "a lordly ship": *N&J1*, 350.
p. 193. "I would not": *L2*, 68.
p. 194. "Tangier Jew": *N&J1*, 368.
p. 194. "After all this": *N&J1*, 367–68.
p. 196. "There is no element": *TIA*, 40.
p. 197. "sat in a great": *L2*, 74.
p. 197. "purification, suffocation": *TIA*, 75.
p. 197. "the great uncultivated": *TIA*, 57.
p. 197. "I was not able": *SP*, 444.
p. 200. "blue theatrical fires": *TIA*, 93.

p. 201. "under the towering massive": *N&J*1, 390.

p. 201. "by moonlight!": *N&J*1, 391.

p. 201. "an eternal circus": *TIA*, 113.

p. 202. "a French gold piece": *TA*2: 18.

p. 202. "We are a handful": *L*2, 85.

p. 202. "Writing addresses": *N&J*1, 407.

p. 203. "impossible Russian dance": *TIA*, 166–67; *N&J*1, 422.

p. 203. "kindness in affording": *L*2, 86.

p. 204. "Apollo and Diana": *N&J*2, 415.

p. 204. "noble ruins": *N&J*1, 415.

p. 205. "The inhuman tyranny": *TIA*, 186.

p. 205. "then south": *L*2, 93.

p. 206. "looked like she": *IA*, 42.

p. 206. "Got enough of": *N&J*1, 419.

p. 206. "A Syrian village": *TIA*, 189.

p. 206. "I can go as far": *N&J*1, 421, 482.

p. 206. "splendid stars": *N&J*1, 424.

p. 207. "The people of this region": *N&J*1, 424–25.

p. 207. "like any other savages": *N&J*1, 425.

p. 207. "rocks—rocks": *N&J*1, 432.

p. 207. "Thought we *never*": *N&J*1, 432.

p. 208. "Mrs. Jane Clemens": *L*2, 95.

p. 208. "took a horse in": *N&J*1, 438.

p. 208. "No second Advent": *N&J*1, 438.

p. 209. "Mrs. Fairbanks thinks": *L*2, 110.

p. 209. "The country is": *L*2, 99.

p. 210. "This pleasure party": *L*2, 101.

p. 211. "the idea of appearing": *L*2, 128.

p. 211. "funeral without": *TIA*, 319.

p. 211. "print the savagest": *L*2, 122–23.

p. 211. "I have some hope": *L*2, 108.

p. 212. "It was scarcely": *New York Herald*, November 21, 1867.

p. 212. "The Jumping Frog book": *MTE*, 148.

p. 213. "I was seated": *L*2, 110.

p. 213. "All I need": William M. Stewart. *Reminiscences*. Edited by George Rothwell Brown. New York: Neal Publishing Company, 1908, pp. 222.

p. 214. "full swing, & abuse": *L*2, 160.

p. 214. "Although we didn't": *MTA*1, 323–24; *SP*, 601.

p. 215. "He never got": *TA*, 26.

p. 215. "the most self-possessed": *TA*, 26.

p. 215. "I am embarrassed": *N&J*1, 491; *MTA*1, 13.

p. 215. "& particularly": *L*2, 119.

p. 216. "Their house is": *L*2, 124.

p. 216. "I am already": *L*2, 136.

p. 217. "Charley Langdon's sister": *L*2, 144.

CHAPTER 8

p. 218. "I want a good wife": *L*2, 133–34.

p. 219. "But I had my mind": *L*2, 160.

p. 219. "gradually getting": *L*2, 161.

p. 219. " 'In matters of business' ": *L*2, 160.

p. 220. "had a very gay time": *L*2, 144–45.

p. 220. "Twain would cut": *L*2, 160.

p. 220. "for a Quaker City book": *L*2, 160.

p. 221. "Puritans are": *L*2, 161.

p. 221. "I have to smoke": *San Francisco Alta California*, March 1, 1868.

p. 221. "I desire to have": *L*2, 166.

p. 222. "I am bound": *L*2, 188–89.

p. 222. "I don't care": *L*2, 188–89.
p. 222. "*could* make": *L*2, 167.
p. 222. "If you can't recollect": *L*2, 184.
p. 223. "was like a steam engine": *L*2, 194.
p. 223. "move again": *L*2, 195.
p. 223. "To be *busy*": *L*2, 197–98.
p. 223. "I hope you *have*": *L*2, 219.
p. 224. "superb contract": *L*2, 198.
p. 224. "If the *Alta*'s book": *L*2, 202.
p. 224. "an excuse to go": *L*2, 202.
p. 225. "I was now quite": *MTA*1, 244.
p. 225. "In my preface": *MTA*1, 244–45.
p. 226. "It is only the small-fry": *L*2, 221.
p. 226 "any of [his] good": *L*2, 209.
p. 226. "to preach in the States": *L*2, 216–17.
p. 226. "every night": *MTA*1, 245.
p. 226. "*homeward bound*": *L*2, 222.
p. 228. "already attained": *L*2, 234.
p. 228. "Train stops": *L*2, 242–43.
p. 229. "Mr. C. had": *L*2, 249.
p. 232. "in very delicate health": *SK*, 83–84.
p. 233. "bore her weight": *SK*, 92.
p. 233. "Livy breakfasted": *SK*, 92.
p. 233. "*for the first time*": *SK*, 92.
p. 234. "I do not regret": *L*2, 247–48.
p. 235. "I *must* not preach": *L*2, 264.
p. 235. "with the happy surprise": *L*2, 250–51.
p. 236. "I am desperately": *MTBus*, 101–2.
p. 236. "There is something": *L*2, 252.
p. 236. "I have been thinking": *L*2, 168.
p. 236. "I could not be blind": *L*2, 255.
p. 237. "just a *little*": *L*2, 256.
p. 237. "Charley [fell]": *L*2, 256–57.
p. 237. "Charley's head": *L*2, 258.

p. 237. "I am here": *L*2, 261.
p. 238. "[He] apologized to me": *L*2, 267.
p. 238. "You do not know": *L*2, 268.
p. 238. "Twichell is splendid": *L*2, 272.
p. 238. "I never put a joke": *L*3, 8.
p. 239. "Get your Browning": *L*2, 274.
p. 239. "Made a *splendid*": *L*2, 280.
p. 239. "simply lecturing": *L*2, 282.
p. 240. "something frightful": *L*3, 259.
p. 240. "The majority of them": *MTE*, 147.
p. 241. "It is a *readable* book": *L*3, 194.
p. 241. "Every one of [these delays]": *L*3, 285.
p. 241. "It is the very handsomest": *L*3, 292.
p. 241. "In the midst": *L*2, 319.
p. 241. "well-balanced": *L*3, 23.
p. 242. "She said she never": *L*3, 85.
p. 242. "She thinks about me": *L*3, 1.
p. 242. "Anybody who could": *L*3, 8.
p. 243. "I *do* wish": *L*2, 284.
p. 243. "of him as a *man*": *L*2, 285–86.
p. 243. "an almost entirely": *L*2, 360.
p. 243. "I never yet made": *L*2, 307.
p. 243. "They all": *L*2, 295.
p. 243. "Much of my conduct": *L*2, 357.
p. 244. "I would rather bury": *L*3, 57.
p. 244. "The friends that": *L*3, 320.
p. 244. "I can state": *L*3, 91.
p. 244. "I am upon": *L*2, 353, 359.
p. 244. "married away down below": *L*2, 301.
p. 245. "I do not wish": *L*3, 91.
p. 245. "much afflicted": *L*3, 91.
p. 245. "the gladdest that ever": *L*2, 370.
p. 245. "The fountains of": *L*4, 50.

CHAPTER 9

p. 247. "This system": *MTA*1, 150–51.

p. 248. "two-thirds of a night": *MTA*1, 150–51.

p. 249. "insultingly contemptuous": *L*3, 440.

p. 249. "I don't know": Mrs. James T. Fields, *Memories of a Hostess*. Edited by M. A. De Wolfe Howe. Boston, 1922, p. 111.

p. 250. "nothing like it since": *L*3, 440.

p. 250. "I like the circulars": *L*3, 292.

p. 250. "a malicious satisfaction": *L*3, 440.

p. 250. "little peevish spirit": *L*3, 289.

p. 251. "I am grateful": *L*3, 304.

p. 251. "I wrote & asked": *L*3, 311.

p. 251. "I have just purchased": *L*3, 297.

p. 252. "The Express proposition": *L*3, 299.

p. 252. "I shall have to work": *L*3, 298–99.

p. 252. "vastly improved": *L*3, 304.

p. 252. "Then we scribble": *L*3, 317.

p. 253. "Although he is": *L*3, 307.

p. 253. "We must board": *L*3, 325.

p. 253. "The book is selling": *L*3, 342.

p. 253. "the pupils did not": *L*3, 426.

p. 254. "what happened to": *L*4, 66.

p. 255. "would rather be": *L*4, 58.

p. 255. "I have at this moment": *L*4, 51.

p. 255. "asked me last night": *L*4, 54.

p. 256. "[She] has undergone the most astounding": *L*4, 67.

p. 256. "Every day I nerve": *L*4, 70–71.

p. 256. "I went & tricked": *L*4, 71.

p. 257. "it takes all": *L*4, 77.

p. 257. "I am a permanency": *L*4, 89.

p. 257. "out of the lecture": *L*4, 120; 94.

p. 258. "I suppose I am": *L*4, 171.

p. 258. "drew the contract": *MTE*, 152–53.

p. 258. "I never had": *L*4, 179.

p. 259. "Glad you have": *L*4, 282.

p. 259. "All my organs": *L*4, 108.

p. 260. "material enough": *L*4, 167.

p. 260. "utterly hopeless": *L*4, 180.

p. 260. "Father died": *L*4, 181.

p. 260. "This is a house of mourning": *L*4, 183.

p. 261. "All the impulses": *L*4, 182.

p. 261. "gave up the fight": MT/Arthur Reade, March 14, 1882.

p. 261. "Have you got": *L*4, 218, 223.

p. 262. "I have told Bliss": *L*4, 221.

p. 262. "The family have": *L*4, 177–78.

p. 262. "I do *resent*": *L*4, 229–30.

p. 263. "try to select": *L*4, 118.

p. 263. "I give her a narcotic": *L*4, 186.

p. 263. "getting along": *L*4, 189.

p. 263. "poor little": *L*4, 191.

p. 263. "During the last two": *MTE*, 249–52.

p. 263. "driveling along": *L*4, 210.

p. 263. "$600 to $700": *L*4, 213.

p. 264. "I have moved her": *L*4, 220–221.

p. 264. "Born to us": *L*4, 226.

p. 264. "I often feel": *L*4, 311.

p. 265. "Sometimes I have hope": *L*4, 329, 331.

p. 265. "2 nights rest": *L*4, 332.

p. 265. "very seriously ill": *L*4, 336.

p. 265. "In my belief": *MTE*, 249–52.

p. 266. "I believe": *L*4, 366.

p. 266. "wholly worthless": *L*4, 362.

p. 266. "I have come": *L*4, 337.

p. 267. "The man that will": *L*4, 338.

p. 267. "We . . . are going": *L*4, 347.

p. 268. "I find myself": *L*4, 379.

p. 268. "Don't fear for us": *L*4, 442.

p. 269. "I do not think": *L*4, 387.

p. 269. "[He] writes by my side": *L*4, 386.

p. 269. *"contemptuous"*: *L*4, 249.

p. 269. "I . . . hate to be accused": *L*4, 316.

p. 269. "a single moment": *L*4, 391.

p. 270. *"so* sick & tired": *L*4, 419.

p. 270. "I admire the book": *L*4, 443.

p. 270. "scarcely any hope": *L*4, 452.

p. 270. "We must take": *L*4, 459.

p. 271. "no notes in lecturing": *L*4, 408, 415.

p. 271. "Nasby prices": *L*4, 455.

p. 271. "I can't talk diamonds": *L*4, 467.

p. 272. *"absolute simplicity"*: *L*4, 471–72.

p. 272. "It is Saturday night": *L*4, 510.

p. 272. "Be bright & happy": *L*4, 530.

p. 272. "a vivid dream": *L*5, 17.

p. 272. "It suits *me*": *L*4, 478.

p. 272. "tip-top lecture": *L*4, 511, 514.

p. 273. "a crisp, bitter day": *L*4, 517.

p. 273. "I haven't a cent": *L*5, 36.

p. 273. "I would like": OLC/OLL, January 19, 1872.

p. 273. "his teeth [had not]": *L*5, 79.

p. 274. "lukewarmness toward God": *L*4, 510.

p. 274. "and sputtering out": *L*4, 485.

p. 275. "the most detestable": *L*5, 43.

p. 276. "deserted stream": *L*5, 15.

p. 277. *"act* [was] indefensible": *L*5, 55.

p. 277. "I am glad": *L*5, 65.

p. 278. "change entirely": *L*4, 510.

p. 279. "born . . . to the wife": *L*5,59.

p. 279. "The new baby": *L*5, 86.

p. 279. "& the suffering": *L*5, 86.

p. 279. "I soon dropped": *L*5, 99.

p. 279. "the little Clemens boy": *L*5, 98.

p. 279. "He kept thinking": *L*5, 98.

p. 279. "Oh, how sweet": *L*5, 98.

p. 280. "in the same room": *L*5, 100.

p. 281. "a splendid night": *L*5, 183.

p. 281. "in respectful silence": *L*5, 183–84.

p. 283. *"a self-pasting scrapbook"*: *L*5, 143.

p. 284. "our kindred blood": *L*5, 120.

p. 284. "leave for England": *L*5, 140.

p. 284. "felt fully convinced": *L*5, 101.

p. 284. "see as many": *L*5, 199.

p. 284. "But as Americans": *L*5, 200.

p. 284. "About one thing": *L*5, 196.

p. 285. "If you & Theodore": *L*5, 213.

p. 285. "I am revamping": *L*5, 208–9.

p. 285. "I hunted that": *L*5, 205.

p. 285. "nicely shaved": *L*5, 208.

p. 285. "I haven't done much": *L*5, 215.

p. 285. "that when affairs": *L*5, 221.

p. 286. "I would a good deal": *L*5, 213.

p. 287. "a filthy subject": *L*5, 236.

p. 288. "the loveliest building": *L*5, 270.

p. 289. "More than any other": *L*5, 249.

p. 290. "I hope you will stand": *L*5, 264.

p. 290. "jam into": *L*5, 346–48.

p. 291. "in the solitude": *L*5, 293.

p. 291. "mutual satisfaction": *L*5, 293.

p. 294. "I am leaving you": *GA*, 9.

p. 294. "pass from the auction-block": *GA*, 7.

p. 294. " 'Providence . . . has placed' ": *GA*, 20.

p. 295. "I can put this money": *GA*, 6.

p. 295. "Beautiful credit": *GA*, 26.

p. 296. "They have done": *MTMF*, 171.

p. 296. "[Warner] has worked up the fiction": *L5*, 343.

p. 297. "You give us a notice": *L5*, 346.

p. 297. "Now just see": *L5*, 348.

p. 297. "I was more than bilious": *L5*, 351.

p. 297. "[Reid] is a contemptible cur": *L5*, 367.

p. 298. "Some people think": *L5*, 324.

p. 299. "My wife": *L5*, 385.

p. 300. "sentences came slow": *L5*, 418.

p. 300. "the glory of English": *L5*, 419.

p. 300. "to be introduced": *L5*, 419.

p. 301. "better not see": *L5*, 430.

p. 301. "probably never see": *L5*, 432.

p. 301. "little odds & ends": *L5*, 435.

p. 302. "I have been here": *L5*, p. 435.

p. 302. "The financial panic": *L5*, 439.

p. 302. "You know if the firm": *L5*, 444.

p. 302. "a comparatively young man": *L5*, 453.

p. 303. "purest": *MTA1*, 140.

p. 304. "the time slides by": *L5*, 474.

p. 304. "everything the neighbors": *L5*, 479–80.

p. 304. "An autograph note": *L5*, 522.

p. 304. "Livy darling": *L5*, 496–97.

p. 304. "thick blue smoke": *L5*, 497.

p. 305. "If I'm not homesick": *L5*, 508.

p. 305. "I am *entirely* idle": *L6*, 23.

p. 305. "two months had made": *L6*, 178.

p. 305. "a quiet, murmurous": *L6*, 173.

p. 305. "so seriously as to scare": *L6*, 178.

p. 306. "It is such a comfort": MT/MMF, November 6–10, 1872.

p. 306. "In America": *L5*, 643–44.

p. 307. "names had become": *CR*, 140.

p. 307. "It is a distortion": *CR*, 133.

p. 307. "Warner felt the adverse criticism": IVL, in *MTP*. Notes, November 1933, on a copy of the agreement between Clemens, Warner, and the American Publishing Company.

p. 308. "not consent": *L5*, 368.

p. 309. *"I entirely re-wrote"*: *L6*, 267–68.

p. 309. "I don't think much": *L6*, 193.

p. 309. "We suppose": *L6*, 359.

p. 309. "a singularly emphatic": *L6*, 359.

p. 310. "quite as good": see *L6*, 319.

p. 310. "Warner's been in here": *L6*, 52.

p. 310. "I saw a good deal": *L6*, 86.

p. 312. "We sleep in Ma's": *L6*, 238.

p. 312. "I have been bullyragged": *L6*, 244–45.

p. 312. "We arrive by rail": *L6*, 280.

p. 312. "some such story": *MTHL1*, 33.

p. 313. "I find I can't": *L6*, 247, 261.

p. 313. "about old Mississippi days": *L6*, 262–63.

CHAPTER 11

p. 315. "You're doing the science": *MTHL1*, 61.

p. 315. "If we can ever": *L6*, 537.

p. 316. "The piloting material": *L6*, 356.

p. 316. "[He] went to his safe": *L6*, 380.

p. 316. "You have the two": *MTHL1*, 55.

p. 317. "a lagging journey": *L6*, 298, 359.

p. 317. "Friend Bliss": *L6*, 395.

p. 317. "a boy of twelve": *L6*, 504.

p. 317. "Yesterday I began a novel": *L6*, 430.

p. 318. "Don't waste it": *MTHL*1, 90.

p. 318. "it would be fatal": *L6*, 503.

p. 318. "it is *not* a boy's book": *L6*, 503.

p. 318. "which loses no charm": *CR*, p. 157.

p. 319. "perfectly superb notice": *L6*, 559.

p. 319. "You see, the thing": *L6*, 559.

p. 319. "was splendid": *MTHL*1, 121.

p. 319. "written & rewritten": *L6*, 378.

p. 319. "and they comb me": *MTHL*1, 122.

p. 319. "I have noticed": *L6*, 350.

p. 319. "Profanity is more": MT/OC, May 14, 1877.

p. 319. "I can see by": MT/WB, August 31, 1876.

p. 321. "quite say": *MTMF*, 207.

p. 322. "He examined my": MT/?, December 18, 1906.

p. 323. "I heard them": *L5*, 315–16.

p. 323. "The present era": MT/OC, March 27, 1875.

p. 324. "not going to cure": MT/OC, March 27, 1875.

p. 324. "a picture of": MT/Frank M. Etting, June 8, 1876.

p. 324. "St. Patrick": MT/Richard McCloud, March 16, 1876.

p. 324. "Get your book": *MTHL*1, 143.

p. 325. "nearly all the people": *SP*, 97.

p. 325. "one of the Republican": *MTE*, 287.

p. 326. "what is called": MT/OLC, January 2, 1874.

p. 326. "I never would": MT/PCM, July 23, 1875.

p. 327. "a sort of father": MT/BT, January 24, 1877.

p. 328. "I have a selfish": MT/Board of Directors, American Publishing Company, June 24, 1876.

p. 328. "This recent bust-up": MT/CWS, September 20, 1876.

p. 328. "We have got": *MTHL*1, 158.

p. 328. "But I have trained": *MTHL*1, 158.

p. 329. "Susie is so large": OLC/OLL, March 21, 1875.

p. 329. " 'This is my wedding' ": MT & OLC/OLL, February 2 and 4, 1877.

p. 329. "has her mother's": *L6*, 288.

p. 329. "I can't encourage": MT/JLC & PCM, April 25, 1875.

p. 331. "I think Harte": *MTHL*1, 162.

p. 331. "divide the swag": *MTHL*1, 157.

p. 332. "is to be": *MTHL*1, 157.

p. 332. "My plot is built": *MTHL*1, 157.

p. 332. "plotting out": *MTHL*1, 172.

p. 332. "study Chinese character": *SCH*, 127.

p. 332. "ineffable idiocy": *SCH*, 127.

p. 333. "[Tell Harte that] I have gone": MT/CEP, May 15, 1877.

p. 333. "If the play's": *MTHL*1, 188.

p. 333. "[Harte] will pay me": MT/OLC, July 27, 1877.

p. 333. "We are so desperately": OLC/MT, July 29, 1877.

p. 333. "It is very short": MT/OLC, July 27, 1877.

p. 333. "every time the audience": *MTHL*1, 193.

p. 334. "was received with great": MT/Francis Millet, August 7, 1877.

p. 334. "a most abject": *MTHL*1, 206.

p. 334. "It is full of": *MTHL*1, 192.

p. 334. "till his entire indebtedness": MT/CEP, August 3, 1877.

p. 334. "cordial enemies": MT/MC, August 6, 1877.

p. 334. "Wherever he goes": MT/WDH, June 21, 1877.

p. 334. "Never mind": MT/WDH, June 21, 1877.

p. 335. "he is poor": *SCH*, 137.

p. 335. "at last one of those": MT/JR, December 28, 1874.

p. 335. "The real health-giving": *N&J*2, 17.

p. 336. "they are a dull lot": MT/WDH, June 21, 1877.

p. 337. "I have always practiced": *MTE*, 207–8.

p. 337. "new, young, spry": *MTHL*1, 196–97.

p. 337. "Her horse is running": *MTHL*1, 196–97.

p. 338. "for one instant": *MTHL*1, 196–97.

p. 338. "seized the gray": *MTHL*1, 196–97.

p. 339. "Delicacy—a sad": *MTHL*1, 203.

p. 339. "jaded, melancholy": *SP*, 111.

p. 340. "My sense of": *MTHL*1, 212.

p. 340. "into which a man walks": *MTHL*1, 213.

p. 340. "I come before you": MT/Emerson, Longfellow, Holmes, December 27, 1877.

p. 340. "The pictures are gone": MT/CWS, March 20, 1878.

p. 341. "Mr Clemens grows": MT & OLC/OLL, February 2 and 4, 1877.

p. 341. "If I can make": MT/OC, December 19, 1877.

p. 341. "You must not": *MTHL*1, 216.

p. 342. "I never did meddle": MT/Dennis E. McCarthy, March 29, 1878.

p. 342. "That young man": *MTE*, 162–65.

p. 343. "a great convenience": MT/Rollin M. Daggett, January 24, 1878.

p. 343. "inexhaustible appetite": OLC/OLL, April 20, 1878.

p. 343. "What a paradise": *MTHL*1, 227.

p. 343. "For I am out of it": *MTHL*1, 227.

p. 344. "5 Fuss 8½": MT/BT, May 7, 1878.

p. 344. "night & day": MT/CDW, June 16, 1878.

p. 344. "She chatters away": OLC/CL, July 21, 1878.

p. 344. "Then, about 5": MT/CDW, June 16, 1878.

p. 345. "I bullyrag Joe": MT/CDW, August 1, 1878.

p. 345. "It is no sort": *MTLP*, 109.

p. 345. "Since Twichell has been": *MTLP*, 109.

p. 345. "announced as a walking": *MTLP*, 109.

p. 345. "When I was talking": MT/BT, December 14, 1878.

p. 346. "what a red rag": *N&J*2, 139.

p. 346. "sharply curtailed": *TA*, 31.

p. 346. "I can't tell": MT/BT, December 14, 1878.

p. 347. "My book is half": *MTHL*1, 246.

p. 347. "Yes, I'm still pegging": MT/FB, February 9, 1879.

p. 347. "I am a great": *MTHL*1, 215.

p. 348. "I *hate* travel": *MTHL*1, 248–49.

p. 348. "Fire, fire": *TA*, 10.

p. 349. "Anywhere is better": MT/General Lucius Fairchild, April 28, 1880.

CHAPTER 12

p. 351. "We were the first": *SP*, 108.

p. 351. "I was lucky": MT/DS, September 1879.

p. 351. "Out of the poverty": MT/Gentlemen [of the Battle-flag Day Committee]. *Hartford Courant*, September 8, 1879.

p. 351. "Personal contact": MT/P.D. Peltier, Esq., October 14, 1869.

p. 351. "strong enough": MT/JHT, October 2, 1879.

p. 352. "I have been knocking": MT/JHT, October 2, 1879.

p. 352. "a house going that": OLC/OLL, November 1, 1879.

p. 352. "I was up at 6 AM": *MTHL*1, 278.

p. 352. "When the head": *MTL*1, 367–68.

p. 353. "carried away": *MTHL*1, 279.

p. 353. "a bullet-shredded": *MTHL*1, 279.

p. 353. "stepped into view": *MTHL*1, 280.

p. 353. "We haven't all had": *SP*, 131–33.

p. 354. "I shook [Grant] up": *MTHL*1, 280.

p. 354. "till every . . . bone": *MTL*1, 372.

p. 354. "It was a memorable": MT/OC, November 14, 1879.

p. 355. "First Citizen": *SP*, 137–38.

p. 356. "invoked the loudest": *MTHL*1, 332.

p. 356. "I couldn't get General Grant": MT/EHH, February 19, 1881.

p. 356. "act just as if nothing": *MTHL*1, 282.

p. 357. "Pride protects a man": *SP*, 135.

p. 357. "been flinging sneers": *MTHL*1, 386.

p. 357. "day & night": *MTHL*1, 387.

p. 357. "almost daily": *MTHL*1, 387.

p. 358. "small mouse": *MTHL*1, 389.

p. 360. "My bitterness against:" *MTE*, 155.

p. 360. "I must speculate": *MTHL*1, 439.

p. 360. "I AM TRYING": MT/OC, December 9, 1874.

p. 361. "I write so much": MT/KJG, March 23, 1882.

p. 361. "Five hundred years": MT/DG, September 23, 1880.

p. 361. "I'm just about": MT/FF, November 22, 1879.

p. 362. "drew out of Dan": MT/FF, December 5, 1879.

p. 362. "a building": MT/PCM, March 16, 1881.

p. 363. "& then failed": *N&J*2, 392.

p. 363. "[Don't] submit picayune trades": MT/DS, January 26, 1881.

p. 363. "quite anxious that": *N&J*2, 395.

p. 363. "If the utility": MT/DS, March 16, 1881.

p. 364. "there was a fortune": MT/DS, March 31, 1881.

p. 364. "complete authority": *MTBus*, 152.

p. 364. "The day that Kaolatype": *MTB*, 160.

p. 365. "on the mere *prospect*": MT/PM, March 1, 1881.

p. 366. "I took $2,000": *MTA*1, 70.

p. 366. "Here was a machine": *MTA*1, 71.

p. 366. "to raise a capital": *MTA*1, 72.

p. 366. "to pay the preliminary": *MTBus*, 180.

p. 367. "the machine [is] now flawless": *MTBus*, 211.

p. 367. "the whole thing": *MTBus*, 308.

p. 367. "I'd rather have $250,000": *MTB*, 308.

p. 367. "the rising gust": MT/OLL, January 9, 1881.

p. 367. "We are curiously": MT/OLL, January 9, 1881.

p. 367. "If she had passed": *MTBus*, 150.

p. 367. "Time is moving": MT/OLC, November 27, 1879.

p. 368. "is thoroughly satisfactory": *MTHL*1, 319.

p. 368. "This is the first time": MT/Elizabeth Warner & SW, June 17, 1880.

p. 368. "Women must be": OLC/OLL, November 30, 1879.

p. 369. "What I have always": *MTL*1, 404.

p. 369. "I don't want to be": MTL1, 405

p. 369. "carpetless & dismantled": MT/KJG, October 9, 1881.

p. 369. "O *never* revamp": MT/EH, October 4, 1881.

p. 369. "A life of don't-care-a-damn": *MTHL*1, 389.

p. 370. "congregational singing": Edwin Pond Parker in the *Hartford Courant*, 1912; quoted in Leah H. Strong, *Joseph Hopkins Twichell*. Athens: University of Georgia Press, 1966, pp.96–97.

p. 370. "There was no time": Edwin Pond Parker in the *Hartford Courant*, 1912; quoted in Strong, pp. 96–97.

p. 370. "I had asked him": *MMT*, 31–32.

p. 370. "It isn't healthy": MT/HKG, August 31, 1881.

p. 371. "I hope you won't": *MTHL*1, 315.

p. 372. "interrupting assistance": MT/JHT, July 20, 1883.

p. 372. "contrived a way": MT/JHT, July 20, 1883.

p. 373. "I might have known": *MTHL*1, 439.

p. 373. "to see whether": MT/CW, August 3, 1883.

p. 373. "It is beautifully done": MT/OC, August 29, 1883.

p. 373. "all the reigns": MT/CW, September 22, 1883.

p. 373. "I thought that": MT/OC, March 5, 1889.

p. 373. "I don't see how": MT/HB, April 23, 1880.

p. 373. "[Howells] has read it": MT/EP, December 24, 1880.

p. 374. "Well, I'll put my name": MT/EP, December 24, 1880.

p. 374. "It isn't good journalism": Quoted in Louis Budd, *Our Mark Twain*. Philadelphia: University of Pennsylvania, 1983, p. 104.

p. 374. "Howells's notice": *MTLP*, 143.

p. 374. "of Mr. Clements's": *CR*, 203.

p. 374. "surprisingly complimentary": MT/AC, March 3, 1882.

p. 374. "which were the reverse": MT/AC, March 3, 1882.

p. 376. "I find myself": MT/HB, January 11, 1882.

p. 376. "some outlines": MT/JCH, June 1881.

p. 376. "Old Uncle Dan'l": *MTL*1, 403.

p. 376. "I would like": *MTLHP*, 158.

p. 377. "Howells is still": MT/GWC, July 17, 1881.

p. 377. "Osgood, remind me to": *MTLP*, 147.

p. 378. "In old days": *LM*, 42.

p. 378. "Next time I make": *MTHL*1, 287.

p. 379. "a magnificent scheme": *MMT*, 53.

p. 379. "the South's finest": *LM*, 44.

CHAPTER 13

p. 381. "a most serene": *LLMT*, 210.

p. 381. "emerge from boyhood": MT/DB, March 20, 1880.

p. 382. "call their names": MT/DB, March 20, 1880.

p. 382. "built yesterday": *N&J2*, 528.

p. 382. "ask about": *N&J2*, 456.

p. 382. "tell, now, in full, the events": *N&J2*, 454.

p. 383. "casks & barrels": *LM*, 41.

p. 383. "chief topic": *LM*, 45.

p. 384. "reduced to lying": MT/OLC, April 29, 1882.

p. 384. "constant stream": *N&J2*, 556.

p. 384. "up the breezy": *LM*, 48.

p. 384. "the big colored": *N&J2*, 546–47.

p. 385. "I must remember": MT/KJG, May 1, 1883.

p. 386. "They do not call": *N&J2*, 574.

p. 386. "Mary's Gone Wid": *N&J2*, 562–63.

p. 386. "At 5 PM got to": *N&J2*, 476.

p. 386. "now in heaven": *N&J2*, 478.

p. 386. "Alas! everything": *N&J2*, 479.

p. 387. "That world which I knew": MT/OLC, May 17, 1882.

p. 387. "delightful days": MT/OLC, May 17, 1882.

p. 387. "a wretchedly poor": MT/OLC, May 20, 1882.

p. 387. "they ate on deck": MT/OLC, May 20, 1882.

p. 388. "always read himself": *N&J2*, 486.

p. 389. "I am a border ruffian": *SP*, 163–64.

p. 389. "set a cheap expert": MT/JRO, June 11, 1882.

p. 390. "I would like him": MT/CW, July 16, 1882.

p. 391. "You are as good": MT/OC, January 22, 1883.

p. 391. "I solemnly swear": MT/OC, January 27, 1883.

p. 391. "I have never seen": OLC/SM, August 13, 1882.

p. 391. "Every body here": MT/JLC, October 9, 1882.

p. 391. "my brain . . . stuffed": MT/JHT, September 19, 1882.

p. 391. "I shall finish": MT/GWC, October 16, 1882.

p. 392. "The spur & burden": *MTHL*1, 417.

p. 392. "What I write": MT/EH, December 2, 1882.

p. 392. "is fallen away": MT/JRO, April 6, 1883.

p. 392. "We have a professional": MT/LH, April 22, 1883.

p. 393. "come right up": MT/GWC, June 4, 1883.

p. 393. "[She] is still a skeleton": MT/HR, July 11, 1883.

p. 394. "Why, it's like": *MTHL*1, 435; MT/JLC, OC, and MC, July 21, 1883.

p. 394. "I wrote 4000 words": *MTHL*1, 435.

p. 394. "I've wrought from": *MTHL*1, 438.

p. 394. "wonderful moonlight": OLC/HW, July 16, 1883.

p. 395. "I had written 50,000": MT/JRO, September 1, 1883.

p. 395. "pigeon hole or burn": *MTHL*1, 144.

p. 395. "give 'em away": MT/Hamlin Garland, July 28, 1883.

p. 395. "I've just finished": MT/AC, September 1, 1883.

p. 395. "full charge": *MTLP*, 158.

p. 395. "deep mourning": MT/JLC, August 20, 1883.

p. 396. "to make herself": MT/JLC, August 20, 1883.

p. 396. "I have never for a moment": *MTLP*, 164–65.

p. 397. "If we haven't 40,000": *MT-Bus*, 249.

p. 397. "If I were": *MTHL*1, 436.

p. 397. "I couldn't enter into": *MTHL*1, 96.

p. 398. "We shall yet write": *MTHL*1, 216.

p. 398. "Your refined people": *MTHL*1, 372.

p. 398. "every bit about Sellers": *MTHL*1, 446.

p. 398. "Go through our": *MTHL*1, 364.

p. 398. "I appreciate all you say": *MTHL*1, 363–64.

p. 399. "illustrate a but-little considered": *MTHL*2, 461.

p. 399. "a burlesque Frankenstein": *N&J*3, 49, 54, 56.

p. 400. "hills are long": MT/JHT, September 16, 1884.

p. 401. "wasted in ineffectual efforts": MT/JHT, September 16, 1884.

p. 401. "To see grown men": *MTHL*2, 501.

p. 402. "Four days hence": MT/EH, October 31, 1884.

p. 402. "Mamma made us": CC/MT, November 21, 1884.

p. 402. "This trip's my last": MT/C&W, November 5, 1884.

p. 402. "[Cable] is a marvelous": *MTHL*1, 419.

p. 403. "He's a bright": MT/EHH, February 27, 1884.

p. 404. "the audience must": MT/JBP, October 27 (?), 1884.

p. 404. "dapper sort": *N&J*2, 63.

p. 404. "Louder advertising": MT/JBP, November 15, 1884.

p. 404. "I never enjoyed you more": *MTHL*2, 513.

p. 404. "merely a starving": *MTHL*2, 539.

p. 405. "This trip's a great thing": MT/OLC, December 6, 1884.

p. 405. "He came into the": Arlin Turner, *Mark Twain & G. W. Cable: The Record of a Literary Friendship*. Lansing: Michigan State University Press, 1960, p. 62.

p. 405. "telling them not": *LLMT*, 231.

p. 406. "to get awry": OLC/MT, November 21, 1884.

p. 406. "littlenesses, like Napoleon": MT/OLC, January 7, 1885.

p. 406. "You will never": *MTHL*2, 520.

p. 406. "$550 to $600 a week": *N&J*3, 88.

p. 406. "is too divinely": *LLMT*, 239.

p. 406. "Mighty good clothes": *LLMT*, 225.

p. 407. "This visit to Hannibal": *LLMT*, 229.

p. 407. "Make a kind of": *N&J*3, 91.

p. 407. "A beautiful evening": *LLMT*, 229.

p. 407. " 'You are a man' ": *MTE*, 118–30.

p. 408. "My four-months platform": *MTHL*2, 520.

p. 409. "personal efforts": *N&J*3, 65.

p. 410. "I mean you shall": *N&J*3, 96.

p. 410. "The directors of": *St. Louis Post-Dispatch*, March 17, 1885.

p. 411. "full of spirit": *CR*, 275.

p. 411. "Mark Twain is having": *New Orleans Daily Picayune*, April 11, 1885.

p. 411. "It is pitched in": *Boston Herald*, February 1, 1885.

p. 411. "wearisome and monotonous": *CR*, 274.

p. 411. "It is possible": Booker T. Washington, *Nation*, June 11, 1910, 454.

p. 412. "He is failing": MT/AC, March 11, 1885.

p. 412. "closed up all": MT/EH, May 13, 1885.

p. 412. "Composition is": *MTBus*, 320.

p. 413. "The General is": MT/OLC, July 1, 1885.

p. 413. "Every step has been": MT/Editor of *Boston Herald*, July 6, 1885.

p. 413. "From now till": *MTHL*2, 539.

p. 413. "I am kept so": MT/unknown, September 23, 1885.

p. 413. "It was immensely amusing": *MTHL*2, 541.

p. 413. "totally free": *MTHL*2, 549.

p. 414. "with a delight": *MTHL*2, 545.

CHAPTER 14

p. 415. "[We] had a riotous time": MT/OC, November 28, 1885.

p. 416. "Livy & I love": MT/JHT, December 24, 1885.

p. 416. "the accumulated riches": MT/CS, August 20, 1886.

p. 417. "if a child": *PA*, 194.

p. 418. "papa and mamma": *PA*, 196–200.

p. 418. "Well, mamma, you know": *PA*, 76.

p. 419. "I have never": MT/unknown, November 30(?), 1885.

p. 419. "May you never be": MT/JCH, November 29, 1885.

p. 419. "It was the pleasantest": MT/My Dear Conspirators, November 29, 1885.

p. 419. "Papa uses very strong": *PA*, 100.

p. 419. "I prized my wife's": *PA*, 102–5.

p. 420. "thunder-stroke fell": *MTHL*2, 575.

p. 421. "We want to go": MT/KJG, May 4, 1884.

p. 421. "[Papa] is a very striking": *PA*, 83.

p. 421. "He glimmered at you": *MMT*, 29.

p. 422. "being a knight": *N&J*3, 78.

p. 422. "noble and simple eloquence": *N&J*3, 159.

p. 422. "He mourns": *N&J*3, 216.

p. 422. "a holiday book": *N&J*3, 216.

p. 423. "a vast amount": *N&J*3, 237.

p. 423. "You did well": *MTBus*, 364.

p. 423. "He ought to have": *MTBus*, 388.

p. 423. "sell a Choctaw Bible": *MTBus*, 377.

p. 424. "the Hartford man": *MTHL*2, 550.

p. 424. "Only two or three": *MTMF*, 257–58.

p. 424. "If I peg away": *MTBus*, 355.

p. 425. "to avoid the awful": MT/OC, June 2, 1886.

p. 425. "We expect to do": MT/OC, June 2, 1886.

p. 425. "four or five days": MT/FGW, July 12, 1886.

p. 425. "I burnt a hole": *MTL*1, 470–71.

p. 425. "I love you": MT/PCM, July 10 (?), 1886.

p. 425. "the pleasantest & completest": MT/FGW, July 12, 1886.

p. 426. "I won't allow": *MTBus*, 356.

p. 426. "It *is* a lunatic": *MTHL*2, 556.

p. 428. "nearly half done": MT/unknown, July 18, 1887.

p. 428. "How stunning are": *MTHL*, 595–96.

p. 428. "without rest or stop": MT/FGW, July 21, 1887.

p. 428. "splendid progress": MT/FGW, August 5, 1887.

p. 428. "I had a sort of half-way": MT/AC, September 17, 1888.

p. 428. "I had had the hope": MT/Thomas Edison, May 15, 1888.

p. 431. "also show the firm's indebtedness": *N&J3*, 286.

p. 431. "not be called": *N&J3*, 320, 322.

p. 431. "I woke up 6 weeks": *MTLHP*, 229.

p. 431. "My valuation": *MTBus*, 376.

p. 431. "We've got a safe full": *MTBus*, 378.

p. 432. "Don't make the mistake": MT/Belle C. Greene, January 17, 1887.

p. 432. "Curse all business": MT/FGW, August 17, 1887.

p. 432. "We did not know": *MTBus*, 385–86.

p. 432. "My duty to wife": *N&J3*, 375.

p. 432. "How long he has": *N&J3*, 374.

p. 433. "I have never hated": MT/OC, July 1, 1889.

p. 433. "[He] left this dying injunction": *N&J3*, 625.

p. 433. "There are no words": MT/Annie Moffett Webster, April 26, 1891.

p. 434. "sell the whole thing": *MTBus*, 308.

p. 434. "a net yearly profit": *N&J3*, 241.

p. 434. "Every expense connected": *N&J3*, 219.

p. 435. "Business sanity": *MTA1*, 76.

p. 435. "There could be no sense": *MTA1*, 76.

p. 435. "a most extraordinary compound": *MTA1*, 72.

p. 436. "If I had half": MT/CH, December 16, 1886.

p. 436. "One doesn't go": MT/William Smith, February 3–4, 1887.

p. 436. "There is a market": MT/FGW, August 14, 1887.

p. 436. "Happy New year!": MT/OLC, December 31, 1888.

p. 436. "At 12:20 this afternoon": *MTL2*, 506–7.

p. 437. "takes a livelihood away": *MTHL2*, 597.

p. 437. "doubtless the only": MT/Charles H. Taylor, March 2, 1889.

p. 437. "*finished*": *N&J* 3, 515.

p. 437. "There are two times": *N&J3*, 433.

p. 438. "I thought she was": MT/FGW, September 3, 1886.

p. 438. "I can have no stoppage": MT/FGW, August 1889.

p. 438. "I want to show": *MTHL2*, 615.

p. 438. "Papers are now": MT/JTG, November 29, 1889.

p. 439. "Jones standing": MT/JTG, November 19, 1889.

p. 439. "Paige & I always": *MTA1*, 78.

p. 439. "Youth . . . I want": OLC/MT, May 21, 1890.

p. 439. "Now here is": MT/JTG, June 22, 1890.

p. 440. "sit by the machine": MT/JTG, June 22, 1890.

p. 440. "I am resolved": MT/OC & MC, August 21, 1890.

p. 440. "Take $75,000 worth": MT/John P. Jones, February 13, 1891.

p. 440. "Mr Clemens . . . desires": MT/JWP, January 3, 1891.

p. 440. "I've forsook the machine": MT/OC, February 25, 1891.

p. 441. "I wish there was": OLC/OLL, October 26, 1890.

p. 441. "I want to thank you too": OLC/OLL, November 8, 1890.

p. 442. "He is known": *PA*, 206.

p. 443. "Mamma and I": *PA*, 187.

p. 443. "he didn't expect": MT/OC, February 25, 1891.

p. 443. "wasted fortunes": MT/OC, February 25, 1891.

p. 443. "completed the first": MT/OC, February 25, 1891.

p. 443. "A book by": *CR*, 329.

p. 444. "I'd rather take": *MTHL*2, 486.

p. 444. "one of the prettiest": MT/JBP, March 14, 1885.

p. 444. "*That* would be nice": MT/EH, December 17, 1886.

p. 444. "I've done up": MT/EH, December 26, 1886.

p. 444. "A few days ago": *N&J*3, 542–45; Paul Fatout, "Mark Twain, Litigant." *American Literature*, March 1959, 30–45.

p. 445. "House seems to have": *N&J*3, 454.

p. 445. "I remember": MT/EH, February 26, 1889.

p. 445. "I must live up": MT/EH, March 19, 1889.

p. 446. "I would naturally have": MT/EH, March 19, 1889.

p. 446. "I *must* have": MT/Daniel Whitford, October 16, 1890.

p. 446. "to stop the present": *N&J*3, 543.

p. 446. "one in the hands": MT/JBP, October 17, 1890.

p. 446. "MARK TWAIN": *New York Times*, January 27, 1890.

p. 447. "Any mention of the stage": *MTHL*2, 362.

p. 447. "Nine months": OLC/GK, September 10, 1890.

p. 448. "Please send me": MT/Rogers Peet Clothing Store, August 15, 1890.

p. 449. "All the poetry": MT/Joseph B. Gilder, May 16, 1886.

p. 449. "I used to explain": MT/Cornelia W. Foote, December 2, 1887.

p. 449. "Shakespeare; and Browning": MT/Rev. C. D. Crane, January 20, 1887.

p. 449. "Mama revolts": SC/EH; September 7, 1887.

p. 449. "a brief little": MT/SB, December 3, 1889.

p. 449. "It is by long odds": MT/JTG, October 4, 1890.

p. 449. "Our train was drifting": MT/PCM, October 12, 1890.

p. 451. "She knew my face": *SP*, 497.

p. 451. "nearest and dearest": *SP*, 497.

p. 451. "Livy Darling": MT/OLC, November 26–27, 1890.

p. 451. "savage attack": MT/RLS, April 15, 1888.

p. 452. "We are all growing": MT/PCM, July 1, 1889.

p. 452. "mental tortures": MT/WW, November 5, 1890.

p. 452. "an infinite pity": MT/OC, January 22, 1888.

p. 452. "admiration & gratitude": MT/OC & MC, August 21, 1890.

p. 452. "It appeased": MT/WW, November 5, 1890.

p. 452. "I ought to be": *MTHL*2, 633.

p. 453. "she got quiet": OLC/MT, November 27, 1890.

p. 453. "I feel so much": OLC/GK, January 14, 1891.

p. 453. "sigh for the islands": MT/Thomas L. Gulick, January 8, 1891.

p. 453. "has determined": *MTHL*2, 645.

p. 454. "in the rush": MT/My Dear Sir, May 11, 1891.

CHAPTER 15

p. 455. "I have been": NBK 31.

p. 455. "the Atlantic ever": *N&J*3, 641.

p. 456. "Come yo' seff": NBK 31.

p. 456. "Huck comes back": *N&J*3, 606.

p. 457. "I could write": MT/RUJ, July 10, 1891.

p. 457. "hour or so at a time": MT/Clarence Clough Buel, August 16, 1891.

p. 457. "all diseases [were] welcomed": "Aix, Paradise of Rheumatics," *Europe and Elsewhere*. New York: Harper and Brothers, 1923.

p. 458. "They fed us": "Aix, Paradise of Rheumatics," *Europe and Elsewhere*.

p. 458. "I was a skittish": NBK 31.

p. 458. "Hell or Heidelberg": NBK 31.

p. 459. "The idiotic Crusades": NBK, 31.

p. 459. "it was wonderful": NBK, 32; *PW*, "Conclusion."

p. 460. "pleasant sunny": OLC/HW, September 23, 1891.

p. 460. "I shall be glad": *MTLP*, 293; MT/FGW, July 18, 1891.

p. 460. "one of the most": OLC/GW, December 1, 1891.

p. 460. "Ah, Louise": SC/LB, October 31, 1891.

p. 461. "At this rate": MT/PB, November 9, 1891.

p. 461. "complained sharply": NBK 31.

p. 461. "any more talking": *MTOA*, 131.

p. 462. "I would like to be": NBK 31.

p. 462. "I was really frightened": OLC/DAY, March 7, 1892.

p. 462. "a state of excited": NBK 31.

p. 462. "I leave Monday": MT/FGW, February 20, 1892.

p. 462. "just us two": MT & OLC/AT, March 8, 1892.

p. 463. "pangs of homesickness": OLC/DAY, March 7, 1892.

p. 463. "Mr Clemens says": OLC/DAY, March 7, 1892.

p. 463. "gigantic fleas": NBK 31.

p. 463. "looking across to": NBK 31.

p. 464. "[We had] great times here": MT/CC, December 25, 1892.

p. 464. "better speed": MT/OC, September 2, 1892.

p. 464. "Don't get used to": OLC/CC, December 11, 1892.

p. 464. "Reading all day": SC/CC, November 4, 1892.

p. 465. "curable & *easily*": MT/CC, June 10, 1892.

p. 465. "in the clouds": MT/OC, June 28, 1892.

p. 465. "Lord protect her": MT/CL, August 7, 1892.

p. 465. "excessive dryness": MT/WB, December 28, 1892.

p. 465. "I do think": SC/LB, December 31, 1892.

p. 465. "her old fascinating": SC/CC, October 7(?), 1892.

p. 465. "one of her lasting": MT/CC, November 10, 1892.

p. 465. "the ever-changing aspects": MT/FGW, October 22, 1892.

p. 465. "had a little more": OLC/CC, December 11, 1892.

p. 466. "Nothing *but* a Co": NBK 31.

p. 466. "I came away": MT/AT, July 18, 1892.

p. 467. "It's a noble": MT/RWG, October 19, 1892.

p. 467. "quite weaned": SC/LB, December 31, 1892.

p. 467. "I have seen": SC/CC, January 24, 1893.

p. 468. "Mrs. Clemens, one": Janet Ross. *The Fourth Generation*, New York, 1912.

p. 468. "It is lonesome": MT/CC, February 5, 1893.

p. 469. "The priests of Church": NBK 32.

p. 470. "the usual brilliant sunshine": NBK 33.

p. 470. "57 yrs. old": NBK 32.

p. 470. "People wonder why": SP, 274.

p. 470. "I dreamed I was": MT/SLC, March 19, 1893.

p. 470. "the dream again": NBK 33.

p. 471. "My dear darling child": OLC/MT, April 13, 1893.

p. 471. "to continue the": NBK 33.

p. 472. "Put all your eggs": NBK 33.

p. 472. "well along in building": NBK 33.

p. 472. "He said it broke": NBK 33.

p. 472. "He could persuade": NBK 33.

p. 472. "grand naval": NBK 33.

p. 473. "All the family here": MT/OLC, May 6, 1893.

p. 473. "& approached the arbor": MT/SC, May 7, 1893.

p. 473. "My trip was merely": MT/William Phelps, May 29, 1893.

p. 473. "Mr C. is much": OLC/HW, June 2, 1893.

p. 473. "We are at heavy": MTLP, 343.

p. 473. "Will Harper": MTLP, 343–4.

p. 474. "went off well": SC/LB, June 8, 1893.

p. 474. "the most unattractive": OLC/DAY, July 8, 1893.

p. 474. "It is just decided": MT/HR, July 20, 1893.

p. 474. "deadly homesick": MT/OC & MC, July 26, 1893.

p. 474. "I feel panicky": MTLP, 350–51.

p. 475. "the murder &": MTLP, 354.

p. 475. "the most difficult": MTLP, 354.

p. 475. "This time it suits me": MT/C&W, July 30, 1893.

p. 475. "I do not sleep": MTLP, 355.

p. 476. "I am not made": MTLP, 346.

p. 476. "to be on this side": MT/CC, September 13, 1893.

p. 476. "Money can not": MT/OLC, September 13, 1893.

p. 476. "Well, when the worst": MT/OLC, September 13, 1893.

p. 476. "I don't feel uncheerful": MT/OLC, September 13, 1893.

p. 477. "bachelorizing": MT/FGW, September 13, 1893.

p. 477. "having good sociable": MT/CC, September 10, 1893.

p. 477. "little or no relief": NBK 33.

p. 477. "mind cure": NBK 33.

p. 477. "Don't know if he": NBK 33.

p. 477. "acquainted with him": MT/CC, September 15, 1893.

p. 477. "President of the Standard": NBK, 32.

p. 478. "We were strangers": MTA1, 256.

p. 478. "The best new acquaintance": MT/CC, September 15, 1893.

p. 479. "There's no telling": MT/CC, September 23, 1893.

p. 479. "No, it would not": OLC/CC, October 15, 1893.

p. 479. "I would rather be": SC/CC, October 1893.

p. 479. "deliciously quiet": MT/CC, September 30, 1893.

p. 480. "beautiful & impressive": MT/OLC, November 14, 1893.

p. 480. "What magnificent weather": MT/OLC, November 28, 1893.

p. 480. "Don't you be troubled": MT/OLC, n.d. (December 1893 or early 1894).

p. 480. "I play billiards": MT/SC, December 27, 1893.

p. 481. "he had seen three": MT/OLC, November 28, 1893.

p. 481. "I must get to work": MT/OLC, October 17, 1893 to December 17, 1893.

p. 481. "I am going to resume": MT/PB, February 11, 1894.

p. 481. "mapped out": MT/OC & MC, November 3, 1893.

p. 481. "though the people": MT/OLC, November 8, 1893.

p. 481. "I said I didn't": *MTLL*, p. 273.

p. 481. "I do not venture": MT/RWG, November 6, 1893.

p. 482. "vigorous indictment": *CR*, p. 364.

p. 482. "clearly & powerfully": *MTLL*, 291.

p. 482. "Mr. Rogers represented": MT/OLC, December 8, 1893.

p. 483. "If Paige finds out": MT/OLC, December 15, 1893.

p. 483. "to demand & receive": NBK 33.

p. 483. "We furnish $120,000": NBK 33.

p. 483. "If you should come": MT/OLC, December 15, 1893.

p. 483. "all jump with jubilation": *MTL*2, 598.

p. 483. "I may as well": MT/OLC, December 25, 1893.

p. 483. "Whenever I have found": MT/OLC, December 25, 1893.

p. 484. "The absence of a message": MT/OLC, December 25, 1893.

p. 484. "At the end": MT/OLC, December 25, 1893.

p. 484. "That ended the Chicago": MT/OLC, December 25, 1893.

p. 484. "I am full of pity": MT/OLC, December 25, 1893.

p. 484. "the great news": NBK 33.

p. 484. "So long as the contract": *LLMT*, 289.

p. 484. "it rain[ed] invitations": *LLMT*, 292.

p. 485. " 'Farewell—a long farewell' ": *MTL*2, 607.

p. 485. "a great date": *MTL*2, 607.

p. 485. "Look out for good": *LLMT*, 293.

p. 485. *"Nearing Success"*: MT/OLC, February 11, 1894.

p. 485. "I & mine": *LLMT*, 293.

p. 485. "Wedding-news": MT/OLC, February 2, 1894.

p. 485. "We rejoice with you": MT/OLC, February 2, 1894.

p. 485. "I mean to ask": MT/OLC, February 7 or August 8 1894.

p. 486. "You have saved": *MTHHR*, 38.

p. 486. "He is fast coming": MT/OLC, February 20, 1894.

p. 486. "let him rot": MT/PCM, February 25, 1894.

p. 487. "I am going to get": MT/PCM, February 25, 1894.

p. 487. "she would lose": *MTHHR*, 49.

p. 487. "hypnotism & mind-cure": OLC/DAY, February 4, 1894.

p. 487. "no mind-curist": MT/OLC, February 11, 1894.

p. 487. "gives me a sense": OLC/DAY, February 4, 1894.

p. 488. "I have lost": MT/HR, April 20, 1894.

p. 488. "Nobody finds the slightest fault": *LLMT*, 301.

p. 489. "separate fortune": OLC/DAY, May 23, 1894.

p. 489. "I for myself": OLC/GK, June 16, 1894.

p. 489. "Mr. Clemens and I": *Twainean* 6, no. 6 (November–December 1947): 2–3.

p. 489. "the most idiotic book": MT/OLC, May 17, 1894.

p. 490. "little chalet": OLC/GK, May 16, 1894.

p. 490. "No, I cannot feel": OLC/DAY, July 1, 1894.

p. 490. "If you get short": MT/OLC, May 17, 1894.

p. 490. "expecting to see": *LLMT*, 304.

p. 490. "Let us be spared": *LLMT*, 304.

p. 490. "Clemens was very kind": *MMT*, 85.

p. 490. "gracious glimpses": *MTHL*2, 533–34.

p. 491. "I cannot, *cannot*": SC/LB, July 29, 1894.

p. 491. "It's Jean's birth-day": MT/LH, July 26, 1894.

p. 491. "I have no authority": MT/FJH, June 1, 1894.

p. 492. "help them in every": *LLMT*, 309.

p. 492. "all day the": *LLMT*, 305.

p. 492. "tortured by a conscience": MT/OLC, August 3, 1894.

p. 492. "venture on house-keeping": *MHHR*, 73.

p. 493. "to drop the lecture platform": *MHHR*, 71.

p. 493. "I drove the quill": *MTHHR*, 73.

p. 493. "The madam": *MTHHR*, 77.

p. 493. "a good while": *MTHHR*, 78.

p. 493. "more comfortable": *MTHHR*, 97.

p. 493. "France hasn't any": MT/Lloyd S. Bryce, October 13, 1894.

p. 493. "I am pretty impatient": *MTHHR*, 91.

p. 494. "I have now lost": MT/Lloyd S. Bryce, November 30, 1894.

p. 494. "healing for sore eyes": *MTHR*, 83.

p. 494. "Mergenthaler people": *MTHHR*, 83.

p. 494. "Things couldn't well": *MTHHR*, 88.

p. 494. "When the machine": *MTHHR*, 89.

p. 494. "account of the machine's": *MTHHR*, 96.

p. 494. "Great guns": *MTHHR*, 96.

p. 495. "Clemens, stand": *MTHHR*, 99–199.

p. 495. "I am catching around": *MTHHR*, 104.

p. 495. "a sudden inquest": *MTHHR*, 107.

p. 495. "I *seemed* to be": *MTHHR*, 108.

p. 495. "*Don't* say I'm wild": *MTHHR*, 108–9.

p. 495. "I couldn't shake off": *MTHHR*, 115.

p. 496. "I ought to have knocked": *MTHHR*, 116.

p. 496. "for money": *MTHHR*, 126.

p. 497. "to Mrs. Clemens": *MTHHR*, 126.

CHAPTER 16

p. 499. "You are in": *MTHHR*, 169.

p. 499. "Look here, don't you": *MTHHR*, 161.

p. 499. "was ill, over": *MTHHR*, 167.

p. 499. "Bliss is an ass": *MTHHR*, 141.

p. 499. "I've signed a lot": *MTHHR*, 149.

p. 500. "I have great hope": OLC/FGW, June 18, 1895.

p. 500. "a big book": MT/?, nd,/ 1895.

p. 500. "If I go on that": *MTHHR*, 127.

p. 501. "I've *got* to mount": *MTHHR*, 129.

p. 501. "After a long period": *MFMT*, 136.

p. 501. "the experts": *MTHHR*, 141.

p. 501. "Livy & Clara go": MT/OC, May 26, 1895.

p. 501. "spare the time": MT/OC, May 26, 1895.

p. 501. "My head is tired": *MTHHR*, 141.

p. 501. "Livy looks young": MT/OC, May 26, 1895.

p. 502. "break the incognito": MT/John David Adams, June 13, 1895.

p. 502. "pretty malignant": MT/HMA, May 30, 1895.

p. 502. "as big as a turkey's": MT/RUJ, May 30, 1895.

p. 502. "I have detested": *SP*, 300–1.

p. 502. "I'm perishing": MT/John David Adams, June 13, 1895; CC/PCM, July 6, 1895.

p. 503. "There is more Clemens": *MTHHR*, 151.

p. 503. "sloughed out": MT/RUJ, May 30, 1895; MT/JBP, June 1895.

p. 503. "to undergo the shame": MT/PCM, July 14, 1895.

p. 503. "I can't make any": MT/PCM, July 14, 1895.

p. 503. "I've got to": *MTHHR*, 165.

p. 504. "dead failure": NBK 35.

p. 504. "Suppose that every": *SP*, 280.

p. 504. "I got *started* magnificently": *MTHHR*, 171.

p. 505. "I am at work": *MTHHR*, 177.

p. 505. "only once a day": MT/FF, August 4, 1895.

p. 506. "a horizon-girdled": NBK 35.

p. 506. "You *must* hire": *MTHHR*, 177.

p. 506. "colored regiment": NBK 35.

p. 506. "Let Jim tell Huck": NBK 35.

p. 507. "one-dollar bills": MT/SM, August 14, 1895.

p. 507. "My eyes have been": MT/SM, August 14, 1895.

p. 507. "Lecturing is gymnastics": MT/SM, August 14, 1895.

p. 508. "splendid house": NBK 35.

p. 508. "a big house": NBK 35.

p. 508. "a kitten walked": NBK 35.

p. 508. "[Sailing] seems quite": CC/SM, August 17, 1895.

p. 508. "I shall arrive": MT/Rudyard Kipling, August 16, 1895.

p. 508. "It is midnight": MT/HHR, August 22, 1895.

p. 508. "threatened a little": MT/HHR, August 22, 1895.

p. 509. "a most disagreeable": NBK 35.

p. 509. "The weather has been": MT/HHR, August 30, 1895.

p. 509. "In a couple of hours": MT/HHR, August 30, 1895.

p. 509. "This first little boat": OLC/SC, August 30, 1895.

p. 509. "luminous blue water": NBK 35.

p. 509. "the vast plain": NBK 35.

p. 510. "was not distinguishable": NBK, 35.

p. 510. "Mr. Clemens seems": OLC/SC, September 5, 1895.

p. 510. "a flight of silver": NBK 35.

p. 510. "splendid half nude": NBK 35.

p. 510. "so *natural*": NBK 35.

p. 511. "My wife is so": MT/H. Walter Barnett, October 3, 1895.

p. 511. "Really I am almost": *MTHHR*, 188.

p. 511. "I think Papa": MT/SC, October 20, 1895.

p. 512. "[At that time] fogs": *SP*, 294.

p. 512. "[He] is so impressed with": OLC/SLC, March 30, 1896.

p. 512. "One of the signs": NBK 35.

p. 513. "There is nothing": NBK 34.

p. 513. "Badly crippled": MT/HHR, November 10, 1895.

p. 513. "It is the strangest thing": NBK 34.

p. 513. "Can't see that": NBK 34.

p. 514. "All savages": NBK 34.

p. 514. "England might be": NBK 34.

p. 515. "the poor exiled Tasmanian": NBK 34.

p. 515. "floating pig-sty": MT/Mrs. Joseph Kinsey, November 23, 1895.

p. 515. "We leave for Auckland": CC/SM, November 12, 1895.

p. 516. "We have had": MT/HHR, December 12, 1895.

p. 516. "I wonder if we shall": OLC/SLC, November 24, 1895.

p. 517. "Everything takes": OLC/SC, December 2, 1895.

p. 517. "We have done steadily": OLC/SC, December 2, 1895.

p. 517. "We get up many": OLC/JC, 2/16 & February 18, 1896.

p. 517. "everlasting peace": NBK 37.

p. 517. "miraculously cured": NBK 37.

p. 517. "dazzling yellows": CC/PCM, February 1896.

p. 517. "sumptuously tropical": *FQ*, 37.

p. 518. "The most amazing": NBK 36.

p. 518. "infernal cough": NBK 36.

p. 518. "Slambang of Gutcheree": NBK, 36.

p. 518. "It carried me": NBK 36; *FQ*, 38.

p. 519. "India does not consist": *FQ*, 39.

p. 519. "row of vultures": NBK 36.

p. 519. "Gaudy & gorgeous": NBK 36.

p. 520. "always like": NBK 36.

p. 520. "everybody came": NBK 36.

p. 520. "[Religion] is the business": *FQ*, 50.

p. 520. "In these countries": NBK 36; *FQ* 50.

p. 521. "I only liked Manuel": *FQ*, , 60.

p. 521. "from head to heel": *FQ*, 60.

p. 521. "I am shut up": MT/SC, February 7, 1896.

p. 522. "& 2 other great peaks": NBK 36.

p. 522. "We have lectured": MT/CHW, February 16, 1896.

p. 522. "We started in rugs": *MTHHR*, 195.

p. 522. "But it has": OLC/SC, March 30, 1896.

p. 522. "rest a week": NBK 36.

p. 523. "splendid full moon": *FQ*, 59.

p. 523. "the *real* summer": *MTHHR*, 212.

p. 523. "I think this": OLC/JC, March 10, 1896.

p. 523. "the most odious race": Swift, *Gulliver's Travels* II; NBK 37.

p. 524. "as large as mice": CC/SM, April 7, 1896.

p. 524. "I feel": OLC/SC, March 30, 1896.

p. 524. "Do you remember": *MFMT*, 179.

p. 524. "We feel now": OLC/SC, March 30, 1896.

p. 525. "the days [were] warm": NBK 38.

p. 525. "came of an undemonstrative": NBK 39.

p. 525. "We seem each": OLC/HW, April 9, 1896.

p. 525. "We don't *call*": NBK 39.

p. 526. "direct descendants": NBK 38.

p. 526. "Of course, of course": NBK 38.

p. 526. "Must pretend that": NBK 38.

p. 527. "the curse of *party*": NBK 38.

p. 527. "Explained to the prisoners": NBK 38.

p. 527. "Everybody says": NBK 38.

p. 528. "Kruger, it is said": NBK 38.

p. 528. "meddle in Transvaal": NBK 38.

p. 528. "I could frame": NBK 38.

p. 528. "*one* blossom in this": NBK 38.

p. 528. "These darkies": NBK 38.

p. 529. "died of heart disease": NBK 38.

p. 529. "tired of the platform": *MTHHR*, 227.

p. 529. "*I don't want*": OLC/SLC, June 21, 1896.

p. 529. "when she found": *MTHL2*, 661.

p. 530. "the luxury & rest": *MTHL2*, 661.

p. 530. "I am often": SC/CC, August 10, 1895.

p. 530. "I have become": SC/CC, September 13, 1895.

p. 530. "to leave Elmira": SC/CC, September 16, 1895.

p. 531. "If I ever can be": SC/CC, September 16, 1895.

p. 531. "one Spiritualist": *Leary*, 134–35.

p. 531. "absent treatments": *Leary*, 134.

p. 532. "full of historionic": SC/CC, December 30(?), 1895.

p. 532. "No! Nobody will": *Leary*, 136.

p. 533. "We have been": *MTHHR*, 232.

p. 533. "The recovery would": *MTA1*, 33.

p. 533. "The calamity": *LLMT*, 317.

p. 533. "dear head [would] be": *LLMT*, 317.

p. 533. "I am not demonstrative": *LLMT*, 317.

p. 534. "Be good & get": *LLMT*, 317.

p. 534. "Susy could not stand": *LLMT*, 326.

p. 534. "MARK TWAIN'S ELDEST": *MFMT*, 171.

CHAPTER 17

p. 535. "The Square & adjacent": NBK, 39.

p. 535. "the rumble": NBK 39.

p. 535. "I cannot believe": MT/SLC, September 30, 1896.

p. 535. "going around with": NBK 39.

p. 536. "I have always had": OLC/GK, March 8, 1897.

p. 536. "nothing in the world": MTL2, 642.

p. 536. "It is a noble poem": MT/MAC, July 20, 1897.

p. 536. "I bear it as I bear": MT/FGW, September 10, 1896.

p. 536. "I cannot always be": *SP*, 362.

p. 536. "Thunderous outbursts": *MFMT*, 179.

p. 536. "Luck has turned": *MTHHR*, 236.

p. 536. "My luck is down": MT/FGW, September 23, 1896.

p. 537. "Up go the trolley cars": *PA*, 51.

p. 537. "I am blind": NBK 39.

p. 537. "[At least] she died in her own": *MFMT*, 173–74; *LLMT*, 322.

p. 537. "the City of Heartbreak": MT/JHT, January 3, 1899.

p. 537. "billiards, and billiards": *LLMT*, 323.

p. 537. "I don't know how": *Leary*, 137.

p. 538. "I shall never see": *LLMT*, 323.

p. 538. "I myself can keep": *MTHHR*, 255.

p. 538. "I work all the days": *MTL2*, 641.

p. 538. "Never did he write": *MFMT*, 178.

p. 538. "We are a broken-hearted

family": OLC/MMF, December 28, 1896.

p. 538. "I work seven days": *MTHHR*, 255.

p. 538. "Susy you know": MT/DAY, September 11, 1896.

p. 539. "If she had had only": *MTHHR*, 255.

p. 539. "the lousy scoundrel": MT/PCM, January 7, 1897.

p. 539. "sinister doctrine": *MFMT*, 182.

p. 540. "Nothing can kill": NBK 40.

p. 540. "While you sleep": NBK 41.

p. 540. "dark-colored": NBK 39.

p. 540. "Waking, I move slowly": NBK 40.

p. 541. "disgusting proposition": NBK 40.

p. 541. "for a long time": NBK 41.

p. 541. "It is my house": MT/ECS, October 16, 1896.

p. 542. "The report of my illness": NBK 41; *MTHHR*, 282.

p. 542. "any faster than anybody": NBK 41.

p. 542. "This way out": MT/JGB, June 1897.

p. 542. "My wife won't allow": MT/JGB, June 1897.

p. 542. "I shall work out": MT/OC, March 28, 1897.

p. 543. "Now if that scheme": MT/FF, May 27, 1897.

p. 543. "go home & lecture": MT/SM, July 7, 1897.

p. 543. "It is like a new": *MTHHR*, 226.

p. 544. "twenty-five years": MT/C&W, March 25, 1897.

p. 544. "Four-fifths of it": MT/OC, March 28, 1897.

p. 544. "sleepy and timorous": *MTHHR*, 272.

p. 544. "This is a strange time": *MTHHR*, 286.

p. 545. " 'Are you an American?' ": NBK 41.

p. 545. "Since bad luck": NBK 41.

p. 547. "the day solitary": NBK 42.

p. 547. "There was no August day": MT/FS, September 9 or October 10 1897.

p. 548. "We are gathering cheerfulness": MT/WM, July 27, 1897.

p. 548. "hang back long enough": MT/WM, August 22, 1897.

p. 548. "I am a cheerful man": MT/JBP, September 17, 1897.

p. 548. "I know more about": MT/C&W, July 25, 1897.

p. 549. "It was the only book": MT/WM, August 22, 1897.

p. 549. "I have mapped out": MT/WM, August 22, 1897.

p. 550. "up to the house": NBK 40.

p. 550. "He was with us 18 years": NBK 39.

p. 550. "Orion as T's uncle": NBK, 40.

p. 551. "the Lev'n boys": NBK 40.

p. 551. "negro smuggled": NBK 40.

p. 551. "Tom is disguised": NBK 40.

p. 552. "The Lincoln of our Literature": *MMT*, 101.

p. 553. "the stillness and solemnity": *OFG*, 28.

p. 553. "I've seen nothing": *MTHHR*, 302.

p. 553. "It was being whispered": *OFG*, 28.

p. 554. "my favorite city": *OFG*, 30.

p. 558. "All anniversaries": NBK 40.

p. 559. "Herr Mark Twain": *OFG*, 35.

p. 560. "der Jude Mark Twain": *OFG*, 166–70.

p. 560. "The difference between": *MTL2*, 647.

p. 561. "be done to dispel": MT/the Editor of *American Hebrew*, March 1890.

p. 561. "rudimental Christian": MT/the Editor of *American Hebrew*, March 1890.

p. 561. "Wild editorials": MT/HH, February 8, 1898.

p. 562. "A grand figure": MT/*New York Herald*, January 30 (?), 1898.

p. 563. "There was hammerings": NBK 40.

p. 563. "[Sixty] policemen marched": NBK 40.

p. 563. "none of the show": *MTL*1, 652.

p. 563. "I & all of us": MT/MC, December 11, 1897.

p. 563. "send to Mrs. Orion": MT/FGW, December 11, 1897.

p. 563. "escape from this life": MT/MC, December 11, 1897.

p. 564. "It does seem": OLC/SM, January 6, 1898.

p. 564. "We are hoping that": MT/TBA, June 29, 1898.

p. 564. "[It is] almost like being": OLC/CL, April 24, 1898.

p. 564. "I think we ought": MT & OLC/Cornelius Cole, May 17, 1898.

p. 565. "I am writing hard": *MTHHR*, 308.

p. 565. "For the first time": *MTHHR*, 310.

p. 565. "Splendid bird": *MTHHR*, 386.

p. 565. "I have abundant peace": *MTHHR*, 316.

p. 565. "You could not": MT/MAC, March 12, 1898.

p. 565. "We own a house": *MTHL*2, 684.

p. 565. "I would like to": MT/Ameila S. Levetus, March 15, 1898.

p. 566. "I was afraid": NBK 40.

p. 566. "I've landed a big fish": *MTHHR*, 327.

p. 566. "a laboratory 3 or 4": MT/RWG, April 2, 1898.

p. 566. "When I hear": *MTHHR*, 342–43.

p. 567. "So, all these months": MT/John Adams, December 5, 1898.

p. 568. "I hold myself": MT/HMA, November 2, 1898.

p. 569. "changed his principles": *MSM*, 190.

p. 569. "he takes Huck": NBK 40.

p. 569. "No—militarism, which": NBK 40.

p. 570. "If I were a citizen": NBK 40.

p. 570. "in red, gold and white": *OFG*, 85–86.

p. 570. "a competent judge": OLC/FC, October 7, 1898.

p. 570. "When Clara is away": OLC/FC, October 7, 1898.

p. 570. "We are all usually": OLC/FC, October 7, 1898.

p. 571. "Sometimes I have felt": OLC/FC, October 7, 1898.

p. 571. "I am not 'making' ": MT/FB, December 10, 1898.

p. 571. "A good deal of": MT/Edward W. Bok, October 10, 1898.

p. 571. "If it weren't for": CC/JRC, December 23, 1898.

p. 571. "does not go well": MT/JHT, January 3, 1899.

p. 571. "[They] contain nothing offensive": MT/FEB, February 27, 1899.

p. 572. "The salt water will": MT/JHT, May 5, 1899.

p. 572. "ordered . . . by the doctors": MT/MAC, June 3, 1899.

p. 572. "We are still in exile": MT/Alice L. Bunner, June 6, 1899.

p. 573. "We are here till October": MT/LH, July 13, 1899.

p. 573. "semi-annual itching": *MTHHR*, 406.

p. 573. "astonishing": NBK 40.

p. 574. "fell in a spasm": NBK 40.

p. 574. "Hell (Sanna Branch)": MT/CC, July 12, 1899.

p. 574. "I take it myself": MT/RWG, July 23, 1899.

p. 574. "this system, like surgery": MT/John B. Walker, July 30, 1899.

p. 575. "being practiced": *MTHHR*, 414.

p. 575. "If only I had found": *MTHHR*, 414.

p. 575. "all books upon": *MTHHR*, 418.

p. 575. "straightening up": *MTHHR*, 418.

p. 576. "that it was about time": *MTHHR*, 436.

p. 576. "The scientific testimonials": *MTHHR*, 436; MT/MAC, March 8, 1900; MT/MAC, March 10, 1900.

p. 577. "I think it would be": *MTHHR*, 440.

p. 577. "I take it in": MT/AC, n.d. 1900.

p. 577. "You are bound to": MT/William James, April 17, 1900.

p. 578. "who did more than": *MTHL2*, 682.

p. 578. "war for humanity": *MTHL2*, 673.

p. 578. "London wild with joy": NBK 43.

p. 578. "the dirtiest dwelling-house": NBK 43.

p. 578. "rather lucky": MT/RWG, July 31, 1900.

p. 579. "our Day of Mourning": MT/MAC, August 18, 1900.

p. 579. "I am getting heart-breakingly": MT/LH, January 1, 1900.

CHAPTER 18

p. 580. "I have intended": *MTHL2*, 698.

p. 581. "as the eyes": *MTHL2*, 667–68.

p. 581. "We are all hoping": *MTHL2*, 677.

p. 581. "You have pervaded": *MTHL2*, 672.

p. 582. "What's the matter with": *Mr. Dooley Remembers: The Informal Memoirs of Finley Peter Dunne.* Edited by Philip Dunne. Boston: Little, Brown, 1963, pp. 250–51.

p. 583. "I think that England": *SP*, 368–69.

p. 583. "according to an anonymous": *SP*, 369.

p. 583. "I'm not expecting anything": *MTL2*, 704–5.

p. 584. "I am only distressed": *MTL2*, 704–5.

p. 584. "to confer the blessings": "To a Person Sitting in Darkness" (1901).

p. 584. "For fifty years": *MTE*, 2.

p. 585. "one or two letters": OLC/Annie Fields, February 19, 1901.

p. 585. "When I hear what": *MTHL2*, 743.

p. 585. "So many dinners": *MTHL2*, 735.

p. 586. "throw out the old": *SP*, 390.

p. 586. "I've been in favor": *SP*, 375.

p. 586. "My axiom is": *SP*, 397.

p. 587. "unreliable": OLC/GK, February 15 and 24, 1901.

p. 587. "We do not oppose": OLC/GK, February 15 and 24, 1901.

p. 587. "whose condemnation": *SP*, 384.

p. 588. "a public enemy": *SP*, 384.

p. 588. "some heavy traveling": MT/JHT, April 24, 1901.

p. 588. "I have done very little": MT/Rudolph Lindau, April 24, 1901.

p. 588. "I judge that nothing": MT/Laura Fitch McQuiston, April 1, 1901.

p. 588. "primeval wilderness": MT/FS, July 29, 1901.

p. 589. "stacks of Literary Remains": MT/JHT, September 8, 1901.

p. 589. "How strange it would be": OLC/CC, July 4, 1901.

p. 589. "It has always brought": OLC/SM, July 17, 1901.

p. 590. "planned to make": MT/JHT, September 8, 1901.

p. 590. "The thing I am": MT/FB, August 26, 1901.

p. 591. "Upon reflection": MT/FB, August 29, 1901.

p. 591. "Jean is getting along": MT/LH, January 1, 1900.

p. 591. "We are ourselves": MT/TBA, December 21, 1901.

p. 592. "the sea was beyond": MT/OLC, March 21, 1902.

p. 592. "fruit debauch": MT/OLC, March 21, 1902.

p. 592. "swam far out": MT/OLC, March 21, 1902.

p. 592. "grunting and blaspheming": SP, 455.

p. 592. "a Brobdignagian tarantula": MT/OLC, March 23, 1902.

p. 592. "the most prodigal": MT/OLC, March 29, 1902.

p. 592. "poker chapel": SP, 455.

p. 592. "very much to go": OLC/Katherine Clemens, May 17, 1902.

p. 593. "He has no time": MTHL2, 735.

p. 593. "rich Chicagoan": MT/FGW, May 19, 1902.

p. 593. "dear old Unreconstructible": MT/William R. Gillis, May 16, 1902.

p. 593. "I shall be 67": MT/JG, May 16, 1902.

p. 594. "Almost every tombstone": MTE, 201.

p. 594. "out again over that": SP, 457.

p. 594. "an intensely emotional week": SP, 435.

p. 595. "it would have been": MTHHR, 489–90.

p. 595. "to be out from": MT/FGW, June 14, 1902.

p. 595. "to be issued": MTHHR, 494–95.

p. 595. "get rid of the house": MTHHR, 499.

p. 595. "five years of constant": MTHHR, 496.

p. 595. "a nightly experience": MTHHR, 496.

p. 596. "violently ill": NBK 45.

p. 596. "She could not breathe" NBK 45.

p. 596. "organic heart disease": MTHL2, 747.

p. 596. "She is low-spirited": MT/SLC, August 15, 1902.

p. 597. "with an allopathic": MTHHR, 497.

p. 597. "It proved . . . good": MTHHR, 498.

p. 597. "Of all the impossible": MTHHR, 498.

p. 597. "The illness drags": MTHHR, 498–99.

p. 597. "on his way to": MT/TBA, September 11, 1902.

p. 597. "I have been—in literary": MT/FAD, September 15, 1902.

p. 597. "very rich": MT/CL, December 26, 1902.

p. 598. "invalid car from York": MT/JHT, October 1902.

p. 598. "[She] isn't strong & some-times": MT/FAD, September 15, 1902.

p. 598. "a vigorous case": MT/PB, October 27, 1902.

p. 599. "a little troubled": MT/FGW, November 5, 1902.

p. 599. "[Livy's] heart is bad": MT/SC, December 26, 1902.

p. 599. "The whole thing would": MT/SC, December 29, 1902.

p. 599. "but a poor clumsy liar": MT/JHT, December 31, 1902.

p. 599. "The house is a hospital": MT/FB, December 25, 1902.

p. 599. "For the first time": MT/JHT, December 31, 1902.

p. 599. "It grieves me so": MT/OLC, n.d. 1902–1903.

p. 600. "wood-carving": MT/LH, November 6, 1902.

p. 600. "I love you darling": MT/OLC, n.d., 1903.

p. 600. "The summer is here": MT/OLC, n.d., 1903.

p. 600. "making fun of that": MT/Frederick W. Peabody, December 5, 1902.

p. 600. "to reconcile the Harper": MT/Stockholders of the American Publishing Company, June 1903.

p. 601. "in the same year": SP, 458.

p. 602. "better side": OLC/MT, n.d., 1902–1903.

p. 602. "What I have tried": MT/CTH, November 26, 1902.

p. 602. "99 parts of me": MT/CTH, November 26, 1902.

p. 603. "witnessed the post": NBK 46.

p. 603. "at $7,000 more": MT/FGW, April 28, 1903.

p. 603. "For the Lord Jesus": MT/FGW, April 5, 1903.

p. 604. "the voyage marvelously": NBK 46.

p. 605. "God himself couldn't": MTHL2, 775.

p. 605. "It transpires": NBK 47.

p. 605. "We have heavy": MT/MAC, November 17, 1903.

p. 606. "Calamity House": NBK 47.

p. 606. "[The countess's] presence poisons": MTHHR, 558.

p. 606. "mind & conscience": MT/WB, n.d., November 1903 to June 1904.

p. 607. "one of those machines": CC/WB, n.d., November 1903 to June 1904.

p. 607. "should have these": CC/WB, n.d., November 1903 to June 1904.

p. 607. "It's a long time": MT/OLC, February 2, 1903.

p. 607. "When we first arrived": MT/FAD, February 8, 1904.

p. 607. "I was seized": CC/Dorothy Gilder, February 5, 1904.

p. 608. "[She] astonished the house": NBK 47.

p. 608. "awful attack": NBK 47.

p. 609. "You will never know": MTHL2, 778.

p. 609. "existing books": MTHL2, 779.

p. 609. "Mrs. Clemens is really": MTL2, 753.

p. 609. "We take not to-morrow's": MTL2, 754.

p. 609. "bright & young": MTL2, 755.

p. 610. "It doesn't look": MTHHR, 566.

p. 610. "It was too pitiful": MTHL2, 787–88.

p. 610. "choking horror": MT/JHT, June 8, 1904.

p. 610. "It does get deadly": NBK 47.

p. 610. "Livy Langdon": MT/SC, September 9, 1904.

p. 610. "I've been awful sick": Leary, 228.

p. 611. "were holding the oxygen": *MTHL2*, 785.

p. 611. "I think I spoke": *MTHL2*, 785.

p. 611. "They put their arms": *Leary*, 229.

p. 611. "How sweet she": MT/JHT, June 8, 1904.

p. 611. "at 4, 5, 7, 8": MT/JHT, June 8, 1904.

p. 611. "The immediate cause": MT/Mr. Mason, July 23, 1904.

p. 611. "the body was embalmed": MT/Mr. Mason, July 23, 1904.

p. 611. "I kept my promise": *Leary*, 229.

p. 611. "An hour ago the best": *MTL2*, 758.

p. 611. "out of a heart": MT/CL, June 26, 1904.

p. 611. "It was heart failure": *MTHHR*, 569.

p. 612. "I was beginning to hope": *MTHHR*, 569.

p. 612. "I am tired & old": *MTHL2*, 785.

CHAPTER 19

p. 613. "The weather, the air": Henry James/Jocelyn Persse, September 6, 1904.

p. 614. "a native of the James": William James/Alice Howe James, July 29, 1889.

p. 614. "I am a man without": MT/CL, June 19, 1904.

p. 614. "if any man who": *MTHL2*, 784.

p. 614. "I thank you out": MT/Laura Frazer [Hawkins], June 1904.

p. 614. "How thankful I am": *MTHL2*, 785.

p. 614. "I wish I could find": *MTHHR*, 565–66.

p. 615. "I made a personal": NBK 47;

MT/Dr. Moses Allen Starr, February 3, 1905.

p. 615. "people who travel": NBK 47.

p. 615. "31 years ago": NBK 47.

p. 615. "I was never in my life": NBK 47.

p. 615. "in a breaking voice": MT/Thomas R. Lounsbury, July 21, 1904.

p. 616. "Sick, heart-broken": NBK 46.

p. 616. "WARM SUMMER SUN": Transcription by Richard Bucci.

p. 616. "The world is black": MT/TBA, June 6, 1904.

p. 617. "With Mrs. Clemens gone": MT/MAC, November 9, 1904.

p. 617. "a long farewell": MT/MAC, November 9, 1904.

p. 617. "I feel like sending you": CC/MT, November 7, 1904.

p. 618. "splendid cat": MT/SLC, January 25, 1905.

p. 618. "[I] expect to stay": MT/MrsANC, n.d., 1905.

p. 618. "hobbled downstairs": MT/SLC, January 25, 1905.

p. 618. "It broke my heart": MT/SLC, January 25, 1905.

p. 618. "What he wants": *MTL2*, 766–67; MT/GH, n.d., 1904, in Willis Fletcher Johnson, *George Harvey, A Passionate Patriot*, 1929, pp. 80–81.

p. 619. "I have never read": MT/David A. Munro, February 8, 1905.

p. 619. " 'Uncle Mark's' savage": IVL in MTP.

p. 619. "I am warned": MT/Samuel M. Bergheim, February 6, 1903.

p. 620. "truthful, honorable": MT/MAC, November 22, 1904.

p. 620. "embossed cut": MT/Ralph Ashcroft, September 2, 1905.

p. 620. "The bearer of this": MT/ Abbott Thayer, February 28, 1905.

p. 621. "We are a very peaceful": IVL/HW, February 6, 1905.

p. 621. "I have led": MT/TBAs, April 26, 1906.

p. 621. "Good place to work": MT/CC, June 8, 1905.

p. 621. "It beats the record": MT/CC, June 11, 1905.

p. 622. "one of those intervals": MT/MP, July 26, 1905.

p. 622. "I'm appointing you": MT/CC, June 18, 1905.

p. 622. "tainted money": MT/JHT, July 13, 1905.

p. 622. "I want her to see": *MTHHR*, 592.

p. 622. "coarse & poor": MT/CC, July 16, 1905.

p. 623. "Dear heart, I am": MT/CC, June 11, 1905.

p. 623. "poor old father": MT/CC, September 3, 1905.

p. 623. "drunk . . . with the autumn": MT/CC, October 15, 1905.

p. 623. "the pleasantest summer": MT/MP, October 11, 1905.

p. 623. "surgical examination": MT/CC, October 20, 1905.

p. 623. "Assume full & sole": MT/CC, October 18, 1905.

p. 624. "a foot-high plaster": *SP*, 462.

p. 624. "I am seventy": *SP*, 467.

p. 624. "Damned Human Race": *MTHL2*, 828.

p. 625. "We must not let": *SP*, 519.

p. 625. "It is less risky": MT/CT, May 18, 1906.

p. 626. "tacitly committed to": MT/TSB, January 8, 1906.

p. 626. "last visit to the State": MT/TSB, January 1906.

p. 626. "young and delightfulish": IVL, March 28, 1906.

p. 627. "I did, and when": Twain Project note to Narodny/MT, April 10, 1906.

p. 627. "beautiful play": MT/CT, June 16, 1906.

p. 627. "& we talked": MT/IVL, July 10, 1906.

p. 627. "You are launched": MT/CT, October 9, 1906.

p. 628. "I am saying these": *MTE*, 201.

p. 628. "You should write": *MTB*, 1261.

p. 629. "Yes, come soon": *MTB*, 1262.

p. 629. "he had hoped": *MTB*, 1263–64.

p. 629. "You really *mustn't* let": *MTHL2*, 803.

p. 630. "in the middle of": *MTHL2*, 811.

p. 630. "dictating some fearful": *MTHL2*, 815.

p. 630. "I'm not overworking": MT/CC, June 18–19, 1906.

p. 630. "The rest of the household": MTAD, June 11, 1906.

p. 631. "[She] mourns": MT/CC, October 9, 1906.

p. 632. *"a purely literary"*: MT/CT, July 31, 1906.

p. 632. "very nice culling": MT/CT, July 31, 1906.

p. 632. "energy enough": MT/Eden Phillpots, April 26, 1908.

p. 634. "The King . . . has always": IVL/HW, June 27, 1907.

p. 634. "I go out frequently": MT/CC, February 24, 1907.

p. 634. "talked in a snow-white": MT/JC, May 14, 1907.

p. 635. "Once I turned": MT/CC, June 30, 1907.

p. 635. "that lovely spirit": MT/Mrs. TBA, March 29, 1907.

p. 635. "I'll sell you the site": *MTHL2*, 819.

p. 635. "I would come": *MTHL2*, 820.

p. 636. "I am really exceedingly":
CC/MT, August 5, 1907.

p. 636. "He walked up and down":
IVL, October 23, 1907.

p. 636. "Evidently there is": MT/JC,
May 21, 1908.

p. 637. "I am 73": MT/Nettie Brock-
ley, December 1908.

p. 638. "It's a frisk-about lot": *MTAQ*,
251.

p. 638. "I wish a person":
MT/Dorothy Quick, January 13,
1908.

p. 639. "She will make": MT/JC, June
5, 1908.

p. 639. "better than Mark": MT/CC,
March 23, 1908.

p. 639. "[He] has been": *SP*, 605.

p. 639. "private papers": IVL in *MTP*,
January 1908.

p. 639. "When Paine discovered": IVL
in *MTP*, January 1908.

p. 640. "I don't like to have":
MTHL2, 828.

p. 640. "should not have hesitated":
MTHL2, 829.

p. 640. "beat the bronchitis": MT/CL,
February 11, 1908.

p. 641. "I realize that I haven't":
MTHHR, 650.

p. 641. "Miss Lyon has": MT/CC,
June 20, 1908.

p. 641. "an old time minstrel":
MTHL2, 831.

p. 641. "You see your": *MTHL2*, 831.

p. 641. "I was gone two": MT/JC, August 9, 1908.

p. 641. "The doctor had half":
MTHHR, 652.

p. 642. "as brisk & active": *MTHHR*,
657.

p. 642. "There is nothing": MT/
General Bingham, September 18,
1908; MT/Notice to the Next
Burgler, September 18, 1908.

p. 642. "Not a woman": *MTHL2*,
835.

p. 643. "was in his long": *MTHL2*,
843.

p. 644. "To me his prose": *MTHL2*,
841.

p. 644. "a religious person": *MTHL2*,
844–45.

p. 644. "try to beat a threatened":
MT/JC, March 3, 1909.

p. 644. "While we are hunting":
MT/CC, March 11 and 14, 1909.

p. 645. "Nothing is as it was":
MT/CC, March 11 and 14, 1909.

p. 645. "Jesus, what a week!":
MT/CC, March 11 and 14, 1909.

p. 645. "It won't make any": IVL/
Hattie Enders, February 16, 1909.

p. 646. "poor old man": Hamlin Hill,
Mark Twain: God's Fool. New
York: Harper & Row, 1973,
pp. 218–19.

p. 646. "You will give Miss Lyon":
CC/MT, April (?) 1909.

p. 646. "Dear child": MT/JC, April
1909.

p. 647. "It's the first time": MT/EW,
August 27, 1909.

p. 647. "She and Mr. Ashcroft":
JC/JHT, June 14, 1909.

p. 647. "was a liar": MT/CC, March
6, 1910.

p. 647. "At this very day": NBK 48.

p. 648. "This is terrible": *MTHHR*,
648.

p. 648. "He had a helpless": *MTB*,
1490–91.

p. 648. "How glad I am": *MTB*, 1492.

p. 648. "Clara has": MT/FGW, June
21, 1909.

p. 648. "necessary for her recovery":
MT/FGW, June 21, 1909.

p. 648. "I have a curious": *MTB*,
1497.

p. 648. "That pain has come": *MTB*,
1498.

p. 648. "It is heart-disease": *MTAQ*, 261–62.

p. 648. "go out of sight": MT/William R. Coe, June 27, 1909.

p. 649. "But it was too lonesome": MT/EW, July 1909.

p. 649. "You would better come": MT/GH, August 12, 1909.

p. 649. "It is an ideal life": MT/AO, September 22, 1909.

p. 649. "Therefore the pains": MT/William Henry Bishop, October 11, 1909.

p. 649. "most thoroughly grateful": MT/AO, October 13, 1909.

p. 650. "decked out": Mrs. Sprague/Dixon Wecter, July 9, 1947.

p. 650. "Everything—weather included": MT/CC, November 26, 1909.

p. 650. "the quality of a command": MT/CC, November 26, 1909.

p. 650. "The doctors are certain": JC/Mayverite Schmitt, November 20, 1909.

p. 650. "I do not seem": MT/CC, December 6, 1909.

p. 651. "What is there about": MT/Helen Picard, August 26, 1909.

p. 651. "two splendid days": MT/JHTs, December 27, 1909.

p. 651. "I hear the newspapers": MT/Manager, Associated Press, December 24, 1909; *MFMT*, 283.

p. 651. "Miss Jean is dead!": *Leary*, 322; MT/WC, December 27, 1909.

p. 652. "How sweet, & peaceful": MT/JHTs, December 27, 1909.

p. 652. "watched the hearse": *MTB*, 1550.

p. 652. "already rejoicing": MT/WC, December 27, 1909.

p. 652. "from the swindle": MT/MLB, January 26, 1901.

p. 652. "so glad": *MTL2*, 835.

p. 652. "If only I had": CC/JL, January 23, 1910.

p. 652. "an indefinite stay": MT/EW, January 1, 1910.

p. 652. "I turn to his books": *MTB*, 1557.

p. 652. "The main thing is": CC/JL, January 23, 1910.

p. 652. "my raft has landed me": MT/MLB, January 26, 1901.

p. 653. "You are nearer": MT/CC, February 21, 22, and 23, 1910.

p. 653. "I shall probably": CC/ABP, February 5 and 7, 1910.

p. 653. "He seems so alone": CC/Mrs. Wilson, circa February 1 to March 30, 1910.

p. 653. "I don't know why": MT/CC, December 28, 1909.

p. 653. "Sometime or other": MT-HA/ABP, March 2, 1910.

p. 653. "Prodigiously pleased": MT/CC, March 12, 1910.

p. 653. "I don't want to": *MTB*, 1562–63.

p. 653. "My father died": MT/CC, March 24 and 25, 1910.

p. 654. "I am sorry for you": *MTB*, 1571.

p. 654. "be stimulated back": *MTB*, 1573.

p. 654. "Father has been": CC/Marion S. Allen, April 18, 1910.

p. 654. "Dear You did not": MT/CC, April 21, 1910.

p. 654. "congeries of contradictions": WDH American Academy of Arts & Letters, November 30, 1910.

p. 655. "They were like one another": *MMT*, 101.

ACKNOWLEDGMENTS

For generous and amiable access to its vast archive of Mark Twain materials, I am indebted to the Mark Twain Project at the Bancroft Library, University of California, Berkeley. Its editor-in-chief, Robert H. Hirst, and its recent and current editors, Dahlia Armon, Richard Pack Browning, Richard Bucci, Victor Fischer, Michael B. Frank, Lin Salamo, Kenneth M. Sanderson, and Harriet Elinor Smith, have done and continue to do inestimably valuable service to American literature. Without their achievements as editors of the Mark Twain Papers and the Works of Mark Twain and the Mark Twain Library, our knowledge of Twain would be impoverished and our access to his life and works significantly decreased. By extension, I am indebted to a large number of archives and individuals who have made their resources available, by photocopy and microfilm, to scholars working at the Twain Project. The chief among these are the Beinecke Rare Book and Manuscript Library, Yale University; the Berg Collection, New York Public Library; Mark Twain House, Hartford, Connecticut; and Vassar College Library. Additional letters are archived in dozens of other libraries and in private collections around the world.

Those tangible remnants of Twain's world that have been preserved and restored are great assets and have been of immense help in visualizing the physical realities of his daily life, particularly the Mark Twain House in Hartford, Connecticut, the various Hannibal, Missouri, Twain sites, and Quarry Farm in Elmira, New York. Memorializing Mark Twain has been and continues to be a scholarly enterprise, a commercial business, and a cultural preoccupation. As a biographer, though often without disclosing my vocation, I have benefited considerably from all the above enterprises, in California, Nevada, Missouri, Connecticut, and New York, as well as from two electronic maps, the on-line Mark Twain Forum and James Zwick's often informative Mark Twain website. Most of my voyaging with Twain, though, has been through unpublished letters and manuscripts, and through books, the most important of which have been the various editions of his letters, especially the ongoing *Mark Twain Letters*. This biography also partly rests on the labors of a large number of scholars who have written about special aspects of Twain's biography. Some of them are quoted in the Notes. Many are not; they are, though, part of the deep background, the hidden substratum, and to those authors I express my thanks for their work.

One of the pleasures of writing a biography of Mark Twain is to become aware of and to share in the goodwill and scholarly comity that characterize professional and nonprofessional Twaineans. I am indebted to many of them for their published work and for their private encouragement. Though I have met most of them only through their publications, I do offer my celebratory testimony to the high quality of so much that they have accomplished, and to the humane spirit that characterizes their discourse. A few of them, by the accidents of propinquity, have been directly helpful, specifically Shelley Fisher Fishkin, who was graciously encouraging, Susan Harris, a former colleague, who was generous and supportive at an early stage, and Richard Bucci, an invaluable resource on all matters regarding Twain (and the helpful reader of an unrevised version of this biography). Everett Emerson, with whom I never had any other connection, had the kindness and generosity to write to me with words of praise for my Henry James biography, and to say how much he looked forward to my Twain biography. I regret that he's not alive to write to me again. A special word is due about Justin Kaplan: he and his work have been a helpful presence over the years. With his wife, he was my host at their home one gray Cambridge day when I was working on a biography of James. I had then, as I have now, great admiration for *Mr. Clemens and Mark Twain*. Though my own emphasis in creating a portrait of Twain is substantially different, there is, at least to me, an admirable and very American irony in having two biographers of Twain with this particular last name. Only in America, as has often been said. Years ago as a young graduate student I sat next to Lewis Leary, the Twain scholar and editor, on a return flight in a horrible storm from Chicago to New York. The plane skidded, veered, and tilted as it landed, almost bringing to a close both a very young and a very senior career. In making frequent use of Leary's edition of Twain's letters to Henry Huddleston Rogers, that memory was strong in my mind. To one of Leary's successors at Columbia University, Carl Woodring, my enduring appreciation for so many professional and personal kindnesses.

For professional assistance, my thanks to Georges Borchardt, Anne Borchardt, Valerie Borchardt, and Hope Richardson at Georges Borchardt, Inc.; to William Thomas, Kendra Harpster, and Karla Roberson at Doubleday, and to two other excellent editors, William Patrick and Alison Kerr Miller; to Robert H. Hirst at the Mark Twain Papers; to the Research Foundation of the City University of New York; to Nancy Comley's attentive ministrations at Queens College; to Joan Richardson and William Kelly at the Graduate Center of the City University of New York, the former for her sympathetic support, the latter for a long-ago helpful conversation. And to Charles Molesworth for his unflagging interest and sharp perception through many conversations about things literary, including Mark Twain. For personal support and hospitality, I thank Murray Baumgarten, Sheila Baumgarten, Ed Geffner, Jane Jordan, John Jordan, Benjamin J. Kaplan, Julia R. Kaplan, Noah J. Kaplan, David Kleinbard, Donald McQuade, Carol Molesworth, Charles Molesworth, Maureen Waters, and Garret Weyr; and Dr. Raymond Matta, for his expert attention to my physical well-being. Rhoda Weyr, to whom praise and thanks are due, is again in a category of her own.

INDEX

ALSO BY FRED KAPLAN

*"Kaplan's book is an invaluable font of research on the
subject, possibly the only one we'll ever need."*
—The Washington Post Book World

GORE VIDAL

A Biography

No writer since Hemingway has lived life on as ambitious or
international a stage as Gore Vidal, and Vidal's work has become
as prominent a landmark in twentieth-century American literature. In this first major, authorized biography we meet the complete and unabridged Gore Vidal, from his privileged Washington
childhood to his army experience, from his television and Holly-
wood career to his work as a novelist, playwright, and essayist.
Acclaimed biographer Fred Kaplan also sheds new light on
Vidal's much-publicized exploration of his own sexuality and
tracks Vidal's friendships and feuds with Tennessee Williams,
Anaïs Nin, Jack Kerouac, Paul Bowles, Norman Mailer, William
Buckley, and Truman Capote.

A revelatory chronicle of a towering literary figure, Kaplan's *Gore
Vidal* ties together the prolific diversity of Vidal's work with his
eventful life in a highly satisfying, utterly thorough study. It will
be the starting point for any critical and cultural analysis of Gore
Vidal for years to come.

Biography/0-385-47704-X

ANCHOR BOOKS
Available at your local bookstore, or call toll-free to order:
1-800-793-2665 (credit cards only)